Countdown to Murder:

Alex Murdaugh

Money, Murder & Deception in South Carolina

Rebecca F. Pittman

Published by Wonderland Productions, LLC 2023

USA

Cover Design: Rebecca F. Pittman

ISBN: 978-0-9983692-6-6

DEDICATION

For Stephen Smith, Gloria Satterfield, Mallory Beach, Margaret "Maggie" Murdaugh and Paul Murdaugh.

For those who shared their stories and memories with me—this book would be nothing without you. So many of you have suffered knee-buckling loss. You deserve answers and healing.

For my husband John Drzemala, who sat with me through 6 weeks of trial during the double murder case of Alex Murdaugh and listened ad nauseum to my reports and theories, I love you dearly. You make a wonderful Watson.

For my family, who support me and give me hours of laughter and love, thank you for understanding the long hours and TMI on each book I write. You're my world.

CONTENTS

Acknowledgments

ACKNOWLEDGMENTS

How do you begin to acknowledge so many people who set aside their time, trepidations, and agendas to help me with tackling this monster of a book? Many, for various reasons, asked that their names be kept from the information they shared with me. They are still living in the area of Hampton, and I understand their need for privacy. In some cases, Confidentiality Agreements had to be signed before these people could share their inside information. When it applied, that new information was turned over to SLED to further their investigations into the Stephen Smith and Gloria Satterfield cases; always with the consent of the person providing it to me. Therefore, sadly, many names deserving of accolades are not mentioned below.

The reports about the different cases surrounding the Murdaugh family came out daily. It required new interviews and new content each time. And so, it is with the biggest "Thank You!" this author can muster that I acknowledge the contributions of the following people and agencies:

Caroline M. Pinckney with the Department of Natural Resources (DNR); Angie Topper (Deputy Coroner); Sargent William Reid (Hampton County Courthouse); Colleton County Courthouse; Clay Emminger and William "Rosco" Towne with the Beaufort Water Search and Rescue; Linda Hiers (Gloria Satterfield's Best Friend); Brian Hariott (Gloria Satterfield's Youngest Son); Nick Ginn (Former Hampton County Sheriff's Office); Jared S. Newman, Attorney Beaufort, SC); Dawn Turner Erwin (Paralegal Assistant, Beaufort, SC)'; (Susanne Andrews (Founder of *Standing for Stephen* and the *SC Hate Crime Bill*); Sandy Smith (Stephen Smith's Mother); Kathleen McKenna Hewtson (Author of *Murdaugh She*

Wrote); Michael Virzi (Ethics Lawyer, Columbia, SC); Michelle Freed (Remote Viewing Instructor); Melissa Kotter (Technical Support). News outlets and media platforms are listed under Recommended Media at the back of this book.

And to John Drzemala, who spent hours supporting my time on this book, watching a 6-week-long trial, and reminding me when the pages climbed toward the 700-page mark, "This Too Shall Pass."

For all the family and friends who called daily and said, "You Got This!" when the stress mounted. "You are appreciated!"

A big Thank You to Nick Ginn with Natural Graphics Photography for his beautiful photos taken in Beaufort, SC and elsewhere. You can hire Nick for weddings and all special events.

See his Facebook page at Natural Graphics Photography/Facebook.

Linda Hiers and Nick Ginn on location in Beaufort, SC on the Beaufort Water Search and Rescue. Photo: Rebecca F. Pittman

Prologue

The Lowcountry tidal plains of South Carolina are steeped in history and mystery. The waters here heave and breathe, undulating beneath the watercraft that have learned their secrets and time their journeys accordingly. With a watchful eye on the moon's cycles, denizens of these estuaries and inlets know when high tide will swell the waters to an amazing 8 feet in height, then drop to boat-bottoming levels.

Rushing in, ebbing out. Covering and betraying. Secrets buried in the pluff mud are suddenly revealed at low tide as the ocean reclaims its briny offspring, leaving stands of salt marsh, cord grass, and hidden treasures. Seashells embedded in the mud are suddenly showcased in ghostly white and pastel colors. At high tide, they can be swept away again, all imprints of their brief stay erased.

It is here that Mallory Beach was swept away on a cold February morning in 2019. The ebb and flow of the tide carried her maddingly out of reach of divers and search and rescue teams. Within reach and then gone. It was not until one such eddying stream pushed her into a small branch off Archer's Creek that miraculously she came to rest in the marsh and was found.

The story of her death and the circumstances surrounding it set off a maelstrom of buried stories surrounding other mysterious deaths and corruption within the legal system of South Carolina. Beneath the gravitational pull of justice, the high tide of secrets and insidious machinations were slowly swept away, exposing an underbelly of entitlement and greed such as the Palmetto State and indeed the world had rarely seen. Five victims—two by gunshot, one by drowning, another beaten and left in the road, and a fifth involved in a suspicious trip and fall "accident." All had one thing in common. All had the misfortune of entering that tide pool of deceit and malevolence. All fell within the crosshairs of one name: Murdaugh.

This is a book that could not have been written without the bravery of so many who shared their stories with this author. These are good people rooted within a small area bordered by farmland, small shops, churches, remnants of plantations, back roads, and water, always water. It licks at the knees of cypress trees in small riverways lining the roads of South Carolina's Lowcountry. The sweet acrid smell of pluff mud and rotting roots permeates the air after a day of baking in the sweltering heat. These ponds and sudden pooling of water run close to thoroughfares, ideal for pitching things into from speeding cars. Things meant to be buried and hidden. Things only the snapping turtles and snakes are apt to find. An occasional alligator may stir them in its passing, yet their secrets may have been around since pirates found their way into the Carolina inlets long ago.

Some 68 islands lay claim to this Lowcountry enclave. The Gullah people still live here, creating beautiful works of art with their salt grass basketry and filling the air with their lyrical cadence. Oyster roasts are a tradition during the "ber" months when it's cold and the oysters are fresh. Locals board their john boats and carefully navigate the myriad fingers of creeks that run like mazes through Beaufort and other tidal plain areas. It is a way of life known only to those who live here. Pat Conroy, South Carolina's native son, portrayed its romance and clandestine underbelly in his famous works such as *The Prince of Tides, Trouble the Water*, *Beach Music*, and *The Water is Wide.*

Hollywood fell in love with the Lowcountry and filmed classics such as *Forest Gump* (1994); *The Big Chill* (1983); *The Great Santini* (1979, based on Pat Conroy's novel of the same name); *GI Jane* (1997); *The Fugitive* (1993); *Forces of Nature* (1999); and *The Prince of Tides* (1991). Other films and TV shows have found their way here, spawning celebrity sightings in local restaurants and hotels.

For this author, who was raised in the south, it was like coming home during the research for this book. It took only moments to remember the unparalleled hospitality and southern manners I remembered in my youth. The soft "Y'all's" and "Bless your heart" that peppered every conversation, the offering of sweet tea the moment you crossed a threshold, and those wonderful larger-than-life personalities that feel as though they have stepped from the pages of a book. You also notice the unashamed road signs declaring Jesus Saves, and the plethora of small churches that dot the counties with their white steeples peeping out from between the tall Spanish oaks. The sway of grey moss, the pitching masts of moored boats, and roadside stores offering boiled peanuts brought familiar memories that have lain dormant for decades.

It lures you here, this gentle yet turbulent area of the country. It portrays an innocence and nostalgia with its front porch rockers and a slower pace of living. Sadly, there are those who will prey on that innocence and remove from this life those who were the best of us. Their lifetime of promise snuffed out simply because they came too close and interrupted some evil agenda that lay beneath the surface like the decomposing rudiments of murky swampland.

This is the story of a family dynasty that set the rules for generations and punished those who broke them. Names of certain people who came forward in interviews for this book have been omitted or changed to assure their anonymity. Hampton and surrounding towns are still their home, and it is understandable that they shield themselves from possible ramifications. Many were grateful to give their information so that justice can be served, and to those amazingly brave and kind souls, I give a heartfelt "Thank you!" If enough is laid bare beneath the spotlight of truth, it may be that Hampton and Colleton County families and businesses can thrive once again.

*I have left many interviews, including those by law enforcement and lawyers, unedited. Therefore, you will see many stop and start sentences, "you know," and creative syntax. I felt I did not have the right to edit testimony. "Bless Your Heart."

Rebecca F. Pittman

May 2023

Chapter One
HEADLIGHTS

The sound of katydids and crickets filled the sticky predawn air with rhythmic thrumming. It was dark out—around 3 o'clock in the morning; the grey Spanish moss a ghostly white barely moving in the 6-mph breeze. A time when most people are asleep and only those out for nefarious motives move through the stillness. Humidity clung to the blades of grass. It would later betray a clue of which few knew.

The sound of mud tires on asphalt had receded hours before, along with the jarring sound of a gate crashing in. Several shadowed silhouettes in the trees had hurried back to their vehicles and roared away toward anonymity. There would be no witnesses here where the farmland and hunting properties spread out for miles. Only an unseen deer camera on an unoccupied hunting acreage might betray a murderer's identity. It was a night of secrets.

Just before 4 a.m. that same morning, a man on his way to work blinked the sleepiness from his eyes and followed the swath of light his headlights cut through the undisturbed back road countryside. He knew Sandy Run Road by heart and still referred to it by the name the locals had always called it—Crocketville Road. Up ahead something was lying in the middle of the road; a nondescript shape that was not that of the typical deer carcasses he was used to seeing. He slowed and as his headlights bathed the horrific scene, his heart pounded. It was a young man, sprawled across the middle yellow line, his blond hair white in the harsh car lights. Blood was running from his head and was spreading across the asphalt.

Nerves straining, the driver looked about him into the shadows of the cornfield to his left and a small dark house nestled in oaks to his right. Realizing whoever did this could still be lurking nearby; he carefully skirted the young man in the road and drove a mile until he came to a stop sign. Only then did he pick up his cell phone and call 911. Little did he know the powerful forces already in play that day that would subvert every effort to find out what happened to the boy in the wee morning hours of July 8, 2015.

A Legacy Begins
Randolph Murdaugh Sr.

Randolph Murdaugh Sr. was born in Varnville, South Carolina on February 28, 1887, the youngest son of Josiah Putnam Murdaugh Sr., a wealthy Lowcountry businessman who made his fortune in the phosphate mining industry and later in real estate. His mother was Annie Marvin Murdaugh (née Davis). His maternal grandfather, Joseph W. Davis, was a cousin of Confederate President Jefferson Davis. Randolph attended the US Naval Academy in Annapolis, Maryland, and graduated from the University of South Carolina (USC) law school in 1910. It was here that the Murdaugh legacy in the legal community began. He put out the word in 1910 that he was open for business and began a one-man law firm in Hampton, South Carolina, a stone's throw from the small town of Varnville, and 78 miles west of the capital of Columbia. It specialized in civil litigation and would spawn the law firm of Peters, Murdaugh, Parker, Eltzroth, and Detrick (PMPED) in later years.

Handling local legal wranglings wasn't filling his time completely, so he ran a local daily newspaper, *The Hampton County Herald.* It served up the daily gossip, events, and occasional tragedy. It also gave Randolph a mouthpiece he could use for his own purposes. His wife's garden parties, and social activities received ink, as well as his own appearances at multiple noteworthy events. He rose quickly in his chosen field of law and in 1920 he became one of what would become three consecutive Murdaughs in the post of solicitor in the 14th Judicial Circuit Court. A solicitor is the same as a prosecutor and is a very powerful position. In this case, the 14th Circuit included five counties: Hampton, Colleton, Allendale, Beaufort, and Jasper counties. The 14th Judicial Circuit is the chief prosecuting agency, covering 3,200 square miles. It is the only five-county circuit in the state. For the majority of the next 86 years, a Murdaugh would hold that title.

RANDOLPH MURDAUGH

Candidate for Solicitor of the Fourteen
Judicial Circuit.

Newspaper clipping announcing Randolph Murdaugh as a candidate for the office of solicitor for the 14th Judicial Circuit

From 1920 until 2006, a Murdaugh held the office of solicitor in charge of prosecuting all criminal cases in the state's 14th Judicial Circuit Court. This led to the locals calling the five-county district "Murdaugh Country." They did more than prosecute cases; a solicitor could nominate people for the position of judge, sheriff, coroner, and other high-profile professions. These candidates were then voted on. The rumors of behind-the-scenes and under-the-table endorsements may have been well founded. If the solicitor also had judges, law enforcement, and medical personnel in their pockets, the power over individual case files would be prolific. Well-respected South Carolina attorney Justin Bamberg summed it up succinctly: "The Murdaughs were not just part of the system. They *were* the system!"

As Murdaugh began feeling his oats, he took on more and more high-profile cases, such as defending a state governor and later prosecuting another. Others to fall beneath his blade were bankers, preachers who were not totally without sin, and murderers. He would begin the long legacy of Murdaugh theatrics in the courtroom, never shy to go beyond dry diatribes.

It didn't take long before the accusations that Hampton County was a "judicial hell hole" tainted the 14th Circuit's Court system's reputation. Jurors typically called in a guilty verdict if a Murdaugh was prosecuting the case. The web of deceit may have been beneath the surface, but it was powerful. If you got on the wrong side of a Murdaugh, you suddenly found yourself tailed by a policeman, fired from a job, and in later years, drugs suddenly appearing in your vehicle or workplace. Locals learned quickly if they were to live within the 14th Circuit, they played by the rules or died by the rules—in some cases, literally.

Randolph Murdaugh, Sr.

In the decade before his election to solicitor, Randolph married, and fathered his successor, Randolph "Buster" Murdaugh II. On February 28, 1940, Randolph I was endorsed for re-election. It was here that Randolph Murdaugh's stars failed to align.

Later in life, around 1939, he began battling an illness that curtailed many of his activities. In April of 1940, after a hospital stay, he was released and convalescing at home. On the evening of July 19, 1940, he rallied himself and left to visit a friend. He stayed, playing cards, and left around 1 a.m. At a railroad crossing, a few miles east of his home in Varnville, he paused and waited for the approaching train. A Charleston & Western Carolina freight train was barreling through the humid summer morning. The train conductor, W.W. Bartlett, later testified that he saw Murdaugh's car waiting at the crossing. He said the man in the car waved at him as the train approached and then suddenly gunned the engine and shot out onto the tracks at the moment the train reached the crossing. *The Hampton County Guardian* reported on July 24, 1940, that "the impact hurled the automobile approximately 900 feet up the track, totally wrecking it," and "Murdaugh's body was found beside the track approximately 150 feet from the crossing." He was only 59 years old.

Rumors began circulating shortly after. Had the solicitor been drunk, or had he, in despair of his failing health, decided to commit suicide while the bright headlight of a speeding train illuminated the horrific scene? Despite the speculation, the coroner deemed his death an accident, which satisfied the medical requirements but not the local gossip mills.

The re-election of Randolph Murdaugh was not to be, but waiting in the wings was his son, Randolph "Buster" Murdaugh II who would take on the role his father forfeited. Wasting no time after his father's untimely death, Randolph Jr., went after the railway company of Charleston and Western Carolina. As executor of his father's will, he filed a summons and complaint against CWC on behalf of Randolph Sr.'s widow Mary, and her children for the "wrongful death of said Randolph Murdaugh, Sr." It would be the first of many lawsuits involving the railway giant that later became CSX Transportation.

According to the lawsuit against CWC, the train was traveling "at a high rate of speed" and failed to blow a whistle or ring a bell at the

Camp Branch crossing. The crossing's poor condition was also attacked saying it "was in rough, washed out and dangerous condition." The suit noted that Randolph's view of the approaching train was blocked by trees and tall ragged underbrush. Added to the early morning hour's foggy condition, this placed the solicitor in "sudden and imminent peril."

Buster filed for a judgment of $100,000 for the wrongful death of his father. The settlement was concluded on September 22, 1941, for an undisclosed amount.

Randolph "Buster" Murdaugh II Jr.

Randolph "Buster" Murdaugh Jr. was born January 9, 1915, in Varnville, Hampton County, South Carolina.

Randolph "Buster" Murdaugh Jr.

During his 46 years in government, Buster faced opposition just twice. He brought a flamboyance to an otherwise dusty courtroom, often acting out for the jury (and no doubt his growing gallery of admirers) how a murder took place. He was known for throwing things across the courtroom, lying on the floor to mirror the dead person, and wrapping a hose around his neck while questioning a witness, often to the pounding of a displeased gavel. The jury loved him; judges reached for aspirin bottles. He was known for his love of chewing tobacco and a spittoon or empty cup was never far away.

Buster skated close to the edge in his typical cavalier manner, resulting in his being on the wrong side of the gavel on more than one occasion. Professor John Blume of Cornell Law School claims that Buster received several reprimands from the state supreme court for his closing arguments in various cases involving the death sentence. In 1956, a federal grand jury reportedly indicted him for allegedly advising a bootlegger to move a still into a neighboring county to elude the police. Not surprisingly, he was found not guilty. This was not to be Buster's only dealing with "White Lightning."

Colleton Whiskey Conspiracy

South Carolina's Lowcountry is a patchwork quilt of ethnicities, religions, affluence, and poverty. Within a mile one could pass a colonial pillared home with sprawling lawns and brick columns, standing in harsh juxtaposition against neighboring shanty houses or rundown trailer homes. It was overseen by a chosen few that favored the rich and influential, and ignored for the most part the downtrodden and "inferior" family lines. Enter Buster Murdaugh who saw opportunity in every caste system. He became a living legend—a Robin Hood of sorts with a bootlegging operation that made no distinction in its clientele.

In June 1956, Buster Murdaugh was indicted by a federal Grand Jury in what became known as the "Colleton Whiskey Conspiracy." Under Buster's helmsmanship, as the solicitor of the 14th Judicial Circuit, his law enforcement community was revealed to be a criminal enterprise. The Grand Jury handed down indictments for 26 people which included the Colleton County sheriff, three of his deputies, two former deputies and a magistrate judge. Included were also a plethora of businessmen and bootleggers. It was a judicial maelstrom of the likes never before seen in the Palmetto State.

When Buster Murdaugh's name was added to the list, it appeared there was no ceiling to this house of cards. He was accused of not only being part of the conspiracy but of personally profiting from the deluge of illicit whiskey flowing throughout the Lowcountry. Prohibition may have ended long before in 1933, but the sale of moonshine was still against the law. Front and center was Buster, filling his pockets with the payoffs from his lucrative trade in fermented beverages.

The News and Courier newspaper in Charleston reported defendants in the case taking bribes, manipulating fines, and staging friendly raids to give the impression law enforcement was cracking down on the backroad bootlegging operations. Buster was quoted as telling the sheriff, "For God's sake, make the raids, even if you have to warn them in advance, catch them and set up fines. I'll take care of them." One bootlegger testified that the sheriff arranged a "friendly raid" on his still, and a pint of whiskey was seized. He then said he and the sheriff drank about half of the pint and the rest was taken away as "evidence."

There were reports of tampering with witnesses, including the U.S. District Attorney. During the trial, two key prosecution witnesses had to be protected by federal marshals. So many people were involved that it was impossible to prosecute them all. One way or another, a network of corruption was revealed with many caught with their hands in the till...or still.

Three miles outside of Walterboro—the Colleton County Seat where the Murdaugh Double Murder Trial took place in 2023—sat a massive distillery in an open field. It was this operation that drew the attention of the U.S. Treasury Department's Alcohol Tobacco Tax Division's attention. Locals nicknamed the distillery "Schenley's" after the world's largest legal producer of alcohol. By the time the dust settled, 32 moonshine stills, producing 90,000 gallons of illicit liquor, were investigated. The trial lasted two weeks, with much name calling and pointing fingers. Many rallied to Buster Murdaugh's defense. Assistant U.S. Attorney Arthur G. Howe of Charleston shouted, "It reaches to the crux of our government and our way of life. It reaches from the swamps of Jackass Pond into the Colleton County Courthouse." He called it "the most important case ever tried in South Carolina." Another Murdaugh would put that quote to the test on January 23, 2023, in that very courthouse Howe had denigrated.

In the end, the purveyor of liquid gold was found not guilty, despite the declarations of heated prosecutors screaming he was the mastermind behind the entire operation. Two other players in this grand scale debacle were acquitted along with Murdaugh: a plantation property manager, and a man from the Green Pond area who could find underground water supplies for bootleggers by using a dogwood branch, or in other words, "dowsing."

The Colleton Whiskey Conspiracy opened the doors for myriad stories of corruption surrounding Buster Murdaugh and his misuse of power in the legal system. Rumors of jury manipulation, threats against witnesses, greed, corrupt law enforcement, and other underhanded actions swirled around the solicitor of the 14th Judicial Circuit of South Carolina. He was indicted for bribery when he was accused of handing out $100 bills to each jury member. He was even seen taking a payoff from the Colleton County Sheriff for his moonshine delivery in a courthouse hallway. Although being found not guilty, the stain of corruption was never really erased from the Murdaugh name afterwards. In a foreshadowing of over 99 cases of insurance fraud that would be brought against his grandson, Alex Murdaugh, Buster was also accused of stealing from his clients.

A photo depicting a still in Hell Hole Swamp in Berkeley County, SC.

During an interview for this book, I was fortunate to find someone who had firsthand knowledge of how the operation worked. We'll call her Nancy. This is her story.

"I was dating; it was in the late 60s, I'd say 68, and the guy that I was dating was living at Almeda on the property where Randolph Murdaugh III's house is today. It's the same house that Miss Libby lives in now and was featured in Alex Murdaugh's murder trial, but at the time, the house hadn't been moved there to its current location. There was a big old barn there. It had a loft and there were cattle and everything and then off to the left of that was a smaller little smoke shed or something and that's where the still was; in there. I was dating this guy and on Fridays he would run these routes. I didn't know what we were doing. He would be out on these country roads around Gifford and Furman. You have to look on a map; it's the backwoods of Estill and he would stop in these people's yards, like these old black people would be sitting out on the porch in rocking chairs and stuff, waiting for him to get there. He would open the trunk and get out these glass jugs, and he would give them like two glass jugs, or maybe 4 glass jugs, you know, and then we would speed away from there to the next place.

"The car was some kind of Ford car with a special fuel injection-type system; something to ramp up really fast. I can't remember what kind of car it was, but I think it was a Ford Fairlane. It was bright red too. So, these people we went to see were giving him money; some of them were putting it on a tab. He either had something in his hand or wrote something down. I could see a little bit of what was going on behind the car, you know, but I was really confused about what we were doing because this was supposed to be a date night. We were eventually gonna end up going to a dance or something, but we always had to run these errands first.

"Looking back, I think that Buster wanted me riding with this guy as a cover, so instead of a man in a red car flying around it was a couple, you know, like on a date or whatever. It was almost two years later that I finally saw the still on Randolph's property and then I was kind of like putting things together, you know? It's hard to explain. Anyway, there were cracks between the boards of that shed I mentioned on Murdaugh's property where you could peek in, and they always made sure to keep this little barn or smokehouse, or

10

whatever it was, locked with padlocks. Nobody was supposed to get around there and, you know, it made me more curious to see how careful they were to keep it locked. None of the Murdaughs were living in Almeda then. This family was living there, and I was dating the son. There was a mobile home sitting there. They put the mobile home there, but it wasn't this guy's job to make the moonshine. I think his father made the moonshine. His father worked for Continental Can Company and was in big with the timber people and I suspect that he was the one running the still, making the moonshine, and the son making these deliveries.

"Buster Murdaugh was the owner. He was the head honcho. He was the ringleader. Back in the 50s, there was a trial, you know, about that. Well Buster was temporarily removed from office and tried for running moonshine. He was tried for tipping moonshiners that they were about to be raided. He continued to run it into the late 70s. They made the moonshine out of corn and sugar, and I don't know what else and then fermented it. I saw just one of them you know, and there were like shelves on the walls with like little quart size jars with clear liquid, and then down on the ground on the floor were big glass jars with clear liquids.

"Mr. Randolph's house that you saw during Alex' murder trial is on the property now where the trailer used to be. It was sitting next door to where Fred's is, where the Dollar Store is now. They actually picked it up and moved it there, maybe seven or eight years ago, 10 years at the most. It hadn't been real long after Mr. Buster died Randolph had the house moved to Almeda."

Buster Murdaugh was said to negotiate with people who wanted someone "taken care of" or a favor needed, no matter the crime. Buster would ask, "What do you have to offer me?" An exchange would be made, sometimes property or cash, or some other arrangement. It was said Old Buster told someone to whom Buster owed a favor, "If you ever need someone to disappear, bring them to Hampton County."

With the mysterious deaths surrounding Alex Murdaugh and his family and reports of other deaths not yet on the radar, it would seem Buster Murdaugh was not just whistling Dixie.

Randolph Murdaugh III

Randolph Murdaugh III was born in Savannah, Georgia, a short drive across the bridge that separates Georgia from South Carolina. Born on October 25, 1939, he would follow in his father's footsteps and his grandfather's, becoming the third Murdaugh to hold the position of solicitor in the 14th Judicial Circuit Court of South Carolina. He graduated from Wade Hampton High School in Hampton, in 1957, where he was very active in sports. It was here he began dating his future wife, Elizabeth. After graduation he attended the University of South Carolina, graduating in 1961 with a BS Degree in Business Administration. That summer, he married "Libby."

In the fall of that year, he enrolled in the University of South Carolina School of Law and graduated in 1964. After graduating he returned to Hampton to work in his father's law firm and became an Assistant Solicitor for the 14th Circuit.

Randolph Murdaugh III

When Buster retired in 1986, Randolph III became the solicitor, where he served until the end of 2005. Thus, stamped upon the annals of South Carolina history is the longest run of one family serving as solicitor for the state: 87 consecutive years. In 2006, he joined the law firm which now bears his name: Peters, Murdaugh, Parker, Eltzroth & Detrick, P.A.

Randolph was President of the South Carolina Solicitor's Association Board of Directors from 1998-2005 and received the Order of the Palmetto (South Carolina's highest civilian honor) from Governor Henry McMaster in 2018. It was a moment of immense pride for Randolph and his family. As he stood on the balcony of the Hampton County Court House, he said humbly, "I want to thank all of you for coming here and I thank the Governor for this honor. There may be people in South Carolina more deserving, but nobody is more appreciate than I am." Over his lifetime he achieved many awards, including induction into the Wade Hampton Athletic Hall of Fame.

Randolph Murdaugh III receiving the Order of the Palmetto award, surrounded by his family and wife Libby, to his right in the photo.
Photo courtesy of the *Greenville News*.

As a solicitor, Randolph tried over 200 murder cases, once convicting two murderers in the same week. Not to be outdone by his father's theatrics, he would show how a murder took place. Ripping off his suit jacket he would ask a medical examiner to place two red ink dots on his pristine white shirt to show the jurors where the bullets entered and exited the deceased. The cost of one ruined shirt paled in comparison to the desired verdict, which he unerringly achieved. He gave to the community in many ways, especially in the sports arena, even coaching alongside his son Alex. He was reelected for five terms, stepping down on December 31, 2005, to return to his old law firm at PMPED, along with his two sons Alex and Randy.

Jeff Purdy, left, of the Beaufort County Sheriff's Office, uses a large map as he describes to 14th Circuit Solicitor Randolph Murdaugh III where the body of James Dillard was found off McPhersonville Road during testimony Tuesday morning.

Testimony begins in Coker trial

Larilyn Fields, sister of James Dillard, reacts as testimony about the condition of Dillard's body is given Tuesday morning.

By CHRIS BENDER
Gazette staff writer

14th Circuit Solicitor Randolph Murdaugh III told the jury in the James Dillard murder trial Tuesday he will present testimony that proves others heard the Yemassee man charged with the crime admit to the May 2000 killing.

Testimony in the trial in front of Judge Jackson Gregory continues today in General Sessions Court. Shameen Coker, 20, of Yemassee, is charged with murder, kidnapping and armed robbery in connection with the death of Dillard, 32, of Yemassee. Dillard's body was found May 24, 2000, in a wooded area near McPhersonville Road in Sheldon.

Ajanae C. Roach, 20, of Colleton County, also is charged with murder, kidnapping and armed robbery in connection with the slaying.

"You will hear the testimony of three people," Murdaugh said in his opening statement. "You will hear the testimony of Michael Curry, a young man who came to the Sheriff's Office and said Shameen

Coker told him (Coker) killed (Dillard)."

Murdaugh also presented witnesses who described the discovery of the body. Michelle Dixon, a State Law Enforcement Division investigator, said Dillard's body was found in a clearing about a mile and a half from U.S. 17 in Sheldon.

"A worker was checking the gates (to Buckfield Plantation) and he smelled this foul smell ... and found our victim, James Dillard," Dixon said. "His body was in a bad state of decomposition."

Dillard's brother-in-law, Ronny Manigo, said he had loaned his 1993 Pontiac Grand Am to Dillard the day of his disappearance. The car was found by Department of Natural Resources officers a day later, submerged in water near a public boat landing in Colleton County.

Inside the trunk of the car, authorities found a billfold with James Dillard's identification card inside.

Murdaugh put Hampton County Sheriff's Office investigator T.C. Smalls (See TRIAL, Page 2A)

One of the many murder trials prosecuted by Randolph Murdaugh III

Randolph and Libby had four children: Lynn Murdaugh Goettee of Summerville, SC; Randolph "Randy" Murdaugh IV of Hampton, SC; Richard Alexander Murdaugh of Islandton, SC; and John Marvin Murdaugh of Okatie, SC. The couple had 10 grandchildren including Buster and Paul Murdaugh.

Randolph Murdaugh III died in his home at Almeda on June 10, 2021, from cancer. He was 81. He took care of his family, often using his powerful position to get them out of trouble. This was never more obvious than the night his grandson, Paul Terry Murdaugh, crashed the family boat into a bridge on Archer's Creek.

3 Generations of Randolph's: Buster (l), Randy & Randolph III (r).

Randolph Murdaugh III with sons Alex (l) and Randy Murdaugh

Chapter Two
Archers Creek

Paul Terry Murdaugh was the grandson of Randolph Murdaugh III. He was the youngest son of Richard Alexander and Margaret Murdaugh. He had an older brother, Buster, named after his great-grandfather. It was a family of privilege. Boating was a big part of the Murdaugh's leisure time, and Paul made full use of the family boats. On one fateful February evening in 2019, Paul set his father's boat on a course that ended in tragedy. It began at a popular gas station and convenience store called Parker's Kitchen.

At 5:30 p.m., Paul Murdaugh, 20 at the time, drove a white pick-up truck with a boat in tow into the parking lot of Parker's Kitchen Convenience Store. It was February 23, 2019. Photos courtesy of DNR.

Lawsuits would ensue over the surveillance footage of an underage Paul Murdaugh buying alcohol that, according to the filings, attributed to his drunken state as he drove Alex Murdaugh's boat through the fog-laden waters of Archers Creek, resulting in the death of Mallory Beach on February 24, 2019. Watching the snapshots of the surveillance video at Parker's Kitchen, the day before Mallory was ejected from the boat, shows someone who has navigated the labyrinth of deceit more than once. In other words, this wasn't Paul Murdaugh's first rodeo using fake ID or his mother's credit card to buy substances that should have been off-limits to him.

Parker's surveillance cameras filmed his movements as he exited the truck and strode across the parking lot to the store's entrance, pulling his wallet from his back pocket to check his fake ID as he neared the door.

He enters the store and goes directly to the refrigerated beer cases. The store's music track is playing "Nobody's Gonna Break My Stride." It would prove to be sadly prophetic before the boating trip is over.

Paul takes his beer to the counter and asks the cashier for a pack of Marlboro Light cigarettes. She turns to the case behind her, selects the pack of cigarettes and returns to the counter. It is here that Paul presents her with his older brother Buster's ID card. This is a card Buster Murdaugh reported missing and had replaced. Just as she takes the ID from Paul, he distracts her by leaning forward and asking a question about the cigarettes. She answers him and holds them up for him to see, forgetting about scrutinizing the ID further.

Paul handing her the fake ID. (DNR)

Cashier showing him the cigarettes. (DNR)

The cashier rings up a 6-pack of Michelob Ultra beers, a 12-pack of White Claw seltzers, and a 15-pack of Natural Light beers. Paul is seen in the surveillance tape pulling nervously on his long sleeves, glancing several times toward the exit, and running a hand over his mouth. He steps back, eyeing the candy counter and throws in a pack of gum. His ID is returned to him as the total is tallied. He then pulls out what has become known as his mother's credit card and inserts it into the card reader. As the cashier goes to bag his items he tells her, "I don't need any bags," but she places the 6-pack of bottles into one anyway. Paul collects his merchandise and exits the store.

Paying with Maggie Murdaugh's credit card. (DNR)

Paul exits the store and as he nears the boat, he holds up
the beer as if to say, "Look what I scored!" (DNR)

Paul climbs up onto the boat's side and flips back the lid of a cooler, where he deposits the beer. Connor Cook exits a black SUV that has pulled up next to the boat, facing the opposite direction. He stands by the boat talking to Paul as he loads the alcohol into the cooler. Paul jumps down and throws the empty beer boxes into the back of his truck. Connor reaches over the boat's side and flips the cooler lid shut. He gets into the truck with Paul. The black SUV leaves, possibly carrying Miley Altman and the others of the party. The white truck and boat exit the parking lot. It is 9 hours before a fatal boat crash will kill Mallory Beach.

Filling the cooler. Photos courtesy of DNR.

Connor Cook flips cooler lid closed as Paul carries away boxes. (DNR)

A group of six young friends meet up at Paul Murdaugh's family riverside property on Chechessee Creek at 6:36 pm. It is a segment of land owned by the Murdaugh family for generations. Small cabins used as guest quarters dot the acreage. The $1.45 million property is called "The Island" and belongs to Paul's grandfather. It is less than two miles away from Parker's in Ridgeland where he purchased the alcohol.

Murdaugh's Chechessee River House.

Here, Paul Murdaugh, Morgan Doughty, Mallory Beach, Anthony

Cook, his cousin Connor Cook, and Miley Altman consumed alcohol before boarding the 17-foot Sea Hunt boat belonging to Paul's father, Alex Murdaugh. Before departing, Paul emptied six beers into a funnel and drained it.

At 7:07 p.m., the group headed out into the maze of small creeks and rivers on their way to Kristy Wood's oyster roast on Paukie Island, which is north of Broad River and nearly 20 miles away from the Murdaugh river house. It was rumored the group chose to go the long distance by boat to avoid alcohol checkpoints on the roadways.

It took them almost an hour to arrive on a chilly February evening. It was 8:00 p.m. when they pulled up to the dock where Kristy Wood, a school principal at Brunson Elementary in Hampton County, along with her husband James, were welcoming "friends and their families." They served oysters, appetizers, and a crab boil. The event was "bring your own beer" for those of legal age, according to Wood. Here the story varies depending on who is telling it. In Kristy Wood's statement to DNR (Division of Natural Resources) and S.C. law enforcement, she stated, "No kids were seen drinking at our house nor were they provided alcohol," Wood said. Morgan Doughty disputed that in a statement of her own, saying they "all ate food and drank alcohol." Whether or not the Woods provided it, it seemed clear the underage youths were drinking during the roast. Most were 19, with Anthony Cook being the oldest...his 21st birthday was only days away. Miley Altman said they went back and forth to the boat during the party to get alcohol from the cooler.

The group that had arrived on Paul's boat played cornhole and sat by the fire. There are Snapchat videos of Miley playing a ukulele and Mallory enjoying her food. Rumors put Maggie Murdaugh and possibly other Murdaugh family members at the oyster roast. Wood said she talked to the kids and none of them seemed to be intoxicated or voiced concerns about being on the boat. "Paul is very familiar with boats," she said in her statement, "and navigating water." As midnight neared, Wood said she invited the group of young people to spend the night at her house because the temperature had dropped and it would be even colder on the water; "not for any other concern," she said. It was also reported that Maggie was later seen at Luther's Rare and Well Done bar and restaurant in downtown Beaufort—Paul's next stop.

Luther's and More Alcohol

At 12:11 a.m., DNR created a timeline of events based on the boat's GPS navigation system. The timeline shows the group of six young adults boated from Paukie Island toward Beaufort's waterfront. Murdaugh and the group left the oyster roast because "Paul wanted to get shots" in historic downtown Beaufort, according to Miley Altman's statement. According to DNR's timeline, the boat almost collided with the Woods Memorial Bridge at 12:35 a.m. Morgan Doughty said in her statement that Connor Cook had to take the wheel because Paul was going to hit the bridge. GPS coordinates show the group arrived at the day dock in downtown Beaufort at 12:39 a.m. A minute later, the group pushed from the dock and traveled away, according to coordinates. It is unclear why, unless the group was trying to dissuade Paul from stopping. It was late and cold, and they all wanted to go home. However, four minutes later, at 12:44 a.m., the boat arrived back at the day dock for a second time. The day dock is a 200-foot-long floating dock accessed by an aluminum gangway at the east end of Henry C. Chambers Waterfront Park. Boats can tie up there and have easy access to downtown Beaufort's nightlife and shopping. It is the long dock seen in so many documentaries about the fatal boat crash where you later see the group walking back to the boat.

The group of six at the day dock by the park. (DNR)

At 12:55 a.m., the group walks along the dock. Paul wants to go to Luther's Rare and Well Done that is a popular watering hole. The others, who don't have fake IDs (with the exception of Connor Cook and Miley Altman) want to wait. Paul insists Connor go with him and the two take the short walk to the bar. The others step into the park and sit on the swings. According to the lawsuit filed by Mallory Beach's mother, the group of intoxicated underage boaters stopped at Henry C. Chambers Waterfront Park, some being served alcohol at the bar, before the boat accident which killed her daughter.

"Morgan was yelling at Paul not to go but he did anyways," Altman said. Miley is Connor Cook's girlfriend. Morgan had been dating Paul for a few years, but she had begun to tire of his treatment of her when he was drunk. Only the year before he had rolled his pickup truck, with her in it, into a ditch. It was not a happy party at this time.

Luther's Rare and Well Done.

Paul and Connor went to Luther's to get shots. Surveillance footage shows the two entering the bar area. Paul steps up to the bar, grabs a seat and pats the one next to him for Connor to join him. The two were in the bar for 12 minutes where they took turns ordering shots. Paul paid for the first round of Jägermeister shots. He and Connor knock them back. Connor then orders two shots of Lemon Drop: a lemon vodka mix. They down those and talk for a few minutes.

Paul (l) and Connor at the bar at Luther's. Surveillance video.

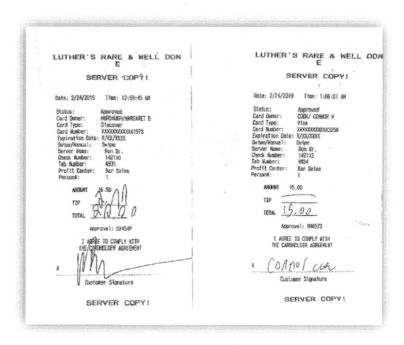

Paul Murdaugh and Connor Cook's bar receipts. (DNR)

Each pays his tab. Miley and Morgan went into the bar to get them. Everyone wanted to get going. Stories vary here. During some depositions of the boating passengers, they claim they all went into

Luther's after Paul asked the staff if "his friends could come in too?" Miley said Paul knocked down a chair on the bar's patio as they exited. A guy standing there jokes, "What did that chair ever do to you?" He and Connor take a few steps before the young man's comment permeates Paul's haze of alcohol. "What did he say to me?" he asks Connor, his temper surfacing. Paul asked the guy if he had "a problem with him?" Connor holds Paul back and steers him toward the day dock to where the others are waiting.

In the security footage capturing the group's movements from here until they board the boat, you see a very intoxicated Paul swaying as he walks along the dock. He holds a small flashlight in his right hand, as he points it toward the waiting boat. It is clear Morgan is angry with him as she walks ahead of him with her arms folded. Miley is holding Connor's hand, and Anthony and Mallory are laughing and walking along together, clearly in love. It was the last image capturing Mallory Beach alive.

Mallory Beach and Anthony Cook, February 24, 2019.

24/02/2019 01:13:38

Miley and Connor holding hands in the lead, Morgan right behind them, and Paul bringing up the rear. Anthony and Mallory are just behind him (out of picture view. See previous photo.)

As the group walks up the gangway toward the boat, Paul grabs Connor's shirt and pulls him away from Miley. Connor hangs back and Morgan joins Miley on the short walk to the boat. As the group goes to board, Anthony begs Paul to let him drive. It is clear that Paul is heavily intoxicated. When Paul vehemently refuses, Anthony admits later that he considered getting a ride home along with Mallory rather than boarding the boat if Paul was driving. He stayed because he did not want to leave his friends alone. He asks again to drive and is rebuffed. He once again hesitates, considering other options to get home. Reluctantly he helps Mallory into the boat and steps in. It was a decision that would forever haunt him.

At 1:13 a.m., the boat pulls away from the dock and they travel south toward Port Royal Sound, in the direction of the Murdaugh river house. According to Miley Altman, Paul was driving the boat. Connor Cook, she said, stood on the right side of the boat at the console next to Paul. Miley and Morgan were seated on the cooler in front of the console facing the front of the boat with Paul and Connor behind them. Anthony and Mallory were in the back of the boat where Mallory was seated on Anthony's lap. According to the group, as they pulled away from the dock, Paul narrowly missed hitting a sailboat. He then began to drive the boat in circles, enjoying the frustration and anger of the group who wanted to get home.

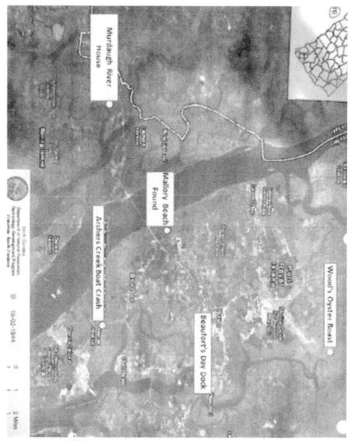

DNR's map of the route the boat took that night.

"We all got irritated," Miley's statement to DNR read. "It was funny at first, but then we ALL got mad and fed up and told Paul to let someone else drive…" Miley yelled at Paul to let Connor drive. At this point, Paul began displaying the traits that the others recognized as his alter ego "Timmy" taking over. Timmy was a nickname Anthony Cook jokingly called Paul once when Paul was really drunk. He would begin doing strange things with his hands. His fingers would splay out as though he could not force them back together. His eyes would stare at you in a penetrating gaze that was unnerving to many. It was usually at this time that a fight would break out.

Once Miley confronted Paul, his Timmy side took over. He "got aggressive" and yelled that it was "his boat and no one else was going to drive it," Miley said in her statement. "Paul drove almost all the way" to Sands Beach in Port Royal, Morgan Doughty wrote in her statement to DNR. "From there, we begged Connor to drive." According to DNR's timeline, the boat slowed down at 2:20 a.m. as Murdaugh moved to the front of the boat to argue with his soon-to-be-ex-girlfriend, Morgan Doughty. According to Morgan, Paul "got close to my face screaming, cussing and saying horrible things." Miley stated she saw Morgan push Paul back and shout, "What? Are you going to hit me like you have all those times before?" At that, Paul slapped her face and she hit him back before crumpling onto the cooler next to Miley and pulling a blanket over her head.

Connor had grabbed the wheel when Paul abandoned it to confront Morgan. He had taken control of the wheel a few times, including when Paul let go of it to strip down to his boxers in his anger; something the group said they had seen him do before. In a white-hot rage, Paul grabbed the wheel from Connor. Morgan had embarrassed him in front of his peers and let them know he had hit her before. Everyone was yelling. Mallory said something to Paul in defense of Morgan. Paul turned to face her at the back of the boat and made a gesture with his hand as though imitating a gun. Anthony said to him, "You better think about that Paul!" With that, Paul turned and pushed the boat throttle all the way over.

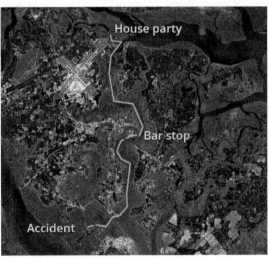

Map of stops that night/morning.

28

30201 11.4 ft W80° 42.717' 59.2 °F	35 ft	0:00:01 24 mph 247.6° true		2/24/2019 2:20:31 AM N32° 21.741'	
30202 14.5 ft W80° 42.723' 59.2 °F	36 ft	0:00:01 24 mph 246.0° true		2/24/2019 2:20:32 AM N32° 21.738'	
30203 17.5 ft W80° 42.730' 59.2 °F	42 ft	0:00:01 29 mph 244.2° true		2/24/2019 2:20:33 AM N32° 21.736'	⚔ ⚔
30204 20.6 ft W80° 42.737' 59.2 °F	197 ft	0:00:06 22 mph 243.9° true		2/24/2019 2:20:34 AM N32° 21.733'	
30205 19.4 ft W80° 42.772' 59.2 °F	30 ft	0:00:01 21 mph 280.8° true		2/24/2019 2:20:40 AM N32° 21.719'	
30206 19.7 ft W80° 42.777' 59.2 °F	18 ft	0:00:01 12 mph 325.7° true		2/24/2019 2:20:41 AM N32° 21.720'	
30207 15.3 ft W80° 42.779' 59.2 °F	14 ft	0:00:01 10 mph 349.2° true		2/24/2019 2:20:42 AM N32° 21.722'	
30208 12.5 ft W80° 42.780' 59.2 °F	25 ft	0:00:01 17 mph 337.5° true		2/24/2019 2:20:43 AM N32° 21.724'	
30209 9.3 ft W80° 42.782' 59.2 °F	24 ft	0:00:01 16 mph 332.7° true		2/24/2019 2:20:44 AM N32° 21.728'	
30210 1.1 ft 21.732' W80° 42.784' 59.2 °F	19 ft	0:00:03 4.4 mph	336.9° true	2/24/2019 2:20:45 AM N32°	
30211 1.7 ft 21.735' W80° 42.785' 59.3 °F	17 ft	0:00:26 0.4 mph	93.1° true	2/24/2019 2:20:48 AM N32°	
30212 21.735' W80° 42.782' 59.7 °F	9 ft	0:00:45 0.1 mph	36.3° true	2/24/2019 2:21:14 AM N32°	

DNR's GPS table shows the speed of the boat at time of impact: 2:20:33 a.m., 29 mph. Its engine finally stops at 2:21:14 a.m.

According to DNR's timeline, the boat's speed increased at 2:20 a.m. The temperature outside was a chilly 58 degrees with a water temperature of only 54 degrees. Heavy sea fog had settled in; a thick blanket of white miasma that the small flashlight Connor was using to navigate with barely penetrated. Wind whipped across the group in blasts of frigid air as the boat ploughed recklessly through the water. Anthony got down on the floor of the rear of the boat and pulled Mallory down on top of him, his feet braced against the boat seat. Morgan was still under the blanket. Only Miley saw what was coming as she faced the front of the boat, fighting to keep her long hair from whipping her face.

Berkeley Bridge connects Port Royal Island to the Marine Corps

Recruit Depot, carrying vehicles over Archers Creek. According to police reports, a boat carrying a group of intoxicated young adults in the early morning hours of January 24, 2019, with heavy fog, struck the pilings of the narrow opening beneath the bridge. Miley was the first to see it: a maze of pilings and dolphin heads with only a mere 12' feet of space between them to navigate beneath the bridge. The high tide was rushing and pulling at the boat, adding to the increased speed until it felt like a runaway train. It was high tide with a water height of 7.5 feet, 58 degrees, and 100% humidity.

According to Miley's statement, the bridge "came out of nowhere." Right before impact, she screamed Connor's name and yelled, "Watch out!" The Sea Hunt hit a dolphin head just to the left of the front bow, deflecting the boat to the right with hull splitting force. Anthony and Mallory were hurled from the boat toward the bridge pilings. Morgan was flung to the left side of the boat where her hand was caught between a piling and the side of the hull. Several fingers split open. Connor, who had been standing next to Paul with the flashlight, was hurled forward where his face hit a bar and broke several plastic rod holders lining the console. His jaw broke in several places and a large gash split the left side of his jawline.

The boat continued its trajectory until it bottomed out on the rocky shoreline to the right of the bridge. Screams filled the night as the stunned group tried to assess the bodily damage as blood coated the floor of the boat. Anthony finally bobbed to the surface on the other side of the bridge, several feet from the boat and began swimming against the strong current to get back. He had a dislocated shoulder. It was then he realized he didn't see Mallory and frantically began searching the water's surface for her. When he didn't see her, he dove beneath the frigid and murky surface again and again, battling the undertow the entire time. He finally pulled himself to shore only to realize he was on the wrong bank of Archers Creek. The wrecked boat was across the water where Morgan and Miley were screaming hysterically, "Where's Mallory?"

Impact transfer on the boat console from hitting two more pilings, after the dolphin head. Photo courtesy: DNR

Chapter Three
Who Was Driving the Boat?

Connor Cook, with a jaw broken in four places and a lacerated chin, called 911 as chaos ensued around him. Screams of "Mallory!" are heard over and over from Miley and Morgan. A scuffle going on between Anthony and Paul can be heard in the background. Anthony, who had been in the fast-moving current for 15 minutes trying to find his girlfriend, has made it back to the shoreline where the boat is grounded. He sees Paul in the water with his arms wrapped around a piling and shouts to him, "Just put your feet down; it's not that deep right there." Once a very intoxicated Paul Murdaugh drags himself up onto the rocky slope, Anthony tackles him and screams, "Is this what you wanted? Is this what you f#@king wanted?" You can hear Anthony screaming at him as Connor tries desperately to give information to the 911 operator. The phone is ringing:

"Paul, what bridge is this?" Connor yells.
"911, what is your emergency?" a tired dispatcher begins her routine but very shortly realizes this will not be an easy exchange. "Hello? Police, fire, EMS."
Miley is screaming at Anthony and Paul to please stop fighting.
Connor: "We're in a boat crash on Archer's Creek."
Dispatcher: "Whereabouts on Archer Street?"
Connor: "In Archer's Creek. The only bridge on Archer's Creek."
Dispatcher: "Archer Street?"
Connor: "Archer's Creek."
Dispatcher: "Archer's Creek."
Connor: "Parris Island."
Dispatcher: "Ok. What's going on?"
Connor: "It's by Parris Island."
Dispatcher: "What's going on?"

Connor: "We're in a boat crash."

Dispatcher: "You're in a what...what kind of boat?"

Connor: "We're in a boat crash."

Morgan is screaming, "Oh my God, there's so much blood!"

Dispatcher: "Did you say a boat crash?" Sounds of yelling are heard in the background throughout the call from the others.

Dispatcher: "So, are you at the docks?"

Connor: "No, we just crashed in a boat."

Dispatcher: "Are you in the water?"

Connor: "We're in the boat. We have someone missing."

Dispatcher: "Hold on one second, ok?"

Connor: "Paul! What is this bridge called?"

Miley: "Mallory!!!"

Connor: "Please send someone."

Dispatcher: (out of breath and typing furiously) "We're coming, we're coming, ok?"

The dispatcher and Connor go back and forth about where they are. He keeps repeating, "There's only one bridge on Archer's Creek." The dispatcher is sounding more flustered as the call continues. She is trying to find out where they are, thinking they are out somewhere in the water.

Morgan is screaming, "There's so much blood!"

Dispatcher: "Who's that in the background?"

Connor had climbed up to the bridge to make the call due to all the screaming on the boat.

Connor: "There's six of us and one is missing," he repeated.

Dispatcher: "Ok...six and one is gone. Do you guys have life jackets on?"

Connor: "Yes, ma'am, we have more than enough life jackets. We're on the bank."

Dispatcher: Ok. Who is missing?"

Connor: "A female, Mallory Beach." Morgan is still screaming about the blood as the chaos continues.

Dispatcher: "Ok, what is your name, sir?"

Connor: "My name is Connor Cook."

Beaufort County Dispatch at 2:29 a.m.: "I'm calling about a disabled boat...a boat crash. It's 6 people on board. They currently have one missing. They are right there on Archer's Creek which is right there near Parris Island. There's a bridge on Parris Island and they're underneath it. They crashed into the bridge."

Other emergency crews are notified.

"I'll be in route to the Bell Bridge. Can you also notify Port Royal and let BMO know as well?"

Beaufort County Dispatch: "It's one female. Uhh…that's all the description I have right now."

EMS 1: "I respond to an accident with injuries, 50 Marina's Drive on Parris Island…There's going to be a change to that location. They're on Malecon Drive, down right before you get to the traffic circle."

Dispatcher: "Ok. County's on scene. Port Royal's on scene. Evidently the girl was sitting on her boyfriend's lap when they hit the bridge at a high rate of speed and now, she's missing. They just keep telling us they hit the bridge. 310 got on scene. He said the fog is pretty thick and he couldn't even find them."

The sea fog obscured everything. Connor was the only one who saw Mallery after she went into the water. He simply said, "I saw her for a minute and then she was gone."

Archers Creek facing the bridge. The rocky embankment where the boat came to rest is at the right beneath the bridge.
Photo courtesy of Nicholas Ginn/Natural Graphics Photography.

Dolphin head (front center) with the bank to the right.
Photo: Nicholas Ginn/Natural Graphics Photography

The embankment where the boat came to rest.
Photo by John Drzemala.

Beaufort Water Search & Rescue boat. Photo courtesy of
Nicholas Ginn/Natural Graphics Photography

Clay Emminger, boat captain for Beaufort Water Search & Rescue.
Photo courtesy of Nicholas Ginn/Natural Graphics Photography

Clay Emminger is the captain for Beaufort Water Search &
Rescue. He and William "Rosco" Towne took my husband, John
Drzemala and I, along with professional photographer Nick Ginn
and my good friend Linda Heir out to see where the boat crash
happened. Along the way he talked to me about the events of that

night and what could have been done differently. As we spoke of Mallory, he said, "Mallory would have had to have been along the shoreline all the way. I was asking dispatch to try to give me information: ask the witnesses what time she went in? The exact time that they got close to was to check the 911 call. That's frustrating. To know the exact time, she went into the water would have been paramount to gauging her location based on the current, wind, direction of the wind, temperatures, etc. And that's what I think; that's the thing that's plagued this whole thing is there's so many inconsistencies.

"As for the kids on the boat, you're not supposed to be drinking, you know you're not supposed to be drinking anyway, right? The most important thing going through your head is you wanna find your friend, right? Get her back. Maybe we can escape this without getting in trouble, right? You know, I get it. But that time frame is critical for us because that matters from where our search starts.

"We use buoys that we put in the water. They call this "dropping data." Drop that data. How long did it take to go from one buoy in that time period to another so that you could take that information? Apply it to what time the water reaches a certain location, or different buoy. A person went in here, then you would calculate that. I know it's been this long. This should be my starting point. OK, according to my set and drift, right? What is the current doing, the winds doing, all that stuff, all those are factors, even the winds are a factor because the tide, like I showed you in the creek, if the tides going out and the winds pushing in, it's gonna affect your setting drift. Second, it's gonna affect how fast an object is moving in the water because the wind may push against it like right now, right?

"There were so many people showing up to help search. They would ask me, hey, we're here to help search for Mallory or search for the girl. They asked me which way do you think we need to go? Of course, I can't tell them which way to go. I can tell them where we're searching from, OK, but she could be anywhere. At this point, we don't know which is true. We don't know. When you have that many people, do you start worrying that you're gonna have to go rescue *them* at some point? I mean, that's always a concern. Because a lot of the people that came down here are not from here. And I hate to use that phrase, "You ain't from around here, are you?" But you got to know what you're doing in this water. This was seven feet right there, right? Tide's gonna drop. How much further? So that's what we just came across in a few hours and they really have a certain amount of time. I can take you in here, but then we have got to go. And they wouldn't know that. My grandfather would say "Tide and time wait for no man."

This author interviews Captain Clay Emminger aboard the Beaufort Water Search and Rescue boat on Archers Creek, Oct. 3, 2022. Photo courtesy of John Drzemala.

Clay went on to tell me how certain GPS systems on boats have "tracks." "They're like breadcrumbs that let you follow the same route back. If they had used that that night, it might have turned out differently."

When we arrived at the bridge where the collision occurred, he pointed out the dolphin head where the boat first hit before glancing off to the right and impacting two other pilings before coming to rest on the shoreline. The boat showed transfer marks from each of those impacts. There had been a swipe of white paint on the metal cable surrounding the dolphin head from the first collision that ripped the hull open. You can no longer see the paint today, but it showed that it was high tide when the boat hit. He also pointed out that it was only 12' feet wide between the pilings holding up the bridge. Only

12 feet to navigate a boat between the bridge pilings to the other side! Paul's boat was 8' wide. That left only 2' on either side for error. You are dealing with a dark night, sea fog lying along the water, high speeds, and a drunk driver.

Rosco, to demonstrate what it felt like to be going the speed the Sea Hunt was traveling when it collided, pushed the throttle to 30 mph. I was shocked! 30 mph on the water is entirely different than it feels like in a car. The front of the boat lifted, and I was pushed over, my hair whipping my face. You could sense the loss of control if the person driving had been intoxicated. It was such a surprise to feel the power of the water and wind at that speed.

William "Rosco" Towne with Beaufort Water Search & Rescue. Photo courtesy of Nicholas Ginn/Natural Graphics Photography.

Rosco shared with me that the night before Mallory was found, several people were gigging along the bank near where she came to rest. So close, but in the dark they did not see her, or the tide had not pushed her to that point yet.

As with many sad outcomes, there may have been actions taken to find Mallory alive. Better communication for sure was needed. The entire 911 call had been so hectic. The boat crash location took valuable minutes to ascertain as dispatchers went back and forth about the name of the bridge and the coordinates. Then there was the timing: a split second where the boat's speed and the pilings' spacing was all that was needed for Mallory to hit a piling head on, but for Anthony to sail through the opening and end up on the other side of the bridge. Paul too had missed hitting the fiberglass sheathing around the poles and ended up in the water. It is one of those senseless things that haunts loved ones. What if? If only…

Low tide at Archers Creek. Photo: Rebecca F. Pittman

Thus began an investigation that would bring the Murdaugh dynasty to their knees. More than the headlights shining on the tragic form of a young man left on a dark back road in Hampton county; more than the headlight of a barreling train hitting the Murdaugh patriarch in 1940; it would be the feeble light from a flashlight trying without success to navigate a speeding boat through impenetrable sea fog that would illuminate a family so corrupt, it would take volumes of case files and man hours to even put a dent in the decades of subterfuge and deaths. Whether fate had also been at the wheel that night, it would be a hollow victory for the Beach family who lost their beautiful daughter at the hands of one who had always been protected and bailed out by his powerful family. While the entire world would give anything to have Mallory back, her death put the stone in David's sling and hurled it at the Goliath called Murdaugh.

Beaufort County Sheriff's Department were the first responders the night of the boat crash. They found a stumbling Paul Murdaugh, bleary-eyed and at times incoherent, wandering around in his wet boxers. Anthony Cook, Mallory's boyfriend, was crying uncontrollably from the seat of a patrol car, his body turned in the open door and running his hand over his face and through his hair. From his right hand dangled a white bandage tied around an injury. He ignored his dislocated shoulder. His shirt was gone, he was only in his jeans. The deputy there with Anthony tried his best to calm him down and get information. Twice he pushed a cigarette on the young man to steady his nerves. Anthony replied that he had "quit smoking three months ago."

During a deposition on June 9, 2020, that would come later when Renee S. Beach filed a lawsuit against Gregory M. Parker—the owner of Parker's Kitchen where Paul had illegally purchased alcohol—Anthony Cook was represented by Attorney Mark Tinsley. Paul's attorney, Jim Griffin, was there to protect Paul's interests, as the identity of the driver of the boat would be crucial in the lawsuit. Anthony Cook gave this statement:

Anthony: "...we argued the whole...the whole way, everybody was fighting and arguing. We drifted around in circles numerous times. We idled long. I mean, it was...Miley was steady hollering that she had to work the next morning. She was ready to go. That she wanted to hurry up and get home and all Paul was doing was making a fool of himself. Paul for some reason acted like he was on drugs or something. He started taking his clothes off during one of the arguments and it is 40 degrees outside and whenever...however long it took us to get to the dock to where the boat took off which from what I saw on the GPS wasn't but a few minutes before we hit the bridge. From downtown Beaufort to there, we didn't do nothing but argue the whole time. And that's when the fight happened, or the argument, or whatever you want to call it, where the boat took off...it felt like 10 hours...but I think it was over an hour."

Jim Griffin asks Anthony:

"You said Paul got mad. What was Paul mad about?"

"Because we was trying to...everybody was trying to talk him into letting me drive the boat and he wasn't having it no different." He said, "It's his boat and don't nobody know the "effing" river like he does, and he is the only one driving the "effing" boat."

Attorney Griffin asks, "Did anybody drive the boat besides Paul?"

"Connor was holding the wheel when he was taking his clothes off or walking circles in the boat. There were numerous times when he would walk to the front of the boat and leave the boat going."

Griffin: "Connor was...when Paul walked off, he could grab the wheel?"

Mr. Tinsley: "Object to form."

Anthony: "Yes."

Griffin: "Is that what he did?"

Tinsley: "Object to the form."

Anthony: "Yes."

Griffin: "And Paul was at the center console also?"

Anthony: "I thought you asked me if Paul was at the center. Connor always stood on the right-hand side of the center console to watch the GPS while Paul was driving."

Griffin: "And Paul was on the left side of the steering wheel?"

Anthony: "Yes."

Griffin: "With the exception of when Paul would walk off?"

Anthony: "Connor was there. But we wouldn't be doing nothing but idling three or four miles an hour."

Griffin: "And Paul started taking his clothes off?"

Anthony: "He stripped all the way down to his boxers."

Griffin: "And you found that unusual?"

Anthony: "No sir. I have seen him do it a few times when he gets drunk. I don't know why he does it."

Meanwhile, Morgan Doughty, Paul's girlfriend, was giving her statement about what happened.

Q. "Did you at any point take any action to take control of the boat?"

A. "No, Ma'am. I don't know how to drive a boat, especially at night."

Q. "Did anyone else?"

A. "Paul was very, like, this is my boat; you're not driving it. That's about it."

Q. "Where were you looking when the crash occurred?"

A. "I had my head in the blanket and then Miley said Connor's name a couple of times and I looked up and in that same second is when we hit it."

Q. "Did you see the bridge before you hit it?"

A. "No, ma'am. Just a split second of it."

Q. "Do you know why Miley screamed Connor's name?"

A. "No, ma'am."

Q. "You said the boat sped up?"

A. "Mm-hmm."

Q. "Do you know what caused it to speed up?"

A. "I've gone over it in my head so many times and, like, is...the only thing I can think of is, like, Paul is an angry drunk, and he thinks he is invincible and so when he's angry, I just feel like—he put it in full motion."

The questions continue, asking if Morgan looked back to see who was driving when the boat sped up? She did not. Did she see whose hand was on the throttle? She did not. Was anyone wearing life jackets? "No, ma'am." She is then asked about the lights on the boat, and she says Connor was holding a single flashlight to try and illuminate the river. She was unclear which hand he was holding it in.

Q. "Did you end up in the water?"

A. "No, ma'am...Mallory, Anthony, and Paul" were ejected when the boat hit the dolphin heads and ended up in the water.

Q. "I think you said you'd been posting to social media at various times during the night. Did you do that using your phone?"

A. "Yes, ma'am." After the crash, "it was dead. When we crashed, everybody was trying to look around and find Mallory and we need to call 911. I think my phone was dead, so we couldn't use it. I think it was Miley's phone that 911 was called off of. But I don't remember."

The statements taken down about the events of that fateful morning left investigators with little to hang their hats on. Conflicting stories of who was at the wheel at the time of impact made some wonder if the real driver was being shielded or had the confusion on the boat really obscured whose hands had hold of the wheel at that crucial moment. The fact that evidence disappeared did not help move the needle. This would not be an easy resolution of facts.

The passengers that night: (Left to right) Connor Cook & Miley Altman; Anthony Cook & Mallory Beach; Morgan Doughty & Paul Murdaugh.

The questions about who was driving the boat had been paramount that foggy morning as EMTs, ambulances, and law enforcement continued to arrive at the crash site. Flashing lights lit up the cold February morning and pierced the fog in an array of white, red, and blue bursts of color. Dash and body cams picked up the voices of myriad responders asking questions and shouting orders. Many were told that all the boaters were present and being looked over by medics, all but the missing teenager. Morgan Doughty had remained seated in the boat and was being attended to for her lacerated fingers. It was her blood seen on the left side of the steering console at the bow of the boat near where she had been seated. To the right of the console was Connor's blood where his face hit an overhead metal bar and broke two hard plastic fishing rod holders in the console.

Miley and Connor were placed in an ambulance and were being attended to. Miley was unhurt. She said when she saw the bridge, she "braced herself," saving herself from being flung about the boat as the others had. Anthony was still seated in the open car door of a patrol car, desperate for them to find Mallory. He called his mother, who was with SLED (South Carolina Law Enforcement Division) and told her to "get to Beaufort quick." It was the wee hours of the morning, close to 3 a.m., when Beverly Cook was awakened from

44

her sleep by her son's frantic phone call. It would be a long hour drive to get to Beaufort from Hampton.

As Anthony is explaining to the deputy, who was treating him with kindness and trying to settle him down, he had "begged and begged and begged Paul to let me drive the boat." He told the deputy that he pulled Mallory into his lap on the floor of the stern when Paul's driving became erratic, and he finally pushed the throttle all the way over. The front of the boat lifted into the air as it hurtled through the frigid water and sea fog. "The next thing I knew, I was in the water," he said.

While Anthony waited for his parents to arrive, weeping uncontrollably, Paul was wandering around in his wet boxers trying to focus on what was happening. The body cam video of a responder is heard talking to him; Paul's answers are slurred and faltering:

"Can I use your phone?" Paul asks the responder.

"I don't got my phone on me, Bubba," he replies.

"You ain't got your phone on you?" Paul asks incredulously.

"No, you dropped yours in the grass right back there."

"That don't surprise me," Paul says undaunted, swaying slightly.

"Have you been checked out by an ambulance?" the responder asks him.

"Yeah, I'm fine," Paul answers, sounding like he has other stuff on his mind.

"What's your last name, buddy?"

"Murdaugh."

"M-U-R.."

"D-A-U-G-H," Paul fills in."

"And your first name?"

"Paul," sounding a little lost and weak.

He finally asks about Mallory.

"They're down there right now looking for her," the responder tells him.

"They got a good search on her, right?" Paul asks, slurring. "They're probably gonna find her easy, don't you think?"

"They're down there right now looking," he repeats.

"You know they got a search, right?" Paul is sounding more under the influence during this conversation.

"Yeah, they got a good team down there looking for her, okay?" The responder is being patient with the repetitive questions.

Paul, sounding like he's begging, repeats his original question, "Hey, can I use your phone?"

"I don't have my phone on me," the responder states again. "Here, stay right here, I'm going to go get that one you dropped on the ground back there." Someone calls out they picked it up. "You got it already?" the responder asks the other officer.

Paul is no longer present during the body cam audio. He has his phone, and he is calling the one person who can get him out of this mess. Not his father Alex Murdaugh, the one who owns the boat he just wrecked. No, Paul brings in the big guns. His grandfather, Randolph Murdaugh III.

The responders discuss what's going on. They discuss the boat impacting the piling and ejecting the "young female from the boat." One mentions the tide is going out and that they have people walking downstream along the marsh in hopes of seeing her. He tells the other officer that the lady still in the boat "is the most severe of the injuries we have of the five that were in the boat."

The conversation now picks up on the car cam where you hear Anthony crying and saying, "I'm f#@*ed." Anthony told his mother that there are 50 cops here, coastguard, everything. He then tells her to call Mallory's parents. He keeps repeating, we can't find Mallory. The officer gets on the phone with Anthony's mother and tells her he is doing everything he can to keep Anthony calm.

Apparently, Paul has wandered over across from Anthony and is looking at him. Anthony suddenly shouts to the officer standing there, "Get that mother#@er away from me!" The officer hangs up from talking to Anthony's Mom, and says to him, "Are you talking about that one with no shirt on?" Noticing how heavy Anthony is breathing and the look on his face, he tells him, "I don't want you to get in any trouble, you hear me? Did you hear what I said? Your parents are on their way." You can hear how heavily Anthony is breathing.

"That motherf#@ker wouldn't let me drive," Anthony says in a low voice.

"I don't want you to get in any trouble," the officer repeats.

"*He* won't get in no trouble," Anthony says.

"Oh yes, he will," the officer assures him.

Suddenly, Anthony explodes. It was reported it was at that moment Paul grinned at him. Perhaps he overheard Anthony say

Paul wouldn't get in any trouble.

"Are you f#@king smiling?" Anthony screams. "You think it's f#@king funny? My f#@king girlfriend is gone, Bo! You think it's f#@king funny?"

The officer is trying to calm Anthony down. "Sit down, sit down, sit down."

"I hope you rot in f#@king hell!" he screams, words that would later haunt him.

"Here. Here," the officer tells Anthony. "Smoke your cigarette. He's going away."

"You know," Anthony says, breathing heavily, but calmer now, "about a month ago, a year ago, him and her got in a wreck together. Only she lived," he said brokenly, meaning Paul's girlfriend lived, but his didn't.

Anthony Cook seated in the patrol car as the others are taken to the Beaufort Memorial Hospital. He alone remained behind. Police dash cam.

He is referring to Paul driving his truck a year prior while intoxicated and missing a turn, rolling the white pickup truck into a ditch with Morgan onboard. Morgan had crawled out and dialed 911. Paul crawled out and sat on the grass, angry that she had called 911. He called his father or grandfather. Within minutes, Maggie, Alex, and Randolph showed up. Without even asking if the two teenagers were alright, they began hurriedly removing guns and beer cans from the truck. Randolph was upset with Morgan for calling 911. Shortly, a tow truck showed up and hauled away the truck to a gentleman who worked on all the Murdaugh vehicles.

At the boat crash scene, Anthony is still in anguish.

"I'll be 21 in three days, man," Anthony said, his voice cracking.

"What about the driver?" the officer asks him. "Is he 21?" Anthony replies, "No." "Has everyone on the boat been drinking?"

"Yeah," Anthony replies.

"The driver...," the officer begins, but Anthony cuts him off.

"I begged and begged for him to let me drive that boat."

"How much has the driver had to drink?" the officer presses.

"I'll tell you this much," Anthony says. "We stopped...I don't even know where the f#@k we were. We stopped in downtown Beaufort and me and him almost fought on the f#@king dock because I told him he didn't need to be goin' into a f#@king bar and we needed to be goin' home."

"So, he was drinkin' at the bar?"

"I reckon...I didn't go in," Anthony said.

He is asked if that was how the boat got going so fast. Anthony answers, "I don't even know. I got to the point to where I grabbed my girlfriend, and I got in the bottom of the f#@king boat. I was holding on with my eyes closed and the next thing I know, I'm in the f#@king water."

There's a pause when the officer asks if he can feel the heater and Anthony tells him he's not cold. The officer tells him he *is* cold, he's just in shock and doesn't know it.

Anthony asks him, "Is anyone in the water looking for her?"

"We got the fire department, DNR's in the water, the coast guard is on the way with a chopper."

"She could be on the bottom of the river, man," he sobs.

"They've got a dive team, we got a bunch of resources, alright? Regardless of the outcome, we will find her, alright? You got to keep faith that she's somewhere on the bank, you see what I'm sayin'?" The officer keeps reminding Anthony that he is concerned about him at that time and tries to keep him calm.

"Where did y'all put in at?" he asks Anthony.

"Chechessee Island, the only island on Chechessee." Anthony says, and then bows his head and cries.

Chechessee Island: Murdaugh's River House.

"Y'all know Alex Murdaugh?" Anthony asked suddenly.
"Yeah, I know that name," the officer responds.
"That's his *son*," Anthony says in a firm tone.
"That's him driving the boat?" the officer asks.
"Good luck!" Anthony declares.

Boat Diagram showing positions of passengers prior to crash.
Connor is seen holding a flashlight. It would have been dark and foggy.
Diagram by Rebecca F. Pittman

Chapter Four
Obstruction of Justice?

1st Sargent Adam Henderson stated in his Supplemental Report the following for the events of that fateful morning:

"At approximately 3:00 am, Sunday 2-24-2019, I received an incident text from CO Austin Pritcher stating that he was responding to a boating accident at the bridge at Archers Creek on Parris Island and that one person was still missing…. On my way, CO Pritcher informed me that it appeared that alcohol may have been involved. I asked if there were searchers out. CO Pritcher informed me that there were multiple vessels searching as well as people looking from the bridge and along the banks. I was getting close to the scene, so I advised CO Pritcher to go to the hospital to interview and get statements from the other passengers to try to determine who was the operator of the boat. I arrived on scene at approximately 3:40 am and went down to the vessel involved in the accident. I photographed the vessel from land, observing blood in the floor of the vessel and what appeared to be the primary impact on the port forward bow."

Photo of damage to the port side of the bow. (DNR)

Boat filmed from front where Morgan and Mallory had been seated on the cooler. Connor's blood from his injury is to the left. (DNR)

"I spoke with Jack Keener with the Beaufort Sheriff's Department and SGT Keven Heany w/PRPD. They advised that one of the occupants Kevin (Anthony) Cook was still on the scene with his mother and was the missing girl's (Mallory Beach) boyfriend. I went and introduced myself to Keith (Anthony) Cook and his mother and asked if I could speak with him about the incident. He was sitting on the ground with a blanket wrapped around him and appeared to be a little distant in thought."

Beverly Cook, Anthony's mother, had been awakened from sleep at around 3:00 am by her ringing cell phone. It was Anthony, clearly distraught and begging her to come to Beaufort "quick." She and her husband drove the long hour drive and found Anthony seated in an open patrol car door, turned to the side, his head in his hands. Beverly placed a warm parka around his shoulders and tried to comfort him as seen in the dash cam video. He is seen walking along the bank, wrapped from the waist down in a white medic's blanket. Finally, he collapses to the ground and curls up beneath the blanket, beyond comfort. His mother and father kneel next to him as Sgt. Henderson approaches and asks him about the events of the evening.

Anthony's recitation of the night and early morning events was the same as he stated before. When asked by Henderson, "Who was driving the boat?" he responded that Paul and Connor were arguing about who should be driving the boat and all he could say was that Paul Murdaugh was driving when they left the dock (day dock after

Luther's bar stop). He looked up at me and said, "Me and Paul have been friends for a long time but no more. I can't forgive him for this." I asked him if Paul was driving. He told me again that he couldn't be sure, but he knew that Paul was driving when they left. I asked him if he would be willing to give me a written statement on paper. He said he would if I would give him a little bit. He said he wasn't going anywhere."

It was a statement of truth. According to his mother, Anthony stayed all day long, and each day after that, at the crash scene, watching as the myriad boats, divers, and helicopters searched for the love of his life.

Anthony with an arm sling for his dislocated shoulder. He refused to leave the bank as the search for Mallory Beach continued.

As Anthony Cook watched and waited from the shoreline, the Emergency Ward at Beaufort Memorial Hospital was dealing with its own chaotic scene. The boat crash passengers had been wheeled in from the ambulances. Only Miley Altman came in under her own steam. She remained steadfast by Connor's side and refused to leave his room. The staff told her she would have to get a Visitor's Pass in order to stay, which she did. Paul, who had given the ambulance EMTs trouble all the way in, was trying to climb off the gurney as they wheeled him to his ER room. He was still clad only in boxers and repeatedly threw off the blanket with which they had covered him. You could hear him down the hallway as he belligerently harassed the staff and shouted orders.

Within ten minutes of the group arriving, Alex Murdaugh and Randolph Murdaugh III strode into the ER. In typical fashion, Alex began gladhanding the staff as if he was running for Mayor. If there was any doubt as to who this guy was, Alex had clipped his shiny Assistant Solicitor badge to his pants' pocket where all could see. As Randolph headed to Room 10, where his red-eyed grandson lay, Alex went into full containment mode.

Alex with his badge in full view at the Beaufort Memorial Hospital as he talks to Pritchard, and while on the stand in his own defense during the double murder trial, downplaying that he ever used the badge to influence others as to the power he wielded as Assistant Solicitor.

Connor's parents were also advised that their son was in the hospital. Marty and Christine Cook drove as fast as they could through the darkness from Hampton to Beaufort. Along the way, Marty's cell phone rang frequently. It was Alex Murdaugh informing him that his son Connor had been driving the boat. It would be the precursor to an all-out effort to pin the boat crash on Connor Cook's drunken driving. At the hospital, Alex corralled each set of frantic parents as they arrived to see their kids. Before they could get into their ER rooms, Alex was already spinning his story of who was driving and telling them all not to say anything to the authorities. He had their backs; he would represent the entire party. Then he was back on the phone, incessantly prowling the

Emergency Ward hallways, putting things into place for a cover-up.

Alex on the phone in the Emergency Ward hallway.

Based on reports from the nursing staff, more than one overheard Alex on his phone, speaking to whom they assumed was his wife. He was heard to assure her that Paul was fine. Then after a pause, he said, "She's gone, Baby, she's gone." Mallory had only been missing for a few hours and Alex had written her off as dead. He made calls to his brother John Marvin and countless other people as he put the wheels in motion to save his son.

They wheeled Connor out into the hallway, headed for a CAT scan. His jaw was clearly broken, probably in more than one place. Alex blocked them, and whispered into Connor's ear, "Don't say anything. I'll take care of this. Just don't be saying anything." Connor, clearly agitated from all that happened, was irritated at Alex's interference, and may have begun to realize that he could be blamed for the crash.

Marty and Christine Cook arrived, out of breath and panicked. Alex made a beeline for them, once again reiterating that he would handle everything, and that Connor was driving the boat. Marty stated later in a documentary that it really upset him. "I was trying to get to my son!" he said, hotly.

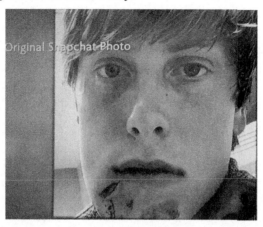

Connor Cook's snapchat photo of his face before surgery.

Morgan had been taken to get her fingers sutured and was finally put into a private room in the ER. Randolph appeared at her doorway, and it unnerved her. Alex also tried to get in. She begged the nurse to keep him away from her. Alex could be heard in the hallway badgering the staff and announcing he was the kids' attorney and needed to speak to them. Several of the staff stated they smelled alcohol on his breath.

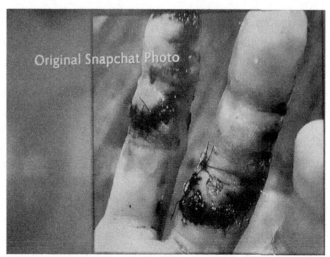

Morgan Doughty's snapchat photo of her sutured fingers, while at the hospital.

In Room 10, things were not going well. Both Connor and Paul had refused to take a Sobriety Test. The hospital and officials were requesting it to gauge their alcohol levels. When law enforcement entered and announced they needed a statement from Paul about the morning's events leading up to the boat crash, Randolph interceded and said, "You can't interview him right now. He's drunker than Cooter Brown."

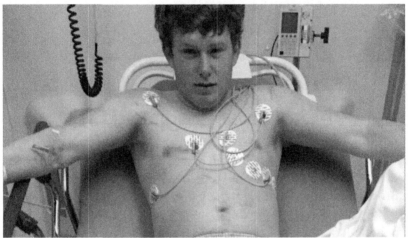

Paul Murdaugh in Room 10. His stomach was covered in scratches, but he was uninjured. For the staff responsible for taking his vitals and overseeing his charts, it would be a long morning.

"Drunker than Cooter Brown," is a favorite Southern go-to when describing someone drunk out of their mind. Cooter Brown lived along the Mason-Dixon line at the time of the Civil War. He had family on both sides, and, not wishing to be drafted by either the North or the South, he decided to get drunk—and stay drunk—so that he wouldn't have to fight in the war. Inebriety has been measured against Cooter Brown's extended binge ever since.

The nursing staff had pretty much had their fill of the Murdaugh's, no matter what badge was hanging from Alex's pocket. He was seen scanning the patient board in the hallway to find where each of the boat passengers were roomed. He was told repeatedly to stay in his son's room and to stop roaming the hallways or attempting to speak to the patients. It did no good. Like father, like son, Paul continually unhooked whatever apparatus was attached to him and also came out into the hallway. They would force him back into his room where his grandfather Randolph continually told him to "Shut Up!" If Paul had hoped that by calling his grandfather, he would get an easier time of it that morning, he was mistaken. Randolph Murdaugh III was clearly angry. Alex had other fish to fry as he continued to try to get at the kids and tell them to keep quiet.

In all the chaos, not one member of law enforcement had called Mallory Beach's parents to tell them their daughter was missing. In a police body cam, you can see Beverly Cook (Anthony's mother) telling the patrolman that someone should call Miss Renee and Mr. Phillip. The police officer can be heard telling her that it was not a good idea. Having them come down there until they knew more would add to the chaotic scene. Beverly tells them that she has their phone numbers, but "I don't want to be the one to make that call." She is clearly concerned that no one has called them.

At some point, Renee Beach heard about the crash. She arrived at the scene at 4:00 am, a full hour after Anthony's parents arrived. She could never have imagined the array of flashing lights, and the noise of sirens and cars pulling up and leaving. Boats were on the water, but it was hard to see them clearly in the fog. You could make out their powerful search lights as they tried valiantly to see anything along the banks or in the water. Hand radios crackled everywhere as reports came in from dispatchers and command centers. But where was her daughter?

1st Sargent Adam Henderson wrote in his report, "I stayed on the scene to secure the vessel and to keep non-essential persons from entering the scene. More family members began arriving on scene. I spoke to the mother and the father (of Mallory) and asked that they stay near where they were parked and not to go down to the water where the vessel was located." He asked his supervisor, Michael Brock, if he should get a chaplain over there for the family.

"I updated Lt. Thomas again at approximately 9:00 am and he indicated he would be on his way to the scene. By approximately 11:00 am, divers were in the water and multiple other SCDNR officers and other agencies had the scene secure." Helicopters were on their way now that the fog had cleared.

Renee and Phillip Beach felt shuttled to the side as they watched helplessly. They begged to go down to the crash site or near the water. "We just wanted to be near it and see what happened," she said sadly. They were refused and told not to go beyond the crime scene tape at the top of the embankment.

Alex had been conversing with Officer Pritcher throughout the morning in the ER hallway. Pritcher was a good friend of Alex's. It did not go unnoticed in later preparations for lawsuits concerning the boat crash, that it was Pritcher who called 1st Sargent Adam Henderson from the hospital to inform him that "Connor Cook may be the Operator based on what he was getting from the hospital." I told him to continue his interviews and try to find out where the trailer for the vessel was located and if it would be possible for us to get it for when we need to remove the boat."

Austin Pritcher, a good friend of the Murdaughs, went to talk to Connor Cook but he was getting an MRI or Xray done. He was told by Investigator Michael Brock to ask the boat crash victims at the hospital to draw where everyone was sitting on the boat. Miley Altman and Morgan Doughty each did a crude drawing.

Morgan Doughty's drawing (l). Miley Altman's drawing (r)
Note where Morgan drew Connor—driving the boat.

After obtaining the drawings, Pritcher was advised by Brock to get an SFTS from Connor. SFTS is a 'standardized field sobriety test' to measure alcohol intake. Connor refused to take one, as did Paul Murdaugh. Due to Paul's crazy behavior, blood was drawn to test for drugs. Every staff member present assumed he must be reacting to some kind of drug. The blood test came back that Paul was 3 times over the legal limit for alcohol. What was most "sobering" is that the blood was drawn almost 3 hours after the boat crash. How high were his levels when the boat hit the bridge?

Morgan Doughty listed her address in Okatie, SC, in the county of Beaufort. Morgan filled out a written statement at the hospital for Officer Pritcher. Her retelling of the outing's events was the same as what had been stated previously. By the time she filled out the report, she had been told by Alex Murdaugh not to say too much. He would handle everything. Paul had repeatedly tried to get to her room but was taken back to Room 10 each time. Morgan did not want to see him. Investigator Brock arrived and stopped Morgan Doughty and talked with her for a short period. The patients would be released soon; all but Connor who was transferred to MUSC for surgery. Morgan's surgery on her hand had taken two hours.

Whether from fear of the Murdaughs or Morgan's genuine recollection of the events, she wrote in her first statement: "We left downtown Beaufort around 2. From there Paul drove, he was very intoxicated as well as Connor. We putted around until Connor took over. We slammed into the bridge." The statement on its own would be damning for Connor. Morgan continued, "Paul drove almost all the way to the Beaufort Sands. From there we begged Connor to drive. Connor took over and the boat was going at a steady speed towards Chechessee. Between the Sands and the Parris Island Bridge, Paul came up from behind and got close to my face screaming, cussing, and saying horrible things. He walked back to the console on the left side. I put my face in the blanket for the rest of the ride. I am unsure of who was driving but the boat's manner was different from when Connor was driving. The speed seemed like the throttle was all the way down."

A nurse reported seeing Miley Altman come up to Morgan and hug her in the hallway as they were being released. The nurse said it looked like Morgan whispered something into Morgan's ear, and she became visibly upset. Whatever Miley said to her, Morgan asked the next day to change her statement. She called Pritcher.

"I saw Anthony on the bank (after the boat came to rest on the rocks)," Morgan stated. "Anthony went back into the water screaming for Mallory.... Connor called 911. 20 minutes later, the police showed up... While Anthony was on the bank, right after he got back out of the water looking for Mallory, Paul kept telling Anthony to "shut up," and to "stop talking." I remember Anthony shoved Paul and hit Paul. Anthony kept screaming Mallory's name in pain. Paul walked away.

"After my surgery," Morgan said, "When I got out, Alex Murdaugh kept trying to enter my room multiple times, but my nurse wound not allow him to. In the hallway, he kept saying I was with him and that he needed to tell me what to say. When I was discharged at 9 am, I went to the bridge and stayed there until 6 when they shut down the search. I have so much going through my head. Last night it all started coming back to me. I have the strongest feeling Paul was driving. Today, Monday morning, I texted Austin (Pritcher) and he allowed me to rewrite this statement now that my head was on right."

Morgan added a few more details. She described how Paul would act when severely intoxicated. "...he would spread his fingers as wide as he could. He would spread his hands and fingers and act real crazy. He walked up one last time before the crash and spit on me and slapped me in the face and walked back around to the console to where he was on the left side when he was driving." Morgan spoke with Investigator Yongue and Investigator Brock again on March 1, 2019. She informed them this wasn't the first time Paul had hit her. She began to cry.

Had Miley whispered to Morgan in that hospital hallway that Alex was trying to frame Connor as the driver? Miley had stayed by his side in the room. Connor may have told her about how Alex stopped him on the way to his CAT scan. Whatever happened to change her mind, Morgan changed her story. She was also through with Paul Murdaugh. Despite his texts trying to get her to talk to him, she held strong. They never dated again.

On March 1, 2019, Investigator Yongue interviewed Anthony. Investigator Brock had done the first interview and wrote Anthony's statement for him due to the injury to his shoulder. Anthony had repeated the same story as the others had about the events leading to the crash. He mentioned that they knew "Paul hit that stage of being drunk," to where "Timmy was out!" Anthony had been the one to give Paul that nickname at a prior party. Paul's fingers would splay out and he became combative.

Paul Murdaugh during his "Timmy" transformation

In Yongue's follow-up interview with Anthony, he gave what might have been the most damning statement concerning who was driving the boat. Younge asked him if he made statements to Paul during their scuffle on the rocks about "killing his girlfriend?" Anthony said, "Yes, I probably did, because Paul had been driving the boat so crazy and that was why his girlfriend was missing."

Miley Altman gave a detailed report, describing how angry Paul became when she told him to let Connor drive the boat. "You think y'all know this river better than me?" he screamed. "This is my boat and I'll be damned if someone else drives my boat!" She described him taking off his clothes and sitting in front of Morgan yelling at her. Anthony told him if he was going to drive, then to let him off at the next dock. Miley described that Paul took her phone and "called his grandad right away. They made Paul, Connor and I ride together in one ambulance and Morgan in a separate one. Paul got aggressive with the EMS people, cussing them and being rude to the point of him almost having to be thrown into a cop car. They strapped him down as Connor and I sat next to each other and rode to the hospital."

It was during the ambulance ride that Miley and Connor overheard Paul on the cell phone saying "Cotton Top" was driving the boat. "Cotton Top" is Connor Cook's nickname. The two of them just looked at each other and shook their heads. Little did they know, it was not a throwaway statement made by a drunken Paul. It was the start of a slew of lawsuits.

Of all the passengers on the boat that foggy February morning, Miley was the only one who said she saw Paul driving. According to Investigator Yongue's report, "She looked over her left shoulder and watched Paul at the steering wheel driving the boat. Ms. Altman stated that just a short time after that is when she looked up and saw the bridge and she screamed. She stated she braced herself and at impact she was knocked down in the seat where she was originally sitting...After the crash, Ms. Altman stated she looked around and saw Connor laying on the right-hand side of the boat, where he had been standing most of the night.

Miley was asked to list the alcohol the group brought with them on the boat. She stated:

Morgan had a 12 pack of White Claws
Miley had a 6 pack of White Claws Mango
Mallory had a 12 pack bottles of Corona Premiums
Anthony had Michelob Ultra and Crown Royal
Connor had maybe a 12 pack of Budweiser
She could not remember what all Paul had to drink.

Investigator W. Ladue interviewed Connor Cook in the presence of his parents at MUSC. When he asked Connor who was driving the boat, Connor replied, "I don't know." He repeated, "I don't know," when asked again. He took Connor's parents aside and told them how important it was to know who was driving the boat. They said they had asked Connor but that they did not know who was driving the boat. Mrs. Cook informed Ladue that she "had raised her boy right" and he doesn't lie. He hurriedly assured her that he believed she had raised him right, but that they needed to get to the bottom of the driver issue.

In an affidavit for a search warrant served on property pertaining to Connor Cook, the description of property sought included:

Any and all instrumentalities of the crimes of reckless/negligent operation of a vessel and unlawful consumption of alcohol by a person under 21 to include but not limited to, medical records and reports, medical staff notes, observations, and recommendations, diagnosis and referrals, X-rays or other imagery, pertaining to Connor Martin Cook, who was a patient in the Emergency Room on or about February 24, 2019.

Boat occupants were unable or refused to identify who was operating. It is believed comparing medical records/documents may assist in identifying who was operating the vessel.

Signed by a judge on February 27, 2019.

Investigator's photo of remaining alcohol in the boat cooler.

As the boat passengers' reports began to fill file folders, there was still one more person to interview. He was one of the 6 passengers. He was the one claiming it "was his boat." Paul Murdaugh had become the bane of the Beaufort Memorial Hospital's Emergency Ward's existence. Getting his statement would not be easy.

Chapter Five
The Murdaughs Are in the House!

Austin Pritcher entered Room 10 at the Beaufort Memorial Hospital Emergency Ward. There he found a highly intoxicated young man lying back in the bed with myriad strobes attached to his chest. His chest and stomach were covered with minor scratches. On his chart was the name Paul Terry Murdaugh. According to Pritcher's report, Paul was wearing only boxer shorts. His eyes were bloodshot, and his speech was slurred. Pritcher asked him to tell him what happened and who was driving the boat. Paul responded, "Why do you need to know who was driving? That isn't going to help find Mallory. What if it was me who was driving the boat?" Pritcher responded with, "Was it you who was driving?" Paul responded with, "I definitely was not driving; these are all my best friends."

Pritcher then went to talk to Miley and Connor in Connor's room but neither would say who was driving the boat. He returned to Paul's room and asked him if he could give him a statement on what happened. "Yes, I can," Paul slurred." Pritcher began to get his forms out when Mr. Randolph Murdaugh III and Alex Murdaugh strode into the room. Pritcher told them he was talking to Paul. Mr. Randolph said, "Well, I am his lawyer starting now, and he isn't giving any statements." It was at this time Randolph made the comment about Paul being drunker than Cooter Brown and was in no condition to make a statement.

Pritcher left the room and went back to Morgan Doughty's room. He was asking her what happened when Alex Murdaugh showed up at the door and tried to walk in. Morgan told the nurse to please not let him into the room; only her mother and Pritcher. She wanted all the doors closed and the curtained windows to the corridor closed where she could see Randolph Murdaugh tapping on the glass to get her attention. Nervously, she told Pritcher she "didn't want anybody to hear what I am going to say." She told about the events beginning with "a party on Paukie Island with friends." She spoke of Paul and Connor going into Luther's bar because Paul had to have a Jager shot. They were the only ones with ID's, she said. She said they left and headed home, and Connor was driving because Paul was too drunk to drive. "We hit the bridge and rode up onto the rocks. Mallory was nowhere to be found." She would later change her statement after Miley whispered something to her in the hallway during discharge.

Perhaps the person that night to receive the full force of Paul's erratic behavior was Laura Kent. In a statement she made to Investigator Michael Brock she said:

"I was working as ED tech the night of the boat crash. I was in and out of the room Paul was in. He did not express any concern about anyone else that was involved in the crash. When I asked him for a urine sample, he smiled at me and asked if I was going to "hold it for him?" When I went back into the room he pointed to my butt and said, "Oh, Wow! That's nice!" I helped the doctor stitch up Morgan's hand. She kept going back and forth from crying and talking about Mallory to talking completely about unrelated things, such as mentioning one of the other police officers was "so hot!" I also heard Paul's father stop Connor on his way over to CT and he kept telling him not to say anything; that he would take care of it."

As parents of the passengers arrived, the wounded and distraught teenagers burst into tears. Reality was dawning, and Mallory had yet to be found. The Murdaughs had badgered them into keeping their mouths shut about who was driving, and they did so. Marty Cook, who had been friends with Alex since High School, was close to punching him out. Alex kept harping that Connor was driving the boat and that he would represent him or find someone who would. Enter Corey Fleming, Alex's close friend, an attorney, and Paul's Godfather.

Miley Altman finally agreed to be looked at after her parents arrived and insisted, she at least get checked out. Paul could be heard yelling for his clothes and that he wanted to leave. The attendants put him in blue paper scrubs as he had only come in wearing his boxer shorts. He made a beeline for Morgan who was in the hallway getting ready to leave. He wouldn't leave her alone until she hugged him, which she finally did, to get rid of him. Paul, Randolph, and Alex Murdaugh left the ER at 0400 (4:00 am.) The ER collectively breathed a sigh of relief. Paul Murdaugh was called the most belligerent and rude teenager to ever enter the ER's double doors.

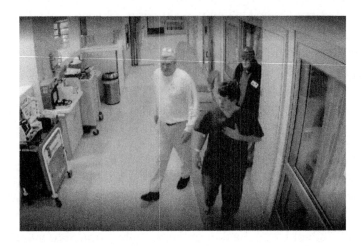

Paul leaving the hospital with his powerhouse backup: his father Alex Murdaugh (l) and his grandfather Randolph Murdaugh III, the former solicitor of the 14th Judicial Circuit of which Beaufort was included.

Snapchat video from the boat with Miley Altman in the foreground and Paul Murdaugh behind her driving the boat.

Back at the bridge, Renee and Phillip Beach paced frantically behind the yellow Crime Scene tape, watching helplessly as law enforcement talked to each other but not to them. Somewhere, in that green murky miasma was their daughter. Yet, they were not allowed to go down to the boat or get closer to the water.

Just then, Maggie Murdaugh and Randolph Murdaugh III, fresh from the ER room, walked up to the yellow tape and said something softly to one of the officers standing there. He lifted the tape to allow them to pass. They walked down to the boat. Renee Beach later said that she was shocked. She was Mallory's mother, but Maggie Murdaugh had meandered down to the boat without anyone stopping her. Had Maggie told the officer that her son needed his clothes, as he was clad only in boxers, and their home was over an hour away? Was it the mention of the fact that the boat belonged to Assistant Solicitor Alex Murdaugh, and they were told to assess the damage? Oh, and by the way…this is THE former solicitor for the 14th Circuit and recipient of the Order of Palmetto Award, just in case you didn't know. But they did know. Most of the law enforcement present at the scene that night were good friends with the Murdaughs, had attended parties at their homes, and been bailed out of messes when the need for a good attorney arose.

An inventory of the boat's contents had been taken along with cursory photos as the vessel sat impaled upon the shoreline.

Boat Inventory

- 1 Yeti Cushion
- 1 Youth Type III PFD
- 4 Adult Type III PFD
- 5 Adult Type II PFD
- 1 Apple Watch
- **1 Flannel Shirt hanging on throttle.**
- 1 Black t-shirt
- 1 blanket
- **1 rain jacket**
- 1 camouflage pullover
- 1 gas can
- 1 pink bag

- 1 flashlight
- 1 fleece jacket
- 1 lighter
- 2 cigarettes
- 1 pair of pliers
- 2 tackle boxes
- 1 filet knife
- Miscellaneous fishing tackle
- Miscellaneous paperwork
- Empty white claw beverage box
  [Bold type is the author's]

After Austin Pritcher had conducted all the interviews with the boat crash passengers, he and Investigator Michael Brock returned to the accident scene. John Marvin Murdaugh called Pritcher and was able to bring the boat's trailer to Paris Island Landing. "I met John Marvin at the landing and took the trailer back to the scene where I assisted on helping the dive team load into vessels. I stayed at the scene of the accident until FSGT Henderson was able to get there in the vessel to tow it to Paris Island Landing. I met FSGT Henderson and Capt. Donnie Pritcher at the landing with the trailer, and we loaded it onto the trailer. Once Investigator Brock was able to get the search warrants completed and signed, we waited on a Beaufort County Forensics Tech to arrive, and he was able to process the boat. I then helped Brock and Investigator Hammond inventory the boat. Investigator Hammond took the vessel to Charleston, and I went home for the evening," Austin Pritcher.

According to FSGT Henderson's report, he stated, "I left the scene to get an additional vessel to join the search. I launched my vessel from Battery Creek Landing and went to the Archers Creek bridge and towed the vessel involved in the accident back to Battery Creek landing where we placed it on a trailer. I then went back to Archers Creek bridge and assisted in the search with the dive team until dark."

Parris Island Landing accesses Battery Creek and according to Search and Rescue, the names are used interchangeably. What is confusing is that there are photos of a white truck towing the boat in a trailer from a landing, and also photos of a black truck towing the boat on a trailer from an area near what looks like Archers Creek bridge. Many people have stated that John Marvin towed the boat away using his white pickup truck. Parents of the boat crash passengers have asserted John Marvin (JM) did pull the boat away. There is footage of it seen in documentaries about the case.

Photo of JM in his white truck towing the boat trailer and boat. Photo courtesy of Netflix: *Murdaugh Murders: A Southern Scandal.*

Boat being towed away by a black truck, presumably Hammond's. Photo courtesy of South Carolina Dept. of Natural Resources (DNR)

According to Hammond's report, he stated: "6:00 pm. I meet Inv. Brock at the Battery Creek boat ramp and inventory the boat. After inventorying the boat, I attached the boat and trailer to my truck to transport it to Ft. Johnson to put the boat into evidence.

"11:00 pm (5 hours later): "I delivered the boat and trailer to Ft. Johnson. After arriving to Ft. Johnson, I backed the boat and trailer into storage shed where I left it for evidence storage." The drive to Ft. Johnson, Charleston, SC is 1 hour and 43 minutes from Beaufort. Fort Johnson is a branch of SCDNR.

John Marvin Murdaugh made several calls to Michael Thomas, one of the investigators at the scene, during the time of the boat transferal. It should be noted Michael Thomas is John Marvin's best friend.

Call log from that afternoon. Highlighted are the calls between John Marvin and Michael Paul Thomas. Photo: *Netflix.*

John Marvin with Michael Paul Thomas (Facebook)

Alex Murdaugh's call log was no less interesting that day. It shows a call to Curtis Eddie Smith.

	Liz Murdaugh	John Marvin Murdaugh	1 min
9:44 AM	John Marvin Murdaugh	Austin Pritcher	7 Mi
9:45 AM	John Marvin Murdaugh	Michael P Thomas	1 min
9:52 AM	John Marvin Murdaugh	Alex Murdaugh	1 min
9:52 AM	John Marvin Murdaugh	Alex Murdaugh	3 Min
9:59 AM	Alex Murdaugh	Curtis Smith	1 min
10:03 AM	Michael P Thomas	John Marvin Murdaugh	2 Minu
10:25 AM	Randolph Murdaugh	Murdaugh	2 Minu
		Alex Murdaugh	1 Minu

From the investigation into Paul Murdaugh. Phone logs from that day.

Photos of the inside of the boat taken before it was towed away show Paul's checked shirt lying on the floor in one photo. In another, it has been placed on the throttle to hang it up. According to attorneys for the boat crash victims, Paul's clothes are missing, as is DNA evidence collected from the boat by the Sheriff's Department in Beaufort. According to Hammond's report: "11:16 am—Arrived at the Beaufort County Sheriff Department to meet with Cpt. Purdy. At that time, Cpt Purdy delivered the reports from the sheriff's deputy that had arrived on scene that night. As well as the report from the investigator with the Sheriff's Department who came to get DNA evidence from the boat."

It is interesting to note that the current 14th Circuit Solicitor's Office at the time, two Beaufort County Judges, and the Beaufort County Sheriff's Office, all recused themselves from the case because of their ties to the Murdaughs. It is also interesting that Paul's clothes disappeared from the boat, including the wallet in his pants pocket containing Buster's fake ID and Maggie's credit card.

Other evidence, including DNA results would also go missing.

As the search continued for Mallory Beach, the anxious families of the passengers waited and prayed. Each day that passed lowered their hopes for a miracle. The sound of choppers filled the air and divers scoured the river bottom for miles. Their logs of hours, days, and depths filled pages. Many volunteers had grabbed their boats and were out hunting. The Beach family handed out supplies and "Thank You" packages to all who were donating their time.

A day or two into the search, Beverly Cook, Anthony's mother, needed a break from all the noise. She walked to their truck and climbed inside, shutting the door against the chaos. As she sat there and prayed for Mallory to be found, she heard the rear door of the truck open. To her surprise, Maggie Murdaugh climbed in. Without preamble she asked Beverly, "What if they never find her?" It was such a shocking and unwelcome statement that Beverly couldn't find the words to answer her. She would not let her mind go there. Maggie exited the truck as quickly as she had come. Later, Beverly would wonder at such an ominous statement. Did it have a darker meaning? An old mantra in law is "No body, no crime."

Anthony Cook stayed on the shore where the rescue efforts were centered every day of the search. Days turned into a week. On that Sunday, he went to church. It was the only day he hadn't been standing vigil by the water. It was on that day that they found Mallory Beach.

Finding Mallory

"Today my brother and I went to look for Mallory," Kenneth Campbell wrote in a report. "We left Broad River landing and went towards Ridgeland direction. I took the first big creek to the right. I was looking only for about 20 minutes before going into a small creek. My brother said, "There she is." (His brother was seated atop the hard top of Kenneth Campbell's 23-foot Hydro Sport boat.) "As we were about 30 yards out, then approximately low tide, I saw a fully clothed person with tan boots on and jeans. My brother Keith could see blond hair. She was face down, high up in the mud, next to marsh grass. I called 911. Two DNR officers called me on the phone. Keith kept the boat next to her until DNR arrived.

__ Kenneth T. Campbell. March 3, 2019, statement. Office of Sheriff of Beaufort County, Michael M. Hatfield.

The Deputy Report for Incident 19S050949 with the Beaufort County Sheriff's Office filed this report:

"I gathered all available information. DNR Officer Pope and I arrived at the Broad River Boat Landing simultaneously. DNR advised that they had several boats in the water and were heading to Kenneth's location. DNR then requested assistance shutting down the boat landing and pier for the recovery of the found body... I requested all the people at the boat landing and pier to leave the area in reference to an ongoing investigation. I requested Kenneth and Keith Campbell to make written statements, which was done."

LCpl Abell with the Beaufort County Sheriff's Office wrote:

"While at the recovery location, my camera was used by LCpl Byrd to take recovery photographs due to him standing on land. The remaining photographs were taken by me from the SCDNR boat. A female body was recovered and transported back to the Broad River Boat Landing by SCDNR and Coroner Ottis took possession of the body and then had her transported to his facility.

"Once back at the boat landing, I spoke with SCDNR Investigator Michael Brock. He advised based on the physical and clothing description that the female recovered was Mallory Beach. I informed Brock that a copy of the photographs would be available for him through BCSO Evidence. The family notification will be conducted by Coroner Ottis and SCDNR."

Mallory had been in the water, the tides pushing her out and pulling her back in for a week. It was a miracle that she was found as the current could have taken her out beyond reach. For her family and friends, it meant the end of keeping vigil by the water and praying she would be found alive. There is no such thing as closure, though the word is often used. The grief of losing someone comes in stages: shock, denial, heartbreaking reality, and the beginning of days without that person. Grief takes its time. It never really abates. It simply moves in with the grieving and dulls over the years. It was a sad day on Archers Creek and one that would tumble the Murdaugh dynasty.

On March 5, 2019, Brock was contacted by Craig Jones to obtain "the victim's Apple Watch in Hampton." An affidavit was filed for one Rose Gold Apple Watch for all incoming and outgoing text/sms messages, social media messages, chats, posts, phone logs, GPS location information, and GPS history/tracking. Photos, videos, or audio which may be contained on the cell phone internal memory and/or memory cards attached to the Apple Watch. Stored voicemail and email.

That on or about February 24th, 2019, this watch was utilized and recovered from the victim Mallory Beach who was involved in a boating accident resulting in her being ejected from the boat and resulting in loss of life. It is believed that there may be information from the watch that will be helpful in the investigation. This was a report filed by SCDNR.

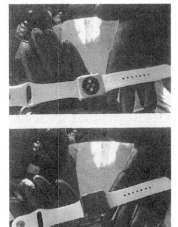 

Mallory Beach's Apple Watch and Cell Phone. Courtesy of DNR.

Finding Mallory. Crime Scene photo. DNR.

Months would go by without any action taken concerning repercussions for the driver of the boat that resulted in a boat crash and the death of Mallory Beach. Many took to Twitter in anger against Paul Murdaugh. Everyone feared the whole thing would be covered up by the Murdaugh juggernaut. Statements such as, "No cuffs!" or "No jumpsuit!" filled social media. Paul was spit on and harassed wherever he went. Newspaper articles pointed out that had it been anyone other than a Murdaugh, they would have been in jail pending a trial.

Finally, on April 18, 2019, the State of South Carolina, County of Beaufort, in the Court of General Sessions, filed an indictment against Paul Terry Murdaugh. The charges were OPERATION OF A MOVING WATER DEVICE UNDER THE INFLUENCE OF ALCOHOL OR DRUGS RESULTING IN GREAT BODILY INJURY TO Connor Martin Cook, all in violation of 50-21-113, of THE code of LAWS OF SOUTH CAROLINA. April 18, 2019, would have been Mallory Beach's 20th birthday.

Paul was also indicted for boating under the influence causing death and two counts of boating under the influence causing great bodily injury. He pleaded not guilty to all of the charges.

Connor Cook, who had in the aftermath of the horror of that fateful morning, remained silent at the hospital when asked who was driving the boat, was acting on orders given to him by Alex Murdaugh. Alex had stopped Marty Cook in the hallway before he could get to his son. Dr. Callaghan noticed the two men talking. Marty went immediately to Connor's room where Pritcher had just begun to interview him. Behind Pritchard's back, Marty made a slashing motion across his throat to Connor, meaning "Don't say anything." Alex must have convinced Mr. Cook that it was not in Connor's best interest to give a statement. Instead, Alex handed them his buddy Corey Fleming who would be sure to keep the lid on if Connor tried to negate his role in the driving of the boat that morning. Only later, when Connor realized he was being set up to take the fall, which would have landed him in prison for 25 years or more, did he speak out.

At Paul's arraignment, the court ordered mediation in the wrongful death lawsuit, which failed on June 4, 2021. This meant the case would now go to trial. It was just three days later that Paul and Maggie Murdaugh were found shot to death at their family hunting lodge.

Renee Beach, Mallory's mother filed suit against Alex Murdaugh, Buster Murdaugh (for supplying Paul with his fake ID), Randolph Murdaugh III (for allowing drinking of alcohol at his river house property), Gregory Parker, owner of Parker's Convenience Store (for selling liquor to Paul, who was underage), Luthor's Rare and Well Done (selling liquor to a minor), and Kristy and James Wood (for serving alcohol to the teens at the oyster roast party). These were filed in two different lawsuits: one in Beaufort and one in Hampton.

There would be more to come in this complicated case. The photographs taken of Mallory's body on the shoreline were leaked or sold to a third party who sold them to a documentary program.

On May 6, 2019, Paul Murdaugh appeared in Beaufort County General Sessions court and pleaded not guilty to the three felony charges related to the death of Mallory Beach in a February boat crash. Jim Griffin and Dick Harpootlian represented Paul as he stood before Judge Steven John of the 15th Judicial Circuit. Paul was dressed in a navy-blue blazer and matching plaid shirt. With his hair neatly combed, he looked like a clean-cut young 20-year-old man. His parents, Maggie and Alex Murdaugh looked on anxiously from the front row. When the judge announced that Paul was officially charged with the death of Mallory Beach, a bailiff approached him with handcuffs. Paul's eyes bulged as he looked to his parents for help. The cuffs were waived, but it had scared the young man who had always been bailed out of trouble by his family. Waiving the handcuffs would not be the only concession for Paul.

This author interviewed Attorney Jared Newman in Beaufort, South Carolina. I asked him about his background:

"I grew up on James Island, South Carolina, went to the University of South Carolina, got a degree in criminal justice, got a job working for the Goose Creek Police Department. I graduated second in the Police Academy class. I had a chance to come to Beaufort. Gonna come down here for two years, and I never left. Beaufort is "Charleston light." Charleston has just gotten so damn big thanks to Southern living and all those Tourism Yankees won't leave."

This author is from Colorado, so I wasn't sure if I qualified as one of those "Tourism Yankees," but I didn't mind.

"I was a detective with the Beaufort County Sheriff's Office," Jared continued. "I was chief detective with the narcotics division of the Beaufort County Sheriff's Office. Got out in '89 and went to work for Randolph Murdaugh III. The old man had semi-retired by then. Randolph was a solicitor. The typical South Carolina way of transitioning power is Old Buster ran his last term, and in 1986, two years and one day into his term, he resigned. And if you're two years or more, there's no special election. The governor appoints the gap. So obviously with their connections, with governors... Point is, son Randolph III became solicitor. Yeah. That's how you transition power. It's a time-honored tradition.

"We all thought that it was gonna be Alex next. But Alex had no interest in wanting to do that. Randolph Murdaugh IV, Randy, was never a chosen one. Or not. He's a very good lawyer. He is very humble, very soft spoken, very shy, very effective. He's a great lawyer. But he's just not a people person. Alex...if he walked into this room, he would meet every one of us and remember our names and little things about us. True politician. That's how Randolph was. The old man could walk up to you and before you could get rid of him, you know, he would know a little something about you. With Randolph IV, Little Randy as we call him, even though he's 6 foot three, it's just, it's not a personality fit. And Randolph and Buster, both told me, you have to have a little bit of son of a bitch in you to be a prosecutor. Because you gotta make, you know, make decisions. The rule in South Carolina is old law is good law, OK?

"PMPED got the big bucks in civil law cases. It's been called "The House that CSX built. They sued the railroad. And what made their firm would help make it so powerful. It's kind of a twisted case that came out of the early 1900s and the Supreme Court got it wrong, and it kept getting it wrong and wrong. They would find a way to get to a venue in Hampton County in a civil case. So, you could have a guy that, say the plaintiffs were from Greenville, SC, the defendants from Wisconsin, and the wreck happened in Arkansas. They could find a way to get it in court in Hampton County because they owned the juries. Because CSX tracks goes through Hampton County, that was enough to get venue because it did business in Hampton. That was one of the South Carolina laws I was talking about that you don't see elsewhere, right? That ended in the case of the Murdaugh law firm called Whaley versus CSX Railroad. And the Supreme Court finally said, "Hey, we've gotten this wrong for over 100 years." Well, it really doesn't work like that. Yeah, just cause those tracks come through here, it doesn't mean they have any case here. That's why you will not find a Walmart in Hampton County. I mean, we sued Walmart probably a dozen times over 25 years, but you won't find one in Hampton."

Jared's Director of Administration/Paralegal, Dawn Turner Erwin, sat in on the interview and would add content. I loved the ease with which the two worked together. Dawn laughingly commented that she had been with Jared for over 20 years. "I can't leave," she said. "He's got half of the files in his head, and I have the other half."

Attorney Jared Newman   Dawn Turner Erwin

Besides being a well-respected lawyer in the Lowcountry, Attorney Newman happened to be in the courtroom the day Paul Murdaugh was arraigned on charges pertaining to the 2019 boat crash. He was there on other court business and just happened to have ringside seats to Paul Murdaugh's arraignment. He told me, "I saw this man come in with a black wooden box and I knew exactly what it was. It was an old-fashioned fingerprint kit.

"They printed Paul Murdaugh right there rather than take him to jail like any other person brought up on charges. They then took his "mug shot" in the courtroom hallway in his nice dress shirt. He might as well have been posing for his Senior Prom photo. I knew right then, Paul Murdaugh was not going to take one step inside a jail house.

"They did it backwards," Jared Newman said. "You are supposed to get booked, fingerprinted (which is digital these days, not a fingerprint kit), put in an orange jumpsuit, and *then* you come before the judge. Nope. Didn't happen for this kid."

Paul was released on a $50,000 personal recognizance bond. Judge John said that he was required by law in non-capital cases to consider a PR bond, and he made a statement prior to setting his bond. "The purpose of bond is to ensure that a person comes to court when they should, not as a punishment."

Paul Murdaugh's mug shot.

Paul's arraignment, May 6, 2019. Jim Griffin (l), Dick Harpootlian (r).

Paul surrendered his passport and signed a waiver of extradition. As a stipulation of his PR bond, Paul was expected to avoid criminal offenses of any kind, and he may not leave the five-county 14th Judicial Circuit without written permission. Harpootlian faced the cameras afterward and declared Paul was "not guilty." He said there was nothing unusual about the court's ruling. Paul would be allowed to continue his education until the trial.

The hue and cry shot through social media concerning Paul's special treatment. Videos of him drinking to excess at college after his arraignment made their way onto social media platforms, and reports of him driving a boat intoxicated filtered in from the Edisto Beach area. For the Beach family, it was a slap in the face. Their daughter had died at the hands of a drunk Paul Murdaugh driving a boat, and yet he was carrying on as if nothing had happened.

The arraignment was in May of 2019. In a little over 2 years' time, Paul Murdaugh would be gunned down at the hunting property he loved so much.

Mallory Beach

Mallory Beach and her love of dogs.

Anthony and Connor Cook (back), Mallory and Miley (front).

Mallory Beach was one of the rare lights in this world. She was as kind as she was beautiful. Her love of dogs was evident in her Facebook posts and friends' memories of her. Her plan was to create a shelter for unloved pets. And, according to Connor Cook's deposition, she had voiced a desire to "flip" houses; making something beautiful out of something neglected. It was a theme that ran through her young life. She had found love with Anthony Cook, and he admitted he would have married her.

Her laughter and bright personality were infectious. Everyone loved her. She had been childhood friends with Miley Altman, their sweet photos throughout elementary school such a touching testament to friendships that last a lifetime. Morgan Doughty had come along later but was no less a part of the pretty threesome. They posed for prom photos, mugged for the camera at parties and outings, and lived life to the fullest.

Anthony Cook has said of her that she could be everything: someone who would join in the tomboy stuff but turn around and be a girl's girl. She worked at Retail Therapy where she decked herself out in their variety of fashions. In a heartbeat, she could change into camo and join in a bird hunt. All of the passengers aboard the Sea Hunt had hunting licenses for deer, turkey, duck, etc.

In Mallory's honor, a non-profit organization called "Mals Pals" was set up to donate to the Hampton County Animal Shelter. It had been her wish, and the donations poured in. Her love of dogs was memorialized on her gravestone with small paw prints.

Mallory Beach could not have known that her death would shine a spotlight on the mysterious deaths of two other people who had ties to the Murdaugh family, or the years of financial corruption that Paul Murdaugh's trial would have uncovered. Like the tide going out exposing the muck and decay beneath it, the boat crash that took this shining light from us, illuminated more than anyone could have imagined.

Chapter Six
When Darkness Comes

There is a certain time of the morning when the katydids and crickets' hand over their watch to the sentinels of the dawn. The constant buzzing of cicadas fills the sodden air of daylight hours and plays like background music throughout the south. As evening comes, it transitions once again to the heralds of the night.

The tragic murder of Stephen Smith on that humid July morning in Hampton County, South Carolina, mirrored the passing of the baton utilized by the insects. He was passed from one law enforcement agency to another, until the chaos of the case overrode any real progress. In the end, at least in the slow-moving months of the latter half of 2015 and early 2016, it would come to nothing. A grief-stricken family was left without answers and friends retreated to the shadows, afraid of the secrets to which they might be privy. Police were left with rumors and hearsay, with one exception. The name Murdaugh rose to the surface of nearly every tip they received.

It began in the wee hours of July 8, 2015; a murder mystery that would weave throughout the Lowcountry, refusing to go away. The whispering continued unabated for 7 long years, each person hoping the other would come forward with what they knew. It would take the death of Mallory Beach and the headlights of a man heading to work down a dark backroad flanked by woods and cornfields to illuminate what the shadows had hidden.

It Begins

3:57:43 a.m.

"Hampton County 911, what is your emergency?"

"Hello, yeah, I was going down Crocketville Road and I see someone layin' out."

"What road?"

The dispatcher goes back and forth a few times with the caller to establish which road he's on. They finally established it is called Sandy Run Road, although many of the older locals still call it Crocketville Road, as it leads to the small town of Crocketville.

"Is he in the road or on the side of the road?" the dispatcher asks.

"He in the road."

"He's in the road? Alright, what's your name?"

The man answers "Ronnie" and gives his last name. He is reluctant to give his phone number. She finally asks if it's the number he called from and he answers "Yes." He explained he was on his way to work. He finally gives his full name: Ronnie Capers.

"Ok, we'll get an officer out there to see what's going on."

"He's layin' in the road. I didn't move him or nothin' like that. But, umm, somebody gonna hit him. It's dark. Somebody gonna hit him."

"Alright. We'll get an officer headed out that way."

"Ok."

"Alright, sir."

Hampton County Dispatch relayed the data to the Hampton County Sheriff's Office. The information that follows is from the Multi-Disciplinary Accident Investigation Team case files, also known as M.A.I.T.

4:07 a.m.

Hampton County Sheriff's Office Officer Michael Bridges is the first to respond to the scene. It is with this initial report that the mystery already begins. His arrival time varies, and his dashcam video and audio goes missing. What did he see when he arrived on Sandy Run Road with only his car's headlights and a search light throwing the bloodied form of a young man into stark relief? Was someone else already there? Was the body of Stephen Smith lying in a different position from what crime scene photographs would later reveal? Had conversations been picked up on the cam's recorder that needed to be erased? It would be the first of years of subterfuge surrounding this case.

5:15 a.m.

The second agency to respond to the scene was South Carolina

Highway Patrol. Lt. Bruce Brock notified J.L. Booker to respond to the scene. He in turn calls in Corporal Michael E. Duncan, also with the Highway Patrol, at **5:18 a.m.** Michael Duncan, along with several other Highway Patrol officers, would be the bulldogs in the case who would not give up.

5:37 a.m.

Corporal M.D. Allen with the South Carolina Highway Patrol (SCHP) calls Sargent Thomas Moore of that same agency. Sgt. Moore is informed that it looks like they have a hit-and-run case in Hampton County on Sandy Run Road. A hit-and-run would involve the Highway Patrol as it is a person vs a vehicle accident and so they begin their investigation. But as the various officers with the SCHP begin looking over the scene, they feel their Spidey sense take over. None of the usual telltale signs of a vehicle hitting a pedestrian are evident. Despite the lack of road debris that typically follows an impact like that, the victim himself looks "off."

Cpl. M.D. Allen turns to Cpl. Michael Duncan and states, "The only injuries to the victim were around the head area." No signs of bumper strikes to his legs. No signs that he was hit and propelled through the air or bounced along the roadway. The only blood was spilling from his head across the asphalt. His legs were bent at an angle with one leg resting atop the other. And the young man's shoes...the shoes would come up again and again in reports and conversation.

"If you have someone hit by a car," Sgt. Moore stated, "their shoes are almost always knocked from their feet. This young man's shoes were loosely tied and still on his feet."

Cpl. Duncan would later walk the road a mile in each direction of where the body had been. There was not one piece of car debris that usually accompanies a vehicular impact. "It was clean," he stated. On top of that, there were no skid marks, no blood drops to show that Stephen might have been hit here and thrown there. It made no sense."

6:00 a.m.

Before Cpl. Duncan arrived at the scene that morning, he called his supervisor Booker and said, "I was just told it appears to be a homicide and SLED is taking over." Booker receives the same news and is told that "there is a possible gunshot wound to the victim's head." So, not a hit-and-run, although most would assume a hit-and-run is a homicide, but nonetheless, South Carolina Highway Patrol (SCHP) are being told, no vehicle involved? You may go.

6:08 a.m.

Now the "Who's on First?" chaos ensues. SCHP Cpl. Allen calls Sgt. Moore and tells him M.A.I.T., the division of the Highway Patrol that deals with complicated vehicle crashes, is in route to the scene and Allen is almost there. Sgt. Moore heads to Sandy Run Road. En route, Allen informs Moore that it is now being ruled a homicide and not hit-and-run. Confused, and wanting to cross all the t's, Moore tells Allen to make sure that Hampton County's Sheriff's Office and the coroner are in agreement that it's a homicide.

6:12 a.m.

Only two hours after Hampton County Sheriff's Office (HCSO) Michael Bridges arrived on the scene, theories are clashing on what happened to this young man. Chief Deputy Billy Jarrell of HCSO requests SLED to assist in the investigation as it now looks like a homicide due to a gunshot wound to the head. SLED stands for South Carolina Law Enforcement Division and is considered the big guns in the state's criminal investigations.

Shortly after, Brittany Burke and James B. Tallon III arrive on scene. They were not the only ones surrounding the body of Stephen Smith and comparing notes. Chief Jarrell with HCSO, Investigator Perry Singleton, and other HCSO personnel were there. Coroner Ernie Washington also arrives.

6:25 a.m.

Sgt. Thomas Moore with the SCHP arrives, not yet ready to relinquish the scene without more information as to the cause of death of the victim, still lying prone in the middle of the yellow line. The harsh light of flashlights and searchlights played over Stephen's body, the blood on the asphalt glistening in the crime scene photographs. In the photos, you see an array of men in varying uniforms comparing notes, seeming somehow detached from the fact a young 19-year-old-man is lying lifeless in front of them, his once handsome face split open on the right-hand side. It would be when they rolled him over, that they would discover the road rash on his back and the wounds to the back of his head. His arms were covered in scratches, some deep. Were they defensive wounds, or had he been lashed by tree limbs as he ran from his attackers?

The coroner bends over the lifeless body and points to a small wound above Stephen's right eye socket. It is an extension of the gaping wound that split his forehead in two from his left ear to his right forehead hairline, running in a crescent shape. Coroner Washington calls the small opening the "entry point" of a bullet wound.

Sgt. Moore takes it all in, still uncertain. Kelly Greene, the Hampton County deputy coroner showed Moore photos of the body, pointing to what they said was an entry point of a bullet trajectory. He was also shown defensive wounds on Stephen's hands. Sgt. Moore asked, "if they were sure, it was a homicide, and their response was 'yes'."

Still unhappy with the turn of events, Sgt. Moore tells the M.A.I.T. crew they are no longer needed. This was now a murder investigation. Still not satisfied, Sgt. Moore played his flashlight into the weeds and roadway of Sandy Run Road as he walked it as the sun began to rise at 6:23 a.m. It was 74 degrees with 88% humidity. Beads of sweat ran along his brow as he looked for any sign of car parts or telltale signs of a vehicle crash. He saw none. He returned to the incident site and "had all units (SCHP) clear the scene."

8:25 a.m.

SLED agents arrive. James B. Tallon III and Brittany Burke begin processing the scene. Tallon says in his report that "an EMS worker stated a projectile wound was located on the victim's head." He also notes that "the HCCO moved the victim prior to SLED Crime Scene arrival." This is probably in reference to the coroner rolling Stephen over. In an interview with Sandy Smith, Stephen's mother, she mentioned that Stephen's arm was behind his back. In all of the crime scene photos shown in documentaries and still shots, his right arm is extended to the right in the road, and his left arm is down by his side. Had one of his arms been originally bent back behind him? In a crime scene photo of Stephen's back, there is a diagonal purple stripe, which has been identified by law enforcement as lividity— the pooling of blood to the lower regions due to gravity. Was this perhaps where his arm had originally been, causing the pooling of blood to go to that area first as it was elevated above the rest of his back?

Tallon and Burke begin the laborious task of documenting the scene. Photos and notes are taken and a sketch showing the position of the body and its relation to the side of the road are now measured off and drawn.

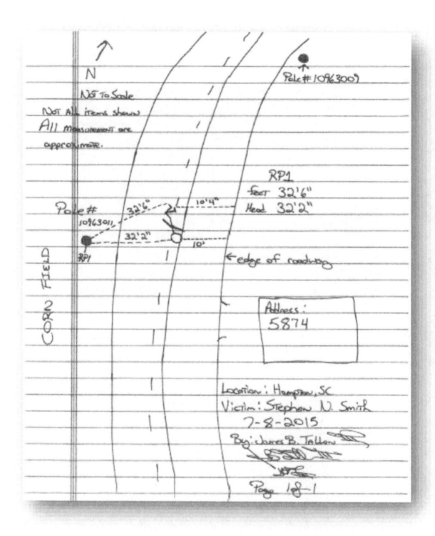

Crime scene drawing of Stephen Smith's body location,
by James B. Tallon III/SLED.

SLED'S log and case files began to fill with the early-stage preliminaries of the case. "Upon entering the scene, agents observed that the scene was secured by HCSO personnel and yellow barrier tape. The victim was covered with a sheet. A hole in the skull was located above the victim's right eye," the SLED report noted. "It was still unclear at this time if this hole was caused by a projectile. The victim's right arm was covered in blood and agents were unable to see any injuries." This arm had been extended and was lying in the blood pooled all the way across the right-hand side of the road.

Stephen Smith was found the morning of July 8, 2015. His right or left arm may have been moved into this position by the coroner before this photo was taken.

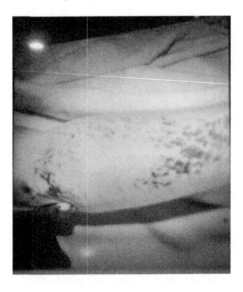

Injuries to Stephen's left arm photographed.

Stephen's shoes in the crime scene photo.

SLED searched the area for cartridge cases. Stephen's hands were then bagged. Ernie Washington, the coroner, searched through Stephen's pockets. He found a vehicle key in his right front left pocket. He handed the key to the Hampton County Sheriff's Office.

An odd entry in the report follows here:

"No other evidence was located at the scene," the SLED agent wrote. It was later stated that Stephen had his cell phone on him. A cell phone and a single car key. Why is the phone not mentioned here? Had it been taken away? Was it photographed later after someone accessed its contents?

Stephen Smith's phone crime scene photo.

"Prior to leaving the scene, agents discussed their findings and completed a walkthrough with Investigator Perry Singleton and Chief Billy Jarrell," according to the SLED report. At this point, they were looking at it as a homicide by gunshot wound. How were the wounds to the back of his head and fractured face taken into consideration? Only that a bullet was the fatal delivery. It was hard to say. It would become stranger as the autopsy was conducted.

9:18 a.m.

SLED's involvement at this point with the body was concluded. They released the victim and the scene to the Hampton County Sheriff's Office and left. Little did they know that the second part of the crime scene was about to be discovered.

9:30 a.m.

Stephen Smith's body is removed from the roadway. At this point, it is not certain that the officials knew the name of the victim. It is possible someone who was there earlier knew exactly who he was.

The Banana Car

Three miles away from where Stephen Smith's body was found, a small yellow car sat a car width's distance from the road near a metal fence bordering a large hunting property. It was bright yellow in color and the family of Stephen Smith had nicknamed it "The Banana Car."

A young man going to help with some manual labor in the early morning hours saw the car up ahead. It was still dark out and he wondered as he approached it what it was doing out there on that lonely street. His first impression as he approached it in his truck was how far off the road it was; practically pressed into the foliage that ran the length of the metal fence. He thought it looked as if the little yellow car had been forced off the road. As he got up closer to it, he could clearly see tire tracks in the humidity-laden grass that bordered both sides of the cement swatch the car was parked next to. The tracks swooped up off the road, ran up close to the car, and then swooped back onto the road in an arc. Forced off the road, he thought again. There was no crime scene tape. He saw the car around 5:30 a.m. The Hampton County Sheriff's Office wouldn't find it until much later.

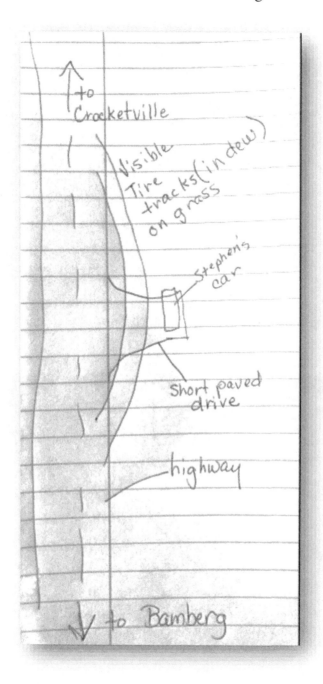

Hand drawn map by the source who shared what he saw that morning with Rebecca F. Pittman—author.

Crime scene photo with tape. Note the cement swatch and grass on either side. It looks as if the car was forced over by the trees.

The metal fence running the length of the hunting property would prove to be a possible clue in what happened the morning Stephen Smith was brutally beaten to death.

9:20 a.m.

SLED agents had been alerted by the HCSO that an abandoned yellow car had been found on the side of the Bamberg Highway.

Although called a highway, this portion of the road is isolated with spread out farms. Houses are set back from the street and are surrounded by acres of farmland. Traffic ranges depending on the day, but in the early morning hours, on a weekday, it is desolate.

"After receiving a search warrant, agents searched the area and the vehicle," the report said. "The gas tank door was open, and the gas cap was hanging on the side of the vehicle. The vehicle doors were locked. The key located in the victim's pocket was used to open the vehicle. The vehicle was in park. The battery was functional; however, the vehicle would not start."

Stephen's car with the gas cap dangling outside. Crime scene photo.

What they found inside the car was even more puzzling. SLED unlocked Stephen's car and found his wallet between the car door interior and a bag of Ritz crackers near the driver's seat. Why would a person who had run out of gas walk away without his wallet? Why would you take the gas cap off to start with? Either you have gas to pour into it, or you don't. You don't peek into the hole to see if you can see any. It looked staged. Sgt. Moore later stated that there was enough gas in the car to make it the short distance to Stephen's father's home on Joe Miley Road, only 3 miles away. It was also stated that someone had tampered with the car under the hood.

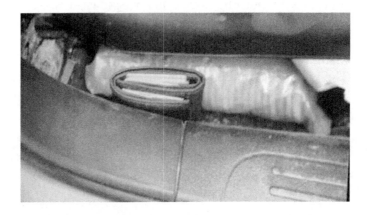

Stephen's wallet locked inside his car. Crime scene photo.

Investigator Perry Singleton took the wallet, according to SLED reports. The car was rather messy. Whether it was messy when they found it, or the photos were taken after law enforcement searched it, is the question. Stephen's books from his courses at Orangeburg College were in the front and back seats. On the floor of the passenger side front, were the motor oil quarts that he kept at the ready due to the car having a small leak. Only his wallet was taken.

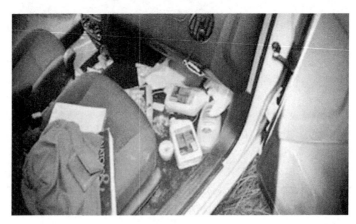

Quarts of oil in the passenger floorboard, front. Crime Scene photo.

9:40 a.m.

SLED did a walk-through of the scene where the car was found with Investigator Singleton and Sheriff Chief Jarrell of the Hampton County Sheriff's Office. The Highway Patrol was informed they would not be needed at Stephen Smith's autopsy according to SLED and the HCSO.

Stephanie Smith Joyner, Stephen's twin sister, talking about that morning:

"I was taking my dad to work. We were taking Sandy Run Road and we pulled up to a scene. We didn't know what it was. We just saw state troopers all around the road. No lights: cars are just sitting there running. Finally, after waiting like 15 minutes, we took the long way. I drop my dad off. I was like, hey, I'm gonna try to take that way back home because this is a small town. If you see something like that, you're gonna be nosy. So, I went back through there and they were still there. So, I took the other back way home."

Sandy Smith (Stephen's mother) also stated what happened that morning: "I think I heard it on the radio at like 7:30. I called, and Stephanie answered. 'I heard that they said somebody threw a body out on Sandy Run Road. Who do you think it is?'"

Stephanie said. "I don't know, but I was like, Mama, did you hear from Stephen any? I was like Steven never came home."

"And that's when I knew. That it was him," Sandy said.

Joel Smith, Stephen's father, was called to go to the Sheriff's Office around 8:00 am. SLED hadn't found Stephen's wallet in his car until around 9:30 a.m. which would have provided some ID. Yet, someone at the Sheriff's Office knew who the victim was already.

Joel waited anxiously inside the Sheriff's Office before the Sheriff got there. While he was sitting there, Randy Murdaugh called him. Randy was doing a workmen's comp case for Joel and so he called Joel and offered to help investigate. At that time, Joel had not talked with the Sheriff or seen Stephen. Investigate what? Joel was still unaware of what had happened. The first thing Randy asked for was Stephen's passwords and all his electronics. His passwords? Did Randy have Stephen's phone and needed to get into it? Why would you need a hit-and-run victim's electronics (laptop, tablet, etc.)? Did he think Stephen had been texting with someone who was going to hit him in the dark and keep going? To Sandy Smith, it made no sense.

After the ID had been made, and the family was given the heartbreaking news that it was indeed Stephen they had found, they began to do what every loved one has done for generations: make plans for a funeral service and burial. Sandy, Stephanie, and Stephen's older brother were driving down Sandy Run Road to the funeral home to make arrangements around 10:30 or 11:00 a.m. that same morning. As they came to where Stephen's body had been found, they saw Randy and Alex Murdaugh standing there. Stephen's body had left the roadway at 9:30 a.m. Why were they there?

Shortly after, Randy Murdaugh called Sandy and asked, "Was that you that just drove by?" Sandy said, "Yes." He said, "I wish I had known that. I would have liked to have met you."

Randy offered to represent Joel Smith pro bono for Stephen's investigation. Randy Murdaugh worked for PMPED at the time. They specialized in personal injury accidents, not murders. And why for free? Stephanie was there when her dad got the call from Randy offering his services for free. She said, "My Dad was kinda iffy about that."

10:30 a.m.

Coroner Washington informed SCHP Sgt. Moore that he has made that dreaded call to Stephen's parents to notify them of Stephen's death.

11:29 a.m.

Only two hours after Stephen's body was removed from Sandy Run Road, an autopsy was underway at MUSC, the medical center at the University of South Carolina. James B. Tallon III and Brittany Burke, the same SLED agents that had been at the crime scene and drawn a diagram and measured the area, attended the autopsy. Absent were any members of the SCHP. They had been released after a possible gunshot entry wound had been identified.

It is now that the revolving door of who would handle this case changed hands once again. During the autopsy, "It was determined that the wound in the victim's head was not caused by a fired projectile." Pathologist Erin Presnell determined "that it appeared the victim was struck by a vehicle." With that, SLED agent Tallon contacted Perry Singleton and told him the Highway Patrol were to be brought back in to investigate the case.

Even though the notification has been made that this is now the Highway Patrol's investigation, SLED collects the Gun Shot Residue (GSR) kit from MUSC at the autopsy. They remain there for another two hours.

12:30 a.m.

According to Dr. Erin Presnell's autopsy report, she begins at this time to further complete Stephen's autopsy. No bullet or bullet fragments were found in his head, and so a gunshot fatality is ruled out. The report went as follows:

- 7.25-inch laceration on the right side of Stephen's forehead along with bruises on both sides of his forehead. Scratches were also noted on his face.
- The right side of his skull has multiple fractures, bruising and contusions.
- His right eyebrow is lacerated.
- His right shoulder is dislocated.
- On the inside of his left arm there are small cuts on in the interior.
- His right hand shows cuts and bruising.
- Cuts are seen on his right arm, including a 6-inch irregular cut on the interior of the right arm.
- He has cuts on his right fingers.
- His right arm showed 12) 3-inch "aggregates" of irregular to angulated abrasions.
- Blood was found in his airway.
- Conclusion: Cause of death due to blunt head trauma sustained by a "motor vehicle crash."

The autopsy summary read: "In light of historical information and the autopsy findings, it is the opinion of the pathologist that the decedent died as the result of blunt head trauma sustained in a motor vehicle crash in which the decedent was a pedestrian struck by a vehicle."

1:43 a.m.

SLED, who had notified the SCHP the ruling was a hit-n-run two hours previously and they were now in charge of the scene, left the autopsy room at MUSC, taking vital evidence with them.

And so, the South Carolina Highway Patrol were now given

Stephen's Smith case, without the benefit of attending the autopsy themselves and without any evidence acquired during the medical procedure. It was a no-win situation to start with and the cloak of secrecy was only just beginning.

A white cross marks the location where Stephen Smith was found murdered on July 8, 2015, on Sandy Run Road in Hampton County, SC. Photo by Rebecca F. Pittman

A somber reminder of where Stephen Smith was found.
As the investigation continued, it would shed doubt that this
location was where he had met his death.
Photo by: Rebecca F. Pittman.

Chapter Seven
An Investigation Begins

For the family of Stephen Smith, it had been a long day of heartbreak, questions, and seeing what had been done to their son and brother. The gash in his face was so wide that reconstruction putty had to be used to fill in the gap. The family had decided on an open viewing to "show the world what they did to him." As the family made funeral arrangements, the Highway Patrol were trying to regain the ground and time they had lost when the case was taken from them.

It was now late afternoon on the day of Stephen's death. He had been autopsied and his body taken to Peeples-Rhoden Funeral Home in Hampton. Whoever was responsible for Stephen's death were no doubt covering any remaining tracks of their crime, whether it was damage done to a vehicle due to striking a pedestrian, or damage of a different kind. The violent injuries to Stephen's body would have left some evidence, some DNA, somewhere. If he had been assaulted by human hands, perhaps they would have left his mark on them as well.

A frustrated Highway Patrol began trying to play catch-up. Every hour matters in a homicide, whether vehicular or not. They had been denied the close-up examination at the autopsy to form their own conclusions, and all evidence had been taken away. It would be only the beginning of a game of cat and mouse, not only by those involved in the investigation, but by witnesses, participants in Stephen's death, and other concerned parties. Precious hours had been lost and the SCHP was trying to solve a puzzle with missing pieces.

4:15 p.m.
Hampton County Sheriff T.C. Smalls calls Cpl. David Rowell with

the SCHP and tells him Stephen's autopsy shows the young man's death is the result of a hit-and-run. Cpl. Rowell calls Sgt. Moore to give him the news. Sgt. Moore calls the Sheriff and Smalls tells him the "doctor was ruling it a motor vehicle accident and they were turning it over to us." Sgt. Moore called Investigator Perry Singleton with the Hampton County Sheriff's Office and "asks for any information he has." Singleton tells Moore he is not at his desk but would get back to him in 30 minutes.

According to the M.A.I.T (Multi-Disciplinary Accident Investigation) case file, a 100+ page document, it would not be smooth sailing for the stalled investigation into Stephen Smith's death. Undaunted, Sgt. Moore tries to make up for lost time. It is still day one of the murder.

4:40 p.m.

Sgt. Moore calls the coroner who oversaw the crime scene that morning. Washington seems evasive. Moore asks Washington if the hit-and-run ruling was his conclusion as well. "He stated he would have to go with the doctor's ruling," Moore wrote in his report. "I then reminded him that earlier that morning they were certain it was a gunshot wound and he told me he had to go by the opinion of the doctor." Frustrated, Sgt. Moore asks the coroner where Stephen Smith's body is now. Washington tells him that after the death notification had been made, "as per the wishes of the family, the body has been taken to the funeral home."

Sgt. Moore calls the Peeples-Rhoden Funeral Home and speaks with a director there. He asks him if they are in possession of Stephen's clothing that he was wearing at the time of the accident. Moore is told the clothes are in a paper bag with the body. Frustrated that preparations have begun to prepare Stephen's body for funerial purposes, Moore orders them to stop, and "cover him up." Sgt. Moore calls Cpl. Rowell and instructs him to go and pick up the victim's clothing from the funeral home.

5:57 p.m.

As the long afternoon turns toward evening, Sgt. Moore calls the pathologist responsible for Stephen's autopsy. "I wanted to try and understand" what made her decide Stephen was killed in a hit-and-run. "She said that it was not a gunshot wound and no bullet or fragments were found during the x-ray, and it didn't look like a bullet wound in her opinion and that since the body was found in the roadway, she could only theorize that it had to be a motor vehicle that caused the death."

When Sgt. Moore asks Dr. Presnell about any other injuries, she tells him "Only a partially dislocated shoulder." With frustration growing, Moore asks the pathologist if she found anything to make her belief he had been hit by a car. "Were there any glass fragments or any other evidence of a motor vehicle collision," and she said, "No." Moore finally put the hammer down. "I then asked her why she was ruling it as a motor vehicle accident and what she thought caused the head injury?" he wrote in his report. "She told me it was not her job to figure that out, it was mine."

6:14 p.m.

Lt. Bruce Brock with the SCHP notifies J.L. Booker with the same agency that "the victim did not have a gunshot wound according to the autopsy." Booker then contacts Sgt. Moore and Burns and instructs them "to gather further information." Sgt. Moore calls Investigator Perry Singleton again with the Hampton County Sheriff's Department who has yet to call him back. His call goes to voicemail. He then calls Hampton County Sheriff T.C. Smalls to see if he can retrieve any information from him. Smalls tells him he'll call him right back but doesn't. When Moore calls Small again, it goes straight to voicemail.

Feeling like he's beginning a case with his hands tied behind his back, Sgt. Moore instructs Cpl. David Rowell to go back to the crime scene and make sure the body's location has been marked. He tells him to look "for debris in both directions." Rowell calls Moore later and informs him he could find "no debris at all."

Sgt. Moore calls Mitch Altman with the SCHP and tells him to go to the scene and see if he can find any debris. Altman goes to the location on Sandy Run Road. After walking it off and searching, he calls Moore and tells him, "He could find nothing." Altman is then given the night shift. Moore tells him to go to the scene and sit there between 3 and 5 a.m. He is to make a report, documenting what type of traffic is moving at that time of morning.

6:30 p.m.

Booker and Duncan with the SCHP (Highway Patrol) get together to "formulate a plan of action." It was a case that had gotten off to a faltering start. One of the first things they did was create and distribute a flyer asking anyone for tips in the case.

7:28 p.m.

SCHP King calls Lt. Moore and tells him that Brock with M.A.I.T. would be calling. He tells Moore to get in touch with someone from SLED to get them to come out the next day.

8:02 p.m.

Moore calls Booker and "explained the scenario to him." They decide to ask SLED to meet them at the funeral home where Stephen's body is being held at 9 a.m. the next day.

Moore calls Croft to get a list of which agents were at the scene that morning.

8:22 p.m.

Lt. Moore calls SLED agent Brittany Burke, who was the first SLED agent to arrive that morning with Agent Tallon. She informs Moore that she and Tallon were notified of the incident at 6:10 a.m. and arrived at the scene at 9 a.m. She told Moore that she didn't think Stephen's injury looked like a gunshot wound and she informed the Sheriff and Coroner of that on the scene at that time. She told him "They were adamant it was a gunshot wound, so they mapped the scene and began to gather evidence as they would normally do."

They located Stephen's car on US 601 (Bamberg Highway) and said that the gas cap was off and dangling. They found engine oil in the vehicle but could not get the car to start. [Lt. Moore would later state there was enough gas in the car for Stephen to have driven it home. It looked as though someone had incapacitated the car by messing with the engine.]

"They believe he was walking home when the incident occurred," the report stated. Moore asks Burke if she can come to the funeral home the next morning.

Thus concluded a long and complex day. The first 48 hours are the most important in any crime. Yet, with Stephen Smith's case, so much time had been wasted. First it was determined to be hit-and-run. Then the hole above Stephen's eye socket was determined to be a bullet hole. When no bullet fragments are found, the pathologist reverts back to a hit-and-run. Each law enforcement agency handed it off to the other depending on their jurisdiction. Case logs differed and the chain of custody for valuable evidence was a nightmare. Stephen's family went to bed that night with no sense of what had happened to their loved one. Nightmares of seeing his once handsome face split in two would haunt them forever. Their only hope was to find out who did this and why.

July 9, 2015

5:50 a.m.

Moore calls Cpl. Rowell and Payne and sends them back out to Sandy Run Road. They are to scour the roadway and look for debris, "anything out of the ordinary."

They call him back, and once again, the results are negative. He asks them to meet him at the funeral home.

It would later be a topic of frustration that no one seemed to have asked the occupants of the small house, only a few feet away from where Stephen was found, if they heard or seen anything that day or the previous night. As it turns out, the house was abandoned at the time Stephen was murdered. This author pulled into the driveway of the tiny run-down home while researching this book. There were people there now, and a service van was in the driveway. Anyone standing near that house could see where Stephen's body lay. Had his killer(s) hidden behind the house, or in the bordering trees, and watched to see if someone would run over the body? Or had they run off into the shelter of their homes and hoped for it to be ruled a hit-and-run, perpetrated by a stranger who was gone with the wind?

8:53 a.m.

Brittany Burke meets Moore at Peeples-Rhoden Funeral Home in Hampton to provide documentation from the original crime scene and to transfer the evidence SLED had collected the day before.

9 a.m.

The sad task of seeing the body at the funeral home fell to Booker, Duncan, and Rowell of the Highway Patrol, and to SLED agent Burke. M.A.I.T, the special sector of the South Carolina Highway Patrol (SCHP), took photos of the body and Stephen Smith's clothing. It is the first time the SCHP officers have seen his body as they were told not to attend the autopsy. They speak with SLED agent Burke and ask her about her findings. Moore examined Stephen's body and wrote "there were no visible injuries to the deceased, other than his head wound and a small amount of road rash on both arms." Booker tried to interview the 911 caller, but he was not at home. Met with the Hampton County Sheriff's Office to gather information and the victim's phone.

Stephen Smith's shoes. Crime scene photo: M.A.I.T.

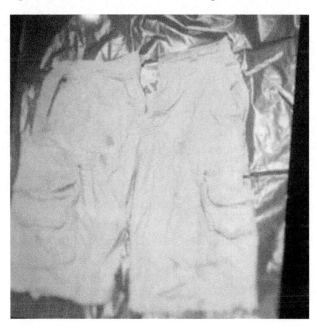

Stephen Smith's shorts crime scene photo: M.A.I.T

Stephen Smith's shirt. Photo: M.A.I.T

Cpl. Duncan speaks with Stephen's family and goes over the pathologist's final announcement: Stephen was the victim of a hit-and-run. They totally reject Stephen would have been hit by a car.

Both Sandy and Stephanie Smith said Stephen would never be walking in the roadway at night. If he saw a car coming, he would hide in the woods. "He always said, 'Nobody's gonna kidnap my sexy behind,'" she said, sadly. He had run out of gas before and always called his twin sister to come and get him.

"And why would he leave his wallet in the car if he was walking to get gas?" Sandy asked, incredulously. "It just don't make any sense."

Sandy and Stephanie were asked if anything seemed different about Stephen in the two weeks prior to his death?

"He was acting a little more secretive," they both said.

"Stephen began cutting classes," Sandy said, "and he never cut classes. He was very studious. He was studying to be a nurse, so that he could go on and become a doctor. He wanted to go to countries that didn't have a doctor and help them."

What happened in the weeks leading up to Stephen's murder? Had he hooked up with the wrong person? Knew something he shouldn't? Talked too much about a new love interest? It was going to be a long road to the truth.

When Moore, Booker, Duncan, Rowell, and Burke arrived at the funeral home that morning, they found Stephen's clothes thrown together in a paper bag, sitting out in the open. There was no chain of custody of who had handled the clothing. It was presumed they had been removed during the autopsy, but oddly, Sheriff Smalls said Stephen's body came in, in a white t-shirt. Had they put a shirt on his body after the autopsy to send him back to Hampton's funeral home—preserving the clothes he was wearing for evidence? The white shirt was never mentioned again.

Lt. Moore wrote in his notes, "I turned the clothing over to Duncan and had a discussion by all parties as to why this did not appear to be related to a motor vehicle."

Moore, Rowell, Booker, and Duncan return to Sandy Run Road to document the scene and "looked for any evidence at the scene for approximately 100 yards in both directions." They found nothing.

Cpl. Rowell received a phone call from Lt. Singleton advising them that they had the phone and wallet of the deceased. Cpl. Rowell, Sgt. Booker, and Lt. Moore met at a substation in Varnville and had a discussion with Lt. Singleton, who stated that he thought a logging truck may have struck him. Lt. Singleton shared with them all his information. Sgt. Booker signed for the cell phone. The wallet was left with Lt. Singleton since it had been unsecured since the previous morning and had money in it. He was advised to return it to the coroner's office. A warrant was obtained in Hampton County for the phone's contents and was forwarded to Sgt. Booker to take to SLED to retrieve the information from the phone.

Cpl. Rowell and Lt. Moore began riding the area around the site where Stephen was found looking for possible logging sites. They were all old sites that obviously had not been used recently. They went to McMillan Farms on the same road Stephen's body had been found. They spoke with Mr. (Jimmy) McMillan who runs the farm. "We asked if we could look at his trucks and he agreed. He had a few seed trucks that we looked at, but we did not see any damage or evidence of bodily fluid or blood. After speaking with Mr. McMillan, he advised us that his trucks weren't running at this

109

particular time since there was no grain to haul." After they left McMillan Farms, Cpl. Rowell was advised to ride the area further to look for farming or logging trucks and Moore went to Bobcat Landing where the deceased had supposedly hung out the night before swimming. Moore did not see anyone or anything out of the ordinary.

July 10, 2015

Lt. Thomas Moore was back at the scene the next day. It had been two days since Stephen was found murdered. He and the other SCHP officers were looking for anything of interest. While they were there, "an investigator from the Murdaugh law firm" showed up. We were still out there combing that scene because no other law enforcement was willing to help. He shows up with a camera and wants to come into the crime scene. I said, 'I'm sorry, you can't come in here. If you want to take pictures, you can take them after we're gone." It wasn't' about taking pictures; it was about seeing what we were doing, trying to get one step ahead. If you wanted to get pictures, you could get those anytime. So, you wonder, "Is a Murdaugh involved in this?"

Later that day, Stephen's clothes and iPhone are sent to SLED. Why the phone wasn't mentioned in the original evidence removed from his body is unclear. But it seems to have resurfaced.

July 11, 2015

At 5:00 p.m., a wake was held in the chapel at Peeples-Rhoden Funeral Home in Hampton, SC. Stephanie and Sandy Smith had decided to leave the casket open. The make-up artist had done their best to reconstruct the right side of Stephen's face with make-up, putty, and cosmetics.

Joel Smith, Stephen's father, could not go near the casket. His boy had been alive and talking to him only four days ago. He had his entire future ahead of him as a doctor. Friends and family poured into the small room, sobbing and still in disbelief. Who would do this?

Stephanie said a man showed up that the family did not know. He was clearly a lot older than Stephen and told the family he was Stephen's boyfriend. Stephanie immediately thought it impossible.

This guy had to be close to 40-years-old. But her father said to go ahead and let him go into the viewing. Stephanie warned the man that Stephen didn't look like he used to. The man paid a hasty visit, made a phone call to someone, and said, "Yeah, it's him," and left. This man would show up later on Cpl. Duncan's radar.

Stephen's obituary was filled with loving phrases and a belief in a benevolent God.

Stephen Nicholas Smith, Graduation Day at
Wade Hampton High School in Hampton, SC.

Stephen Nicholas Smith

January 29, 1996 – July 8, 2015

Our Father, which art in heaven, hallowed be thy name…

The Angel of death has visited again, and a Godly life ended on Wednesday morning, July 8, 2015. Mr. Stephen Smith was taken from our sight. We know he is at rest with our Heavenly Father…

Stephen, the son of Fred Joel Smith and Sandy Smith was born January 29, 1996, in Lexington County, SC. He was a 2014 graduate of Wade Hampton High School. He was attending OC Tech of

Orangeburg studying to become a Registered Nurse. Stephen was predeceased by his brother Joseph Smith.

Stephen leaves, to cherish his fond memories, two sisters, Stephanie Smith and Melissa Smith, two brothers Christopher Smith and David (Christina) Wingate, two nieces, Mercedes Jackson and Caitlin Wingate, and a host of friends and family. Funeral services will be 5 p.m. Sunday in Sandy Run Baptist Church conducted by Rev. Paul Reid and Rev. Paul Creason, with burial in the Gooding Cemetery directed by Peeples-Rhoden Funeral Home in Hampton. Friends may call at the Chapel located at 300 Mulberry Street West in Hampton, Saturday evening after 5 p.m.

Stephen was buried at Gooding Cemetery; just up
the road from where his body had been found.

Stephen Smith's grave marker. A magnificent marble one would replace
it in later years due to a campaign called *Standing for Stephen*.

The funeral formalities were over, but the grieving was still at a fever pitch. The family would be dealt another blow when the first of three death certificates were issued by Coroner Washington and given to Stephen's parents.

Hampton County Coroner's Office:

- Date of Injury: July 8, 2015
- Actual or presumed Date of Death: July 8, 2015.
- Time of injury: 0300
- Actual or presumed time of death: 0300
- Cause of death: Blunt force trauma (probably pedestrian in motor vehicle accident possibly struck by side mirror)
- Manner of death: Pending investigation
- How injury occurred: Subject was apparently hit by a motor vehicle, possibly a truck.

According to the reckoning on this document, Stephen was murdered only one hour before Ronnie Capers drove up that dark street and called 911 at roughly 4 a.m., July 8, 2015. We do not know how the pathologist and coroner arrived at such a precise time as 3:00 a.m. Photos of Stephen lying in the road show a great deal of blood around his head. You can see that it is still very wet, as though his injuries have just happened. Yet, the photos of him were taken over an hour later. The death certificate states time of death as 3:00 a.m. The 911 call came in around 4:00 a.m. by the man who found him, and the first responder was there at 4:07 am. The photos were after that. Something seems off. This author spoke with a retired officer in Hampton, and he said blood coagulates rather quickly once exposed to the air, even with high humidity.

Hampton County Sheriff's Office Michael Bridges was the first to respond at 4:07 a.m. Within 10 minutes he was at the scene. As stated earlier, his dashcam footage is missing from that morning. The crime scene photos show it is still dark out, and Stephen's blood is still wet and shiny in the harsh glare of camera flashes and headlights. If Ronnie Capers had driven by on his way to work, only minutes earlier, would he have seen the perpetrator(s)? We know he was too nervous to remain by Stephen's body in the dark. He drove a mile to make the 911 call.

SCHP trooper Todd Proctor stated he thought the body looked like it had been placed in the middle of the road. No hit-and-run victim would land that way. Based on the road rash, the positioning of his arms, and his bent legs, it appeared to him that someone lifted him, possibly from the back of a truck, and put him in the road. Perhaps they changed their minds as to where was the best place to put him to guarantee a car would strike him and cover their damage to the boy's body, and so they pulled him to the center of the road, leaving tell-tale signs of road rash. We do know no alcohol or drugs were found in Stephen's system. Very little else was known other than a grocery list of injuries.

An empty house was the only witness to Stephen's death that morning. It sat only a few feet away from where he was found.

Chapter Eight
Rumors and Secrets

Sandy Smith proudly posing with her son, Stephen Smith.

One of the highlights of my journalistic career was having the opportunity to interview Sandy Smith. She is warm, intelligent, and kind. She has amazing comic timing, and she touched my heart. As she shared her stories of Stephen, I laughed, and I cried. Here is that interview:

Sandy: "Steven was my angel child. When he was born, he weighed 2 lbs. 12 ounces and they gave him a 50/50 chance to live. They called me and they said, 'Well this is probably it; you need to come up here, because once we put him on this machine, he probably won't come back off.' And so, I went to the ICU, and we kangarooed: skin to skin, chest to chest. I held him for about 30 minutes. And he started breathing on his own. So, he's my miracle baby."

Me: "That's amazing. 2 pounds and he came back around. No wonder your bond with him was so strong."

Sandy: "There was never a dull moment with him. He was a jokester. He was just a beautiful person inside and out. Mama's baby of course."

Me: "What were some of his favorite things to do as he was growing up?"

Sandy: "Reading. All his money he spent on books. Didn't matter if it was fiction or nonfiction. If it was a book, he was gonna read it. Once a year or something, the County Library would sell all the books that they didn't need anymore. And he would go buy them. When you walked into his room, it was a library. He loved his books. He would read Greek Mythology, it didn't matter."

Me: "How old was he when he started reading Greek Mythology?"

Sandy: "Ten."

Me: "That's incredible. Was he above average intelligence?"

Sandy: "Yes. He wanted to be a doctor. He wanted to be a doctor for children that don't have insurance. And, I mean, he was always like, if there was a hurt animal, he would bring it home and hide it in the barn, so his Daddy couldn't find it. He would care for that animal, whatever it was.

"His favorite holiday was Thanksgiving. He always looked up a new recipe for sweet potato pie, and that was his job.

Me: "Oh, he made it himself? Was it good?"

Sandy: "Always!"

Me: "Stephen and Stephanie are twins, correct? How far apart were they born?

Sandy: "30 minutes because Stephen was breach. I had my kids natural, and I said, "This is my last!" Stephanie was 2 pounds 6. She could breathe on her own. Stephen just had that struggle with his lungs because I had him in my 27th week."

Me: "Did he excel in school? Because I remember hearing something that you said in an interview that he never missed school, but he missed that day, or sometime in the two weeks leading up to his death? Because school sounds like it was a big deal to him."

Sandy: "Yes. He could have graduated in the 10th grade. But he didn't want to leave Stephanie. He wanted to graduate with his twin sister. He would just go to school and do extracurricular activities, work in the office, or sometimes they would send him to work in the

Fed's office or the hospital.

"Stephen was an athletic trainer at school. He didn't' like sports but he was there to help whoever was injured and all that. Any kind of medical matter. He could tell you what was wrong with you, know what you needed to do because he never took medication. He made his own medication out of herbs."

Me: "You're kidding? Did he grow herbs or buy them?"

Sandy" "He grew them. He loved walking through the woods and collecting herbs, and he would grow his own."

Me: "What an amazing young man. What was his biggest fear?"

Sandy: "Strangers. If he doesn't know you, he's not talking to you. Walking down the road, if he heard a car coming, he would hide in the woods because he didn't want nobody to stop. When he was little, he stuttered, and he had to do speech therapy. So, he would whisper in Stephanie's ear, because they were in the same class in the beginning, because he wouldn't talk to nobody. So, he would whisper into Stephanie's ear and Stephanie would tell what he said, because he was embarrassed that he stuttered. He overcame it, but he didn't' overcome the "don't talk to strangers" part."

Me: "The whole thing with the herbs—he would have been an incredible doctor because he's actually coming at it from a holistic standpoint, as well."

Sandy: "Oh yes, he would make lots of things with herbs. I was his guinea pig. He came in once with a biscuit he made and asked me to try it. I said, "Well, who made it?" He said, "I did, just try it." So, I did, and I said, "This is good, son!" He said, "So, you don't feel funny or anything?" "What do you mean? No, I don't feel funny." "Ok, I had to make sure it was safe before I gave it to my dog."

Me: I am in hysterics. I'm lost in her stories and wish I could have met Stephen. "I don't want to make this worse, but you must miss him terribly. I'm trying not to choke up here. I'm just so sorry."

Sandy: "I miss him every day. All day long, you know? I'll get a chance to be with him again. Sometimes when I'll be washing dishes or something, I'll feel him sneak up on me. He used to sneak up on me all the time. And I'll know he's here.

"He was just totally amazing. I mean, I can't really explain Stephen. I don't think they make enough words to describe him."

Me: "How long did he have left to go to become a doctor or a nursing student? How many more years?"

Sandy: "He was about to start his clinicals. After his death, that following week, he would have started his clinicals. In Charleston and Columbia hospitals to do clinicals. There was only one class he did not like in High School. Spanish. But he learned it. He did learn it, but he didn't like learning it."

Me: "I can tell you, I'm not usually at a loss for words. I've interviewed a lot of people. But I was really dreading this because I did not want to bring you any pain. And I hope I haven't."

Sandy: "No. I love talking about Stephen. I can talk about him all day long. He loved to joke We were at Walmart near here and he saw a group of Mexicans. And he was saying, "Mama, say this to those guys," and he would tell me something to say in Spanish. I said, "Oh no you don't, buddy. I'm not saying something to them, cuz I know you're trying to get me in trouble!" He would have made me look stupid." (Sandy is laughing at the memory.)

"He and Steph wanted to go to this little carnival we had in Barnwell. He wanted a funnel cake or something. It was cold, so I told them I was going to stay in the car and he and Stephanie could go get a funnel cake. I'm sitting in the car, and he comes over and says, "This guy wants my number." The concession stand guy wanted his phone number. OK, so Steven gave him a number and when he got back to the car, he said, "Mama, if you get a call, don't answer it. I gave that guy your number." I said, "*What?* Why did you give him MY number?" He said, "Well, I had to give him a working number!"

Me: It took me several moments to stop laughing. I felt so privileged to understand how wonderful Stephen Smith was.

"Well, I just can't thank you enough, Sandy for speaking with me. I feel cheated that I didn't get to meet your son. I feel the world was cheated out of the doctor he would have become. Everyone that I mentioned you to said you're just the most loving, humble, and kind person, and you certainly are."

Sandy: "Oh, thank you."

I ended the interview with offering to send her something we Coloradoans make with "herbs." I asked her if she wanted me to send her brownies from the Rockies—the regular kind, or the kind from Boulder. Her infectious laugh filled my heart. I would like to thank Susanne Andrews for setting up this interview for me. I will never forget it.

Stephen Smith

CALLED BY: Stephen
FAVORITE QUOTE: "You can have all the money in the world...but one thing you will never have...is a dinosaur!" ~Homer Simpson
MOST LIKELY TO: Become a medical physician or rule the world

Stephen's Senior picture at Wade Hampton. His favorite quote above summed up his humor, and his outlook on life: "You can have all the money in the world...but one thing you will never have...is a dinosaur." --Homer Simpson

So many of Stephen's friends spoke of his kindness and courage. He lived life large and was always true to himself. He danced, roller skated, laughed, and joked, but mostly what they remember about him was his compassion. He lifted them up. He encouraged them to dream big. Many of his friends came from modest beginnings. He reminded them that their current conditions were only temporary. Stephen encouraged other gay friends to "come out" and not be ashamed of who they were. He was the light for them, shining through the prejudice and fear that surrounds people who live differently than us.

It would be to many of these peers that law enforcement went to in the early days of the investigation into Stephen's death to try and find some answers. But the wagons had circled. The fear ran deep in Hampton regarding the names they would have to implicate. Others, who knew more than they should about the heinous events that took place in the early morning hours of July 8, 2015, went underground, or lied during police interviews. Some left town. Lt. Thomas Moore said he wondered if some "had been incentivized" to leave, meaning they had been paid to take a quick "vacation."

The Highway Patrol would not have an easy time of it.

July 13, 2015.

An audio interview is conducted with the 911 caller Ronnie Capers. He states he never stopped. He at first thought it was an animal in the road but as he got closer, he could see it was "a white guy" lying in the road.

July 14, 2015.

Cpl. Duncan travels to the impound lot to see Stephen's car. He would comment later that the SCHP never got to see the car at the location where it was found, which would have been helpful. The gas cap was still off and dangling.

Duncan contacted the man by phone who showed up at Stephen's wake claiming to be his boyfriend. Mark claimed he and Stephen were in a relationship. He said he talked and texted with Stephen the morning Stephen was killed. Mark told Duncan that on the night of the murder, Stephen was being harassed at Snider's Crossing by two "rednecks," one with a tattoo, on his way to Walterboro that night. He told Duncan that Stephen was often "harassed in his town" and that people screwed with Stephen's car battery. He rambled on that at one point while talking to Stephen he heard dogs barking and trucks going by. He asked Stephen, "Are you walking?" Stephen replies, "No." "The last thing I heard before the call dropped, was BIG mud tires," Mark says.

The problem Duncan was having with Mark was that he was clearly disjointed in his thoughts. He admitted he was on heavy medication for some brain injuries. He repeatedly calls Duncan throughout the day, leaving messages that he might be wrong about his timelines, etc. but reiterating he did not do this to Stephen. He even offers to take a lie detector test. His best guess as to when he spoke to Stephen last was 3:30 a.m. The coroner put Stephen's death at 3:00 a.m.

Duncan contacts Cpl. Rowell and asks him to get Stephen's iPad and laptop from the family.

July 15, 2015.

Duncan travels to Troop 7 Headquarters where he meets with Lt. Taylor and Lt. Moore. Moore transfers Stephen's laptop and iPad to Duncan.

July 17, 2015.

Cpl. Duncan interviews Stephanie Smith (Stephen's twin) at the DMV where there was a patrol substation. She said Stephen had been more "secretive" in the two weeks prior to his murder. She stated she didn't know of anyone who had a problem with Stephen. She said she was sure he had classes at Orangeburg Tech the night before his murder, July 7th. Note: Sandy Smith said Stephen had morning classes. It appears his schedule was at different times of the day. Stephanie said Stephen had gone to an Exxon and bought cigarettes for his dad. He called her from the gas station and said his car "wouldn't crank." When she got there, she found someone had loosened his battery cables. She tightened them back up and followed him home. She said this was at 5:30 p.m. He jumped in the shower and left at exactly 6:00 p.m. It was the last she heard from him.

Stephanie told Duncan that Stephen would usually leave at 6 to be at his 8 -10 pm. night classes at Orange Tech. She said in the past two weeks he had not only begun to act secretive, but he was coming home late. There were times he skipped school and stayed at his mom's all day. She said he had been spending more time at Bobcat Landing, and that once, he sent her a picture while he was supposed to be in class. One of his shoes was off. When she questioned him about it, he said he had taken it off to get mud off of it. She told Duncan she didn't believe it was muddy at the college. It seemed Stephen had begun skipping classes and was living a clandestine life where he confided less in his family than was normal, kept later hours, and was very careful about letting people know his address.

As Duncan recorded the session, Stephanie went on and said that Stephen didn't talk about his boyfriend a lot. She said he didn't get into relationships usually because he didn't trust people. He was in gay chat rooms online, but it was not to meet someone; it was just to have someone to talk to. She admitted he was on Craigslist and had begun "putting himself out there," sometimes for money. There was one person Stephen confided to her about. She said that all Stephen would say is that the new friend was "a prominent person in the community and that he was taking him on a deep-sea fishing trip soon." According to Sandy Smith, that trip was to be the weekend after he was killed in the Florida Keys. A friend said that

Stephen told her, that if she knew who the person was, it would rock Hampton. Note: photos of Buster, Paul, Maggie, and Alex on a fishing trip surfaced the same month Stephen was murdered.

Buster, Paul, Alex and Maggie Murdaugh during fishing trip

Buster and Paul. Paul is showing off his catch.

The 2015 Megadock Billfishing Tournament was July 8-11, and the Carolina Billfish Classic that year was July 18-20th. These are part of the SC Governor's Cup competitions in South Carolina. The Carolina Billfish Classic was "the weekend after he was killed."

While conducting interviews for this book, I spoke with one of Stephen's closest friends about the fishing trip. I asked her, "If Buster was trying to keep a possible gay relationship secret, why would he have invited Stephen to a fishing trip where his family was going to be joining them?" Her answer was, "Maybe it was his way to "come out" to his family." [It has to be mentioned again that there is no evidence that the rumors surrounding Buster Murdaugh are founded by fact. Police reports and witness statements are all we have to go by.]

Stephanie tells Duncan that Randy Murdaugh was the second person to call her father after Joel was called by the Sheriff's office to come in to identify Stephen's body. He told Joel he would take Stephen's case for free...before there even was a case. She said her dad "was iffy" about the offer. [Duncan does not include this in his report.]

Stephanie Smith tells Duncan that she officially left the house for the first time since Stephen's death the day before (July 16) and went to a store. She said a bunch of people came up to her saying, "Did you know the Murdaugh boys are behind it, saying Buster Murdaugh, the one we went to school with, did it, and some of his friends." It was hard for Stephanie to believe that. "I'm just sitting here like 'why?' It makes no sense," she said. "He's never said anything bad about Stephen. He's never been around Stephen."

[In truth, Alex Murdaugh had coached Stephen and Buster in baseball when they were younger. They played on the same team. It was also said that Stephen tutored Buster in High School.]

Duncan asked Stephanie who told her the rumor. She said, Stephen's friend, another kid she called Taylor, and "a couple of other people."

[This was also not included in the case notes, but it was a recorded interview at the substation at the DMV, July 17, 2015.]

Duncan returned Stephen's laptop to Stephanie. The iPad was sent to Charleston, SC with Trooper Proctor. Duncan then went to speak with Stephen's mother, Sandy Smith. Sandy confirmed what Stephanie had said: he was being more secretive in the weeks prior to his death. He was also skipping classes, which was not like him. Sandy said the family was skeptical of Mark, the man who showed up at the funeral and said he was Stephen's boyfriend. Sandy tells Duncan that Stephen was going to school and hung out at Bobcat Landing a lot recently. (Bobcat Landing is a lake and hook-up spot on 601, the same highway on which Stephen's car was found.)

Sandy tells Duncan that she keeps hearing rumors about the Murdaugh boys. "The thing going around Hampton, that everybody keeps coming up to me and saying, is it was the Murdaugh boys." Duncan repeats, "The Murdaugh boys?"

"Yes. Whoever they are," Sandy stated. [This conversation concerning the Murdaugh boys was not listed in Duncan's case notes. The audio has aired on several TV documentaries.]

Sandy mentioned a friend of Stephen's named James who worked at the local Bi-Lo store. She said they had had an argument a while back but had become friends again.

Duncan speaks with Rowell about tracking down James at Bi-Lo and seeing the store surveillance video. Duncan reports that Mark (the man purporting to be Stephen's boyfriend) was seen hanging around the accident site that morning. [Where Stephen was found in the road.]

July 21, 2015.

James admits he and Stephen had been in a relationship, but he hadn't seen him in a while. No store video surfaces.

The Interviews Begin

According to Cpl. Duncan's case notes, July 21st duties continued. He contacted Lt. Johnson at SLED and was told there was still no luck in unlocking Stephen's phone. Duncan contacted Sandy Smith, Stephen's mother, but she had no new information to give him.

July 28, 2015

On July 28, Duncan reviews the download from Stephen's iPad on the dates pertinent to the investigation. The information does not reveal much.

iPad download:

- Media: 7/5/15. 14:44:33 EDT
- 11:50 – 1:00: do not come…& nbsp.
- Francamente me quiero ir a casa, la color me esta matando
- Tuesday 3:30
- 1955

Not much to go on. Stephen was killed on Wednesday, July 8th. The sentence in Spanish is equally confusing. It translates to: "Frankly I want to go home; the color is killing me." The 'nbsp' is said to be texting slang for 'no bulls%$t please.'

July 22, 2015

Investigator Proctor with the SCHP said this in his file report:

"I went down to MUSC on this date to meet with Dr. Erin Presnell, she is the pathologist that performed the autopsy on the victim in this case. The reason I went and spoke with her was due to a preliminary report where she stated that the victim was possibly struck by a motor vehicle mirror, which was the cause of death. F/Sgt. Moore had already had, from my understanding, a heated conversation with her about this issue. The M.A.I.T team has always had a good working relationship with MUSC, so I wanted to see if I could go down there and get some sort of clarification.

"As soon as Dr. Presnell came into the room she began in a negative tone stating that I did not have a meeting scheduled and that she was very busy. She stated that she could not even begin speaking with me about this case without the coroner's consent. I advised her that I had spoken with Coroner Washington the day before and she basically called me a liar and said she would call him right then. When I asked if she wanted me to call from my cell phone, she backed off. I asked her why she stated that in the report and her answer was "because he was found in the road." She had no evidence other than that for the statement being put in the report. She asked why we did not think it was a vehicle strike and I explained to her that we had no evidence of this individual being struck by a vehicle. I asked her if someone with a baseball bat could do that, and she said "No". When I probed further, asking what about someone in a moving car with a bat, she stated. "Well, I guess it's possible." She then asked if we found a bat as evidence.

"I could see that this conversation was not going to yield any positive results. As I was leaving, she stated that the report was preliminary, and it was my job to figure out what it was that struck him, not hers.

On 8-18-2015, "I spoke with Coroner Washington today in

reference to the final autopsy report issued from MUSC. He faxed me a copy of the report and told me that he does not agree with the pathologist stating that the victim was struck by a motor vehicle. We discussed the fact that the report states the cause of death as blunt head trauma, motor vehicle crash, pedestrian v. vehicle. Then the manner of death was "undetermined." I would think that the blunt force head trauma would be the cause of death and the motor vehicle crash would be the manner the trauma was delivered to cause the death. The pathologist also states in the report, that "in light of historical information along with the autopsy, these conclusions were made." To what historical information she possessed, I am unaware.

SCHP Incident Report listing no sign of vehicle contact.

I attempted to speak with Dr. Presnell at an earlier date to go over information that had been discovered throughout the investigation, and that was ill received. The coroner did tell me that the deputy coroner, (Kelly Greene, who was responsible for the transfer of evidence and who was fired sometime between July 22-August 18, 2015) had gone down to MUSC the morning of the autopsy and spoke with the pathologist; she has since been fired from his office. I spoke with Deputy Coroner Greene, and Agent Burke with SLED, as both of them were present at the time of the autopsy. Both stated they made no reference to the pathologist about the victim being struck by a vehicle, only that he was found in the road. The coroner stated that he had made contact with the pathologist, Dr. Presnell and she stated that she would be willing to change her report to read however he wanted it."

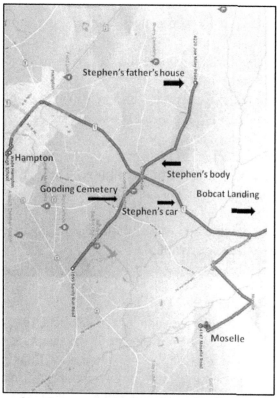

Map showing pertinent locations for Stephen's case.

Chapter Nine
Evasion

July 29, 2015.

Forensic scientist Michael Moskal of SLED sent a letter to J.D. James of SCHP with the results of trace evidence results from Stephen's clothing:

- One black Nike short sleeve shirt: No automotive paint found.
- One pair of khaki Union Bay cargo shorts: No automotive paint found.
- Cutting taken from item 3: No automotive paint found.
- One pair of blue Airspeed Footwear shoes: No automotive paint found.
- Debris collected from items 2 – 4: "Several single-layer metallic blue paint chips were found. Due to the condition of the sample, no make, model, and year information was available.
- "These paint chips are suitable for comparison should a standard become available."

August 3, 2015.

Cpl. Duncan contacts Lt. Johnson with SLED to make arrangements about getting Stephen's phone back on Tuesday.

Duncan contacts Sandy Smith to see if she can help them unlock the phone. She tells him she is the secondary fingerprint for the phone and that she will meet him in Orangeburg on Tuesday.

M.A.I.T with the SCHP's investigator J.D. James wrote in the case file notes:

"I received a message to call SLED agent Michael Moscal in

reference to discussing trace evidence located on the deceased's clothes in this case. During our conversation, Mr. Moscal advised he located around 10, 1mm single layer blue paint chips. Mr. Moscal advised he needed more paint layer evidence to pinpoint a particular vehicle. Mr. Moscal advised that the PDQ database indicated the paint could be from an industrial tool, dumpster, or signpost. Mr. Moscal added that Toyota used this particular paint on its vehicles from 1982 to 1988."

August 4, 2015.

Duncan picked up the iPhone from SLED. Notes no chain of custody with the phone. A report from SLED noted that Duncan did sign a chain of custody form on August 4, 2015, and that he transferred the phone to L. Conley of the SCHP on Highway 1-95 the next day.

Duncan meets with Sandy and Stephanie Smith in Orangeburg to see if Sandy can unlock Stephen's phone. She is unable to. He then gives it to Conley the next day, August 5, 2015.

Duncan contacts Rachel, Stephen's best friend. She said the last time she spoke with Stephen was by text July 7, 2025, around 7 – 8 pm, the night before he was murdered. She said they just talked about school stuff. She didn't know where he was or what he was doing.

"He was very likeable," Rachel said. "Not to my knowledge did anyone not like him. I heard it was a hit-and-run and then it wasn't'." Those were the only rumors she had heard. No other information provided.

August 5, 2015.

Cpl. Lance Conley meets with Duncan and gives him Stephen's iPad. Duncan then returns it to Stephanie Smith, Stephen's sister.

A billboard is placed on Sandy Run Road asking for any information on Stephen Smith's case. Cpl. Rowell states, "We haven't really found anything that would indicate to us that it's vehicle involved."

August 6, 2015.

Stephanie Smith contacts Duncan by phone and says she has some information to give him. Duncan asks her to email him the information she just talked to him about. She emails him the information.

Sandy Smith calls Duncan and says she went out to the scene and found a footprint about 200 feet down from where Stephen was found. The impression was in an ant mound. She said another footprint had been obscured by the rain.

The Buster Murdaugh and Stephen Smith Rumor Begins

August 7, 2015.

Duncan contacts a girl named Angela. She is the source Stephanie Smith emailed to Duncan. She tells Duncan that Angela came to her at church and told her about something she was told. Angela tells Duncan a boy, "another friend of mine," named Brenden had texted her and asked if she ever heard that Buster and Stephen were in a relationship? Angela replied, "No, not that I know of. Why?" He said he heard it. She asked him who told him, and he said he just heard it. Angela tells Duncan she was aware that Stephen was gay.

Duncan calls Brenden and receives no answer.

August 10, 2015.

Brenden's father calls Cpl, Duncan, and askes "What's going on?" Duncan tells him. Brenden's father says he'll have Brenden call him.

August 11, 2015.

Duncan alerts Trooper Moore to the rumor from Brenden that suggested he heard Buster and Stephen may be in a relationship.

Brenden calls Cpl. Duncan and confirms he did send a text to Angela. He said he only "heard the rumor." He tells Duncan he doesn't know anything else about Stephen's death. That was the only rumor he heard. He does not say from whom he heard it.

It is here we see what would become a common thread concerning the young men who became implicated in Stephen's murder. Brenden had two different lawsuits pending with someone in PMPED, the Murdaugh law firm, concerning car accidents. These suits were filed against him later in July of 2015, shortly after Stephen's murder. Both lawsuits were dropped in 2016. We will see this level of influence occur again against two others whose names appear in police reports.

Duncan notes in the case files that he is still looking through the downloaded information from Stephen's iPad. "Still trying to get a timeline. No new information," he writes. He notes that the iPad was at Orangeburg Technical College the night before Stephen's death, according to the iPad breadcrumbs. This is the college Stephen was attending. (Stephen was killed in the early morning of June 8th.)

SCHEDULE Course/Description	Days	Times	Lc
BIO-211-02 Anatomy & Physiology II	W W T	10:15AM 12:20PM 01:30PM 03:35PM 01:00PM 05:10PM	
HIS-202-01 Amer Hist: 1877 to Pres	TTH	08:00AM 10:05AM	
BIO-210-01 Anatomy & Physiology I	M M T	10:15AM 12:20PM 01:30PM 03:35PM 01:00PM 05:10PM	
AHS-106-35C Cardiopulmonary Resuscit	MW	01:00PM 09:00PM	
AHS-106-92 Cardiopulmonary Resuscit	MW F	05:00PM 10:00PM 09:00AM 03:00PM	

EXPLANATION OF CHARGES

Term   Date   Invoice #   Code   Description

Stephen's course schedule and description from Orangeburg Tech. Courtesy of the SCHP M.A.I.T files.

The Rape Kit

One of the many odd circumstances concerning Stephen Smith's murder is the ordering of a rape kit. If this was a hit-and-run, as the pathologist stated, then why was a rape kit needed? The autopsy report doesn't mention a rape kit was obtained during the autopsy, yet Deputy Coroner Kelly Greene was given rectal, penis, and oral swabs taken from Stephen's body at the time of the autopsy. Green was in charge of the evidence collected during the procedure. The Hampton County deputy coroner transferred the rape kit from MUSC to Trooper Proctor on July 22, 2015, two weeks after Stephen's death. Proctor gave the kit to Laura Lynn Hydrick. She moved the evidence from Highway Patrol 6A to the Highway Patrol Central Evidence Facility on August 11, 2015.

Hydrick left the Highway Patrol not long after that and went to work at the Yemassee Police Department where Gregory Alexander was Chief. Alex Murdaugh reportedly gave Alexander $5,000 a few weeks after Stephen's murder. Alex also defended Hydrick in a lawsuit she was involved in from Midland Funding LLC in 2016. Gregory Alexander also communicated with the Smith family during the Smith investigation, and he was one of the first people Alex Murdaugh called on the night Alex found his wife and son shot on the Moselle hunting property.

Deputy Coroner Greene was fired sometime before August 18th as we've noted earlier in the book. What was going on with the rape kit evidence? Why were the two people responsible for it fired or removed themselves from the Highway Patrol shortly after it was transferred to evidence? We never hear about the rape kit again until 2023.

August 17, 2015.

At 10:54 am and 1:10 pm, Duncan calls the man named Mark who had claimed to be Stephen's boyfriend. It goes straight to voicemail. Duncan leaves messages. Duncan calls Mark again on August 18th and August 26th, both times getting only his voicemail. He has suddenly gone underground after hounding Duncan shortly after he was interviewed concerning Stephen's death.

August 26, 2015.

Sandy Smith calls Duncan and gives him the name and phone number of someone who might know something. His name is Cecil.

Duncan calls Cecil and it goes to voicemail.

Sandy gives Duncan another name and phone number to contact, a person named Nora. Duncan calls her and it rings several times. There is no voicemail recording. Duncan doesn't note that he ever called her again.

Duncan reaches out to Stephanie Smith and asks her about Nora.

Stephanie tells him that Nora and a guy named Dale saw a green Jeep following Stephen on or the day before his death. Duncan does not note that he ever called Dale to follow-up on the Jeep tip.

August 27, 2015.

Duncan interviews Cecil, the boy Sandy told Duncan about the day before. Cecil worked at Hardee's in Hampton. He told Duncan that he went to school with Stephen, but they never hung out or anything. Cecil said a white man in his 30s or 40s came looking for him, and Cecil called the police and told them about him. Cecil's co-worker said the man came into Hardee's again looking for Cecil. He told the co-worker that he knew Cecil from hanging out with him and Stephen before.

Duncan asked Cecil if he heard any rumors about Stephen's death. He said he heard "he was running in the woods from somebody." He then added he thought he was running from an older guy. "Maybe it was some guy he was messing with, and nobody knew, and Stephen was going to bring him out."

August 28, 2015.

Stephen's car was returned to the family. While Sandy Smith was looking through it, she found a gate pass to an upscale gated community in Hilton Head. It had the name of a man on it. She called the SCHP about it. Cpl. Lance Conley interviewed the man. He said he was an older man and recently divorced. He met Stephen online and had a one-night stand with him. When asked if money exchanged hands, he paused, and then said, "No." He hurried on to say that he "doesn't do this kind of thing often." He said they hooked up on June 28, but that was the only time. The man said he texted Stephen a few times later but didn't realize he had passed away until he was contacted by Stephen's mother, Sandy. Conley did not ask the man where he was the night/morning Stephen was killed. He is never contacted again by the authorities.

5:02 pm.

Proctor calls a young man on the phone whose name was given to him through the rumor mill. Proctor tells him that through a "he said, she said" rumor, this young man's name was mentioned. We will call him David. David seemed to have a lot of information about the events of July 8th. He said he heard that past weekend that "certain young men" were riding down 601 (Bamberg Highway), saw Stephen broken down on the road, passed Stephen and turned around and "stuck something out the window," that ended up hitting Stephen. David tells Proctor, "I will help you in any way possible."

David tells Proctor that he heard three names. "I don't want to say the names over the phone," he said. He asks if he can meet Proctor in person. He lets Proctor know he's in a tricky position. He's sort of "torn" because he hates relating news based on the "he said, she said" situation. But the more he has thought about the situation, what he heard "makes sense."

Proctor tries to soothe David's reservations. He tells him his office is out of Charleston and "there's no big name in Hampton that worries me, and I want you to feel at ease about this as well." Proctor tells David that he's heard that "people associated with this name (a big family) have been around kind of not, well, kind of threatening, putting the heat on people" to keep their mouths shut.

David tells Proctor that he knew "this person" and went to school with him. He says, "It kind of all makes sense." He is still reluctant to make unfounded accusations. He tells Proctor he would feel better if they could meet in person rather than discussing this over the phone.

Sept. 2, 2015.

Video from the interrogation room where Proctor and David meet show them seated across from each other at a small table. Proctor has his notes spread out across the table and takes additional notes as David tells what he knows. David's face is blurred to maintain his privacy. His hands move in sync with his words.

David says he first heard Stephen was shot but then heard it was hit-and-run. He says that recently, in the past week, week and a half, he heard that "two, maybe three people were riding down 601 and saw Stephen on the side of the road. They were, I want to say, messing around with him, and stuck something out the window. I heard names, well a name, and that name was Buster Murdaugh." David goes on to say, "It was kind of out of character to who I knew." He said the person who told him this said Buster was high on drugs.

David went on, his hand lifting and falling onto the table as he spoke. "I hate to only be able to give you hearsay. I hate it because the main thing is whether that is the case or not the case, there is still somebody who lost a child, lost a brother, lost a family member and that's just not right." Proctor asks David where he heard this from, and he gives him a name we have heard before: Brenden. David says Brenden told him that Buster and another guy tried to sell him cocaine at a party at Moselle. He then says that this guy suddenly moved to Oklahoma. "It's just weird to me," David says. "All this could be a very strange coincidence, but it's just weird to me." He tells Proctor that the other guy with Buster pushing drugs on Brenden was "bad on drugs."

Proctor asks David if he thinks this guy who was "bad on drugs" was in the car with Buster. "It fits the mold," David said. "There's some part inside me that says there's a possibility," he says, pertaining to this other guy being in the car with Buster.

Proctor asks David how he found out that this guy moved to Oklahoma. He says he saw it on his Facebook page. David then brings up Brenden again as the source of the rumor and says he doesn't understand why law enforcement hasn't gone straight to Brenden to find out.

As David willingly tells all he knows, it becomes apparent that he knows a good deal. Proctor tells him that he heard Buster, and the guys were coming back from a baseball game when the events took place leading to Stephen's death. David says Buster and whoever was with him were actually coming from the Murdaugh's house in Moselle on 601. Rumors of a party at Moselle after the game have surfaced before. Stephen's car was found less than 10 minutes down 601 from Moselle. Proctor asks David if he knows if Buster was driving. "I would imagine so," David says, stating Buster usually drove when he and his friends were driving around. He says Buster used to drive a Suburban but would sometimes drive a black F-150 or an F-250. Kevin backs away from naming any other names that may have been in the car with Buster.

David reiterates that the only name given to him was Buster's. "Everyone is shy to say anything because, I don't want to say power, but the name brings a certain standard with it. I think that's why people are hush hush about it."

David admits he has heard that "they have gone to certain people and told them to keep their mouths shut," he says. He tells Proctor that three people at a party were talking about Stephen's death and a guy said, "I feel nothing will come of it." And that's how the Murdaugh's name was brought up. "I feel they wouldn't want anything to happen to their reputation," David says. He admits he's even gone to South Carolina games with them. "I hate to throw names out there but then again, what's right is right, what's wrong is wrong.

Proctor says to him, "I think it's a situation when you grow up and your family is kinda high profile and you get away with some things because of your family name, and you're given, given, and given things. You become invincible in a way, and you get a little liquor, and you think you're untouchable."

"I think that it happened, they freaked out and maybe it's just trying to get it covered up at this point."

David says the Smiths "deserve the truth. I'd want to know the truth."

Proctor tells him that "Buster was on their radar long before you were...the Murdaughs know that. They know he's on our radar. What you're telling me is valuable information." He then shares with David a separate chain of people who gave information to the SCHP concerning Buster's involvement.

The subject returns to Moselle. David tells Proctor that the Murdaughs have "big parties" at their houses "every weekend or every other weekend. Kids from Varnville and Bamberg, anywhere you can think of" would come. That is where the party spot was in Hampton," David says of Moselle. He says he's gone to one party there. It's known "for a lot of fights, alcohol, drugs kind of thrown in there at the same time."

David goes on to tell Proctor that he was surprised to hear Buster's name associated with Stephen's death. At first, he thought they meant Paul, Buster's younger brother. "I don't want to say troublemaker, but Paul's more the 'my last name is Murdaugh, I can do whatever." Proctor asks him Paul's age. "Is he 15, 16?" David says Paul is either a junior, or possibly a senior, in high school. They used to call him "Little Paul."

David makes a plea to Proctor. "I'm not scared of those people, but I definitely don't want them knowing that I had anything to do with this. I just don't want to get into all that because Hampton is a small town. I really can't say anything bad about them," David says.

"They were nothing but nice. I hate it that I have to say anything towards them. I can't help it if it's the truth. Your name can't carry you but so far."

Hoping for more information, Proctor dangles the "maybe it was an accident" ploy. He tells David that the way he understands it they didn't go out there to intentionally kill Stephen.

"I feel very strongly about that," David says. He says he doesn't believe Stephen was killed on purpose.

Proctor says, "That's the thing. That night. If they were playing around..." If people are hiding it and lying about it, "How do you expect me to take mercy on you when you left this family for months not knowing what happened to their loved one? Typically, you don't see the Highway Patrol working a murder and that's what this is. We're not classifying this as anything other than a murder. There's a reason why Hampton County Sheriff's Office is not handling this, and I'll leave it there."

It was an ominous statement to make. It intimated the Sheriff's Office was in Murdaugh's camp.

David plays his card. "Someone at work said the Highway Patrol is looking for 'the Murdaugh kid'." Proctor tells him, "I'm not saying the Murdaugh boy did it because I don't know yet but if we're going to start throwing out names, I'm not going to withhold his name because of who he is. His name's going to be out there just like anybody else's name that is on my radar, and I don't care who knows it."

David says he hopes Murdaugh didn't do it. "But when you start throwing puzzle pieces in there...it makes more sense than not."

Proctor tells him "There had to be more than one." If Buster was driving, then someone else was responsible for hitting Stephen. "It's not all on Buster Murdaugh," he says. "There's more people involved here."

Other rumors that turned up during the interviews of Stephen's friends were that "he was beat up and thrown out of a truck," "he was pulled from his car," "two or three boys were involved," and a possible "party at Moselle following the softball tournament." One person said the reason the boys may have been coming down 601 was that "the only place to go for food nearby is Hampton and you would go down 601 to get there." One name that came up over 40 times during the investigation in those early days was Buster

Murdaugh.

No one has been arrested yet, and all names mentioned are innocent until proven guilty. As of the writing of this book, a new investigation into the murder of Stephen Smith is underway. His body was exhumed April 1, 2023, and an independent autopsy done in Tampa, Florida. SLED has released a statement saying they have "cracked" Stephen's phone. One report said the rape kit is still missing.

Chapter Ten
New Evidence in the Stephen Smith Case

During the research for this book, this author was privileged to interview a number of people who echoed David's thoughts: Hampton is a small town, and it is hard to share evidence to which they may have been privy. In some cases, I had to sign a confidentiality agreement before some sources would speak with me. One in particular was associated with a name that would make it very hard to come forward. Others were frightened to talk. It was only when I promised not to use their names that they told me the following stories. All people mentioned are presumed innocent until proven guilty. Some of the names mentioned are being questioned again by SLED in the Spring of 2023.

The Softball Tournament

I am guarding the anonymity of the people who gave me the information listed here in the new evidence section. I will use only the first names of those implicated in the reports:

According to my source, they report an eyewitness who was in the parking area after a softball tournament the night before Stephen's body was found. He said he saw several boys get into Buster Murdaugh's truck with him:

"I was told by someone who was at the game that the people who reportedly left the game with Buster that night was a young black man, possibly named Donterrio or Brendan, a boy nicknamed "Ro," and someone named Kelly. Kelly wasn't seen getting into the truck, but he was standing there with them. The witness thinks he left the game with them. And Shawn, who is Jimmy McMillan's grandson."

Reports coming up will see these names surface again, except for Kelly and "Ro."

The Tire Tracks

As reported earlier, a young man was driving down 601 early in the morning of July 8th and saw a small yellow car pulled "a full car-width" from the roadway. "It was on a cement swatch with grass bordering it on both sides. The grass was wet with dew, and you could clearly see a set of tire tracks leave the road, 'swoop' up by the little car, and then swing back onto the highway in an arch. It looked like whoever was driving the car that left the tire tracks forced the yellow car off the road or pulled up next to it. It was odd to see this car a mile from anything out in the middle of nowhere in the early morning hours."

[You can see the hand-drawn map provided to me on page 29.]

The Broken Gate

On page 30 is a crime scene photo of Stephen's car. I circled the metal fence behind his car. This fence runs the parameter of a large parcel of land used as a hunting property. The owner lives out-of-state, so it is probably not occupied year-round. A source told me the following:

"Just up from Stephen's car on 601 is a rural road that turns to the right. It's the same direction Stephen's car was facing. It's called Corbin Lane. If you turn right onto Corbin Lane from 601, there is a gate there that goes to the hunting property. It's not far from Stephen's car—maybe one quarter of a mile. Well, the morning Stephen was murdered, somebody crashed into that gate. I heard there were cameras by the gate…maybe deer cameras. Anyway, I heard that Jimmy McMillan from McMillan Farms paid to have that gate replaced. I'm thinking, 'Why is Jimmy paying for this other guy's gate?' Now, Jimmy is Shawn's grandfather. And Shawn's uncle leases the farmland next to the property where the gate was busted in. It could be the hunting property owner saw the deer cam footage and recognized Shawn and told Jimmy he owed him a gate."

We know that Shawn will come up in reports surfacing later in

2015 in early December. He and his friend Patrick are written up in a police report by Cpl. Duncan.

Basically, a tip came in on December 9, 2015, saying Shawn went to his friend Patrick and told him he was drunk the night of July 7th and "hit something" in the road. He went home, but the next morning, he went back to see what he had hit. He saw a lot of police and got scared. He later heard a young man had been struck on Sandy Run Road and was dead. The location of Stephen's body is right down the road from the McMillan Farms where Shawn lives with his grandfather. Patrick goes to the man dating his mother, Darrell, and tells him what Shawn has told him. Darrell calls his ex-stepson Nick, who was with the Hampton County Sheriff's Office at the time, to get his advice.

Darrell tells Nick that the odd thing is, is that after Patrick tells Darrell about what Shawn told him, he went out back and threw up. Darrell says to Nick, "Why would Patrick get so upset that he would go outside and throw up, unless he was with Shawn?"

This is all written down in Cpl. Duncan's report, with one ominous statement written at the bottom. It says that Randy Murdaugh told Darrell to tell all of this to the police.

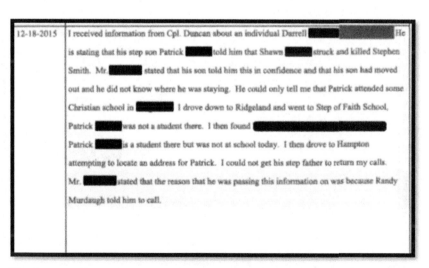

| 12-18-2015 | I received information from Cpl. Duncan about an individual Darrell ████████ ██ He is stating that his step son Patrick ████ told him that Shawn ████ struck and killed Stephen Smith. Mr. ████ stated that his son told him this in confidence and that his son had moved out and he did not know where he was staying. He could only tell me that Patrick attended some Christian school in ██████ I drove down to Ridgeland and went to Step of Faith School, Patrick ████ was not a student there. I then found ████████████████ Patrick ████ is a student there but was not at school today. I then drove to Hampton attempting to locate an address for Patrick. I could not get his step father to return my calls. Mr. ████ stated that the reason that he was passing this information on was because Randy Murdaugh told him to call. |

The bottom line of Duncan's report concerning the Shawn tip says: Mr. _____ stated that the reason he was passing this information on was because Randy Murdaugh told him to call.

Courtesy of the SCHP case files.

What is interesting, is that a tip was called in two days earlier on December 7th, implicating 'Murdaugh' and a young man named Donterrio. Was the Shawn tip two days after the Buster tip meant to offset the blame against Buster? Why is Randy Murdaugh's name involved with the information about Shawn hitting something? Later, Darrell would retract his statement and say he never said Randy Murdaugh told him to call. Later, the following year, Shawn was told to say he hit a deer.

Shawn and Patrick were involved with lawsuits with PMPED in 2015 for various crimes. Shawn's were related to vehicle infractions, while Patrick's were more serious. He was being sued for shooting three times at a car with civilians inside during a dispute. Patrick was given an attorney name we have become familiar with later in the Murdaugh saga: Corey Fleming. Both young men were facing prison time. Strangely, both of their cases were dropped the following year in 2016. Had they been blackmailed or "incentivized" to tell the "Shawn was drunk driving and hit something" story? Once the cases were dropped, Shawn was allowed to say it was a deer he hit. There were rumors that there was damage done to Shawn's side-view mirror on his truck. Again, was this staged?

Report from Cpl. Duncan referencing the email tip he was given saying Donterrio along with another black male and a white male (Murdaugh) are the ones involved in death. Duncan passes this on to Proctor who tries to reach Donterrio but is unable to find him. Courtesy of SCHP case files.

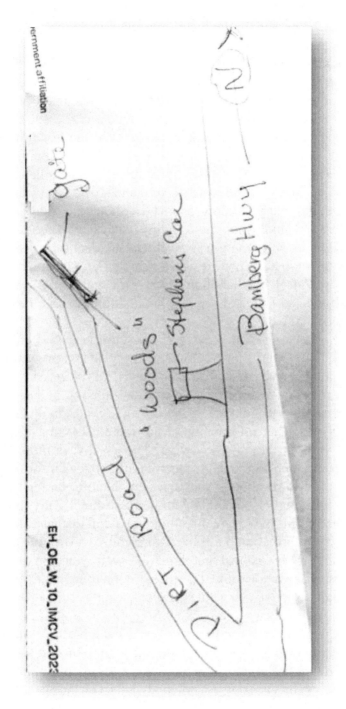

Drawing of gate & Stephen Smith's car locations.

The drawing on the previous page was given to this author by the person who passed on the 'gate' information.

This author interviewed Nicholas Ginn who was the officer Cpl. Duncan contacted concerning the tip about Patrick and Shawn. He said the following:

"I worked for the town of Hampton at the time that I got involved in this case. I wasn't involved in it much at all, but when I got involved, it was because of my stepfather at the time; that's really the only thing that I did. Not that it's any less important than any other case, it was simply not in my enforcement jurisdiction. But he called me because he trusted me and because I was in law enforcement, but you know, as I said, I didn't have any jurisdiction over that area and by that time Highway Patrol was conducting their investigation, so to me it was a vehicle accident type deal, whether it was intentional or not. It was a vehicle issue for me because the Highway Patrol was handling it when it came to me; it was out of town limits, so I didn't have any jurisdiction over the investigation or any of that work.

"But one thing I do know is, even inside a law enforcement agency, not every law enforcement agent is privy to certain information. Even though the Highway Patrol was investigating, and you know these officers were investigating and the Sheriff's Office and everybody, all of these people were involved, but that doesn't mean that information is not there. They may have found things without the other knowing. There's always more to it than what comes out. Because they're not going to leak information, you know, everything about whoever leaked the information that did get out is going to be somebody who was not directly involved in that case, because if they were directly involved in that case, they would let *all* the information out if they were going leak a little bit.

"A lot of things just get kind of, well you're a writer, you understand, that you know I could say something and leave out one word and it can mean a whole different, a completely different thing than if I added that word back in. So, you know, it's kind of one of those things. It's kind of like you get bits and pieces of information and then maybe it's not juicy enough and you know a lot of people want attention. I'm not out here looking for attention but both you and I know, that as soon as somebody gets a chance to get on TV or in a newspaper, in a book, they are going to do whatever it takes to get there, and you know a lot of times you really don't have to do that. I've got like a grain of salt part of this case compared to other people. But you know, look how many people have contacted me, so you really don't have to do anything to get that exposure if that's what people are looking for."

One of my interviews was with a person whose friend was at a bar, seated at a table with a young black male named Brenden. Brenden was talking to his best friend and had been drinking too much. He blurted out, "We beat the ^%$# out that little $#@@." This person said he was talking about Stephen Smith. Is Brenden the other black male listed with Donterrio and Buster in the report above? Oddly, it's a young man named Brenden who started the rumor train that Buster was in a relationship with Stephen. And those rumors began circulating within the week of Stephen's death. The name Brenden is also mentioned earlier in police reports.

Gloria Satterfield's Statement

Gloria Satterfield was in a rare position to know most of what went on at the Murdaugh's homes. She had worked for them in several capacities for over 20 years. She was a housekeeper, nanny, party server, errand runner, and pretty much anything they asked of her. She practically raised Paul and Buster. Paul was only two when she came to work for Maggie and Alex. She worked at their home on Holly Street in Hampton, and she would be asked to clean at Moselle, especially after party nights.

It was the day of Stephen's death that Gloria went to someone with whom she was very close. She was clearly distressed, and it was obvious she had something to disclose that was upsetting her. Gloria was a very religious woman who attended church and loved reading the Bible. It was said she loved Paul and Buster as much as her own children and would do anything for them...to a point.

The person that Gloria went to on July 8, 2015, was kind enough to give me an interview but asked that their name be kept private. Here is what I was told:

"Gloria came over and she seemed really upset. Word of Stephen's death was just starting to circulate through Hampton. I asked her what was wrong, and she said, "Buster turned his truck in today to the repair shop. He is borrowing Maggie's Range Rover until it's fixed." It was her demeanor as much as her words that struck my source as something significant. The truck wasn't in for engine trouble; it went in for damage to the truck. This was before anyone knew of a broken gate. In fact, until that information was turned into SLED and other authorities by this author in March 2023, the gate and tire mark information had never been shared. What was going on was that Stephen had been in a hit-and-run accident. It may be that Gloria's angst was due to the damage done to Buster's truck on the same day a young man was found murdered not far from Moselle.

Paul Murdaugh on Facebook

I was told about a post Paul Murdaugh made on his Facebook page the day of Stephen's death. He posted, "We took care of our problem." According to my source, a lot of people saw it before Alex demanded that Paul "take it down." The information came from someone privy to Alex's comment.

The Parties

An interview for this book was with one of Stephen's closest friends. I asked about the famous parties at the Murdaugh's. I had always assumed the parties were inside the house at Moselle, which they may have been often. But according to Stephen's friend, in the summer months, they would often be down by the dog kennels. They would have a bonfire, and music. There was drinking, marijuana, sometimes heavier drugs, and fights...always fights. This is what was told to me by this friend, who wishes to remain anonymous:

"There was always a fight going on at the parties. Whether it was at Moselle or the Holly Street house. The person who usually initiated the fights was Paul. Almost every time. Yeah, well, OK. So, we went to a party out in Moselle, and well, it was this big field. And then there is a big, big shed. Right beside the beginning of the road. Like when you first came in. When we went to this party there were so many people. I mean, and it was pitch black dark out there.

146

The only thing we had were like big truck lights. And a fire, and there were just so many fights going around. It was insane. Paul didn't start every single fight, but he would just instigate things. It was just what he did. I mean, like he would just start things, you know what I mean? Like he just had his friends with him and if he told his friends that he felt disrespected or he wanted to jump this person, there didn't have to be a reason. It was just what he did. He was just mean like that, especially under the influence, I'd say.

"And then there was another party that we had went to. They had this one at an actual house on Holly St. It had an inground pool in the backyard. Maggie was there, which I didn't know until the very end of the party that anybody was there parent-wise. Paul had his friends and stuff. This one boy there was openly bisexual. Stephen Smith was not here on this night. There were other people there that were close to Stephen. There are some mutual friends, and so on and so forth.

"We were smoking weed, but there were all kinds of people smoking weed, and drinking, and probably doing God only knows what. Paul got mad because we were smoking weed there. He told one of his friends, basically to tell all the "potheads" and the "Ni$#rs" to go. Like he actually said the "N" word and when he said the "N" word, wow, other people heard him. And it caused a big fight because all of a sudden there were a bunch of people of color getting mad. I've never seen nothing like it. There are a bunch of white people and people of color. Again, it's like all of these white country people. Like, literally like they were all facing each other about to fight because Paul was being so racist. But even his friends he invited were pissed.

So, his mom…this is where Maggie comes out the door, and she was like "Party's over! Party's over! Everybody go home!" Because she knew Paul was about to get beat up. Because I guess she was watching from the house. One of Paul's friends came around to where the bi-sexual boy was, and he said, "Watch where you walk to go to your car because if you come around this way, Paul told a bunch of us to jump you." And he said, "I don't wanna do that, but I'm Paul's friend, so I'm gonna have to do it." That's what he said. I thought about it after Stephen was killed. You know people were saying the Murdaugh boys did it. It sounded like what would have happened to that guy at the party if he hadn't been warned to go a different way to his car."

Other stories about parties at Moselle were highly consistent. Kids came from all around. It was the party place. The Murdaugh's had money. They were said to be very generous with their money. Kids were invited to big trips, to hang out at all three places: Moselle, Holly Street, and the Edisto Beach house. One source told me Paul's nickname was "Gas money," because he always had a credit card at the ready. It was found out during the boat crash that Maggie Murdaugh often handed him her credit card.

Aerial view of the Murdaugh Holly Street house with pool.

Finding Out Stephen Had Been Killed

The following is from a source who related to me a personal view of what happened the morning Stephen died:

"It was so early, but I had already heard that the Murdaughs are the ones who did it. That's how fast and like everybody knew. Everybody. I found out because we were at MUSC. Which I later found out was where Stephen's body was at. Getting his autopsy. I had no idea, but that's where I was with my grandma and my mother cause my granny was getting breast cancer surgery. So, it was supposed to be a very good day for us, you know, because of her going through all that, and this was supposed to be the day where, you know, she gets it removed and everything hopefully would be great. And we were about to cross the street to get lunch, because she had just gone in, and my sister called me and she said, "I think that Stephen, they think that it was Stephen at the time just passed away from getting shot." And that's what I was told. I didn't even know how to react to it, so I told my sister, "If you're telling me this, and you're serious, then you need to please know that it is for real, that you're really telling me this and that it's true!" I'm just like "whoever you're talking to, please, call them back and get like a confirmation."

"And so, we hung up and I was just, my world was spinning, but I was trying to be optimistic because please, no, you know? Like no, no, no! She called me back and then she told me, "Yes, it is him." But then again, you know, this was where they weren't sure because again, he's getting an autopsy and this is where they were trying to say like hit-and-run, you know? Accident, you know, versus straight up murdered. And I think, yeah, so I heard that he got shot and then, I think it was the very next day when I was told. Something about the hit-and-run. I had already been told that the Murdaughs were involved. Yeah, by two different people that were not around me at the same time. I mean, just, Why? I mean, you know, that's crazy. And then it's like if I know this, you know how many other people knew at that point? And I mean this was, it probably wasn't even lunchtime, on that same day he was found in the road. It was so early, and everybody already knew! About the Murdaughs. They took his body away at, what, 9:30? So, it was early so that's why it's just stuck with me, and stuck with me, and stuck with me.

"Then something happened, like a month after that. Please don't laugh at me, but I kept feeling Stephen around me. He was one of my very best friends. We had just gone out with some friends a couple of days before he was murdered. So, I went in this little store. This was when Coke was putting names on their cans. I just walked up to the cooler to get a can of Coke, and there was two cans side by side in the cooler. One said Stephen and right next to it, it said Paul, sitting right beside each other. And I looked at it and I couldn't believe it. And that just gave me goosebumps. There's just, yeah, there were just so many things. Like there's just so many things that I felt like Stephen was trying to say, and that might sound crazy to someone else, but I believe in messages from people who have passed on."

Many reports were given to this author about how fast the word spread through Hampton the day of Stephen's death that "the Murdaugh boys were involved." It needs to be stated here, that no arrests have been made in Stephen's death—as of this writing. Everyone is presumed innocent until it is proven otherwise in a court of law.

Alex Murdaugh in front of a blue ATV 5 months after
Stephen's death. Photo courtesy Maggie Murdaugh's FB page

A report was later released from SLED that the blue paint chips found on Stephen's Smith's clothing could have come from a blue ATV, like a "Gator or Mule, etc." The previous photograph is of a *blue* ATV. In the photo, taken just five months after Stephen's death, is Alex Murdaugh (standing), Randolph Murdaugh III (seated inside), John Marvin Murdaugh with his children (in the back). We know the Murdaughs had Rangers at Moselle. A green one is mentioned in Gloria Satterfield's 911 accident call. Most of these

ATV's are similar. It is interesting to note that they are very loud on the open roads. The tires are large with wide tread and made for off-roading. Most in Hampton were sold for farm work and hunting. One of the people investigated in Stephen Smith's case said he was on the phone with Stephen and heard "big mud tires" just before the call was dropped and Stephen was never heard from again.

Other than Stephen's electronics—of which we are still not sure what was extracted—it seems the only tangible evidence SLED has in their possession are the 10 miniscule chips of blue paint. They stated if they had something to compare them to, it would help.

The Investigation Staggers On

The year 2015 ended with the family of Stephen Smith receiving no answers as to what happened to him. Michael DeWitt with the *Hampton Guardian* offered to work with Sandy Smith and post an article at Thanksgiving, literally begging for anyone with information to come forward. They had high hopes that the article would make its way into someone's conscience, but no one came forward. It may be that it did jolt a few people into action, as it was just a couple of weeks later that the two tips came into Duncan: one saying Shawn hit something in the road, and the other naming Murdaugh, Donterrio, and another black male as Stephen's killers. Even with that, Thanksgiving and Christmas came and went.

"The hardest part was that first Thanksgiving looking at Stephen's empty chair," Sandy Smith said. It was not just Stephen the family had lost that year. Stephen's father Joel died just three months after Stephen's murder. According to his family, he never recovered from the death of his son. He stayed in the house and was "a broken man." He finally died in his sleep of what was termed a heart attack. Sandy said, "I think he died of a broken heart."

January 26, 2016.

SCHP Todd Proctor obtained a search warrant for Stephen's phone records from Cellco/Verizon wireless. The warrant covered texts, calls, cell tower pings, etc. for the period of June 9, 2015 –

July 9, 2015. It covered one month of data. The result of that cell phone data investigation was never revealed. In April 2023, SLED released a statement saying they had "cracked" Stephen's phone. This is different from obtaining Verizon call and text information that was done in 2015. This is an announcement that they opened Stephen's physical phone. No information pertaining to what was found was included in the statement.

June 13, 2016.

Highway Patrol Trooper J.D. James interviewed Donterrio, the young man mentioned in the tip Duncan received that named him, Murdaugh, and another black male as Stephen's killers. Trooper Hoffman accompanies James for the interview. When asked how Donterrio found out about Stephen's death, he answered, "I heard he was killed on FB. RIP Stephen. I heard he got hit by a car."

"He didn't get hit by no car," Trooper James says emphatically.

"He didn't?"

"No!"

Donterrio answers questions and tells the troopers how he knew Stephen. "He was my trainer in football in High School. Stephen didn't talk a lot. I heard about it on Friday when I got home."

When asked about how well he knows the Murdaugh boys, he distances himself from them. He doesn't admit to "a party with a Murdaugh who graduated with Stephen." (Buster graduated the same year as Stephen.)

Trooper James starts applying pressure. He tells Donterrio that his name has come up a lot. He finally drops all pretense of this just being an interview. "Do you have an attorney?" he asks him.

That was it. It was the end of any case notes or advancement in the investigation. From the middle of 2016 until the double murders of Maggie and Paul Murdaugh in 2021, Stephen's case went cold. There were many rumors that certain boys were paid to leave town, or they were suddenly involved in lawsuits handled by PMPED that were later dropped. One rumor was that Alex Murdaugh paid for Brendan's college tuition. Another pointed to Donterrio owning an expensive transport business with semi-trucks. Shawn is slated to inherit his grandfather's farm on Sandy Run Road.

So many lives were impacted by this tragedy. Friends of Stephen's were left devastated. Some moved away. His family is still dealing with an open wound that won't heal. For Sandy Smith, it would only get worse.

Sandy filed for Freedom of Information Act (FOIA) information. She combed through reports, hounded law enforcement, and prayed for a miracle. In 2018, out of desperation, she sent a letter to the FBI begging for help.

Sandy's Letter to the FBI

"It has been apparent from the first week of this investigation that authorities are covering up critical evidence and we no longer know who to trust. This investigation is being deliberately derailed. The first call my family received after the murder was from authorities notifying us of Stephen's death. The second came very quickly the same morning from solicitor Randolph Murdoch. In fact, he called my ex-husband cell phone as we waited in the police station for a positive identification. He said he heard of the case and was interested in working pro bono as a liaison between the family and investigators. Stephen's father accepted the offer, although we were unsure why Mr. Murdaugh wanted to help us. We also weren't sure how he found out so quickly, even before it was confirmed to be our son. Surprisingly, after just a few interactions, Mr. Murdaugh stopped returning our calls. As a family, it was suspicious to us since he had taken such an immediate interest in the case and then became unreachable so quickly.

Several weeks later, an unnamed witness told yet another member of her family that he was present when Stephen was murdered, and that the killer was Buster Murdaugh. According to this witness, Buster Murdaugh allegedly beat Stephen to death with a baseball bat because Stephen was gay. The witness said they were out smashing mailboxes when they came upon Stephen, and Buster seized the opportunity. The young man said that Buster threatened to kill him if he ever spoke up. This information was given to investigators, but nothing has come of it. There is also an alleged conversation between a schoolmate of Buster's littler brother Paul and school officials. I was told the schoolmate claimed to have knowledge of the murder and implicated Buster as the murderer. There was no further follow-up on this information. The Murdaughs are probably the most prominent family in Hampton County. Stephen had on more than one occasion mentioned to friends and his twin sister that he was involved romantically with someone from a prominent family in the county who was hiding his sexuality. He said it would shock people to know this person was gay. We suspect this could be the young man Stephen was referring to, though he never named him. Buster Murdaugh got rid of his old vehicle following the murder, which according to her, was critical because I and others believed there was DNA in Buster's old vehicle. A year before, I submitted a plea for help to former SC governor and current 2024 presidential candidate Nikki Haley. To my surprise, Haley not only responded but made the case an investigative priority. She responded promptly and assigned new investigators to the case. While it appeared to be the answer to our prayers, very little progress was made, and they say they have exhausted their leads."

Nothing came of Sandy Smith's letter to the FBI.

It wasn't until the boat crash in 2019 that took young Mallory Beach's life that Stephen's case suddenly came back into the spotlight. As the rage over the young woman's death, attributed to an intoxicated Paul Murdaugh, made headlines, tips started pouring in saying, "Look into the Stephen Smith case."

In the summer of 2020, two investigators hired by Parker's Kitchen, who was now embroiled in a lawsuit concerning Mallory's Beach's death, came knocking on Sandy's door. Henri Rossato and Max Frutatti said they were interested in Stephen's death. They asked if they could borrow his iPad that the SCHP hadn't found much on, other than it pinged at Orangeburg Tech the night before Stephen was found beaten to death. Hoping they would help her, she let them borrow her son's iPad. They never returned it.

June 7, 2021, the Lowcountry was rocked by the double murders of Paul and Maggie Murdaugh. Alex Murdaugh, of the Murdaugh dynasty legacy, came back to his hunting property at Moselle after visiting his invalid mother, and found his wife and son shot to death near the dog kennels. Suddenly, stories of Stephen Smith's death rattled the cages of the local law enforcement. People brought up that Buster Murdaugh, the only surviving son of Alex Murdaugh, and Paul's older brother, was implicated over 40 times during the investigation into Stephen Smith's death. Buster was never interviewed. Not once. Buster received one phone call from the SCHP during their investigation into Stephen's death. It went to voicemail. The email also went unanswered. It was rumored that his mother Maggie Murdaugh had taken him out of the country shortly after Stephen's murder. The most prevalent rumor was that they went to the Bahamas. You cannot compel someone to testify in our country. If a Grand Jury were to subpoena them, that would be a different matter. But if they don't wish to talk, they don't have to.

On June 17, 2021, Sandy heard SLED was looking into Stephen's case. They were working on the double murders of Maggie and Paul at the time. Sandy was elated. Something was actually going to happen. She got a knock at her door and found a SLED agent standing there. Rather than ask questions about Stephen, he told her he was there to take a buccal swab to eliminate her as a suspect in the Murdaugh murders. After all, Buster had been linked to her son's death and she might have a motive for murder. She said it felt "like a slap in the face!"

She later got a letter from SLED stating they were looking into her son's death. Once again, she got her hopes up. On June 22, 2021, they officially announced their involvement in Stephen's case.

During this new focus on her son's death, the media was relentless. "They were everywhere," Sandy said. "Everybody was trying to make money off Stephen's death. The *New York Times* knocked on my door at 1:30 in the morning!" Her dog Mercedes would go nuts each time someone approached her home.

As her hopes began to falter again, it seemed an angel had been sent to her. An attorney out of Charleston came calling. Andy Savage said he had heard about her case and was touched by it. He offered to represent her for only one dollar. He immediately began setting the rules for his involvement. She was not to talk to the media anymore—at all! He shut her down from doing interviews to try and keep her son's case alive and beg the community for tips. She was not to mention the "Murdaugh boys" anymore. She agreed and he became her attorney in July 2021. Mr. Savage immediately hired an investigator named Steven Peterson. Peterson was hired to work on the Smith case over the summer. Sandy would later say that she communicated with Peterson more than with Andy Savage. She almost never heard from him. Little did she know that Savage had partnered with Dick Harpootlian on the Charleston Church shootings. Dick not only represented Paul Murdaugh in the boat crash lawsuit before he died, but he would be Alex Murdaugh's attorney as well.

Whether or not Savage may have been sent into Sandy's camp to shut her down from seeking help for Stephen or not, it was his next move that hit her like a brick. On October 27, 2021, Andy Savage released an article with *ABC News 4* whose headline read, "Focus on the Murdaughs and Stephen Smith's Death May Be Unfounded." Savage had not talked to Sandy about the article or that he was about to exonerate the Murdaughs in the death of her son. This was her own attorney, which would give the world the impression she sanctioned the article. She was furious. "I felt betrayed," she said. Her voice was a mixture of sadness, resignation, and anger. She had been used.

Steven Peterson, the investigator Savage had hired to work with Sandy, told Sandy they had a suspect in the case and the Murdaughs weren't connected. They absolved the Murdaughs, although Peterson made it sound like it was only Paul they absolved. Peterson said he interviewed Shawn and he "came undone." He said he told Shawn he had photos of the damage to his truck. Shawn said he hit a deer. When Peterson approached Darrell about Duncan's report on Shawn, Darrell now says he never said Randy told him to tell the police about Patrick and Shawn. Peterson seemed uninterested in the names of the boys said to be seen with Buster that night.

Shortly after this, Andy Savage went live and said the Murdaughs had nothing to do with Stephen's death.

Three days after Andy Savage released the *ABC News 4* article, something wonderful happened to Sandy Smith and her family. This is the story of one woman who heard of the family's sadness and wanted to do something that might make a difference. She called it, "Standing for Stephen."

Standing for Stephen

"I was lying in bed one-night last September and was just scrolling through Facebook," Susanne Andrews told this author. "All of these different Murdaugh pages came out about last summer when Maggie and Paul were killed and as I was scrolling through. I just saw a picture of Steven's gravesite. It's just this little plastic placard and it just had his name and year of birth and year of death. There was this little pitiful looking ceramic cat. But I just saw that and thought of my son—he'll be 18 next month. I cannot imagine in six years that my child would not have a better headstone. No one had come to help her get him some type of monument; something to memorialize his last resting place.

"My dad owns the Capital Club here in Columbia, which is a gay bar, a gay club. It's the longest open gay club in the southeast. I immediately called him because obviously Steven was gay and I was like, "Dad, if I can get in touch with this woman and get permission from her, would it be OK if we host something at the club to try to raise some money to get this kid a headstone?" He said, "Yeah, let me talk with my board members."

"That all turned out OK. I Facebook-stalked Miss Sandy until I found her and sent our message and introduced myself and explained to her what I was wanting to do and gave her my phone number. I asked if she wanted to call me, and I'd be happy to speak with her. Long story short, we planned the auction. We had national media there: *20/20, Dateline, Netflix*, etc. We planned it all within 4 1/2 weeks! It was crazy! We have raised, as of today, well over $40,000. Steven's headstone just went in in July 2022. Everything was on back order because of the supply chain issue so it took a while to get it in and then once they did get the monument in, there was an issue with the laser machine they had. So, they had to order a part for that.

"The first time I met Miss Sandy was before the fundraiser and I met her down in the Crocketville Cemetery. Sherrie Alcorn, she's now in Atlanta but she is the Greenville SC *Fox News* affiliate anchor, and she asked for us to meet her down there, so she and I met. I didn't know when I got there that to the left of Steven's grave is his father's grave who passed away three months after he did. Miss Sandy said it was from a broken heart and Mr. Joel did not have a headstone either. To the right of Steven's grave was a 2-month-old baby boy Miss Sandy lost several years ago. I mean this woman has just been through total hell. So, we raised enough money not only for Steven's headstone, but we got his dad a headstone and that just went in a couple of weeks ago.

"It has definitely been one of the most awe-inspiring challenges. I have a real job too and I was actually moving and closing on a house while in the process of getting this fundraiser together. It's just been one of the most amazing things I've ever been a part of and I'm going to stand by Miss Sandy through the rest of her challenges. I've become really close to Miss Sandy. She comes up here and stays with me; she stayed late numerous times and she's like a part of my family now and it's just been a great little experience."

"I believe we're here to help people and oddly enough I get a lot of flak for it, like there's just some people saying things like "Well, there's a lot of people out there that don't have headstones." OK, then how about you raise money? I mean I can't do it for everyone. I mean gosh, if I could take in every stray animal I would but you can't."

Susanne continued her friendship with Sandy Smith. Miss Sandy has touched the hearts of many who have seen myriad documentaries where Sandy is asked to retell her story about the events of July 8, 2015. It is her hope that by telling the public of Stephen's unsolved murder, perhaps someone will finally come forward with information. As she has often said, "Someone out there knows something." And while, at the writing of this book, in May 2023, SLED is announcing progress is being made, many wonder if a resolution in this young man's murder will ever be found.

Sandy Smith stands proudly behind Stephen's beautiful new headstone during the revealing ceremony at Gooding Cemetery. Photo courtesy of "Standing for Stephen."

Susanne Andrews wanted to do more. She, like many, thought Stephen's death was attributed to his openness about his sexuality. She looked into Hate Crime bills for South Carolina and found none.

Susanne Andrews. Founder of "Standing for Stephen."

The Hate Crime Bill

"DID YOU KNOW SOUTH CAROLINA IS 1 of 2 STATES IN THE NATION THAT DOES NOT HAVE A HATE CRIME LAW? 48 out 50 states have passed a Hate Crime bill - what is the common denominator?" Susanne Andrews said in her petition to South Carolina government officials.

"Yes, there are laws already in place for crimes, however, there should be preventative measures in place to deter people from committing hate crimes in the first place.

"Stephen N. Smith was a gay 19-year-old young man found dead in the middle of the road in the early morning hours of July 8, 2015, in Hampton County. There is a huge coverup to Stephen's death with law enforcement and other influential people in Hampton County. Stephen's death was not the cause of a hit and run. We know that Stephen was brutally murdered and then placed in the road to appear as if it was a hit and run.

"**StandingForStephen** was founded in October 2021 to raise money for Stephen's family so they could purchase a headstone for him – 6 years after his death. Please follow Stephen's story on Facebook.

"Standing For Stephen has accomplished what it originally set out to do…but we are by no means done.

"If Stephen's family cannot get answers about his death, the least we can do for his family is to get a Hate Crime bill passed for the State of South Carolina in Stephen Smith's name or at the very least have StandingForStephen honored as an advocate for helping to get the bill passed this year!

"StandingForStephen is begging the Senators of South Carolina to step up and do the right thing and pass this bill. We will not stop, we will not waiver, we will not allow for this to be swept under the rug any longer.

Susanne Andrews
Founder of StandingForStephen

While the search for justice in Stephen's case continues to roll forward in the year 2023, Sandy is hopeful that her new attorneys Eric Bland and Ronnie Richter can accomplish what others have not. SLED has promised to work together with them to share new information and evidence. At the time of this writing in March 2023, there are rumors of a Grand Jury investigation. Sandy Smith has also started a "Justice for Stephen" fundraiser to raise money to have her son's body exhumed. She wants to put to rest once and for all that his death was the result of a hit-in-run, something she negated from the beginning. It is possible a new autopsy will bring evidence that was overlooked before. Tips continue to come in. After almost 8 years of waiting, we are all praying the Smith family gets some answers. [Update: Stephen's body was exhumed April 1, 2023, and an independent autopsy done. Results of that investigation are yet to be released as of May 11, 2023.]

Stephen Smith will be remembered for so much more than his heartbreaking death. So many people shared this about him:

"He never had a bad day. He was the friend who would sit and listen to you and lift you up." "He walked into a room, and it was a light coming in. Everyone would turn and look at him." "He was unabashedly himself! No excuses! This is me!" "He could dance! Whether we were roller skating, or hanging out, he had moves!" "We were at a football game once at High School, and we were in the bleachers. Stephen started acting like a cheerleader and had the whole section doing the routine with him. He was like that. People admired the fact that he was himself with no apologies. He was real! There was nothing fake about him." "Yeah, he grew up without a lot of money, but it never stopped him. He worked and saved, and he went to college. He would have been an amazing doctor because he cared so much about everybody! He would take home things that got hit by cars and try to nurse them back to health. I will never meet anyone like him again." "You know how you can have a really bad day, or even a really bad year, and you can't see how it will ever get any better? Stephen knew it would get better. He shared that optimism with those around him. He taught us that you can make your world whatever you want it to be. He didn't just say it, he lived it. Why such a wonderful person was taken from us...I just don't know. Maybe the song is right, "Only the good die young."

"RIP, Stephen. You showed us the light. We still feel you. We will never forget you!"

A unique "view" of this tragic case it found in Chapter 40.

Stephen Smith: An amazing light gone too soon.

Chapter Eleven
What Happened to Gloria Satterfield?

Gloria Satterfield. So much more than a "housekeeper."

Gloria Harriott Satterfield was so much more than the media portrayed. Her family was her world. She worked hard for menial pay to keep a room over the heads of her two sons, Brian "Little B" Harriott and Michael "Tony" Satterfield. As a widow, life had not been easy. Yet she is remembered for her love of church and her friends and family.

Gloria worked as a housekeeper and nanny for the Murdaughs for nearly two decades. The 57-year-old was incredibly proud of her profession because it allowed her to create a stable life for her family, all the while caring for others. Gloria is also survived by three brothers — Eric, Wayne, and Scott Harriot — along with three sisters — Sandra Manning, Glenda Pike, and Ginger Hadwin — all of whom seemed close to her.

The Satterfield's during an interview for *NBC*. Front row left to right: Brian Harriott and Tony Satterfield. Back row: Ginger, Eric, and Scott, Gloria's siblings. Photo courtesy of Daily Mail.

Gloria helped raise Buster and Paul Murdaugh. By the time Paul could walk, he would follow her around the house holding onto her skirt. She was paid $10 an hour to cook and clean. She was also asked to help serve at parties, run errands, and other miscellaneous chores. She worked mainly at the Murdaugh's home on Holly Street but would also clean at Moselle. The Murdaughs sold the Holly Street house in 2020 (two years after Gloria's death), making Moselle their permanent residence. Maggie would also spend time at their home at Edisto Beach, about an hour from Moselle. Maggie posted on her FB page that she had moved to Edisto Beach in June of 2020.

Gloria with her two sons Tony and Brian.

This author was told that on the morning Gloria fell she had borrowed her sister Sandra's car. Gloria had been in a wreck the day before and her truck was being worked on. Here the story becomes complicated. Many rumors in the early days of her accident reported she had fallen at the *Holly Street* house. Many referred to it as the Hampton house. Moselle was in Colleton County. Many earlier reports about Gloria's fall say the Hampton House, and many people miss the significance. Supposedly, she arrived for work at 8 a.m. as she always did. Yet, the tragic events that took place the morning of February 2, 2018, at 9:24 a.m. tell a different story all together.

The 911 Call

9:24:38 AM. February 2, 2018.
Dispatcher: 911, where's your emergency?"
Maggie Murdaugh: 4147 Moselle Road.
Dispatcher: Can you give me the address, again?
Maggie: 4147 Moselle Road."
Dispatcher: What's going on out there?

Maggie: I'm sorry?

Dispatcher: What's going on out there?

Maggie: My housekeeper has fallen, and her head is bleeding. I cannot get her up.

Dispatcher: OK, you said she's fallen and she's bleeding from the head?

Maggie: Yes.

Dispatcher: How old is she?

Maggie: I'm not sure. Like 58, maybe? (Maggie sounds strained and a bit put out)

Dispatcher: Do you know if she fell from standing or not?

Maggie: No, no.

Dispatcher: Where did she fall from?

Maggie: Uh, she fell going up the steps, up the brick steps.

Dispatcher: Is she inside or outside?

Maggie: She's outside.

Dispatcher: How many steps are there?

Maggie: Uh, 8.

Dispatcher: OK, is she on the ground or up near the top?

Maggie: She's on the ground. She's on the ground. She's on the ground.

Dispatcher: Is she conscious?

Maggie: No, not really.

Dispatcher: Is she awake at all?

Maggie: Yes.

Dispatcher: Is she just not like responding appropriately, but she is awake?

Maggie: Ma'am, no, she's not. She's not responding. (Irritable)

Dispatcher: OK. I've already got them on the way. Me asking questions does not slow them down, ma'am. Knowing if she's conscious is one of the things that the medic needs to know. Is she responding at all to you?

Maggie: No.

Dispatcher: Ok, so she's not responsive *at* all?

Maggie: Well, I mean she's mumbling.

Dispatcher: So, she is somewhat conscious. Is she breathing, okay?

Maggie: Yes.

Dispatcher: Is she bleeding from anywhere?

Maggie: Yes, her head.

Dispatcher: Ok, are you guys able to control the bleeding?

Maggie: No.

Dispatcher: Can you put a clean rag or anything on it?

Maggie: Yes, I got...

Dispatcher: (cuts her off) Ok, is she bleeding from her face or the back of the head?

Maggie: (To someone else) I've got an ambulance coming. Uh? Ma'am, what, Ma'am, what?

Dispatcher: Where exactly is she bleeding from on her head?

Maggie: I'm not sure, the top of her head.

Dispatcher: (Begins to speak)

Maggie: (Suddenly moans)

Dispatcher: What happened?

Maggie: She just fell back down. Can I please get off this phone and get down there?

Dispatcher: Can I have your name and phone number? Are you able to bring the phone down by her?

Maggie: What?

Dispatcher: Are you on a cell phone where you can walk down there and...

Maggie: I'm not on a cell phone, no.

Dispatcher: Can you bring it with you so we can ask her some questions about what kind of pain she's having?

At this point Maggie has given up trying and is possibly going down the steps to Gloria. We now hear some faint voices in the background. She has handed the phone over to Paul, but before he gets on the line with the dispatcher, we can faintly hear the following:

A male voice asking a question that is indecipherable. Then you hear Paul saying, "We didn't give her *anything*," in response to the question we can't hear. A pause, and then Alex Murdaugh is clearly heard saying, "Good!" Apparently, Alex has arrived on scene. It is probably Alex that Maggie informs that she has called an ambulance, as Paul is already there and is aware of that. Alex is asking for an update from Paul. The question is, what did Alex ask Paul? Was it, "Did you give her anything?" which could be what an attorney trained in Personal Injury cases would want to know. A lawsuit can transpire if a victim is given something that exacerbates their condition. Or did he ask Paul if he gave the dispatcher

167

anything…like details? All we know is that Paul responds, "We didn't give her *anything*," and Alex says emphatically, "Good!"

Paul now jumps on the 911 call:

Paul: Hello?

Dispatcher: Yeah, can you ask the patient what kind of pain she's having?

Paul: Ma'am, she can't talk.,

Dispatcher: OK, do you know…?

Paul: She's cracked her head and there's blood on the concrete and she's bleeding out of her left ear.

Dispatcher: She's bleeding out of her ear?

Paul: And out of her head. She cracked her skull.

Dispatcher: Alright, the other lady said she tried to stand up and fell down again?

Paul: No, I was trying to hold her up, but she told me to turn her loose and then she fell back over.

Dispatcher: Ok. Do you guys know who she is?

Paul: Yeah, she works for us.

Dispatcher: Ok, do you know if she's ever had a stroke or anything before?

Paul: Ma'am, can you quit asking all these questions? (Clearly agitated)

Dispatcher: I already have them on the way. Me asking questions does not slow them down in any way. These are relevant questions that I have to ask for the ambulance. One of my questions is, has she ever had a stroke?

Paul: I don't believe she's ever had a stroke. Not that I know of. (Calming down a little)

Dispatcher: Ok, is she able to talk to you guys at all or is she unconscious now?

Paul: She's not unconscious. She's just mumbling. I believe she's hit her head and maybe has a concussion or something. (Sounding subdued)

Dispatcher: Do you know what her name is?

Paul: Gloria Satterfield.

Dispatcher: Did you say Sanderfield?

Paul: Satterfield.

Dispatcher: Ok, what's the house look like out there?

Paul: It's offset from the road. It's a big house. It has a long driveway.

Dispatcher: Is there a gate down there they have to go through?

Paul: There's two brick columns they have to come through.

Dispatcher: Ok. There's no gate code they need?

Paul: No, Ma'am, and tell them to look for a fella on a 6 x 6 Ranger, waitin' on them in the road. It's green. They probably know what a Ranger looks like.

Dispatcher: Yes. (Sounding amused)

Paul: He's got on a black sweater, a hat, and pants.

Dispatcher: If anything changes with her, if she loses consciousness or anything like that, I need you guys to call me right away, okay?

Paul: Ok. How long is it going to take...

Dispatcher: I've had them on the way since Maggie first told me. I think they're coming from Bells Highway in Ruffin, okay?

Paul: Thank you.

Dispatcher: Ok. But like I said, if something changes, call me back.

Paul: Ok.

We know by the timestamp on the 911 call that Maggie announces she has called an ambulance to someone standing nearby at 2:22 minutes into the phone call. At 3 minutes into the call, we begin to hear male voices in the background, one of them Alex Murdaugh.

Here is Alex being questioned by an insurance investigator concerning Gloria's fall:

Insurance investigator: "My name is Brian McGowan. I'm in Moselle, South Carolina. Today is Thursday, March 29th. The time is approximately 11:15 AM. I'm meeting with Alexander Murdaugh. Mr. Murdaugh, you understand I'm recording this statement?

Alex: Yes, Sir.

Investigator: "And I'm doing so with your permission.

Alex: Yes, Sir.

Investigator: May I have your full name, please?

Alex: Richard Alexander Murdaugh.

Investigator: And do you go by Alexander?

Alex: I go by Alex.

Investigator: OK. And that's short for Alexander, obviously. Yes, Sir.

Investigator: What's your home address?

Alex: It is 515 Holly St. Ext. Hampton, SC 29924.

Investigator: Is that your primary residence address?

Alex: Yes, Sir.

Investigator: OK how? How long have you lived there?

Alex: Since January 2000. So, 18 years?

Investigator: And so, like you and I have been meeting to talk about an occurrence that happened here at the property involving a Gloria Satterfield back on February 2nd of this year, which was a Friday? And you recall the incident I'm referring to?

Alex: Yes Sir.

Investigator: Alright. So, I wanted to ask you some questions about that. So, why don't you just go ahead and start off by filling me in as to how your day unfolded that day?

Alex: I went to work that morning and I received a phone call from my wife that Gloria was injured, seriously injured. And she asked me if I could come home. I immediately left and headed to Moselle. It's about a 12–13-minute ride under normal circumstances and I appreciated the fact that this was a serious injury, so I would estimate that I made it in probably 10 minutes or so.

Arriving I found Gloria, my wife, my son Paul, and my employee Ronnie Freeman. Gloria was on the, we call it a patio. For lack of a better term, landing area at the bottom of the steps. Gloria was there sitting up. Big pool of blood. A lot of blood on the side of her face. Shortly after I arrived here, EMS arrived and tended to her.

Investigator: Did you know Gloria was coming to your house that day?

Alex: I didn't.

Investigator: OK. But was that uncommon? Was that uncommon for Gloria to be here at your house?

Alex: Uncommon for her to be here?

Investigator: Yeah. Was it? I mean, you said when you left for work that morning, you didn't know that Gloria was gonna be coming to work? I mean, come in for any purpose to the house.

Alex: I didn't know that that day, right? My wife knew she was coming.

Investigator: OK? Did you? And when you talked with your wife, you understood that she was coming? For what reason?

Alex: Gloria was coming to be paid. My mom inadvertently left town without paying Gloria for work and she asked Maggie to pay her on her behalf.

Investigator: And so, Gloria was coming here to get paid? And were you able to speak with Gloria before she was taken away in the ambulance?

Alex: I was.

Investigator: Did you ask her what happened?

Alex: Sure. I asked her what happened. I mean, the first thing I was making sure that Gloria.... I was trying to assess her mental capability at the time. Did she know where she was? Did she know what was going on? That type of thing. And you know, asking her if she knew me, did she know Maggie? Did she know Paul? Did she know Ronnie? Did she know where she was?

Investigator: So how was she responding?

Alex: She knew. She knew those things. She knew where she was. She knew who I was. I mean, she, she obviously was not functioning at full capacity, but she did, she, I mean, she knew those things.

Investigator: OK and then the ambulance removed her, and did you follow the ambulance after that?

Alex: I did. I followed the ambulance to Colleton Hospital, and they were a little bit ahead of me. They lost me going through town. I was able to keep up with them in the rural parts, but in town they kept plugging away and I slowed up, you know, for the speed limits and traffic. And I'd say they got a few minutes ahead of me. So, when I arrived at the hospital, they were actually loading Gloria onto the helicopter.

Investigator: OK, now here at your home, I know you and I covered a lot of information regarding the dogs you got, so why don't you just go down the line? I think you said you have four dogs.

Alex: Four dogs. We have Bubba who is a yellow lab and he's the oldest. I estimate that he's probably six years old. We have Bourbon who is a chocolate lab, who I estimate is probably a year and a half old, maybe younger than that. And the youngest we have is Blue, who I estimate is a year old. Blue is a Labrador Poodle mix or a Labradoodle. And then we have Sassy, who is a German shorthair, who is six months, no more than six months old.

Investigator: OK. And in particular, I think you had expressed that Bourbon, the female chocolate lab, I believe she was purchased from Lazy Lab kennels. And we'll button up all that data. But she had been away at obedience school, is that correct?

Alex: That is correct.

Investigator: And how long had she been back when this incident occurred?

Alex: I think it's been a day. I think she has been back. A little more than a day.

Investigator: OK? And when you were talking with Gloria before she was taken away, did she, did she describe the chain of events in any way to you? Obviously, she was out of it.

Alex: She indicated that the dogs had caused her to fall.

Investigator: She was at the base of the front steps?

Alex: She was, and she was sitting on the base of the steps when I arrived. Now my understanding from my wife when she found her, she was unconscious. Unconscious and her head was on the landing area and her feet were up the steps.

Investigator: So, she was like she was upside down?

Alex: Well, I think she was laying on her back or on her side, but her feet were up on like the second step and her head was on the ground, so she was literally on the steps. With their head down on the brick landing area.

Investigator: Did Gloria live here at the property?

Alex: No, she did not. I don't know her exact address, but I know that Gloria lived in Furman, SC. OK, so that's about 20 minutes, 20 minutes, 25 minutes. It's in Hampton County.

Investigator: And how long would you estimate that Gloria had been doing work for you and all your family?

Alex: She's been working for our family for close to 20 years, I would estimate. I know she babysat my children when they were, when my youngest was an infant. So, he's 19 now.

Investigator: So, and she was paid how?

Alex: Paid as she went along. She was not like a full-time employee. She was an hourly I mean. She would be paid by the hour when she would work.

Investigator: OK, alright. And I know, I know we had, we had gone over that. The obedience school is run by Brett Lawson. You're gonna tie down the rest of that information for me.

Alex: I'm gonna get Brett Lawson's. I'm gonna get what paperwork he has. I'm gonna get vet records and I'm gonna get the genealogical papers on Bourbon.

Investigator: OK, and when was the last time you would estimate that Gloria had worked for either you or your wife Maggie, here at the house prior to this event?

Alex: I mean, Gloria did some things. I mean, she was routinely doing things for us. So, whether it was running errands, whether it was doing something at the Hampton house or doing something out here it would have been, it would be in the very recent past. It would have been within 14 days, probably less than that.

Investigator: Alright. And she was familiar with Bubba, Blue, and Sassy? Did she ever have any problems with any of those dogs?

Alex: No. She was familiar with, yeah, she was familiar with them, and I mean she would have been familiar with Bourbon before she went off to obedience school? I don't know if we ever had her. I'm trying to think. I don't know that we ever had Bourbon at home before, but she was certainly familiar with Bubba, Blue, and Sassy.

Investigator: During the course when she would be working for you, would she feed the dogs?

Alex: Sure, I mean, there's been occasions where she did.

Investigator: Did you ever have any other incidences involved in any problems with the dogs being aggressive or anything similar? I guess any kind of incident with a complaint about the dogs.

Alex: Never had any issue with any of the dogs being vicious or aggressive in the sense of violence or biting or attacking or any of that. And the problem is and why we sent Bourbon to obedience school is, as I told you earlier, she would, I mean, she's so hyper she would stir all the dogs up and they compete to be petted and to get attention and so. You know, what I'm assuming happened is when Gloria pulled up the dogs are, you know, rushing her for affection. And you know Bourbon had only been back for a day or so. So, you know the way they all do when Bourbon's here is different than they do when it's just them.

Investigator: OK, so the people that were, that were on site when the ambulance came were you, your wife, Maggie, your son, Paul, and an employee of yours, Ronnie Freeman.

Alex: That's correct.

Investigator: And was anybody with Gloria, when she drove up, I assume she drove her own car here.

Alex: That's correct.

Investigator: Was there anybody in the car with her?

Alex: No.

Investigator: OK, so there was no witness to the chain of events to the event itself, right?

Alex: No, Sir. Not that I'm aware of.

Investigator: OK. And do you have any surveillance cameras around the exterior of the home?

Alex: No, Sir.

Investigator: I've tried to go over everything. Think of anything else you'd like to add?

Alex: I don't think so.

Investigator: Alright, nothing else to add. I'll be concluding the interview at this time.

Gloria Satterfield.

Chapter Twelve
So Many Lies

What is most notable in Alex's interview with this insurance investigator at the end of the previous chapter is that he never anchors himself to a timeline. Not once did he give the man a time: not when he left for work, not when Maggie called him, not when he left work to go home...not once. It's all ambiguous. Yet, the insurance investigator never tries to pin him down for details. He seems more interested in hearing about the dogs and their history. That interview by McGowan is March 29, 2018. Gloria fell February 2nd and died about 3 weeks later on February 26, 2018. Note how fast Alex is moving on getting this claim going. He's talking with insurance investigators in roughly 4 weeks' time.

A Lloyds of London attorney hired to question Alex Murdaugh in the case concerning Gloria's death was a man named Scott Wallinger. He interviewed Alex, Maggie, and Paul concerning the accident. Lloyds of London was the insurance holder for Alex's Homeowner's Policy and would pay on things related to that. Someone falling on the property, especially due to the property owner's dogs, would fall under that policy. Let's look at the timeline and all the inconsistencies concerning Gloria's fall that morning. The full payout amount for this policy is $505 thousand dollars. Wallinger's report is very interesting. Let's compare it with the 911 call.

Maggie calls 911 at 9:24 a.m. and says her housekeeper has fallen from "walking up the brick steps," "outside," and is "on the ground."

According to the interview Maggie gave to Lloyd's of London's investigator, Maggie "was asleep and was awakened by the sounds of the dogs barking in an usual tone" which alerted her to go outside.

She went out the front door and saw Gloria "lying on her back, head toward the bottom of the steps, with a bleeding head wound." She tells him Satterfield's "eyes are open. She was conscious and mumbling gibberish." Maggie said she yelled "Oh my God" and called 911. Maggie also says she calls for Paul who was "in his bedroom asleep."

Moselle house with the 8 brick steps leading up to the front door.

Maggie also added in the report that she "saw the dogs outside around Gloria." Maggie said she expected Gloria to come by "some time that day." She made a point to talk about their chocolate lab Bourbon, saying the dog "was just horrible, seeking attention, and always whining." They had just picked him up from obedience school a few days before. This jives with what Alex told McGowan in the interview at the end of the previous chapter. They also agree that there are four dogs: Bourbon, Bubba, Sassy, and Blue. Maggie says the dogs were "roaming free."

While interviewing Gloria's close friend, Linda Hiers, for this book, this author was told that "the dogs were never allowed to roam free." Linda also said that "Gloria hated dogs and would kick at them if they got around her." She doubted very much that the dogs were loose in the first place, and secondly, they knew better than to come to Gloria "for affection," as Alex stated in his interview with McGowan.

During the double murder trial of Alex Murdaugh in February

2023, we learn there is an electric fence around the front portion of the Moselle house for the dogs. We also heard they had dog beds on the porch as they weren't allowed inside due to allergies. But we also heard Maggie would go down to the kennels to "run the dogs" and let them out of their cages for a while. Maggie was said to favor two of the dogs.

In the 911 call, you hear no dogs barking. Maggie and Paul never mention that dogs tripped her, which would be something you would think they would mention when describing the fall. It is Alex who begins the "dogs tripped her up" theory. Paul at one point confirms it during his interview with Lloyd's investigator Wallinger.

In this same interview with the Lloyd's of London's attorney, Alex tells him Maggie called him at PMPED at 9:45 a.m. The 911 call is at 9:24 a.m. As mentioned in the previous chapter, if you listen to the 911 call, you can hear Maggie tell someone who has apparently just arrived on the scene that "I called an ambulance." This is roughly at 9:26:22 in the call. There are the sounds of male voices in the background, but you can't tell what they are saying. Then about a minute later, just when Maggie quits responding to the dispatcher's questions, you hear a male voice say something, and then Paul replies to it, "We didn't give her *anything*." You then hear Alex say, "Good!" That puts Alex arriving at the scene around 9:26 – 9:27 a.m. In Alex's interview with McGowan, he is careful to give no timeline. Yet, here he tells Wallinger, Maggie called him at 9:45 at work to alert him of Gloria's fall. That means he is saying he left work almost twenty minutes *later* than he arrived at the house!

He tells Wallinger that he "immediately left work and got to Moselle before EMS arrived." According to the dispatch log, EMS arrived on the scene at 9:41 a.m. If Maggie called him at 9:45 a.m. at work, and PMPED is a 20-minute drive to Moselle, how does he arrive before the EMS team gets there at 9:41 a.m.? Even if you speed, you can't get there four minutes *before* your wife calls at 9:45 a.m. to alert you there has been an accident!

Let's get back to the questions about the series of events leading up to the 911 call. Wallinger interviews Paul, who says, "I was asleep in my *downstairs* bedroom, and I heard dogs barking" and then his mother calls "down" to him. He said, "I knew something was wrong."

Yes, there is definitely something wrong. Paul's bedroom is

upstairs at Moselle. Maggie and Alex had the master bedroom on the main floor where the kitchen and rec room are. In the double murder trial, their housekeeper in 2021, Blanca, said that when SLED came in, they looked in Alex and Maggie's room on the first floor. She then said they went *upstairs* to Paul's bedroom and found a shotgun shell on his nightstand. There is no bedroom beneath Maggie and Alex's bedroom on the first floor. Did Paul slip up? Was he describing the Holly Street house? Many rumors circulated that Gloria's "accident" was at the "Hampton house" which was their primary residence until they sold it in 2020.

Alex tells Wallinger that when he arrived at Moselle, Gloria was "sitting up on the landing to the stairs." Maggie tells 911 Gloria just "fell back over." When Paul gets on the 911 call, he explains that he was trying to help Gloria sit up, but she told him to leave her alone. She put her arm down to try to help herself up, but she fell back over. Paul told Wallinger that "Gloria started throwing up, so he and Alex sat her up" while waiting for EMS to get there. So, which is it? Was Gloria lying flat, throwing up, and Alex and Paul sat her up? Or was she already sitting up when Alex arrived? Alex told McGowan that she had blood on her face and there was blood on the landing. Alex told him as well that she was sitting up when he arrived.

Paul tells Wallinger that when he went outside to see what his mother was yelling about, he saw Gloria on the ground with her feet up on "the 2nd or 3rd step from the bottom, and she was lying on her back." He said she was bleeding from a head wound and blood was on the brick landing. He said she was awake, making weird noises, and not making any sense.

Maggie tells Wallinger that Gloria was able to tell EMS her name, but when asked, she said the current president was Bill Clinton. Yet, we have both Paul and Maggie telling the 911 dispatcher that "she can't talk; she's just mumbling." Another comment was that she "was talking gibberish that didn't make any sense." Yet, Paul tells Wallinger that he heard Gloria tell his dad that "the dogs tripped her up." Interestingly, that is the exact phrase Alex used in his interviews. Paul will be the only one to collaborate Alex's story about the dogs. Alex and Maggie state later that Gloria's relatives said the dogs made her fall, yet they didn't say which relative. As Gloria's family stated, she said little at the hospital during her 3-

week-stay, and the medical staff said Gloria told the admitting staff in the Emergency ward she "didn't know what made her fall," yet Alex's dog story persisted. Alex told anyone he ran into that his "dogs tripped her up."

Alex told Wallinger that Gloria was semi-conscious when he got there that morning. The medical report at the hospital stated "she fell from a standing position down a few stairs. She does not know why she fell."

As if the story isn't confusing enough, we have a phone interview with Ronnie Freeman, one of the two work hands on the property that morning. Maggie makes a point to say they were "nowhere near the house" during the incident. In *Netflix's* documentary, *A Southern Scandal*, an investigator gets Ronnie Freeman on the phone to ask him if he ever overheard anything about Stephen's Smith's death while working at Moselle? He answers, "No," but then goes on to begin commenting on Gloria Satterfield's death:

"Been getting to work at that time at 7:30 am, so Gloria probably come through there at about 8:30 am. Walkin' up to the house, she's got a McDonald's cup in one hand, her purse on her shoulder, like she does every mornin'. Maggie calls me about 15 minutes later. I asked her what the hell happened, and she was hysterical. 'Ronnie, you got to get up here. Gloria fell. There's blood everywhere.' Her feet were above her head. We needed to at least get her body horizontal. So, Paul, you know, grabs her legs. I grab both of her shoulders to get her horizontal."

The investigator then asks Ronnie, "So EMS arrives and it's you, Paul, and Maggie? Investigative reports say Alex talked to Gloria and she said the dogs tripped her."

Ronnie replies, "That's not true. He wasn't there."

Investigator: "So then, you're saying that Alex is still not there when EMS leaves?"

Ronnie: "Correct."

Are you happy with the guided tour of the rabbit hole yet? So now, we have Ronnie Freeman, who Maggie said was one of the two workers that day on the property, but not near the house, stating he saw Gloria drive in and was close enough to see her carrying a McDonald's cup and her purse over her shoulder, "like she does every mornin'." Yet, according to Alex, Gloria was not coming to work that day, she was only coming by to pick up a check from his mother that Miss Libby owed her for some work. According to Alex, Gloria would sometimes act as "a personal assistant to his mother."

If Gloria is just there to pick up a check, why take in your McDonald's drink and your purse? And if Ronnie wasn't close to the house, how did he see all that? And if Ronnie was close enough to see all that, why didn't he hear the dogs barking that startled Maggie and Paul when Gloria fell? Why not see the fall? It would have happened within seconds of Ronnie seeing Gloria walk to the steps?

Gloria worked primarily at the Holly Street house. Her friend Linda Hiers told me that she would be called out to the Moselle house to clean up after a party, but she worked at Holly Street. But we have the Moselle property worker saying she showed up with her drink and purse "like she does *every mornin*." Alex told the insurance investigator that the last time Gloria had worked at Moselle was maybe "14 days ago." But Ronnie is saying Gloria showed up just like "every mornin." Perhaps, the question is, where was Ronnie working that morning? Holly Street or Moselle?

Why would Ronnie say Alex wasn't there? It may have been Ronnie who Paul told the 911 dispatcher would be waiting for them in the street at the end of the long driveway to the house. You can hear male voices in the background of the 911 call. Was it Alex telling Ronnie, or maybe Travis, the other farmhand there that day, to go wait for the emergency drivers? Paul knew during the few short minutes he was on with 911 that someone on a "Green Ranger" was already heading down there to wait for them, so someone told a workman to go. It is possible Maggie told him to go in the seconds before she hands Paul the phone, but we hear Alex's voice within the seconds before Paul talks to 911. Why would they lie? Maggie lied about when she called Alex at work. Alex lied about leaving when he got the call at 9:45, only to arrive at 9:41, four minutes *before* he got Maggie's call, and we know he was actually there by 9:26 a.m.

If this is a simple, clearcut accident, why all the lies? Why no sound of dogs barking during the call? And...if Maggie called Ronnie 15 minutes after Gloria arrived at 8:30, *why* does she wait until 9:24 to call 911? None of this makes sense. There is no mention of Gloria's McDonald's cup hitting the bricks and going everywhere. And the first rumors to hit Hampton was that Gloria fell *inside* the *Hampton house*. There is one other thing to consider: Gloria's friend Linda told me Gloria never used the front door. She always went in through the back door.

So many discrepancies. Thanks to the 911 call, we know when Alex is there. We hear his voice. He may have come even earlier than 9:26 a.m. I'm basing his arrival on Maggie telling someone other than Paul or Ronnie, "I called an ambulance." In the Alex Murdaugh murder trial, his employees at PMPED said he typically got to work around lunchtime. But according to Alex, not *this* morning.

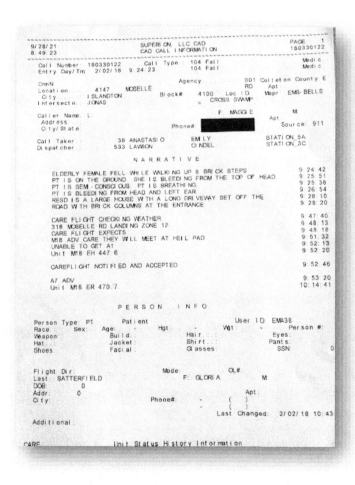

Emergency Services call log Pg.1 for Gloria's 911 accident call.

```
  9/28/21                      SUPERION, LLC CAD                  PAGE    2
  8:49:23                      CAD CALL INFORMATION               180330122

   2/02/18   9:47:33    4  Dispatched            D
   2/02/18   9:48:40   33  Enroute to Scene      ES
   2/02/18   9:51:45    6  At Scene              AS
   2/02/18  10:15:14   16  Reset Unit Time Chec  RS
   2/02/18  10:49:33   16  Reset Unit Time Chec  RS
   2/02/18  11:35:47   16  Reset Unit Time Chec  RS
   2/02/18  11:51:38   16  Reset Unit Time Chec  RS
   2/02/18  12:11:30   20  Available             AV

                    U N I T   L O C A T I O N S

       1      501    ROBERTSON                      BLV  Apt        02/02/1
              City:  WALTERBORO         ST:    ZIP       Block#:   500  9:51:5
              Common Name  COLLETON MEDICAL CENTER


 E18                       Unit Status History Information

   2/02/18   9:26:43    4  Dispatched            D
   2/02/18   9:26:44   33  Enroute to Scene      ES
   2/02/18   9:29:27   30  Enroute to Headquart  EQ
   2/02/18  10:15:14   16  Reset Unit Time Chec  RS
   2/02/18  10:47:22   20  Available             AV


 E23                       Unit Status History Information

   2/02/18   9:29:23    4  Dispatched            D
   2/02/18   9:29:25   33  Enroute to Scene      ES
   2/02/18   9:41:54    6  At Scene              AS
   2/02/18   9:54:11   30  Enroute to Headquart  EQ
   2/02/18  10:08:01   20  Available             AV


 M18                       Unit Status History Information

   2/02/18   9:25:17    4  Dispatched            D
   2/02/18   9:25:17   11  Assigned as Primary   PR
   2/02/18   9:26:02   33  Enroute to Scene      ES
   2/02/18   9:41:22    6  At Scene              AS
   2/02/18   9:42:07   59  Unit with Patient     WP
   2/02/18   9:52:20   34  Enroute To Hospital   EH
   2/02/18  10:14:41   26  Out at Hospital       ER
   2/02/18  10:33:01   30  Enroute to Headquart  EQ
   2/02/18  10:47:22   20  Available             AV


                    D I S P O S I T I O N S

      1  028  Fire Report                Case#  1 - 18-000866 Unit:  M18



                 COLLETON CO. SHERIFF'S OFFICE
```

Page 2 of the Emergency Service call log. You can see exactly what time EMS arrived on scene, and when the helicopter was ordered.

Linda Hiers was Gloria Satterfield's best friend. They had known each other since elementary school and did everything together. It was Linda who Gloria would confide in and vice versa. During a lengthy interview with Linda, she shared several things with me, including her thoughts about the morning Gloria "fell."

"I will tell you this," Linda said. "Gloria, from what I understood, Gloria was supposed to be at Maggie's at 8:00 o'clock to *work* that morning that she fell. From what I understood, she was supposed to be in there at 8:00 o'clock because I've questioned it. Why didn't Maggie check on her when she didn't show up at 8:00 am? If I'm supposed to be at someone's house around 8:00 o'clock, and if you're not there by 10 minutes after, I'm calling to see where you're at. But the point of the matter is, Gloria laid out there for a good 30 minutes, I want to say. Maggie called 911 at 9:24 am. The Murdaughs also said too that she went out there to pick up a check for someone, for someone else. I know she was going there to work because she had to borrow her sister's car; she had to borrow Sandra's car to go to work out there. She had to drop her truck off up here at Scott's to have him work on it and that's why she had to take her sister's car to go to Maggie's. Those dogs should have been in those kennels. The dogs weren't allowed to run free on the property.

"One thing with Gloria," Linda continued, "Gloria did not like dogs, and she did not like cats, point blank. If a dog came up around her, she was gonna kick the daylights out of him because she didn't want him up around her. She loved horses but she did not like dogs, and she did not like cats, so for supposedly the dogs tripping her up or something, I don't believe that; I don't believe that the dogs tripped her up because I knew her too well. No dogs were gonna get close enough to her to trip her up.

"As for the 911 call Maggie made when Gloria fell, if you come up on someone that is injured or whatever, I know I keep my calm about things, but you can tell the tone in the person's voice that they're very concerned. I did not get that feeling with Maggie in that 911 call. It was almost like it was an inconvenience. When I was doing that thing for *Discovery*, one of the other guests on the show, Kim told me, I'm not sure exactly, but they said Buster had been at that house that day also. That is what the housekeeper said. So, I don't know which housekeeper. I don't know if it was Miss Blanca, or Miss Barbara, I don't know. Sometimes Barbara would do for them and sometimes Blanca. Gloria was pretty much full-time and always on call. She was a personal assistant to Alex's mother, Miss Libby, and she worked for Miss Olivia also. She would go out there to Miss Libby's (Alex's mother) and actually her and Barbara would go. It was sometimes just Gloria, sometimes Gloria and Barbara, sometimes it's Barbara. It all depended on who was needed.

"I think it was more or less Barbara that would sit with Miss Libby. Blanca did work over at the law firm, from what I just read a few minutes ago, not too long ago. Blanca translated for one of their clients because they couldn't speak English. Blanca was Hispanic. I don't know what else she did for them, but she did clean for them. Gloria made about $10 an hour. She also cleaned for one other person, and she did Maggie's, and Miss Libby's and Mr. Randolph's. She was cleaning for Miss Vivian. Vivian and Maggie were supposed to have been real good friends, sorority sisters and stuff like that, and something happened between those two. The next thing I know, Gloria said that Vivian told her as long as she's working for Maggie, she didn't want her to work for her.

"Brian (Gloria's son) came over—I can't remember what day--he came over and he was happy. We talked and then he broke down, and he, you know, he has his moments and stuff since she died, and then he told me, "It just makes me so happy that you are my mom's best friend." He and I were talking, and he would say, "My Mama would come home and sometimes, you know, she'd sit down and try to rest and then they're (Murdaughs) calling her again. And I said, "Mama just don't answer your phone or tell them no."

"But, you know, she had to survive," Linda said. "And sometimes you do things that, you know, you have to do. Gloria, when she was living at Furman, it would take probably a good 20 minutes to get to the Murdaugh's house. They would just snap their fingers and she would go running."

"Paul would follow Gloria around when he was 18 months old and hang onto her skirt. She was with Paul since he was a baby; she more or less, you know, raised him. His nickname for Gloria was "Go Go."

A prevalent rumor at the time of Gloria's fall was that Paul had pushed her in some kind of rage. Those close to Paul say, "No way."

Anthony Cook was Paul's close friend, until the boat crash that killed Anthony's girlfriend Mallory Beach. Despite that, Anthony has spoken kindly of Paul in the several documentaries in which he's appeared. In the *Netflix* special, *A Southern Scandal*, Anthony said,

"There was no way in the whole wide world" that Paul pushed Gloria down the stairs. "He would never hurt her."

In the same documentary, Morgan Doughty, Paul's girlfriend at the time, said he was very hurt and sad. She said after Gloria's funeral, Paul sat in his truck and told Morgan stories and his memories of Gloria. Many people said Gloria's picture was the only one Paul carried in his wallet.

In that same documentary, Morgan stated something ominous. She said shortly before Gloria's fall, Gloria found some baggies of pills taped underneath Alex's bed. Paul told Morgan that Gloria told him because she was afraid to tell Maggie for fear that Maggie might think she was snooping, and she would lose her job. This was at the beginning of 2018. Gloria fell February 2nd. Had one of the Murdaughs become angry about Gloria discovering Alex's drugs? Was there a confrontation that morning, and something happened to her? She knew about Buster turning in his truck the day Stephen was murdered. What else did she know? Did it come to a head that morning? Morgan didn't believe the dogs tripped Gloria either.

Gloria was airlifted by helicopter from Colleton Hospital to Trident Medical Center in Charleston. Alex told Wallinger that the medics handed him Gloria's purse as they lifted her into the hospital helicopter. Her injuries were more severe than what appeared on the surface. The head wound was only a fraction of what the hospital medical staff found. According to the report filed by Lloyd's of London insurance investigator:

"She had several severe injuries being managed which together created a greater risk of a downward decline. After a few days, she was moved out of ICU. She appeared by nurse observation to be doing better, then she declined and was returned to ICU and placed on a ventilator. She developed pneumonia of unknown origin, although doctors were aware of sinusitis, they never diagnosed the source of the pneumonia. She developed fluid in her lungs and had a heart attack and coded.

"She appears to have sustained an anoxic brain injury and went into a deep coma. Her brain activity was evaluated by EEG and the family was told she had a slim chance of survival."

Wallinger's report stated that Gloria sustained a right-sided head laceration, a right-sided subdural hematoma, a traumatic brain injury, multiple left-side posterior rib fractures, a partially collapsed lung and a pulmonary contusion. Mr. Wallinger stated, "As you know, a traumatic brain injury can cause amnesia of the *pre-incident* [italics are the author's] activity and some post-incident activity." In other words, Gloria may not remember what happened to her seconds before she sustained the head injury. Did that lead to her telling hospital personnel that she didn't "remember how she fell?"

Gloria underwent surgery to repair her broken ribs and to reconstruct her chest wall, and to remove significant blood in her chest cavity. Wallinger's report continued stating: "The subdural hematoma was evaluated to not be operable," the report said. "Doctors also suspected but never located a bowel perforation. She developed a pleural effusion and already had the partially collapsed left lung. She had bilateral chest drains. *There is charting by radiology to the effect that at one point her endotracheal tube was positioned too far in (touching the carina) and that an arterial line was in the wrong place, both of which eventually were rectified." (Was that suspicious? Nothing was said about it. Italics are the authors.)*

Gloria died February 26, 2018. According to Linda Hiers, Maggie visited her once in the three weeks she was hospitalized while Linda was present. Alex came by two days before she died. Some were suspicious of her hospitalization and what occurred after her death.

According to Wallinger's interview with Maggie Murdaugh, we have the followings statements from Maggie:

Maggie drove to the hospital and met with the Satterfield relatives. "Maggie saw Satterfield in the ICU; she was sleeping but occasionally woke and stated her head hurt and she was cold. Maggie said she never visited Satterfield *alone*. Maggie recalled that at the time of Satterfield's admission it was the peak of flu season and patients were on gurneys in every hallway. Satterfield never told Maggie why Satterfield fell." (Italics are the author's)

According to the report, Maggie visited Satterfield five or six times but never *alone*. She was not surprised to hear Satterfield died.

Something that jumps out in two of these statements is that Maggie makes it a point to say she never visited Gloria "alone." Why? Was there something suspicious going on at the hospital? It seems an odd thing to underscore, twice. Nor does she say who went with her. Wouldn't you just say, "Paul and I went," or "My sister and I went?" Just to make it a point to say that she never went alone to visit Gloria is really odd, in my opinion.

"My daughter and I went to see Gloria in the hospital after the fall," Linda Hiers told me. Linda went every day to see Gloria and sit by her bedside. "She was trying to take the oxygen mask off because I told her, "Bo, you know, you gotta get out of here now, we've got more adventures to go and do," and she was moving her legs and stuff like that. A male orderly came in and saw her moving her legs and I said, "Look at her! We're going to do it. We're going to walk out of here and have more fun times." He said, "It looks like she wants to do that right now," and he smiled. The next morning, she was dead.

"When Gloria was trying to take her oxygen mask off, my daughter said, 'Mama, I think Miss Gloria was trying to tell you something.' I said, 'I think you're right.' I honestly thought that she was going to pull out of that but then the next thing I know, I get the phone call and I can't recall if it was Tony or Sandra, Gloria's sister, I think it was Sandra that called me, and told me "Gloria's gone." I'm like, "What?" I just was in shock because I mean I just thought for sure, she was going to make it when her legs were moving, and she was trying to move her oxygen mask."

"I started to question things, like why was she put into just a regular room? (She was in a coma and hooked up to a ventilator). Should they not have kept her in there to keep monitoring her, but what I understand, she was put into another room. This was still at Trident Hospital. When they had the visitation for Gloria at the hospital, Maggie came once, and she didn't speak to me. I thought that was odd because she knew well that Gloria and I were best friends, but maybe she didn't want to have anything to do with me because maybe she was afraid that I would say something, or you know, ask questions. I think she had the idea that I really didn't care for her to start with. Gloria was working for them once and the morning that I found my daddy had passed right here at the house, you know, right off the bat, Gloria heard, and she said that she had to go to Mr. Lewis and Miss Marianne's house, and she left Miss Libby's house and Mr. Randolph's house, and she come straight here to this house. Maybe Miss Maggie didn't like her taking her off like that."

The strange occurrences surrounding Gloria Satterfield's death did not stop with the inconsistent accounts surrounding her fall, and her surprising death. Gloria's sister Ginger said Gloria had told her the night before her death, "I love you." Gloria was talking. Was that something that was too dangerous to allow? She was dead by the following morning.

The strange things concerning Gloria Satterfield's fall keep mounting. For instance: Maggie tells the 911 dispatcher that "she fell going up the steps, up the brick steps." If Maggie was asleep when Gloria fell, how does she know that? If someone is laying at the bottom of a set of stairs, with their head on the landing and their feet resting on the 2nd or 3rd step, isn't your first thought they fell on the stairs? Not going up, necessarily, just fell at some point? The injury was to the *top* of her head. How do you get that from falling backwards after only climbing two or three steps? How do you land on the top of your head? Is that why there was no notice to the coroner and no autopsy? Her injuries did not match the crime scene.

Angie Topper was the deputy coroner at the time of Gloria Satterfield's death. From the beginning, she saw things that concerned her, beginning with the death certificate. The cause of death was listed as "Natural." Not "Accident," or "Undetermined," but "Natural." There is nothing natural about a fall that resulted in hospitalization, culminating in death. While a heart attack might be considered a natural occurrence based on her injuries, there were extenuating circumstances. There were other things. Angie tried to get answers, and when none were given, she went to SLED.

The letter reads:

Dear Chief Keel,

I would like to request the assistance of SLED in the investigation of the death of Gloria Satterfield on February 26, 2018.

According to a "Petition for Approval of a Wrongful Death Settlement" in the Court of Common Pleas in Hampton County, South Carolina, the decedent, Gloria Satterfield died as a 'result of injuries sustained in a trip and fall accident, in Hampton County.' The defendant in this action was Richard A. Murdaugh.

The decedent's death was not reported to the coroner at the time, nor was an autopsy performed. On the death certificate the manner of death was ruled "Natural," which is inconsistent with injuries sustained in a trip and fall accident.

In light of the inconsistencies noted above, I feel that it is prudent to pursue an investigation into Gloria Satterfield's death.

Chief Mark Keel
4400 Broad River Road
Columbia, SC 29210

Dear Chief Keel,

I would like to request the assistance of SLED in the investigation of the death of Gloria Satterfield on February 26, 2018.

According to a "Petition for Approval of a Wrongful Death Settlement" in the Court of Common Pleas in Hampton County South Carolina, the decedent, Gloria Satterfield died as a "result of injuries sustained in a trip and fall accident, in Hampton County". The defendant in this action was Richard A. Murdaugh.

The decedent's death was not reported to the Coroner at the time, nor was an autopsy performed. On the death certificate the manner of death was ruled "Natural," which is inconsistent with injuries sustained in a trip and fall accident.

In light of the inconsistencies noted above, I feel that it is prudent to pursue an investigation into Gloria Satterfield's death.

Thank you for your consideration.

Respectfully,

Angela Topper, Coroner
Hampton County, South Carolina

Thank you for your consideration.

Respectfully,
Angela Topper, Coroner 9-15-2021 Hampton County, South Carolina

Angie Topper's letter to SLED concerning Gloria Satterfield.

Angie's bravery in coming forward with her concerns over the handling of this case would have dire consequences.

Chapter Thirteen
Smoke and Mirrors

Angie Topper was the deputy coroner when Gloria Satterfield died. During a phone interview with Ms. Topper, she told this author the following concerning the events of Gloria's passing:

"How I came involved in the situation is, and what a lot of people don't know, but I have been treated for cancer. Some days, you know, I was doing my chemo treatments. I would not go to the office that day because they didn't make me sick and nauseated, just made me tired. So, I had a chemo treatment that day, but I was looking for an autopsy report coming in through my fax. You know, I was going to the office on my way home, and just stopped and checked the fax machine. So, I stopped by my office. There were SLED units there at my office within the EMS building. So, I thought it had something to do with EMS dispatch or something. When I walked in, my deputy that was working with me, handling the administrative duties for me, was there and approached me and I asked him, "What's going on up here?" He said, "Don't worry about it, Miss Angie, they're here to see me." I asked, "Why are they here to see you, because you're attached to me? This is the Corners Office. Why are they here?" I said, "Why didn't you pick a phone up and call me? It affects my office. If they're talking to you, it affects my office." He said he thought I wasn't coming in. I said, "But still I should have been notified. If I had not come in, I wouldn't know anything was going on, on the coroner side."

"I went to my office and a SLED agent saw me. She said, 'Well, hey, Miss Angie. We're actually here to see you.' I said, "What can I do for you?" She said, 'We have a subpoena for all Stephen

Smith's and Gloria Satterfield's files.' She told me my employee found the Smith files. I went in there and I was looking for the Satterfield case because like I said, in 2015, I was not in the Coroner's Office... Stephen Smith died in 2015. Glory Satterfield died in 2018 and I was the deputy coroner at that time, and I didn't recall a Gloria Satterfield.

"So, I went behind them and I looked for the file for 2018 and all files for 2018 that were in my office. I went through every file, and I didn't find anything. I went to SLED and told them I didn't have a file on Gloria Satterfield and "Mr. Washington, he would have a file somewhere in that file cabinet. He would have something, even if it's a notification." "I said there's nothing here," so I had to type a paper, saying, I didn't have a file on Satterfield. It was typed up and I signed it and gave it to the SLED agent. She asked if I found anything, to notify them and I said I would.

"After everyone left, I was approached by someone, whose name I cannot share with you at this time. This person told me to "leave it alone" and "there's no file in that office." I was told by this person "You ain't got nothing to worry about. You don't wanna get mixed up in this."

"That threw up a red flag in my head. You know, I'm going do what I can. If I find something, I'm going to turn it in. So, I put on my investigator hat and sent out some subpoenas. I subpoenaed the medical records because she was a Hampton County resident. At the time, I didn't know exactly who she was, though I knew the woman all my life, but I didn't know her as Satterfield. I knew her as Gloria Harriot. I didn't find out her name was Satterfield until later on. So, I had her death certificate in my hand. I had the file, I had her medical records in a file, and I recognized that her trip and fall was in Colleton County, I just kind of let it go.

"I was home, a week later. I was cooking and my husband was watching the news and he called me, and I came out, put my glasses on, and I was reading the screen. There was a court document on the screen about the Gloria Satterfield case where they, I guess, took it to Hampton County and did a hearing or whatever, and it was from a trip and fall accident in Hampton County not Colleton County. That's not right.

"The death certificate said, "Natural" causes. I mean you can't just it say "natural", and you have a court document that says she died from a trip and fall accident. That's two different things. So, I took a picture of the TV screen and uploaded it. Well, first I called another corner, because I've never heard of anything like this. I didn't know what to do with it. And so, the lady that I called was a coroner for 25 years. She went over it with me for about 45 minutes to an hour. She asked me, "Do you know what to do?" I said, "Yes, I want to turn it in, what I've got." She told me, "You are learning."

"So, that's when I picked up the phone and I called SLED and told them what I had found out. They told me I had to send a letter in asking for their assistance. So, that's what I did. Nobody knew about my letter. I didn't tell anybody at the EMS building. I didn't tell anybody. SLED told me I was part of their investigation now and if anybody asks, just tell them you can't talk about it, because you are working with SLED.

"So, I didn't say anything for a while, and I received a phone call from SLED stating that my letter was going to be released to the media. They just wanted to give me a heads up. I said, "That's fine. I don't have anything to hide. I don't care. You know, do what you got to do." And so, I thought I had little time to get prepared. Well, when I left my office that same day after talking to SLED, I went by a little store, grabbed a few things, and went home. I went to the front door and had a bag in my hand. I put it down on my bench. I went back to my car, grabbed my second bag, brought it in, and my phone started ringing. It was someone asking if I "forgot to tell them something?" I said, "What are you talking about?' And they said they were watching the news. I said, "Oh, are you talking about the Satterfield thing?" She said, "Yes." I said, "Oh, I'm sorry. I can't talk about it, it's an on-going investigation." She said, "We will pray for you, and you just lost your entire staff."

"This was when SLED was looking into Stephen Smith's and Gloria Satterfield's deaths after the world found out about the murders of Maggie and Paul. So, it was the summer of 2021.

"I feel something is fishy here. September 15, 2021, is when my letter was released to the media. It went through every channel it could possibly go through. After the day the letter was released, every step of my work, to the end of my tenure, was made more difficult. I lost the respect and support of certain county employees and co-workers, to include the county administration, who treated me with disrespect and made it hard for me in every way.

"The beginning of the downfall resulting in my losing the election started in March 2022. The first election was in June. I lost a primary, and with me running Democratic, that hurt. All three coroners running for the seat were Democrats. The female that ran against me was actually my part-time deputy. I had another deputy, also part-time that worked with me who was a male deputy. He was approached by a county employee and asked to run against me. He told my husband first because he didn't want to hurt my feelings. It didn't hurt my feelings, but it made me mad. And then somehow a rumor was circulated that I was dying of cancer."

Angie Topper is going strong today. She lost the election, and while the pain is still there, amazingly, she is optimistic about the future and has been offered another deputy coroner's position.

"It's for deputy coroner, and yes, it's hard to accept a position that is a step down for me, since I was lead coroner before all this happened, but I'm grateful for it. I just want to do what I love doing."

This author is very grateful for Mrs. Topper's time and candor. She is a very sweet, religious, and humble person. She was one of many to fall beneath the sword during the subterfuge for the cases surrounding the Murdaugh name.

Something Wicked This Way Comes

Alex Murdaugh had two insurance policies at the time of Gloria's "fall." Lloyds of London, which held his "underlying insurance" policy for $505,000, and Nautilus, which held his "extra" or "umbrella" policy for $5 million. The rumor was, Alex took out extra insurance on Moselle only a month before Gloria's "accident."

The thing that must be remembered here, is that in order for Alex to tap into his Nautilus policy, all of the underlying policy with Lloyds of London had to be paid out. Alex had to convince Lloyds of London that he, *or his dogs*, were responsible for her death in order to get to the big bucks with Nautilus.

Let's back up a minute. We have not mentioned why Alex needs to be represented by Scott Wallinger with Lloyds of London in a case against him. Who filed a lawsuit against Alex Murdaugh regarding Gloria's fall? Why, Gloria's sons, Brian and Tony. And who put the idea into their head? I'll give you a minute... Alex Murdaugh!

At Gloria's funeral, Alex came up to the two broken-hearted sons of his former housekeeper/nanny/errand-runner/cook/server employee. He told them the reason their mother fell was because his dogs had tripped her. Therefore, he felt badly and since technically, as they were his dogs, he felt responsible. He offered to "sue himself" on behalf of the Satterfield boys, so that they would have some money. Gloria had been the breadwinner, and that was now taken from them. The boys were in their early 20's and had been living with their mother in a trailer home. She was all they had in the way of support.

Knowing their mother had considered the Murdaughs as "family" and their name was included in Gloria's obituary as part of her extended family, they saw a glimmer of hope in the midst of their sadness. They eagerly agreed to let Alex go forth with his plan to "help them." And now, a plan is hatched so diabolical that the term "evil" doesn't even dent the surface, Alex Murdaugh put the wheels in motion to fill his coffers with the boys' insurance payout. Here's what he did:

Alex told Tony Satterfield, Gloria's oldest son, that Tony would act as the representative in the case, meaning he would be in the loop and the money would go through him when it was awarded. All good. He then said, "I need someone to be the attorney to sue me, so I've got a good one for you, a guy I highly recommend—Corey Fleming." Or words to that effect. He did not tell Tony that Corey was a longtime friend and Godfather to Alex's youngest son, Paul. Tony says, "Fine with me," or words to that affect, and the wheels begin to turn.

Next, Alex comes to Tony and says basically, "Look, this is going to get complicated, and I think you need a guy who knows numbers and can handle all the financial stuff coming, so I recommend you step aside as representative, and we let Chad Westendorf fill that role. He's VP at Palmetto State Bank and there's nobody better to handle the money side of things." Tony says, "Ok."

Now the lawsuits go forward, and the insurance investigators and attorneys ask their questions. Corey Fleming also goes into action. A week after Gloria's death, at the end of February 2018, Corey sends a Letter of Intent to sue Alex Murdaugh on behalf of the Satterfield's. On May 24th, Alex has his assistant send a letter to Gloria's healthcare provider in the guise of discussing the $13.65

filing charge for providing Gloria's records. Alex's assistant writes, "We'll pay $6.50, and you have 30 days to give us the information." Tony Satterfield had tried to get his mother's records but was unsuccessful. On May 27th, a fax with PMPED's letterhead arrived requesting the records. It is amazing how quickly after Gloria's funeral Alex was playing hardball to get the money coming in.

As the year waxes on, Alex needs things to start happening. On Oct. 30, 2018, Corey Fleming goes after Lloyds of London. He sends a policy limit demand giving them until November 12th to fulfill the claim. If it was not obtained by then, they would sue them in excess of the policy limits of $505k. Keep in mind, Alex can't go after Nautilus for the big payout in the millions until Lloyds has paid the full $505k. Lloyds replies and asks for a one-week extension. They only received Scott Wallinger's extensive report on Nov. 6, 2018. They've barely had time to look it over and follow-up on the assertions or do a medical review. Lloyds' representative, T. David Reney was not happy.

Wallinger sends Lloyds of London a statement saying, "Mr. Murdaugh does not want to be sued over this matter if practical and possible to avoid that as he sees that a wrongful death lawsuit would be detrimental to him personally and professionally in that small rural community." This was in effect offering support for the reason they should give Mr. Murdaugh via Corey Fleming a full payout.

If the soft touch didn't work, a little reminder of how much power Murdaugh and his firm had was included in the report. It was not a subtle reminder that if this was tried in Colleton County or Hampton County, the Murdaughs were not embryos when it came to suing insurance companies. It was widely known that any suit tried before a 14th Circuit jury would go in Murdaugh's favor. The final nudge came with the sentence, "The Fourteenth Circuit has two resident judges, Judge Perry Buckner and Judge Carmen Mullen. These judges know Mr. Murdaugh and Mr. Fleming well."

The fact that Alex made sure Gloria's fall was due to an accident caused by his dogs was no "accident." He was careful to say Gloria was not working that day but only stopping by to collect a check from his mother for her services for Miss Libby. Thus, he avoids only a workman's comp claim which is not the big bucks. He is also careful to negate her fall could have come from any injuries sustained in her car crash the day before she fell. If she simply fell out of clumsiness or from an aftermath from the car incident, this would not fall within the insurance company's purview. Enter Alex's dogs causing her fall on the Moselle property, which just had new insurance coverage added one month before.

Three months before Corey Fleming's intimidating letter to Lloyds of London on November 6, 2018, Alex opened a second bank account called Forge, with the Bank of America. We will hear a lot more about Forge in the chapters concerning his insurance fraud. For now, let it suffice to say that Alex created a bank account as Richard Alexander Murdaugh dba (doing business as) Forge. It was a devious plan. There was a legitimate business in South Carolina called Forge Consulting. They were a respected company that handled large settlements for their clients in the way of protecting them against foolish spending and making smart decisions, such as annuities that would pay out over the years and actually make them more money. This fake Forge account would be where Alex's ill-gotten gains would be deposited when the money started rolling in.

The two insurance companies paid up. Lloyds paid the full amount of $505k and Nautilus paid almost $3.8 million. It totaled $4.3 million in damages. Judge Carmen Mullen signed off on the settlements in an "off-the-books" proceeding. The usual avenue of bringing in the recipients for the money was avoided. Normally, Tony and Brian would have been in court to verify they had been treated fairly by their representatives and that they understood the procedures before agreeing to the payouts. They would not be able to come back later and claim more. But the boys were never told, and no such procedure happened.

As the months passed since their mother's death, Tony Satterfield would try and find out how the insurance claims were progressing. Since Tony had been removed as the representative in the case, it meant no one had to include him in anything. Chad Westendorf was now the representative. Tony tried in vain to get information from Chad, and continually reached out to Alex, who told him "Things are progressing." Tony would send him the mounting medical bills coming in from his mother's prolonged hospital stay. He also sent Alex something "from the trailer company." That last statement may have been a notice to evict. The two boys did lose the trailer home. The boys' relatives took turns taking them in. At the time Tony was begging for money, Alex had deposited some of it into his Forge account. The boys never got a dime of the money.

According to Gloria's close friend, Linda Hiers, Gloria, despite rumors to the contrary, was not in a car accident the day before her fall. "Her brother Scott was just doing regular maintenance on Miss Gloria's truck the day before she fell. He doesn't do body repair. Her son Brian said the same thing when those rumors started. He said his mother was never in a car wreck the day before she fell."

It was not until a newspaper article the next year, October 2019, came out that the Satterfield boys saw for the first time that they had been awarded any money. The article was spurred on by the boat crash, and while researching records associated with the lawsuits resulting from the crash, the $505k payout to the Satterfield boys surfaced. They were shocked. No one had told them. It would be the beginning of the fall of the House of Alex Murdaugh and his fake Forge accounts.

Chapter Fourteen
Gloria's Gift

Brian Hariott is Gloria Satterfield's youngest son. At first, he was hesitant to talk to me, and very protective of his dear friend, Linda Hiers. He wanted to make sure my intentions were pure in interviewing her for this book. He spends a lot of time at Miss Linda's. He agreed to speak with me if Miss Linda could be there too. When Linda answered my phone call, she put me on the speaker phone so Brian could hear and talk with me. They were on the front porch playing Scrabble. I asked who was winning. Linda said she was at the moment. I said, "I see missing tiles in your future." Brian's laughter was like sunshine. "Yes, Ma'am," he laughed. "That could happen." Here are segments of that interview:

Brian: "My mom was the kind of person that told you like it is, like it or not, she would tell you how it is. Whether people like it or not, she told them. She and Miss Linda were both feisty. When they got together, if we saw them comin', we'd say, "Oh, oh…here comes Double Trouble!

"Mama loved food. BBQ. Me too. So, I don't know if you would like it. It sounds gross, but she liked peanut butter and banana sandwiches, with mayonnaise. It is so good. And she liked it for a snack. She was like my grandma; she would always overdo it. You'd think she was cookin' for ten families. Her favorite place to go was the Golden Corral. We'd go for breakfast and still be there for lunch.

"Her favorite color was purple. She liked yellow too. She worked really hard. When she did sit down for a bit, she liked to read her Bible. Yeah, she liked to read the Bible. She did that the most. Most of the time I'd be in my room. I had a TV in my room, my bedroom, my own bedroom, and I look at TV most of the time in there. Then I'm going to watch it in the living room and look at it with her. I enjoy looking at TV with her, but she liked Westerns. Westerns and Soap Operas. She liked the show Andy Griffith, too.

"She'd wear pants and stuff. Like jeans and stuff but as she got older, she started and got to church, she started wearing dresses and skirts and stuff like that.

"I would go with Mama sometimes when she was at the Murdaughs cleaning. I was more around Paul than I was Buster. Paul and Buster were nice to me. I think she was there not long after Paul was born. At my Mama's funeral, I, the whole family came there, and I saw him breakdown, Paul. He had tears comin' out of his eyes at my mama's funeral, Paul did. Everybody says that her picture was the only one he carried in his wallet. Paul would call my Mama before he would call his own Mama. If he was in trouble or not doin' well. She would shut up and help him not get in trouble with his mom and daddy. She got on Paul about his drinkin'. Yes, she would. She got on to him about that. Times, I think she told, she told Alex also. Sometimes about how she felt about some of the stuff he did. He didn't tell her to mind her own business. I think most of the time he went on about his business."

Linda Hiers was on the phone call with Brian and I and would add to the memories he was sharing with me.

Linda:" I can tell you, Brian, we would go to the fair, to the haunted house. Brian liked to run all over me. You remember that, Brian? Smashed the heck out of me. I thought he was gonna throw me down. Somebody, something jumped out. I was leading the way and he about mowed me down. I don't know what Brian was trying to do. I talked to Gloria, I said, "Brian tried to kill me in there." (Brian's wonderful laughter filled up the next several moments.)

Brian: "My mom wasn't a beach person. She liked the mountains. My mom would go to the beach, and she said, "I'll go see it." But she was getting out of there. She didn't go in. One time we went, and we didn't even stay an hour, did we? She went down to the water and said, "OK, I've seen it. Let's go." She mostly sat in the shade at the beach while the rest of us went in the water."

Linda: "She liked John Deere and horses and all. That was two of her favorite things. And she, she has some dolls. But most of them were porcelain dolls. Well, let's say if there was a percentage on it, 90% of her would be country. Because like I said, it doesn't matter if I called her. She was here. She called me. I was there. It really didn't matter. That is a one-of-a-kind friendship. She comes here in the afternoons and sits in the rocking chairs in the living room, and we'd talk and laugh."

Brian: "Her number one music band was Alabama. But they're not my number one thing. I like their music and their songs and everything. Every time I hear them and it's a song she liked, I breakdown, because I know my Mama liked them."

Brian talked about people talking to him about his mother. He works at a store, and people come up to him and ask him about Gloria. It's hard for him, but I was so impressed with how he handled it all:

Brian: "I've had to cut some of them off. Sometimes because they asked me stuff that they shouldn't be asking me. Things like, "I heard they're gonna dig your Mama up." You know, exhume my Mama's body. I've had former friends of my Mama's asking me "When are they gonna do it?" And I told them, "I'm sorry, I don't mean to cut you off. But I don't wanna talk about it.

"There's the nice ones, though. You know about this one customer, she's black. I don't know who she is, but not long ago she came into the store. I was on one of the aisles trying to pull up the food to the front. They call it "blocking." It's stocking the shelves. And I was like squatting down and she comes walking up. She looks at me kind of funny and I'm looking at her, like, "Who are you?" And she's like, "Well, are you Gloria Satterfield's son?" I'm like, "Yes, ma'am," and she said, "I'm so sorry with what you've been having to put up with and what you are going through," and stuff like that. And I'm like "Oh, thank you." And I give her a hug and I don't even know who she is."

This interview means so much to me. Thank you, Brian, for trusting me with your memories.

I spoke with Linda Hiers in a separate interview. Her years with Gloria spanned decades: from elementary school up until the day Gloria passed away.

Linda Hiers top left, and Gloria, top right.

Gloria and Linda top back. Photos courtesy of Linda Hiers & Nick Ginn.

Linda: "I really didn't date much; she didn't date much. I mean, we were just basically just hanging out. Basically, either she was staying at my house, or I stayed at her house. We weren't your typical teenagers; we didn't go out partying, we didn't do all kinds of stuff. It was just sleepovers, watching movies. I love horror movies. She would go along with me. She was right along with me, I mean she was alright with scary movies, but if her sister stayed, they would close their eyes or whatever.

"We weren't Betty Crocker... I'm gonna tell you that right now. When we got older and stuff, we would have cookouts, or we would go shopping or we would go to the fair when it came around. There was our one thing we always did. It was our tradition every year; we did Relay for Life. We never failed; we did it. We would walk and they would have vendors out there. They would have luminaries out there for, you know, loved ones that you've lost to cancer, or you know ones that have survived cancer. It was in Hampton. It was at the track field at Wade Hampton. That was our one thing, and if one of the kids had a doctor's appointment or I had a doctor, whoever had a doctor's appointment, we all loaded up and we all of us would go to whoever had a doctor's appointment.

"We would go out to eat. Our favorite place was Golden Corral. But, you know, we had birthday parties. We were not blood related but even her sister said that I was more like her sister, you know. I mean we were there for each other for the good times and bad times and whatever other times. Whenever, you know, someone was mean or ugly or nasty I was the one that would always speak up about it. I always said Gloria was the saint and I was a sinner because I would just let it go, you know, I just let him have it right then and there. Oh yeah, I am on the feisty one. My daddy would always tell me "That mouth of yours is gonna wind you up in jail one day or left for dead."

"I think there were six kids in her family. Let me see, Gloria, Glenda, Sandra, Wayne, Ginger, and Scott. They were all as hard working as she was. They were all raised with that work ethic. The thing is, if I stayed over at her house, her Mama would say, "Just because you're a guest doesn't mean you go sit over there not doing anything" Of course, they'd come over here and they had to do chores and I told Gloria, I said "We can't get away from it!" Miss Elizabeth was her mother and she'd say that—"You're not just gonna sit over there."

"Whatever Gloria's family went and did, you know, I'll drive along with them and whatever we did they were riding along with us. But like I said, she loved Christmas. Her favorite color was purple. Everything was purple. She loved Clemson University. We always had a good time. She would call me up and say, "Let's go eat" and you know, I'm like, I don't have the money to go. She's like "I didn't ask you that; let's go!" But then if I had extra money, I would call her, and we go. We never kept tabs on each other as to who bought. It wasn't like that. I'll tell everyone she was my one true friend because if we tell the other something, I wouldn't go back and say something and she wouldn't go back and say something, so you know, it was between us. I could be up front and honest with her. If she was wearing an ugly dress and I thought it was ugly I would tell her, "That dress is just downright ugly!" She would say, "OK whatever." Or you know, if I had something on, she would tell me, "I really don't like this." She was there when I was in my first marriage and then my second marriage, and that one was a doozy, so one night I called, and I said my husband sold my car. She said, "I'll be right there." So, she came over and I jumped in the van with her. She holds up a wrench and says, "This is all I had was a wrench." I said, "Well, all I got is a hammer. Let's go find him!"

"I went to meet Gloria and she had Buster and Paul Murdaugh in the back seat. Buster was mouthing off about who his Daddy was and who his Grandaddy was. I think I told him to fasten his seat belt or something and he didn't like it. The way I was brought up, the way I was raised, you know, you don't talk back, and you respect your elders. He was a kid, I'm an adult. No child is gonna talk to me the way he talked to me. I can't remember what all he said at that point in time because you have all these nerves running through your body and he was on that one last nerve. I told him "You call your dad, you call your granddaddy, I don't care. You will not disrespect me." And that's when Gloria said to him, "This is one you don't mess with." Buster was at least 12 or 13, something like that.

"Gloria's nickname was 'Tootie.' That's what her Mama, Miss Elizabeth called her. Now if Miss Elizabeth was mad with Gloria, she'd yell her middle name, which left no doubt she was in trouble. Paul Murdaugh called her "Go Go." Miss Elizabeth always called me Lynn.

"57 is just too young to die, and you know, on Gloria's Mama's side of the family, most of them passed away at 52. So, when Gloria's 52nd birthday was coming up, I'd say to her, "You know 52 is coming up. I suppose you got this alright." So, she passed it too. I said, "I told you, you know, and then I told her, "Well, you should be able to draw off Mike's Social Security and stuff when you get 60." She never made it to that.

"It hurts, it does. I miss her, but I guess I have a different outlook on things than other people do. Our memories, what we did together, you know, and we did not judge each other; we were there for each other. That goes for Gloria, and that goes for my daddy, because people ask me how I cope losing my daddy. I always answer because of the wonderful, beautiful memories. There's no regrets in anything; nothing. But, number one, if you go back to my daddy, and my daddy found out that I was sitting around moping, he kicked me square up the ****. You carry on, you know. With Gloria, you know, she told me, "Oh, you better get up and go; you better go do what you gotta do."

"We knew each other so well, if she was going to make homemade macaroni and cheese, she said, "Bo, you know what I'm making today?" I'm like, "What you making?" She said, "Mac and Cheese, you coming over?" I said, "Yeah, I'll be there in a little bit." She knew that that's my favorite thing, homemade Mac and Cheese.

"The boys are still struggling. Brian has told me he's tired of these people coming up wanting to know "When they're going to dig up my momma's body?" I told him, "Brian you know I have mixed feelings about this, but I have to look at it both ways. You know number one, you really don't want to disturb her but number 2, if it proves that it was something that was done on purpose, or natural causes, or whatever, you know it's gonna be hard. I know it'll be hard on you, but when the day comes and it happens, I said, I'll be there for you. I think you need some closure one way or the other." At first, I was a little ticked. No, they don't need to disturb her. But I thought about it, and I says yeah, somebody purposely caused her death. I know Paul's not here but it's the point of the matter."

With the money the Satterfield's received from a lawsuit settlement against Alex Murdaugh in 2021, the family set up something to honor Gloria's memory. Her favorite holiday was

Christmas. The Satterfield's wanted to give back to the community in Gloria's honor, and "Gloria's Gift" was created.

"Gloria's Gift is a special program to raise money for underprivileged families; for kids, so kids could have Christmas because that was Gloria's most favorite holiday," said Linda Hiers, Gloria's closest friend. "I mean, it didn't matter if she had money, she was gonna make sure everybody had a happy Christmas. I mean, it could have been something that cost $5 but she was gonna get you something for Christmas, no matter what. She was also the type of person that, say if I needed a sweater or something, and she knew I needed that sweater, yeah, she would go take it out of her closet and say, "go take this," you know. She loved giving things to people. She wasn't a taker; she was a giver."

Gloria's son Brian added, "It's supposed to be for the families that can't buy Christmas for like their kids and stuff. They can go and get money from the foundation and buy Christmas presents and stuff for the family and the kids."

"Gloria's Gift" during a ceremony celebrating its creation.

"Gloria's Gift" is a wonderful tribute to a truly caring and selfless person. But after talking with her son Brian and her best friend Linda, I feel Gloria's biggest gift was her sons, her family, and her friends. She was truly loved, and she left behind two amazing young men with huge hearts who have weathered an unimaginable storm and come out of it with grace and kindness. They lost their mother and their home, while entrusting someone they thought was their friend. Alex Murdaugh, the man their mother had worked and slaved for, for over 20 years, devoting herself to *his* sons, robbed hers of the money they desperately needed to pay Gloria's medical bills and to keep a roof over their heads.

They were lied to, manipulated, and used in order to fill Alex Murdaugh's coffers. Yet, when you see them today, you sense no malice. They speak without bitterness and want to do good with what they ultimately received through a court battle. Brian's laughter peppers his conversations, and he is a genuinely fine person. Tony Satterfield took the witness stand and testified about what Alex Murdaugh did to him and his brother, but it was through short answers to the prosecutor's questions. He was forced to point out Alex in the courtroom, which could not have been easy. Those who were present in the gallery said that of all the witnesses in that long trial, it was Tony Satterfield who elicited the most emotion from the jurors. He conducted himself with poise. These two young men will do much with their lives. That to me is Gloria Satterfield's biggest gift to the world.

Tony and Gloria Satterfield

Chapter Fifteen
Land Deals and "Square Grouper"

Richard Alexander Murdaugh had his fingers in so many pies, a bakery would be jealous. Assistant Solicitor, lawyer, hunting aficionado, boating enthusiast, opioid expert, occasional coach, and landowner. During deep dives into his personal filings, it appears he was doing a little more behind the scenes than was realized on the surface.

This author did some digging, and it turns out Alex held more properties and post office boxes than seem necessary. Here's what I found:

Alex's employment as a lawyer is listed as active between September 11, 2012 – August 19, 2022, with the law firm PMPED. He is listed as a private attorney beginning August 8, 2008. It is widely known that he was fired from his position with PMPED in September 2021. He was also disbarred, so it's unclear why he is shown as still practicing in August of 2022. It may have been a natural license renewal end date.

He owned a couple of businesses:

Murdaugh Charters LLC in South Carolina. The company may also have had a branch in Florida. The filing date was May 24, 2007, Alex Murdaugh was the Registered Agent. It was still in "Good Standing" as of October 15, 2021.

Eclipse Landscape and Design, LLC. Filing date was January 11, 2010. Again, Alex Murdaugh is the Registered Agent, and it is listed as in "Good Standing" as of Oct. 15, 2021.

A company with a name smacking of piracy, Redbeard LLC, was filed on May 21, 2007, in South Carolina with the red-headed Alex

Murdaugh as the Registered Agent. It is shown as "Good Standing" as of Oct. 19, 2021.

Alex has 19 locations listed, beginning in 1997, all in South Carolina. These can be past and present residences and places of work. The final residence is 4157 Moselle Road, terminating on March 8, 2023. He has 6 P.O. Boxes scattered across the Lowcountry. Who needs 6 Post Office boxes?

Court records show a history of Alex buying up properties with the late Barret T. Boulware. Boulware was the current owner of the Moselle property where so much misfortune seems to have occurred. Boulware sold it to Murdaugh in 2013. Their interest in outlying islands around Beaufort, South Carolina, has many wondering if the purchase of these properties was strategic for other than land investments.

One of the duo's land acquisitions was a Beaufort County Island titled "Island A." It's a 22-acre island in the "Williams Islands," also called the Cherry Knoll Islands. It's the largest of the three islands and is located off the coast of Beaufort. While the waterfront view is appealing, the property has seen better days. The dock is unusable due to past hurricane damage and could only be accessed during certain tides when it was in good repair. The only way to reach the property was via boat. According to the filings, Murdaugh owns 50% of the island through Murdaugh Holdings, and Barrett Boulware's estate owns the other 50%.

According to court filings, Alex owns seven islands around Beaufort, ranging in size from 20 acres to .08. These islands are jointly owned with Barrett Boulware or with other investment entities. With the history that South Carolina has with drug running, it gives the positioning and ownership of these islands an ominous overtone. Barrett Boulware and his father Barrett Boulware Sr. were caught up in indictments for drug smuggling and made the papers more than once.

According to property records, here's the number of investments Boulware and Murdaugh made together:

R300 025 000 0017 0000 Boulware Barrett Murdaugh Alexander
R300 025 000 0018 0000 Boulware Barrett Murdaugh Alexander
R300 025 000 0021 0000 Boulware Barrett Murdaugh Alexander

The following partnerships show Alex filing as Murdaugh Holdings, LLC:

R300 037 000 0005 0000 1 Station Creek Island Boulware & Murdaugh Holdings with % each.
R300 038 000 0003 0000 Boulware & Murdaugh Holdings % each
R300 038 000 0004 0000 Boulware & Murdaugh Holdings % each
R300 038 000 0005 0000 Boulware & Murdaugh Holdings % each
R300 038 000 0006 0000 Boulware & Murdaugh Holdings % each
R300 038 000 0007 0000 Boulware & Murdaugh Holdings % each
R300 028 000 0008 0000 Boulware & Murdaugh Holdings % each

These strange bedfellows may have had some father figures that were already "dabbling" in illicit drug smuggling. Boulware and his father were certainly no stranger to newspaper headlines. Was this possibly a reason for so many Murdaugh P.O. boxes across South Carolina? Drug money? During the Murdaugh double murder trial in February of 2023, Alex admitted on the stand to a location he owned with the dubious street cross sections called Redbeard and Union. It appeared to be an isolated location that was not one of his listed residences or places of work. Rumors of drug drop-off locations had been drifting around the Lowcountry for years, including the Moselle property Boulware sold to Murdaugh. How many hunting properties have a private plane landing strip and hangar? Curtis Eddie Smith supposedly was very familiar with the area around the hanger on the Moselle property. It was mentioned in connection with payments he received from Alex Murdaugh.

Operation Jackpot

"Operation Jackpot" was a federal drug task force based in South Carolina that captured and convicted more than 100 marijuana smugglers from 1983 to 1986 during President Ronald Reagan's "War on Drugs." Among the chief targets of Operation Jackpot were South Carolina marijuana kingpins Barry Foy and Les Riley, who stood accused of smuggling 347,000 pounds of marijuana and 130,000 pounds of hashish into the United States. Known as the 'gentlemen smugglers' because of their college educations and aversion to violence, Foy, Riley, and their associates regularly sailed drug-laden boats from Jamaica, Colombia, and Lebanon through the marshes of the Eastern Seaboard. Because of lax drug coastal patrols, hometown familiarity, and a plethora of inlets, South Carolina was the gentlemen smugglers' most frequent destination for offloading drugs.

Les Riley grew up just a few miles from downtown Columbia. His upbringing was typical of the South, with plenty of time spent hunting, fishing, and escorting the occasional debutante. In college at the University of South Carolina, Les was known to take his dates to the roof of Cornell Arms to smoke marijuana and enjoy the sunset. He spent his free time between classes his senior year burning up the road between Columbia and Key West, Florida, where he worked as a doorman. After college, Les moved to Key West and started a landscaping business, cutting grass for $5. He counted playwright Tennessee Williams as a client and musician Jimmy Buffett as a friend.

Growing up a few miles from Les in Columbia, Barry Foy spent his youth delivering newspapers and eggs, working on construction crews, and pumping gas. After brief attempts at college, first at Newberry College and then at USC, Barry began selling marijuana in Five Points. Later, he moved into a Hollywood, Florida, beachside hotel frequented by men who participated in, among other activities, drug dealing. In 1971, they asked Barry and another hotel guest to sail to Jamaica to bring back 400 pounds of marijuana. With that, Barry's career as a drug smuggler launched, and he enjoyed legendary status among Columbia's marijuana enthusiasts. Some even volunteered to come along, enticed by the idea of cruising the Caribbean and returning on mattresses of marijuana bales.

Barry and Les met in Key West where, in 1973, Barry persuaded Les that smuggling grass was much more lucrative than cutting it. Barry flew to Jamaica to meet with suppliers, while Les and three others struggled to sail there in storms, high seas, and high winds. The return trip home was worse, especially when they were fired upon when straying too close to Cuba. [*South Carolina Jackpot: A South Carolina High*; Columbia Metropolitan; by Lynn Pagett Beard.]

Smugglers Barry Foy, Les Riley, and Wally Butler at a
Hilton Head Mackerel Tournament. The so-called
"Gentleman Smugglers."

Organized by U.S. Attorney Henry McMaster, Operation Jackpot
was one of the first federal drug task forces to use newly enacted
federal civil forfeiture laws to combat drug smugglers by seizing the
gentlemen smugglers' assets, including homes, cars, money and
boats. Operation Jackpot was also one of the first federal task forces
to combine investigators from a variety of federal agencies,
including the Internal Revenue Service, U.S. Customs, Federal
Bureau of Investigation, Drug Enforcement Administration and
U.S. Customs Patrol. Ultimately, Operation Jackpot would indict
four smuggling rings operating in South Carolina. Many of the
smugglers and kingpins evaded arrest for years, resulting in
manhunts across the United States and the world through the early
and mid-1980s, and captures in Antigua, Australia, Miami, New
York, and San Diego. The last fugitive from Operation Jackpot was
arrested in 2007.

In time, the drug trade grew crowded in South Florida. Barry and
Les decided to look for a quieter entry point for their product. As
native South Carolinians, they did not take long to settle on the lush

211

Carolina coast, with its virtually endless waterways and, in the 1970s, undeveloped seclusion. In most areas, major highways were within an easy distance, aiding quick distribution to major cities like Atlanta; New York; Washington, D.C.; and Chicago. Les bought a home on Hilton Head, as well as other property, and used it for offloading his merchandise. The smugglers also "borrowed" plantations along the coast owned by rich Northerners who rarely visited. McClellanville's creeks were popular, too. Other choices included an abandoned oyster shelling company on Hilton Head and West Bank Plantation on Edisto Island, owned by Ella Seabrook, grandmother of Barry and Les' friend, Skip Sanders. The property had a deep-water dock. Unbeknownst to his grandmother, Skip charged the smugglers a fee to offload their product there. [*Columbia Metropolitan*]

A task force was put together under Reagan's "War on Drugs." In South Carolina, it included SLED. It was a long, grueling ordeal to round up all the offenders, including extradition of Les Foy and Wally Butler from Australia. When all the Operation Jackpot trials were over, more than 100 smugglers went to jail. "It's the most amazing story going on in law enforcement in the United States today," said Henry at the time. The longest sentence went to Lee Harvey, who received 40 years for drug smuggling, possession of machine guns and silencers, intimidation of a grand jury witness, and racketeering, among other charges. Bob Byers got a 25-year sentence plus eight years for his escape. Tom Rhoad received a 15-year sentence, Barry Foy got 18 years, and Les Riley was sentenced to 21 years.

Square Grouper

According to a source I interviewed for this book, the following information was given concerning the smuggling operations in the Lowcountry around Beaufort, Hilton Head, and Myrtles Beach, South Carolina:

"The drug money and Hampton County is apparently very thick and deep. A person here was associated with this drug boat and this guy Tony. They got "square grouper" and they brought it back to

Hampton in coolers. Underneath the ice covered with real fish was what they called "square grouper." That was the nickname they gave the drugs. It was square packages of drugs, but the ice and the fish covered it. They called it "square grouper" after the fish, but there were drugs underneath. Whatever kind of drugs, God only knows. Someone I know went out twice on this drug boat before he figured out what was going on and he was told "Once you leave this town limit sign you forget anything you see."

"The boat went out from Myrtle Beach, and this is still going on today. They also brought in illegal aliens who had paid a fee and the captain of the boat pretended that he was paying these illegal aliens to work for him and then he would bring them into the inland.

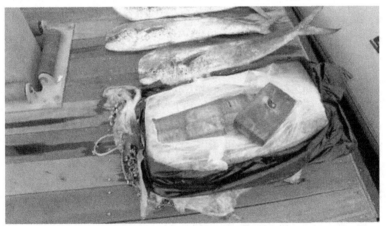

A "catch" of Square Grouper in the South Carolina waterways.

Barrett Boulware died of cancer in 2018, ending what had been a very lucrative partnership with the Murdaughs. While nothing had been proven against Alex Murdaugh in relationship to drug smuggling, the allusions to his participation were rampant. One member of a drug ring in Columbia said, "Alex Murdaugh ran half the drugs in this state."

The Timeline of Events

The dubious relationship between the Boulware's and the Murdaughs began back in 1949. Old Buster Murdaugh was the solicitor at the time. He and Thomas M. Boulware were working on a civil case: Ridgeland Box Manufacturing vs Sinclair. They paired up again in December of 1951 for a Supreme Court case: Beaufort County vs Jasper County.

In August of 1977, Barrett Boulware married Jeannine Morris. Her name *Jeannine Anne* would adorn a boat of dubious reputation three years later.

According to *The State* newspaper, in January of 1980:

- 11 Miami area men were rescued 50 to 60 miles off the coast near St. Helena Sound.
- The men claimed to have been rescued by *The Waterworld* and *Miss Kathy* boats. *The Waterworld* was taking on water. The men claimed to have been traveling from Miami to New York.
- The *Miss Kathy* was owned by Joel E. Morris of Beaufort and operated by Edward E. Legree (who was later arrested in another drug bust).
- *The Waterworld* was owned by Barrett Boulware of Allendale and operated by Johnny Morris.
- Apparently, no one was arrested.

The Tallahassee Democrat newspaper reported in February of 1983, that seventeen tons of marijuana were seized in the Bahamas. A shrimp boat was the carrier; a custom that would be used regularly as a means to transport drugs. E.J. Lewis and William O. Lane (nicknamed "Red") were sought as participants in the capture. Lewis was a Panama City attorney. It seems the legal system spawned a few drug-laden seafaring men.

The list of names of those charged with conspiracy to possess and distribute 34,000 pounds of marijuana ranged from Florida to South Carolina. The men were also charged with conspiracy to import the illegal drug into the United States. Among the list of names was Barrett Boulware of Allendale. Franklin Branch of Eastpoint was the captain of the *Jeannine Anne*, named after Boulware's wife. Others indicted were Sarah J. Wyatt and Sandra G. Clark, both of Carrabelle, Florida; Saxby C. Chaplin of Frogmore and Richard M. Harriott of Frogmore, South Carolina.

214

Before the trial date for the drug bust arrived, in April of 1983, the captain of the *Jeannine Anne*, Franklin Branch, was killed when a car struck him as he was on his way home from a bar one night in Tallahassee, Florida. According to the local newspaper, the *Tallahassee Democrat*, Branch "walked into the path of an oncoming vehicle." Branch was to be the star witness in the case against the Boulware's concerning the drug bust. The *Democrat* stated he was "scheduled to testify in a drug trial at the time of his death."

Not long after the "star witness" died, the charges against both of the Boulware's were dropped. The other four indicted on the drug charges did not fare as well: they were convicted.

Only one month after the tragic pedestrian vs vehicle death of Branch, in May of 1983, U.S. District Judge Falcon B. Hawkins barred the government from re-indicting Barrett Boulware and his father. It was basically calling on the double jeopardy caveat. "The Grand Jury could not present the same charges against Boulware to a Grand Jury a second time."

In what would be seen as precursor for the actions of his son, Alexander Murdaugh, Randolph Murdaugh III was indicted on tax evasion charges in June of 1983. Judge Thomas G. Heyward sat on the bench for the Fourth Circuit Appeals Court as Murdaugh argued unsuccessfully against infractions. Drug trafficking charges were involved and ominously, a plane. (Hint: there is a plane landing strip at Moselle, Alex Murdaugh's hunting property.) In April of 2023, his son, Alex Murdaugh, while sitting in prison after being found guilty of the murders of his wife and son, was also brought up on tax evasion charges. Aren't family traditions wonderful?

Barrett and Jeannine Boulware went about enjoying their drugs and looking for inventive ways to transport them, including a rented car they were driving in the late 1980s. They were pulled over for speeding. A search of the car revealed drugs in the glove compartment and marijuana in Jeannine's purse. Both were convicted: Barrett for trafficking cocaine and Jeannine for possession of marijuana. Although they appealed and lost, there is no record that either did any prison time.

Fast-forward to early 1997. It appears the Murdaughs and the Boulware's are in business. Murdaugh Holdings and Barrett T. Boulware purchased property owned by James L. Ilhy for $115,000.

In March of 2000, Barrett bought 4157 Moselle Road from Don Houck for $257,000. That address would play across television screens in 2023 when the murders of Paul and Maggie Murdaugh are showcased at the airplane hangar location on the property. Later that year, in December, Alex Murdaugh and Barrett Boulware again bought property from James L. Ilhy for $115,000. In July of 2004, Boulware and Murdaugh are on the books for the purchase of property from William H. Gay for $150,000.

Barrett Boulware's luck begins to run out in 2006, when a breach of contract is filed against him by Salkehatchie Woods LLC. Barrett is represented in the lawsuit by his good buddy and attorney, Alex Murdaugh. Two years later, in May of 2008, Barrett is hit with a foreclosure judgment in the amount of $408,664.78. It was brought out in the Alex Murdaugh murder trial that it was about this time in 2008 that some of Alex's properties were floundering and his money problems began. Barrett transferred the deed to 4147 Moselle Road to his wife and partner in crime, Jeannine in March of 2009 for $1.00, a ruse Alex would mimic later in an effort to keep the property away from collectors.

In September of 2012, Barrett Boulware Sr., Randolph Murdaugh III's friend and co-conspirator, died. Randolph would outlive him by 11 years.

Barrett Boulware Jr. transfers 4157 Moselle Road to Alex Murdaugh in April of 2013 for $5.00. Alex would later testify that Barrett owed him money that Alex had given him on past land deals. Following Barrett's example, Alex transfers the deed to Maggie Murdaugh, his wife, in December of 2016 for $5.00. It was obvious this was to remove it from any lawsuits filed against Alex. The boat crash wouldn't happen for another three years, so it makes one wonder, was this for tax purposes or was he in the crosshairs in 2016 for nefarious reasons?

On July 6, 2018, Boulware granted power of attorney to Alex Murdaugh – authorizing his attorney and business partner to "lease, let, take possession, bargain, sell, assign, convey, pledge, mortgage and encumber, repair, insure and generally manage any and all property, both real and personal, which I own, or may hereafter acquire from any source."

The instrument Boulware signed just prior to his death also authorized Murdaugh to "sign, execute and deliver any and all legal documents" in his name, and to "deposit any monies received from any source whatever for me, and in my name with any bank, and to draw and deliver checks in my name against said monies and other monies to be deposited in my name or to my credit."

Boulware further authorized Murdaugh to "do all things necessary concerning any insurance policies, including the right to change beneficiary," and was even granted control over "decisions regarding my health and healthcare."

Finally, the document made clear any decisions made by Murdaugh regarding Boulware's assets would be "binding on myself and my heirs."

Barrett Boulware's granting of Power of Attorney to Alex Murdaugh.

Barrett Boulware died in September of 2018.

We will probably never know the extent to which the Boulware's and Murdaugh's were involved with drug smuggling and the suspicious circumstances that surrounded them. Throughout the Alex Murdaugh murder trial, the question of where all that money went rattled the courthouse walls. Many surmise, it has to do with drug smuggling.

Witness dies in accident

Democrat staff report

EASTPOINT — A 33-year-old federal witness was killed early Saturday morning when he walked into the path of an oncoming vehicle.

At about 1:20 a.m., Franklin C. Branch, of Eastpoint, was apparently making his way to the Wonder Bar in St. Joe Beach when he was stuck by a car driven by T.J Whitfield.

Whitfield, returning home from Gulfport, Miss., was questioned by authorities and released.

Branch was one of nine people arrested in February when authorities seized about 17 tons of marijuana from a shrimp boat in Beaufort, S.C.

According to Trooper Millard Gillman of the Florida Highway Patrol, Branch had a high blood-alcohol level at the time of death.

Gillman said FBI agents were investigating the case as Branch was scheduled to testify in a drug trial.

Funeral services are scheduled for 3 p.m. today at First Baptist Church of Eastpoint. The body may be viewed from 2 to 3 p.m. Burial will follow the services in Eastpoint Cemetery.

A native of Eastpoint, he was a Vietnam War veteran and a member of First Baptist of Eastpoint. He was a shrimper.

Survivors include his daughter, Rose Branch of Eastpoint; his father, Wesley Branch of Apalachicola; two brothers, Edward Branch of Apalachicola and Stephen Branch of Eastpoint; three sisters, Kathy Johnson of Bayou LaBatre, Ala., and Mary Williams and Brandi Branch, both of Apalachicola; his grandfather, Roy Branch of Apalachicola; and his grandmother, Era Segree of Eastpoint.

Middlebrooks Funeral Home of Apalachicola is in charge of arrangements.

There were other suspicious deaths surrounding the drug smuggling operations. A man mysteriously washed overboard while taking a fishing trip with his sister and her husband off the coast of South Carolina. It seems people randomly meet their demise in this southern coastal community. Perhaps Old Buster Murdaugh wasn't kidding when he told a man to whom he owed a favor: "If you need someone to disappear, just bring them to Hampton County."

If you think drug smuggling in South Carolina is relegated to the past, think again. *Channel 7* posted this article as recently as Aug. 18, 2021, by journalist Bethany Fowler.

ANDERSON COUNTY, S.C. (WSPA) – South Carolina Acting Attorney said 12 people were arrested for their roles in the "largest of its kind ever" drug trafficking conspiracy in Anderson County.

The attorney said a joint team of 130 federal, state, and local law enforcement officers executed 20 federal search warrants and charged 12 suspects on 34-count federal indictment charges.

During the operation, agents located approximately 15 kilograms of cocaine, with a street value of approximately $500,000, 5 ounces of heroin, 18 pounds of marijuana, 10 guns, hundreds of rounds of ammunition, $245,000 in cash and 3 cars.

The 34-count indictment charges the defendants with various drug trafficking and firearms-related offenses that include: drug trafficking conspiracy; possession with intent to distribute cocaine, crack cocaine, and marijuana; distribution of methamphetamine, cocaine, and crack cocaine; maintaining a stash house; felony for possession of firearm and ammunition; and possession of firearms in furtherance of drug trafficking.

According the to AP, drugs are also smuggled into jails and prisons. The latest was drugs being smuggled into correctional facilities in shampoo. In 2020, this was reported:

SC prison guard fired, accused of smuggling in drugs

November 3, 2020

COLUMBIA, S.C. (AP) — A guard at a South Carolina prison has been fired following her arrest on drug trafficking charges, the state Department of Corrections said.

Ashley Nickole Williams, 33, of Greenwood, was fired after her Saturday arrest, the department said in a news release Monday.

Williams worked as a correctional officer at McCormick Correctional Institution, a high-security prison located about 80 miles west of Columbia, The State reported. On Friday, she was searched as she entered the facility and investigators found four packages filled with substances that tested positive for methamphetamines, marijuana, and cocaine. The drugs were hidden in food containers, according to arrest warrants.

Alex Murdaugh's dealings in property would be used as a catalyst for the beginning of his financial struggles and his descent into insurance fraud schemes. According to Prosecuting Attorney Creighton Waters, who would lead a team of lawyers in South Carolina vs Richard Alexander Murdaugh, for the double murders of Murdaugh's wife and son in on June 7, 2021, it was the recession of 2007 and 2008 decimating Murdaugh's property deals that pointed the compass needle at what would eventually lead to murder.

Chapter Sixteen
Countdown to Murder

When Creighton Waters, the State Prosecutor who went head-to-head with Dick Harpootlian during the double murder trial of Alex Murdaugh, outlined his game plan for Murdaugh's motive for murder, it was minute, and hammered down. He stood before Judge Newman Dec. 6th, 2022, in a Motion Hearing before the trial began to argue an exception to 404 B leading to motive and intent. It showed literally a "Countdown to Murder:"

Creighton Waters Timeline

SC vs Alex Murdaugh Motion Hearing

Creighton Waters pleading his case to Judge Newman to allow Murdaugh's financial frauds in as a motive for murder.

Creighton Waters before Judge Newman:

221

"In this particular case where you have a man who is accused and indicted for the murder of his own wife and son, the motive might be the most important fact that any jury would want to know. It's not an element of the defense, but it is the most important fact that any jury is going to want to know in this case. And for a jury to understand that, for them to really understand what the motive is in this particular case, they're going to have to understand that there was a huge difference between who Alex Murdaugh professed to be to the outside world and how important that was to him as a central figure in this prominent family and who he really was, that only he knew, that no one else knew. Over and over again, I've interviewed witnesses before, witnesses on the stand, who thought that they knew this man, and they, over and over again said," I didn't know him, I didn't know who this man was." So, for a jury to understand that they're going to have to understand not only that distinction between who he professed to be and who he was, and how important that was to him, but also how that allowed him to avoid accountability for defrauding victims of almost $9 million since 2011, that we've been able to detect.

"I think when this case started, a lot of people assumed that this was a murder case and then a few months later there was some white collar thrown in there. But the reality is, is we have done this extensive investigation, a State Grand Jury investigation, and we've realized that this is a white-collar case, that culminated with two murders. And so, if you look at the development of this particular case and the evidence in this particular case, what we see is, is that the defendant in the late 2000s, and that's a long time to go back, and I recognize that this Your Honor, but I think the important point to realize is that this is an unbroken chain of constant lies, and misappropriations and thefts, that has been going on for so long; a hamster wheel on which this man has been on constantly having to borrow, to earn, to steal millions of dollars just to keep kicking the can down the road and staying above water—an exhausting hamster wheel. A slow burn that was heating up and heating up, and so, June the 7th, 2021. [The day of the murders of Maggie and Paul.]

Alex Murdaugh's reaction during Water's layout of his frauds at Hearing.

"It all started with land deals. In 2007, 2008 the recession hit, and he really ended up upside down on those land deals, and it materially changed his financial picture. The reason why we know that Your Honor, is that in the early part of this past decade, in 2011, he had some *big* cases. He had a big case, he had the Pinckney case, he had the Thomas case, he had the Badger case. And these cases...the people around him thought they knew he had some issues and had some problems, but they thought that those recoveries and those *really* high fees that he had obtained—six figures or more—had fixed the financial problems that Alex Murdaugh had, but they didn't. They weren't enough. And not only did he have huge fees from those particular cases, but he also stole money from the clients as well.

"Your Honor, if I look at the unbroken chain that I'm talking about here, of these thefts that went on, they start in 2011. And every single year from 2011 to 2021, he stole money from clients. It is an unbroken chain. Because even though he was making six and sometimes seven figures of legitimate income in his law practice, it was not enough to sustain a lifestyle he had and the debts that he had. Even though he was borrowing *millions* of dollars from Palmetto State Bank from his buddy Russell Lafitte, borrowing close to $1,000,000 from this law partner, borrowing hundreds of thousands of dollars from his father, borrowing hundreds of thousands of dollars from Russell Lafitte's father, Having Russell Lafitte loan him close to $1,000,000 from the Plyler money, for which he had Russell appointed conservator. It still wasn't enough. It wasn't enough to keep Alex Murdaugh's head above water. And he couldn't stop. He couldn't stop.

"I've detailed in the filing Your Honor that you're generally familiar with the State Grand Jury evidence of the four manners in which he was stealing money, including from his own family and his law firm. And he'd been doing that for a long time, but one thing happened that caused the slow burn to finally heat up. And that was the boat crash in February of 2019. I've done a lot of white-collar crime and like every Ponzi scheme, theoretically, Ponzi can last forever as long as there's new money coming in. But the second that money stops or slows down, it's inevitably going to crash and burn.

"And that is what the boat case meant here. And so, what we see after the boat case is we see a huge uptick in the amount of money that he is stealing and the biggest one of that was the Satterfield's. And that was different because he's actually the defendant in that particular case. He's not the plaintiff's attorney there. And what he does is conspire with his buddy Corey Fleming to get a recovery against his own insurance company for her fall at his house. And then ask Corey Fleming to write the check out to the fake Forge account. $2.9 million dollars! And unlike prior to the boat crash case, where he's able to pull off a slight of hand of stealing money from clients in plain sight with stuff on the disbursement forms and the sheets that they're signing. Because at the same time he's handing them a huge check of life-changing money and they're shaking hands as they walk out the door.

"Here with the Satterfield's, after the boat case, he takes it all. He takes every dime. Every dime. What does that mean? Well, one thing it means is that he doesn't have that umbrella policy anymore. (It was used up for the Satterfield's, so he can't use it for insurance for the boat crash. In fact, the insurance companies turn him down.) And so, the boat case becomes very significant because the plaintiffs in the boat case made it very clear that this was not just about recovering from an insurance company or recovering from the deep pockets of the convenience store or the bar. The plaintiffs wanted a specific personal recovery from Alex Murdaugh because they believed, like everyone, that he had a lot of money. It was the principle of the thing that they wanted him to pay. Personally, that there was going be any settlement. And as that time went on, the boat case plaintiffs made it very clear to Alex Murdaugh's civil attorneys that we want a *personal* recovery from Alex. And his attorneys finally told them that he doesn't have any money and they're incredulous. They don't believe that because like everyone, they believe he's wealthy and they file a motion to compel him to disclose his accounts, disclose his finances, disclose all of that.

"That hearing is initially set for May of 2021, but it gets continued because Mr. Murdaugh's attorney, John Tiller, is, of course deceased now, but was having medical treatments. What else is going on at this time—we're now in spring of 2021—the State Grand Jury subpoenas are being issued as well about the boat case. What else is going on at this particular time? Alex Murdaugh has an opportunity for a big recovery in a case he has with Chris Wilson. And he actually argues and agrees to get the defendants for a big automotive company. And it gets them to agree to what seemed like a really good move at the time. He gets them to say he's going to waive punitive damages if they waive the right to appeal. So that is going to be a bench trial (judge only; no jury), so whatever decision is made, it's tried on just damages, then that money is going to be *instantly* available.

"That might seem like a good strategic move, but the reality is Alex Murdaugh needs that money *right* now. Because the way the law firm worked, as I say, you don't get your bonus until the end of the year. Other than that, you just get $125k salary spread out over the course of the year. For a person like that, the second he gets the fusion of cash in the 6 high six figures, that's gone within a couple of months.

"So, that case happens. The judge issues his ruling, and ultimately, it's a pretty good recovery. And there's $792,000 in fees for Mr. Murdaugh. But what he does is, he convinces his Co-counsel in that case (Fleming) to write those fees directly to him instead of writing it to the firm. And why is that? So that he can get that money. By the way, I have bypassed the problem where it's supposed to go. And so, he does that. 3/4 of a $1,000,000, and it's gone within a very, very short period of time.

"In May of 2021 though his staff, Mr. Murdaugh's staff becomes suspicious because they get the expense check and they don't have the fee check and they call up the other attorney's office and they said, "Where's the fees?" And initially they said, "Well, we gave it to Alex." And then, they're trying to figure it out and they can't get a satisfactory answer, and they go up and talk to financial staff and they're trying to get a straight answer, and they can't get a straight answer. And one of the attorneys calls that other attorney and they can't seem to figure it out. Where are these fees? Where's the $792,000 in fees? He's already got it. He's already spent it. He doesn't have the means to pay it back.

"So, what happens on June 7th? All of this is finally coming to a head. That morning, a PMPD staffer comes at the direction of the partners and says, "Alex, I need an answer today, where is that money? I need an answer today!" And Alex is in his office working on the boat case. Because that hearing is scheduled for June 10th, and Judge Hallows made it very clear there's going to be no more continuances and that's going to expose everything as well. And the only thing that stops the conversation about "I need an answer right now" is that Alex, unfortunately gets a call that Mister Randolph had gone to the hospital with a very poor prognosis. This is his father, who repeatedly had loaned him hundreds of thousands of dollars when he needed it. All of those are happening on this very day. It's a day of reckoning for him. The very day that Maggie and Paul were murdered.

"And what happens in the wake of that, what happens is the exact opposite happens. Everybody immediately rallies to his aid. Immediately. That hearing is cancelled. It's not even rescheduled anytime soon. The PMPED people, the last thing they're worried about is where these fees are. They're not. They don't care about that anymore. They're all rallying to his aid. All of the things that were about to happen *stopped*. And what does he do in the interim? The first thing he does, one, the first thing he does, at least business wise, is get more money from one of his law partners, get more money from Russell Lafitte from Palmetto State Bank in order to send enough money to Chris Wilson, so that Chris Wilson will incentive PMPED and say "Yeah, these funds were there." Everything's cool. He's covered his tracks.

"That would have never happened if it wasn't for the deaths of Maggie and Paul. And the only thing that changed was that in September, a PMPED staffer happened to find a copy of the check that was written directly from the other lawyer, written directly and made out to Alex. And she knew right then that he had been lying about it. And she takes it to another staffer. And that triggered another staffer to think about some of the others, some other Forge checks that have been made out, that didn't seem quite right. And they go look at those checks. Then they run it through the system and all of a sudden, all those Forge checks start popping up. And they go take it to the partners and they're like, "Oh my God, he's been stealing from us. He's been stealing from clients."

"They eventually confront him, and he resigns on September 3rd. September 4th, his best friend, who he had convinced to send back those fees to PMPED, and to cover $192,000 with his own money, that Alan couldn't borrow enough to pay. He is trying to get ahold of Alex and finally gets to meet with him on the doorstep of the front porch of Alex's mother's house. Alex confesses to him that he's been using pills and he's been stealing. He doesn't have the $192,000.

"All that accountability is starting to crash down on Alex again. And what happens within a couple hours? Right after the conversation with his best friend confronting him about $192,000? Alex is the victim. On the side of the road. And accountability is coming on him again and suddenly there's a gunshot and he's a victim again. And everybody rushes to his aid again. Except this time, it doesn't take long for people to figure out something's not right here. But the symmetry there is very, very telling. Your Honor, this is an unbroken chain of financial crimes that highlight what has happened here. This is a white-collar case that culminated in murders, and we've cited a number of cases here, of very, very similar circumstances in which courts have admitted evidence of motive just like this.

"And I would actually point to one case that was cited and this is the Segal case, and this was written, I believe by Judge Traxler on the 4th Circuit and there's a number of cases that we've cited in our brief. And this is a quote from that particular case. Because Segal has been defrauding multiple victims for the last, at least 20 years, and had never taken such extreme action, it's really important for the government to be able to explain to the jury why it was suddenly necessary for Segal to resort to murder.

"This is not propensity evidence. Evidence of all this fraud and abuse of his law license is not propensity evidence. It doesn't show that he's more likely to engage with fraud, because murder is a much different thing than fraud. But what it does show is what may be the most important factor in this entire case, and that is why this particular individual would murder his own wife and son. And the answer is because it is to escape the accountability that was coming upon him that he's never had to deal with in his entire life. Never had to deal with it in his entire life. And it worked!

"And if there wasn't for that check showing up in September, it might be still working to this day. I think the case file is clear on this Your Honor. This is in admissible evidence in this particular case because of the how important the motive is and how singularly important it is to the jury, particularly when you have an individual accused of killing his own family members, where there's typically an affectionate relationship, the probative value. far outweighs any prejudicial effect. And I would also point out that all of this is established by more than clear convincing evidence, which is a part of the standard as well. All of us, the vast majority of them, are the subject of State Grand Jury evidence. The evidence has been gathered by subpoena and sworn testimony. And it's already out there in all of these indictments, so the prejudicial effect is minimal, but the probative value is extreme in explaining what led this to happen. And that was that the day of reckoning was upon him. And he was out of cards to play after he's been playing every card he could. Thank you."

State Prosecutor Creighton Waters sums up his argument.

Any who watched the double murder trial of Alex Murdaugh for the murders of his wife Maggie Murdaugh and his son Paul Murdaugh, know Judge Newman's final ruling was in favor of Mr. Water's plea to allow the jury to hear about Alex Murdaugh's history of insurance fraud, lies, avoidance methods when he was about to get caught, and the lives he ruined.

The biggest hurdle the jury would have to overcome is believing a parent could kill his own child just to buy time before the boat case and it's probative accounting of his financial standing would go forward. In this author's opinion, based on many interviews for this book, I believe two things that fly in the face of the State's case and the final outcome of the trial:

I don't believe Alex Murdaugh knew Paul was there that night. I know, what about the kennel video, what about Alex's words about what Paul was doing at the kennels and his speaking to him? I will explain it during the chapter on why I think Paul was in the wrong place at the wrong time. The reason I mention it here, is that I believe if the State had shown reasonable doubt that Alex killed his son on purpose, it may have predisposed the jury to rule for a verdict of Guilty, which luckily, they did anyway.

There were also rumors of not one, but three mistresses Alex Murdaugh was seeing at the time of Maggie's murder. Her own sister said on the stand that Maggie had never quite gotten over Alex's affairs many years before. One of the so-called mistresses was actually at Maggie's funeral and posted a photo of herself with wet hair, beaming, saying she was at the funeral. The rain had come down in torrents during the funeral service, causing it to end prematurely. One of my sources was at the funeral reception at Moselle where food was served and saw this particular woman at the gathering...Maggie's memorial gathering.

The receipt SLED found in the trash bag the day after the double murders was passed over quickly during the trial. The bodycam footage of two SLED agents opening and going through a large black bag of trash showed a credit card receipt with the word Gucci circled with the word Charleston next to it. There is a Gucci store in Charleston and Maggie was in Charleston that day for a pedicure. Next to Gucci was a purchase in the amount of $1,200. It is ripped in half, like most of the other papers in the trash. In the bodycam footage you can see them pull it from a bag of kitchen trash that includes torn up bills and décor catalogues.

Gucci was circled by someone other than themselves. Who? And why? Had Maggie found it and circled it to show it to Alex to explain it to her? Or, had Maggie purchased an expensive item and Alex circled it to show it to her? He was in deep financial trouble. Maggie had purchased a Mercedes Benz SUV for herself only 7 months before her death. She posed happily with it at the dealership on her FB page, saying, "Merry Christmas to me!" It is dated December 10, 2020.

Brad at Dick Dyer Mercedes Benz & Volvo is at **Dick Dyer and Associates (Columbia, SC)**.

December 10, 2020 at 10:49 PM · Columbia, SC · ⬤

Congrats to Margaret (Maggy) Murdaugh Fir buying her MB. GLS from me.

Lakesha Douglas
Congratulations

9 mos   Report

Maggie Murdaugh posing at the Mercedes Benz dealership, with her new SUV. December 10, 2020.

Or… was it the purchase of Gucci Ammo 300 Blackout Harvest 04 for shooting?

SLED discovering Gucci receipt in kitchen garbage bag.

SLED discovering Gucci receipt in kitchen garbage bag.

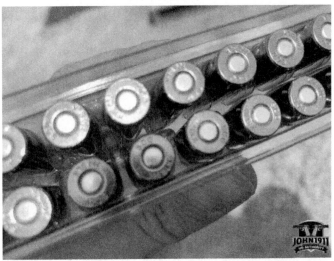

Gucci Ammo 300 Blackout package Harvest 04 cartridges.

It seems odd someone would circle cartridges or would spend $1200 on ammunition. The question is why was it circled on the receipt? We do know SLED put it in the "to keep for further investigation" pile, as is witnessed in the bodycam footage.

Chapter Seventeen
Holly Street, Moselle & Edisto Beach

Not surprisingly, the three main residential properties the Alex Murdaugh family owned were as controversial as the man himself. Let's start with 515 Holly Street Ext, Hampton, South Carolina.

The Holly Street house, or "Hampton House" as the friends and family of the Murdaughs called it, to differentiate it from the Moselle property, was a lovely dormered home set back from the road with a Private Property sign posted at the roadway. It was a dirt road leading back into a dense population of pine trees. In many ways it mirrored the remote setting of Moselle

The only view of the Holly Street house is a dirt road leading into pines.

515 Holly Street Ext., Hampton, SC

515 Holly St Ext, with pool, surrounded by trees.

515 Holly Street is 6,752-sf home boasting 4 bedrooms and 3.5 bathrooms. It came with secluded acreage and an in-ground swimming pool. It was up for sale in 2020 and sold on May 1st of that same year. While valued at $607,200, it garnered far less—

$375,000 due to an outstanding mortgage of $283,492. Alex Murdaugh and his family had lived there for 18 years before he put it on the market in 2020. He said so in his third interview with SLED. What he failed to mention was a mysterious fire that had been set at the house years earlier.

On July 9, 2009, a local newspaper, the *Hampton County Guardian*, published a story that raised eyebrows in the small community. "Local and state police are still searching for a suspect in connection with an apparent arson attempt at the home of a local attorney," wrote Michael M. Dewitt, Jr.

That local attorney was none other than Alex Murdaugh, and the home where the attempted arson took place was 515 Holly St. It was 7:30, Friday morning, July 3rd, in a setting far removed from the street. A perfect location for clandestine motives. The fire was quickly extinguished, in fact, it hadn't caused much damage at all. Hampton Police Chief Perry McAlhaney made it known he was instigating an investigation based on evidence he said was acquired from the scene.

On July 16, 2009, just 13 days after the suspicious fire at the Murdaugh home, the Hampton Police Department made an arrest in connection with "the arson incident that occurred last week and an armed robbery that occurred last year."

Michael David List, 40, of 2304 Cross Swamp Road in Islandton, was arrested for arson after being arrested on five counts of failure to pay laborers. The allegations of the arson fly in the face of the local gossip saying gasoline was poured around the house on the outside. Here, List is accused of spraying accelerant on the furniture and the walls of Alex Murdaugh's house and then attempted to ignite the building. The words "attempted to ignite the building" are interesting. Did it not catch fire? Had Alex found another patsy like he did for all the crimes pertaining to him and his family members?

During an interview for this book, I was told by a local the story that had been going around at the time. It was said Alex Murdaugh, in the early morning hours, took cans of gasoline and circled the outside of the residence, soaking its foundation. He seemingly concentrated a large amount of the flammable liquid onto the back porch steps doormat. According to this source, it was the doormat that went up in flames when Murdaugh struck the match. The rest of the building didn't seem to catch very well. All of this, of course, is hearsay.

This fire is set in 2009. If Alex was responsible for it, was it for insurance money? As we've seen in the prior chapter, Alex would do things when the money was running out. Were his land deals still tanking after the 2007-2008 recession? Many investors never recovered after the devastating effects of that shutdown. Building stopped, no one was investing in property or commercial excavation.

The Holly Street house comes back into the spotlight when it hits the market for sale in late 2019/early 2020. What do we see happening around these dates? The boat crash of February 2019. A boat crash that was the catalyst for Renee Beach, Mallory's Beach's mother, to launch a formidable lawsuit against the Murdaughs, Parker's Kitchen, Luther's Well and Rare Done, Kristy Woods, and others. They made it known they were going after $30 million from Alex's estate alone. Yet, due to the upside-down mortgage on the house, it went for roughly half of its value. Not nearly enough.

Was there another reason to put the house up for sale at this time? It sold on May 1, 2020. Maggie Murdaugh, only two months later posts on her FB page that she has "moved to Edisto Beach." Alex moved into the Moselle house full-time. Marriage issues? The rumors had swirled around s possible split. Were they keeping up appearances until Paul Murdaugh's boat crash trial was over? Showing the world, a united front? In all fairness, it was also stated that Maggie was having renovations done at Edisto and was there to oversee the operations. It is hard to say. They seemed to still care deeply for each other. Perhaps an ultimatum had been put down for Alex to stop the drug use, or else?

In South Carolina, they have specific guidelines for the pathway to divorce. According to the South Carolina Bar: "In South Carolina, the only way to obtain a no-fault divorce is to live separately for one year. Living separately occurs when spouses live in two different locations. Living in separate bedrooms in the same house does not qualify as living separately. Spouses do not need an Order of Separate Maintenance and Support to live separately, but it can help the spouses protect their financial interest and resolve visitation and custody issues during the separation period."

Posting a public notice can act as evidence of the beginning of an important process. It is now on record, with the exact date of separate living conditions proclaimed. Chillingly, when Maggie was murdered on June 7, 2021, she was less than a month shy of that one-year separation period, and a no-fault divorce.

Alex told law enforcement at the murder scene, "Whoever did this has been planning it a long time." Had Jennie Seckinger, PMPED's CFO, cornering Alex in his office on the morning of the murders, escalated his plot to kill Maggie before the "no-fault separation period" was over? It seems an odd coincidence. Was it part of the "countdown?"

Maggie Murdaugh's FB announcement of her move to Edisto

Another Suspicious Fire

Another strange fire that might be attached to the Murdaugh's is one that rivaled most magic tricks on the Las Vegas Strip. One day after the murders of Paul and Maggie Murdaugh, fire engines roared out to a fire on Highway 278. A small, abandoned house near the road and the railroad tracks was on fire. The officiant of the Lighthouse Church across the street from the fire saw the smoke and phoned it in. The small building stood on property adjacent to other houses and a Murdaugh family acreage that may have been used for hunting.

Fire crews responding to a 911 call about a fire.
Photo courtesy of Danielle Renea.

This author reached out to the man who called it in, asking for the photos and video he took that morning. He said he had sold it and had no copies. "Sold it whom?" I received an evasive answer.

Photos of the fire and the large number of responders resurfaced on Facebook after the murders of Paul and Maggie Murdaugh on June 7, 2021. One day later, smoke rose from the trees at a driveway leading into property adjacent to the Murdaughs: specifically, to Randolph Murdaugh IV, more commonly known as Randy, Alex' older brother. According to spectators, the fire engines watched as the house burned to the ground. It was said no attempt was made to put it out. More strangely yet, all mention of the fire was buried. There are no reports of it ever happening or that firefighters were called out.

All the responders in the Lighthouse Church parking lot responding to a fire that never happened. You can see the smoke still rising into the sky.

A posting of a map of the property where the small house burned down the day after Maggie and Paul's murders. The yellow arrow at the top points to Randy Murdaugh's property. Other houses have been blocked out to maintain the owner's anonymity. Map courtesy of Danielle Renea.

The media did not report on this disappearing fire. It's timing so close to the murders and in such close proximity to Randy Murdaugh's property is what gives one pause. Add to that, the total redaction by the fire departments of any log records or documented response to the fire is odd. We do know that John Marvin was at the Moselle property the day after the murders at the feed shed where Paul was murdered. He claimed on the witness stand during the double murder case that he "had tried to clean up the mess, but just couldn't do it." He said his older brother Randy had told him to stop and he would send out a cleanup crew to do it. It seemed very fast when you consider SLED was out there that same day still looking through trash, checking measurements, and looking for Maggie's cell phone, which John Marvin help to facilitate.

So, what burned down? Just an old shed or small abandoned house that spontaneously combusted the day after the murders. Was it innocuous or had perhaps remains from the feed shed been disposed of in that fire? But why burn an entire building down? It's just another mystery to add to so many others when a Murdaugh is around. Again, there is no proof of what happened or if a Murdaugh was involved. Any "evidence" went up in smoke.

The Edisto Beach House

Alex and Maggie Murdaugh purchased the four-bedroom, three-bathroom Cape Cod-style estate at 3606 Big Bay Drive at Edisto Beach in 2002 for $415,000. While the property was not beach front, it was close enough. The covered portico beneath the house housed a boat that was seen in numerous photos of the Murdaughs enjoying the ocean. This was Maggie's sanctuary. When the Holly Street house was sold in 2020, she made Edisto her residence of choice. Moselle was a hunting lodge, surrounded by tree-dominated acreage, a swamp, dove field, kennels, deer feeders, and even a private fish-stocked lake. In the summer, the yellow flies from the swamp were a plague. Maggie's sister, Marion, said she loved the beach and Edisto was her refuge.

It became more of a refuge after the 2019 boat crash of Mallory Beach. Hampton, a small community to begin with, became a rather unfriendly place to be after rumors of Paul's drunk driving resulting in Mallory's death, and his apparent differential treatment by the justice system, made the news. When Maggie shopped at the local Piggly Wiggly, whispered conversations went on behind her back. Michael DeWitt, editor for the local paper said he was present at a store when Maggie walked by and he heard two women whisper, "There goes Maggie Murder." When he asked them why they called her that, they said it was rumored Maggie pushed the housekeeper down the stairs. And so, as far back as Gloria Satterfield's tragic fall in 2018, while at the Murdaugh home, the small town of Hampton and surrounding areas was becoming a lot smaller. Many said Maggie was spending more time in Edisto Beach to escape the obvious malice against her family, especially with the boat crash trial looming.

Maggie Murdaugh's Edisto Beach retreat.

One of the videos shown during the double murder trial of Paul and Maggie Murdaugh was taken only a week before the murders. It was a Memorial Day weekend party doubling as a surprise birthday party for Alex. In it, his friends and family surprise him with a cake. It is heartbreaking to watch now, especially to see Paul and Maggie, and Chris Wilson giving Alex a big hug. Chris was a broken man during his time on the witness stand, still coming to grips with "the friend" he thought he knew.

The patio beneath the Edisto house where the Memorial Day/Alex's birthday party was held. Photo: Real Estate posting.

Paul Murdaugh carrying his dad's birthday cake.

242

Chris Wilson hugging Alex at the party.

As the video plays, a rousing chorus of Happy Birthday is heard. Alex beams and says, "Thank you all SO much! Thank you, Baby!" His "Baby" would be shot five times at the Moselle property in just over a week.

Chapter Eighteen
Shots in the Night

The 79-degree heat that had permeated the day dropped to a doable 73 shortly after nightfall on June 7, 2021. Humidity still wrapped around one's face like a damp washcloth leaving the grass glossy with its moisture, moisture that would later spotlight telltale tire tracks and sodden shoes. A misty rain had begun closer to 9 p.m. that evening, teasing the Moselle property with its lapses and then sudden bursts. It would come into play later in a double murder trial as a possible contributor to the drenched area around one of the murder victims executed that summer evening.

Angela Stallings, 911 Dispatcher the night of June 7, 2021

The 911 Call

911. 10:07 p.m. What is your emergency?

Alex (gasping and emitting short cries): This is Alex Murdaugh at 4147 Moselle Road. I need the police and an ambulance immediately. My wife and my child have been shot badly.

911: Ok, you said 4147 Moselle Road in Islandton.

Alex: Huh?

911: 4147 Moselle Road in Islandton.

Alex: Yes, sir. Please hurry.

911: Ok, stay on the line with me, ok?

Colleton County dispatcher is patched in: "Colleton County Dispatch."

911: Colleton, I have an Alex Murdaugh on the line calling from 4147 Moselle Road. He's advising his wife and child were shot.

Colleton: Ok, sir. Give me the address again.

Alex: 4147 Moselle Road. I've been up to it now. It's bad!

Colleton: Ok and did they shoot themselves?

Alex: Oh no! *HELL* no!

Colleton: Ok, and are they breathing?

Alex: No ma'am.

Colleton: Ok, and you say it's your wife and your son?

Alex: My wife and my son.

Colleton: Are they in a vehicle?

Alex: No ma'am. They're on the ground out at my kennels. (Oh, oh) I can tell that she's shot in the head, and he's shot really bad. (Softer) He's shot really bad.

Colleton: Ok, and where is he shot at?

Alex: Ma'am I don't know. There is blood everywhere. I can see his brain. She's on her side, I turned her a little bit. She's got a hole in her head.

Colleton: Is he breathing at all?

Alex: No. Nobody.

Colleton: Do you see anyone in the area?

Alex: No Ma'am.

Colleton: Is there any guns near them at all?

Alex: NO! (Alex says "Here." Dog barking) If that's what you're asking, they didn't shoot themselves, Ma'am.

Colleton: What color's your house on the outside?

Alex: It's white, but you can't see it from the road.

Colleton: Ok, is it a house or a mobile home?

Alex: It's a *house*! (Yells it)

Colleton: Ok, and what is your name?

Alex: My name is Alex…Murdaugh.

[This sounds like the same 911 operator who took Maggie's 911 call when Gloria Satterfield fell down the steps. Does she recognize this is again a Murdaugh calling with an emergency from the Moselle address?]

Colleton: Ok, did you hear anything, or did you come home and find them?

Alex: No ma'am. I've been gone. I just came back. (Alex is wailing)

Colleton: And was anyone supposed to be at your house?

Alex: No ma'am. (Pause as she types. Dogs barking in background.) Please hurry! (Pause. Dog barking) Paul! Oh Paul (maybe Paw Paw). I should have known. (Sobbing. Dog barking)

Colleton: We're getting someone out there to you. (Dog barking is louder here) What is her name?

Alex: Maggie. Maggie and Paul.

Colleton: Maggie is her name?

Alex: Yes, Ma'am.

Colleton: When is the last time you talked with Maggie?

Alex: Hour and a half ago, probably. Two hours ago.

Colleton: Ok, you said about two hours ago you talked to them?

Alex: Yes, Ma'am…approximately…approximately.

Colleton: Did she say what they were doing at all?

Alex: No, I talked to her in person.

Colleton: You talked to her in person?

Alex: Please hurry.

Colleton: We're getting somebody out there to you. Me asking you these questions don't slow them down in getting to you, ok?

[The sounds of dogs are not heard here. Alex is breathing hard as though he is walking.]

Colleton: And you're sure they're not breathing? Is he moving at all, your son? I know you said she was shot in the head, but what about your son?

[Alex is panting and sobbing. No sound of dogs here]

Alex: Nobody. Neither one of them is moving.

Colleton: What is your telephone number? (Redacted number)

Alex: I'm going back to my house just to get a gun just in case. I'm about a hundred yards from my house.

Colleton. And does anything look out of place? (Silence. Pause.)

Alex: Ma'am. I…Not particularly, not really, no ma'am. (Sounds calmer)

Colleton: I know you're upset Mr. Murdaugh but I don't want you to get a gun and have a gun out when my officers get there, ok?

Alex: I will not do that. He's been threatened about a boat wreck for months and months and months. He's been hit several times.

Colleton: Do you know who was threatening your son?

Alex: Hold the phone. One second.

Colleton: You don't know the name of who was threatening him at all?

Alex: My son knows.

Colleton: Your son knows who was threatening him?

Alex: I have another son, Ma'am. (Long pause and typing from dispatcher) Alright, I'm going back down there. (Radio chatter)

Alex: Are they close, Ma'am?

Colleton: They've been in route to you ever since you got on the phone with me. I have multiple people coming out there to you.

Alex: (unintelligible)

Colleton: Ok, can you turn on the flashers on your car so they can see where your kennels are? (Dogs barking) Do you have your flashers on for me, Mr. Murdaugh? I don't want you to touch them at all. I don't know if you've already touched them. I don't want you to touch them just in case they can get any evidence, ok?

Alex: I already touched them trying to…to see if they were breathin'. (Dogs are barking again)

Colleton: Ok. I just don't want you to move anything just in case they can get any evidence, ok?

Alex: Ah. (Dogs barking. Alex groans)

Colleton: I know you said your son had been threatened. Did your son make reports of this at all?

Alex: Um, yes ma'am.

Colleton: He did? And what's your son's name?

Alex: Paul. Ma'am, I need to call some of my family.

Colleton: Ok. Do me a favor for me, when you see the officer or the medics, cuz they're all coming to you, can you put your gun in your vehicle for me?

Alex: Absolutely.

Colleton: They're coming. Turn on the flashers on the vehicle for me. Do you have your flashers on?

Alex: I do.

Colleton: Ok, whenever you see them put your gun up for me, ok?

Alex: Ok.

Colleton: How old is your son?

Alex: 22!

Colleton: Ok, we're getting them out there to you, ok?

Alex: And I'll --------------- car.

Colleton: Alright.

The last sentence we hear from Alex says something about the car. Radio chatter is talking over him and it's hard to understand. The dispatcher asks him to put the gun in the car and he says, "Absolutely." Yet when the first officer arrives, we see from his bodycam that Alex has placed the shotgun leaning up against the outside of the driver's side door. He immediately alerts the officer that he has a gun and it's over there against the car. It's curious that he didn't put it inside the car as he promised.

Moselle hangar (center) and dog kennels (right, long narrow building with white roof)

Alex pointing at the shotgun leaning against his SUV as the first officer, Greene, arrives on the scene that night. Police bodycam video still.

But what happened on that lonely, remote hunting property that night? Towering South Carolina pines hide the area near a large airplane hangar from Moselle Road. Its red roof can be seen from the road at the end of a white sand and gravel driveway. At the entrance to that driveway sits an old shed and a rustic cabin, alongside a mailbox.

As one travels up the gravel path they will circle around the hangar and arrive at a row of dog kennels next to a chicken coop sitting at a perpendicular angle. In the overhang of the hangar, directly across from a small feed room attached to the dog kennels sits a side-by-side Polaris ATV and some small farm equipment. A neon green hose, anchored to the dog kennels, is hastily wrapped around its holder.

Alex Murdaugh arrived at his house at Moselle at 10:00 p.m. that night. He had been to see his invalid mother at her home in Almeda, roughly a twenty-minute drive from 4147 Moselle Road. Miss Libby, as she was fondly called, had dementia. She had round-the-clock caregivers who sat with her and attended to her needs. They were to provide valuable evidence in the double murder trial that would come almost two years later. Alex sat with his mother and watched part of a game show with Miss Libby's caregiver, Shelley Smith. He left after staying 15-20 minutes, and returned home, driving up one of the two driveways to access the hunting property.

One weaved around the airplane hangar and kennels, the other went directly to the main house. He took the main drive.

4147 Moselle Road at the end of the main driveway.

According to Alex's story, he checked inside the house, looking for his wife and son. They were not there. He said he had dinner with them earlier and then fell asleep on the couch as Maggie headed for the kennels to "run the dogs." He didn't know where Paul went...just outside somewhere. When he didn't see them in the house, he got in his SUV and went down to the kennels to look for Maggie. As his headlights turned from the gravel driveway, pointing toward the kennels, he saw in their glare a horrendous sight. His wife of 30 years lay face down in front of the Polaris ATV, one arm in front of her, the other beneath her abdomen. There was blood all around her head and what appeared to be brain matter a few feet in front of her. It was not the last of the horrors. Looking to her right, just a few feet away, lay his 22-year-old son, Paul Murdaugh. Light was pouring out of the feed shed, illuminating the carnage splayed out on the cement walkway of the kennels. Paul was lying face down, his feet inside the small feed shed, his torso on the walkway, and his face in the white gravel drive. The back of his head was missing, and his brain lay near his left leg. Blood was everywhere,

250

spreading out from the head area and from his torso.

Moselle hangar overhang and dog kennels with feed shed.
Maggie was shot near the small doghouse (left) & Paul was
shot as he came out of the feed shed (right).

Rain was falling intermittingly, mixing with his blood as it spread out in various stages of thickness. Anyone standing anywhere near him would have blood on his shoes. According to Alex, he tried to "turn him over...then figured it out." He also said, "I picked up his phone and was going to... then I didn't..." He said Paul's phone "popped out of his back pocket" when he tried to turn him over. He finally placed it on Paul's bottom near his pocket. A bloody fingerprint was found inside Paul's back pocket, and it was surmised someone either took the phone out of his pocket, or tried to return it and gave up. Text messages and calls were coming in from Paul's friend, Rogan Gibson, as Paul lay dead on the concrete. Alex would no doubt have heard it ringing or seen the texts coming in as he bent over him.

The dogs were highly agitated and barking throughout the 911 call Alex placed at 10:07 p.m. The volume of their barking would vary as Alex moved away or moved closer to the kennels. At times, it was only his panting and intermittent sobs that broke the silence during pauses in the 911 calls. Law enforcement radio chatter and the beeping of the dispatch controls obliterated some of his statements to the operator. She would, at times, talk over him before he could finish answering her question. His time at the house lasted only

251

about a minute or two. He said he went up there to get a gun "just in case." The gun room is a separate door at the side of the Moselle house and the guns are just inside the door.

When the first responders arrived, it was beginning to rain. It can be seen in the bodycam footage. It is very dark by the kennels. The headlights from Alex's SUV are the only lights, except for the arriving emergency vehicles' own headlights, and the light coming from the feed shed where Paul Murdaugh is lying. Up ahead, like a ghost in his almost luminescent white t-shirt, Alex Murdaugh waits for them. It is not until they get closer to him that they see there is light coming from the large hangar tool area. They walk past Paul and Maggie to get to him. He is standing only a few feet from Maggie's body.

Alex is agitated, but responsive. He is quick to tell Officer Greene that he has gotten a shotgun from the house and it's right there against his SUV. Officer Greene pulls up his shirt to check for other weapons and does a quick look at the cargo shorts Alex is wearing. Alex tells him the gun is loaded. Officer Greene carefully carries it to his own police car and locks it inside the front passenger seat.

He returns to Alex who is pacing and sobbing. Alex asks if someone has checked on "them?" He is told, they have. "Are they dead?" Alex wails. He is told they are in fact deceased. "Are you sure? Are they officially dead?" he repeats. Officer Greene begins writing down Alex's name, and the names of his wife and son. He asks him for Paul's birthday and Alex seems to need to count back from Buster's birthday. He is rocking and turning in circles. Just then, another officer walks behind Officer Greene and Alex stops crying and in a nonchalant manner says, "How ya doin'?" It struck Officer Greene as odd—how quickly Alex turned off the hysteria and greeted the second officer calmly, as though it was just a gathering. It was brought up during the trial.

As Officer Greene continues to speak to Alex, Alex begins wailing, "It was the boat crash! That's what this is!" He then relays the details of the boat crash and how Paul has been getting threats. He breaks off as he looks over to where other officers are covering Maggie and Paul with sheets. "Are they covering them?" Alex asks. Officer Greene is heard telling the other officers he wishes they weren't putting sheets over them, as he feared it might contaminate the crime scene. Shortly, a canopy arrives to be put up over Maggie as the rain picks up. Most of Paul's body is under the metal overhang from the kennels, but his head is exposed. Mark Ball, an attorney and friend of Alex's arrived that night as one of the many people Alex called. He said it upset him to see the rain falling on Paul's head. He thought it was disrespectful and it "bothered me a lot."

Besides Mark Ball, Alex had called Ronnie Crosby, another PMPED attorney and friend, his brothers Randy and John Marvin, and his "clean-up" guy, Chief Gregory Alexander, who was out of his Yemassee jurisdiction. He was somehow always at Alex's side and had been for many years. He was present during the Stephen Smith investigation, again, not in his back yard, and was a fixture at Murdaugh BBQ's and parties.

Alex walked a distance away from Officer Greene and called Randy Murdaugh. Alex is seen by the other large shed, head bent and pacing, his white shirt bobbing in the darkness. As Alex walked back to Greene, he said he had just called his brother who was on his way. Randy arrived shortly after. He was the first to arrive of the family, friends, and attorneys. He pulled up behind Alex's SUV, whose headlights were still on. Alex walked back to him, away from any police officers who might have found their conversation interesting. Another officer, who had been looking at the .300 Blackout casings, approached Officer Greene and said, "Do you know the name Alex Murdaugh?" It was scarily reminiscent of Anthony Cook's question to the DNR officials at the scene of the boat crash on February 24, 2019. It was a question that said volumes.

Officer Greene hooked his thumb over to where Alex and Randy were in the shadows. "He's talking to his brother over there," he said in response. At the end of the kennels, down toward the driveway entrance, more and more medics and officers were arriving; their headlights turning the small area into a glaring crime scene. They walked carefully between Paul and Maggie's bodies, noting ".300 Blackout shells." They began putting down markers so that no one would disturb them.

Back at the cavalcade of responding law enforcement, one officer calls to another that "Alex Murdaugh's brother is here and wants to know if he can come in?" The officer tells him, "Tell him to go around the other way. He doesn't need to go through here." His tone suggested that no family member should see this, as well as preserving the crime scene. John Marvin drives around to the right of the hangar, away from the bodies and joins his brothers. Attorney friends, many awakened from sleep, begin showing up. The large group is finally moved to the main house so the officers can do their jobs. SLED has arrived and things are getting buttoned down.

At the house, some of Paul's friends begin to arrive. Alex called them as well. He was especially eager to get Rogan Gibson there— the young man he had seen trying to get Paul on the phone as Alex knelt over his son's body. They all came in crying and hugging Alex. Nolan Tuten's DNA was found on the shoulder of Alex's white t-shirt when it was analyzed by SLED. It was chaos. Phone calls were made, including one to Buster Murdaugh, Alex's surviving son. Buster was in Rock Hill with his girlfriend. They threw some things together and began the 3-hour drive to Moselle. Later, it would be discovered that some of the people at the house had moved things. The dinner the housekeeper Blanca had made for the family that night was still sitting in pots and pans, the leftovers growing stale. Someone put the pots and pans in the refrigerator. Blanca had gone before the family arrived to eat. She was not witness to what transpired that night.

Buster and his girlfriend, Brooke, arrived. He testified during the double murder trial that he was sad and crying. He hugged his father. One can only imagine the shock of it all. People sat around on the couches and chairs, staring in disbelief and trying to console Alex who was "broken," according to most reports. Finally, close to 3 am, Alex, John Marvin, Buster and Brooke left for Miss Libby's to spend the night there. No one wanted to stay at the house that night. SLED agents had already come through, looking at guns, and asking questions as discreetly as they could. They would be back the next morning, as would many of the Murdaughs and their friends.

Alex called Blanca early the morning after the murders from his parent's house and asked her to come back the next morning to "the Moselle house and put things back the way Maggie would have had them." In other words, clean up. The housekeeper found the remains of the dinner, pots, pans and all, in the refrigerator. Maggie's pajamas were found neatly folded on the floor inside the laundry room door, with a pair of her freshly folded panties laying on top. Blanca would testify during the trial that Maggie didn't wear underwear with her pajamas. A few of Maggie's clothes were sitting near the bathtub. Maggie had been staying at Edisto Beach. Who put them there, and why?

When the small party loaded into cars and left the house to head to Alex's parents' home, they turned right onto Moselle Road, rain falling in the early morning hours. Only a quarter of a mile from the Moselle driveway, along the road to Almeda, Maggie Murdaugh's cell phone lay glinting in the weeds and pine needles just 15 feet from the road. As they passed it, had Alex turned surreptitiously to see if it was still there in the darkness?

Maggie Murdaugh's cell phone as it was photographed the morning after the murders when it was found near Moselle Road, 15-20 feet from the road.

Chapter Nineteen
Changing Alibis

The night of June 7, 2021, would begin the building of a double murder case. From the initial 911 call, Alex was locking himself into timelines and alibis. If one listens carefully to that call, it can be somewhat determined where he was, at least in the vicinity of the dog kennels. The constant barking alerted the listener to whether he was close to Paul's body or had moved away. It is fainter when he is closer to Maggie's body, and then the barking completely disappears in other segments of the call. What was he doing? We know he said he went up to the house to get a gun, but there are several times during the call when he is not driving to or from the house that it is eerily quiet.

After SLED arrived the night of the murders, they finally isolated Alex away from the others and placed him in Agent Owens car. Colleton County Deputy Laura Rutland and Alex's friend Danny Henderson, sat in the back seats of the car. Danny was an attorney and wanted to be present as Owens questioned Alex.

SLED agents David Owen & Deputy Laura Rutland were present at Alex Murdaugh's first interview on June 7, 2021.

During the interview in Agent Owen's car, midnight has recently passed. and it is now June 8, 2021. The interview takes place at 12:57 a.m. You get a sense of the humidity as Owen wipes his face several times. It has also been raining. Owen clipped his body camera to his visor and adjusted it to focus on himself and Alex. You can also see Rutland and Henderson in the back. As Owen makes notes, Alex glances over at his writing several times during the interview. Rutland is also taking notes.

Alex Murdaugh's First Interview on June 7, 2021

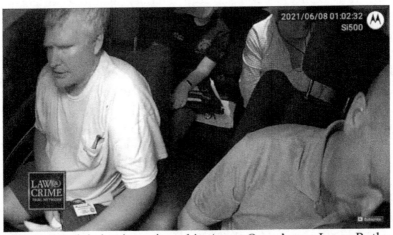

Alex Murdaugh being interviewed in Agent Owen's car. Laura Rutland sits behind Alex and Danny Henderson is behind Owen. Photo courtesy of Law & Crime.

12:57 a.m. Alex is handed a SLED business card.

Owen: Alright, sir. State your full name for me, please.
Alex: Richard Alexander Murdaugh.
Owen: And spell your last name so I can get it correct.
Alex: MURDAUGH.
Owen: And you go by Alec?
Alex: Yes, Sir.
Owen: And your date of birth?
Alex: May 27, 1968.
Owen: Phone number for you? (redacted) And sir, what was your

name?

Danny: Yeah, Danny Henderson.

Owen: OK. Alright, as I stated, I'm David Owen. And Laura Rutland. We're with Colleton County SLED. I hate to have to do this...

Alex: I totally understand. So, you don't...You don't have any problem with it.

Owen: Just start at the top, take your time.

Alex: Like when I came back here? I mean, I pulled up and I could see them and, you know, I knew something was bad. I ran out. I knew it was really bad. My boy over there, I could see it was... (Alex falls apart weeping. Both Deputy Rutland and Danny Henderson reach over from the back seats and place a hand on Alex's shoulder.)

Rutland: I'm sorry, Mr. Murdaugh.

Alex: (wailing) I could see this brain on the sidewalk. And I ran over to Maggie. Actually, I think I tried to turn Paul over first. You know, I tried to turn him over and I don't know, I figured it out. His cell phone popped out of his pocket. Started trying to do something with it, thinking maybe, but then I put it back down really quickly. Then I went to my wife, and I mean, I could see...

Owen: Did you touch Maggie at all?

Alex: I did. I touched them both. I tried to take; I mean... I tried to do it as limited as possible, but I tried to take their pulse on both of them. And you know, I called 911. Pretty much right away and she was very good. I talked to her. I told her I was gonna get off the phone to call some family members. I did that. And...

Owen: What family members did you call?

Alex: I called my brother Randy. And I called my brother John. And I tried to call the little boy, real good friend, that's right around the corner from here, but I didn't get him.

Owen: What all was around, Paul when you walked up?

Alex: Blood.

Owen: Anything else?

Alex: (Calm) I mean, there was some other body parts, yes, Sir.

Owen: I mean, like any other evidence? I know you said his phone fell out of his pocket, but did you see anything else that didn't belong or shouldn't belong, or that wasn't part of Paul?

Alex: No, Sir not, no not. No, Sir.

Owen: What about Maggie? You didn't see anything around her?

Alex: No, sir.

Owen: What made you come out here tonight?

Alex: I went to...my mom's a late-stage Alzheimer's patient. My dad's in the hospital. My mom gets anxious when he does. I went to check on them, and Maggie's a dog lover, she fools with the dogs, and I knew she'd gone to the kennel. I was at the house. I left the house and went to my mom's. For just a little while. Tried to call her when I left, texted her, no response. When I got back to the house, the house was obviously, nobody was in there, so figured they're still up here fooling around here. Paul was going to set up to plant our sunflower seeds. They got sprayed and died and he was refiguring to do, to plant the sunflower seeds. So, I came *back* up here. And drove up and saw...and called. (Italics are the authors. He said, "came *back* up here." His story was he was never at the kennels that night. In fairness, he was there earlier driving around with Paul.)

Owen: Had Maggie and Paul been arguing over anything?

Alex: No.

Owen: What was their relationship like?

Alex: Wonderful.

Owen: Wonderful? How about yours and Maggie's?

Alex: Wonderful. I mean, I'm sure we had little things here and there, but we had a wonderful marriage, wonderful relationship.

Owen: And yours and Paul's relationship?

Alex: As good as it could be. (Emphatic)

Owen: How old was Paul?

Alex: 22.

Owen: You know his date of birth?

Alex: I do. April 11, 96 is his brother's, April 14th, 99 is Paul's.

Owen: What's Maggie's full name?

Alex: Margaret Branstetter Murdaugh.

Owen: Her date of birth?

Alex: September 15th, 1968.

Owen: Have you been having any problems out here? Trespassers, or people breaking in?

Alex: None that I know of. The only thing that comes to my mind is my son Paul was in a boat wreck a couple of years ago and there's been a, you know, he was charged with, being arrested for being the driver. There's been a lot of negative publicity about that and there's been a lot of people online, just really vile stuff. But when Paul's out and about, I mean people routinely, I don't think I know the full story. So, I don't think they gave it to me, but I mean. He's been punched and hit and just attacked a lot, so. You know, but I mean nothing like this.

Owen: Yeah. Any one person in particular or group of people?

Alex: I don't know. Not that I, I don't know, Sir.

Owen: Other than being assaulted has he received any direct threats related to the boat accident?

Owen: Oh yes, all the time, he gets threats. Yes, Sir. I mean, he gets them all the time.

Owen: What kind of threats?

Ales: I'm gonna kick your ass, you know. I've never been privy firsthand, you know?

Rutland: Is that through social media or...

Owen: No, ma'am. It's mostly like if he goes out places is what you know, what he goes out like somewhere. He's in college, so if he goes out, that's what I understand. I can find out better details from some of his younger friends on that.

Rutland: Who's his best friend?

Owen: His best friend in Colombia is Wills Chapman and Will Loving. Bobby Boyle. Bobby Boyle, Wills Chapman, and Paul were getting ready to move into a house together. In Columbia. Around here, his best friends are clearly Nolan Tuten and Rogan Gibson.

Owen: Have you talked with any of these guys tonight?

Alex: I talked with Nolan, yes Sir.

Owen: Is he out here?

Alex: Yes, Sir. I tried to call Rogan. He was one of the people that he's the boy that I told you lives around the corner that's there. You know, he's just a good, helpful young man. Do you mind if I open the door?

Owen: Do what you need to do. (Alex leans out the door and spits) So is there anybody that you can think of that we need to talk to tonight? Is there a name that comes to mind?

Alex: I mean, I can't tell you anybody that I'm overly suspicious of. Off the top of my head, you know, I mean, this is such a stupid thing, I'm even embarrassed to say it. But it just didn't make any sense. I just hired a guy out here and he really, he wasn't cutting the mustard, but I hadn't told him this yet. Paul's been working with him a lot. He killed the sunflower seeds in our dove field just recently, which is why Paul was here doing this. He told Paul the story the other day about how when he was in high school, he got in a fight with some black guys. And an FBI undercover team observed him fighting those guys and put him on an undercover team with three Navy seals and that their job was to kill radical Black Panthers and they did that from Myrtle Beach to Savannah. And now I really don't think this guy. you know, is probably the person, but that's just so freaking farfetched story, but he was off today. He took his daddy to the doctor.

Owen: What's his name?

Alex: C.B. Rowe. And I sent him a message to text me earlier today about the sunflowers, and he called me back when I was on the way to my mom's house.

Owen: Did you talk to him at that time?

Alex: Briefly. I was on the phone with a lawyer friend of mine named Chris Wilson from Bamberg, so I told him I'd call him back tomorrow, see him in the morning.

Owen: When you briefly talked to Mr. Rowe, what was his demeanor or attitude?

Alex: I mean, it seemed normal. I mean, I asked him about the sunflowers and so, you know, I mean. I'm sure he's a little bit...

Owen: (Cuts Alex off from finishing his sentence) Where does he live?

Alex: I don't know exactly but I know somewhere in Brunson.

Owen: Do you have his phone number? You got it with you?

Alex: Yeah. (He looks through his phone and finally finds the number from when C.B. called him around 9 p.m. that night as Alex left for his mother's.) You know, but I do think he and Paul got along pretty well. That's just really, really weird.

Danny: (Leaning forward) You need to get that phone on a charge, if you can.

Owen: (hands Alex an iPhone charger and he plugs it in.) When did you tell that story to Paul?

Alex: Sometime last week. My son Paul, actually. And I really do not think in all honesty that it's him but you've gotta check it out. But Paul was so taken aback by it. Then he sent it, I'll find it. I got it on my phone. He recorded him saying bits and pieces of it. But for all this weirdness, I mean, I do think they like got along pretty good. (Alex is holding his phone but he makes no effort to look for the audio Paul took of C.B. killing Black Panthers. We never hear of the story again until the trial.)

Owen: How long has he been working here?

Alex? I guess about three or four pay periods, so... 8 weeks, couple months.

Owen: Going back to the boat incident. Anybody on that boat, really have a hard on for Paul? That you would think would come after him or know of any direct threats from people on the boats?

Alex: I don't know of any direct threats between any of the people on the boat, specifically but I do think there's been a small amount of Yip Yap between a couple of them, but not recently. Most of this was stuff from people that Paul didn't really know. It was some people that he knew distantly, but more times than not, when I learned about it, it was somebody that he didn't know. It's like, for example, he went out in Charleston a couple months ago, came back, you know, he got a black eye, and you know, he can't defend himself right now because he has these charges. So, you know, he would pose a real tough man's man, you know he would.

Owen: He would defend himself, but he hadn't been?

Alex: That's right.

Rutland: But how is he handling that case over everybody?

Alex: As far as what?

Owen: How was he handling it?

Alex: I've never been prouder of him than the way he has handled the pressures and the adversity. In that situation. But I think I've told Danny that before. I mean, Paul is a wonderful, wonderful, wonderful kid. He can do almost anything. He gets along with almost anybody.

Owen: Do y'all store any weapons out here?

Alex: We don't store them, but they're, you know, they're frequently out here and I need to find out if there were any out here because I know there was a shotgun; there was a 12-gauge shotgun out here. I will have to find out exactly when that was. I think it got put up. But I'm not positive.

Owen: What did that shotgun look like?

Alex: It was a camouflage. I wanna say it was a Benelli or maybe a Beretta. I can't remember which brand it is. I don't think it was out here recently. But I'm not positive.

Owen: And the shotgun that you had when deputies pulled up, where did that come from?

Alex: I went to the house, and I got a gun. Probably overreacting, but...

Owen: And was that when you pulled up and saw them?

Alex: And no, I mean I came out and I called 911 first. Talked to them for a little while, and then I told her. Told her that I was, that I was gonna go to the house. That I would let the authorities know when they got here that I had a gun.

Owen: Do you happen to have a list of all your guns?

Alex: I can make one. I don't have one, but I can make one.

Owen: OK. Well, I'm just saying, you know, so we could compare if that shotgun was out here and now it's missing.

Alex: Absolutely.

Owen: Trying to figure that out.

Ale: Absolutely.

Owen: And I know living out here in the country, you probably have more than one or two.

Alex: We do. We probably have 20-25 guns.

Owen: Any rifles?

Alex: Yes, Sir.

Owen: What kind of rifles?

Alex: All kinds. I mean you name it, across the board, we have them I mean, all of them we have are in a hunting room, in our house.

Rutland: What was their schedule today? When did they get home?

Alex: My son works for my brother, and he was coming home to deal with the sunflowers. He got here pretty early, because he and I rode around looking at everything for a good little while, probably 45 minutes to an hour. Maggie had things she did in Charleston. She had a doctor's appointment in Charleston. And she got back here. It was fairly late.

Rutland: Was it dark yet when Paul got home?

Alex: No, Paul got home early.

Rutland: Early? OK, so before dinner time?

Alex: Oh yes, ma'am.

Rutland: Lunchtime?

Alex: No, ma'am.

Owen: What brother? What brother does Paul work for?

Alex: John Marvin.

Owen: What does Paul do for him?

Alex: Everything.

Owen: Handyman?

Alex: Yes, Sir. (Opens door and spits)

Rutland: Was it unusual for Maggie to feed the dogs this time of night or check on them?

Alex: Oh, no. I mean, she played with those dogs all the time and it was especially common for her to, you know, if she's been gone for a while, to come and let, especially two of them, out to run.

Rutland: OK, so she pretty regularly comes out here in the evening?

Alex: Very regular. She comes out here a lot.

Rutland: You have any cameras on your property?

Alex: I have deer cameras, but none, you know around up here.

Rutland: Where are they at?

Alex: Oh, different deer stands.

Rutland: OK, so deep in the woods.

Alex: Well, not necessarily deep in the woods. Some of them are in the fields. But there's none that are near here.

Owen: What doctor appointment? What doctor did Maggie see today?

Alex: I forget the guy's name. Maggie's been having trouble with her... She's been having trouble with her stomach and her tooth. I'm not positive. It was sort of a routine visit, and I can't remember. She told me the name of him, and I can't... I want to say Gordine, Gordeen, Gordine? is who I think she saw.

Owen: So, was she back home around suppertime? Or six o'clock, 7:00 o'clock?

Alex: I don't think she got back quite that early. I think she got back a little bit later than that.... umm.

Owen: What did you do today? Where you were in the office or no?

Alex: No. I was home. Paul and I messed around. I, I. I was up at the house. I laid down, took a nap on the couch, probably, I don't know, 25-30 minutes. I got up. I called Maggie. Didn't get an answer. And I left to go to my mom's. She said she might ride with me, but she normally doesn't when I go over there. And I think I texted her. And she's very good about answering the phone, so that was odd, or calling me back. So that was odd, but it wasn't that big a deal.

Rutland: About what time was that?

Alex: What time was what? (Sounds a little harsh)

Rutland: You sent her a text message?

Alex: (Alex puts his glasses on his head and looks at his text messages on his phone) Alright, I checked, texted her at 9:08, "Going to check on M, be right back," and then I texted her at 9:47. That must be when I started to come back. I think I called her before that. Let me make sure. Pretty sure that I called her. 9:45. And then I tried Paul. And then. No, I think that was riding'. I think that might have been riding' over there. 10:03… I mean, my calls are right here. Yeah, so. Obviously, this is when this is when I at 10:06... (Spits out the door) Can I have a piece of gum?

Owen: Yes, Sir. There you go. Anybody else want some gum?

Alex asks Danny if he has some water. He says, "Sorry, I don't.

Alex: That's okay. I don't need it.

Owen: If you look behind Denny's head, there's a case of water. (Rutland hands Alex a bottle of water and he thanks her.) I'm sure we're going to have much more questions…

Alex: I'm available at… you know, you let me know.

Owen: What's another number in case I can't get you on your cell?

Alex: I don't have a house phone. I have an office number. I can give you my brother's cell phones. (He gives them their numbers.)

Owen: And you said your dads in the hospital? Charleston or Savannah?

Alex: Savannah. St. Joseph.

Owen: Is he doing OK or what?

Alex: He's having a really, really hard time. He's got a lot, lot, lot, lot going on. He's doing OK, giving everything, but he's got a lot going on.

Owen: How about Maggie's family, were are they?

Alex: Summerville.

Owen: Have you been in touch with them?

Alex: Yes, I have. My brother called Bart, the wife of his sister, and I mean the husband of Maggie's sister. So that they could go and tell Maggie's parents. I felt like they needed to hear from them in person and they are going there and calling me. I'm telling you they must not be there yet.

Owen: Maggie's parents are in Sommerville?

Alex: Yes. And she, her mom just had a knee replacement surgery.

And her dad really has trouble getting around nowadays.

Owen: Do you have any other children?

Alex: I do. I have a 24-year-old.

Owen: Right. You said. What's his name?

Alex: Well, Richard Alexander Junior. Buster. He goes by Buster.

Owen: Is here tonight?

Alex: He's on his way.

Owen: OK? Laura, you got anything else?

Rutland: This one's hard, but when you first saw Paul, you said you tried to flip him over. Was he lying on his back or on his stomach?

Alex: Just like he, just like he is.

Rutland: You weren't able to move him? OK, and did he help Maggie a lot out here with the animals?

Alex: He helped everybody with everything,

Rutland: OK. So, it was kind of routine for him to be out here as well?

Alex: This place is his absolute passion! I tried to turn him and then I tried and then I checked him, and I mean. I think I already knew, but I checked them.

Rutland: And when you first pulled, first pulled into the property, did you come from this direction where all our police cars are, or which way did you come in?

Alex: I went to the house, and then I came from the house just like straight here. I mean where my vehicle was parked.

Rutland: (she cuts him off) Is probably where it was, OK.

Alex: Well, no, maybe not exactly, but it was pretty close cause I came back the same route.

Rutland: That's right, cause you went back to get your shotgun...

Alex: When I came back.

Owen: I can't think of anything else right now, but you know, we'll certainly be in touch.

Alex: Thank you all for everything for all you're doing.

Owen: Just so, you know, just to kind of let you know what's gonna go on. We're gonna be out here for quite some time. The coroner will take custody of Paul and Maggie.

Alex: (His phone rings) Can I answer that?

Owen: Yeah.

Alex: What? No, Lenny, (breaks down) we're finished. Let me come out there. I'll be there when he gets here. No, don't let him come up here. OK. Yeah, I think we're about done. Alright, thank you.

Owen: Buster? (Inquires if the call was that Buster was almost there)

Alex: I'm sorry. Yes, Sir. I dropped my card. Sorry.

Owen: (Hands him a SLED business card.) There you go.

Alex: Thank you.

Owen: The coroner will come over and talk to you, you know, they'll do the autopsy and everything and go from there.

Alex: Thank you.

Owen: But we'll come to you before we leave.

Alex: Thank you very much. Thank you. Thank you very much. (Alex exits the car.)

Owen: Here, you want this water?

Alex: Yes, please. Thank you.

There is so much to unpack with this initial interview with Alex. As always, he is never pinned down on times, except for a few texts and calls. He does not commit to what time Paul arrives that night. Has no idea when Maggie got there. When asked if he went into the office, he outright lies and says, "No." He may not have wanted SLED to ask questions about his time at work that day. It was while in his office that Jeannie Seckinger CPA, and PMPED's CFO, confronted him, demanding to know where the missing fees were from a case over which he had been dodging her. A phone call from Randy telling him their father has just been sent back to the hospital fortuitously interrupts that confrontation and he is off the hook…temporarily. Jeannie quickly drops the subject and tries to comfort him about his father. He leaves work around 6:30 p.m. and heads home.

It is very interesting to look at Alex's words in this interview when referring to Paul and Maggie. When he speaks of Paul it is almost always in the present tense—as if he cannot come to terms with the fact, he is dead. Maggie is a footnote. His answers about her are perfunctory, and without much emotion. He can't remember why she had a doctor's appointment or who the doctor was. We find out later that Maggie was actually in Charleston sitting in the doctor's office waiting area when Alex texted her to come home because Randolph III was going back into the hospital. She also got a pedicure and foot massage.

Perhaps the most important takeaway from this interview is the segment concerning the sunflowers and Paul's role in their care. Here, we hear where Alex assumes Paul will be that night. Twice, he says Paul was here to "refigure" the sunflowers that C.B. Rowe had killed by over spraying them. Alex tried several times to get hold of Rowe in the early evening. Was it to get him out to the dove field where the sunflowers were to help Paul? It seems Rowe is avoiding his calls. His excuse for not being at work that day was that he was taking his father to the doctor's.

In Kathleen McKenna Hewton's book, *Murdaugh She Wrote*, she interviews C.B. Rowe about that night. He said Paul called him at 7:20 pm the night of the murders. This would be when Paul is riding around the property with Alex. Rowe said Paul asked him, on behalf of Alex, to meet Paul out there at Moselle that night to help them plant sunflowers. Ms. Hewton said Rowe told her in the interview that he told Paul "No," saying he was busy and would deal with it the next day as it was growing late, and it was going to rain. We found out later that he was really looking for another job and didn't want Alex to know. Alex doesn't mention this to SLED during the interview. (My thanks to Ms. Hewton for her permission to reprint this segment of her interview with Mr. Rowe.)

It is obvious that Alex is trying to set up C.B. Rowe in the interview as a bad guy, capable of violence. Was the plan to get Rowe out there to the sunflower fields and set him up for Maggie's murder? As I mentioned before, I don't think Alex knew Paul was in the feed shed that night, and I will go over my theory later in the book. We know from Blanca, the Murdaugh housekeeper, that she had a phone conversation with Maggie earlier in the afternoon that day. Maggie tells Blanca that Paul is coming home to look after some dead sunflowers. Maggie says she left some food out in the refrigerator and asks Blanca to fix dinner. Maggie says she is coming home too. Alex asked her to because Randolph is back in the hospital.

If we look at the timeline here, we see Alex asking Maggie at the last minute to come to Moselle to go see his dad with him. Maggie loved "Handsome," and she reluctantly decided to go. Her plans were to be at Edisto overseeing the work being done there. Maggie's sister, Marion, would later testify that she regrets encouraging Maggie to go. Since Alex only found out in the afternoon at work about Randolph's collapse, then it makes sense he got hold of

Maggie later that day. Maggie asks Blanca to make dinner at Moselle. The texts between Maggie and Blanca are around 3:30 pm.

Shortly before the night of the murders, Maggie had found pills in Alex's computer bag as she waited for him in the car while he was seeing a doctor for cataracts. She told Paul, who had been monitoring his father's drug abuse. Paul texted him and told him they needed to talk. Was the dinner at Moselle the first opportunity Paul and Maggie had to sit down with Alex and confront him about his ongoing addiction? Is that why Alex was never able to answer, "What did you three talk about at dinner?" He was always evasive. He stumbled over his words, and finally said, "Normal stuff." If that was the last meal you had with your family, who would be found murdered only a couple of hours later, wouldn't that last dinner conversation be burned into your mind?

So, Alex says Paul shows up, sometime around 7, which is about right. John Marvin said Paul left Okatie around 6 p.m. Alex says he and Paul rode around the property for 45 minutes to an hour. At other times, he said it was two hours. Each time he was asked where they went, he could not be pinned down. "All over," was all he would say. Someone finally pinned him down to mention the dove fields (where the sunflowers are), and he finally talked about a duck pond where Paul showed off how his planted corn was doing better than Alex's. Thanks to Paul's Snapchat video, we do see Alex with him, playing with a tree, as Paul laughs in the background. It was taken at 7:36 p.m. and sent to friends at 7:57 p.m.

When did Alex come up with needing the sunflowers handled that night? Why was he so urgent to get hold of Rowe and get him out there to take care of it? If Paul is there, does Alex make sure he will be way over in the dove fields hoeing under the dead flowers when Maggie is shot near the kennels?

During Alex's time on the witness stand during his trial for the murder of his wife and son, he says in his "new story" that he and Paul washed off a bulldozer. He is never asked "Why?" Had they used the bulldozer while they were running around the property that night? The point is, was Alex's plan to have Rowe there with Paul, running a loud piece of farm equipment to till under the ruined sunflowers, while Alex is shooting Maggie at the kennels? And, then throw Rowe under the bus for being on the property. A minute amount of Rowe's DNA was found under one of Maggie's nails. It could have gotten there from her touching anything at the hangar that Rowe worked with, including the Polaris she may have leaned against when she was shot in the thigh. Or, if you have a suspicious mind, as this author does, did someone in law enforcement that was in Alex's back pocket, take the buccal swab taken from Rowe and rub it under her nail at Alex's request? And don't forget, Curtis Eddie Smith, Alex's drug runner and distant cousin, would later start a rumor that Maggie had been fooling around with C.B. Rowe in the hangar shed. Could Alex have put him up to that? Everyone who heard the rumor thought it was ludicrous. Just a thought.

But Rowe didn't show up. In fact, he finally called Alex at 9:00 p.m. that night as Alex was leaving to go see his mother. The murders were over by then. Alex tells Rowe not to worry about the sunflowers. He can come in the morning.

The other patsy mentioned during the 911 call, the announcement to the first officer on the scene that night, and to SLED in the first interview that evening, was the boat crash. "The boat crash...that's what this is!" Alex now has two possible murderers of his wife and son. Someone associated with the boat crash and C.B. Rowe. Seems very familiar. Like throwing Connor to the wolves with the boat crash and possibly setting up Shawn Connelly for the murder of Stephen Smith. For the Murdaugh's, it was not enough to have an alibi for themselves, they had to have someone to roast on the spit. Curtis "Eddie" Smith would find that out in the coming months. The list of patsies was long and varied. The saddest part would be that none of them mattered to Alex. They were all expendable, just like the clients from whom he stole.

Chapter Twenty
What Was Supposed to Happen?

So many rumors swirled around this double murder case. In the end, all we have are the facts. It seems phones would be Alex Murdaugh's undoing. Whether it was texts and phone calls made by him (many mysteriously erased), or the evidence found on his son Paul's phone. they would ultimately be his downfall.

Below is the timeline of June 7, 2021, showing Alex, Maggie, and Paul's phone history. Let's see if we can piece together what was supposed to happen that fateful day. My suggestions are in brackets.

Timeline of Phone Logs of Alex, Maggie and Paul

JUNE 7

12:06:47 p.m.: Alex Murdaugh's vehicle leaves the Moselle property headed to the PMPED law firm in Hampton.

12:24:06 p.m.: Alex Murdaugh arrives at the PMPED law firm.

[Sometime after Alex arrives at work, PMPED's CFO Jeannie Seckinger corners Alex on the second floor as he is leaning against a file cabinet. He shoots her a dirty look and asks, "Now what do you want?" She tells him to go into his office where she confronts him about the missing Ferris fees. During that surprise meeting,

271

Alex supposedly gets a call from Randy telling him their father is worse and is returning to the hospital. Alex relays the bad news to Seckinger who terminates the discussion about the fees and instead tries to comfort him. He tells her his dad is now "terminal." What we do not see in these log reports is a record of that call coming in from Randy. Where is it? It doesn't even show up as one that was later erased. We know Alex's friend Chris Wilson said Alex called him that night on a number he didn't recognize as the one Alex normally used. Was the call from Randy on a different cell phone? Or did the call come to Alex's office phone, which is possible. It seems odd Randy would not call his brother's personal phone. Was Randy right there in the building? He was a law partner there. We see a lot of silence between 12:24 and the next log at 3:28.]

3:28 p.m.: Murdaugh's housekeeper Blanca Turrubiate-Simpson finishes cooking dinner at Moselle. She texts Maggie, who is in the Charleston area, "Dinners on the stove, just left."

3:40 p.m.: Maggie texts Blanca "Thank you."

3:41 p.m.: Alex Murdaugh places a FaceTime call to his wife Maggie. It goes unanswered. A SLED agent testifies that the record of the call is later manually deleted from Alex's phone.

Before 4 p.m.: Roger Dale Davis arrives at Moselle to feed the dogs, chickens, and clean the dog pens. He said no one else was at the property when he arrived, and nothing was out of place.

3:55 p.m.: Maggie texts Blanca, "I'm waiting at doctor. Alex wants me to come home. I have to leave the door open at Edisto. I trust Mexicans to shut and lock for me. His dad is back in hospital. No cancer. It's pneumonia."

[Look at this message. Maggie is telling Blanca "Alex wants me to come home. I have to leave the door open at Edisto." Blanca has already told Maggie at 3:28 p.m. that "dinner is on the stove." Maggie texts her back at 3:40 p.m. "Thank you." Wouldn't Blanca already know Maggie was coming home at 3:28 if she was expected for dinner? It sounds like this is the first time Maggie is telling her she's coming, and she's concerned about the Edisto Beach house door being left open after the workers finish that day.]

Marian Proctor, Maggie's sister, later testifies that Maggie thought she was going to Moselle to see Alex's dying father.

3:57 p.m.: Maggie texts Blanca regarding Alex having a lot of pressure on him to care for his ailing parents, "Alex is about to die. Hope he doesn't go down there to sleep. Alex needs to take care of himself as well."

[Again, this sounds like Maggie has received the news about Alex's father in the past few minutes.]

3:57 p.m.: Alex texts Maggie, "How's your doctor appt?"

Maggie responds: "Waiting as usual."

4:06 p.m.: Maggie texts Blanca, in reference to the ailing Randolph Murdaugh, "I'm scared for him and Alex and all of us."

Blanca texts Maggie, "I know just pray about it. Just pray about it and hope he gets a little better. Alex and you really need to relax. Always being on the go with little to no sleep is not healthy. I have a doctor's appointment in the morning in Beaufort. If I go to Moselle, I will let you know."

4:10-6:25 p.m.: Alex Murdaugh's phone places him at the PMPED law firm in Hampton.

[Jeannie Seckinger testified that Alex contacted her around 4 p.m. while he was still at the office to ask about his 401K plan. She said she was surprised that he was still in the office as he had received a call during their talk that sounded like his dad was terminal. In

273

reality, Randolph was back in the hospital for pneumonia, not the cancer this time.]

4:25-7:05 p.m.: Maggie's phone places her in the West Ashley area, near Charleston.

4:30 p.m.: Roger Dale Davis leaves Moselle after caring for the dogs and chickens.

4:35 p.m.: Alex places a FaceTime call to Maggie. It goes unanswered. **A SLED agent testifies that the record of the call is later manually deleted from Alex's phone.**

5:30-6:09 p.m.: Paul Murdaugh's phone places him in Okatie.

6:04:11 p.m.: Paul Murdaugh calls Will Loving.

6:04:25 p.m.: Will Loving calls Paul Murdaugh.

6:08:57 p.m.: Paul Murdaugh calls "Dad." **No record of the call is found on Alex Murdaugh's phone.**

6:09:48: Maggie Murdaugh texts Paul saying she's getting a foot massage.

6:20:53 p.m.: Marian Proctor calls her sister Maggie's phone. Maggie texts Marian saying she can't talk and she's getting a foot massage.

6:23:27 p.m.: Paul texts his mom asking what Blanca cooked for dinner. She replies, country fried steak and macaroni and cheese.

[Paul obviously knows Blanca has made dinner at this point. Was it during the deleted phone call to his "Dad" at 6:08 or just because Blanca always fixes dinner for Alex? Was that call to Alex the first time Alex knew Paul was coming along with John Marvin, and would be coming to Moselle while John Marvin took his dad to the hospital? COVID was still limiting access to the hospital and only essential people were allowed in. Paul took John Marvin's truck to Moselle while John Marvin loaded his father into Miss Libby's car for the drive. It was hard for Randolph to step up into the truck.]

6:24 p.m.: Alex Murdaugh's vehicle leaves the PMPED law firm, headed to Moselle.

6:25:35 p.m.: Alex Murdaugh's phone receives a call from Jay Parker.

6:17-6:53 p.m.: Paul's phone shows him traveling from Okatie to Moselle.

6:40:01 p.m.: Paul Murdaugh calls "PA" (Alex Murdaugh's phone). The call lasts 2 minutes and 29 seconds. **There is no call log for it in Alex Murdaugh's phone.** (Note: The first call Paul makes to Alex shows in the log as "Dad." This second call shows in the log as "PA." Did Paul call two different phones for his dad?)

6:42 p.m.: Alex Murdaugh's vehicle arrives at Moselle.

6:43 p.m.: Alex calls his wife's phone. The call lasts 104 seconds. **There is no call log for it in the data extractions of Alex's phone.**

6:53:44 p.m.: Paul Murdaugh's phone calls John Marvin Murdaugh.

7:04 p.m.: Paul Murdaugh is at Moselle.

[Alex is repeatedly asked by investigators what time he and Paul arrived at Moselle. He is always evasive and never gives them a time frame. He only says, "I'm not sure. I may have got there before him, or he may have gotten there before me. It was around the same time." We now can see from the phone data that Alex arrived at 6:42 p.m. and Paul arrived 22 minutes later.

7:05 p.m.: Alex texts Maggie, "Paul says you are getting pedi!! Call when you get done."

[Paul has probably now hooked up with his dad at Moselle. According to Alex's interviews, it was around 7 that they started riding around the property. What's interesting, is what happens next.]

7:10:06 p.m.: Paul texts CB Rowe asking if he's coming to Moselle to help with the sunflowers tonight.

7:18:40 p.m.: Alex texts CB Rowe stating "Call me pls."

[Paul had only been at Moselle for 6 minutes when he tried to get C.B. Rowe on the phone to come and help plow under the dead sunflowers. It is possible Alex and Paul traveled to the dove fields in 6 minutes and looked at the damage. One investigator stated that Rowe told Paul he was busy, and as it would be 8 p.m. before he got there, and it was supposed to rain, he wasn't coming. Alex texts Rowe 8 minutes later and tells him to "Call me pls." Rowe does not call him.]

7:07-7:50 p.m.: Maggie's phone places her traveling from the North Charleston area, taking Highway 17, towards Moselle.

7:09:43 p.m.: Maggie Murdaugh calls Courtney Shelbourne. The call lasts 3 seconds.

7:09:43 p.m.: Maggie Murdaugh calls "Mom." The call lasts 8 minutes and 17 seconds.

7:14:13-7:22:19 p.m.: Paul Murdaugh's phone records 208 steps taken. (Are they walking the sunflower rows here?)

7:15:35-7:21:52 p.m.: Alex Murdaugh's phone records 200 steps taken.

7:18:40 p.m.: Maggie Murdaugh calls "Barbara." The call lasts 2 seconds.

7:25:03-7:34:47 p.m.: Paul Murdaugh's phone shows 139 steps taken.

7:28:35-7:37:11 p.m.: Alex Murdaugh's phone records 47 steps taken.

7:31:13 p.m.: Maggie Murdaugh calls her sister Marian Proctor. The call lasts 7 minutes and 39 seconds.

7:35:10-7:41:43 p.m.: Paul Murdaugh's phone records 171 steps taken.

7:37 p.m.: Paul Murdaugh receives a Snapchat message from "michellebeck" stating, "BC I have short term memory loss."

7:38:34 p.m.: Paul receives an iMessage from Meagan Kimbrell stating, "Paul."

7:39:48 p.m.: Maggie Murdaugh calls "Barbara." There is no answer.

7:39:55 p.m.: It appears Paul Murdaugh records the video of his father here. He sends it as a Snapchat video about 15 minutes later.

[This SnapChat video shows Alex in his office clothes of a pale blue dress shirt and khaki pants. He is wearing shoes that Blanca identifies as his house shoes, not the ones he wears outside. This video would become an important piece of evidence in the trial. It is clear that Alex and Paul are surveying the property. Their steps seem to match up as they get out and move around Moselle's back acreage.]

7:41:23-7:48:49 p.m.: Alex Murdaugh's phone records 29 steps.

7:45-7:56 p.m.: Paul's phone places him by the kennels on the Moselle property.

[Paul is now back at the kennels. We do not see Alex's phone placing him at any location at this time.]

7:50 p.m.: Maggie's phone is in Walterboro, roughly a half hour away from Moselle. It's the last location data pulled from her phone.

7:50:03 p.m.: Maggie calls "Barbara." The call lasts 8 seconds.

7:55:44-8:05:28 p.m.: Paul Murdaugh's phone records 262 steps.

7:55:32-8:05:07 p.m.: Alex Murdaugh's phone records 270 steps. [It appears Paul and his dad are still together as their steps and time lapse are almost identical.]

7:56 p.m.: Paul sends a SnapChat video. A still shot of the Snapchat video is shown below. Paul laughs as Alex is seen standing by a little tree at Moselle as it flops over.

8:05:35-8:09:52 p.m.: Alex Murdaugh's phone records 54 steps.

8:05:46-8:15:24 p.m.: Paul Murdaugh's phone records 303 steps.

Paul's SnapChat video showing Alex with a drooping tree. He is wearing a "seafoam green Columbia polo shirt, light brown khaki pants, and his brown house shoes. (Testimony by Blanca Simpson)

8:06 p.m.: Paul's phone begins moving from the kennels to the main house. (The previous log shows Paul taking 303 steps during this time. Did he walk back to the house? Alex left before him. Which of the two trucks was he driving? John Marvin's white truck that Paul drove to Moselle is seen at the house after the murders.)

8:07:20 p.m.: Paul Murdaugh sends a Snapchat message to several friends.

8:09-9:02 p.m.: Alex's phone records no steps, indicating he was not moving with the phone in his possession. He later told investigators he was sleeping during that time.

[For almost a full hour, Alex's phone is void of movement or any phone data.]

8:11:08-8:31:15 p.m.: Maggie Murdaugh's phone is locked. She unplugs it from her car at about 8:15 p.m. It is probably when she arrives at the Moselle house.]

8:14-8:35 p.m.: Paul Murdaugh's phone puts him at the main house.

8:15:55-8:21:45 p.m.: Paul's phone records 140 steps.

8:17-8:18 p.m.: Maggie Murdaugh's phone records 38 steps taken.

[This may be when she exits the car and walks up the steps and into the house.]

8:19:23 p.m.: Paul Murdaugh receives a Snapchat message from "Ansley Wilson," stating "He's got the magic touch."

8:23:33 p.m.: Paul sends a Snapchat message to "Marlene Robinson," stating, "He's hurt."

8:24:08 p.m.: Paul sends an iMessage to Meagan Kimbrell stating, "Meagan."

8:28:07 p.m.: Paul receives an iMessage from Meagan Kimbrell stating, "We're u avoiding me."

8:28:35 p.m.: Paul responds to Meagan Kimbrell with, "When?"

8:28:54 p.m.: Paul receives an iMessage from a Mrs. Morgan stating, "I have not received anything back yet. Did you get the lease email?"

8:29:06 p.m.: Paul receives an iMessage from Meagan Kimbrell stating, "You didn't send me any movie recommendations."

8:29:36 p.m.: Paul responds, "Haha I didn't have a good one. Wills might."

8:30-8:33 p.m.: Maggie Murdaugh's phone records 43 steps taken.

[Here we may have Maggie leaving the house to probably get into a vehicle to go down to the kennels. It appears dinner is over. Paul looks as if he spent the dinner texting back and forth to friends and a Mrs. Morgan.]

8:31 p.m.: John Marvin Murdaugh sends a text to several family members, including Alex and Maggie, which reads, "I plan to go over to visit dad tomorrow afternoon. Is anyone else planning to go?" Maggie Murdaugh's phone did not unlock for the notification until 8:49:26 p.m. Alex Murdaugh reads his text from John at 1:44 p.m. the following day. [Maggie may have left the phone in the Mercedes or whatever she drove down in, or somewhere else at the kennels. It is obvious that Alex is not very worried about his dad's health at this time. He waits until the next day to read his brother John Marvin's text concerning their father.]

8:32:10 p.m.: Paul receives a call from Lucile Boyle. The call is not answered.

8:32:25-8:42:11 p.m.: Paul's cell phone records 283 steps taken. (Is Paul walking back down to the kennels?)

8:38 p.m.: Paul's phone places him by the kennels.

8:40:20 p.m.: Paul calls longtime friend Rogan Gibson asking if something is wrong with the tail of Gibson's dog, who was staying in the Murdaugh kennels. The call lasts 4 minutes and 14 seconds. It is during this call that Rogan hears Alex's voice in the background, so Alex is at the kennels by 8:40:20 p.m. He testified in court he took a golf cart down after Maggie left the house.)

Rogan Gibson testifying at Alex's murder trial.

8:41:38 p.m.: Paul receives a Snapchat message from Rogan Gibson.

8:44:34 p.m.: Paul Murdaugh initiates a FaceTime call with Gibson. It lasts 11 seconds and fails to send.

8:44:55 p.m.: Paul records a video for Gibson at the kennels, showing the dog. Three voices are heard in the video. Multiple witnesses testify that those voices are Paul, Maggie, and Alex Murdaugh.

8:47:55 p.m.: Paul sends an iMessage to Meagan Kimbrell stating, "Haha kidding."

8:48:05 p.m.: Paul again sends an iMessage to her, stating, "Star was born is the movie."

8:48:29 p.m.: Meagan Kimbrell texts Paul, "No I need something happy" and "Don't like watching sad movies."

8:49:01 p.m.: Paul Murdaugh's phone is locked. [He will be shot in the next several seconds.]

8:49:26 p.m.: Maggie Murdaugh's phone unlocks, and she reads another text in the group chat about Randolph Murdaugh.

[This is the last time Maggie reads her phone messages. It is now that she probably hears shots coming from the feed shed.]

8:49:28 p.m.: Maggie Murdaugh's phone accesses an application and implements orientation change to landscape.

[Landscape mode on a phone is lying flat. Maggie dropped the phone and hurried to the feed shed where she was shot in the thigh. As she backs away, she is shot three to four more times and dies by a small doghouse at the hangar overhang.]

8:49:31 p.m.: Maggie Murdaugh's phone is locked and not unlocked until it's found a quarter mile away the next afternoon.

8:49:35 p.m.: Rogan Gibson texts Paul about the dog's tail, "See if you can get a good picture of it. MaryAnn wants to send it to a girl we know that's a vet. Get him to sit and stay. He shouldn't move around too much." The text goes unread.

Investigators believe Maggie and Paul Murdaugh are killed around 8:50 p.m. near the kennels. Paul is shot twice with a shotgun, once in the chest and once in the head. Maggie is shot 4-5 times with .300 Blackout ammo from an AR-style rifle. Two of those shots struck her in the head.

8:53 p.m.: The orientation on Maggie's phone changes, waking the screen to activate its Face ID security feature. But the phone remains locked, thus implying it is picked up by someone who is not her.

8:53:15-8:55:32 p.m.: Maggie Murdaugh's phone records 59 steps. (Testimony during the murder trial opines the shooter was walking with Maggie's phone, possibly with the phone in his pocket.

8:55:48 p.m.: Maggie Murdaugh's phone takes a snapshot of an open app, Facebook, running in the background.

9:02:18-9:06:47 p.m.: Alex Murdaugh's phone comes to life, recording 283 steps, about 70 steps per minute.

[It is now that Alex's phone, which has been inactive for almost an hour, is back in use.]

9:04:23 p.m.: Alex Murdaugh calls his wife's phone. **There is no record of the call in the data extraction from Alex's phone.**

9:05:15 p.m.: Alex Murdaugh calls his father Randolph Murdaugh. The call lasts 18 seconds. **There is no record of it in the data extraction from Alex's phone.**

9:06 p.m.: The orientation of Maggie Murdaugh's phone changes.

9:06:14 p.m.: Alex Murdaugh calls his wife's phone. There is no answer. **There is no record of the call in the data extraction from Alex's phone.**

9:06:51 p.m.: Alex Murdaugh calls his wife's phone. There is no answer. **There is no record of the call in the data extraction from Alex's phone.**

9:07:06 p.m.: Alex's vehicle leaves Moselle headed to Almeda.

9:08:36 p.m.: Alex Murdaugh's vehicle drives by where Maggie Murdaugh's missing cell phone would be found the following day. After passing the location, the vehicle quickly increases speed.

[This is probably the time that Alex throws the phone from his truck window as he drives toward his mother's home in Almeda.]

9:08:58 p.m.: Alex texts his wife's phone, "Going to check on M be rite back."

9:10:47 p.m.: Alex calls his son Buster Murdaugh. The call lasts 60 seconds. **There is no record of it in the data extraction from Alex's phone.**

9:12:14 p.m.: Alex calls longtime friend and fellow attorney Chris Wilson. Wilson was busy and asked if he could call Alex back. The call lasts 2 minutes.

9:18:46 p.m.: Alex calls John Marvin Murdaugh. The call lasts 106 seconds. **There is no record of the call in the data extraction of Alex's phone.**

9:20 p.m.: Chris Wilson calls Alex back. Alex says he's getting close to his mom's house and asks if he can call him back. The call lasts 3 minutes.

9:22:06 p.m.: Alex's vehicle arrives at his mother's Almeda property.

9:22:39 p.m.: Alex's vehicle parks by the wood line, near the smoke house, away from the home.

The speed of the trip is faster than any trip he took that day, reaching 74 miles per hour.

9:24:13 p.m.: Shelly Smith, Libby Murdaugh's caregiver, testifies that Alex calls her from outside the home and asks to be let inside. She's able to get to the door 5 minutes later. Smith testifies that Libby, in the advanced stages of dementia, is asleep during the visit and that Alex is looking at his phone a lot. She later testifies that he is wearing a white t-shirt, cargo shorts, and Sperry shoes… "soft covered shoes."

9:34 p.m.: Rogan Gibson, after not hearing back from Paul, texts Maggie Murdaugh, "Tell Paul to call me." The text goes unread.

9:35:55-9:45:37 p.m.: Alex Murdaugh's phone records 60 steps taken.

9:43:05 p.m.: Alex's vehicle is taken out of park at Almeda.

[This shows Alex only stayed with his mother for roughly 20 minutes; less if you count when he begins walking at 9:35 p.m.]

9:43:59 p.m.: Alex's vehicle is put into park.

9:44:54 p.m.: Alex's vehicle is taken out of park. (He paused at the end of the Almeda driveway for close to a minute before exiting onto the street.)

9:46:35 p.m.: Alex calls Paul Murdaugh's phone. The connection lasts 18 seconds. **There was no record of it in the data extraction from Alex's phone.**

9:47 p.m.: Alex texts Maggie, "Call me babe." The text goes unread.

9:52:15 p.m.: Alex texts Chris Wilson, "Call me if u up."

9:52:59 p.m.: Chris Wilson calls Alex. There is no answer.

9:53:55 p.m.: Chris Wilson calls Alex again. Alex picks up. Chris wanted to talk about some cases, but Alex said he was almost back home and would call him back.

9:54:24 p.m.: Alex Murdaugh's vehicle reaches 74 miles per hour as he returns to Moselle.

9:56:57-10:06:57 p.m.: Alex Murdaugh's phone records 231 steps taken.

[Alex is obviously out of the SUV now and walking around. This is when he tells law enforcement he went to the house, didn't see anyone there, went to the kennels, saw his wife and son shot, checked their pulses, and called 911.]

9:57:09 p.m.: Rogan Gibson calls Paul Murdaugh. There is no answer.

9:58 p.m.: After not hearing from Paul or Maggie, Rogan Gibson texts Paul "Yo."

10:00:36 p.m.: Alex returns to Moselle and places his vehicle into park at the main house. On the drive back from Almeda, the vehicle reached 80 mph where the max speed limit was 55 mph.

10:01:17 p.m.: Alex takes the vehicle out of park.

10:01:29 p.m.: Alex puts the vehicle into park.

10:01:30 p.m.: Alex takes the vehicle out of park.

10:01:43 p.m.: Alex puts the vehicle into park at the main house at Moselle.

10:04:49 p.m.: Alex takes the vehicle out of park.

10:05:04 p.m.: Rogan Gibson calls Buster Murdaugh. The connection lasts 2 seconds.

10:05:06 p.m.: Alex Murdaugh's vehicle drives to the kennels from the main house.

10:05:55 p.m.: Alex puts the vehicle into park by the kennels.

10:06:14 p.m.: Alex calls 911 from the Moselle property. The call is received by Hampton County dispatch before being transferred to Colleton County.

[According to Alex, he checked Paul and Maggie for signs of life, turned Paul almost over, puts Paul's phone on his bottom, and calls 911, all within 20 seconds after putting his car in park at 10:05:55 p.m.]

In the 7-minute call, he says he found Maggie and Paul shot and neither were breathing.

During the call, he notes he is not presently by the bodies. He said he touched them after finding them but only to see if they were still breathing.

He hangs up after saying he needed to call family members.

10:06:57-10:16:37 p.m.: Alex Murdaugh's phone records 594 steps. (Why all the steps in this ten-minute time?)

10:11:45 p.m.: Alex takes the vehicle out of park at the kennels and returns to the main house.

[This is probably when Alex tells 911, he is going back to the house for a gun. This author believes it is also when he changes his shoes from the Speery shoes to the neon-colored tennis shoes.]

10:12:38 p.m.: Alex puts the vehicle into park at the main house.

10:13:39 p.m.: Alex takes the vehicle out of park at the main house, returning to the kennels.

10:14:30 p.m.: Alex Murdaugh's vehicle returns to the kennels.

10:17:49 p.m.: Alex Murdaugh calls Randy Murdaugh. He is finished with the 911 call. The connection to Randy lasts 16 seconds. **There is no record of the call in the data extraction of Alex's phone.**

10:18:45 p.m.: Alex Murdaugh iMessages Randy Murdaugh, stating, "Pls call me. Emergency."

10:18:53-10:28:05 p.m.: Alex's cell phone records 525 steps taken. (All those steps taken. The first responder shows up at 10:25 pm. What was he doing before the police arrived?)

10:19:32 p.m.: Alex Murdaugh calls Randy Murdaugh. The connection lasts 1 second. **There is no record of the call in the data extraction of Alex's phone.**

10:19:44 p.m.: Alex Murdaugh calls John Marvin Murdaugh. The call lasts 40 seconds. **There is no record of the call in the data extraction of Alex's phone.**

10:21:25 p.m.: Alex Murdaugh calls Rogan Gibson. There is no answer. Gibson testified he was already asleep.

10:21:57 p.m.: Alex Murdaugh calls Christy Murdaugh. The call lasts 53 seconds.

10:24:43 p.m.: Alex Murdaugh texts Rogan Gibson, stating "Call me."

10:25:49 p.m.: Alex Murdaugh attempts to FaceTime Rogan Gibson. There is no answer.

[Why is Alex so desperate to get hold of Paul's friend? Had he seen Rogan's texts coming in on Paul's phone as he bent over his dead son's body, and is concerned that Paul may have said something to Rogan about Alex being at the kennels? One officer who took the witness stand in the murder trial said, "The last thing on my mind would be calling my son's friend. I'd be on the ground."

10:25 p.m.: The Colleton County Sheriff's office arrives at the kennels. The South Carolina Law Enforcement Division is contacted for assistance.

10:28:54-10:37:27 p.m.: Alex Murdaugh's phone records 320 steps taken.

10:29:17 p.m.: Alex Murdaugh calls Randy Murdaugh. The call lasts 42 seconds. **There is no record of the call in the data extracted from Alex's phone.**

10:30:31 p.m.: **Alex Murdaugh again attempts to FaceTime Rogan Gibson. There is no answer.**

10:34 p.m.: Nolen Tuten calls Paul Murdaugh's phone. Paul Murdaugh's phone dies.

10:35 p.m.: Alex Murdaugh calls John Marvin Murdaugh. The call lasts 28 seconds.

10:36 p.m.: Alex Murdaugh calls Randy Murdaugh. The call lasts 56 seconds.

10:40 p.m.: Alex Murdaugh searched "Whaley's Edisto" in Safari browser.

[This was a curiosity brought up at the trial. It was finally filed under a "butt dial" kind of thing, meaning Alex had probably accessed the popular restaurant at a different time. I was not aware you could butt dial Google.]

10:40:19-10:50:02 p.m.: Alex Murdaugh's phone records 244 steps taken.

10:44:20 p.m.: Alex Murdaugh calls Buster Murdaugh. The connection lasts 8 seconds.

10:45 p.m.: Alex Murdaugh calls Brooklyn White. The connection lasts 13 seconds. **There is no record of the call in the data extraction of Alex's call**.

10:46 p.m.: Alex Murdaugh calls Tracy White. The connection lasts 14 seconds. **There is no record of the call in the data extraction of Alex's call.**

10:46 p.m.: Buster Murdaugh calls Maggie Murdaugh. There is no answer.

10:47 p.m.: Alex Murdaugh texts Buster, Tracy White, and Brooklyn White stating, "Call me urgent."

10:47 p.m.: Buster Murdaugh calls Alex. The call lasts 162 seconds.

10:55 p.m.: Alex Murdaugh calls Brian White. The connection lasts 8 seconds.

10:56 p.m.: Buster Murdaugh calls Alex Murdaugh. The call lasts 216 seconds.

11:17 p.m.: Alex Murdaugh calls Bart Proctor. The connection lasts 14 seconds.

[Bart is Maggie's brother-in-law. He's married to Marion, Maggie's sister.]

11:19 p.m.: Randy Murdaugh, using Alex's phone, texts Bart Proctor stating, "Bart this is Randy Murdaugh. There has been a terrible tragedy and I need you to call me phone number XXX-XXX-XXXX immediately."

11:28 p.m.: LaClaire Lafitte texts Alex Murdaugh, stating, "Our hearts hurt for you and with you Charlie and LaClaire."

11:56 p.m.: Tracy White texts Alex Murdaugh stating, "I am so so sorry!!!! Let me know how I can help!!! I am here for you all!"

11:47 p.m.: SLED arrives to the scene.

According to testimony during the trial, SLED investigators found Alex had deleted over 75 phone and texts messages by the time they retrieved his phone in September, after he was arrested. His phone was taken during the third interview on June 10, three days after the murders, but they only did a logistics download, which means what you can see on the surface. The download done in September was an advanced search that shows deleted data.

Why were so many of Paul's calls to his "Dad," while Paul was on his way to Moselle, deleted by Alex that night? Why so many of Maggie's? Why was the flurry of calls to C.B. Rowe sent only after Paul arrived at Moselle close to 7 p.m. that evening? Alex wanted the groundskeeper there badly. If you were planning on murdering your family, would you want a witness around? Two reasons you might: one being you were going to shoot Paul and Maggie and blame it on C.B. Rowe—that Black Panther murdering nut job; or you needed him there to babysit Paul in the dove fields while you killed your wife by the kennels. Did Alex need a way to make sure Paul was on the other side of the property handling dead sunflower acreage? Alex may have only found out C.B. hadn't shown up for work that day when Alex and Paul arrived that night. Hence, the flurry of texts and calls to C.B. from Paul and Alex around 7:06 pm. Later, after Maggie is dead, Alex can say Rowe was on the property...hint, hint. The problem with that is that Paul would be Rowe's alibi when gunshots were heard, unless you're operating a big bulldozer while plowing under dead sunflowers and you don't hear anything. It's complicated.

We do know the autopsies revealed both Maggie and Paul had the same stomach contents, so we know they ate together. We have only a sketchy account by Alex that he was even at dinner. Paul spent his time on the phone. At one point, Maggie looked at a Posh Mark app, possibly to check on things she was selling. That was around 8:30 when the dinner looked like it was wrapping up.

It's odd to know a person's last movements were the innocent enjoyment of a meal with your family and checking online sales platforms. Within less than 20 minutes of her Posh Mark entry, she would be dead. And that very phone she was holding would be the subject of a concerted search effort.

Chapter Twenty-One
The Investigation Presses On

On the morning of June 8, 2021, many things were happening. Tired SLED agents had grabbed a few hours' sleep and were back at the crime scene at 4147 Moselle Road. Fresh crime scene specialists were scouring the blood-soaked areas where Paul and Maggie Murdaugh had been gunned down. Cartridge casings from .300 Blackout bullets had been marked the night before. Looking at them in the fresh light of morning, it was evident they formed what was called a "candy cane pattern" leading up to Maggie Murdaugh's body. It was an eerie trail of breadcrumbs showing where a killer, or killers, had advanced on the helpless 52-year-old woman.

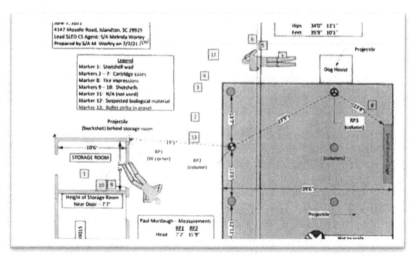

SLED diagram of shell and cartridge casings for Paul and Maggie.

Cartridge casing markers around where Maggie Murdaugh was murdered. Her body was found in the circled area in front of a small doghouse.

While measurements were being taken by SLED members, John Marvin was assisting the investigation. He gave agents a tour of the house and when asked about Maggie's cell phone, he answered that he could ask Maggie's surviving son Buster, who had his mother's phone on his phone's Find My Phone app. This was accomplished and Maggie's phone location pinged. John Marvin and three of the SLED team began walking to the bottom of the hangar driveway, following the app's map. When they arrived at Moselle Drive, they realized it was farther away than they thought.

John Marvin (center) w/SLED following Buster's *Find My Phone*.

In the previous photo, John Marvin Murdaugh (center in white) walks with SLED agents as they follow Buster's Find My Phone app pinging the location of Maggie's missing phone.

They took separate cars and drove to the proximity of the map location, about a quarter of a mile up the road. Two teams spread out: one to the right of the road on the Moselle property side, and others to the left. John Marvin was on the right and combing through tall grass when a SLED agent on the left called out that he had found it. It was lying in pine needles and leaves, the prior evening's rain still beaded on its glassy face. They flagged the location with orange landscaping flags and took photos before anyone picked it up. They put it into Airplane mode to keep unwanted data from coming in and placed it in an evidence bag. The team would later be castrated during the trial for not placing the phone in a Faraday bag, commonly used by law enforcement to keep any signals or outside electronic devices from deleting or tampering with the phone's data.

The location of Maggie's phone as it would have been seen from Alex's driver side window after he threw it. He just missed getting it into the woods.

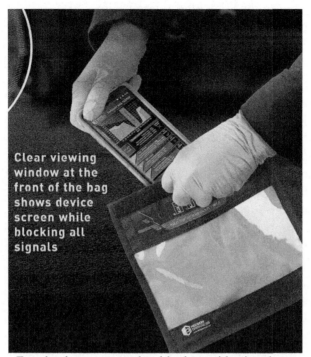

Clear viewing window at the front of the bag shows device screen while blocking all signals

Faraday bags are used to block outside signals.

When the SLED team could not unlock Maggie's phone, John Marvin called Alex to ask him if he had Maggie's cell phone password? Alex gave it to him, and they unlocked her phone. Can you imagine Alex getting that call? They found her phone, and he just gave them the keys to a wealth of information.

When Hampton locals awoke to the news that two members of the powerful Murdaugh family had been gunned down on their hunting property the night before, they were in shock. Adding to that news bombshell came a second one. On that same morning, SLED released the confusing news that the community was in no danger. No danger? Two people were just brutally gunned down on their own property, no word of a suspect (or suspects), and there was nothing to fear? As they were processing that tidbit, another statement was released with SLED's phone number asking for anyone with information to call in. So...the public has nothing to fear, there is no danger, but just in case, call us if you know who the suspect or suspects are. It looked like the invitation to the rabbit hole had begun only one day after the murders.

Alex called Blanca, the Murdaughs housekeeper, who had filled the vacant position left by the late Gloria Satterfield and asked her to please go over to the house and clean it up "the way Maggie kept it." The poor woman fell apart when she heard her employer and friend was murdered, along with Paul. She had just fixed dinner for them the day before. She canceled her doctor's appointment in Beaufort and went dutifully to the house at Moselle. It was very early, and she said during her testimony that no one stopped her as she entered the house. She was obviously very distraught during her testimony. Alex Murdaugh sat only a few feet away from her as she told of the morning's events.

"Entering the house was the hardest part," she said. She walked slowly through the first floor, numb with pain and disbelief. When she got to the kitchen, she was surprised to see someone had put the night's dinner in the refrigerator, still in the pots and pans. It was usually left for her to clean up the next morning. As she walked on, she came to the laundry room and found it strange that Maggie's pajamas were neatly folded inside the door on the floor. A pair of fresh panties lay atop them, still folded as though no one had worn them. She would testify that Maggie didn't wear underwear to bed, so she found the whole thing odd. What she didn't say was that Maggie didn't sleep there much anymore. She stayed at Edisto.

In the master bedroom on the first floor, she saw a pair of khaki pants, the same kind Alex had worn to work on the shower floor, next to a puddle of water. When asked on the witness stand, she admitted he had many of the same kind of pants. Was the question meant to infer that perhaps the khakis had been placed on the bathroom floor by water to look like someone had showered and left them there? Alex would later tell investigators, when they surprised him in the third interview by showing him Paul's Snapchat photo and asking him when he changed his clothes, that he must have changed before dinner. Nowhere was the blue shirt he had been wearing, or the Sperry shoes. It was not clear if the khakis on the floor were the ones he had been wearing or planted there.

She said on the stand that she did not want to mess with Miss Maggie's things and had a hard time straightening up after the people who had been sitting around the night before.

Blanca Turrubiate-Simpson, the Murdaugh housekeeper and friend.

Blanca's testimony would take a more sinister turn during her testimony on the witness stand two years later. Her loyalty to Mr. Alex only went so far. Lying for him went beyond the pale.

The Second Interview

As SLED continued with their investigation of the murders of Maggie and Paul Murdaugh, Alex stayed away from Moselle. He alternated time staying with his brothers Randy and John Marvin. It was reported he never stayed another night at the hunting lodge home. He also stayed away from his law office at PMPED. According to testimony by the firm's CFO, Jeannie Seckinger, "Everything pretty much shut down in the days following the murders. We rallied around Alex and tried to help where we could. Obviously, there was no mention of the missing fees at this time."

According to Blanca Simpson's testimony, the Murdaugh housekeeper, "There was a little house between Mr. Randy's and

Mr. Parker's house. Alex asked that all his clothes and toiletries be moved there so he could get to them. When asked if the clothes she saw Alex wear to work that morning were among the clothing at "the little house," she said, "No. I never saw them again." It would be at the "little house" where Alex asked Blanca to lie for him in the days to come.

As with the delay of business at PMPED after the murders, a complete halt came to the boat crash motion on June 10th that had loomed over Alex, Maggie, and Paul's heads. Paul was dead. He was the one to go on trial for Mallory Beach's death and was looking at a possible 25 years in prison. Maggie was dead, and the Beach lawsuit had recently added her estate to the names on the suit, especially after finding out Alex had moved Moselle and Edisto both into her name. Plus, who was going to continue with a motion hearing to look into Alex's finances only three days after his wife and child were brutally gunned down? The world stopped in Hampton County. Locals and the rest of the country poured over newspapers, both in print and online, over their morning coffee, hoping for some news of who would kill these two people...and Murdaughs no less?

Alex went into hiding. He sometimes went to Summerville to see Maggie's grieving parents, but he basically laid low. That is until the necessities of funeral arrangements and a second SLED interview brought him back into the spotlight.

On June 10th (the day the boat crash motion hearing should have taken place), Alex, Randy, John Marvin, and Buster Murdaugh are asked by SLED to meet at John Marvin's hunting lodge "Greenfield" not far from Randolph and Miss Libby's home in Almeda. Each of the men were put into separate SLED cars at the same time and interviewed. Once again, Alex is with Agent David Owen. Agent Jeff Croft is present, and Jim Griffin. It is just before 4 p.m.

Agent Owens begins by telling Alex, "One thing I'd like to do is get a cell phone exam just so we can collaborate everything." Alex looks decidedly put out when Owen's says he "has a guy out here now that's going to do it." Jim Griffin, Alex's attorney is in the back seat and asks, "So they're going to do it now?" Owen answers, "Yes, sir." Alex says, "So I'm going to get to keep my phone?" He seems relieved that he will have it returned before the interview ends.

Alex is a different person in this interview. He looks annoyed, shoots furtive glances at Agent Owens throughout and shifts in his seat continually. This is three days after the murders. He has obviously heard the announcement the day after the double homicide that "the public has nothing to fear," indicating to all who heard it that SLED must already know who did it and it was probably targeted to only the Murdaugh family. Alex is also aware they found Maggie's phone that he was careful to toss out the window into the roadside brush. He had to supply the password. The boat crash was delayed, but it would rear its head again at some point. And now, a second interview. The old Murdaugh charm and theatrics were not working this time. SLED was back for more.

He was scrambling to come up with the $192,000 he owed Chris Wilson so that Jeannie Seckinger could have the fees back in the firm where they belonged. Chris Wilson and Alex had split the fees for a recent case called the Ferris case which involved a truck company they went after for their clients, Mr. and Mrs. Ferris. Alex told Chris to make his share totaling $792,000 directly out to him, not to PMPED, where it should have gone. These are the missing fees Jeannie Seckinger confronted him with on June 7th, only hours before the murders. Alex figured if he could send the fees back to Chris and have Chris tell Jeannie, "Hey, we're all good. The fees are right here. We just structured them differently. I'll send them right over," that all would be okay, and he could pivot and probably keep cheating clients, or think of another way to enrich his ever-shrinking bank account. He did manage to get $600,000 of it to Chris, but he was $192,000 short. Chris eventually had to pay the balance out of his own pocket.

Chris Wilson's testimony on the witness stand during the double murder trial in February 2023, focused on the case known as the "MAC Trucks/Ferris" case. According to Wilson, their clients were awarded a total of $5.5 million from the case. Murdaugh's fees were $792,000, and Wilson's were around $791,000.

As Agent Owen took Alex's phone from him and walked it back to his data "guy," Alex is visibly agitated and pulling on his khaki pants continually. He and Jim Griffin warn Agent Owen that there are probably client confidentiality issues with them downloading his phone data. Owen assures them they have a way to redact privileged information. Jim Griffin seems to understand that a "taint attorney" will go over it and he gives his consent. Alex is abrupt and impatient as he signs the consent form. Alex is still agitated and says, "I text a lot of clients," as they try to play it down that it will mostly be the emails. He gives them his passcode to his phone and Owen runs it back to the data expert.

When Owen reenters the car, the interrogation begins. He asks Alex, "Let's start with Monday morning and walk me through your day."

Alex: "Monday? Uh. What did I do Monday? My wife and my older son had gone to the baseball games that weekend. You know, I really can't remember what I did Monday. I know I went to work. But, you know, I think I was dragging a little bit from the weekend and then I went to work. I usually mess around on the farm and then I go to work. I was at work…at my office in Hampton. Uh. You know, I mean, I was just at my office doing…legal work. I'm sure I can go back and probably recreate some specifics if you need me to, but I can't like sit here and recall on the top of my head exactly what I was working on. I know one thing I was working on. Was we had some big motions coming up and a Dominion Energy case. I was getting ready for those.

"And I was getting ready for some motions. I'm a defendant in a civil case involving my son. I told you about the boat wreck. And there were some motions coming up in that on Thursday. And I was mostly just getting ready for those things.

Owen: What time did you leave the house?"

Alex" "For the office? I'm not sure."

Owen: Who was at the house when you left?"

Alex: "To go to my office that morning?"

Owen: "Or when you got up, who was at the house?"

Alex: [Scratching his head.] "I'm sure my wife was. And I can't remember if Blanca had made it out there yet or not. Blanca is our housekeeper, and she comes different times. She doesn't have set hours, but she comes most days. She'll be able to tell you if I was there and when I, when she left or not. I just… I can't remember."

Owen: "And so you went to the office, you did, you know, some motions. What time did you leave the office?"

Alex: "I left a little bit earlier than normal because my son Paul was coming home. Because he had not been with us during the weekend and he was coming home, we were going to, we were going to

302

replant some sunflowers the next day and so he was calibrating and doing and getting everything ready. But he got home a little early. I left a little early so he and I could knock around and we knocked around for, you know, just doing things we like to do out there, you know, riding around, looking at... all over the place looking, you know. Look, looking for hogs. A little bit of target practice. Just bullshit, yeah."

Owen: "You said Paul wasn't with you over the weekend. Where does he live... with you? At the house on Moselle?"

Alex: "Oh, I mean, that's his home. He has an apartment in Columbia. And he goes to Charleston a lot of weekends with his buddies, and he had been in Charleston for the weekend. And then Paul worked for my brother John. Just out here... you met John. So, Paul works for him. So, Paul decided to go to...he went to spend the night with my brother, his Uncle John. They are very, very close. Sunday night. And then he worked for John Marvin, and he came home Monday afternoon.

Owen: "OK. Roughly what time in the afternoon?"

Alex: "You know, I would think it would be somewhere in the five o'clock range a little bit. It was, it was broad daylight when we were... it wasn't dust or dark yet. We rode, you know, we just rode around, we rode around our dove field looking at how the corn was doing. He and I planted corn in the dove field, and he planted the corn in the duck pond, and he was, you know, showing me how much better his corn was doing than mine was. And we rode around the duck pond. I mean, we just, you know, we rode the property. Just so you know, we just, we rode the property then, you know, I mean we rode around so much. We just rode probably... it was a good little while. It was more than 20 minutes. Thirty minutes. And, you know, was it 2 hours? I don't know. I'd say it was more than an hour. And it wasn't, you know, it wasn't getting dark. Mama wasn't home yet. She'd gone to a doctor's appointment So, yeah."

Owen: "Just out of curiosity, target practice, what did you shoot at?"

Alex: "Just a little bottle. Do you mean what gun?"

Owen: "Yeah."

Alex: "22 Magnum... I think he shot two times, and I shot one time."

Owen: "So after y'all got finished riding around. Try to take me through the rest of the evening."

We see in this interview Alex's continued refusal to be pinned down to specific times. Agent Owen rarely gets a straight answer about the timeline that day. Unlike the first interview, Alex admits he did go to work. He has probably decided SLED has checked out his fuzzy alibi. We see here that he found out Paul was coming home, which may be the call Paul makes to Alex on his way home from Okotie. We hear about the sunflowers again. Was that where Paul was supposed to be that evening after dinner? "Calibrating" or "refiguring" the dove field? Is that the need for urgent phone calls to get C.B. Rowe out there that night? The interview continues with Agent Owen asking what the rest of the evening was like.

Alex: "Alright. You know. At some point we were all back at the house. Maggie had gotten home, and you know, we sat down, we ate supper and, we usually eat supper together, so. The one thing I remember, I don't know how much detail y'all want. So, if I start talking about something that you don't need, just tell me and I'll move to something else."
Owen: "The more detail, the better."
Alex: "So, Paul has been having high blood pressure and his Mama was worried sick about it, so we were actually trying to get him... he doesn't like to go to doctors, making him go get his blood pressure checked. His feet have swollen up recently. So, you know, that was, it was a, it was a big, huge deal. You know, we hung around the house for a little while. I know that Maggie went to the kennels. I don't know exactly where Paul went, but he left the house."
Owen: "OK, how did Maggie get down to the kennels?"
Alex: "I don't know exactly, but on normal occasions she would drive, drive a buggy, drive a four-Wheeler, or very common for her to walk."
Owen: "OK. How about Paul?"
Alex: "Paul wasn't much of a walker, but he would use all of the others. OK, but I mean, could be anyway, you know? I don't know exactly; I wish I could help you with that."
Owen: "So, so they left and went down to the kennels?"
Alex: "Well, Maggie went to go to the kennels and Paul left and I'm assuming, you know, I'm assuming Paul left because of, you know, what happened. I mean, I'm assuming Paul, yeah, went to the kennels."

Alex is reciting the string of events as if it was scripted, until Owen begins to ask specifics about how Maggie and Paul went to the kennels and where Paul went when he left the house. Alex is squirming continually; the robotic answers are now filled with pauses and "you know." It is also apparent there is an issue with how they got to the kennels. Maggie's car was found at the house after her murder. A golf cart is seen in a crime scene photo parked haphazardly near the front steps of the house. Maggie's Mercedes is in front of the cart, as if it has been driven back to the house *after* the golf cart is parked. The golf carts are usually parked to the right of the main steps. John Marvin's truck that Paul drove from Okatie is parked at the house, so he didn't drive it down to the kennels.

Owen: "OK. And what did you do once Maggie and Paul left?"

Alex: "I stayed in the house. Just watching TV. Looking at my phone and I actually fell asleep on the couch.

Owen: "OK. And what time did you, you know...?"

Alex: "I don't know exactly what time I woke up. But when y'all get my phone, you know, I think one of the first things I did when I got up was call Maggie because I was going to my mom's. And I know I texted her because I checked my phone. So, you know, I texted her. So, I called her just before that. And I mean, she, she didn't answer at that point, and I left to go to my mom's. Y'all just have to look. I'm not sure if I called Paul."

Owen: "Well, and that, and that's why we're getting the phone so we can nail down the times and everything."

Alex: "So, I left and drove well, you know, I'm gonna tell y'all this even though I think it's kinda crazy. You know, I was certain that I heard them pull up. I mean I was positive that I heard... and people don't just come out there you know, we don't get like people passing through. I was certain that I heard them pull up, but they didn't."

Owen: "So, if you heard something pull up. What did it sound like?"

Alex: "You know, I don't... I can't tell you what it sounded like. I just know that I thought they, I thought that...that my wife had pulled up. The car had pulled up."

Owen: "Would it have been the buggy that she normally drives? Or would it be a car?"

Alex: "No, no, I had the impression that it a car pulled up."

Owen: OK, and have you woken up by that time but hadn't left for your moms?"

Alex: "Yep. But it wasn't much time in between there because I left pretty damn close. It wasn't much time between me waking up and me leaving the house. *And* when I went outside... (big pause) You know. There's a cat, a wild cat that lives around that house. I'm pretty sure it was the cat that ran from my car. But you know, I never had the impression it was a person, but there was something, you know, but I really don't think. You know, I'm just throwing that out there because it was in my mind."

Owen: "Totally fine."

Alex: "I left. I drove to, I drove to my mom's. Checked on my mom talked with Shelly for a few minutes. Shirley is the caregiver. And, you know, I know that I called some people on the way, that I know I returned the call from my brother John. I know I called Chris Wilson. I know that I talked to Buster. So, I made a few phone calls and..."

Owen: "Where was Buster?"

Alex: "Buster was in Rock Hill. He lives in Colombia, but he just started a new job. He's going back to law school in January. OK, so he's working a little part time job with Wild Wings through January. You know, just kind of killing time and he was in... His girlfriend lives in Rock Hill. She's studying for the bar exam, so she had to be in Charlotte. So, he was staying with her in Rock Hill, her and her mom. Can I open the door?"

Owen: "Sure." (Alex spits out tobacco and asks where he left off) "Left your mom's, making phone calls?"

Alex: "I left my mom's, and I went back home. I got to the house. I went inside. Nobody was there. I got in the car; I went back to the kennels and.... you know."

Owen: "And you, when you went back to the kennels, besides Maggie and Paul, did you see anybody? Any cars?"

Alex: "I didn't see anything... No, Sir." (Becomes a little emotional)

Owen: "Take your time."

Alex: "You know, I saw Maggie, and I saw Paul laying down. I knew. You know? I didn't know. You know, I knew it was bad. I went over there and, you know, I saw it. You know, I called 911."

Owen: "What made you decide to go back to the house and get a gun?"

Alex: "Yeah, this thing, the whole scene had me freaked out."

Owen: "Did you take your car back out there? Did you run up there?"

Alex: "I drove up."

Owen: "OK? And of course, the shotgun that we have is the one you brought back."

Alex: "They were asking me earlier. I'm not sure which one it was, Jim?

Jim Griffin: "It was a 12 gauge. Yeah, Ronnie had the question if it was 12 or 20, it was a 12 gauge. It was a Camo."

Owen: And it was a Camo Benelli."

Jim asks Alex: "But that's about all you got out there is Benelli, right?" [Alex doesn't answer him. He stares straight ahead.]

Owen: "And we talked about this a little bit the other night, too. And I know Paul had been getting some threats and getting some, some being assaulted from, you know, the boat. Who? Who stands out in your mind besides the boat incident, who stands out in your mind? That would want to come after, after Paul, and or Maggie?"

Alex: "I mean, Sir, I can't think of anybody who would wanna go to that extreme. You know, I mean, he got a bunch of threats, mostly from, you know. I mean, I have *no* idea."

Owen: "How did he receive most of those threats?"

Alex: "What do you mean?"

Owen: "I mean would people call and hang up on him?"

Alex: "No, no. It was mostly like in person. Confrontations are the ones that I learned about now. I suspect his friends can probably tell you about more, cause I doubt Paul told me about all of them. But I knew about a lot of, you know, there were a lot of times where people would come up to him and he'd be like they'd say something about, you know, "You gonna tell me who was driving that boat?" Or "You, you little piece of shit, were you driving that boat?" you know, stuff like that.

Owen: "Who did he go to Charleston with that weekend?"

Alex: "I don't know exactly. I know that. I mean, I know who his buddies are, but specifically who was on the boat with him, I'm not sure you know. But I can give you a list of names of who it probably was."

Jim Griffin: "Put your pens down, but a good buddy of mine's son went fishing with me yesterday and he has a best friend and his dad's name is Lee Chapman. Lee's son said that Paul's slept on his couch in Charleston two nights before he was murdered. I can get his name. I learned that yesterday.

Alex: "There was a bunch of Chapman cousins that Paul was very close with. Closest one being Wills Chapman and Frank Chapman. Wills is Lee Chapman's son."

Jim: "Will Chapman…that was his name."

Alex: "And those boys are, you know, they're just really good boys and friends of Paul's. I'm telling you now, I can promise you that, I mean, those boys love Paul. It's absolutely none of them."

Owen: "Well, you know, I just want to talk to them about their weekend."

Alex: "Sure. I can tell you this that riding around with Paul, he was his normal bright. You know. Just. He was really a great kid."

Owen: "So being a dad myself, what was the biggest issue you had with Paul? When you had, when you had to call him down and scold him or correct him, what was the biggest issue you had with him?"

Alex: "You know, I mean, irresponsibility. You know he has ADHD. He was bad about jumping from… And he had so many wonderful qualities now. But he was bad about jumping from… he'd start this. Maybe not quite. Finish it. Do something else and you know, you'll find out from his friends. He had clothes strung out all over the state. He did that with clothes. He did that with guns. He did that with my boats. Everywhere. Everywhere. I mean, he would go off for the weekend. Sometimes he wouldn't pack clothes because he's got clothes in somebody's house. Paul was one... He wouldn't understand how you go out; you know? Like you and the girl go out on a date. He liked the crowd."

Owen: "Who is his girlfriend?"

Alex: "He didn't have a girlfriend right now."

Owen: "And you said on Monday, Maggie had a doctor's appointment in Charleston, now that we talked about this on Monday, do you recall the doctor that she went to or for what the reason was?"

Alex: "Maggie had a couple little things going on and I personally think she was going to see Doctor Gordine, but I'm not positive, OK? I'm pretty sure that's who it was. I can find out. Specifically, though, her mom will know."

Owen: "OK? And you said she and Buster were at the ball games all weekend with you?"

Alex: "Football Games, Carolina regional. Paul was in Charleston."

Owen: "So he didn't hang out with y'all that weekend?"

Alex: "No, Sir."

Owen: "And what time did Maggie get home that night?"

Alex: "It was after Paul, and I had gone. She was not there when Paul and I left to go mess around. OK, so you know it was sometime after that. There was a point when, you know, she got back; we got back."

Owen: "Y'all got back from messin' around on the farm. She was home?"

Alex: "Yes."

Owen: "OK"

Alex: "And I don't believe she'd been home too long when…"

Owen: "What's her car? That Mercedes that's out there?"

Alex: "Yes, sir."

Owen: "OK. Blanca cooked dinner that night cuz Maggie cooks when the boys are home. Course, she tries to really, for me, but she wasn't going to be there that day, so she had Blanca cook a meal."

Owen: "How is your relationship with Maggie?"

Alex: "Very good. As good as it could possibly be, I mean, you know, we had our issues, but wonderful."

Owen: "And I'm just trying to understand the family dynamic."

Alex: "I understand. You gotta do what you gotta do. I promise."

Owen: "What were your biggest arguments? What were your biggest things that y'all would argue about the most? What would they be over?"

Alex: "I mean, we really didn't argue, but the basic, I'd say the really the only thing that caused any friction between us is and she was always wanting us to go… And I love her family. I mean, they're wonderful people. I love her, but she was always wanting to go there, stay there a little longer than me and the boys wanted to stay. That was really… and it really, you know, she'd get really ticked off. I mean, we really didn't argue about much, didn't have much to argue about. I mean, I'm sure there was an occasional thing that came up that we argued about, but I mean, tell you what it is, I can't think of it."

[Alex breaks downs sobbing]

Alex: "I'm sorry. She was a wonderful girl, wonderful wife, and mother. She, you know, didn't work, and she always said it was her job. She was privileged enough not to work. She was gonna make sure she took care of me, and the boys and I mean she did everything. She did absolutely everything." [Sobs] I'm sorry. I'm good. You go ahead."

Agent Croft: "That afternoon. During the time you and Paul were riding, did you go up to, around the kennels for anything? Did y'all do anything around the kennels?"

Alex: "I'm sure we did. You know that's where our main shop is, you know, right there. But you know, I mean we're normally in there for long times tinkering and I will say that particular day, we did not tinker around there a bunch, you know?"

Owen: "When y'all rode around the farm, what were y'all ridin' in, a truck or…?

Alex: "Actually in two trucks, we rode in one truck and then we rode in another truck some. One was the black one and one was the white one that was *out* there."

Croft: "Mr. Alex? You know, the other day when we were there, we came in and we were talking with John a little bit. Y'all obviously got a lot of weapons…20-25 weapons. Do you know what kind of weapons you got as far as any kind of, what kind of weapons you have?"

Alex: "I'm pretty much, yes, Sir."

Croft: "I know you don't know them all, but can run down kind of what you have, what you got there?"

Alex: [sounding testy] "What I own or that's in there *now*? "

Croft: "That you own."

Alex: "Alright. That I own. You know, I mean, Paul has guns scattered all over the place, so, you know, some of our guns aren't there, but so you want to know all of them, or you want to know what I think is in my house? What was in my house on Monday?"

Owen: "Yeah, let's start with what was in your house on Monday."

Alex: "OK? Whatever was in my house on Monday is exactly what was there, minus one shotgun that I got, that y'all got. [The one Alex retrieved from the house during the 911 call.] No guns had been moved for, you know, that been any guns moved in and out of there other than when Paul was home. You know, when Paul came home, he would ride around, and shoot hogs a lot."

Owen: "What did he shoot hogs with?"

Alex: "You know, I mean primarily he would shoot them with Buster's gun. Paul had a 300 blackout and it got, you know, he says it got stolen. It has been gone for some time. But anyway, he would use his brother's Blackout a lot of times. Buster also had a .300. I gave them both one."

Owen: "OK, when was that?"

Alex: "Years ago, more than a year ago. Alright, so, but he would do anything. **Paul had this, Paul had this little light that I used that night. Paul would take that thing up to, you know, to my .308. And I mean he was, he was always rigging something.**"

At 34:27 into the interview, Alex Murdaugh makes the above statement. "Paul had this little light that I used that night..." Not a flashlight similar to the one Paul moved from gun to gun, but the same one Paul attached to guns. Why does Alex have it when the first responders show up shortly after the 911 call? Shouldn't it be attached to a gun? Was it attached to one of the two weapons used in the murders that night and Alex popped it out of the mount afterwards to use as a light source as he moved all over the place during the 911 call? (Author highlighted the sentences in bold above.)

Officer Greene's body cam showing Alex with a flashlight as Greene arrived on the scene.

311

Alex did retrieve a shotgun during the 911 call. It was leaning against his SUV when Officer Greene arrived on the scene. Alex points it out immediately and tells him he got it from the house, and it's loaded. Officer Greene carries it to his patrol car and locks it into the front passenger seat. This is all picked up on his body cam.

Officer Daniel Greene holding up the shotgun Alex retrieved from the house during the 911 call.

In Officer Greene's bodycam video, as he arrived on the scene that night, Alex is waving around a handheld flashlight. He does say in the highlighted area of the interview that Paul would take the light, like the one he "used that night" and attach it to his .308." Paul moved the flashlight from gun to gun. Was it on the shotgun used to kill him that night? The gun that is missing. At this point, we will never know.

When Will Loving took the stand to describe the AR-15 that Maggie and Alex bought Paul to replace the one he lost, Loving said that gun had an optic scope on it, not a thermal scope like the original one had that was lost. Buster's old AR had a thermal scope, but it had loading problems. It is the replacement AR-15 with the scope that Will Loving and Paul try out by the side door at Moselle as they sight it in. Those cartridge cases were still lying in the flower beds around that side door and at the Moselle shooting range when SLED agents found the casings during the double murder investigation. According to their testimony, those cartridge cases were from the same AR-15 that murdered Maggie Murdaugh.

The gun that killed Maggie was never found. Nor was the shotgun that killed Paul. If the AR-15 that Paul rigged when he got it as a replacement was used to kill Maggie, it still had the red dot optic scope on it, not a flashlight or thermal scope.

Continuing on with the interview:

Alex: "You know, so, sometimes shotguns for when he would go try to kill the hogs, cause you know piglets would be grouped up, but normally he would have a rifle when he went to shoot pigs. So. Alright, so going back to the guns, you want me to tell y'all what was in there? Like an inventory?"

Croft: "I took a video. But the thing is, I didn't write down everything that you had. I just took a random, just like recording, of what was on the gun rack or on the gun wall."

"Alex: "And they're probably, there are some more guns that aren't in that gun room, you know? I don't know how many, but you know, like I do know there's a shotgun in my bedroom."

Croft: "Katie, Agent Katie saw that one when she walked the house with John."

Alex: "OK. And I imagine there's probably some in some... I know that... I think it was the night we had two, two gun cases, one small one and one big one, and I moved some guns from the little case to the big case just cause, you know, her mom and dad were in there and I just took all the guns to the back room. But that's after the fact."

Croft: "Would those guns have been in the room, in the gun room, when we came over with John?"

Alex: "I can't remember exactly when y'all came, but probably, I think y'all came a little bit, because it was a good while before y'all came that afternoon."

Croft: "It was probably around 2:00 that afternoon before we came.

Owen: "Did you keep any guns out at the kennels?"

Alex: "We didn't *keep* guns out there, but there were always guns out there, you know? I mean, and I'm gonna be honest with you, we were all a little bit bad about it, but Paul was the worst. He would leave a gun out there. He would leave anything, anywhere. It was not unusual for there to be guns out there. I can tell you that, I mean they told me that .300 Blackout was used in this, that .300 Blackout, you know it was, it was not out there."

Owen: "So y'all didn't use that at target practice or he didn't have it out there with him on Monday?"

Alex: "No."

Owen: "No, that's right because it was in the house. [Possibly a trap that didn't work] So Paul said that one was stolen or lost, and it was some time ago. Was that reported anywhere?"

Alex: "It wasn't officially reported because I wasn't totally convinced it was stolen, you know, as opposed to lost, but I mean, you know. People told me about it, yeah. I know that I told John Benningfield about it. Um. I know that I told some other local officers about it, you know, just in case it turned up in a drug thing but, I didn't do an official report."

Owen: "The two that you bought for the boys, that each one of them had one, and the one Paul had was lost. Is that the only ones that you have?"

Alex: "Well, I'm gonna tell you this. I thought we replaced it. I thought that Paul got another one replaced. Buster said we didn't. But I was certain that we did. But I mean my memory is, it's been gone for a substantial while, too."

The John Beddingfield mentioned above is a **South Carolina Department of Natural Resources agent and a custom gunmaker.** He also has a firearm license, and he is Alex's cousin. It is explained by Bedingfield that Murdaugh approached him again in April 2018 for a third .300 Blackout rifle saying that Paul had lost his. Alex Murdaugh paid $9,188 for the first two .300 Blackout rifles in 2016 and the third one cost him $875. The change in price was due to the absence of a thermal scope or suppressor. Moreover, Bedingfield further claims that it was Maggie who picked up the guns when they were ready.

Owen: "Do you remember anything about them as far as, were they the same colors?"

Alex: "They were identical except for colors. Buster's is the one we still have. Paul's is the one that he lost his. They are black and tan. Buster's is black. Paul's was tan."

Owen: "And you say you thought you replaced it after you lost it? But Buster says you didn't?"

Alex: "I believe that we did. There'll be a record of that one. It should be, yes. I know the place. But you know I wouldn't. Yeah, I know he replaced it cause I wouldn't replace it again. Maybe I just think that now. I don't know. But I'm certain we replaced it."

Owen: "Have you talked to C.B. Rowe since Monday or Tuesday?"

Alex: "Yes, Sir."

Owen: "Because I know we talked about what he had done on the farm. Have you all, is he still employed?"

Alex: "He's still employed because I gotta have somebody keeping it clean. But I mean I can't keep him, he's an idiot. You know, I know I told you; I don't know why that story seemed important to me the other night. [Alex's telling Owen about Rowe shooting Black Panthers.] I really can't see C.B. Rowe doing it, I just can't. I really do not believe that."

Owen: "Well, it's, I mean, it's an odd story."

Alex: "It's a messed-up story."

Owen: "Being in law enforcement for so long and working on these type cases and I don't know the Islandton area, but talking to Colleton County and seeing the property and how isolated it is, finding somebody that's just gonna randomly come up there that late at night, that doesn't know the property. You know, that's... So of course, I have to look within and then start working my way out."

At this point in the interview, as soon as C.B. Rowe is brought up again, Alex is laser focused on Agent Owen. Up until this time, he has always looked straight ahead. His eyes are trained on the agent like a hawk. Here is where Owen starts showing SLED's hand to Alex, and he is all ears. Jim Griffin from the back seat is also listening intently.

Alex: "So you feel like it's not random? Do you feel like it's intentional, I mean planned?"

Owen: "I don't know what to feel right now. And I hate to say that, but I don't know what to feel right now."

Alex: "So do y'all have any good clues?"

Owen: "All of the evidence that we collected Tuesday morning, and we collected additional evidence on Tuesday afternoon. They collected evidence at autopsy today. So, we we're trying to put a rush on that to get an answer quick and then hoping that's going to tell us something."

Alex: "By evidence, do you mean you think its things that are going to be helpful?"

Owen: "Well, like the shot shells out there, the casings, the DNA swabs that we took from the door handle to see if anybody touched the door handles, any other places that we think somebody may have touched while they were out there, you know, we're trying to collect DNA from that and analyze that. Which at the conclusion of this, what I'm gonna also ask is that we get a buccal swab, DNA swab from you. Your DNA is gonna be there, but we need to eliminate it once it's developed. We have talked to close to 100 people trying to track people down and we're still tracking people down and that's why you know…"

Alex: "I wanna tell you one thing while I'm thinking about it, Paul. was really an incredibly intuitive little dude. And I mean he was like a little detective. And I mean Paul would you know he... You know what I'm trying to say?"

[This is an interesting statement. There is no lead-up and no resolution to the statement about Paul being intuitive and a "little detective." Just wondering why Alex interjected it here.]

Owen: "Yeah. Which leads me to, let's go back to Paul right quick while we're on him… so we have his phone. Do you know his passcode?"

Alex: "I'm telling you this right now. There's a few people I can point you to, yeah, but I can tell you that he was super, super, *super* secretive with that, I mean, cell phone. I asked his brother if he knew it. Did the ones that they got the other day didn't work?"

Owen: [Turning to Jeff Croft in the back seat] "Did y'all get any the other day?"

Croft: "Not for Paul's phone. I know they got Maggie's, and it works. Or it worked. I have not gotten it [Paul's passcode], but there's a lot of people out, moving parts that you know may have gotten that information. So, we'll follow up on that.

Owen: [To Alex] "Do you believe somebody gave us a code for Paul's or possible code for Paul's?"

Alex: "You know, maybe it was Maggie's. I don't know. But I'll find out. I will try to find out. [Pause] But it will surprise me greatly if somebody knows it. I mean…"

Owen: "Certainly, you know, talking about the investigation, certainly we were looking at every angle, trying to figure out what fits. We're talking to, you know, people that were involved in the boat case. We're talking, trying to track down people that Paul knew, was friends with. That's why I asked who he was in Charleston with so we can go try and see if they might know something or try to figure something out. We're trying to get into his phone. Let's see if there's any information, see if he got like a direct threat from somebody there. I mean, the people that are here are not the only ones working on this. We've got people out doing things right now. We're trying to pull everything in. It's just the area, Islandton, unfortunately they don't… There's not a lot of people moving around. I mean, I've got somebody looking at videos right now back at the office. Three hours of videos that we've gone out and collected."

Alex: "Well, thank you. Yeah, very much."

Jeff: "Mr. Alex, so Paul got back to the house, Miss Maggie's there and y'all eat supper which has been prepared, and you say you said you lay down and you took a little nap and when you got up, they left, or did they leave when you lay down.?"

Alex" "I believe that…. I'm not. I'm not sure."

Croft: "But they weren't there when you woke up around 9:00 o'clock mark or so when you made the call to Maggie, to let her know you're going to your mom's house?"

Alex: "No. You know, nobody was in that house when I left."

Croft: "I'm just trying to narrow down that the last time that you saw Paul and Maggie was when y'all were eating supper?" [Alex becomes restless here and looks agitated.]

Alex: "Yes, Sir."

Jeff: "…up until you came back from your moms, then found what you found?"

[Alex doubles over here is and is sobbing. Jim Griffin talks without taking much notice of him.]

Jim: "Alex probably told y'all this, he did check their pulse."

Owen: "Yes. [Alex pulls himself together again. There are no visible signs of tears] When you tried to turn Paul over, do you know if you tried to turn him towards the kennels or away from the kennels and his phone fell out?"

Alex: [Agitated. While he was crying, a conversation had been going on in the back seat between Jeff and Jim. Jeff says that's why they want the DNA from Alex, because he says he turned Paul. Alex is listening and becomes more agitated.] "Away, I think I turned him away."

Owen: "Was he left-handed or right-handed?"

Alex: "Right-handed."

Owen: "Where did he normally keep his phone?"

Alex: "Usually in his hand. [Owen chuckles] But I mean it was always on him, you know, pocket, hand, truck."

Owen: "Where did Maggie carry her phone?"

[Alex doesn't answer. He looks straight ahead. After a long pause, Alex slaps his leg, like he doesn't know. Owen fills in the silence]

Owen: "Anywhere she could?"

Alex: "Yes, Sir. [Pause] Did y'all get fingerprints on her phone?"

Owen: "I haven't gotten that back yet. When Paul's phone came out, did you just pick it up and put it on, you know, place it back down on him or?"

Alex: "You know. I did not try to open it or anything, you know, I just...don't know how I had it in my mind I needed to not mess anything up. I had that. I had that. You know. Somehow, I had that presence of mind that I needed to not mess anything up. And so. I tried not to."

Croft: "And you definitely saw a traumatic picture and I know it's not hard, or not, not easy. [Alex breaks down again] I know it's hard. Sitting here talking today is tough."

Alex: [Wailing] "It's just so bad. They did him so bad. And he was such a good boy. [He pulls himself together] I'm sorry, go ahead."

Whether or not Alex says, "They did him so bad," or if he said, "I did him so bad," became a big contention during the trial. Some believed he said "I" and a fewer number heard "They." This author believes he said, "They" and the transcript with the YouTube video picked up "They." You can listen for yourself at the 51:00 marker in the interview.

Croft: "And but you know, it's the little things that we can get a little better picture to what may have happened."

Alex: [Sounding like he wants to wrap up the interview] "Well, I just thank y'all for everything, you know? My in-laws, my parents, my in-laws... I would like somebody to update me or my brother or somebody so that I can tell them as y'all discovered things. Unless there's some reason y'all don't do that... I mean, they just have so many questions. And I mean they may even... Well, no, they don't...Well, I mean."

Owen: "I know I know Maggie's mother just had a knee replacement. How was their health overall other than that?"

Alex: "You know, they're a little bit, they're getting on up there. Daddy has some neuropathy, but I mean, they're in good physical health. They're in good... You know, their fortitude is good. They're just, you know, they're just getting age on them, you know?"

Owen: "Ok, are they in Summerville? Are they at the house on Moselle?"

Alex: "No, they live in Summerville. I mean, they're here now, they're in Moselle."

Owen: "I'll go by and speak with them and meet with them. If you think that would help."

Alex: "I think that would help a *tremendous* amount if you would just be willing just to sit down and let them. I mean, you know, hearing from me and John, Marvin, and Danny and whoever, what little tidbit y'all get, I'm just, you know what I think it would give them peace of mind to know that y'all got a team of people out there on it. And, you know, just to really, have something you know, a tangible person, instead of being told..." [Alex breaks down again]

Owen: "We got a contact number for them? What are their names?"

Alex: "My father-in-law's name is Terry. My mother-in-law's name is Kennedy Branstetter. And my sister-in-law, and then my sister-in-law, who was closest to Maggie in the whole world, is Marion Proctor. Her husband is Bart Proctor. And they live in Charleston. I'm telling you, man, I've been the luckiest person in the world with in-laws. I mean, they are wonderful people. I tell people all the time."

Owen: "Let me, let me grab a piece of paper. I'll be right back."

[Alex glances up at the bodycam and breaks down again]

Owen: [Re-entering the car] "Alright, so we have a victim's advocate. This is Marian Walker. That's her cell number. There's some information for you on the back. And the Victims Advocate program, they, I mean, they help with different things. I think more specifically, what would be more beneficial, especially for you and Buster on this is some counseling down the road. Grief counseling.

Alex: [Alex cuts him off] "You know I do some assistant solicitor work."

Owen: "Yeah. You're familiar with it."

Alex: "But thank you so much."

Owen: "I know y'all planned out the funeral today. When is the funeral?"

Alex: "Tomorrow. We're doing a service tomorrow. Maggie and Paul aren't gonna be ready until next week, so we're doing a service tomorrow and then we're gonna have a private family thing one day next week."

Owen: "OK. Are y'all doing anything tonight? Because I can run by and talk to Terry and Kennedy tonight…"

Alex: [excited] "I think the sooner you can come and talk to them, the peace of mind that… that would really help them. That's convenient for you. So, we're just out at the house tonight but.... And if for some reason they go back early because of the service tomorrow. That they... They may be staying tonight. They may not be. I'm not sure. All of their cousins and family on the Branstetter side and the Hubbard side are coming in from Kentucky. And so, they may be going back to stay with them. I'll find out and call you. I think you called me. I'll find out and call you in just a minute." [The most enthusiastic Alex has been during the interview]

Owen: "Alright. Do you have any other questions that I might be able to answer right now that we haven't gone over?"

Alex: "No, Sir."

Owen: "As soon as I get something and if it's OK with you, John Marvin asked me to go through him. So, I'm not bothering you in case you're doing something. What time, what time is the service tomorrow?"

Alex: "12:00 o'clock."

Owen: "OK, where is that gonna be?"

Alex: "Hampton Cemetery."

Owen: "So, if I get something around that time, I won't bother you. I'll, I'll wait…

Alex: "If you get anything important, you can call me anytime, OK, anytime."

Owen: "Are you all gonna publicize the service or is it just gonna be for family and friends?

Alex: "No, Sir. It's gonna be, you know, it's gonna be open. But I've got TC [Sheriff] and those making sure there's no... I don't want any press anywhere near."

Owen: "They don't deserve to be near."

Alex: "They're gonna make sure you know. And the town of Hampton, that's, you know, there's no press."

Owen: "Alright, well y'all got my numbers."

Jim Griffin: "Are they done with that phone?"

Owen: "I'm gonna go check on it. Ya'all go back in the house, when it's done, I'll bring it to you. Let's do the buccal swab right quick."

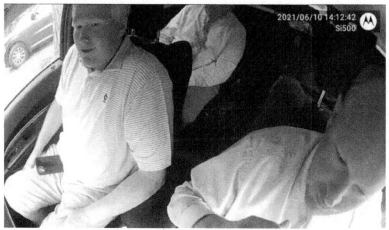

Alex Murdaugh's 2nd SLED interview, June 10, 2021.

Chapter Twenty-Two
Funerals and Alibis

Shortly after Alex Murdaugh walked away from the ordeal he endured during the second SLED interview, the news broke that his father, Randolph Murdaugh III passed away at his home in Almeda. It was the third strike for Alex that day. His wife and son had been autopsied earlier, although when Agent Owen mentioned it during the interview Alex didn't even flinch. He had sat through an hour-long interrogation carefully disguised as a fact-gathering mission, where he felt the net gathering around him as the prime suspect in his wife and son's murders. And now, the patriarch of the Murdaugh family, the man who had always bailed them all out, was dead.

Randolph was a much-respected solicitor in the 14th Circuit Judicial Court area. We covered his legacy in an early chapter, including winning the coveted Order of the Palmetto Award. But personally, for Alex and his sons, Randolph had used his influence and his piggy bank to rescue them numerous times. In Sandy Smith's letter to the FBI begging them to help her find the murderer(s) of her son Stephen, she mentions "Solicitor Randolph" as someone who had reached out to "help" her. Had "Handsome" (his grandchildren's nickname for him), been involved in Stephen Smith's case? We know he is at Paul's side at the hospital immediately after the boat crash. He remains by Paul's bedside advising him to "Shut UP!" as the coverup begins in the death of Mallory Beach.

Over and over, Randolph III bailed Alex out as he loaned him money to cover overdrafts and upside-down land deals. It may have been the knowledge that his father was going downhill fast that added to his impetus to murder Maggie. He desperately needed that $192,000 to give to Chris Wilson and it was now apparent that Randolph was in no condition to help him out this time.

And so, on that muggy hot day of June 10th, the day the boat crash motion would have taken place, the Murdaugh family was dealt another blow. Three deaths in three days. It was a lot to bear.

Randolph Murdaugh III's Obituary

Randolph Murdaugh III, June 10th, 2021, Varnville, South Carolina - 81,

Mr. Randolph Murdaugh, III, 81, of Varnville, died peacefully Thursday afternoon, June 10, 2021, at his residence. Mr. Murdaugh was born October 25, 1939, in Savannah, Georgia, son of the late Randolph "Buster" Murdaugh, Jr. and Gladys Marvin Murdaugh. Randolph graduated from Wade Hampton in 1957 where he was very active in sports. It was here that he began dating his future wife, Libby. After graduation he attended the University of South Carolina, graduating in 1961 with a BS Degree in Business Administration. That summer he married Libby. In the fall of that year, he enrolled in the University of South Carolina School of Law and graduated in 1964. After graduating he returned to Hampton to work in his father's Law Firm and became an Assistant Solicitor for the 14th Circuit. Upon the retirement of his father in 1986 he became

323

the Solicitor of the 14th Circuit where he served until the end of 2005.

For 87 consecutive years three generations of the Murdaugh family served as Solicitor of the 14th Circuit. This 87 years of service in one office, by the same family, is the longest in the history of the United States. In 2006 he rejoined the law firm, which is now Peters, Murdaugh, Parker, Eltzroth & Detrick, P.A. Randolph was President of the South Carolina Solicitor's Association during 1995-1996, he served on the National District Attorney's Association Board of Directors from 1998 - 2005 and received the Order of the Palmetto (South Carolina's highest civilian honor) from Governor Henry McMaster in 2018. Over his lifetime he achieved many awards including induction into the Wade Hampton Athletic Hall of Fame.

Left to cherish his memories is his wife of 60 years, Elizabeth "Libby" Alexander Murdaugh; his daughter, Lynn Murdaugh Goettee (Allen) of Summerville; his sons, Randolph "Randy" Murdaugh , IV (Christy) of Hampton, Richard Alexander "Alex" Murdaugh of Islandton and John Marvin Murdaugh (Liz) of Okatie; grandchildren, Mills Goettee, Trey Goettee, Buster Murdaugh, Reeves Goettee, Mary Elizabeth Murdaugh, Caroline Murdaugh, Mary Marvin Murdaugh, Liza Grace Murdaugh and Randolph Murdaugh, V; sister, Brenda Young (Tommy); sister-in law, Janet Cotter; brother-in-law, Don Alexander (Lisa); and special family member, Barbara Mixon, as well as a number of nieces, nephews and cousins. Mr. Murdaugh was predeceased by his daughter-in-law, Margaret "Maggie" Branstetter Murdaugh; grandson, Paul Terry Murdaugh; and brother-in-law, Arlen Cotter. A private service will be 1 PM, Sunday, June 13, 2021, at Varnville United Methodist Church for family members. Friends are welcome to attend the burial service at 2 PM at Hampton Cemetery conducted by Rev. John Culp and Rev. Tyler Strange and directed by Peeples-Rhoden Funeral Home. Visitation will be at Randolph's home, 2175 Yemassee Highway, Varnville, SC, following the service at the cemetery.

The family suggests that those who wish may send memorials to Varnville United Methodist Church, PO Box 45, Hampton, SC 29924 or The Randolph "Buster" Murdaugh Scholarship Fund, c/o PMPED, PO Box 457, Hampton, SC 29924.

Before Randolph's funeral came Paul and Maggie's. Their service was held at Hampton Cemetery. Over 100 people showed up in the sweltering heat. An ambulance was called during the memorial to aid two elderly people for whom the heat had been too much.

Entrance to Hampton Cemetery Friday, June 11, 2021.
Photo courtesy of *The Island Packet.*

At the packed Hampton Cemetery on Friday, grief, pain, and fond memories laced the community's uneasiness. "The tight ring of uniformed law enforcement officers surrounding the ceremony was a stark reminder that the killings are still unsolved," reported *The Island Packet.*

But the unusual circumstances of the Murdaughs' violent deaths were not mentioned by any of the speakers at Friday's funeral service.

Elizabeth Murdaugh, Alex's sister-in-law and John Marvin's wife, spoke of the family's closeness and her love for Maggie. Ronnie Crosby, a lawyer at the family law firm, described Paul as an outgoing —albeit messy — person who left clothes lying around at "houses across the state." Paul had often hunted on Crosby's property and helped him get rid of troublesome hogs. Crosby was clearly emotional during the murder trial when he spoke of how often Paul spent time with him hunting, and how good Paul was with his kids. He loved him. To lose him in such a violent manner made it all the harder.

Elizabeth said the two were "well lived and well loved." They had annual family reunions at "the river," and traveled all over the state. Elizabeth also spoke fondly of Alex and Buster Murdaugh, the two remaining members of the immediate family.

Elizabeth spoke about how Maggie and Alex met. She finally agreed to attend his fraternity's formal in Savannah, "and the rest was history," she said. Alex was "the one." He had an "almost un-human devotion" to Maggie, she said. One can only imagine the thoughts going through Alex's mind as he heard his sister-in-law's tearful tribute to him and praise his "un-human" devotion to Maggie. Knowing what we know now, a better word would have been "in-humane."

And "Buster," she said, "your strength this week is so very amazing." Alex and Buster were seated in the front row of the service. Alex wiped tears from his eyes throughout most of the memorial. He did not speak during the ceremony but embraced those who approached.

Buster hugging who is reportedly his girlfriend, Brooklyn White.
Photo courtesy of *The Island Packet.*

Alex "actively pursued" Maggie while they were college students at the University of South Carolina. But she always turned him down, Elizabeth said. Those words of "actively pursuing" Maggie brings different images to us today. We see a man armed with an AR-15 rifle "pursuing" his bride as she tried to escape the barrage of bullets.

The service was cut short as the heavens opened and rain poured down on the crowd. While it was a welcome relief from the stifling heat, it quickly became a Lowcountry downpour, and the mourners hurried to the protection of their cars. Throughout, police watched those present with the trained eyes of law enforcement. It was not uncommon for a killer to attend his/her victim's funeral. More than that, many wondered if the Murdaugh family had been targeted. It was also to keep the media at bay.

Rain-soaked mourners hurry to their cars. Photo courtesy of
The Island Packet.

A reception was offered at the Moselle house following the service. To many, it seemed odd, if not downright inappropriate to host a gathering at the very property where Maggie and Paul were murdered. Even more inappropriate was the rumor that a mistress of Alex Murdaugh's had not only been in attendance at the funeral, but she had also shown up for the buffet provided at the house.

The Peeples-Rhoden Funeral home had let it be known the two murdered Murdaugh family members had been cremated. Many of those with suspicious minds muttered about the speed with which

Maggie's and Paul's bodies had been cremated rather than interred. Those whisperings would escalate when two years later, there were still no elegant headstones at their graves. Only the ubiquitous basic ones can be found throughout the cemeteries everywhere. No marble. No beautiful etching such as the one adorning Stephen Smith's grave. Even if the wealthy family had ordered ornate head stones, people gossiped, it was doubtful it would take two years to create them.

Paul Murdaugh's marker at Hampton Cemetery.

Maggie Murdaugh's marker at Hampton Cemetery.

Over 100 people filled the hunting lodge at Moselle where a spread worthy of southern cooking was laid out. According to one attendant, there was fried chicken, beans and rice, casseroles, and myriad desserts. She mentioned to this author that this after-funeral gathering was a bit different. There was a receiving line as guests entered the home that Maggie Murdaugh had decorated. All of the law partners, along with Alex Murdaugh, greeted everyone who arrived. Most such occasions were usually less formal, with people arriving at different times and mingling with a plate of food. Many could not resist going down to the kennels, which according to some reports, had been somewhat sanitized for the occasion. It was also whispered that the reason for having the reception at the house, only four days after the murders, was so that all those people would trample over any remaining evidence.

It was a surreal ending to a surreal murder case for Maggie and Paul Murdaugh. Not many could remember a funeral reception being hosted on the very grounds where the victims had been mowed down. Worthy of a Pat Conroy novel? Maybe. Truman Capote? Definitely.

Randolph III's funeral followed two days later on June 13th. 200 people filed into the same Hampton Cemetery in a macabre sense of Deja vu for the funeral of one of South Carolina's most prominent lawyers. It was more a celebration of a life of a man who seemed larger than life to most who knew him. He had donated profusely to the community, was heavily involved in sports for youth groups, and donated to government officials as well as charities. Most of the funeral service was dominated by two of Randolph's friends who regaled the crowd with stories of this legendary man.

Donnie Meyers, former 11th judicial circuit prosecutor stood before those present and said, "A man who can count his friends with all five fingers is a lucky man. Randolph counts for three of mine." Despite all the accolades and honors Randolph III had amassed, Meyers said it was his family he valued most. He didn't have a favorite child, Meyers said, but he told each one: "Let me tell you something. You know you're my favorite." (He may have gotten that from the Lowcountry's own Pat Conroy who used the same line in his book *Prince of Tides*.) It was with Randolph's first grandchild that he acquired his nickname "Handsome." The little girl asked what she should call him, and he said, "Call me

Handsome, because I've never been called that before by a woman."
And it stuck.

Emotionally, Donnie Meyers concluded by saying, "Goodbye, my
loyal friend. Goodbye, my brother."

Randolph Murdaugh III's funeral service at Hampton Cemetery
June 13, 2021. Photo courtesy of Sophia Sanchez.

Perry Buckner, a retired 14th Circuit judge, told those attending
the funeral that Murdaugh had a way of making everyone feel
special. After people had spoken with Murdaugh, they would say, "I
may not agree with him, but I sure do like him."

Murdaugh cherished his friendships, and, in turn, Buckner said,
they cherished their friendships with him. "I do not know anyone in
my life who loved their family more than Randolph Murdaugh,"
Buckner said.

According to *The Island Packet,* "Murdaugh once told Buckner
how happy he was to have his grandchildren living with him while
son Alex and daughter-in-law Maggie were remodeling their home.
Murdaugh reaped the benefits of having his grandsons so close,
Buckner said, as the grandfather and two grandsons fished and
hunted together, even trapping raccoons."

Buckner said he learned so much from his friend. Murdaugh taught him he didn't have to be a pit bull in the courtroom to be successful — and to never assume he was smarter than a jury. "I can't tell you how many lawyers I've seen in my courtroom that have made these mistakes, and everyday I'm grateful for the lessons Randolph has taught me."

Buckner concluded his eulogy with a story about a church service he attended where the pastor used four worms. He put one in a jar of cigarette smoke, another in a jar of alcohol, the third in a jar of soil, and the fourth in a jar of chocolate syrup. All the worms except for the one in soil died.

"If my friend Randolph Murdaugh had been there," Buckner said, "he would have quickly raised his hand and said, 'As long as you drink, smoke and eat chocolate syrup, you'll never have worms.'"
The tearful crowd nodded in agreement as they roared with laughter.

It was an afternoon filled with beautiful memories of a man who had been well-loved and served his community. True, he had also dabbled in some nefarious enterprises, and ran interference for his family's continual criminal actions. But those present were there to honor what would be the last of the Murdaugh Solicitors of the 14th Circuit legacy. Duffy Stone filled that seat when neither Randy nor Alex Murdaugh wanted it. Alex was content to carry the Assistant Solicitor badge and use it when needed.

I Need You to Lie for Me

The reception for Randolph III was held at his beloved home at Almeda. It was an outdoor set-up to accommodate the crowd who came there following the service. It was a catered affair this time, and canopies and catering trucks filled the left side of the house. Shelley Smith was inside the house, sitting with Miss Libby as she usually did. The Murdaughs had asked her to work extra hours in the days following Randolph's death.

Following the reception, Alex went into Randolph's and Miss Libby's house and entered her bedroom. The windows to that room faced out onto the lawn where the reception had been. It could be accessed through the side door on the same side of the house as the canopies and food trucks. There was Randolph's "smoke house" out to the side and an old shed.

Randolph and Miss Libby's house side door. Their bedroom windows are to the right behind the small tree. It is at this door that Alex arrived on the night of the murders and after Randolph III's funeral service.

Alex entered his mother's room to check on her after the "repass" as Shelley Smith called it. It was her name for a reception following a funeral where people come to eat and pay their respects. During Shelley's testimony on the witness stand, during the trial for the double murders of Maggie and Paul Murdaugh, she became visibly emotional when Attorney Meaders asked her what happened when Alex came into the room to check on his mother. Swallowing repeatedly, and looking incredibly strained, she finally said he had come in to check on his mother. She also said he mentioned the night of the murders. She said he told her that he was there that night for "30-40 minutes." "And was he there for 30 or 40 minutes?" Meaders pressed when Shelley couldn't get the words out. She finally said, "No." "Miss Shelley, why are you crying?" Meaders asked her kindly. "Because they're a good family," she cried. "A good family."

It was clear she did not want to lose her job, and that she was sick about having to testify against Alex, but she would not lie for him. She was very distressed over the situation. Meaders asked her what happened after Alex left. She said she called her brother who was in law enforcement for advice.

Shelley Smith crying as she testifies that Alex wanted her to say he had been there 30-40 minutes the night of the murders, when he she remembers him being there only 15-20 minutes.

When asked if Alex said anything else to her during this same visit, she said he mentioned her getting married soon and that weddings were expensive. She answered him," Yes, sir. Thank you." Meaders asks her if Alex offered to help pay for the wedding and she said "Yes." Alex also mentioned that he was good friends with the head of the school where she worked part-time when not taking care of Miss Libby, and hinted he could put in a word for her. It was "hush money," if she would lie about how long he was there at his mother's bedside the night of the murders. It was not lost on anyone in the courtroom. It was also apparent that this time, Alex did not call to ask her to let him in the door. He needed that phone call as an alibi that he was at his mother's house the night of the murders. He just walked on in this time.

One or two days after the "repass," Alex was back. This time he slapped the side of the house under Miss Libby's bedroom window and announced, "I'm here." The next thing Shelley Smith noted was he came in the door and headed straight up the main staircase at the front of the house that led to the second floor that no one used anymore. She said he was carrying a "blue tarp…like the kind you cover a car or truck with." Attorney Meaders had her demonstrate how Alex was holding it in his arms. It looked like the way someone might carry a baby—cradling it. Meaders asked her if she could tell if there was anything in it, and she said, "No." She said it was "blue and looked to be vinyl." Later that morning, she saw it unfolded on a chair in Miss Libby's old bedroom upstairs.

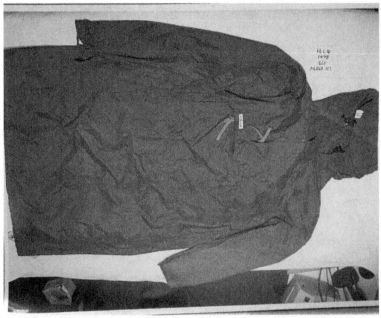

Blue raincoat in vinyl-type material that the prosecution would later say was found balled up in an upstairs closet at the top of the staircase at Randolph's home. It would have sinister implications during the trial.

Shelley said she left at some point that day. When she came back the next day, it wasn't there.

"Did you see Alex Murdaugh leave that day after he went upstairs with the blue vinyl thing?" "Yes. He said, "I'm goin'. I thought he'd gone."

"Did you see him after that?" Meaders asks her."

"He came back to the house. The blind was open, and I saw him come through the driveway." [Again, the blinds in Miss Libby's room face the side yard where the smoke house and old shed are located. There are also several old wells on the property.] "He was drivin' a white truck. I thought it was Mr. Randolph's. He has a white truck also."

"Were there 4-wheelers or ATV's out on that property?" Meaders asked.

"Yes."

"What if anything did you observe about a 4-wheeler, that morning?" Meaders asks the caregiver.

"It was at the house."

"Where had it been previously?"

"At the smoke house," Shelley answers.

"When did it get moved?"

"The same morning Mr. Murdaugh was there," she replies.

"And what did he do when he came back in the white truck?"

"He got in another truck," Shelley answers.

"How long was he gone?" Meaders asks.

"About 10 minutes...15 minutes."

"He got in a black truck."

"Had you seen this black truck before?"

"No, because the catering truck was in the way, and I couldn't see. It blocked my view...he left in a black truck." She didn't know whose truck that was.

Alex Murdaugh looking at Shelley Smith during her incriminating testimony. Was he angry that she was betraying him?

335

Shelley was asked if Alex had ever come to the house at 6:30 a.m. before, and she said, "No." Her regular shift ended at 8:00 a.m. and she would know if he had been there at that early hour before.

"When you saw Alex Murdaugh that morning at 6:30, did you notice anything about his face?"

"He had a little bruise or something. High on his forehead."

Shelley is asked to step down and point out to the jury on the ELMO where the main house at Randolph's property is. She shows the jury where the smoke house and ATV were. When he finally left, he went down the driveway and across the railroad tracks to the road.

Shelley Smith would not go as far as to say Alex had asked her to lie for him. It was implied. He may have simply thrown it out there while talking to her that night. A kind of, "You know there may be questions coming up on this thing. I know I was here 30-40 minutes. I laid on the bed, watched a TV show with you while checking on Mom…no big deal…" To Shelley's ears, it was anything but a simple retelling of the night's events. He was telling her the story she was to tell law enforcement, should they ask. And it was not true. He had placed her in an impossible situation, and it showed while she was on the witness stand. Alex would broaden the minutes he spent with his mother that night even more during his third SLED interview a couple of months later, on August 11th.

The bruise on Alex's forehead was never mentioned again. Its implication may have been that he bumped it while disposing of the two missing weapons. It was left dangling for the jury to digest.

Chapter Twenty-Three
SLED Comes Back for More

Several things happened in the same month, as Maggie and Paul's murders. Some helped Alex, others caused him great concern.

On **June 17, 2021**, four days after Randolph's funeral, Alex's brothers Randy and John Marvin made an appearance on *Good Morning America* insisting their brother was not involved in the murders of Maggie and Paul. It is an emotional interview with each taking a turn to describe how lowing and close their family was. John Marvin would pat Randy's leg as Randy put a protective arm around him. It was a poster child for family solidarity, and it felt very authentic. When Randy stated that the Murdaugh's were just like any other family, many in the poverty-riddled Hampton area were offended.

Randy (L) and John Marvin on *Good Morning America*.

"I see words like dynasty used and power," Randy Murdaugh said during the interview. "And I don't know exactly how people use those words, but we're just regular people and we're hurting just like they would be hurting if this had happened to them." Many did not see the Murdaugh juggernaut as "regular people."

As this interview was going on, SLED was searching a swamp near the murder scene. There is a swamp directly behind the Murdaugh home where Alex went that night to "get a gun" during the 911 call.

On **June 22**, five days after the brothers made their tearful appearance on *Good Morning America*, SLED shocked the country by announcing they were reopening the Stephen Smith investigation into the youth's death in 2015. It said the reason for this sudden move was "based on information gathered during its investigation into Maggie and Paul Murdaugh's murders." The rumor mills in the Lowcountry went into overdrive. What had SLED found while investigating the Murdaugh murders? Did they find a murder weapon used against Stephen? Was it something they found on the family's electronics? A vehicle that matched the blue paint chips found on Stephen's clothes. It kept the FB chat rooms and local podcasters fueled for the next two years.

On that same day, **June 22nd**, SLED released the 911 call made by Alex the night of the murders. It was now out there for armchair sleuths to dissect. And dissect, they did! They picked up Alex crying near the dog kennels, saying, "Paul...Paul...I should have known." Someone picked up hearing Alex say, "Here.." and wondered if he was calling a dog or handing something to someone else. Yet Alex told the 911 dispatcher there was no one else around. He repeated that assertion during each SLED interview. It is a timeline of his movements during that call, at least as much as we can make out. There is a lot of movement, panting, dogs barking going in and out as though he is moving away, and then moving closer to the kennels. There is the trip to the house for the gun he felt he needed for protection. Alex must have felt things were not going well for him. A new investigation into Stephen's death, and now, his 911 call had been released. Was this fear that prompted his next move only one day later on June 23rd.

Ten days after Randolph Murdaugh III's funeral, on **June 23rd**, Lowcountry residents found new headlines glaring back at them over their morning coffee. Alex and Buster Murdaugh were offering a $100,000 reward for any information resulting in an arrest for the murders of Maggie and Paul Murdaugh.

"I want to thank everyone for the incredible love and support that we have received over the last few weeks," Alex Murdaugh, Maggie's husband, and Paul's father, said in a statement released Friday. "Now is the time to bring justice for Maggie and Paul. Buster and I, along with Maggie's mother, father, and our entire family, ask that anyone with helpful information immediately call the SLED tip line or Crime Stoppers."

While the announcement of a reward from the family of the victims for information was not unique, the deadline hit a nerve with many. It gave a September 30, 2021, deadline for tips. Some said they had never heard of a deadline before for a reward. It typically ended when someone was apprehended, unless it went on for years and years. There are some rewards still standing for decades-old cold cases. Yet, the Murdaughs gave the public roughly two months to cough it up. Odd.

According to WCSC, Colleton County: A release states the South Carolina Law Enforcement Division, which is investigating the killings, agreed to identify anyone who provides information that leads to an arrest and conviction of the killers if that tipster wishes to claim the reward.

To be eligible for the reward, which the release states will be administered through the law firm of Peters, Murdaugh, Parker, Eltzroth and Detrick, the tip must be called in to SLED's tip line at 803-896-2605 and must be received by Sept. 30.

The law firm declined to provide additional comment on the reward Friday morning.

The total reward will be allocated equally among all people who provide information that leads to the conviction of the killers, the release states.

SLED spokesman Tommy Crosby said Friday that SLED authorized attorneys Jim Griffin and Dick Harpootlian to provide the SLED tip line. SLED committed to them that they will provide information on any tips to the attorneys so they can evaluate the potential payment of the reward.

"In order for SLED to maintain our independence we cannot be involved with facilitating or adjudicating any potential reward claims," Crosby said.

Crosby did not say how many calls the tip line has already received, saying it would be inappropriate to comment on specifics during an active ongoing investigation. He did, however, confirm SLED had received calls and that agents continue to pursue all leads they are receiving.

The fifth paragraph of this reward announcement by SLED struck me as interesting. "SLED committed to them [Griffin and Harpootlian: Alex's attorneys] that they will provide information on any tips to the attorneys so they can evaluate the potential payment of the reward." Hence, Alex' attorneys will get a heads-up on all tips coming in and know what's going on. Is this another way for Alex to have a ringside seat during the investigation? Just like he asked Agent Owen to tell Alex's in-laws what information they had as the investigation went along. Does it give him a chance to approach any potential witnesses and buy them off or shut them up? True, SLED would have already seen the tips. But witnesses can change their minds, and rumors had circulated since Stephen Smith's death that some members of law enforcement were in Camp Murdaugh.

Nathan Tuten on the witness stand, February 2023.

The next time Alex seems to surface is for the 4th of July holiday. During his testimony on the witness stand, Nathan Tuten said he drove Alex to the airport. "I believe he was going to the Florida Keys with Maggie's family," Tuten testified. During the ride to the airport, Alex told Nathan, who was not only a good friend to his sons, but a "runner" for the PMPED law office, that "He wanted to clear Paul's name" concerning the boat crash." He also said, "he wanted to beat the boat case." Attorney Fernandez asks Tuten, "So a month after the murders with Paul gone, Alex tells you 'He can beat the boat case'?" Tuten answers, "That's correct."

SLED's 3rd Interview with Alex

As July melted into August, SLED had been busy. Paul's phone and its contents had been accessed. Unbeknownst to Alex, they hit the mother lode with the data retrieved from his phone. It is perhaps the most compelling and poignant part of the testimony that would bury Alex Murdaugh in the end. His own son's phone. Without the evidence found there, it might have been possible to persuade the jury to have just a fragment of reasonable doubt concerning Alex's involvement that night. It was Paul speaking from the grave. And he did it through a device that was "never out of his hand."

The third interview with Alex was not in a car but at a SLED office on **August 11, 2021**. He came in accompanied by his good friend Corey Fleming, who was there for support, but also acting in his role as an attorney. He came out swinging before the interview could even begin, asking Agent Owen if they were there for Owen to give them information and update them on the case. When Owen waffled, Fleming doubled down. "We were told we were here for you to give *us* information," Fleming said, leaning across the table. "We will do that in the form of asking questions," Owen countered. "That information will come out in the questions." Fleming pressed further, and finally played his trump card: "Are you asking him questions to further your investigation, or are you asking him questions because you think that he's a suspect? I need a straight answer."

Agent Owen responds, "I am asking these questions to further my investigation."

Fleming says, "Then does that mean you're *not* asking him questions as a suspect? Because I'm not comfortable with you asking him questions as a suspect when I came here with the thought that you were going to be telling *him* where you are in the investigation. What it is you've seen, done, uncovered or whatever. That's why we came here!"

Owen: "Let me answer your question, and I've told Alex this since we first met. Any homicide investigation, you start with the closest person, and/or the person who found the deceased, in this case, that's Alex. Everybody stays in that investigation, until we can get them *out*. And right now, because of the questions I have, that I need explanations for, I cannot get Alex out."

Fleming backs down as Alex nods his agreement. "That's a reasonable statement," Fleming says. "I don't have any problem with that."

With that, after a discussion about all the stuff on the internet popping up about the case, Agent Owen gets started. For the sake of brevity, as this interview is almost two hours long, some of it will be in bullet point or summarized. Places where Alex is changing his story will be included.

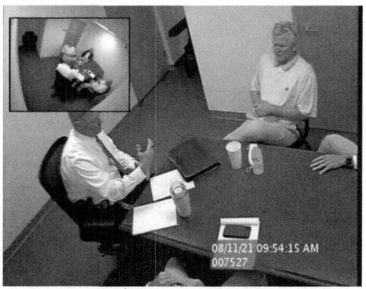

Alex Murdaugh's 3rd Interview with SLED. Corey Fleming's hand can be seen at the right next to Alex.

Owen begins with Monday morning, the day of the murders. He asks Alex what time he left for the office. Once again, he waffles, but finally says 8:30 or 9:00…10 at the latest. "If you need to know exactly what time I went, there will be a keypad that tells exactly what time I got to my office," Alex says, head bobbing. In the first and second interviews, he is vaguer, "kicking around the farm first," etc. We know now that Alex arrived at 12:30 pm that day, after noon.

"Maggie got up a little earlier because she had an appointment in Charleston. I just don't remember if I left right after she did, or I piddled around."

Owen: "We already know that Paul stayed with John Marvin that night, so it's just you and Maggie in the house?"

"That's right," Alex says, head still bobbing. He forgets to mention Blanca was there and even straightened his color for him as he left the house. That collar and the shirt he was wearing would become an important detail in the upcoming murder trial.

They talk about what Alex was working on at the office that day. Alex says he was working on the boat crash civil case.

Owen asks what time did he leave the office to go home?

Alex: "Earlier than normal. I'd say 5:30." We now know he left at 6:30 pm.

Owen: "What time did Paul get home that night?"

Alex: "Um…me and Paul got there about the same time. Maybe he was a little bit later than me or a little bit earlier than me, but it was close to the same time.

Owen: "And y'all road around the farm in, I believe you said two different trucks…two different vehicles. What were those two different vehicles?"

Alex: [Alex starts crying] "Umm… we rode in the white pick-up truck, and we rode in the black pick-up truck."

Owen: "And in any of those, did you see any long guns? Did you see any rifles or shotguns?"

Alex: "I don't remember seeing any that day. We did have pistols." He goes on to say they "were just shooting," not really target practice. "We rode around for a couple of hours. We looked at everything. We just spent some time together." Cries harder and Agent Owen goes to get him some tissues. Corey Fleming asks him if he can do this, and Alex says he can. His time with Paul has now gone from 45 minutes to an hour, to two hours. What comes next is important.

Alex: "We started out looking at the sunflowers. He was worried about the sunflowers and that was the first thing we looked at, and we just rode."

Alex and Paul seem to set off riding the property close to 7 p.m. Within minutes of them heading out, Paul is trying to get C.B. Rowe on the phone. This fits with them going to the sunflowers in the dove field first. It is only a few minutes' drive from the kennels where Paul's phone data puts them. Shortly after that, when C.B. doesn't respond, Alex tries him several times and texts the worker to call him. C.B. does not respond. As stated earlier, did Alex need Rowe there to A) keep Paul occupied at the dove field and away from the kennels, or B) to set Rowe up as the possible murderer of Maggie by having him there on the property at the time she was killed, or C) all of the above. The sunflowers seem to come up in every conversation.

Alex tells Owen that he and Paul talked about his blood pressure and his feet swelling up. Paul didn't want to see a doctor. "We talked about that, we talked about the farm...just everything," Alex says, his voice cracking. Interestingly, there is no mention of them talking about the boat crash case motion that will occur in only three days. It would seem to be something they would be going over.

Owen: "What time did Maggie get back home that night?"

Alex: "Later. Umm...I'd say, best guess, a couple of hours after we got there." [Maggie arrived around 8:15 p.m. which would be about an hour after Paul and Alex arrived that night and began riding around.]

Owen: "When you and Paul arrived back at the house, was Maggie there?"

Alex: "I can't remember if she came by the shed when Paul and I were up there, or we met her at the house." [This is new] "It's not unusual if we're messing around for her to swing through."

Alex's next statement is zeroed in on by Agent Owen:

"Maggie wasn't supposed to be coming home. I just found out she was worried about me, and me worried about my dad, and so she came home."

Owen: "Where was she supposed to stay that night?"

Alex: "At Edisto. We were having work done out there and I wasn't 100% sure, but I was pretty sure she was going to stay at Edisto."

Owen: (zeroing in): "Did it kind of surprise you that she came back then?"

Alex: "It didn't totally surprise me; she'd let me know earlier that she was coming home. I found out later why she came home."

Owen: "Because she was concerned for ya..."

Alex: "Yes, sir."

[Maggie told her nail technician, her sister Marion, and Blanca that Alex asked her to come home that night. Here, he tells Owen it was her idea. No mention is made of him asking her, or of the FaceTime call and others to her before she got to Moselle, that he deleted from his phone.]

"So not too long after that," Alex picks up when Maggie arrived for dinner, after his usual tactic of avoiding a timeline. He cried and went off on Maggie being concerned for him. "Blanca had made dinner. So, the three of us sat down and had dinner."

Owen: "What was the conversation around the dinner table?"

Alex: "Normal. Regular stuff. I mean I can't tell you exactly."

Owen: "How was Maggie's appointment in Charleston that day?"

Alex: "I think it had gone good. I mean, we didn't really get the chance to talk about it in detail. She'd been having a couple of little medical issues. I can't remember which one. It wasn't anything huge she went for."

Owen: "And after dinner, Maggie and Paul went to the kennels, or..."

Alex: "You know, I don't know exactly how that went. Uh...I stayed on the couch, and I dozed off. And then I got up..."

Owen: "Did you watch TV that night?"

Alex: "I know...I believe the TV was on. But I wasn't watching it."

[In Alex's first two interviews, he says Maggie left and went to the kennels after dinner, and Paul went outside. He didn't know where he went. He also said in his 2nd interview that "I stayed in the house. Watched some TV. Looked at my phone and fell asleep." Is he changing his mind about watching TV in case they ask him what he was watching? That would give them a timeline and test what he's telling them. But now...the TV is a maybe.]

It was now that Agent SLED catches Alex off-guard. He tells him they have a Snapchat video found on Paul's phone showing him playing with a tree wearing dress clothes. Alex is completely taken by surprise.

"There is a video on Paul's phone of you and him on the farm that night and you are in khaki pants and a dress shirt. You were playing with a tree..."

"I don't remember playing with a tree?"

"Owen: "My question is, when I met you that night, you were in shorts and a t-shirt. At what point in that evening did you change clothes?" [Alex is looking off in the distance, surprised.]

Alex: "I'm not sure...it would have been..."

Owen: "Before dinner...after dinner..."

Alex: "It would have been...what time of day was that? I would have thought I'd already changed."

Owen: "There's not a timestamp on it because there were so many posts on it, but it looks to be about dusk. So, that would have been 7:30 or 8:00."

Alex: "I guess I changed when I got back to the house."

[Alex's body language is very closed off. His arms are folded tightly across his chest and his legs are crossed. Oddly, Corey Fleming never shuts down the interview, even when it's apparent they are zeroing in on Alex. Alex asks Owen for a time stamp on the video before he answers the question, probably to make sure he won't get caught in a lie. We know the short video was taken around 7:36 p.m. Paul sent it at 7:59 p.m., possibly when they got back to the hanger area where there was cell phone service.]

Owen: "Earlier when we spoke and you got up from your nap and you were going to check on your mother, you tried to call Maggie and you tried to call Paul, and you sent Maggie a message text that you were going to check on your mother. You also told me that Maggie didn't normally go to check on your mother but that she might rather that night. Did you go by and check on her?"

Alex: "Go by and check on my mom?"

Owen: "Maggie, before you left to go..."

Alex: "No, I didn't."

Owen: "With her not responding to you, and you thinking she might ride with you, why didn't you?"

Alex: "I don't remember having plans with Maggie going with me, but maybe she had told me that she was that night. I don't recall that...I don't remember that specifically...I mean it wasn't she didn't normally go with me. It's not like we had plans she was going to ride with me, or she was going..." [He breaks off. Agent Owen is looking through his files for something.]

He pulls out Google maps to show Alex and asks him what route he took to see his mother. Alex describes how he got there while looking at the map. Corey Fleming leans forward to look at the maps.

Owen asks Alex how often he visited his mother.

Alex: "I mean, it wasn't infrequent. It wasn't all the time, but all times of the day." He tells Owen that Miss Libby has Alzheimer's "really bad" and that she got particularly agitated with Randolph not being there. I checked on her more in the days and weeks following my dad's passing, several times a week, anytime." [Which is true. Alex came several times, including telling Shelley to say he had been there for 30-40 minutes. Another time he brought something that was blue vinyl, cradled in his arms. He also did something with an ATV while "visiting his mom." The truth is, according to Miss Libby's caregivers, she didn't know when someone was there or not. She had to be changed and slept a lot.]

Owen: "How long did you stay while at your mother's that night?"

Alex: "45 minutes to an hour."

[Shelley Smith, the caregiver who was sitting with Miss Libby the night of the murders, said Alex was there 15-20 minutes. She had been interviewed by SLED by the time of this interview. Alex's previous interviews had varying times; the last one being 30-40 minutes. He has now stretched it to 45 minutes to an hour! Why? Because now he knows Rogan Gibson heard him at the kennels during a phone call with Paul at 8:40 pm. This is not the famous kennel video, which Rogan never received, because Paul was murdered before he could send it. This was a phone call. Rogan asked Alex about it. So, in this interview, with that new knowledge, Alex has to make sure he is at his mother's long enough to have an alibi for 8:40. It isn't clear how he thinks he is going to convince Rogan he was wrong.

The problem with this new alibi is that he couldn't possibly have left the property at 9:07 when he got up from his nap, driven 20

347

minutes one way, stayed 45 minutes to an hour, driven 20 minutes back, and had a time stamp of 10:06 pm for a 911 call. It belies the laws of physics.

Owen: "Did you make any stops going or coming from your mother's?"

Alex: "Stops? No, I didn't go anywhere. I went straight back."

Owen asks Alex if he and Paul did anything with the dogs pertaining to any injuries while they were at the shed before dinner? Alex tells him no, but that Rogan Gibson told him there was something wrong with his dog's tail and it "had a broken leg." Paul was looking out for Rogan's dog and keeping him at the dog kennels near the hangar at Moselle while he was staying with his girlfriend in Beaufort. He tells Owen that Rogan's dog is a chocolate puppy.

Owen: "Was the leg broken?"

Alex: "Not that I know of."

Owen asks Alex which driveway he went through when he got back to Moselle after visiting his mom. He says he went in through the brick gates, which would be the main drive to the house, not the one that leads to the hanger and kennels.

Owen: "And Maggie and Paul weren't there? Were their vehicles at the house?"

Alex: "Yes sir."

Owen: "How did they get down there that night?"

Alex: "That's still something I don't know. I was hoping you were going to be able to tell me that."

Owen: "The only thing I can come up with is that black truck, Buster, Buster's old black truck. Does it normally stay down at the farm, or does it stay at the house?"

Alex: "Both."

Owen: "Did Maggie ever walk down there?"

Alex: "Maggie walked down there a lot, but Paul had this…if you showed me that Paul walked down there that night, I would be surprised. Absolutely surprised."

Owen: "Well, thinking about Paul's health, do you think Maggie could have gotten him to walk down that night, to come along and walk with me this one time?"

Alex: "It's possible but again, that would be highly, highly unusual. He would have talked her into riding. It's unusual for him to walk."

348

What has been hard to understand is why didn't Alex take either of the two options Owen gave him for how Paul and Maggie got down to the kennels that night? The black truck or that they walked. Why leave it dangling and unanswered? It was getting dark at 8:30 pm when Paul's data said he was making his way to the kennels after dinner. Maggie would not be walking in the dark, let alone with a new pedicure. The answer may be, Alex was smart enough not to commit to a theory. Better to stick with he has no idea how they got down there.

Owen: "So when you were at the kennels, you were just down there with Paul, and you left and went back to the house for dinner…"

Alex: "You know, Paul and I were just knocking around at the shop, the shed, the kennels… the whole property…and that was before dinner, yes, sir."

Owen: "And you didn't go back down there until your return trip from visiting your mother…"

Alex: "Yes, sir."

Owen: "I've got information that was on Paul's phone, and Maggie was heard in the background, and you were heard in the background, and that was prior to you leaving."

Alex: "Rogan Gibson asked me if I was up there. He said he thought it was me."

Owen: "Was it you?"

Alex: "At 9 o'clock?"

Owen: "Yes, sir."

Alex: "No sir, not if my times are right."

Owen: "Who do you think it could have been?"

Alex: "I have no idea."

[This segment, where Owen drops his bombshell that Alex is heard on Paul's phone, goes awry. Paul's first call with Rogan was at 8:40 pm. It is that phone call where Rogan says he heard Alex's voice. Yet Owen just agrees with Alex when he says 9:00. He should have asked if it was him at the kennels at *8:40* during Rogan's phone call, not 9:00. It's a mess.

At this point in the interview, Alex (and everyone else) is unaware of the kennel video where you can distinctly hear his voice calling for Bubba, Paul's lab, as the dog runs off with a chicken in its mouth. Alex was leaving the property right around 9 o'clock. The murders are believed to have happened four minutes after the kennel video was shot on Paul's phone at 8:45 pm. Therefore, Alex is correct. He was in his car and getting ready to leave the property. His phone has been off for an hour, but when he fires up his car around 9, they are already dead.

At the time of this interview, Agent Owen had not gotten the kennel video. He was unaware there was a definite video that could not be disputed. It wasn't found until April 2022.

Owen: "And Rogan's been around your family for pretty much all of his life."

Alex: "Absolutely."

Owen: "He recognizes your voice, and you have a distinct voice. Can you think of anyone who has a voice like yours that he may have misinterpreted?" [Alex is rocking with his arms crossed.]

Alex: "No, sir. I mean he, he told me that he thought I was up there."

Owen: "Did that surprise you?"

Alex: "Yes, sir."

Owen: "So, when you returned back to the kennels, when you returned back from your mom's, where were the dogs?"

Alex: "They were like they were when…I didn't put the dogs up…"

Owen: "So they weren't running loose?"

Alex: "However, where they were…" [Alex breaks off and just nods]

Owen: "On one part of the 911 call you say, "Here," like you're talking to somebody else or something else…"

Alex: "I say, "Here"?

Owen: "Yes, sir."

Alex: [Long pause, staring straight ahead. Owen reads the 911 transcript and tells him where he says, "Here". "I don't have any memory of saying that. I guess I'd have to listen to it. You know, I don't recall a dog being out. I'm certain that there was not a dog out. Um…there's other things people told me about that 911 call I don't remember. Um…I don't know…Here…like I was calling a dog?"

Owen: "I don't know…calling a dog, talking to a person, that's why I'm asking."

Alex: "Obviously, there was nobody else out there. I'm certain that there was not a dog…loose. But I don't remember saying anything. Buster would know...something about threats... [Alex switches the subject] if Buster had information about threats, he would know... [long pause]"

Owen: [goes with change of topic. It is clear Alex is surprised by all the new information and is trying to think. He is also not commenting much.] "Have you learned any new information about the threats?"

Alex: "Nothing really new...no, sir. Outside of things that Randy's told you. There was just so many things on the internet, you know...but nothing new, no, sir." [Alex has gotten very quiet]

Owen: "So during the 911 call, and we also talked about it that night, you went back to the house to get a shotgun..."

Alex: "Yes, sir."

Owen: "What door did you enter?"

Alex: "The best that I can remember, I went in the side door. And I went straight to the gun cabinet..."

Owen: "Were you focused on any particular shotgun or just...grabbed one?"

Alex: "I just grabbed one."

Owen now goes over with Alex how he would normally load a shotgun. He tells him that the shotgun Alex retrieved from the house that night had two different loads chambered, which is unusual. He asks him if he would load buckshot and birdshot in one load, and Alex says not normally.

Owen: "The reason I'm asking, is the shells we recovered that night, one was a buckshot, and one was a turkey shot..." [These are the two shells found behind the door near Paul's body.]

Alex: "I understood that..."

Owen: "The shotgun that you had with you that night...there was a birdshot and a buck shot. When they went back the next day, an attorney, I'm not sure which one it was, said there had been a shotgun laying on the pool table, that he put back, and the ammunition that was with that, it was a buckshot and a birdshot, and the shotgun that we took for potential comparison, it was also loaded with a buck shot and a birdshot, so, I have all of these consistent loads, and its consistent with what we have in the feed room...I call it the feed room at the kennels."

Alex: "That night, I grabbed the shells that I could get my hands on, I had no idea exactly what I had..." [Rocking and nodding his head]

Owen: "Also when we talked, I asked if was usual to keep guns down at the kennels, and you said you had to check. Have you been able to check to see what was missing from your collection?"

Alex: "I have, yes, I know what's missing from our guns...there's three guns that I think are missing. It would be a Benelli shotgun, a Browning shotgun, and a pump shotgun. The Benelli and the Browning are automatic. The pump is a Remington, I believe, but I'm not positive. The Benelli is black, the Browning is camo, and the pump is camo."

Owen: "Would you have those serial numbers recorded anywhere?"

Alex: "I don't have them recorded, but I'm sure...I don't know where the pump shotgun came from, but I should have the Benelli and the Browning."

Owen: "We don't know if they're stolen or where they are so I really can't get them entered into NCIC, so I can alert the ATF to be on the lookout for that gun, and they can alert the person back to who may have had it."

Alex: "Absolutely."

Owen: "If we could work on that to get that back as soon as possible..."

Alex: "I understand, also that a .300 was used that night and I know that John Benningfield said he only had two of those..."

Owen: "Actually, John has told us he sold Maggie a third gun. The story is that she paid for it, and she was supposed to tell you so that you could go sign the paperwork form, and that never occurred. He has a number; he just doesn't have a sale on the final paperwork. Both of the other two .300's are numbered and in the system so that ATF can flag them should they turn up." [This is Buster's black .300, which is accounted for, and the tan one Paul lost.]

Owen: "So we talked about the shotgun shells. The .300 Blackout casings that were thrown around Maggie, match the casings found by the back door to your gun room, and at the shooting range. [This is first time Alex is being told that the old casings by his back door match the ones found by Maggie's body. The casings by the back door were left there when Paul and Will Loving sighted in the new replacement Blackout gun that has gone missing since the night of the murders.] The ones by the house, and some of the ones found at the shooting range are confirmed matches to the ones found by Maggie, which gives another concern. I've got multiple guns loaded with the same shotgun shells, and the Blackout casings matching those around Maggie."

2021/06/08 15:05:40
Si500

SLED bodycam showing 3 of the 5 .300 blackout casings found at the landing of the back staircase to the gunroom on June 8, 2021.

Alex: "So that would mean those guns, of Paul's were used…"
Owen: "Yes and missing."
Alex: "And I understand somebody had seen that gun recently, and I asked Buster about it…I believe that that gun has been gone since before Christmas."
Owen: "Nolan Tuten recalls Paul's first .300 going missing around Halloween at Hampton…the Christmas of 2017, the Halloween of 2018 is when Nolan believes it was taken out of Paul's truck. There were 100's of people at this Halloween party and he knows the gun was in Paul's truck, and after the party, the gun is missing. So, that's the timeline of when that gun goes missing. I'm thinking April of 2019 is when they sighted in the replacement gun. Another part in the 911, you say, "I should have known." What are you referencing in that statement?"
Alex: "I don't know. I guess all the threats and I had been convinced that it had something to do with the boat wreck and all of that."

Owen asks Alex if Paul or Maggie ever got physical with him. Alex says Paul had too much to drink one time and that was the only time. "It had been awhile."

Owen: "When you turned Paul over and his cell phone popped out, and you picked it up, your statement was 'I thought about doing something, but then I put it back down.' That was our first interview. What were intentions with the phone?"

Alex: "I don't know. I mean it, when I went up to him, the phone came out, I don't remember of having any intentions of doing anything with the phone."

The other agent, Agent Croft, who has been sitting in on the interview asks Alex about dinner after he and Paul got back from riding around. He asks Alex if he can guesstimate how long they were at the dinner table?

Alex says, "I mean, it wasn't any long, drawn-out dinner."

He tries to get Alex to comment on how long they sat at the dinner table. He shakes his head, and says, "15...20 minutes, however long it takes...best guess."

He asks about the pistol Alex and Paul had while riding around the property, how long had it been since he had seen guns in that vehicle. Alex answers that Paul always had guns.

Owen brings up that the truck Paul usually drove went into the shop the Friday prior to the Monday murders. He tells Alex there is video of Paul dropping the truck off and not taking any rifles from it. Alex is not sure about Paul switching out trucks prior to the murders. He tells Owen that that Friday he had gone to stay in the hospital with his dad. He said he didn't see Paul that Friday or Saturday at the games. "He wasn't into ball as much," Alex says.

Owen now goes over Alex's timeline again for the morning of the murders. He reminds him that he says he left the house at "around 8:30, 9:00, no later than 10:00 am. And that he left the office early, around 5:30 pm to come home. Other times Owen talked with Alex, he said he didn't remember any times. Owen tells him that during the 911 call, the dispatcher asks Alex when the last time was he saw Maggie...you said an hour and a half to two hours ago.

"You know to me, that's a set time that you rattled off without even thinking about it. We're sitting here trying to figure out a timeline, and you're having trouble coming up with a specific time."

Alex: "Tell me again what I said to the dispatcher..."

Owen: "You said an hour and a half to two hours…"

Alex: "And what time was that?"

Owen: "10:06 pm. Given two hours back, that would have been 8."

Alex: "I think that's probably about right… you think I'm giving you an inconsistent answer?" [8:00 pm was before Maggie even arrived or that they had supposedly sat down and had dinner together. Paul didn't leave for the kennels until 8:30 when dinner ended. An hour and a half would not have been too far off, as that was the time dinner ended and Alex said he went to take a nap. If he hadn't killed them, 8:30 would have been the last time he saw Maggie.]

Owen: "I'm just trying to get a timeline… You said you left the law firm at 5 or 5:30 pm. I have a time readout card from the law firm that shows you coming in the door at 5 or 5:30…"

Alex: "Coming in the door?"

Owen: "Yes, sir, and Randy said when he left at 6:00 pm, you were still there. So, the times aren't matching up."

Alex: "That's not the first time I was at the office that day."

Owen: "There were several readings but your card to your office wasn't working. Somebody had to actually let you in. But I have your card opening the door to the *law firm* at 5:30. And then Randy saying he left at 6 and you were still there. I'm just trying to understand."

Alex: "You know, I left the law office earlier than I normally do. I mean, it's not unusual for me to be there until dark. You know I try to get home when Maggie's home, you know, before dark."

Owen: "She doesn't like staying out there by herself after dark?"

Alex: "That's right. So, you know, 5:30 or 6… I don't think I was still there at 6 o'clock, but, you know, if I was, it wasn't long after that, so…I *believe* that I went straight home. Have y'all been able to check the Chevrolet, to download me…?"

Owen: "We're still working on that. It's a long process."

Alex: "I got home early enough for Paul and I to ride the property for a substantial length of time, you know…more than an hour, I thought a couple of hours that we were together."

Owen: "Did you go down by the river?"

Alex: "We rode down all the roads, I believe that we, I mean we rode all over, we rode all over." [Alex is always vague on exactly where they went.]

Owen: "Have I been able to answer all your questions?"

Alex: "I do know more than I did before."

Owen: "What other questions do you have?"

Alex: "I would like to know exactly what happened."

Owen: "Me too. The best that I've been able to put together…"

Alex begins to cry again. "Go ahead, I'm sorry."

Owen: "I believe Paul was shot first. [Alex is crying and moving his legs in and out like scissors.] For the simple fact of where he was located."

Alex: "How many times was he shot?" [Barely able to speak]

Owen: "Twice."

Alex: "I thought they shot Maggie first because I thought they told me they shot her in the back of the head."

Owen: "We may honestly never know who was first. But I think it was Paul for the simple fact if he saw his mother getting shot, he wouldn't have run to that feed room, unless that's where one of the guns was. We've already established that family guns were used and if they came from Paul's truck, Paul's truck was at the house. Where were they and how did they get down there? It's normal for y'all to leave your keys in cars. However, if somebody showed up and did this, they are not going to take Paul's truck back to the house and leave the key in it."

Alex: "I mean, do you know that the guns were in the truck? Could they have been somewhere else?"

Owen: "I mean they could have been somewhere else. He didn't have his normal truck."

Alex: "I understand that Nolan Tuten believes he saw the other gun three weeks before hand, but I have talked to him, but does he believe it was not the one that was at the house?"

Owen: "It was the Benelli that Paul always kept with him?"

Alex: "Yeah, one of a couple of Benellis…"

Owen: "It was the camo Benelli that was the last one that Nolan saw. And an HDD…some kind of semi-automatic rifle. Do you have that one at home?"

Alex: "Yes, sir. That's what he saw? Because I was told by somebody that Nolan saw a .300…"

Owen: "He told me that he had not seen a .300 since March." [The murders were June 7.] Those were the go-to guns and those were the last ones he saw."

Alex: "So, he definitely saw it during turkey season? Because there was some point back when it was missing at Christmas time…"

Owen: "The *third's one* missing at Christmas time?"

Alex: "Yes, sir. Anyway, if he saw it in March…"

Owen says they got plenty of DNA from the scene. "It's Nolan's, it's Rogan's, it's Alex, it's Paul's, it's Maggie's, it's Buster's…"

Alex breaks down weeping and asks between sobs, "Can you tell me for sure, did either one of them live after they were shot the first time?"

Owen: "Not at all. The shooting happened very quickly."

Alex: "Is this one person, two persons, three persons?"

Owen: "We've got two guns. We've got two different kinds of ammunition. It's hard to say. It is hard to say."

Alex: [Crying hard] "Did either one of them live very long?"

Owen: "Only seconds."

Alex: "Thank you."

Corey Fleming tells Owen that Randy says they have a lot of friends in the community from the wealthy to the lowest economic levels. They think they can ask people to keep their ears out. Owen tells him that he is not going to ask anyone in the law firm or anyone else because it might get misconstrued that they are working for SLED. Owen said he talked to Randy and told him he could not stop him from asking questions, but that they should be told to call SLED.

Alex: "David, you don't have anything substantive that makes you think, hey, this isn't good?"

Owen: "Like I said, the only DNA we have are family and close friends. We don't have any fingerprints. Unfortunately, we don't have any shoe wear or tire wear impressions because it rained that night. The only thing that we can go off of are the cell tower dumps and the FBI was out on your property Friday trying to get some cell phone data. Unfortunately, that all takes time.

Owen explains to Fleming the two different systems on Alex's car for data: OnStar and the infotainment system. He also tells Fleming that they have done a partial download on Paul's phone because they don't have the passcode. Fleming tells Owen that he thinks Maggie owned Paul's phone. Alex says Maggie did back hers up to iCloud, but Paul didn't. Fleming recommends they get the personal representative to get a search warrant to get Paul's phone open. Alex does not look happy. The last thing he wants is for Paul's phone to be opened. He knows Rogan was texting Paul a lot at the time of his murders hinting he was waiting for a photo of the dog's tail.

Corey Fleming asks if they have looked into the whackos on the internet. He tells him they've weeded out a lot of crank calls.

Alex, who has not been participating in this latest conversation, breaks in and asks, "David, how far apart were they shot? Did one of them know the other one was dead, or shot?"

Owen: "I think it's impossible to answer that question."

Alex: "But, you're certain Paul was shot first."

Owen: "I believe he was. I'm not certain, but I believe he was."

Alex: "Maggie would have known that, then, wouldn't she? You don't know how far apart she was shot?"

Owen: "It all depends on how many shooters were there. If we're looking at two shooters, it could have happened at the same time. If we're looking at one shooter, it would have happened... And I know you can't help but think about it, but don't beat yourself up over getting an answer. It's not going to do anything for you."

Alex: "Now that you've talked to me, are you willing to talk to Maggie's family?"

Owen: "Yes, sir. I'll meet them wherever they want to."

Alex: "Thank you. I know y'all are doing everything you can. And I don't take any personal offense at you asking me these questions. I know you need to do what you gotta do."

Owen: "The media keeps throwing you in there. I need every possible evidence..."

Alex: "When you get my car stuff, maybe that will help."

SLED agent Jeff Croft asks Alex about Maggie not liking to stay out there by herself. He asks if there were any cameras. Alex says he never had any issues with stuff missing. He said they had talked about it but hadn't done anything yet. The agent asks if Paul or Maggie ever mentioned stuff missing. Alex said some tools went missing a couple of...it was since C.B. got hired. Alex said when Paul was looking for them, he was going to ask C.B. Alex mentions a boy working out there named Matt Luce. He was there to keep things from getting out of control. He was working for a friend and came in to help Alex late fall. He lives between Beaufort and Barrett

Boulware Jr. plantation. He says Matt is about 35 years old. Alex offers to get Matt's number.

Agent Croft asks Alex if the replacement AR-15 had a thermal scope on it like the original two, or any kind of scope.

Alex: "It didn't have a night vision scope. You know, Paul put something on it. It was new. He moves scopes around from gun to gun to gun, but I'm not sure about a specific scope on it."

Croft: "When was the last time *that* gun had been seen?"

Alex: "I know we looked for it around Christmas holidays. I asked about it Christmas holidays…2020. That was the replacement."

Owen: "I'm still trying to figure this out. I cannot exclude the boat accident and those involved. I know y'all are currently going through the civil motion. How far had that progressed? Were you all in the talks? Was it breaking down?"

Fleming interrupts and says he shouldn't be talking about the boat case unless Alex's lawyers are present and are representing him in that case. Alex says he doesn't mind. He just says it's made some progress. It isn't in its initial stages. Owen says he is just trying to see if someone in that case could be pissed off.

Alex: "I know one of the Daddy's of one of the kids in the boat wreck went to lengths to say you can't be friends with Paul and the Murdaughs and still be friends with us. It may have been the son." Alex says Nate Tuten told him that.

[Alex gets a call from Buster and leaves the room to get a good signal. Owen follows him out. When Alex returns, Fleming says to Owen, "If you don't have any more questions…"

Owen shows them the Snapchat video and Alex explains that he was trying to get the tree to stand up. Owen asks him if it was that night because some of Paul's friends said it was posted that night. Alex says he isn't sure.

Owen: "Anybody from the boat or their family that y'all have heard or know having issues with them recently or prior to this incident?"

Alex: "David, you know I told you about Treehorn. She called me all out of sorts saying the family from the boat wreck…it was so over the top that I didn't pay it a whole lot of attention. I asked her about it, and she didn't know who the people were, but it was a friend, and she would take y'all to the friend. Has she talked to you about that?"

Owen: "She's given us very little."

Alex: "You think she's being evasive? I tell you what I'm trying to do. I know y'all have to look at me. I know some people have said I had something to do with the boat wreck. So, I'm trying not to have conversations with any people you need to talk to. [Alex is referring to the accusations that he interfered with the boat crash investigation and now he's going to great lengths to not be perceived as doing that with this investigation by talking to people.]

Owen: "The problem that I encounter, and every law enforcement encounters is people on the street talk, and they run their mouth and they'll talk to family, and they'll talk to friends, but when police show up, they keep their mouths shut. She has given us some information."

Alex: "Is there a problem with me going to her and you know…"

Owen: "I'm not going to answer that."

Alex: "I'll get someone to talk to her to get her to talk to you."

Owen: "Do you have any other questions… I'll call the Brandstatter's and Marion and get them there at the same time."

After a pause, Owen blindsides Alex and blurts out:

"Did you kill Maggie?"

Alex, looking surprised answers, "Did I kill Maggie? Did I kill my wife? No, David."

Owen: "Do you know who did?"

Alex: [Defensively] "No, I do not know who did. Do you think I killed Maggie?"

Owen: "Did you kill Paul?"

Alex: "No, I did not kill Paul."

Owen: "Do you know who did?"

Alex" "No, I do not know who did."

Owen: "I have to go where the evidence and the facts take me…"

Alex: "I understand that. And you think I killed Paul?"

Owen: "I have to go where the evidence and the facts take me. I don't have anything that points me to anybody else at this time."

Alex: "So does that mean you think I'm a suspect?"

Owen: "It's like I told Corey earlier, you were still in this. With everything we've talked about, with the family guns, with the ammunition, nobody else's DNA, I have to put my beliefs aside and go with the facts.

Alex: "Well, I understand, I mean…"

Alex Murdaugh had just been told he is a suspect in the murders of his wife and son. All pretense was off. His changing stories had not worked. It was a mountain of "evidence and facts" that made it highly unlikely someone outside the family did this. The smoking gun was yet to come, and it would come from Paul's phone and the serendipitous chance that a dog grabbed a chicken and ran.

Chapter Twenty-Four
It All Falls Apart

In the weeks following SLED's interview with Alex Murdaugh, he seemed to make erratic decisions and his lies mounted. Like his son's decision to push the boat throttle over to full blast, Alex raced recklessly into his attempts to get out of the mess he was in. Not just in being a suspect in his wife and son's murders, but in the financial abyss of fraud that was being uncovered at his own law firm; a law firm that his great-grandfather had founded.

Annette Griswold was Alex's paralegal at PMPED and described him as the "Tasmanian Devil" when he came into work each day. He was a whirl of motion and fast talking, cracking the whip at those who had been there hours before him. Alex mentioned in his second interview that Paul had ADHD. It could be that apple hadn't fallen fall from the tree.

Annette Griswold on the witness stand, Feb. 2023.

When Annette Griswold took the witness stand in February 2023, she gave the world a view of Alex's decline in the days of September 2021, following the murders of Paul and Maggie.

"He was more distant, even when he was in the office," Griswold testified. "He was absent, he was hard to get him to sit still and sign our documents that we put in his office to sign. It got much worse after the boat accident; he was rarely there and when he was the door was closed. It was almost impossible for us to reach him. He was always on his phone; he was always dealing with something bigger than what we had going on."

As 2021 wore on, she said, "He was worse. He was not his normal self, or what his normal self used to be. He was very tense. You could tell the boat crash was weighing heavy on him and it was consuming almost his life. He was harder to reach and there were a couple of incidences where I referred to him as having his ass on his shoulders because that's how I felt. He came in and yelled our names and didn't treat us the same way he did before the boat accident.

"He was protective of anyone going into his office. He would like come in on a Monday and yell 'Who's been in my office?' I said 'I don't know, maybe the cleaning ladies. I have no idea.' It was very cluttered, very unorganized, but he said he knew where his stuff was, it was organized in his way."

Annette testified that over the years Alex had told her to put the fee disbursements of his into a "Forge" account, and she, thinking it was for a legitimate company called Forge Consulting, did so. Forge Consulting was a respected company in Charleston that handled large settlements for customers who wanted help in controlling the money, especially if it dealt with a minor, or if they wanted to be smart with the windfall and put part of into an annuity that would garner interest over the years. Alex had created a bank account with Bank of America called Richard Alexander Murdaugh dba Forge. It was a smart move to cover up what was technically his private piggy bank.

Annette would ask Alex when the checks made out to Forge came in from their accounting department if she should mail them over to Michael Gunn, who was their contact at Forge Consulting. Alex would say, "No, you know what? I'm seeing Gunn this weekend. He's coming out to the farm, or we're going to meet halfway and have dinner…" He always said he'd hand deliver it. When Michael

Gunn was approached about this, he said he hadn't done work with Alex for years and had not set up any settlement accounts.

At PMPED, any attorney fees are made out to the firm. The individual attorneys receive their fees at the end of each year in December. But it was suddenly to come to light that fees were made out to him personally or to his fake Forge. As Annette Griswold began noticing these discrepancies, she took her fears to Jeannie Seckinger, the CFO at PMPED. Jeannie told Annette she would talk to Alex about the recent issue that fees from the Ferris case were not in the firm's accounts. Typically, when a case is settled, there are expense fees and there are attorney fees. The Ferris case had been split between Chris Wilson who was co-counsel with Alex in the case. Wilson's firm sent over the expense fees. But Annette noticed the lawyer's fees for Alex were not there. She called Chris Wilson's secretary, Vicki Lyman, and Vicki assured her the fee check had been mailed at the same time as the expense check.

On **May 27, 2021**, emails began going back and forth between Jeannie Seckinger, Annette Griswold, and Vicki Lyman, trying to nail down where the fee check to Alex was. On June 2nd, only five days before the murders of Maggie and Paul, Annette sent another email to Vicki. They wanted copies of everything to clear it all up. They were hoping their suspicions were wrong. Vicki said she would forward the information to Chris Wilson.

After the murders on June 7th, Annette said the law firm rallied around Alex. The Ferris fees were not brought up again until **September 2, 2021**. Annette was looking for a file and thought it might be in Alex's office as he would tend to get a file and leave it in his office.

"I went to his office to look for the file," Annette testified. "When I found the file on his desk, I picked it up, and when I did, a check kind of floated like a feather to the ground. And when I bent over to pick it up, I saw the check and what it had on it, and I instantly became very upset. Because it happened to be one of the checks from the Ferris case that "didn't exist." [Annette means that Alex had denied getting the attorney fees check concerning the Ferris disbursements. He had denied it many times and told them it was being held in a trust at Chris Wilson's firm.]

"It was from Chris Wilson's office. It was written to Richard Alexander Murdaugh, and at the bottom it said Ferris fees, and it was dated March! I said, he's been lying this whole time. He had these funds. That feeling in the back of my mind was correct, because when I flipped the check over, I also saw that he had deposited it by mobile deposit. It has his signature and deposit to Bank of America only.

"I went back to my desk...I called Jeannie and said, 'I just found something.'" Annette went to Jeannie and gave her the check. Jeannie told her that she had just run a report the day before, on September 1st, and one of the attorneys is going to call Michael Gunn today. Jeannie thought there might be other cases such as the Herschberger and Thomas Moore cases. She was finding other issues with stolen funds.

"He was fired the next day," Annette said. "We spent months upon months of going through the files. Lots of manpower of putting everything together. We were in awe at how much had been going on and we had no idea about it." A lot of the checks were ones he had told Annette to have made out to Forge, not Forge Consulting.

PMPED released a statement on Friday, **September 3**, 2021, making sure the public understood why Alex Murdaugh was let go. With the maelstrom about to hit the law firm, it was the first of many volleys on their behalf to assess the blame where it belonged. They wanted the public to understand Richard Alexander Murdaugh was no longer associated with them.

"His resignation came after the discovery by PMPED that Alex misappropriated funds in violation of PMPED standards and policies," the announcement read. "A forensic accounting firm will be retained to conduct a thorough investigation. Law enforcement and the SC Bar have been notified by PMPED. This is disappointing news for all of us. Rest assured that our firm will deal with this in a straightforward manner. There's no place in our firm for such behavior. Due to the ongoing investigations into these matters and client confidentiality, PMPED cannot comment further at this time. We encourage any client with questions to contact our offices regarding their file."

It was a low point for a firm that had begun more than 80 years ago by Alex's great-grandfather, Randolph Murdaugh. The Murdaugh name was represented by the 'M' in the firm's name, PMPED. Their LinkedIn page would now be an embarrassment due to the current situation. It read:

"PMPED's lawyers have served the local communities as solicitor of South Carolina's 14th Judicial Circuit for eighty-six years, and, for over seventy years, represented the members of the Palmetto Electric Cooperative."

On Monday, **September 6**, PMPED's website went dark with only a message stating "This website is temporarily unavailable."

A Confrontation and Gunfire

Chris Wilson, Alex Murdaugh's friend & Co-Counsel.

Alex Murdaugh's carefully constructed network of fraud and lies that he had fought so hard to keep away from the Beach family lawsuit, was now exposed. With each new investigation into Alex's past cases for his law firm, more money was found missing. Many wondered, and still do, how did the accounting office miss this? It would total in the millions of dollars. For Alex, disgraced and realizing he may have killed his family for nothing, he was running for his life. It was about to get worse.

On **September 4**, 2021, the day after Alex was fired from PMPED, his friend and co-counsel on the Ferris case, had reached the end of his rope. Alex still owed him $192,000 dollars that he had covered with his own personal money when Alex needed his firm to see that the Ferris money was still intact. Alex had scraped together $600,000 of what he needed to give back to Chris, but he was still short on the balance. It was D-day in Wilson's mind.

A broken and distraught Chris Wilson took the witness stand during Alex's trial for the double murders of his wife and son. Often breaking down, he looked like someone who had been betrayed at the deepest level. It was his image on the surprise birthday video on Memorial Day weekend hugging Alex fiercely around the neck. That video was taken only a week before the murders.

Chris saw Alex as a brother. He'd known him since High School and went to law school with Alex where they roomed together.

"He was one of my best friends. I thought he felt the same about me." Wilson describes that they went into different law firms but did cases together since 1998.

On **August 17, 2021**, Chris, who had been assured by Alex that everything concerning the Ferris fees had been cleared up with the law firm, wrote out a rudimentary note stipulating that Alex still owed him $192,000. Everyone was worried after the murders of Maggie and Paul, that Alex might want to kill himself. Chris wanted Alex to sign it so if he should do something to himself, his estate would pay the owed money. It was to be paid within 60 days of the signing of this document. Alex signed it.

A few weeks later, **September 3, 2021**, Lee Cope, one of PMPED's attorneys called Wilson and said he needed to know what happened to the Ferris fees. Wilson said it hit him "like a thunderbolt." Alex had told him it had been settled with his firm. When Wilson tried to get hold of him, he dodged him. He finally talked to him that evening. Alex told him he couldn't talk about it right then. Wilson said, "I need to talk to you in person."

Chris recalled what happened on that muggy **September 4th** morning, the day after Alex was fired.

"He said he would meet me at his mom and Daddy's house, late morning. I got there before he did. I waited in the road until he came. We pulled into the driveway. We went in the side door. The caregiver was there. We went out onto the front porch. The first thing I asked him was, 'Alex, what the H is going on here. Have you done something else to me or about me that I don't know about? Because I know about this and I gotta deal with this, but is there something else going on that I need to be concerned with?'

"He broke down crying. He said I can't right this second. He went inside and came back out with some paper towels. He told me he had had a drug problem. That he was addicted to opioids, and that he had been addicted for twenty years or so. He told me he had been stealing money. He told me, 'I shit you up.' He said he had 'shit a lot of people up.'

"I don't remember exactly how the conversation ended, Mr. Waters," Wilson cried on the stand. "I mean, I'd loved the guy for so long, I still love him a little bit, but I was so mad! I left. I mean, I asked him, 'How did I not know these things?' He told me he was concerned about getting me my $192,000 back. I told him I wasn't concerned about that now. I'm sure I raised my voice and hollered, but I didn't when I left. I wasn't happy, but we didn't part fighting or anything. It was sometime around lunchtime. I rode through Hampton, grabbed something at Hardee's and went home to Columbia. I stopped at my office in Bamberg before I got home. I got a call from Lee Cope saying Alex had been shot in the head and was in a helicopter on his way to Savannah."

"I've Been Shot in the Head!"

1:34 p.m., September 4, 2021.

"911, where's your emergency?"
Alex: "I'm on Salkehatchie Road."
911: "Ok, what's the address on Salkehatchie Road?"
Alex: "I'm by the church.'
911: "What church? What church are you talking about?"
Alex: "Uh, I don't know the name of it. With the red roof."
911: "Ooookkk…What end of Salkehatchie Road, cuz I don't know where you're talking about."
Alex: "At the Hampton County side."
911: "Ok, what's goin' on?"
Alex: "I got a flat tire, and I stopped, and somebody stopped to help me, and when I turned my back, they tried to shoot me."
911: "Ohhh, ok, were you shot?"
Alex: "Yes. But I mean, I'm ok…"
911: "You shot where? Where were you shot?"
Alex: [A car can be heard speeding by] "Huh?"

911: "Did they actually shoot you or did they try to shoot you?"

Alex: "They shot me, but…"

911: "Ok, you need EMS?"

Alex: "Well, I mean yes, I can't drive. I can't see and I'm bleedin' a lot."

911: "What part of your body?"

Alex: "I'm not sure…somewhere on my head."

911: "Your head?"

Alex: "Someone just stopped for me, ma'am."

911: "Ok, let me talk to him and see if he can tell me where on Salkehatchie Road…"

Alex can be heard asking someone where they are on Salkehatchie Road. The man goes to see what the name is on the Church marquee.

911: "I'm still here with you. What's your name?"

Alex: "Alex Murdaugh."

911: "Alex Murdaugh? And you say you were driving and got a flat tire, and someone stopped and tried to help you and shot you?"

Alex: "Well, they pulled over, yes, ma'am, like they were going to help me."

Maggie Murdaugh's Mercedes SUV Alex was driving the day he said he got a flat and was shot in the head.

911: "Ok, stay on the line with me and we're going to get somebody…"

911: "Ok, stay on the line with me and we're going to get somebody..."

Alex: "I'm bleedin' pretty bad... St. John Missionary Church," Alex says as the man returns with the name of the church that sits just up the road about ¼ mile, on the same side of the road where Alex's car is found with a flat tire. The church sits in an isolated area with no homes or other buildings around for over a mile. It was a place with little traffic.

St. John's Missionary Church on Old Salkehatchie Road
in Hampton, SC. Alex's car would have been up the road.
in this photo and on the right. Photo by Rebecca F. Pittman.

911: "St. John Missionary Church? Ok, can you give me a description of the man who shot you or shot at you?"

Alex: "Yes, ma'am." Here, he seems to fumble for words. "He was, uh, a white fella, uh, I'd say a fair amount younger than me, really, really short hair. Um...do you have an ambulance comin, ma'am?"

911: "Yes, sir, yes, sir. Stay on the line. I have them on the way."

Alex can be heard saying, "Hey, do you think one of y'all can drive me to the hospital?" A woman is heard saying, "Yes sir, but you might want to get your truck cuz I got a baby in back." "Can one of y'all get in this car and drive me?" "Yes, sir, I can." Alex returns to the 911 operator and says, "They're gonna drive me to the hospital." There is dead air for a few seconds. "Ma'am? Ma'am?"

911: "I'm still here. They're on their way. Don't hang up."
There is nothing more, except a female's voice saying, "I got ya, I got ya." The call is terminated.

Alex's police sketch (L) of the person who shot at him that day. Many armchair sleuths called attention to how much the composite resembles Anthony Cook (R), the boat crash survivor who might have a grudge w/Paul.

The car heard zooming past Alex during his 911 call, also called 911 and said a man was standing on the side of the road with blood all over him, trying to wave them down. They thought it looked staged and did not stop. The 911 operator said, "I don't blame you."

The Good Samaritan loads Alex into her car and is driving down Salkehatchie Road with Alex in the passenger seat who is saying he hoped he didn't get blood on her car. They are met on the road by the EMS team and Alex is airlifted by helicopter to Memorial Health University Medical Center in Savannah, Georgia. SLED later said he was taken there for "treatment of a superficial gunshot wound to the head." T.C. Smalls, the Hampton County Sherriff, and Alex's good friend, asked SLED to take over the case, although he continued to insert himself into it with amended reports.

SLED agents who visited Alex in the hospital said he seemed alert and got out of bed a couple of times. The first of two reports listed the roadside shooting as "an attempted murder," yet the report filed had a box checked that stated, "No visible injury." Sheriff Smalls called it a "clerical error, and a corrected report had been issued." He stood by his friend, saying, "There is a visible injury to his head."

Sheriff Smalls stated that no field sobriety or drug tests had been

371

taken at the scene by law enforcement and went on to say an amended report would show that the boxes checked indicating there was "no alcohol or drugs present in Murdaugh's body" were also a clerical error. Obviously, it was important that people thought Alex was on opioids to back up his upcoming alibi for the mess he was in. He had just confessed to Chris Wilson only an hour before he was "shot" that he was an opioid addict.

Photos would surface, along with hospital records, stating Alex had a superficial head wound that had caused a minor brain bleed, and a fractured skull. According to Alex' faithful attorney, Dick Harpootlian, "there is a definite entrance and exit wound" in the injury.

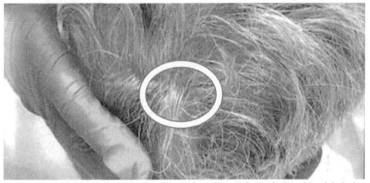

Alex's head wound. A medic is holding his hair back which is stained with blood. The small hole is shallow and red. It is hard to tell if it's a bullet wound or some other injury.

Alex remained in the hospital for two days. At 2:30 in the afternoon of his second day in Savannah, a Murdaugh spokesperson posted this statement:

"The murders of my wife and son have caused an incredibly difficult time in my life. I have made a lot of decisions that I truly regret. I'm resigning from the law firm and entering rehab after a long battle that has been exacerbated by these murders. I am immensely sorry to everyone I've hurt including my family, friends, and colleagues. I ask for prayers as I rehabilitate myself and my relationships."

Alex's brother, Randy, later clarified that it was a drug rehabilitation center.

Chapter Twenty-Five
September's Wrath

The roadside shooting of Alex Murdaugh was just one more twist in an already twisted and convoluted story of deceit. What actually happened on that desolate stretch of road? Alex said he was on his way to Savannah when the incident happened, but all who knew the area said you would not take that road to get to the nearby city of Savannah, Georgia. SLED said in a statement at the time that he was shot on Old Salkehatchie Road near Varnville, South Carolina. He was transported to a hospital in Savannah, Georgia, for "treatment of a superficial gunshot wound to the head."

The family's spokesperson [(Dick Harpootlian) later offered clarification regarding the shooting, saying, "Alex had an entry and exit wound, his skull was fractured. and it was not a self-inflicted bullet wound. Alex pulled over after seeing a low-tire indicator light. A male driver in a blue pickup asked him if he had car troubles, as soon as Alex replied, he was shot."

Meanwhile, Alex's troubles snowballed during the month of September as almost each day brought new headlines. On **September 8, 2021**, Alex's brother, Randy Murdaugh issued a statement. Randy was still employed at PMPED, and knew his name, as well as the firms was under fire. Randy said he was "shocked" to learn of his brother's "settling of money," as well as his "drug addiction."

"I love my law firm family and also love Alex as my brother. While I will support him in his recovery, I do not support, condone, or excuse his conduct in stealing by manipulating his most trusted relationships. I will continue to pursue my client's interests with the highest degree of honesty and integrity, as I always have," he said.

A double whammy came that day when the South Carolina Supreme Court also issued an order suspending Alex Murdaugh's license to practice law in the state.

On **September 13, 2021**, a couple of things went down. SLED announced they would now be looking into the missing money from the law firm. Alex's ticking clock to hide his assets had run out of time. Also on that day, SLED agent Ryan Kelly arranges a phone interview with Alex Murdaugh as his attorneys Dick Harpootlian and Jim Griffin sit in. Agent Kelly first interviewed Alex while he was being treated at Savannah Hospital and Alex gave him his version of events, which was that someone stopped to help him, and when his back was turned, they shot him in the head.

Jim Griffin, Alex's attorney, is the first to chime in as the phone interview begins on September 13. Jim lets Agent Kelly know that he, Alex, and Dick Harpootlian are in an office in Atlanta, Georgia. He lets Kelly know they only have 30 to 40 minutes, and that the two attorneys are in the office to have "a long interview with Alex." Alex is supposedly at a drug treatment clinic at this time. Agent Kelly puts it on the record that they don't normally do telephone interviews but since the attorneys requested it, "we don't have a choice."

Agent Kelly asks Alex, that since he has been receiving treatment, "Are you of sound body and sound mind?" Alex affirms he is and that he is talking to them willingly.

Dick Harpootlian jumps in and says, "We are going to talk about the shooting incident a week ago Saturday, about his being shot in the head and why that happened. We don't want to talk about what happened at Moselle and we don't want to talk about finances and the law firm."

Alex begins by saying he met with Chris Wilson the morning of the shooting, and then admits he has been taking oxycontin for over 20 years. He says on the day of shooting, he had taken some oxycontin, but he had given all he had to someone else. He said he had taken some at 4 a.m., so he was having some withdrawals. Harpootlian leads Alex by doing all the questioning, effectively running the show with what must have been previously structured questions and answers.

Harpootlian recaps that Alex had been fired the day before from his law firm for embezzling funds. "How was your state of mind?" he asks, referring to the day of the roadside shooting.

Alex: "I was in a very bad place. I thought it would be better for me not to be here anymore. I thought that it would make it easier on my family for me to be dead. I had a fair amount of life insurance, um, about $10 or $12 million dollars."

Harpootlian: "And so you decided to end your life?"

Alex: "That's correct."

Harpootlian: "And tell me how you went about, how you went about arranging that."

Alex: "I called Curtis Eddie Smith on the telephone…Curtis Eddie Smith is my primary person I would purchase pills from for years. There would be weeks where there would be $40-$50-$60,000 that I would give him for pills…"

"I called Eddie after I met with Chris Wilson, and asked him to meet me, not too far from my mom's house, at the side of the road at the funeral home. He followed me to the Sunoco gas station in town. I don't think we got out of our cars. I was in my wife's Mercedes, and he was in a grey pick-up truck. I told him that things were getting ready to get really bad and that I would be better off not here. I asked him to shoot me. At first, he was a little surprised, but then he said, "Ok." I told him I wanted him to shoot me in the head. I told him to follow me out and I would make a flat tire, and that he would go past me, and turn around and come back and do it.

Photo of knife found in the weeds Alex used to puncture his car tire.

"I gave him the gun. We stopped somewhere on Salkehatchie Road, I believe, and I gave him the gun. I was worried about cars coming, so it was a very fast thing. I don't think there was much discussion. I gave him a .38 revolver pistol. It was my gun. He followed me to Salkehatchie Road. I stopped, and made my tire flat with a knife, my knife. I threw the knife across the road in the thick grass. The flat was the back driver's side. I think that he'd already passed me, went down the road, and turned around and came back."

Harpootlian: "When you gave him the pistol and he turned around and came back, what was your intent?"

Alex: "For him to kill me. He pulled up and stopped."

Harpootlian: "When he pulled up, did you look in his face?"

Alex: "I don't think so. I went close to his car, and he shot me. He missed and hit me in the very back of the head. I lost my vision for a little bit. I'm not sure if it knocked me to the ground or not. I was disoriented. It took me a minute and a half, two minutes, for my sight to come back. I'm not sure I heard him drive off. I remember there were two cars that came, and one didn't stop. One of them didn't stop, and one of them did stop. They tried to help me. They were crowded in their car. The young lady got in my car and was going to drive me to the hospital. I wasn't thinking about the flat tire. And so, we got out of that. We worked it out somehow for me to get in their car in the front passenger seat. They drove me to meet the ambulance. I called 911."

"My intent was for him to kill me so my son could collect my life insurance. We were about to lose everything, and I figured he was better off that way than living with me." Alex says again Eddie was driving a gray truck. Alex told 911 the shooter was driving a blue truck. Harpootlian asks Alex if he had ever talked to Eddie before about shooting him? "No, sir. When I first asked him, we were at the Sunoco gas station in Varnville. However long it takes to drive to Salkehatchie Road was how long it took for him to shoot me."

Harpootlian: "Did he ever ask you to reconsider…to say 'things aren't that bad…try to convince you to do otherwise?"

Alex: "No, sir."

Harpootlian: "You don't find that strange?"

Alex: "I was focused on…being gone."

Agent Kelly now gets to ask some questions. He asks Alex how long he had known Eddie Smith. Alex stops him, and says, "Officer

Kelly, I just want to apologize to you for lying to you at the hospital. I was in a very bad place.

"I represented Curtis once. He knew my dad from playing softball. He came to my dad with a lawsuit, and I handled that case, so I would guess 10 or 12 years. We talked on the phone very frequently about getting pills. I paid him money to get me pills. I paid him frequently. It varied sometimes but usually several times a week. I paid in cash but mostly checks. The vast majority of them would come from the Bank of America account and some from Palmetto Bank." He tells them about the two accounts at Bank of America, including his dba as Forge.

Kelly: "Did he tell you where he was getting the drugs from?"

Alex: "No, sir."

Jim Griffin stops him, saying, 'Alex…' (It was a warning to tell the truth, all of it.)

Alex: "Oh, I was told he was getting them from a black fella in Walterboro and he had some connection in Beaufort. I never saw those guys, I never dealt with those guys…that's what he told me."

Kelly: "Who else did you give money to for drug?"

Alex: "I gave money to Kenny Hughes. He's a guy that I called up and asked him if he knew of anybody, I could buy pills from. I told him that I had a client who had issues and couldn't get them medically and I would pay him as well. I have no idea how much I gave him. It was cash and checks. It was just Curtis Smith and Kenny Hughes."

Jim Griffin again catches Alex, and says, "Think about it."

Alex: "Oh ok, in the past I have paid other people. I have a lady that worked at our mom's house that I paid…Barbara Mixon, but that was on very few occasions. I'm not sure how I paid her. It was on very limited occasions. I can't think of others right now."

Kelly: "Where did you get the .38 revolver from?"

Alex: "It was at my mom's house. I got it when I went up there that day. I don't know what Curtis did with it."

Kelly: "Has anyone in your family talked to Curtis lately?"

Alex: "I'm not sure, why?" (There is a sharp tone when Alex says, 'Why?')

Kelly: "When we went to talk to Curtis, he wanted an attorney, and he listed you. We told him that's not possible, so he listed Randy. I'm just trying to figure out why."

Alex: "Randy is not going to represent him." (He is sounding more defensive.) Jim Griffin goes to say something, but Kelly raises his voice and hurries on.

Kelly: "I've got one more question. Does Randy have any knowledge of this? Of this attempted suicide/agreement with Curtis?"

Alex: "I told both my brothers and my son yesterday after I knew I'd be talking to you. I wanted them to hear it first. Randy had no knowledge of this. I lied to him too."

Jim Griffin tells Kelly that they told Alex's family around 4 in the afternoon the previous day.

Harpootlian asks Alex: "Here's the important thing—since the shooting, have you talked to the shooter?"

Alex: "Yes. I don't remember what I talked to him about because I had just started detox."

Kelly: "From the hospital?"

Alex: "No, from detox here."

According to Agent Kelly's testimony during the murder trial, Alex did call Eddy from the hospital using a staff member's phone. Once again, Jim Griffin tries to do damage control, and asks Alex, "Are you sure you didn't call him from the hospital, using a nurse's phone? I thought I heard that."

Alex: "Maybe I did do that. Randy said that I called him, and he asked me…Randy did say that I did that. I don't remember phoning Curtis, but I will tell you from past experiences, that when withdrawals start, you will do just about anything to make them quit. I was probably calling him for that purpose. For pills."

(That's a very convenient reason to be trying to get Curtis Eddie Smith instead of the real reason which was to cover his butt and get Eddie to match stories on the roadside shooting.)

Kelly clarifies that the *last* time Alex saw the gun, it was in Eddie Smith's possession.

Alex: "I gave it to him, yes, sir."

(If Eddie shot him in the head and took off, did Alex never see the gun after he handed it to Eddie earlier on the road before he pulled over and flattened his tire? It seemed odd.) Alex repeats that he does not know where it is.

When Kelly reiterates Alex's bank account information and that he was writing checks out to Eddie from those accounts for drugs, he steps into the red zone.

Kelly: "And where did that money come from?"

Harpootlian: "We don't want to get into that. But let's just say the funds were not legitimately obtained."

Kelly: "Ok, I'm not trying to be coy. It's just that Mr. Murdaugh is independently wealthy."

Harpootlian: "Not anymore."

Kelly: "Did you pay Curtis any money for this?" (The shooting)

Alex: "No, sir."

He just did it as a favor.

Kelly: "When was the last time you made a payment to Curtis? Would it have been before the shooting?"

Alex: "It would have been...uh...I mean not like right before the shooting...I mean...several days. The last few times I paid him, it was all in checks."

Kelly: "Do you owe any drug dealers?"

Alex: "No, sir."

Kelly: "So there's not a threat out there we need to worry about?"

Alex: "No, sir."

Kelly: "I got to be honest with you, that doesn't make any sense to me" that Alex didn't pay Eddie any money to shoot him.

Alex: "I understand."

Kelly: "Who is the policy with? Where's the policy at?"

Alex: "I don't know exactly where the actual policy is."

Kelly: "Did you intend to have that paperwork with you in the Mercedes...the will and all that, was that left in there intentionally?"

Alex: "I'd been down to meet with some lawyers about some things, and it was in there from that...Buster's girlfriend's employers, Kathy Alavetti...just to get things cleaned up. I did that with Annette before."

Harpootlian chimes in and says that if you've had a policy for two years, the suicide clause does not apply. He may have thought it would be a problem, so he needed someone to shoot him so that it didn't look like a suicide attempt.

Alex now says that Curtis Eddie Smith gave him the knife that he used to slash his tire. Earlier, he had said it was his knife. Alex said he punctured the tire with the knife. And then he threw it across the

379

road from where the Mercedes was parked. Alex says the gun used should be registered to him. He doesn't remember where or when he purchased it.

Alex is asked if he's had any dealings with Eddie's friends or girlfriend. Alex admits he knows Eddie's girlfriend, Donna Eastman. He said he helped her with some little legal issues over the years. He said she didn't help with the pills.

Kelly: "Do you own any property in Eugie? Up 41."

Alex: "Outside Charleston? Yes, Sir. There's a piece of property that I own with a bunch of other people that nobody else, um, would pay, and so, I've been paying for it, and, um, he did some work up there digging some ditches. (Eddie) He started within the last couple of months. It's off United Road, United Drive, I think it's called... Redbeard and Zero Union Drive." [Redbeard and Zero Union are the names of two of Alex's LLCs.]

Kelly: "So, you communicate with Smith by cell phone?"

Alex: (pausing) "Uh, yes."

Kelly: "How many phones do you have, Alex?"

Alex: "I have one phone. 1227 was my primary phone, and then, um...

Jim Griffin jumps in and tells Ryan that he had to take that phone and turn it in to have it downloaded, and that he got Alex a different phone." Y'all seized both of those, if I remember."

Kelly: "Ok, and so he got a third phone prior to going to the treatment center?"

Jim: "Yes, from Walmart. It's a burner phone."

Kelly: "What's your expected treatment time there in Alpharetta?"

Harpootlian: "It's unclear right now, but he'll go for periods at rehab..."

Kelly asks Alex again if Curtis tried to talk him out of it. Alex answers 'No.' Kelly asks if anybody else was told about it. Alex says the first time was yesterday, because he'd been really sick and yesterday was the first time he could think clearly.

Kelly: "You're right-handed, correct? And you did not shoot yourself?"

Alex: "I'm right-handed, and I did not shoot myself."

Kelly asks Alex when did Eddie give him the knife. Alex says, "I think I got it from him when I gave him the gun.

"When you turned your back to him, about how far away were you from the car?"

Alex: "I don't know. About four or five feet." Alex says he just stood there and waited for Eddie to shoot him. He fired once. Alex says he's not clear if he stumbled off or fell. He says he is sure he lost his vision for a minute and a half to two minutes.

Alex tells Kelly he has no reason for lying to them at the hospital, except he "was in a bad, bad, bad place."

The interview ended. Eddie's version was that Alex called him from Salkehatchie and said he needed help. Eddie was Alex's go-to guy for a lot of things. According to Eddie, he didn't question it. He just went. He said when he pulled up in his truck, Alex jumped out of the Mercedes waving a gun, and said he wanted Eddie to shoot him. Eddie said he was shocked and jumped out of the truck trying to reason with Alex. Alex turned his back and Eddie grabbed the gun and twisted Alex's arm behind his back. When he took the gun from him, it went off. He said he was scared and took the gun and jumped back into his truck and sped away. According to Eddie, he said, "There was no blood on me. There was no blood on him. If I had wanted to shoot him, he'd be dead. He's alive."

When interviewed later, a very emotional Eddie Smith said he felt betrayed by Alex's story. He said he thought of Alex like a brother. Chris Wilson had said the same thing and Alex stole from him and set him up.

St. Joseph's church surveillance camera faces Salkehatchie Road. When its video from that day was taken by SLED, it showed Eddie's truck zooming by, followed quickly by Alex's Mercedes. A few minutes later, Eddie's truck is seen heading back by the church in the opposite direction. Alex did say Eddie passed him; he may have meant as they drove down Salkehatchie for whatever transpired there after Alex pulled over.

St. Joseph's video showing Alex's car and Eddie's truck going by. In the actual video, you see Eddie's truck (which appears blue, not gray) going first, with Alex behind him.

SLED moved quickly after the phone interview with Alex on September 13. The following day, **September 14, 2021**, SLED announced the arrest of Curtis Edward Smith, 61, in connection with the shooting incident involving Alex Murdaugh on Sept. 4th in Hampton County. Smith was charged with assisted suicide, assault and battery of a high aggravated nature, pointing and presenting a firearm, insurance fraud and conspiracy to commit insurance fraud.

Agents had spread out in an attempt to find the .38 revolver that had been used in the shooting. Smith stubbornly said he had "gotten rid of it," and that's all they could get out of him about the location of the gun. There were so many rivers, inlets, swamps, and forest areas, that it was looking for a needle in a haystack. He'd had 10 days to get rid of the gun before he was taken into custody.

The following day, **September 15**, Alex's dream team put their own spin on the story. "Alex Murdaugh enlisted Curtis Smith to shoot and kill him while in his mentally ill, drug addicted, and grieving state," Murdaugh's attorneys Jim Griffin and Dick Harpootlian said in a statement on Sept. 15, a day after Smith was charged.

"On September 4, it became clear Alex believed that ending his life was his only option. Today, he knows that's not true. For the last 20 years, there have been many people feeding his addiction to opioids. During that time, these individuals took advantage of his addiction and his ability to pay substantial funds for illegal drugs. One of those individuals took advantage of his mental illness and agreed to take Alex's life, by shooting him in the head," the statement said.

"Fortunately, Alex was not killed by the gunshot wound. Alex is fully cooperating with SLED in their investigations into his shooting, opioid use, and the search to find the person or people responsible for the murder of his wife and son. Alex is not without fault, but he is just one of many whose life has been devastated by opioid addiction," the lawyers' statement continued.

As more bad news hit that day, Alex's attorneys must have felt like they were the plate spinning act in a circus. They had to keep all the plates spinning atop slender wooden rods before one could stop spinning and crash to the floor.

The old spinning plate act.

Before Alex's dream team could catch their breath, news broke about the fraud Alex had perpetrated on his ex-housekeeper's sons. According to *ABC 7*:

Also on Sept. 15, the sons of a former Murdaugh housekeeper, Gloria Satterfield, filed a lawsuit against Alex Murdaugh, Corey Fleming, and others for allegedly swindling them out of receiving settlement money.

Satterfield reportedly died after a falling accident in the Murdaugh family home in February 2018, the lawsuit states. In the civil lawsuit, Satterfield's surviving sons claimed Alex Murdaugh approached them after she died, proposing the sons sue him so they would get a life insurance settlement on their mother's behalf, the complaint states.

The court papers said that Murdaugh personally introduced them to fellow attorney Corey Fleming with the recommendation that Fleming should represent them "in filing legal claims against Murdaugh for the wrongful death of their mother." The alleged conspiracy led to a $505,000 settlement, but Satterfield's sons claim they haven't gotten any of that settlement money, which was agreed upon in December 2018, the lawsuit claimed.

SLED then said they were opening the investigation into Satterfield's death at the request of the Hampton County Coroner's Office and due to information gathered during the course of other ongoing investigations involving Alex Murdaugh.

The ghost of Gloria Satterfield's "trip and fall accident" was coming back to haunt him. Thanks primarily to Deputy Coroner Angie Toppers letter to SLED at the time of Gloria's death, stating basically, as they say in South Carolina, "Something in the milk ain't clean."

Alex is Arrested

The next day, **September 16, 2021**, the first of Alex Murdaugh's arrests took place. He turned himself to the Hampton County Detention Center. It had been a swift fall once he admitted to conspiring with Smith to an attempted roadside suicide scheme.

He was arrested in connection to the Sept. 4th shooting incident "in which he conspired with Curtis Edward Smith to assist him in committing suicide for the explicit purpose of allowing a beneficiary to collect life insurance," SLED said in a statement.

The affidavit said Murdaugh provided a statement to SLED on Sept. 13: "Admitting to the scheme ... for the purpose of his son collecting a life insurance policy valued at approximately $10 million." A day later, Smith admitted to being present during the Murdaugh shooting and disposing the firearm afterward. Murdaugh was charged with insurance fraud, conspiracy to commit insurance fraud, along with filing a false police report. The case will be prosecuted by the attorney general's office.

"I can assure you that SLED agents will continue working to bring justice to anyone involved with any criminal act associated with these ongoing investigations," said SLED Chief Mark Keel. "The arrests in this case are only the first step in that process."

Alex Murdaugh is arrested on Sept. 16, 2021. Photo courtesy of *The Daily Mail.*

It is apparent in the police photo above that Alex had lost a great deal of weight since the murders of his wife and son three months earlier. Many studied the back of his head as he sat for his bond hearing, trying to find where the bullet wound had been. Only an odd part in his hair seemed to be present. In a bond hearing in Hampton County court on Thursday, **Sept. 18.** Alex Murdaugh was ordered held on a $20,000 personal recognizance bond. Murdaugh will return to rehab, according to his attorney, and will change to an out-of-state rehab facility afterwards. If he leaves the rehab facility, there will be a bench warrant issued for his arrest, Judge Tonja Alexander said. Alex ended up at a rehab center in Orlando, Florida.

Earlier on **Sept. 16**, Curtis Edward Smith appeared in front of a Hampton County judge for a bond hearing on charges where he agreed to a having a public defender represent him. His bond was set at $55,000 for the attempted assisted suicide of Alex Murdaugh. His next hearing was set for Oct. 25, 2021.

Eddie Smith at his bond hearing. Photo courtesy of *The Daily Mail.*

Chapter Twenty-Five
Goliath Has Fallen

If Alex Murdaugh thought he was safe while hiding out in Orlando, Florida at a rehabilitation center, he was unaware of the wheels turning in the investigations into his many crimes. PMPED was continuing to find fraudulent settlements and stolen money. It was beginning to feel like the well of theft and deceit Alex Murdaugh had created was bottomless. One insurance fraud case in particular came roaring back like the mud wheels of a Ranger.

On **October 14, 2021**, as Alex was exiting the Florida Rehabilitation Center at which he'd been hiding, he was arrested in the parking lot on charges that he stole insurance settlements totaling more than $4 million intended for the sons of his longtime housekeeper, Gloria Satterfield. The boys had received not one red dime of the money Alex promised them as he stood as their friend and savior at their mother's funeral. Instead of rescuing them from the sudden loss of their mother and her income, he assured them the insurance case was progressing as they begged him for money for Satterfield's medical bill and to keep a trailer roof over their heads. They lost their home as Alex used the money to enhance his own affluent lifestyle.

There would be no cushy rehab clinic with zen music and decent food. Richard Alexander Murdaugh was now in a dingy cell with the ever-present sounds of clanging bars and angry inmates as his meditation background. He was probably nonplussed, figuring it was a temporary stint until he could get bond again. He was in for a surprise.

Judge Clifton Newman began his long and harried journey that day as he sat over Alex's bond hearing in what would become a long relationship with Murdaugh. The judge listened to the prosecutors stating that not only did Alex have to have money hidden away somewhere, making him a flight risk, but that this was just the tipping point in the insurance fraud schemes. To ice the cake, a SLED agent stepped forward and told the judge there were other deaths they were investigating that could implicate Murdaugh. He was referring to the mysterious death of Stephen Smith in 2015, and the newly reopened investigation into the mysterious fall and consequential death of Gloria Satterfield.

Judge Newman, in his calm, yet no-nonsense manner, made his ruling. No bond! A hush went over the spectators. Had a judge really just denied bond to a Murdaugh? Not only that, but he ordered Alex to undergo a psychiatric evaluation. It was a one-two punch that sent Alex back to jail and immediately dialing the family to mitigate the repercussions.

On **October 28, 2021**, Randy Murdaugh, Alex's own brother, sued him for $46,500 Alex owed him. John E. Parker, Alex's former friend and law partner, sued him for $477,000 of borrowed funds. It was a smart call that any attorney worth his shingle would know how to do. With lawsuits guaranteed to be coming down the pike, the first horse to the trough gets to drink. In other words, they wanted to be near the front of the line when the payouts were made by their former brother and friend.

In a plethora of recorded jailhouse phone calls, Alex tells Buster and John Marvin to sell anything they can. Sometimes couching the words in careful language, he got his message across that they needed to take action fast.

The calls did not go without notice. On **November 2, 2021,** Judge Newman ordered Murdaugh's assets frozen. He appointed two receivers who would oversee any purchases or financial maneuvering. Buster would have to ask for his rent money, and anything else he needed. Alex was furious, filling his daily phone calls to his surviving son with diatribes against the unfairness of it all. Buster was not exactly bursting with happiness either. John Marvin tried to be the voice of reason, begging Alex not to cash in his 401K, as it was the only financial security he had left.

November 17, 2021, brought more bad news for Alex. Prosecutors revealed 27 new charges against him. His total for stealing from clients was climbing. They now had him at $5 million in stolen settlement money. That number would double before the dust settled. Prosecutors alleged Murdaugh was hiding money from the lawyers who sued him over the death of Mallory Beach. The mantra, "Where is all the money?" would follow him into 2023 and beyond. Many believed he had offshore accounts, or that it was hidden on one of many vast Murdaugh properties, or on one of his islands, or it was tied up in drug running. Whatever he did with the millions, it was the only secret he had that did not eventually surface, as of the time of this writing.

Additional indictments against Alex were filed on **January 18, 2022.** The new year brought only more bad news for the disgraced attorney. He was now facing 71 charges and his tally was up to $8.7 million in stolen money from more than a dozen former clients and victims.

In March, the Satterfield case heated up as the gavel came down on others involved in the fraudulent lawsuit Alex instigated on behalf of Gloria's sons. Alex had involved a longtime friend, and Paul Murdaugh's godfather, Corey Fleming in the scheme. Fleming was the attorney brought on board to sue Alex on behalf of the Satterfield boys in an effort to cash in on Alex's property insurances. It worked. Both insurance companies paid out to the tune of over $4 million. But the boys never got any of the money. Fleming got a cut of the payouts. And so, on **March 16, 2022**, Corey Fleming was indicted for insurance fraud in that same case.

Fleming wasn't the only fly in Alex's web of fraud. He also pulled in his good buddy Russell Lafitte, the CEO of Palmetto State Bank in the Lowcountry. Lafitte was eventually fired from his own family-run bank when Alex's plots came to life. He was indicted on **May 4, 2022,** on charges that he conspired with Murdaugh to defraud victims of $1.8 million. One of the victims was the family of a deaf man who became a quadriplegic after a car crash: Hakeem Pinckney.

On **May 4, 2022**, Lisa Weismann with *Channel 5 News* out of Charleston published an article listing assets and equipment being sold off by Buster Murdaugh, who was acting at the time as Alex's power of attorney, shortly after Alex was arrested at the Orlando, Florida rehab facility.

CHARLESTON, S.C. (WCSC) - Assets belonging to prominent Lowcountry attorney Alex Murdaugh were recently sold with the money applied to loans and medical bills associated with his opioid addiction treatment.

A court filing states Murdaugh's brother, John Murdaugh, assisted Alex Murdaugh's son, Buster, in the sale of more than $700,000 of assets. Heavy machinery and equipment, totaling $171,500, were sold to buyers, including Alex Murdaugh's brother, Randy, to whom Alex was indebted to the tune of $75,000. Some proceeds were earmarked for Sunrise Rehab facility in Orlando, where Murdaugh received treatment for opioid addiction.

Murdaugh's share of Green Swamp Hunting Club was sold for $250,000. Real estate website Lands of America describes the club as a 7,000-acre plot of land in Jasper County.

A stake in "2TI" island was sold for $30,000, and an equity buy-out from his former law firm's building and property totaled more than $188,000.

The court filing is part of a lawsuit filed by the mother of Mallory Beach, who was killed in a boat crash in 2019.

After the murders, Maggie's estate was in the crosshairs. While both Edisto Beach and Moselle had been put into her name, when she died, those properties reverted to Alex as witnessed by her will. From jail, he maneuvered to sell the properties for some much-needed cash. Buster was given just enough to live on until the two properties could be put up for sale. In jail house phone calls to his brother John Marvin, Alex pushed him to hurry and sell off the farm equipment and other assets from Moselle before it was all seized by the courts to repay the victims of his fraud cases and to satisfy any of the Beach family's lawsuit. There were rumors that Moselle's heavy equipment, loaded onto flatbeds, roared up the road through Varnville shortly after the murders. Many believed John Marvin facilitated that convoy as he owned heavy equipment rental companies and would have the conveyance methods at hand.

As the one-year anniversary of the murders of Maggie and Paul neared, that humid 2022 summer, more indictments against Alex made headlines. On **June 28, 2022**, prosecutors outlined an 8-year money laundering and painkiller ring in in new indictments. Alex

Murdaugh and Curtis Eddie Smith were charged with possessing, manufacturing, or distributing narcotics. The word manufacturing is interesting. Were Alex and Eddie running their own backcountry pharmacy, brandishing a mortar and pestle? Of course, the word manufacturing could have been included as a catch-all, just in case.

On **July 12, 2022**, the ultimate humiliation and disgrace came down on Alex Murdaugh's head in the form of a formal disbarment. The South Carolina Supreme Court tore up his hard-won credentials and placed a permanent scar on the legacy his great-grandfather had begun 87 years prior. It was a fall worthy of Goliath, and the resounding crash was heard far and wide.

The disbarment was not to be the only unbelievable news handed out that day. Alex's attorney, Jim Griffin announced that investigators had told Alex's family members that they plan to pursue murder charges against Murdaugh for his wife and son. The Palmetto State was rocked to its core. Yes, he was the worst of the worst, a liar, a fraud, and an embezzler, but could he really blow the brains out of his wife and youngest son?

The answer to part of that question came shortly after this announcement was made. On **July 14, 2022**, Richard Alexander Murdaugh was officially charged with murder in the deaths of Maggie and Paul Murdaugh. The Grand Jury handed down the four indictments: one each for the murder of Paul and Maggie; and one indictment for killing Maggie with a rifle, and one for killing Paul with a shotgun.

Alex Murdaugh, with a shaved head, pleads, "Not Guilty" to the charges of murder of his wife and son. Photo courtesy of *Court TV*.

With the murder charges now in place, Prosecutors Creighton Waters and Attorney General Alan Wilson went into a full court press. Alex had his formal arraignment and pleaded "Not Guilty." When asked by Waters, "How shall you be judged?" Alex gave the age-old answer, "By God and my country." In the end, he would be judged by a jury of 12, and an international audience of millions.

November 22, 2022, Russell Lafitte, Alex's friend and accomplice in many of the fraudulent settlement schemes, was found guilty by a federal jury. The former CEO of Palmetto State Bank, whom prosecutors accused of conspiring with Alex Murdaugh was found guilty on all six charges. Each charge held a sentence of up to 30 years in prison and a $1 million fine. The charges are:

1. One count of conspiracy to commit wire fraud/bank fraud.
2. One count of bank fraud and aiding and abetting bank fraud.
3. Wire fraud and the aiding and abetting of wire fraud.

4-6. Misapplication of bank funds and aiding and abetting misapplication of bank funds.

The fifth charge alleged that Lafitte extended a $750,000 loan to Murdaugh for the Edisto Beach house renovations without proper collateral and knowing the money was used for other means. As of March 6, 2023, Russell Lafitte had yet to be sentenced. His appeals for a new trail have been denied. He is under house arrest at this time.

Russell Lafitte leaving court during his trial.

Chapter Twenty-Seven
Hollywood Comes to Walterboro

The Murdaugh saga and the myriad scandals that surrounded that name, would continue on as each day seemed to bring "Breaking News!" Curtis Eddie Smith made headlines with his array of creative ways of bringing in revenue. He was charged with multiple crimes, including four counts of money laundering, three counts of forgery, trafficking methamphetamine 10-29 grams, one count of unlawful possession of marijuana, and two counts of criminal conspiracy. The criminal conspiracy was his duplicity in helping his good buddy Alex try to shoot himself.

Judge Newman originally set bond in June of 2022, but revoked it in August after prosecutors accused Smith of violating his house arrest and misrepresenting how much money he had at a prior bond hearing. Prosecuting attorney Creighton Waters, the bulldog who was the protagonist in Alex Murdaugh's undoing, stood before Judge Newman and asked him to revoke Smith's bond. The request was based on repeated house arrest violations and also on lying about his finances.

Newman had set Eddie's bond for $250,000 with conditions of house arrest, GPS monitoring, and drug testing after Smith was indicted by a grand jury in June. He was released from jail on July 5th, after making bail. The non-repentant Eddie quickly eradicated all the constrictions of his bond agreement and got back to business. According to Water's filing, the GPS data for Smith shows he broke the terms of his house arrest 26 times during his first two weeks of freedom, beginning just hours after his release from jail. He first went to an unauthorized private residence.

Waters also cited the GPS data shows Smith visited seven total private residences in Colleton County on nine occasions during the first 14 days out of jail. He made repeat visits to Meadow Street in Walterboro and the areas of Clydeville Road and Junkyard Road in Cottageville. The tracking also showed Smith made 10 unauthorized trips to the Dorchester Biomass power plant in Harleyville on three different days at odd times. Five of those visits happened in the early morning hours between 1 a.m. and 5 a.m. When questioned about those stops, Smith said he made "deliveries" there and they were open at all hours.

Other of Eddie's routes found him at Fort Jackson military base in Columbia, and local stores in Colleton County. It would appear that Eddie racked up the mileage as he scurried around like the Energizer Bunny immediately upon exiting the detention center.

Waters also wanted Smith's bond revoked because he said Smith lied about his finances when he said in court, "I ain't got no money." According to Waters, Smith had more than $58,000 in the bank at that moment. Smith had apparently gotten a $78,000 insurance settlement three weeks earlier.

And so, back to jail Eddie went, and where he remained for 265 days, until April 5, 2023, following the double trial of Maggie and Paul. He was granted a new bond set at $250,000 with conditions of house arrest, GPS monitoring, and drug testing. Perhaps it was a ploy to tail Eddie and see where he would go now, as the State was still looking for where Alex hid all those millions. Eddie Smith reportedly received in excess of $2.8 million from Alex over the years. Those payments escalated in the months leading up to the double murders, with Alex paying Eddie $160,000 between October 2020 and May of 2021. The murders were June 7, 2021. If anyone knew where all that money went, the State was probably hoping Eddie would know, and perhaps lead them to it.

Motions and hearings concerning Alex Murdaugh would fill Judge Newman's dance card as the prosecution team prepared for the trial of the century, at least where South Carolina was concerned. Waters outlined to Judge Newman in a motion's hearing his reasoning for including Alex's financial crimes as a means to prove motive in the upcoming double murder case. This was hotly disputed by Alex' attorneys, Jim Griffin and Dick Harpootlian as a violation of Alex's rights under the 401 ruling.

A 401 objection means the court may exclude relevant evidence if its probative value is substantially outweighed by a danger of one or more of the following: unfair prejudice, confusing the issues, misleading the jury, undue delay, wasting time, or needlessly presenting cumulative evidence.

Alex's legal team clearly did not want all of Alex's insurance frauds introduced as evidence as it would not be great optics for their client. He had lied, stolen, left families and friends destitute, and showed the world there was nothing he would not stop at to save his own skin and way of life. The State wanted it introduced to show exactly that: this man would screw over anyone, and with the boat crash motion hearing looming only three days after the murders, where all those financial crimes and ill-gotten gains would be revealed, he was capable of murder to delay that happening.

Judge Newman said he would percolate on it. At the beginning of the murder trial, he finally gave his ruling: he was allowing it in. It took a good portion of the morning to cover his decision and the objections from Alex's team, but in the end, Creighton Waters and his legal convoy of attorneys won, and that convoy was about to roll all over Alex Murdaugh.

Lights, Camera, Action!

Walterboro, South Carolina is a sleepy bedroom community that also serves as the county seat of Colleton County. It is located 48 miles from the metropolitan city of Charleston, and a mere 20 minutes from the double murder scene at Moselle. The house and kennels at Moselle fell on the Colleton County side of the map, while other parts of that sprawling 1,700 acreages fell inside Hampton County. The site of the murders was left to Colleton County's jurisdiction, and hence, the courthouse in Walterboro was chosen as the location of the South Carolina vs Richard Alex Murdaugh murder trial.

With a population hovering around 6,000, Walterboro had been the location of the Walterboro Army Airfield and served as a training ground for Army airmen, including a group of Tuskegee Airmen, during World War III. In May 1977, a monument honoring their bravery was placed at that site. It was also the site of a POW camp and base hospital.

Walterboro's logo was The Front Porch of the Lowcountry. Filled with BBQ restaurants, sweet tea, a museum, boutique shops, southern architecture, parks, and flowers, it was an Andy Griffith setting. It was not the kind of place you would associate with drug running. Yet drug gangs were said to dominate the area due to the proximity of I-95 that ran from the bottom of Florida all the way up into Maine. It made the small, unassuming town a perfect drop-off and pick-up spot. Throughout the televised 6-week trial of Alex Murdaugh, one can hear sirens daily zooming past the courthouse. Testimony was often stopped to allow the cacophony of noise to pass. It seemed an odd juxtaposition to this otherwise southern hamlet.

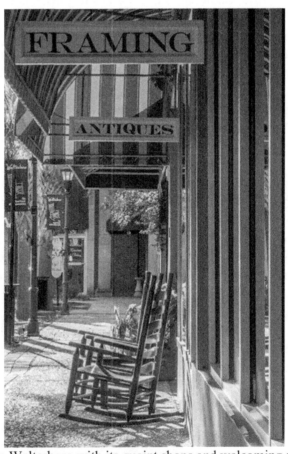

Downtown Walterboro with its quaint shops and welcoming rockers.

In the early months of 2023, Walterboro was going to need more rocking chairs. As more and more headlines spread throughout the United States and across the ocean to other continents, what started as a local hushed-up event with the death of Stephen Smith, made the evening news, podcasts, newspaper headlines, and radio broadcasts on almost a daily basis. Each network vied with the other for Breaking News. Documentaries, which began in the previous year, rolled out under the influential helmsmanship of *Dateline, CNN, Netflix, 48 Hours,* and *HBO.* By the time of the double murder trial, which began January 28, 2023, it was hard to find a U.S. citizen that didn't know a little something about the Murdaugh scandals and suspected murders. The fear was that finding an untainted jury pool would be a trick worthy of Houdini.

Colleton County Courthouse, Walterboro. Photo courtesy of AP.

Front stage and center of this worldwide spotlight was the Colleton Courthouse in downtown Walterboro. It is an imposing edifice, with a double horseshoe staircase leading to the upper gallery and main courtroom. The original section of the courthouse was completed in 1822. While additions and renovations continued throughout the years, it was clear during the televised trial that it was an old building. The TV cameras were trained on the state seal on the back wall behind the judge's bench when the court was not in session. One watching the tube (or cell phone, laptop, or computer) would get a small hint when Judge Newman's clerk, followed by the judge himself, stepped up onto the dais. The camera's feed would shake ever so slightly due to the age of the room. Within a few minutes, the camera would swing away from the seal, and Judge Newman's calm and benevolent grin would signal the beginning of a new session.

Judge Newman sitting before the SC state seal during the Murdaugh murder trial. Photo courtesy of the *San Diego Union-Tribune.*

Walterboro looked at the international interest in the trial, and the crowds of people expected to descend on their fair city, and thought, "What the heck are we going to with all of them? Where will the gallery go to eat at the lunch recess?" The city officials knew Walterboro didn't have nearly enough dining accommodations for the waves of people expected to pour in for the Murdaugh trial. The trial would not only draw hundreds of the curious public, but the media blitz expected to camp outside the courthouse would be formidable. They would need to eat too.

The solution for filling all those bellies? Food trucks. It was a controversial move from the beginning with many complaining it was literally a murder trial hawking burgers. In the end, the food trucks won out. They would offer a variety of Southern comfort foods such as barbecue and mac and cheese. New spins on classics, like a barbecue parfait – a stacked cup of pulled pork, baked beans and coleslaw – also were on the menu. With the temperatures fluctuating from thunderstorms to knee-buckling heat, the cold drinks went 'like hotcakes,' according to one purveyor of sodas.

It was hard to argue that the food trucks were a pragmatic move. Only three of the city's five restaurants serve lunch. "And those three restaurants wouldn't have the capacity to handle the volume of people coming out of the courthouse during lunch breaks," said Scott Grooms, Walterboro's director of tourism and downtown development.

According to the *Carolina News and Reporter* newspaper, Grooms went on to say, "Now, 120 people plus are getting out at 1:10, and they've got to be back in by 1:30 or 2:30 or whenever it's going to be," Grooms said. "(Walterboro) can't do that."

To tackle the problem, Grooms sent out a call on Facebook for food truck owners across the state to come and help. These purveyors of tasty delights had to get a business license from the city. The application process only took five minutes, according to "Ms. Mikki," the owner of Mamma Mikki's food truck. She said she was one of the first ones to respond to Walterboro's post. Those who have eaten at the trucks appreciated Mamma Mikki's presence, with one passerby saying that she served "the best burger I've had in a long time."

The trucks are rotated in and out to allow many vendors to take part. Half of the trucks were from Walterboro. The others came from nearby towns like Bluffton, Estill and Moncks Corner.

Near the food trucks, lined up with colorful outdoor canopy tents, was the media. Thousands upon thousands of dollars in broadcasting equipment was protected with the shade of the tents when not in a reporters and cameramen's 'hands as they sprinted across the courthouse lawn to capture a prized interview with a departing attorney, witness, or promising attendee. The trial launched a bevy of new faces that would become household names as many attorneys tied to the Murdaugh saga were interviewed by *Court TV, Law &*

Crime, FitsNews, local TV outlets, *Fox Nation,* and more. They offered their opinions on the day's testimony and opined on a possible verdict. Nancy Grace with *Fox Nation* was in attendance in the courtroom on numerous occasions, at one point sitting directly behind the Murdaugh family's bench. She gave her commentary with an insider's view of the case.

Nancy Grace at the Alex Murdaugh Murder Trial.
Photo courtesy of Yahoo News.

While cash registers were ringing at Walterboro hotels and Bed and Breakfasts, the local boutiques and tourist sites fared equally well. Many of the spectators from out-of-state took the opportunity to spill over into Hampton and visit the gravesites of Maggie and Paul Murdaugh, Stephen Smith, Mallory Beach, and Gloria Satterfield. Locals were asked for inside information. One gas station attendant reported a woman accosted him for 15 minutes demanding details of the brutal murders that had occurred a short drive from his business. "How would I know what happened?" he stated haplessly. "Good grief, this town will be forever associated with those murders. We used to be known for our Watermelon Festival."

Anyone who had face time on documentaries, news channels, podcasts, etc. was hunted down by the visiting media, hoping to get new details and garner viewership. My friend Susanne Andrews, who founded Standing for Stephen, was even approached by a correspondent from France for *Vanity Fair*. As the trial neared, many residents of the Lowcountry hunkered down, as though an impending hurricane was on the horizon. For many connected with the trial, it would be just that.

Crowds lined up at the Colleton County Courthouse each morning, hoping to get a coveted ticket with a number allowing them a seat in the gallery. Only a certain number were allowed in each day. As some gallery spectators left, others were allowed in to fill their seats. Media, family members, and legal players were given precedent, including SLED agents who were seen on front rows throughout the trial. Journalists, authors, and newscasters scribbled madly, as no cell phones or recording devices were allowed during the trial.

Crowds lining up each day outside the courthouse during
the Murdaugh murder trial.

An interesting factoid was the antics of the Murdaugh family members. Initially, the family of Alex Murdaugh, which included his son Buster and his girlfriend Brooke, Alex's sister Lynn, Lynn's daughter, and Alex's brother John Marvin were seated on row three behind Alex's defense table. They were there daily throughout the 6-week-long trial. Occasionally, John Marvin's wife Liz would join him. Randy Murdaugh made an appearance three or four times, usually during the testimony of members of his law firm. He was noticeably absent during the verdict reading and sentencing of his brother. As the trial progressed, it was noticed that the Murdaugh family was being moved farther and farther back from the defense table. It came to light that Alex's sister, Lynn, had passed Alex's attorney a note. It was also reported that a member of the Murdaugh family handed Alex a paperback book as he was leaving the trial during a break. It is illegal for a prisoner to have anything given to them outside the jail and without it being thoroughly searched. Contraband can be concealed in books, and some have even contained drug-laced pages.

So, back they were pushed. A bailiff reprimanded Buster Murdaugh when he kicked a water bottle in anger when the family was told to move back several benches from the front row.

The alleged flipping of the bird by Buster Murdaugh to Mark Tinsley during the attorney's time on the witness stand. Photo courtesy of *Meaww.*

During the testimony of Mark Tinsley, it was caught on camera that Buster Murdaugh appeared to be flipping off the attorney. While the still shot does indeed show a raised middle finger, if one watches the videos of Buster throughout the trial, he is constantly biting his nails, occasionally raising that finger to his cheek. Why flip Tinsley off to start with? He is Mallory Beach's family's attorney, who was the bane of the Murdaughs' existence with his $30 million demand in Mallory's wrongful death suit. It was his case and his motion to compel Alex to turn over his finances that many thought pushed Murdaugh to murder.

The Murdaugh family was initially seated up front, just behind the security guards for Alex. Photo courtesy of the *Daily Mail*.

The Murdaugh family moved three rows back. Photo courtesy of *Law & Crime*.

Chapter Twenty-Eight
"A Storm Was Coming!"

The anticipation leading up to the double murder trial for the murders of Maggie and Paul Murdaugh was at fever pitch. Myriad documentaries on the mysterious deaths surrounding the Murdaugh name had been airing since the previous year. Networks worked overtime to be the first to market with any new development or lead. *Facebook* groups built solely on the Murdaugh murders grew in numbers overnight. In all candor, a lot of the people commenting in posts in those groups were sharp. This author has no doubt that interested lawyers read many of them to not only gauge the temperature of the public concerning Alex Murdaugh's guilt or innocence, but also picking up a few tidbits of information along the way. Podcasts abounded, each vying for that key witness to bring in the listeners, and *YouTube* channels with new faces popped up on a regular basis as armchair detectives went after their moment in the spotlight. Many were extremely well done; others would become one-shot wonders.

Walterboro hunkered down, not quite sure how many of the masses would descend upon its limited parking spaces. The food trucks rubbed their hands in anticipation of what they saw as the opportunity of a lifetime. Security details surrounded the courthouse, media techs did sound checks as broadcasters checked their hair and makeup before stepping before the cameras. It was as if the whole of South Carolina took a collective breath and waited for that first gavel.

As millions of eyes glued themselves to their televisions and devices, the South Carolina seal appeared in the lens. The camera shook as Judge Newman took the stand and looked out upon the gallery with the kind of calm with which he ran the entire 6-week trial. To his immense credit, no one would have known he had just lost his 40-year-old son only two weeks before. I know this author wondered if the loss of a beloved son would color how he felt about presiding over a trial where the defendant was accused of blowing away his own?

Many of the tube watchers were surprised to see a half-empty courtroom. It was not packed to the rafters. It may have been because the beginning of a trial is consumed with "housekeeping" matters, jury selection, and other details that make up the less dramatic portions of a murder trial. The numbers would gradually grow over the coming days, until it was "grab a number" for a chance at a ringside seat for the action.

Three days of jury selection started with a pool of around 700 prospects and was finally narrowed down into four groups. The groups were then qualified, and 122 jurors were brought in on Wednesday. They were asked a multitude of questions to judge their views toward murder, domestic violence, etc. They were asked if they had any affiliations with the key players in the trial, if they had ever been represented in a lawsuit by PMPED, or tried by any of its lawyers, specifically Alex Murdaugh. Translation: did they have any axe to grind with the Lowcountry legal giant? Many who answered yes were excused. Finally, the customary jury of 12 was chosen with six alternates. Interestingly, 8 of the original 12 were female. Did that give Alex Murdaugh, accused of gunning down his loving wife, pause?

The witness list was posted and consisted of more than 200 names. Not all would be called, but if there was a chance someone might be, they were put on the list to cover the legal criteria of discovery for both sides of the courtroom.

Before jury selection could begin, Murdaugh's defense team sought to block testimony of potential blood evidence. Murdaugh was wearing a white T-shirt when he arrived at the property and discovered his murdered loved ones. That t-shirt had become a point of contention between the State and Murdaugh's Defense team after the latter said forensic tests failed to show stains on the shirt were from human blood.

Attorneys Jim Griffin and Dick Harpootlian asked the court to block the testimony of Orangeburg County Chief Deputy Kenneth Lee Kinsey, a recognized expert in bloodstain evidence. The defense argues that Kinsey said after reviewing a report and analysis from Thomas Bevel, a prosecution witness, he could not form an opinion on whether the blood stains on Murdaugh's shirt were consistent with back spatter from a gunshot.

Without such an opinion, Kinsey's testimony would only unfairly confuse and mislead the jury. Kinsey repeated Bevel's findings of more than 100 stains and that the smaller stains that are present after a chemical treatment appear to be high-velocity impact stains that are caused from a gunshot or high-speed machinery. The Defense says Kinsey then pivots away from that, saying that he can't render an opinion.

That motion and the Defense's motion to block testimony from another blood spatter expert were heard on Tuesday after the final panel of potential jurors were qualified.

Both sides agreed to hold a counsel hearing once that evidence is set to be presented and whether either expert will be called as a witness.

The next motion up for consideration was the hotly debated admittance of all of Alex Murdaugh's financial crimes as the State's motive for his murdering his wife and son. The motion was laid out in a previous chapter when Creighton Waters went over each of Alex's settlement frauds and the timeline of each, leading up to the night of the murders. At the time of the motion, the previous November of 2022, Judge Newman said he'd think about it. Now was the time to hear his thoughts. Both tables waited anxiously to hear his decision. For Alex, it would show the jury a devious, narcissistic man that would steal from orphaned children, from quadriplegics, from people with severe medical issues who desperately needed the money Alex had won for them from various insurance companies. It would show a man who looked them in the eye and took their money to finance his lavish lifestyle. It was not good optics.

Judge Newman argued that a motion in "limine," a legal term that means "a motion at the start," is typically used to exclude evidence from a trial rather than add to it.

"I'm not prepared to grant a motion to admit evidence in limine," Newman said. He was basically telling the two teams of lawyers that they could try to introduce the evidence at the right time, and the other team had the right to object, and he would decide on an objection-by-objection basis. The State agreed to introduce the evidence as needed.

The Prosecution argued that the murders were a cover-up for Alex Murdaugh's financial misdeeds. Previously, the Defense said the State turned over millions of pages of documents during discovery about these financial crimes alone. They felt the motive was completely fabricated.

"His theory is, he knew the jig was up, so he went home, and butchered, blew the head off his son, and butchered his wife," Murdaugh's defense attorney Dick Harpootlian said. "There's not one shred of evidence there were any problems between any of them. There are texts, pictures, people that were with them the previous weekend at a ball game, video from that day with Paul and he's having a good time. There is no dispute anywhere that they were the perfect family in terms of their relationships."

If Alex felt things were already not going in his favor, it was about to get worse. The State proposed to allow a ballistics expert that had some rather damning testimony. He said the casings found around Maggie Murdaugh's body matched .300 casings found at the back door of the Moselle residence and at their private shooting range across the street. It would basically mean the weapon that murdered Maggie was a Murdaugh gun. And to top it off, that gun was now missing.

Before giving his decision about whether or not he would allow the ballistic evidence, Judge Newman had the expert take the stand, without the jury present, to hear what he had to say.

South Carolina Law Enforcement Division (SLED) Agent Paul Greer was called to the stand. He told the court he had been called to testify in 25 cases as a forensics firearm expert. The motion revolved around a series of bullet casings that were found around the body of Maggie Murdaugh.

During cross-examination by Murdaugh attorney Jim Griffin, Greer was asked how confident he was that the mechanism markings from both sets of casings can be from the same weapon. Greer responded that those were his findings.

Newman ruled that Greer could testify and the evidence could be submitted. He said any questions about the qualifications of Greer or science would be heard in cross-examination and should be heard by a jury.

Bam! Right out of the gate, each of Alex's dream team of lawyers had their objections tabled. The jury would hear evidence of his financial crimes, of evidence Kenneth Kinsey found at the crime scene during his reconstruction, and now, evidence showing it was family guns used during the murders of Maggie and Paul Murdaugh. The only caveat Alex's team won was that the testimony of a much-publicized blood-spattered T-shirt would not be allowed due to the conflicting events surrounding its testing.

The nod for opening statements went to the prosecution. It was, after all, their case. The atmosphere outside the courtroom was as thick and atmospheric as it was inside. Dark clouds were moving in, and the barometer was registering an encroaching storm. Creighton Waters used that turbulent weather condition to his advantage.

The Prosecution's Opening Statement
[The Opening Statements are not edited. They are as follows:]

Prosecuting Attorney Creighton Waters during Opening Statement.

"On the evening of June 7th. 2021, at the defendant's property off Moselle Road in Colleton County, his son, Paul Murdaugh, was standing in a small feed room at some kennels that they had on the property. About 8:50 PM, the defendant over there, Alex Murdaugh, took a 12-gauge shotgun and shot him in the chest and the shoulder. With buckshot. And the evidence is going to show it was a million to one shot he could have survived that, but after that another shot went up under his head and did catastrophic damage to his brain and to his head.

"And the evidence is going to show that Paul collapsed right outside that feed room. And just moments later. Just moments later he (Alex) picked up a 300 Blackout, which is a type of ammunition but an AR style rifle, and the evidence is going to show that the family had multiple weapons throughout the property, he picked up that .300 Blackout rifle and opened fire on his wife Maggie, just feet away near some sheds that used to be a hangar. *Pow Pow!* Two shots to the abdomen and in the leg took her down and after that there were additional shots. Including two shots to the head that again did catastrophic damage and killed her instantly.

"The evidence is going to show that neither Paul nor Maggie had any defensive wounds. Neither one of them had any defensive wounds. They didn't see a threat coming from their attacker. And the evidence is also going to show that both Maggie and Paul were shot at extremely close range. The evidence is going to show it's called "stippling." It's almost like a tattoo that when you get shot very close to a weapon, it leaves marks that the forensic pathologist can see. They were shot at close range, and they did not have defensive wounds.

"And the evidence is going to show that the defendant Alex Murdaugh over there told anyone who would listen that he was never at those kennels, but the evidence is also going to show, from these things that everyone of us, most of us carry around in our pockets [holds up a cell phone], that he was there, and he was there just minutes before with Maggie and Paul… just minutes before their cell phones go silent forever and ever. Despite what he told people, he was never at the kennels. The cell phones are going to show otherwise.

"Ladies and gentlemen, my name is Creighton Waters. I'm with the Attorney General's office, and I'll be the lead prosecutor. I introduced myself before. With me is David Fernandez, Savannah Goude, John Meaders, Don Zalinka, John Conrad, and Johnny James. A lot of lawyers. This is a big case. It's a very complicated case and that's why there's so many people working on it. Sitting in back in the next row, we have David Owen, who's the lead investigator. We have Lieutenant Agent Charles Gent who is one of the agents. Special Agent Ryan Kelly, Special Agent Peter Widowski, some of the agents that are working on the case as well as Investigator Isaac Toledo, who's working on the case as well. They're some of the witnesses that you'll hear from."

Waters reminded the jury that they took an oath and that they have the most important job in the courtroom. The judge is the judge of the law, but the jury is the judge of the facts. The State's burden is to present the evidence beyond a reasonable doubt. The emphasis is on "reasonable" doubt"---it is a doubt that causes a reasonable person to hesitate to act.

He reminds the jury of the four charges against Alex Murdaugh that they will rule upon. The four indictments are:

1. For the murder of Maggie Murdaugh.
2. Murdering Paul Murdaugh.
3. Possessing a firearm during the commission of a violent crime against Maggie Murdaugh.
4. Possessing a firearm during the commission of a violent crime against Paul Murdaugh.

Waters tells them the difference between circumstantial evidence and direct evidence. "So, specifically we have the storm out here from what I'm told. Direct evidence is if it's raining outside and a witness goes outside and it's raining and they come here and they get on the witness stand and because they saw it raining, they sit on the stand and say, 'I was just outside and I saw it raining. I saw it raining'. That's direct evidence. They actually saw it rain.

"But to give you an example of what circumstantial evidence is—is if the witness goes into a room. A room where all the curtains are drawn, and when they go into that room, it's sunny outside and everything's dry. And while they're there in that room, they see it darken behind the shades, they hear thunder. They hear the wind blowing. They hear the sound of raindrops on the roof. And then they open up the door and it's not raining, but everything is wet. There's puddles in the driveway, there's puddles in the street, there's puddles in the yard, there's limbs down all over the ground. And then they come in here and say, 'Yeah, it was raining.' Didn't actually see it raining, but those circumstances are beyond any reasonable doubt that it was actually raining. Now, I guess it's possible that somebody could have been standing outside their window and beat the drum to create thunder, and blowing the fan to make it seem like it was the wind, and somehow got enough water to cover the entire neighborhood, but that's not reasonable. Everybody understand that distinction?"

Creighton Waters admonishes the jury to decide credibility of the witnesses. "Rely on that good old-fashioned common sense."

"You're going to see video of him at the scene when law enforcement arrives. You're going to see the police bodycam video and hear what he says about that night. You're gonna hear 3 recorded statements on video that he gave with law enforcement and you're gonna hear how things progress about what he says he did that night. Watch those closely. Watch his expressions. Listen to what he's saying. Listen to what he's *not* saying. Use that common sense."

"I mentioned Maggie was killed with a .300 Blackout rifle, an AR style rifle that was chambered in .300 Blackout ammunition. And you're gonna hear evidence that back in Christmas of 2016, Alex Murdaugh over there bought two .300 Blackout AR-style rifles and that not long after that, one of them went missing from Paul's truck. And time went by and in April of 2018. Alex Murdaugh replaced that rife with another one. Three total Blackout rifles that they had. One of them went missing years ago and a replacement was bought.

"You're gonna hear evidence that Paul and his friend were using that replacement gun. They were standing right outside the side door to the gun room of the house, and they were sighting it in, firing down into a field. And the cases were ejecting. The cases are the empty shell from a bullet, and they were ejecting out into the flower bed right there. And then there's a range across the street and they shot it there. There's cases ejected there as well. And they were shooting that third replacement gun just weeks prior to the murders. Prior to June 7th, 2021, when Maggie and Paul were murdered. And you're gonna hear forensic evidence that the cases that were found in that flower bed and the cases that were found across the street at that range were ejected out of the same weapon that fired all the cases that were around Maggie's dead body that killed her. It was a family weapon that killed Maggie.

"You'll also hear that those three Blackouts that Alex Murdaugh purchased, when law enforcement arrives at the scene on June 7th, 2021, he can only account for one. He can only account for one. And that replacement gun is nowhere to be found.

"You're gonna hear evidence that the type of ammunition, the exact brand, the exact model of ammunition that was used to kill Maggie, S and B .300 Blackout ammunition, 147 grain bullets — that exact ammunition, boxes of that ammunition is found *all over* the property. That very same make and model ammunition that was used to kill her is found in multiple locations throughout the property. And you're also going to hear evidence, the same thing about the shotgun shells that killed Paul. The Federal double buckshot and unfired rounds were found on the property, as well as Winchester #2 Turkey rounds and buckshot that killed Paul. Family weapon, same ammunition found on the property.

"You're also going to hear evidence that about a week after the murders, Randolph III died. And about a week after the murders, Alex shows up early in the morning at his parents' home, where his mother is in late-stage Alzheimer's. It's uncharacteristic for him to show up early, uncharacteristic for him to show up at all like that. And he comes in, he's carrying something in a blue tarp. And he takes it upstairs. And eventually, law enforcement finds out about that. And they go upstairs, and they find upstairs, they find a wadded up, very, very large raincoat in a blue color that could look like a tarp. And you're gonna hear evidence that it was coated with gunshot residue on the *inside.*

"Other evidence is the gunshot residue evidence. You're gonna hear that there was gunshot residue at the scene. There was gunshot residue on the seat belt of Alex's car he was driving. You're gonna hear evidence that when law enforcement got to the scene, he had gone and gotten a shotgun, Paul's shotgun, and that Maggie's DNA was on that shotgun. You're gonna hear other evidence from DNA gunshot residue firearms examiners. There's gonna be a lot of forensic evidence in this case. I'm not gonna get into every single bit of it right now.

"And I will say that a key piece of forensic evidence that you're going to hear in this case is the cell phone. Alex's cell phone, Maggie's cell phone, and Paul's cell phone. It really allows us to do a lot of things and get a lot done, but this cell phone keeps track of who we're talking to. Who we're calling. Who we're texting, whenever we access apps. And every time you do that, there's a record kept in this phone unless it's deleted somehow. If you're using certain apps, you can even get GPS information, where you were, when you did that. On these phones, you can hear evidence that when you make a call and it pings off cell towers, that location information can be gathered from that as well. And so, it allows an investigation to take this and piece together what someone was doing on a particular day, and not only what they were doing, but who they were interacting with and how they were interacting with them. This is gonna be crucial outlets for you to consider.

"That particularly Alex and Paul, and also Maggie were prolific cell phone users to the point where Paul's friends even had a nickname for him.

House at 4147 Moselle Road.

"Before I talk more about that, there's three family properties I need to talk about, OK. The first one I've mentioned is Moselle, Moselle in Colleton County. It's called Moselle, it's off Moselle Road and everybody refers to it as Moselle. And that property is large, this is a lot of acres. There's a main house on it, and there's a driveway that goes to that main house, but it used to be an airstrip. And there's an airstrip that goes down and then down the way just less than 1/3 of a mile away. Just a 3-minute walk, 4-minute walk, 45 second drive is the kennels and the shed that used to be a hangar where Paul and Maggie were murdered. The main house is just less than 1/3 of a mile away; you can see the kennels from the main house. You can see the main house from the kennels.

House at Edisto Beach.

"There's a house in Edisto at the beach. And the evidence is going to show that that is where Maggie preferred to stay, particularly in the summer months. She liked the beach. She was not a hunter. She didn't want to be in Moselle. She didn't want to be at the lodge where it was hot and buggy. She liked being in Edisto.

Randolph III and Miss Libby's house in Almeda.

"And then you're also, I've already mentioned the house in

Almeda, which is where his parents live. On June 7th, 2021, you're gonna hear evidence that his father went into the hospital and the prognosis was not good. And in fact, he died a few days later and his mother was in late-stage Alzheimer's. And that that house was being cared for by caretaker; you're going to hear from that caretaker.

"The main house has a driveway, but the kennels also have a driveway, and the evidence is going to show that that was actually as commonly used as the main driveway. In fact, the mailboxes are by the kennel driveway, driving right past those kennels on the way to the main house.

"I told you that you would hear evidence that Maggie did not like being at Moselle, as much as she liked Edisto, the beach house. But June 7th, 2021, she came back to Moselle. And the evidence is going to show that she arrived about 8:15 pm. And the evidence is going to show that from the cell phones that Paul was there at the house, with Maggie at the main house. Alex Murdaugh himself says that they ate dinner, and the autopsies are gonna reflect both Paul and Maggie having similar stomach contents, indicating that they recently shared a meal altogether. About 8:30 pm, 15 minutes after they arrived, Paul's phone shows he starts moving toward the kennels.

"This evidence again will show that the defendant said he was never at those kennels, that he was napping after they ate, and he was at the main house and never went there. You're also going to hear evidence about how much Alex uses his cell phone, and it would be unusual for him to be anywhere without a cell phone. At 8:44:55 seconds, Paul recorded a video. He was down at the kennels because he had been talking to a friend of his, and you're gonna hear from this friend, because his friend's dog was in the kennels, and they thought there was something wrong with the tail. Paul was recording a video of it to send to his friend. And you'll see that video, you'll hear from witnesses that identify Paul's voice, Maggie's voice, and Alex's voice. To anyone who would listen, he was never there. And at 8:44:55 seconds there's a video, the evidence will show that he was there. He was at the murder scene with the two victims and more than that, just over 3 minutes later, 8:49:01second, Paul's phone locks *forever*.

"Paul never sends another text. He doesn't answer calls. 3 minutes

415

after that video has the defendant at the murder scene with the two victims, Paul's cellphone goes silent forever. And, in fact, another communication comes in from the very friend that he was talking to about the dog at 8:49 and 35 seconds. Just 35 seconds later and he doesn't answer. He never answers another thing. Forever. On top of that, Maggie's phone locks at 8:49 and 31 seconds, around that same time, and she never answers another text, or sends another text. Never makes another phone call. Never received another phone call. 3 minutes, ladies and gentlemen. 3 minutes. After a video shows he's at the scene with the victims and told everybody he was never there. Credibility, ladies and gentlemen. Credibility.

"After that? Well, you'll hear evidence that Alex's phone was conspicuously silent. You have a lot of activity from about 8:09 PM until 9:02 PM. And if he was at the kennels, which the evidence will show, why is this phone not with him? Why is it not showing active? But you will hear that at 9:02, all of a sudden, his phone does start to pick up activity. At 9:02 he calls... He starts moving at 9:04. He calls Maggie's phone. She doesn't answer of course. He calls his father Randolph in the hospital. Doesn't appear there's an answer there. He calls Maggie again at 9:06. Remember, he's just a third of a mile away. You can see it at 9:06 pm. She doesn't answer. At 9:06, he turns on his car. The Suburban. And he texts Maggie that he's going be right back. I'm gonna go check on Mom. And he doesn't drive down to the kennels, even though that's where the mailbox is. That's a common place to me, even though you can see it. He's called his wife two times and in texts and she hasn't responded. Why didn't he just drive down there, say, "Hey, I'm heading. You guys wanna go? What's up? What's up?" Right there, you can see it.

"And he heads out to Almeda where his mom's suffering from Alzheimer's and the caretaker is there. And he starts calling people. He's talking to people. It's up to you to decide whether or not he's trying to manufacture an alibi. He gets there to Almeda. You'll hear evidence about whether or not that was usual. You'll hear evidence about how he was acting when he got there. And he's only there for 20 minutes. Because he's back underway at 9:44. And he makes more phone calls on the way back. Calling friends, calling people who will answer. It will be up to you to decide whether he's trying to create an alibi. And he gets back to Moselle at 10:01. He calls 911 at 10:06 pm.

416

"911 call. Listen to what he says. Listen to what explanations he may offer. You're gonna hear that 911 call, but you're also gonna see the body worn camera of the officers who arrived at the scene. The video camera they wear that records what they're doing. And you're going to see what he did. It's going to be gruesome. There's no other way around. That's what *he* did." (Pointing at Alex Murdaugh)

"On that 911 call on the body worn cameras, pay attention to what he says. Look at how he's acting. But he says within a few minutes of each one of those, he says this is about the boat case. This is about the boat case. And you're going to hear some of what was going on in Alex Murdaugh 's life leading up to that day. Stuff that happened that very day, stuff that was leading up to a perfect storm that was gathering. Much like the storms are coming outside today. Listen for that evidence. Listen to that gathering storm that all came to a head on June 7th, 2021, the day the evidence will show he killed Maggie and Paul.

"This has been a long, exhaustive investigation. It's going to be a fairly long trial because it's complicated. It's a journey. There's a lot of aspects to this case. There's a lot of factors in this case, but a lot of things that are complicated when you start to put them all together, piece them together like a puzzle, all of a sudden, a picture emerges and it's really simple. Once we get to the end of that journey and you have a chance to deliberate, the evidence is going to be such you're going to reach the inescapable conclusion that Alex murdered Maggie and Paul. That *he* was the storm, that the storm was coming for *them*. And the storm arrived on June 7th, 2021, just like the storms that are heading here right now. That they died as a result. Beyond any reasonable doubt. Thank you."

Chapter Twenty-Nine
"It is Our Honor to Represent Him."

Without delay, Judge Newman merely said, "For the Defense." And with that, the jury and the world as a whole, learned what Alex Murdaugh's lead attorney Dick Harpootlian had up his sleeve in his pursuit to get his client out of this mess.

Dick Harpootlian in his opening statement.

"Ladies and Gentlemen of the Jury. My name is Dick Harpootlian. I think I introduced myself to you and all of our attorneys, the three other attorneys: Jim Griffin, Philip Barber, and Margaret Fox.

"It is our *honor* to represent Alex Murdaugh. I say it's our honor because I submit to you what you have heard from the Attorney General as facts, are not. Are *not*. They're his theories, his

419

conjecture. Alex. Stand up." (Alex stands up)

Alex Murdaugh stands at Harpootlian's request during Opening
Statements. Alex's family is one row behind him, his sister.
Lynn is on the far right.

"This is Alex Murdaugh. He was the loving father of Paul and the loving husband of Maggie. You're not gonna hear a single witness say that their relationship, Maggie and Alex's relationship, was anything other than loving. You're gonna hear about how they went to a baseball game the weekend before, you're gonna hear about their relationship. You're gonna see text and emails indicating a loving relationship. Paul was the apple of his eye. You're going to see a video somewhere between 7:30 and 8:00 the night of the murders. With Paul and Alex riding around looking at some trees they planted. It's a Snapchat Paul sent to other people because the trees were not planted very well, they're cantilevering over. They're laughing. They're having a good time. That would be about an hour before the Attorney General says he slaughtered them. When I said he slaughtered them, they were slaughtered and no question.

"Paul was shot twice with buckshot, 12-gauge buckshot, once in the chest. And by the way, that shot would indicate it was in the chest and came out under his arm like somebody that might have been holding up their hands, so when he said no defensive wounds, he perhaps is being held at shotgun. I mean, I can make the same sort of speculation that the Attorney General can, because that's all he's doing, is speculating. What we do know is a 12-guage, at fairly

420

close range shot to the chest. He must have been turned because it comes out under his arm. The wadding, if you're familiar with a shotgun, under his arm. The second shot ended up, and there's going to be some question about the direction of that shot but ended up entering his skull cavity. And the gases from that shot? Well, it exploded his head like a watermelon hit with a sledgehammer. All that was left was the front of his face. Everything else was gone. His brain exploded out of his head, hit the ceiling in the shed and dropped to his feet. Horrendous. Horrible butchering. So, to find Alex Murdaugh guilty of murdering his son, you're gonna have to accept that within an hour of having an extraordinarily bonding... you can see it in the Snapchat, and then that he executes him in a brutal fashion. Not believable.

Dick Harpootlian with his arm up showing that the first shotgun blast went across Paul's chest and under his left arm. His left arm had to have been up in order for the wadding and pellets to go under and out his arm.

"Now, Maggie is shot running and no defensive wounds because she was shot running and after she falls to the ground and has one bullet that has hit her and probably traveled up and hit her brain, she's on the ground and whoever the perpetrator was walked up, took that AR and put one in the back of her head. Executed! Executed!

"*Why?* It's going to be interesting because we don't know why; he doesn't know why. (Meaning Creighton Waters.) They've got telemetry from his car. He left the house at 9:06 and returned at

10:01 after seeing his mother, who has dementia. Now remember, that day his father, who is dying, is taken to the hospital. Mom's home alone with the housekeeper… perfectly reasonable for him to want to go see her. And later than usual. Because his father's not there. He's in the hospital. He dies two days later. His father dies two days later. So, the question is, if he leaves at 9:06 and he's back at 10:01, he literally, I mean, you know, he can account for the car and the cell phone records account for where he was between 9:06 and 10:01. Now this cell phone records, and you're gonna hear this from their own experts, are incomplete. They're incomplete.

"And we submit one of the reasons they're incomplete… And by the way, how do they find Maggie's phone? Maggie's phone was thrown out on the side of the road about 1/4 of a mile away from a little bit more, maybe a half a mile from the Moselle property. Going on the side of the road, they found it by using Find My iPhone. The way they did that, they had to open it or have access… who gave them the code to open the phone? Alex Murdaugh! And he's destroyed. It's just thrown out on the side of the road. If it was him calling that phone at 9:06… As he leaves the house, he did call her twice and texted her. And we also know that at 9:06 as he cranks up his car, as the cell phone records show that as the telemetry data from this shows, the cell phone linking up with the car, that phone (Maggie's phone) is being thrown on the side of the road. Almost a half a mile away. Now that is Houdini. That is magic, that is inexplicable.

"Now I was making notes while the Attorney General's talking. But let me tell you what is more believable. That night, he comes home and finds his wife and son butchered. And when I say butchered, you're gonna see these photographs. When I see them now, after having seen them for the last four or five months, it's still tough to look at. It still bothers me. And he comes home and finds his son lying in his own blood with his brain laying at his feet. Shot to hell. He walks over. He checks to see if there's any life there. Although, I mean, he's seeing this brain laying outside his body. He knows there's nothing there. He goes over and tries to get a pulse out of Maggie. He calls 911. I want you to hear that 911 tape. It is a man hysterical in grief, trying to figure out what's going on and he tells the 911 operator. But he's concerned and he drives up, back up to the house. By the way, you can't see, I've been out there, you can't

422

see the shed. You might see the top of the shed, they're pine trees between the front porch of the house, and the dog pens. And it's not a third of a mile at all, maybe by the way the crow flies, but it takes a little bit longer to drive down there. And this is not unusual for them to communicate by cell phone or text, even when they're all on the same property. It's 1,700 acres, big property, they hunted. So, what I'm trying to say to you is that the Attorney General has given you his view. And again, you can't see the shed. And I'm gonna ask the judge at some point during this trial to ask you, the jury, to be able to go to the scene so you can see it. You can understand the proportions, you can understand the details.

Aerial view of Moselle house (upper left at end of tree-lined drive) and the kennel area, middle of far right where the buildings can be seen.

"Let me give you another fact. You're gonna hear their witnesses explain the catastrophic injuries to Paul. His head literally exploded. And whoever shot him with that shotgun was probably no more than three feet away. His head exploded! You would be covered in blood from head to foot. In blood. They seized his clothes that night. SLED did. And they tested it, well… First of all, you're going to see in the videos from the agent, the officers that arrived that night. There's no blood on him. They didn't find any blood on him. SLED's testing indicated 12 different places on his shirt and pants. No human blood detected. You'll see pictures with him in a white T-shirt, no blood on it. Those are facts. Those aren't theories. Those are the facts.

"Another fact. It is, I think, the reason we're here today. When you hear those questions on the videotapes on the night he's found his wife and son brutally butchered. You can hear on the 911 tape he is hysterical. He comes in and out. It's consistent. If any of you have ever suffered the catastrophic loss of a friend or a family member. It's numbing. So, anything you said that night is, is in the context of just an hour or two before finding his wife and son butchered. He drove back up to the house while on the 911 call saying "I gotta get a gun, that whoever did this might be out there," and he gets a gun. What's fascinating about that is he gets a 12-gauge shotgun, and he grabs some shells. These people hunt a lot. They have guns everywhere. He grabbed some shells. He grabs a 12-gauge gun and put a 12-gauge buckshot in and then he put a 16-gauge buckshot. That's how shook up he was.

"These people have shot all their lives. He knows you can't put a 16-gauge in a 12-guage. Their witness will tell you the little amount of GSR found on him is consistent with him picking up the shotgun he got from the house. You wanna talk about GSR? Again, if you fired a shotgun twice and a rifle six times, you'd be *covered* in GSR. Those are the facts. That's not just theory. The facts.

"These ARs again. You're gonna hear testimony. A lot of guns. They had a gun room. You know, I don't live in Colleton County. I live in downtown Columbia. And there are no gun rooms in downtown Columbia. But apparently, if you live on 1100 acres and you hunt deer and you hunt…whatever, they were planting their sunflowers for... quail? Again, not a hunter. You have a lot of guns. The truth is in 2017…and you'll hear the testimony that Alex bought two Blackouts, one for Paul and one for Buster. Buster is the other son who is sitting out in the audience. And Paul had one stolen. He bought another one for Paul.

"Now Paul was very irresponsible with guns. I think he'd leave guns around and in cars. He oftentimes left guns down at the dog pens in the feed room. Now, I can't tell you whether he was shot with his own weapon or not, or his mom was shot with his weapon or not, but I can tell you that they weren't shot by Alex. They don't have the guns. There's no way to tell conclusively without having the weapons what weapons those were fired by, and we'll be talking a bit with experts about that.

"And why, if they are murdered June 7, 2021, is it September 2022 before they charge him? And I'll tell you what happened that night. And it's a problem. Because each question, and the questioning is aggressive. He's traumatized. They suspected him. They show up, he's got a shotgun, they suspect him and the next morning, after two people are found butchered here in Colleton County at Moselle Road, the police announce, "Don't worry. There's no danger to you all. There's nobody out there that could pose a danger to you." Because, you see, they decided that night he did it.

"Cell phones, without any forensics, and they've been pounding that square peg in the round hole for the last, you know, since June of 2021. Resulting in charges in September of 22. And so, you'll hear it, the accusatory fashion he's being interviewed in. He may not have dealt all the facts, but by the way, whether he'd been down to the dog pens that night or not, really doesn't matter. Really doesn't matter. Because you're gonna see cell phone activity. Let me put it to you this way. Paul's phone at 8:50. Maggie's phone later than that at 8:54. Clearly, it's still being used. At 9:06, he's up at the house, getting in the car, cranking it up. To drive over and see his mom. He would have had to execute both of them, get back up to the house. Get the bloody clothes off. And by the way, they seized his closing that night. They've never searched his house for any other clothes that we know of. Although that night he gave permission, and they got a search warrant. "Go to my house. Go look through everything." Where are the bloody clothes? Where are the bloody clothes?

"There's no eyewitness. There's no forensics tying him to the murder. When I say forensic, I mean fingerprints. Why? Whatever tying him to shooting anybody that night, the cell phone records would indicate he would have had less than 10 minutes to kill them and get up to the house. Get in the car and crank it up, maybe covered in blood. No, if they think he was beginning to establish an alibi. There's no evidence of that. The evidence is consistent with him seeing them earlier at the dog pen and by the way, that audio they have of him and Maggie. They're talking about one of the dogs killing a *chicken*. And they were debating whether it was a guinea hen or a chicken. No animosity. Very normal discussion. Nobody's threatening him and he's not pulling out a shotgun. You know, 10 minutes after that, Paul's texting a girl about going to the movies.

"Ok, big question: One shooter or two? 2 guns: a shotgun and an

AR. And by the way, Maggie has no defensive wounds and she's running. What's she running from? There's a little shed on the other side. Perhaps she heard a shotgun blast and came around and saw two people. And whoever was there opened up. And was there enough time to kill Paul? And then find the AR and then ambush Maggie? Much more likely, there were two people. Again, we don't have to prove anything. As you sit there right now, you have to presume he is innocent. He didn't do it. The law is he is presumed innocent. He didn't do it. They have to prove it beyond a reasonable doubt. You cannot convict him unless the State proves his guilt beyond a reasonable doubt.

"There's no eyewitness. There's no camera. There's no forensics. There's no fingerprints. None! I say that without any fear of contradiction. Now this smoke they've created is about suspicion. They've ignored some witnesses. Another was shown a blue rain jacket when the witness said it was a blue tarp. (An objection was voiced that he was giving testimony. The judge sustained it.)

"No witness is going to say they saw him kill them. All of you have indicated that you will follow the law. (He points to Alex.) He didn't do it. You were picked because you said you would be fair. You would follow the law. If I do something that will anger you or irritate you, don't hold it against Alex, hold it against me. As you sit there right now, in your mind, he didn't do it, he is innocent. He requires a verdict of Not Guilty from you. That's your duty. That's your oath. Thank you."

Chapter Thirty
Testimony Begins

The Opening Statements were, in a way, a Table of Contents for the trial that was to follow. The burden of proof was on the State with Creighton Waters and his team of lawyers in the crosshairs. Waters had made promises to the jury that he would provide the evidence he put before them. If any of that evidence was not presented during the trial, it would make the prosecution look like they were hiding something or couldn't deliver the goods. The defense side as well had made their bullet list of things they would show. There was not as much pressure on them to produce, as there was to defend. Alex Murdaugh's reputation was on the line. And if you look at it in the bare light of day, that is pretty much all that was on the line here for the defendant. The Death Penalty clause had been removed. He would already be in prison for the rest of his life when found guilty for over 100 indictments for fraud, money laundering, conspiracy to commit suicide, and too many others to list. This trial was to prove to the world that he may be a monster for what he did to his clients, friends, and co-workers, Alex Murdaugh could not kill his wife and son. And to this author, it was Paul's death that mattered the most to him.

Week One of the Trial

The first witness to take the stand on Day 4 of the trial, January 26, 2023, was the first officer to arrive on the scene: Officer Daniel Greene. Prosecuting attorney Creighton Waters led him through his testimony. It is his bodycam video that is the first to give the world a view of what he walked into that night. He arrives through the kennel-side driveway. When he parks, his headlights are shining directly up the drive between the kennels and the hangar. Paul's body, lying outside the feed room, was immediately visible up ahead. It is tactfully blurred for online use. It seems it was not for the jury, as monitors for Alex and the State's table are covered to keep the gallery from seeing the footage.

At the end of the driveway, not far from where Paul is lying face down on the cement walkway, is a black Suburban with its headlights and flashers on. The odd thing is what Officer Greene's bodycam captures as he approaches those headlights. Alex darts from the left of his car and hurries over to the right where he is standing when Greene finally gets to him. What was he doing over there? It was very near the chicken coops that are within a few feet of Paul's body. In the bodycam, Alex appears like a ghost flitting about the property, his pristine white T-shirt almost phosphorescent in the darkness.

When Greene gets to Alex, he is standing within a few feet of his wife's body, also lying face down, in the grass near the hangar, a small stand-alone doghouse, and a Polaris ATV. Alex is waving a small flashlight, and immediately tells Officer Greene that he has a loaded shotgun leaning against the Suburban by the driver's side door. Officer Greene described on the stand what he saw:

Officer Daniel Greene holding up the shotgun he retrieved from Alex Murdaugh the night of the murders.

428

Greene: "It was dark, hot, humid, raining off and on that evening." He had arrived 20 minutes after Alex's 911 call. Fire and Rescue pulled up almost immediately behind him. He first checked Alex to make sure he wasn't concealing a weapon. He took Murdaugh's gun to his patrol car and locked it inside. "I did not unload it or manipulate it in any way." When SLED arrived, he turned the shotgun over to them.

Within minutes of telling Greene there was a loaded gun, and Greene securing that gun in his patrol car, Alex launched into his theory, "It was the boat crash! That's what this is!" He tells Greene, "It's a long story…but Paul has been getting threats about the boat crash." Greene testified he saw no tears, but that Alex was somewhat hysterical. He went into sobbing fits and asked several times if the bodies had been checked for signs of life, despite the fact that both of them had gaping holes in the back of their heads. Alex stops in the middle of Greene's questions to say, "Are they covering him up?" Officers are placing a sheet over Paul's body.

Greene testified that there was water around Paul's body, and it did not appear to be from rain. He told the officers he wished they were not covering the bodies, as "We should protect all we can." They were covered anyway, and Deputy Rutland arrived with a canopy to put over Maggie to protect her from the rain.

Greene continues to question Alex, who breaks into sobs at various times when the question hits too close to home. He did say he went to the house to get a gun during the 911 call. He tells how he rode around with Paul for 2 hours "in the truck" earlier. He is sobbing again. Just then, a fireman walks behind Officer Greene. Alex breaks his emotional outburst and in a calm voice says, "Hey, how ya doin'?" Greene said he thought it was odd.

The dogs in the kennels next to Paul's body are barking continually. Deputy Pruitt is putting up crime scene tape, including around Alex's vehicle. Light is pouring out of the open tool shed door, just to the left of Maggie's body. Light is shining out of the small feed room door, illuminating the sheet-draped body of Paul Murdaugh. Those are the only two natural lights at the scene. All else is from myriad headlights and flashlights. Officer Greene's latex-gloved hands are apparent throughout his interview with Alex.

Greene testified he could see the .300 Blackout casings and warned officers to watch where they stepped. He shines his flashlight to the right of Alex's SUV and asks him about the several fresh tire marks clearly visible in the wet grass. He asks Murdaugh if he made all those marks? Alex tells him he only made the ones where he came and found them dead and calls 911, and when he went up to the house to get a gun. It is obvious to the officer, that it seems there are more than that seen in the grass. He later walks in front of the hangar looking for more, occasionally commenting to the officer with him, "Those look old."

Alex excuses himself to call Randy and walks a short distance away to make the call. It is far enough away that no one can hear his conversation. In the meantime, Deputy Pruitt has started a crime log. Greene: 22:26 arrival. Fire and Rescue about the same time. Medic 18 22:27; Badge numbers at 22:30 and 22:39. (These are all before 10:30 p.m.)

Alex returns from his call and stands smoothing his hair at the back of his head over and over. It is a self-soothing motion that we see often throughout the trial.

Greene: "They wanted to look under the sheet where Paul was, so I put on latex gloves. The other gloves (seen when he first arrives, before he puts on gloves to handle the shotgun) are tactical gloves. They were trying to see if a Blackout rifle was under him to see if Paul could have shot Maggie and then himself." None was found. They did find Paul's phone lying on his backside, near his short's pockets. "Dad did say he came over and checked their pulse."

Officer Greene said he left the scene several hours later. SLED had already arrived and taken over. They were still there when he left.

Defense attorney Dick Harpootlian stands for cross examination:

Harpootlian asks Greene if there is water inside and outside the dog pens? He is trying to minimize the amount found mainly to the right of Paul's body.

Greene: (looking at a still of the bodycam footage showing the dog kennels as he walks by them) "That's what it looks like."

Harpootlian: "Are you familiar with washing a pen out when a dog defecates in the pen?"

Greene: "I've never personally done it, but I'm sure that's what you would do to clean out a pen."

Harpootlian: "Ok, so it shows water on the concrete outside these dog pens, correct?"

Greene: "Yes."

Harpootlian: "Those pens are occupied by dogs. You can see water inside the pens and outside the pens, as though someone has been washing them out, correct?"

Greene: "There is water inside and outside the pens, yes."

They go over the ammunition found inside the shotgun Greene collected from Alex at the crime scene. The fact that there were two different ammunitions found in the gun are brought up: a 12-gauge and a 16-guage.

Harpootlian: "Can you fire a 16-guage from a 12-guage shotgun?"

Greene: "I wouldn't recommend trying it. I don't know if it would actually work or not. It could cause damage to the person using it."

Harpootlian tries to get Greene to say that Paul's brains were all over the ceiling. Greene says he was not aware of that, and it was not his part of the scene. "I don't recall saying that, but the other officers said it looked like the shot was fired upward at Paul."

Harpootlian tries again to get him to say that there was brain on the ceiling, and he reiterates he did not say that.

Harpootlian asks him what did he do to preserve the tire tracks he saw in the grass? Did you take pictures? "No, sir, not my job." Did you tell SLED about them? "No, sir. Not my job." You never took SLED over there to point those out to them?" No, sir." Footprints were seen but none of the Colleton County took pictures. They were turning the scene over to SLED.

He then asks about the footprints found behind a trailer by Fire and Rescue. Greene says he doesn't recall.

Harpootlian points out that Deputy McDowell and Deputy Pruitt are walking around Maggie's body where bullet casings are.

Harpootlian goes over Alex's statement about the boat crash, saying Paul had been punched once. "So, on the scene he believed it was related to his son's involvement in the death of the young lady and the others injured in the boat crash?" Greene: "That's correct."

In Creighton Waters re-direct of Officer Greene, he brings up the tire tracks found in the grass near Alex's SUV. Alex told Greene only two tracks are his, the rest "may have been from *earlier*."

(Granted, Alex has already said he and Paul used two trucks earlier in the evening to look around the property. The tracks you can clearly see in the bodycam video are deep impressions in the wet grass that look as though they have not been there long, and, since it started to rain, which was later that night.)

Corporal Chad McDowell being cross-examined by Dick Harpootlian.

Next on the stand is Corporal Chad McDowell. He is a K-9 officer and road patrol. This is the person who crossed behind Greene during his interview with Alex, and Alex says, "Hey, how ya doin'?" McDowell said he had never met Alex before. He goes over what he did to secure the scene, trying not to disturb anything. McDowell said one of the reasons they covered the bodies with sheets is that one of the family members had shown up. This may have been either Randy (who was the first to arrive and parked behind Alex's SUV), or John Marvin, who arrived later and asked if he could come in.

McDowell testified they marked the casings with yellow markers. He recognized the casings as .300 Blackouts because he owns one. (Dogs continue to bark throughout McDowell's bodycam footage.) He says that Paul's hands were underneath him.

Dick Harpootlian approaches McDowell in cross:

McDowell admits that Officer Greene is his supervisor. His job was to help secure the scene for "our investigators" and SLED. He pulled the sheet back to see if there was a weapon under Paul. He stepped into the feed room to do that. (You can clearly see him step into the feed room on Greene's bodycam.) Harpootlian points out he is not wearing footies or protective shoe coverings.

McDowell: "To my knowledge, I did not disturb anything."

In the bodycam footage, you can see the kennel hose neatly wrapped around its holder outside the cages of the kennels. He notes he did not see any blood on Alex's clothes.

During Waters re-direct, he asked if Alex was free to move around and was never placed in a patrol car. "That's correct."

The 911 call is played. We went over this in a previous chapter.

Harpootlian gets in one more question to Corporal McDowell:

"Chief Barry McCoy found 3 rows of tire tracks under the hangar" and he turned his bright crime scene lights on them. There were tire tracks on the sandy part, and one set about 20-30 feet from the bodies. When asked about the civilian cars that continued to arrive, it was stated that none of those tracks were run over. At some point in McDowell's bodycam, it began to rain harder.

Captain Jason Chapman with Colleton County.

Captain Jason Chapman with Colleton County was questioned by Attorney Fernandez. He was asked if SLED was asked to take over due to Colleton County's dealings with the Murdaughs. He denied this. He said it took SLED about two hours to arrive that night. They needed to obtain a search warrant. Chapman said he got there about 10:35 that night. He was not wearing a bodycam.

Chapman said he got Deputy Rutland to begin a search warrant at the office and find a judge to sign it. She also rounded up a canopy for Maggie, which delayed her in arriving at the scene. He stated it was 79-89% humidity during the time they were there. It was hot and sticky. Rain set in within 45 minutes to an hour of their arrival. The canopy tent was put over Maggie to preserve evidence. Paul was under the kennel overhang. (It did still leave Paul's head and shoulders exposed to the rain, but he was under a sheet.)

Colleton County did not collect anything. They secured the inner parameter...the outer parameter, "not so much."

Chapman stated that Paul's brain was lying by him. He was saturated in blood. He did not recall seeing water or blood on the phone. Perhaps the biggest statement Chapman made on the stand was that he felt the house should have been secured as an extension of the crime scene. He is shown photos of the footprints found inside the hangar and a photo of the bottom of Maggie's shoes. They appear to have made the impressions in the soft dirt.

He said they did do a GSR kit on Alex because of the time limit of 6 hours before most GSR is rubbed off. Chapman says there was aerial footage by a drone used for reference.

Chapman says that his impression of Alex's 911 call was that he found it unusual for someone to end a call for help to call their family members. He noted that Alex would be crying one minute while they were there investigating, and then stop when they got close to things. For instance, he stopped crying when they went to take a closer look at the tire impressions in the grass. He was watching them intently. As soon as they moved on, he started crying again.

During Harpootlian's cross of Chapman, he tried to play down Alex's demeanor when they were looking at the tire tracks. "Couldn't his change of demeanor be because he was hopeful it was about the killer(s) of his wife and child?"

The tracks that were found in the hangar, presumably made by Maggie's shoes, looked as if "she was packing back and forth." The point was made that the picture of the footwear prints was taken later. You can see where possibly two people with an REI symbol in the middle of their shoe prints stood close to the tracks thought to be Maggie's. Her prints were not stepped on.

Harpootlian points out that the photos of the water around Paul were taken that night. He points out the water in the pens and two buckets of water for the dogs. He also pointed out that it was dripping water from the kennel overhang onto the area around Paul's body.

Chapman says he took the drone footage the next morning. In answer to Harpootlian's statement about the public being told the next morning that "There was no danger," he said that release did not come from Colleton County. It had been handed over to SLED. It was also SLED who had a search warrant for the house. If they didn't search it for clothes, the drains for blood, it was not their jurisdiction to do so. He was not sure if SLED went to the house or not.

Day 2 of Testimony. January 27, 2021.

Detective Laura Rutland with the Colleton County's Sheriff's Office was called to the stand. Captain Chapman is her supervisor. She had a ringside seat for most of the night's activities. She stated she did not know the Murdaughs. She had briefly heard about the boat crash incident in 2019.

Rutland mentioned that upon arriving and seeing Paul, she was overcome by the smell. She said there was a lot of water around him. She noted seeing skull, brain matter and blood all over the shed and ceiling. She saw Maggie. Alex was standing by his SUV behind Randy's truck. Danny Henderson was introduced to her as Alex' personal attorney.

Shoe impressions matching Maggie's sandals in hangar.

Rutland testified to seeing shotgun wadding on the floor of the feed room and several holes in the feed room window. It was late at night and dark. She used a flashlight. She noted the fresh footprints in the dirt between the tractor and the wall in the hangar. They were going forward and back. They were flat, like flip flops or sandals, she said. She said Maggie's body was to the right of the impressions.

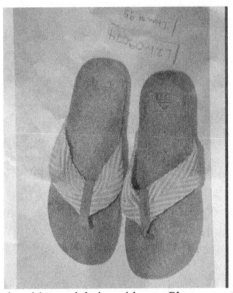

Maggie Murdaugh's sandals in evidence. Photo courtesy of the Courtroom Pool.

Rutland said Alex wanted his attorney Danny Henderson to sit in the SLED patrol car with them during his interview. That interview was listed in a previous chapter and tagged "the first interview."

At the end of the first interview recording that was played for the jury and the courtroom, Rutland was asked for her impressions of the interview. She said she thought it was strange he would go see his mother that late at night. She said as Alex sat in Agent Owen's car in front of her, that he appeared "clean." She said there was a smell of detergent coming from the shirt. She noted his hands, arms, shirt, pants, and shoes. She saw no knee prints or footprints near Paul's body that should have been there if Alex tried to turn him over or check for a pulse. She saw Alex 2-3 hours after the 911 call and his shirt appeared fresh and dry, despite the humidity and all his running around during the 911 call.

Deputy Laura Rutland on the witness stand.

Rutland testified that SLED got his clothes that night. She waited inside the doorway of the Moselle house as Agent Owen took Alex into the master bedroom to change out of his clothes and hand them to him. Owen did say, "I gave him some privacy in the bathroom."

During the cross, Griffin got Rutland to admit she didn't see Greene or Chapman's prints around Paul's body either as they were lifting his sheet. Rutland testified that she saw several clumps of Maggie's hair and a broken earring near the ATV by Maggie's body. Griffin points out there were 20-30 shotgun pellets left behind in the feed room, again pointing out the sloppy crime scene investigation.

On June 10th, three days after the murder, she was with SLED when they interviewed Alex, Randy, John Marvin, and Buster at John Marvin's hunting lodge near Varnville. She said they all gave voluntary interviews. On June 16th, she was with SLED when the diving teams searched another pond on the Moselle property. They used ATVs to search the 1,700 acres. On June 17th, they searched another pond. June 19th, they looked at the autopsy reports of Maggie and Paul. It was stated that Maggie had long brown hairs in her hands. There were injuries on Paul's face: bruises and a scratch on his cheek.

During this time, a BOLO went out in search of Paul's truck that John Marvin had been driving to get to Moselle when it broke down on the side of the road the night of the murders. It was finally cleared up by John Marvin and the truck was located. On June 12th, the black box was removed from Alex's Chevy Suburban. On June 14th, Maggie's Mercedes was processed. It had been towed in. The tire tracks in the hangar shed were found to belong to Mr. Davis, the man who cares for the dogs.

Rutland wraps up her testimony by agreeing to the question, "Did it look like someone (Alex) who just changed his clothes?" "Yes." Like they just came out of the dryer?" "He's sweating and they are dry, so yes," they looked fresh.

SLED agent Delilah Cirencion was next. She is with the Behavioral Science sector at SLED. She testified that on June 8th, buccal swabs were collected from the victims. She collected an iPhone with a clear case at the crime scene. She was with the crime scene unit at the time of the double murders.

Cirencion was asked if a Faraday bag had been used to collect Maggie's cell phone the next morning when it was found up the road from Moselle. She said that Captain Ryan O'Neal gave her the phone and she placed it into a brown paper bag. The passcode, which had been obtained from Alex Murdaugh, was on a piece of paper. She wrote it directly onto the bag. She was unaware if it was turned off or not.

SLED agent Delilah Cirencion identifying the cell phone evidence at trial.

Next up for the prosecution was SLED agent Melinda Worley who took a beating by the defense over the handling of the crime scene. She is a footwear and tire print specialist. She stated they always wear gloves, but not always shoe protection, especially when the crime scene is outside.

Worley said she took the camo shotgun Alex had grabbed that night and unloaded the gun before placing it into a box. She took a buccal swab from Officer Greene to eliminate him as a source of DNA since he handled the shotgun.

Worley stated she took photos of the feed room and other evidence. She said Paul was face down beneath a sheet. After he was removed by the coroner, she went into the feed shed to process it. She identifies Paul's cell phone from the photo shown her. She testifies that she did see bits of Paul's hair and blood on top of the feed room door. There were two shotgun shells behind the door with markers 9 and 10 placed next to them. She identifies the shells in court as two different shells: Winchester and Federal. Marker #1 is next to the shotgun wadding lying on the floor near a large bag of dog food and a partial footprint. She says one print was consistent with Paul's shoes. The shoe prints are facing the window, she said.

Worley notes 6 defects in the window of the feed room. She collected pellets and swabbed the doorknob for touch DNA.

She stated that Maggie was covered with a pink sheet and was lying next to an ATV. Her right arm was bent toward her face and her left arm was bent beneath her. Her legs were straight out behind her. She was lying on top of a casing where her right knee had been. It was a .300 Blackout casing marked #7. Five casings were recovered from the scene that were .300 Blackout casings that were marked with #'s 2-7 markers. Marker #12 showed possible brain matter from Maggie. Marker #13 showed disturbance in the gravel very near the feed shed. There were bullet fragments recovered from that "gravel strike."

Worley testified there was a bullet defect in the small doghouse to the left of Maggie's body. She said there were two ATVs under the hangar overhang. The one nearest to Maggie's left side had biological matter on it. A projectile was collected from the dog shed near Maggie.

Agent Worley made a diagram of the crime scene that has been seen in almost every documentary and broadcast concerning the case. She admits it is not to scale. She mentions that marker #8 shows a projectile that went all the way through the hangar.

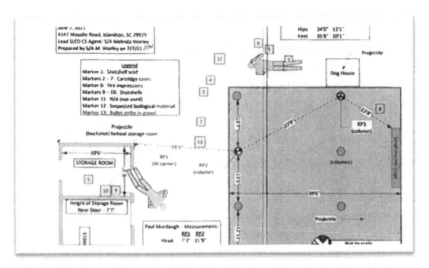

Agent Worley's diagram of the Murdaugh crime scene. The markers mentioned in her testimony can be seen.

Worley took custody of the GSR kit done on Alex. On June 9th, she collected items from Agent Katie McAllister: 3 shotguns, a rifle, spent and unspent cartridges, boxes of ammo and empty boxes. There is a night vision scope on the rifle, and a 30-round magazine with the AR-15. Three empty ammo boxes were discovered in the trash. In Alex Suburban, a 16-guage unfired shotgun shell is found on the floorboard to the rear of the driver's side seat.

Worley testifies that the Suburban is towed from the scene the morning following the murders, on June 8th. On the 9th, it is processed. They checked for blood, swabbed ten areas: driver's armrest, lock buttons, steering wheel, seats, and seat belt. The swabs were presumptive for blood. They completely removed the seat belt unit in order to test it for blood, GSR, and touch DNA.

In the white Ford F150, the found .300 Blackout cartridges in the center console. On Paul's truck and Maggie's car, swabs were taken on the interior and exterior door handles. Worley testified that they took fingernail clippings, clothes, and bullet fragments from Maggie's body. Paul had his fingernail clippings, the wadding in his left shoulder area, and pellets from his body. It is noted that Maggie was wearing a dress. Paul's shoes are now held up for the court. (Alex is seen rocking and crying throughout the testimony concerning the findings for Paul and Maggie.)

Agent Worley testifies that Agent Owen handed them Alex's clothing. "We tested the shirt and shorts with LCV liquid. It will turn purple for blood, bleach, and rust. The T-shirt had some on the front and back of the shirt, and some on the shorts.

Agent Worley holding up the seat belt unit from Alex's Suburban.

A search of Moselle was done on September 13, 2021. The entire residence including the gun room on the main floor. The workshop area near the kennels was also searched. There was a lot of ammo in the gun room...mixed ammo in the bookcase. There was ammo found in the workshop in a wire tub. Shotgun Federal cartridges and Blackout cartridges in the workshop at the kennels were found. Winchester ammo was also found in the gun room bookcase at the house. A single Winchester 12-guage shell was found on Paul's nightstand in his upstairs bedroom at the house.

Worley begins to state that a cartridge was found under the driver's seat of the black Ford F-150 when Dick Harpootlian jumps to his feet and objects to evidence concerning the black truck, stating it is not relevant. It is overruled. Worley goes on to say the black Ford F-150 is usually found in front of the Moselle residence or off to the side of the workshop at the hangar. .300 Blackout cartridges were found in the truck.

Before wrapping up her testimony for that Friday afternoon, Worley said they swabbed the camo shotgun Alex brought down from the house that night during the 911 call. Two swabs were taken from the barrel and from the loading area on the gun. There was visible blood on the gun. Before any other comment is made about these findings, the court recesses until Monday, and week one of the Richard Alexander Murdaugh trial comes to an end.

Chapter Thirty-One
SLED Agents Take Center Stage

On January 30, 2021, Week Two of the Alex Murdaugh murder trial began. The jury was back in place after a weekend of absorbing the previous week's testimony. Only the most obtuse would miss the defense's platform of showing the crime scene contamination and sloppy police work. Cue the O.J. Simpson tactics.

SLED agent Melinda Worley was back on the stand. As the camera panned over the courtroom, it was a decidedly different scene than the prior week when the gallery was half-full. Now, it was packed, and all eyes and ears were on the calm agent with the short brown bobbed haircut.

As Dick Harpootlian arranged his notes and walked toward her, it was obvious that Agent Worley looked a bit less calm than when the Prosecution led her through their questions on Friday. Then, she had been rapid fire with the answers, never hesitant and rarely smiled. As Harpootlian lined up in front of her, a nervous smile played across her face and her answers came with a temerity we had not witnessed before.

Worley stated she had arrived on the scene at 12:07 a.m. the morning after the murders, about two hours after Alex's 911 call. She said the Colleton County Sheriff's office was supposed to secure the scene and they had marked some evidence. Harpootlian pointed out to her that someone had walked into the feed room and that one of the footprints had been linked back to law enforcement.

The defense attorney then goes over Worley's diagram of the crime scene. In the diagram (presented in the previous chapter) you

443

can see the date it was rendered as July 7, 2021, a month *after* the murders.

Harpootlian: "This is not to scale, correct?"

Worley answers in the affirmative. They go over the projectiles that missed their mark: one that entered the small doghouse next to Maggie, one that entered the side of a quail pen inside the hangar, and another that sailed through the hangar. Interestingly, no one seems to care about the bullet strike in the gravel just outside the feed room marked #13 on the diagram. Worley states that RP1 and RP2 on the diagram means "reference points."

At this point in Harpootlian's questioning, he fumbles around in his paperwork and seems disorganized. It goes on long enough that Judge Newman asks him if he needs more time to get organized. It is something that beleaguers the veteran attorney often during the course of the trial. Harpootlian is often at a loss with the ELMO monitor, tape recordings, and other technical equipment during exhibits, often saying, "I apologize, Your Honor. Technology is not my strong suit."

After Harpootlian gathers his notes, he continues with the diagram. He clarifies that the small pen inside the hangar is for quail and not chickens. This had confused many people who heard there was a bullet that went through the chicken coop, when in fact, it was a small cage inside the hangar overhang against the wall of the tool shed used for quail.

Even though Worley admits to the later date of July 7, she said she took the measurements the morning after the murders on June 8th. She also said she took additional measurements on July 16, 2021. She testifies that the bullet hole that entered the small doghouse by Maggie's body was on the kennel side and went into a dog bed inside. A photo of the doghouse on July 16th is shown.

(Testimony is given later in the trial by the pathologist, Dr. Riener, that the shot to Maggie's ribcage shows the bullet went through her body and exited. It could be this bullet that went through the exterior doghouse wall and imbedded in the dog bed inside. There is no casing assigned to the doghouse bullet in Worley's diagram, just an arrow pointing to a projectile entering the small doghouse behind Maggie's body. It may be that a casing left from firing into her body also represented the defect in the doghouse. It is harder to explain which marked casing belonged to the projectile that entered the quail pen.)

The small doghouse is at the left of this photo. Maggie's body was found just to the right of it. Beneath the hangar overhang to the left is the quail pen, against the wall of the tool room or workshop. The kennel door where Paul was found dead is at the right center of the photo.

Harpootlian asks Agent Worley if a FARO was used for her measurements? FARO provides the most precise 3D measurements, imaging and realization technologies. "We used a FARO on July 16th. We couldn't do it on June 8th because it was raining." The FARO gives a 3D image of the scene. Harpootlian asks if Worley provided the FARO as evidence at trial. He points out that Waters didn't ask her about in his direct. It is found and admitted and shown to the jury.

During the video, Harpootlian points out that the small doghouse is not perpendicular to the feed room where Paul was shot and that it sits up on 2' x 4' slats.

Harpootlian: "You took measurements of the quail cage. Let me show you the diagram of the quail cage. Defect interior side wall and back wall of cage. Entry and exit." A flight rod that Worley used to show the bullet trajectory angle going into the wall of quail pen is shown at a 41-degree angle. The bullet went through the back wall of the quail pen and into the tool shed or workroom of the hangar.

The Defense attorney next points out that the bullet hole to the doghouse was on its side facing the kennels (the right side of the doghouse showing in the photo above and on the next page) and the entry was at an 84-degree horizontal angle. "So, the AR was fired from way up here?" he asks emphatically. Worley is repeatedly pressing her lips together nervously and is trying to keep up with all the questions about trajectory that he is hurling at her. He points out that the shots are far away from the feed room, especially the quail pen shot.

"Were the two projectiles (the quail pen and the doghouse bullets) tested for blood?" he asks.

"I don't know," Worley says nervously.

"If I told you they didn't, would that surprise you?"

He then went in for the, pardon the term, kill shot. It was the entire reason for the discussion about bullets and different trajectory ranges. It was the theory they would hang their hat on throughout the trial, no matter how ridiculous the scenario some of their diagrams portrayed.

"Is it a possibility there were two shooters?" he asked.

"It could have indicated movement," Worley said calmly, spiking back her best volley of the cross-examination,

The quail pen can be seen center behind the doghouse. The bullet entered the paper paneling showing on its left side, went through the pen, and entered the wall behind it, which abuts the tool room. Circles show where the two bullets entered the structures.
Photo courtesy of the *Daily Mail*.

Harpootlian's next attack was the footprints in the feed room where Paul was shot. How had she photographed those? He pulled out his Crime Scene Protocol 101 data and stated the photographs taken of the prints should have included: 1) Good lighting; 2) Lay a scale down next to the impression for reference in the photo; 3) Shoot straight down on the print, not at an angle.

Harpootlian: "Was that done on any of these?" he pounded.

Worley: "No, we didn't recognize footwear at that time."

Speaking of footwear, was that a possible footwear impression in mud on the back of Maggie's calf? Worley is a footwear expert, so the question was a valid one. She could only say it could have been a footwear impression…it had a pattern to it. As Harpootlian puts the photo of Maggie's calf with the mud impression up on ELMO for the jury to see, Alex is bobbing his head and grimacing.

Worley: "I wasn't able to attribute it to a particular type of shoe."

Harpootlian: "And again, no proper scale, no proper procedure to show Maggie's calf."

Worley: "It would have been better to take a proper photo with a scale," the agent admits.

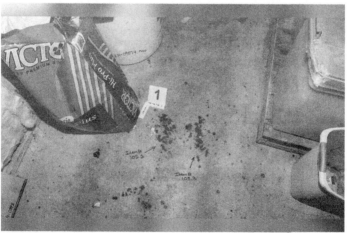

Paul's blood pattern from the blood dripping down his left arm after the first blast. It shows he is moving toward the door. The wadding from the second shot is seen in front of marker #1.

Harpootlian points out that Paul was alive for some period of time after the first shot. His brain was beside his left leg, and he was right at the door during the second shot. "How did he get from facing backwards to how he ended up?" She did not know. He further points out that if he's facing the back of the room, it's bloody, so he had already been shot, and buckshot is found imbedded in a tree outside the back of the window. Worley admits he was dripping blood. (It can be seen near the wadding that came from the second shotgun blast.)

Chief Kenneth Kinsley's reenactment photo of the feed room using a digital mannequin to show where Paul was standing during the first shot. In this illustration, he is not facing backwards as much as he is standing perpendicular to the door (seen at the right).

Next in the crosshairs was Alex's T-shirt worn that night. Harpootlian goes over how it should have been tested including photographing what they found with a scale. Worley says the shirt was not completely clean—it had some stains and smudges. (You can see Alex wipe his face with the shirt in the bodycam footage of Officer Greene). They did grid the shirt to show each section that was tested with Hematrace. No human blood was found on the shirt. There were some traces found on the shorts which Harpootlian had pointed out earlier that he said were when Alex wiped his fingers there after checking their pulses. No tests were done on the tennis shoes he was wearing.

Harpootlian takes his final shot at Agent Worley during his cross, by pointing out that on her official notes of the doghouse, she wrote 84 degrees for the bullet trajectory angle, but on the diagram, she put 94 degrees. She admitted to the error.

It was an obvious relief to SLED Agent Worley when Savannah

Goude with the prosecution stood up for re-direct. She led Worley through some follow-up questions based on Harpootlian's cross. There was stippling found on Maggie's calf which indicated she was shot at close range.

"The shooter could have moved around?" Goude asks.

"Yes."

"One person could have two guns?"

"Yes."

Those bloody footprints in the feed room...Exhibit 35 shows Paul's bloody footprints. Other prints there showed one closer to the door that was Paul's. The other prints could have been made by SLED later as these photos weren't taken until June 15 and 16th.

Goude then points out that an ATV was very near Maggie on her left side and that biological matter was found on the vehicle. Harpootlian objects, saying it could be deer blood; they hunt. That blood was never tested.

Harpootlian was on his feet for re-cross:

"Did you swab it or take it to the lab for testing for Maggie's blood?" (Meaning the blood matter found on the ATV.)

Worley: "No."

Harpootlian: "Did you test the water around Paul—was it tested for human blood?"

Worley: "No."

He pointed out again the lack of protocol in the imaging and measuring tactics used by Worley and ended his questioning.

A relieved Agent Melinda Worley stepped down from the stand. The camera panned to TV personality and True Crime aficionado Nancy Grace who was seated in the audience. The jury took a 10-minute break where one of them must have been on their phone. A tweet was posted by a local podcaster who had been in attendance at the trial. She mentions a juror's number and name in the tweet. At the end of the break, Judge Newman addresses the courtroom to remind everyone present that the names and identities of the jurors are to remain anonymous. Another request from the jury was to please remove a cart that was blocking their TV.

Creighton Waters for the prosecution called his next witness: SLED Agent Jeff Croft who had been present during Alex Murdaugh's second and third interviews. He was called out to the crime scene on June 8, 2021, at 5:30 a.m., missing the first interview with Alex which was held in Agent Owen's car around 1:00 a.m. that morning.

Agent Croft testifies that he interviewed Rogan Gibson. (Alex is riveted during this testimony.) Croft asked Rogan if he had any phone communication with Alex, Maggie, and Paul the night of the murders? Screen shots of Rogan's cell phone usage are put up on the ELMO. Rogan is holding the phone in the screen shot. A timeline of calls and texts are shown:

June 7, 2021:

- 8:40 pm call w/Paul—4 minutes
- 8:44 pm—communication with Paul
- 8:49 pm text to Paul "See if you can get a good picture of it..." No response from Paul
- Outgoing calls to Paul from Rogan: 9:10 pm, 9:29 pm, 9:42 pm, 9:57 (4 seconds). No answers.
- 9:58 pm. Text to Paul "Yo."
- Rogan texts Maggie at 9:34 pm. "Tell Paul to call me."
- Rogan calls Alex at 10:21 and 10:24 pm. No answer.
- Missed calls from Alex to Rogan at 10:25 and 10:30 pm.

Rogan would later testify that he turned his phone off and went to sleep after his last call to Alex. He did not speak with him that night. When Rogan is calling Alex at 10:21 and 10:24, law enforcement is starting to show up and so Alex is a little busy.

Croft testifies that Special Agent Katie McAllister was with him when he interviewed Rogan. A buccal swab was taken.

Agent Croft talks of going to the Moselle residence June 8th around 2 p.m. to secure firearms, shell casings, and ammo. Anthony Sampon and Katie McAllister accompany him. They are looking for firearms that could have fired the ammo found at the crime scene: a 12-guage 3" Magnum, and an AR rifle chambered for .300 Blackout. (Alex appears calm during this testimony.)

The disk of a bodycam worn during the agent's entry into the house is shown to the jury. In it, you can see him step outside where he notices objects on the ground by the back steps leading from the gun room. He and Agent Sampon collect 5 .300 Blackout casings that look weathered, laying in the flower bed by the steps and in some grass at the base of the brick landing.

Flower bed where a .300 Blackout casing was found the day after the murders. It was weathered. 4 more were found in close proximity. Photo courtesy of *Law & Crime* and Courtroom Pool photos.

Croft and Sampon go back into the residence where they find .300 Blackout bullets right next to the door in the gunroom area. Attorney Lee Cope, who works with Alex at PMPED is present. Also present from PMPED at the time are attorneys Mark Ball and Ronnie Crosby. Mark Ball points out a .300 Blackout rifle sitting in a gun wall case. Crosby points it out as well. Mark Ball brings attention to numbers on the bottom of a magazine stamped .223. The magazine can hold .300 Blackout. .300 is bigger than the .223. It has more stopping power, Croft points out on the stand.

Agent Katie McAllister is talking to John Marvin by the pool table in the room. The gunroom is really a gun wall with a bookcase next to it for ammo. It is part of a large recreation room with a pool table, couches and a television. There are half a dozen people in the room, not including law enforcement. McAllister goes over the paperwork for the search warrant. She mentions Alex has given his consent for them to search the house and property. Blanca is there in the kitchen during this time and sees the agents go upstairs to Paul's bedroom where they find a shotgun unfired shell on his nightstand.

The gunroom as seen in Croft's bodycam footage. People are sitting around on the couches in the rec room to the right. Photo courtesy of Law and Order and the Courtroom Pool photos.

Alex's beleaguered friend, Chris Wilson also shows up during the search. The room is teaming with lawyers, who appear to be doing their best to be helpful. Mark Ball is pointing out other ammo and Croft collects them. An empty box of S & B .300 Blackout, grain weight 147 is collected, and 12-gauge shells like those found in the feed room near Paul's body. Croft puts on latex gloves and begins collecting guns and ammo. He picks up an AR-15 chambered for .300 Blackout with the magazine removed. It has a thermal scope on it for night vision, meaning it is Buster's gun. Paul's, that had the thermal scope, was stolen, and the replacement AR had a red dot optic scope on it. The courtroom TV pans over to Buster during the testimony, but he sits expressionless.

As Agent Croft demonstrates for the jury the AR-15 collected from the house, he points out that the .300 Blackout casings found in the flower bed next to the stairs to the gunroom, and later at the family shooting range across the street, are the same as the casings found by Maggie's body. Jim Griffin objects, saying there's no proof that is the gun. He is overruled.

A 12-guage Browning from the bodycam video is shown. Item #90 is a 12-guage pump action shotgun, with the breach open, with a shell ready to be chambered. Exhibit #91 is a Benelli 12-guage similar to the one Paul had that is now missing. It is held up for the court to see.

Agent Jeff Croft demonstrates the thermal scope on the AR-15 that was Buster's gun to the Creighton Waters and the courtroom.

Agent Croft testifies to something that will become important as the ballistic evidence is gone over. These guns fire and eject to the "right and back." When looking at the .300 Blackout markers on Worley's diagram, it is helpful to know that the location of those casings is where they fell probably to the right and slightly behind the shooter.

An interesting object was pointed out in the bodycam footage inside the house the afternoon after the murders. Sitting atop a box on the bookcase next to the gun wall is a "shiny thing." It turns out to be a Capri Sun juice box that Maggie had asked Blanca to pick up from the store for Alex the day of the murders. Blanca was unable to find any at the Food Lion she stopped by.

Mark Ball and Ronnie Crosby both testify later that the SLED agents coming into the residence that day were very respectful and offered to remove their guns and badges if it would be less intrusive to the people in the room who were still grieving.

Agent McAllister (bottom right) talking with John Marvin at the pool table about the search warrant procedures. Chris Wilson and other attorneys are seated around the room.

The rest of the afternoon was spent going through garbage from the house where empty containers of Texas Toast, a small trash bag of cooked spaghetti with tomato sauce, Styrofoam cups of spit tobacco, shopping catalogues, and the credit card with Gucci circled in the amount of $1021.00, were found. Maggie's cell phone had already been located ¼ mile up the road from the house. It was now in evidence with SLED.

The shooting range owned by the family across the street from the Moselle property was searched. There was a "shoot house" there with benches to lean your weapon upon and fire at targets across the field. A dirt berm was behind the targets to catch the bullets or pellets as a precaution. They also searched a pond next to the shoot house where they found mostly shotgun shell casings. These came from a 12-guage shotgun. (Paul's friends would testify that Paul shot his Benelli shotgun here often.)

The remainder of testimony that day was the prosecution playing the recording taken during Alex Murdaugh's second interview inside Agent Owen's car at John Marvin's hunting property. This was covered in a previous chapter, so we won't repeat it here.

A dirt berm behind a shooting range target.
Photo courtesy of Casey Pittman.

January 31, 2021. Day 4 of Testimony

Jim Griffin took on Agent Jeff Croft on Tuesday of Week Two of the trial. Croft admitted that other agents went through the house the day after the murders with family members.

Griffin: "Did anyone look for bloody or dirty clothes?"

Croft: "I was in the gun room."

Griffin: "Aren't AR-15's common guns in the area?"

Croft: "Not as common as other guns."

Griffin: "None of the guns brought to the courtroom killed Paul or Maggie, right? Have you ever found the murder weapons?"

Croft: "Not that I'm aware of, sir."

Griffin tries to get Croft to say that none of the other guns he collected had two different kinds of shells. Croft tells him that is not correct.

The two talk ammo and turkey loads. Croft testifies that a thermal scope has to be charged. It is heat sensitive. He said the shots fired that night would likely be on the left-hand side of the markers as bullets eject to the right and slightly behind.

Griffin makes a salient point when he brings up the fact that SLED did not search Randolph III and Miss Libby's house in Almeda until September of 2021. "Wouldn't that be a good thing to do?" he asks Croft. Many armchair detectives in this saga have asked the same question. Murdaugh went there the night of the murders. He was the first to find the bodies and he was the spouse of one of the victims. That usually puts you "in the circle" right away. Yet SLED did not go to the place he went to upon leaving Moselle at a time that the two victims were probably shot. The weapons were missing from day one, yet they did not go look at Almeda. Was it partly because Randolph III was such a powerful presence in Hampton? But Randolph had passed away only three days after the murders. Was the name Murdaugh still wielding power?

Croft again brings up the .300 Blackout magazine clip found in a black Ford F-150 on the property.

Griffin: "Who last drove the F-150?"

Croft: "I don't know.

Griffin: "Any analysis done?"

Croft: "It doesn't look like it."

Griffin mentions that no one at SLED went to the berm at the shooting range and dug out .300 Blackout projectiles to compare them to the ones found at the crime scene. Did anyone shoot Buster's AR-15 to compare those projectiles to the ones found? Croft was left with egg on his face.

Griffin now zeros in on the time during the second interview in Owen's car when Croft was present. Griffin disputes that Alex says, "I did him so bad!"

Croft: "I made a note of it."

Griffin: "Well, isn't that a significant thing? And yet you don't ask him what he meant by "I did him so bad," in your third interview on August 11th."

Croft said they have a transcript of him saying, "I did him so bad."

Griffin plays the clip again for the courtroom as Exhibit 243. He has Phillip Barber, their tech attorney, play it again at 1/3 speed.

Croft listens and says, "I heard 'I'."

Many, including this author, have listened to that portion of the tape several times. It's a close call. I do think I hear him say, "*They did him so bad.*" You can judge for yourself.

Croft said he did go and interview the Branstetter's (Maggie's parents), and the Proctors (Maggie's sister). They asked about Alex. They said Alex and Maggie had a loving relationship, also with Paul. Barbara Mixon and Tina Treyhorn's names are mentioned but we are left unclear as to their importance in this conversation. Barbara is Miss Libby's caregiver during the daylight hours. Alex did say she bought him drugs a few times. Tina Treyhorn is a mystery.

On Creighton Water's re-direct, he asked Croft about the stippling found on Maggie. It was also determined that stippling was also found on Paul, meaning both had some gunshot wounds that would have been made at three feet or less. Croft confirms that they got two projectiles: one from the dog bed and one from the area by the tire tracks in the hangar. Again, the bullet fragments in the gravel strike are not mentioned.

Michael Kinech with Verizon Wireless was the next witness. He went over data sessions and downloads for pertinent cell phones by various people of interest in the murder case. They were listed as exhibits for the State:

- Ex. 268 Alex Murdaugh's phone records
- Ex. 269 Paul Murdaugh's phone records
- Ex. 265 Maggie Murdaugh's phone records
- Ex. 262 CB Rowe's phone records
- Ex. 263 Marti Cook's phone (Connor Cook's father)
- Ex. 264 Rogan Gibson's phone records
- Ex. 266 Connor Cook's phone records
- Ex. 267 Buster Murdaugh's phone records
- Ex. 270 Key found for each CD (PDF). A key allows someone to read Verizon's records. The records were listed in Greenwich time and local time. It was a four-hour difference between the two.

Maggie's phone records were searched from May 1, 2021 – June 10, 2021. It was reported that Verizon keeps records on file for 18 months.

Sergeant Paul McManigal, with the Charleston County Sheriff's Cyber Fraud division was next. He testified that in June of 2021, Dylan Hightower gave him the data from Alex Murdaugh's phone that was extracted during the June 10th interview with Agent Owen at John Marvin's hunting lodge. He was asked to redact any client privilege information. The redacted version of Alex's phone was then returned to Hightower. There were no call logs redacted.

McManigal testified that Paul's Apple iPhone 11 was locked, and they couldn't unlock it. He said the phone was powered off when he received it and he had to charge it. Paul had let it get to 2% the night of the murders. Sometime that night, as it lay on his body, it finally died.

John Vanhoughten with the Secret Service took the stand and brought a moment of subdued levity to the stuffy diatribe of data and ballistics. He works as a Digital Forensics Investigator for the Secret Service. He received Paul's cell phone from Lt. Dove on March 21, 2022. It was brought to him to see if he could unlock it, a full 9 months after the murders. He testified that you could force your way into a locked phone using Cellebright, which he called brute force. There is a trick to trying to guess at someone's passcode. If you enter the incorrect code too many times incorrectly, it will shut down. A 4-digit code, if you did 146 code variations a day, would take two months to unlock it. If it's a 6-digit code, it could take 18 months.

With that daunting information hanging above the courtroom's heads, he delivered one of the few lighthearted statements in this grim trial. After all the attempts to open Paul's phone; and after Alex's dire warning that no one would ever guess the password because Paul was so secretive, Vanhoughten announced they opened the phone "rather quickly" by typing in Paul's date of birth. A warm chuckle went through the courtroom, but one with a touch of melancholy.

Vanhoughten testified that he did the extractions from the phone, but SLED did the analysis. On March 24, 2022, he returned the phone to Lt. Dove and a chain of custody form was duly filled out.

Lt. Britt Dove identifying the disk with his phone data for the trial.

Lt. Britt Dove would provide the cell phone data that many had been waiting for. The detailed accounts of Maggie's and Paul's last communications and movements would be laid bare for all to dissect. And dissect they did. Many a FB Murdaugh super sleuth went to it with detailed charts and timelines. My hat is off to a few of them that turned in some amazing work.

Lt. Dove's testimony began in the afternoon with a list of Maggie's data. The following day, he did Alex's and then Paul's. In the interest of time, I will combine them in the next chapter as we head into Day 5 of testimony.

Chapter Thirty-One
Cell Phones Paint a Timeline of Murder

Below is a compilation of Alex, Maggie's, and Paul's cell phone records the day of June 7, 2021, beginning with Alex's departure for work. It has never been proven that Maggie Murdaugh spent the previous night there. We only hear about Blanca helping him adjust his shirt collar and that he slips on his loafers and leaves for work.

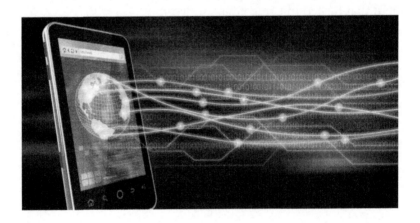

JUNE 7, 2021

Sometime between Alex's arrival at work at 12:24 pm and his call to Jeannie Seckinger at her office at 4 pm, Jeannie confronts

Alex about missing funds. He also receives a call from his brother Randy that their father is going back to the hospital.

12:06:47 p.m.: Alex Murdaugh's vehicle leaves the Moselle property headed to the PMPED law firm in Hampton.

12:24:06 p.m.: Alex Murdaugh arrives at the PMPED law firm.

3:28 p.m.: Murdaugh housekeeper Blanca Turrubiate-Simpson finishes cooking dinner at Moselle. She texts Maggie, who is in the Charleston area, "Dinners on the stove, just left."

3:40 p.m.: Maggie texts Blanca "Thank you."

3:41 p.m.: Alex Murdaugh places a FaceTime call to his wife Maggie. It goes unanswered. A SLED agent testifies that the record of the call is later manually deleted from Alex's phone.

Before 4 p.m.: Roger Dale Davis arrives in Moselle to feed the dogs, chickens and clean the dog pens. He said no one else was at the property when he arrived, and nothing was out of place.

3:55 p.m.: Maggie texts Blanca, "I'm waiting at doctor. Alex wants me to come home. I have to leave the door open at Edisto. I trust Mexicans to shut and lock for me. His dad is back in hospital. No cancer. It's pneumonia."

Marian Proctor, Maggie's sister, later testifies that Maggie thought she was going to Moselle to see Alex's dying father.

3:57 p.m.: Maggie texts Blanca regarding Alex having a lot of pressure on him to care for his ailing parents, "Alex is about to die. Hope he doesn't go down there to sleep. Alex needs to take care of himself as well."

3:57 p.m.: Alex texts Maggie, "How's your doctor appt?"

Maggie responds: "Waiting as usual."

4:06 p.m.: Maggie texts Blanca, in reference to the ailing Randolph Murdaugh, "I'm scared for him and Alex and all of us."

Blanca texts Maggie, "I know just pray about it. Just pray about it and hope he gets a little better. Alex and you really need to relax. Always being on the go with little to no sleep is not healthy. I have a doctor's appointment in the morning in Beaufort. If I go to Moselle, I will let you know."

4:10-6:25 p.m.: Alex Murdaugh's phone places him at the PMPED law firm in Hampton.

4:25-7:05 p.m.: Maggie's phone places her in the West Ashley area, near Charleston.

4:30 p.m.: Roger Dale Davis leaves Moselle after caring for the dogs and chickens.

4:35 p.m.: Alex places a FaceTime call to Maggie. It goes unanswered. A SLED agent testifies that the record of the call is later manually deleted from Alex's phone.

5:30-6:09 p.m.: Paul Murdaugh's phone places him in Okatie.

6:04:11 p.m.: Paul Murdaugh calls Will Loving.

6:04:25 p.m.: Will Loving calls Paul Murdaugh.

6:08:57 p.m.: Paul Murdaugh calls "Dad." No record of the call is found on Alex Murdaugh's phone.

6:09:48: Maggie Murdaugh texts Paul saying she's getting a foot massage.

6:20:53 p.m.: Marian Proctor calls her sister Maggie's phone. Maggie texts Marian saying she can't talk and she's getting a foot massage.

6:23:27 p.m.: Paul texts his mom asking what Blanca cooked for dinner. She replies to country fried steak and macaroni and cheese.

6:24 p.m.: Alex Murdaugh's vehicle leaves the PMPED law firm, headed to Moselle.

6:25:35 p.m.: Alex Murdaugh's phone receives a call from Jay Parker.

6:17-6:53 p.m.: Paul's phone shows him traveling from Okatie to Moselle.

6:40:01 p.m.: Paul Murdaugh calls "PA" (Alex Murdaugh's phone). The call lasts 2 minutes and 29 seconds. There is no call log for it in Alex Murdaugh's phone.

6:42 p.m.: Alex Murdaugh's vehicle arrives at Moselle.

6:43 p.m.: Alex calls his wife's phone. The call lasts 104 seconds. There is no call log for it in the data extractions of Alex's phone.

6:53:44 p.m.: Paul Murdaugh's phone calls John Marvin Murdaugh.

7:04 p.m.: Paul Murdaugh is at Moselle.

7:05 p.m.: Alex texts Maggie, "Paul says you are getting pedi!! Call when you get done."

7:00:06 p.m.: Paul texts CB Rowe asking if he's coming to the property the next day.

7:07-7:50 p.m.: Maggie's phone places her traveling from the North Charleston area, taking Highway 17, towards Moselle.

7:09:43 p.m.: Maggie Murdaugh calls Courtney Shelbourne. The call lasts 3 seconds.

7:09:43 p.m.: Maggie Murdaugh calls "Mom." The call lasts 8 minutes and 17 seconds.

7:14:13-7:22:19 p.m.: Paul Murdaugh's phone records 208 steps taken.

7:15:35-7:21:52 p.m.: Alex Murdaugh's phone records 200 steps taken.

7:18:40 p.m.: Maggie Murdaugh calls "Barbara." The call lasts 2 seconds.

7:18:44 p.m.: Alex Murdaugh texts CB Rowe stating, "Call me pls."

7:25:03-7:34:47 p.m.: Paul Murdaugh's phone shows 139 steps taken.

7:28:35-7:37:11 p.m.: Alex Murdaugh's phone records 47 steps taken.

7:31:13 p.m.: Maggie Murdaugh calls her sister Marian Proctor. The call lasts 7 minutes and 39 seconds.

7:35:10-7:41:43 p.m.: Paul Murdaugh's phone records 171 steps taken.

7:37 p.m.: Paul Murdaugh receives a Snapchat message from "michellebeck" stating, "BC I have short term memory loss."

7:38:34 p.m.: Paul receives an iMessage from Meagan Kimbrell stating, "Paul."

7:39:48 p.m.: Maggie Murdaugh calls "Barbara." There is no answer.

7:39:55 p.m.: It appears Paul Murdaugh records the video of his father he sends as a Snapchat video about 15 minutes later.

7:41:23-7:48:49 p.m.: Alex Murdaugh's phone records 29 steps.

7:45-7:56 p.m.: Paul's phone places him by the kennels on the Moselle property.

7:50 p.m.: Maggie's phone is in Walterboro, roughly a half hour away from Moselle. It's the last location data pulled from her phone.

7:50:03 p.m.: Maggie calls "Barbara." The call lasts 8 seconds.

7:55:44-8:05:28 p.m.: Paul Murdaugh's phone records 262 steps.

7:55:32-8:05:07 p.m.: Alex Murdaugh's phone records 270 steps.

7:56 p.m.: Paul sends a Snapchat video. In the video, Paul laughs as Alex is seen standing by a little tree at Moselle as it flops over.

8:05:35-8:09:52 p.m.: Alex Murdaugh's phone records 54 steps.

8:05:46-8:15:24 p.m.: Paul Murdaugh's phone records 303 steps.

8:06 p.m.: Paul's phone begins moving from the kennels to the main house.

8:07:20 p.m.: Paul Murdaugh sends a Snapchat message to several friends.

8:09-9:02 p.m.: Alex's phone records no steps, indicating he was not moving with the phone in his possession. He later told investigators he was sleeping during that time.

8:11:08-8:31:15 p.m.: Maggie Murdaugh's phone is locked.

8:14-8:35 p.m.: Paul Murdaugh's phone puts him at the main house.

8:15:55-8:21:45 p.m.: Paul's phone records 140 steps.

8:17-8:18 p.m.: Maggie Murdaugh's phone records 38 steps taken.

8:19:23 p.m.: Paul Murdaugh receives a Snapchat message from "Ansley Wilson," stating "He's got the magic touch."

8:23:33 p.m.: Paul sends a Snapchat message to "Marlene Robinson," stating, "He's hurt."

8:24:08 p.m.: Paul sends an iMessage to Meagan Kimbrell stating, "Meagan."

8:28:07 p.m.: Paul receives an iMessage from Meagan Kimbrell stating, "We're u avoiding me."

8:28:35 p.m.: Paul responds to Meagan Kimbrell with, "When?"

8:28:54 p.m.: Paul receives an iMessage from a Mrs. Morgan stating, "I have not received anything back yet. Did you get the lease email?"

8:29:06 p.m.: Paul receives an iMessage from Meagan Kimbrell stating, "You didn't send me any movie recommendations."

8:29:36 p.m.: Paul responds, "Haha I didn't have a good one. Wills might."

8:30-8:33 p.m.: Maggie Murdaugh's phone records 43 steps taken.

8:31 p.m.: John Marvin Murdaugh sends a text to several family members, including Alex and Maggie, which reads, "I plan to go over to visit dad tomorrow afternoon. Is anyone else planning to go?" Maggie Murdaugh's phone did not unlock for the notification until 8:49:26 p.m. Alex Murdaugh read it at 1:44 p.m. the following day.

8:32:10 p.m.: Paul receives a call from Lucile Boyle. The call was not answered.

8:32:25-8:42:11 p.m.: Paul's cell phone records 283 steps taken.

8:38 p.m.: Paul's phone places him by the kennels.

8:40:20 p.m.: Paul calls longtime friend Rogan Gibson asking if something is wrong with the tail of Gibson's dog, who was staying in the Murdaugh kennels. The call lasts 4 minutes and 14 seconds.

8:41:38 p.m.: Paul receives a Snapchat message from Rogan Gibson.

8:44:34 p.m.: Paul Murdaugh initiates a FaceTime call with Gibson. It lasts 11 seconds.

8:44:55 p.m.: Paul records a video for Gibson at the kennels, showing the dog. Three voices are heard in the video. Multiple witnesses testify that those voices are Paul, Maggie, and Alex Murdaugh.

8:47:55 p.m.: Paul sends an iMessage to Meagan Kimbrell stating, "Haha kidding."

8:48:05 p.m.: Paul again sends an iMessage to her, stating, "Star was born is the movie."

8:48:29 p.m.: Meagan Kimbrell texts Paul, "No I need something happy" and "Don't like watching sad movies."

8:49:01 p.m.: Paul Murdaugh's phone is locked.

8:49:26 p.m.: Maggie Murdaugh's phone unlocks, and she reads another text in the group chat about Randolph Murdaugh.

8:49:28 p.m.: Maggie Murdaugh's phone accesses an application and implements orientation change to landscape.

8:49:31 p.m.: Maggie Murdaugh's phone is locked and not unlocked until it's found a quarter mile away the next afternoon.

8:49:35 p.m.: Rogan Gibson texts Paul about the dog's tail, "See if you can get a good picture of it. MaryAnn wants to send it to a girl we know that's a vet. Get him to sit and stay. He shouldn't move around too much." The text goes unread.

Investigators believe Maggie and Paul Murdaugh are killed around 8:50 p.m. near the kennels. Paul is shot twice with a shotgun, once in the chest and once in the head. Maggie is shot 5 times with 300 Blackout ammo from an AR-style rifle. Two of those shots struck her in the head.

8:53 p.m.: The orientation on Maggie's phone changes, waking the screen to activate its Face ID security feature. But the phone remains locked, thus implying it is picked up by someone who is not her.

8:53:15-8:55:32 p.m.: Maggie Murdaugh's phone records 59 steps.

8:55:48 p.m.: Maggie Murdaugh's phone takes a snapshot of an open app, Facebook, running in the background.

9:02:18-9:06:47 p.m.: Alex Murdaugh's phone comes to life, recording 283 steps, about 70 steps per minute.

9:04:23 p.m.: Alex Murdaugh calls his wife's phone. There is no record of the call in the data extraction from Alex's phone.

9:05:15 p.m.: Alex Murdaugh calls his father Randolph Murdaugh. The call lasts 18 seconds. There is no record of it in the data extraction from Alex's phone.

9:06 p.m.: The orientation of Maggie Murdaugh's phone changes.

9:06:14 p.m.: Alex Murdaugh calls his wife's phone. There is no answer. There is no record of the call in the data extraction from Alex's phone.

9:07:06 p.m.: Alex's vehicle leaves Moselle headed to Almeda.

9:06:51 p.m.: Alex Murdaugh calls his wife's phone. There is no answer. There is no record of the call in the data extraction from Alex's phone.

9:08:36 p.m.: Alex Murdaugh's vehicle drives by where Maggie Murdaugh's missing cell phone would be found the following day. After passing the location, the vehicle quickly increases speed.

9:08:58 p.m.: Alex texts his wife's phone, "Going to check on Em be rite back."

9:10:47 p.m.: Alex calls his son Buster Murdaugh. The call lasts 60 seconds. There is no record of it in the data extraction from Alex's phone.

9:12:14 p.m.: Alex calls longtime friend and fellow attorney Chris Wilson. Wilson was busy and asked if he could call Alex back. The call lasts 2 minutes.

9:18:46 p.m.: Alex calls John Marvin Murdaugh. The call lasts 106 seconds. There is no record of the call in the data extraction of Alex's phone.

9:20 p.m.: Chris Wilson calls Alex back. Alex says he's getting close to his mom's house and asks if he can call him back. The call lasts 3 minutes.

9:22:06 p.m.: Alex's vehicle arrives at his mother's Almeda property.

9:22:39 p.m.: Alex's vehicle pauses halfway up the driveway and parks by the wood line, away from the home.

The speed of the trip is faster than any trip he took that day, reaching 74 miles per hour.

9:24:13 p.m.: Shelly Smith, Libby Murdaugh's caregiver, testifies that Alex calls her from outside the home and asks to be let inside. She's able to get to the door 5 minutes later. Smith testifies that Libby, in the advanced stages of dementia, is asleep during the visit and that Alex is on his phone a lot. (Possibly deleting messages & calls.)

9:34 p.m.: Rogan Gibson, after not hearing back from Paul, texts Maggie Murdaugh, "Tell Paul to call me." The text goes unread.

9:35:55-9:45:37 p.m.: Alex Murdaugh's phone records 60 steps taken.

9:43:05 p.m.: Alex's vehicle is taken out of park at Almeda.

9:43:59 p.m.: Alex's vehicle is put into park.

9:44:54 p.m.: Alex's vehicle is taken out of park.

9:46:35 p.m.: Alex calls Paul Murdaugh's phone. The connection lasts 18 seconds. There was no record of it in the data extraction from Alex's phone.

9:47 p.m.: Alex texts Maggie, "Call me babe." The text goes unread.

9:52:15 p.m.: Alex texts Chris Wilson, "Call me if u up."

9:52:59 p.m.: Chris Wilson calls Alex. There is no answer.

9:53:55 p.m.: Chris Wilson calls Alex again. Alex picks up. Chris wanted to talk about some cases, but Alex said he was almost back home and would call him back.

9:54:24 p.m.: Alex Murdaugh's vehicle reaches 74 miles per hour as he returns to Moselle.

9:56:57-10:06:57 p.m.: Alex Murdaugh's phone records 231 steps taken.

9:57:09 p.m.: Rogan Gibson calls Paul Murdaugh. There is no answer.

9:58 p.m.: After not hearing from Paul or Maggie, Rogan Gibson texts Paul "Yo."

10:00:36 p.m.: Alex returns to Moselle and places his vehicle into park at the main house. On the drive back from Almeda, the vehicle reached 80 mph where the max speed limit was 55 mph.

10:01:17 p.m.: Alex takes the vehicle out of park.

10:01:29 p.m.: Alex puts the vehicle into park.

10:01:30 p.m.: Alex takes the vehicle out of park.

10:01:43 p.m.: Alex puts the vehicle into park at the main house at Moselle.

10:04:49 p.m.: Alex takes the vehicle out of park.

10:05:04 p.m.: Rogan Gibson calls Buster Murdaugh. The connection lasts 2 seconds.

10:05:06 p.m.: Alex Murdaugh's vehicle drives to the kennels from the main house.

10:05:55 p.m.: Alex puts the vehicle into park by the kennels.

10:06:14 p.m.: Alex calls 911 from the Moselle property. The call was received by Hampton County dispatch before being transferred to Colleton County.

In the 7-minute call, he says he found Maggie and Paul shot and neither were breathing.

During the call, he notes he is not presently by the bodies. He said he touched them after finding them but only to see if they were still breathing.

He hangs up after saying he needed to call family members.

10:06:57-10:16:37 p.m.: Alex Murdaugh's phone records 594 steps.

10:11:45 p.m.: Alex takes the vehicle out of park at the kennels and returns to the main house.

10:12:38 p.m.: Alex puts the vehicle into park at the main house.

10:13:39 p.m.: Alex takes the vehicle out of park at the main house, returning to the kennels.

10:14:30 p.m.: Alex Murdaugh's vehicle returns to the kennels.

10:17:49 p.m.: Alex Murdaugh calls Randy Murdaugh. The connection lasts 16 seconds. There is no record of the call in the data extraction of Alex's phone.

10:18:45 p.m.: Alex Murdaugh iMessages Randy Murdaugh, stating, "Pls call me. Emergency."

10:18:53-10:28:05 p.m.: Alex's cell phone records 525 steps taken.

10:19:32 p.m.: Alex Murdaugh calls Randy Murdaugh. The connection lasts 1 second. There is no record of the call in the data extraction of Alex's phone.

10:19:44 p.m.: Alex Murdaugh calls John Marvin Murdaugh. The call lasts 40 seconds. There is no record of the call in the data extraction of Alex's phone.

10:21:25 p.m.: Alex Murdaugh calls Rogan Gibson. There is no answer. Gibson testified he was already asleep.

10:21:57 p.m.: Alex Murdaugh calls Christy Murdaugh (Randy Murdaugh's wife.) The call lasts 53 seconds.

10:24:43 p.m.: Alex Murdaugh texts Rogan Gibson, stating "Call me."

10:25:49 p.m.: Alex Murdaugh attempts to FaceTime Rogan Gibson. There is no answer.

10:25 p.m.: The Colleton County Sheriff's office arrives at the kennels. The South Carolina Law Enforcement Division is contacted for assistance.

10:28:54-10:37:27 p.m.: Alex Murdaugh's phone records 320 steps taken.

10:29:17 p.m.: Alex Murdaugh calls Randy Murdaugh. The call lasts 42 seconds. There is no record of the call in the data extracted from Alex's phone.

10:30:31 p.m.: Alex Murdaugh again attempts to FaceTime Rogan Gibson. There is no answer.

10:34 p.m.: Nolen Tuten calls Paul Murdaugh's phone. Paul Murdaugh's phone dies.

10:35 p.m.: Alex Murdaugh calls John Marvin Murdaugh. The call lasts 28 seconds.

10:36 p.m.: Alex Murdaugh calls Randy Murdaugh. The call lasts 56 seconds.

10:40 p.m.: Alex Murdaugh searched "Whaley's Edisto" in Safari browser.

10:40:19-10:50:02 p.m.: Alex Murdaugh's phone records 244 steps taken.

10:44:20 p.m.: Alex Murdaugh calls Buster Murdaugh. The connection lasts 8 seconds.

10:45 p.m.: Alex Murdaugh calls Brooklyn White. The connection lasts 13 seconds. There is no record of the call in the data extraction of Alex's call.

10:46 p.m.: Alex Murdaugh calls Tracy White. The connection lasts 14 seconds. There is no record of the call in the data extraction of Alex's call.

10:46 p.m.: Buster Murdaugh calls Maggie Murdaugh. There is no answer.

10:47 p.m.: Alex Murdaugh texts Buster, Tracy White and Brooklyn White stating, "Call me urgent."

10:47 p.m.: Buster Murdaugh calls Alex. The call lasts 162 seconds.

10:55 p.m.: Alex Murdaugh calls Brian White. The connection lasts 8 seconds.

10:56 p.m.: Buster Murdaugh calls Alex Murdaugh. The call lasts 216 seconds.

11:17 p.m.: Alex Murdaugh calls Bart Proctor. The connection lasts 14 seconds.

11:19 p.m.: Randy Murdaugh, using Alex's phone, texts Bart Proctor stating, "Bart this is Randy Murdaugh. There has been a terrible tragedy and I need you to call me phone number XXX-XXX-XXXX immediately."

11:28 p.m.: LaClaire Lafitte texts Alex Murdaugh, stating, "Our hearts hurt for you and with you, Charlie and LaClaire."

11:56 p.m.: Tracy White texts Alex Murdaugh stating, "I am so so sorry!!!! Let me know how I can help!!! I am here for you all!"

11:47 p.m.: SLED arrives to the scene.

During the testimony given concerning the phone data, a long discussion had to do with phone orientation. Basically, phone orientation is whether it is being held up vertically (portrait mode) or horizontally (landscape mode). Much was made of Maggie's phone changing orientation after she was supposedly dead. It indicated that someone was carrying it around and manipulating it. It was also recording steps after the time she was believed to be dead. The Defense pounced on this piece of information, asking if Maggie and Alex's steps were ever in sync with their phone data, and the answer was, "No." (Note: Alex's phone is inactive until 9:02 pm, when it suddenly comes to life after being silent for an hour. Therefore, it is not recording his steps during the time we see someone carrying Maggie's phone which *is* recording steps. This is just before he heads to Almeda to establish his alibi.)

The other hiccup was the timing of when Maggie's phone was supposedly tossed out the window of Alex's SUV on his way to his mother's house. Maggie's phone did not show an orientation change at the time it would have been thrown. The expert had an explanation for this. He testified that if the phone was thrown in the landscape mode, meaning flat like one would throw a Frisbee, it might not show an orientation change. If, however, the person threw it end over end, it would. This issue was never fully resolved to the satisfaction of all, and it remained a sticky wicket throughout the remainder of the trial.

One of the more eerie moments was when it was pointed out that there seemed to be a short instant with Maggie's phone where it looked like the camera on her phone was accessed as if for face recognition to unlock the phone. It was only a second long, and it was admitted that was too short a time for someone to hope for face recognition. If it was Alex, and this camera swipe was after the time Maggie should have been dead, it didn't seem to make sense. It was Alex who gave SLED Maggie's passcode to unlock her phone the next morning when it was found by the side of the road. Of course, it may be he had found where the passcode was kept by then.

The biggest blowout of the case was finding the kennel video on Paul's phone. Each time it was played for the court, Alex would hunch over, bob his head, and sniff. Many witnesses listened to the video and identified Alex's voice as he calls for Bubba, the Labrador, who is running around with a chicken in his mouth.

Other points brought out about the phones, especially Paul's, were that a text can be partially seen on a phone without opening it. Even though it was the Defense team's Phillip Barber that pointed it out, it seemed like an odd point to make. If Alex had seen Rogan Gibson's text messages coming on Paul's phone, when Alex said it "popped out of Paul's back pocket," then wouldn't that mean Alex knew there was a possibility Rogan might have found out through Paul that Alex was at the kennels? We do know Alex tried multiple times to reach Rogan after that.

Lt. Dove said he got Maggie's phone on June 9th and the intake log created for Maggie's phone was on the same day. Again, Alex's phone is silent from 8:09 pm that night until 9:02 pm, when it suddenly comes to life. It was surmised he had left it deliberately at the house or in his car so that there was no record of his steps of phone log data during that time. This is one of the few pieces of evidence that shows premeditation by 8:00 pm that night. Of course, calling and texting Maggie, asking her to come to Moselle, showed premeditation.

At 9:02 pm, one second after Alex's phone is suddenly active again, and until 9:06 pm, it records that he made 283 steps. Attorney Barber with the Defense points out again that Maggie's phone isn't recording matching steps with Alex's phone, meaning, he wasn't carrying it. One theory posited by a witness was it could have been because her phone was in his pocket and recorded steps as he moved. Another was that his phone was lying inactive in the golf cart. This is the first time a golf cart has been mentioned and a lot of people, including this author, perked up.

Rogan Gibson pointing out Alex Murdaugh during his testimony.

Rogan Gibson was a very close friend to both Paul and Buster Murdaugh. Paul was letting Rogan's dog, Cash, stay in the Murdaugh kennels while Rogan was staying with his girlfriend and working a job in Beaufort. It was this chocolate brown puppy that caused Paul to be at the kennels that night. Paul said he thought something was wrong with Cash's tail, and Rogan asked him if he could take a photo of it. Paul walked down to the kennels, leaving the house around 8:30 p.m. He is on a phone call with Rogan at 8:40 when Rogan hears three voices, Paul's, Maggie's, and Alex's. This is not the famous kennel video. This is a phone call when Rogan hears Alex.

Paul attempts to do a FaceTime chat with Rogan to show him the dog's tail, which seems to show a lump about mid-way up the tail. The FaceTime call does not work. The cell phone coverage is spotty in this area of the property and his battery is down to nearly 5%. Paul tries for a phone video instead, and it is this 54-second video, filmed at 8:44 pm, that is Alex's undoing. Witness after witness identified his voice on the video calling for Bubba. If it had only been Rogan's word that he heard Alex during a phone call, that only he and Paul were privy to, Alex may have wiggled out of that one, or asked Rogan to lie. But the video put it out there for all the world to judge. Not one witness, from Paul's friends to Alex's co-workers and friends, denied it was his voice they heard. It was the most damning evidence of all. He had lied when he said he was never at the kennels. And Paul and Maggie were shot less than 3 minutes after that video was filmed.

It was obvious that Rogan Gibson did not want to be on that witness stand. He was somber and gave short answers, never elaborating. He had spent copious hours with the Murdaugh family and thought of Maggie and Alex as second parents. He seemed to still be grieving the loss of his friend, and perhaps, coming to terms with the fact that Alex had shot him.

Rogan made a statement during his testimony that was treated as a throwaway sentence, and it has stupefied this author that more was not made of it. He was asked if the kennel area could be seen from the house at Moselle. He said, "If the lights are on in the kennel area, you can see all over." I will go over this in a moment.

Rogan agreed with other testimony that Paul would leave his clothes everywhere. Paul was staying all over in the time before the murders. He would couch surf at friends' places, stay at John Marvin's, etc. One minute he was in Charleston with a friend, then at his apartment in Columbia, then down at Okatie. It was posited that Paul was doing this due to threats he had gotten about the boat crash and was trying to keep his whereabouts unknown. That was a point the Defense was happy to hear. It underscored their position that Paul was shot by someone other than Alex Murdaugh.

Paul's habit of leaving guns everywhere was also commented upon. Rogan was then asked if the Murdaughs had always welcomed him and the boy's friends into their homes. He said they did. At Moselle, the Holly Street house before it was sold, and at Edisto. They were always treated like they were part of the family.

When asked, if based on what he knew now, did Rogan still think he knew who Alex was, he answered sadly, "He's still Mr. Alex."

The Murdaughs in the hangar overhang at Moselle.

Back to Rogan's testimony about the lights at the kennel area. He said, "When they are on…you can see all over." In the photo above, we see the Murdaughs posing proudly in front of the tractor parked beneath the overhang at the hangar, right next to the dog kennels where Maggie and Paul were shot. You can see behind Alex that it is dark outside, but the lights inside the hangar are as bright as day. People I've interviewed for this book spoke of parties at Moselle in the hangar area, where the lights were really bright.

In all of the bodycam footage taken that night, immediately after Alex makes his 911 call, it is pitch black in the hangar area. The only light is that of the feed room spilling out over Paul's prostrate body, and from the open tool room at the back. The bright hangar lights are not on. All of the responders leave their headlights on to illuminate the area, until a SLED agent rigs up a tripod light to take photographs.

Why aren't the hangar lights on? Why is it never mentioned once during the trial? It seems pretty significant. Did it mean the shooter

479

wanted darkness to cover what he was doing? It seems implausible that Maggie would be running the dogs at 8:30-ish, when the sun was setting, without light. The feed room light was on. We don't know if the light to the big workshop area of the hangar at the back was on at that time. It was when the first responders arrived and found Alex there. Yet, if you look at the kennel video, taken at 8:44:49, it does appear that it is getting dark out. It probably wasn't full dark until a few minutes later. The question is, why aren't the hangar lights on? Had Alex disabled them ahead of time?

Will Loving on the witness stand.

Will Loving was led through questions by Creighton Waters as Paul's close friend took the stand. Will graduated from High School in 2015, the same year as Buster, and the same year Stephen Smith was murdered. He said he met Paul at Edisto Beach, and even though Paul was two years younger, they hit it off. Before the murders, he and Paul had lived together in Columbia at college. He testified they had plans to get a small house together with another friend for the college term.

Perhaps Will's biggest contribution to the case was his testimony concerning the replacement AR-15 that was believed used in the murder of Maggie Murdaugh and was now missing. Will was with Paul when they went to Ace Hardware and bought a red dot optic scope for the gun. It was put on Alex's tab. He said the scope "doesn't zoom in." They bought it March 6, 2021, he said, and

480

sighted it in to calibrate it with the gun the same day. They sighted it at the back steps leading into the Moselle house by propping it up on the stair banister and shooting it into the field behind the house.

"We learned it on the right stair railing because we're both right-handed," he said. Will said it was early March 2021, when they did this. That would put the AR-15 on the property, and ejecting casings that matched those around Maggie's body, only 3 months before the murders. He said the scope was not a thermal scope used in hog hunting, when you're looking for heat imaging from the hogs. Will said he didn't recall seeing the tan AR-15 again after the night they used it for turkey hunting season on March 21st or 22nd.

Waters has Will identify photos showing the stair railing leading into the gun room and the flower bed and brick landing to say that is the area where they were firing from. It is this area where SLED found the .300 Blackout casings. Will describes Paul's favorite shotgun as a black Super Eagle 3 Benelli shotgun. "It had a camouflage cryptic, sort of blueish purple camouflage, more of a distinctive color camouflage. Waters brings up a shotgun for Will to identify and he confirms it was Paul's favorite shotgun. He says they did have two shotguns that looked like that.

Will testifies that an AR is louder than a shotgun and that Paul didn't want to put a suppressor on it because it decreased the shooting distance and accuracy.

Paul called Will the night of the murders saying he would like to get a hot tub for the house they were going to get together. The only other time he heard from Paul was when Paul sent a SnapChat of Paul and Alex looking at a tree that was "swooped down."

"Miss Maggie would go down to the kennels either by riding her bike, her car, or walking. She liked to walk their two labs around the property, so it was not uncommon for her to go down there. She would go down there and mess with the dogs. She would like to ride her bike right before sunset; she was a dog lover for sure. I only saw her go down in the daytime. She might have been down there just as it got dark, but she wouldn't be down there after dark."

"Paul used his cell phone a lot. He usually kept his phone in one of his front pockets."

(Is this why Alex was trying to roll Paul over? The phone was buzzing in Paul's front pocket. Or was the phone under him?)

Waters asks Will why he thought the Murdaughs sold the Holly

Street house (which was shortly after the boat crash).

"It was just through the grapevine, it was to help pay for some of the lawsuits they were under," Will acknowledged, over objections from Jim Griffin that it was hearsay. Waters plays the kennel video for Will, and he identifies Alex as the voice on the video.

Jim Griffin, during cross, asks Will when was the last time he saw Paul? He testified it was at the Memorial Day/Birthday party for Alex at Edisto. When asked, he said Paul had an awesome relationship with Alex. He said Alex and Maggie were loving and laughing at the party.

Jim Griffin asks Will if Paul had left a .300 Blackout at the Columbia apartment for a month, and he answered "Yes." "Was it the one showed to you here in court with the thermal scope?" "Yes, sir." (This is Buster's AR-15.) And a deer rifle Paul thought lost was found in Will Chapman's closet.

Griffin questions Will about the night of the murders. Will says he got the call around midnight that they had been shot and high-tailed it out of the apartment. "Were you fearful for your safety?" Griffin asks. "Yeah, at first I wasn't, but after some friends said stuff, I decided to get out of there." Griffin asks if he locked the apartment door where he and Paul were rooming in Columbia when he hurried out? "I honestly couldn't tell ya," Will admits. (SLED agents went to Paul's Columbia apartment immediately after the murders and found the door to his apartment open. Rumors were everywhere that maybe SLED was looking for a bat that may have killed Stephen Smith. It was probably to secure Paul's electronic devices.)

Griffin plays the short video of all of them at Edisto where everyone is singing "Happy Birthday" to Alex. (Alex is weeping with his head bobbing as the video is played. Dick Harpootlian looks over at him after several minutes of this and says something to him.)

Will is asked about getting to Moselle that night and hugging Alex when he entered the house. There are about 10 of Paul's friends there and there is crying everywhere. "It was a tough time, wasn't it?" Griffin asks. "Yes, sir."

Creighton Waters stands for re-direct. He plays the Birthday party again and asks Will who the guy is in the green shirt hugging Alex. Will states it is Chris Wilson, Alex's best friend.

. Alex breaks down during the birthday video. Harpootlian puts his hand on his arm and says something to him.

Waters asks Will about the SnapChat video where Paul and Alex are riding the property and looking at a tree. The video is played. Will said he watched the video in real time when it came in that night and says those are the clothes he saw Alex wearing in the original SnapChat.

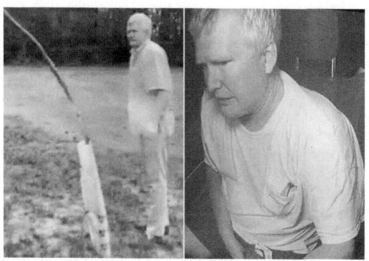

Alex in SnapChat video wearing a blue dress shirt, khaki pants, and brown loafers (left) taken around 7:30 pm the night of the murders by Paul Murdaugh as they "rode the property." On the right, Alex as he was dressed when law enforcement arrived 15 minutes after his 911 call. A white T-shirt and cargo shorts, & neon tennis shoes.

In the photo on the previous page, Alex is in a pale blue button-up dress shirt with long khaki pants and brown loafer-like shoes. This shirt is not the one Blanca described as a seafoam green polo shirt with three buttons at the top that he was wearing when she helped him with his collar as he left for work the afternoon of the murders. The pants and shoes seem to be the ones she said he wore as he went out the door to work, but not the shirt.

Will is asked by Waters if he knew anything about Alex's finances and the $792,000 missing funds. Will answered "No, Sir." Will is dismissed and Day Five comes to an end.

Day 6 of Murdaugh Murder Trial

Day 6 of the trial would bring a few faces to the gallery who had been there infrequently; notably, Randy Murdaugh. Today would be the financial information concerning Alex's myriad frauds and the impact it had on his law office at PMPED. Randy Murdaugh, Alex's brother was still a partner there and he had been grossly affected by his younger brother's behavior. The firm was now called The Parker Law Group.

The Judge began by going over the 404-B ruling. This ruling is basically one that shows whether a defendant's other acts are admissible to show motive—namely Alex's financial crimes. The testimony from a few of the people involved in Alex's financial frauds would be heard first "in-camera," meaning, the jury would not be present, so that the judge could rule if their testimony would later be heard by the jury.

Jennifer Seckinger, CFO for what was the PMPED law firm, but is now called the Parker Law Group, after Alex's frauds came to light and he was let go, is first up. Creighton Waters leads her through each of Alex's settlement frauds and asks her each time what his actions meant to the firm. She answered, "He stole it."

Seckinger found out from Alex that he was trying to defer payments to himself and put them into Maggie's account to hide his revenue from the boat crash lawsuit. She said PMPED did not want any part of it.

The rest of Seckinger's testimony had to do with information already stated in this book. It came to her attention that fees from the Ferris case had not come in, only the expenses from that case, and she and Alex's paralegal, Annette Griswold, began hunting for it. During that process, they found other missing funds. It all came to a head the afternoon of the murders when Seckinger confronted Alex in his office.

During the month of September, following Alex's dismissal and fake roadside shooting, the firm found payments through Palmetto State Bank converted into personal use for Alex. They found the fake Forge account. They compiled a spreadsheet of money they found he had stolen and met with the affected clients. The law firm personally paid them all back to the tune of $2,841,000 dollars. They traced his fraudulent movements clear back to 2015. Later, they found others that went as far as 2008. He started the fake Forge account in 2015.

Russell Lafitte's part in Alex's schemes was brought to the foreground. Palmetto State Bank was a Lafitte family run business with Russell holding key positions. It was found that he had been filtering checks to Alex and re-cutting checks at Alex's request to break them down for Alex's personal benefit. Russell received a substantial fee for acting as conservator in Hakeem Pinckney's settlement where Alex kept the paraplegic's money.

After going over this information, Jeannie Seckinger ruefully admitted that Russell Lafitte was her brother-in-law. "He's married to my husband's sister," she said.

Jeannie finished her lengthy time on the stand by stating Chris Wilson, the co-counsel with Alex in the Ferris case, called on September 3rd, 2021, and said he was missing a couple of hundred thousand and wanted PMPED to "pony up." It was the next day Wilson confronted Alex. Less than two hours after that, Alex was "shot in the head" on Old Salkehatchie Road.

Captain Ryan Neal with SLED was on the stand briefly to say the crime scene tape had been taken down the next day, on June 8th, and the scene had been released. He said a lot of the law firm people were there along with family members. He took drone footage that day.

Next was Dylan Hightower, an investigator for the 14th Circuit Court. He went over finding Maggie's phone on June 8th after John Marvin Murdaugh helped them by using Buster Murdaugh's Find My Phone app. He went over the collecting of the phone and placed landscaping flags around the location of the phone. He was also on

485

the scene at John Marvin's hunting lodge on June 10th to download data from the cell phones belonging to Alex, Randy, John Marvin, and Buster Murdaugh. He stated it took less than an hour per phone to download the information. Their phones were returned to them before they left that day.

Dylan Hightower on the stand.

The phone files were sent to Agent McManigal who used a more advanced data retrieval system called Cellebrite. He said 73 phone calls and two FaceTime's had been deleted from Alex Murdaugh's phone during the June1-June 10 timeline. "You cannot delete records from Verizon," Hightower testified. He said there was a large gap of deleted phone calls on Alex's phone.

When Harpootlian faced off with the unflappable Hightower, he said he went over to Maggie's phone and that it was about 15-20 feet from the road. The Defense attorney pressed that it was too far away from the road for someone to throw it from a car window. With complete confidence, Hightower unflinchingly said, "I could throw it to that location—100%. I'd throw it sideways." (Like a Frisbee.)

Hightower testified that he put Maggie's phone in Airplane mode when it was discovered to prevent the data from being overridden from an outside signal. He said that if someone had her passcode, they could open it and delete messages. He also said the battery was very low.

He finished by saying there was no vandalism reported or anything missing at the crime scene.

SLED agent Katie McAllister

SLED agent Katie McAllister, Senior Special Agent in the Lowcountry was next. McAllister testified that it was she who typed in the passcode to Maggie's cell phone on June 8th and it worked. She did not delete or alter any data. They locked it back and put it in Airplane mode. Captain Neal took it.

McAllister said they arrived at the scene shortly after lunch time. When she and Agent Croft entered the house, there were about 20-25 people. She asked for consent to search, that they were looking for firearms and ammunition. John Marvin and Lee Cope (a partner at PMPED) accompanied them as they searched every room. They searched bathrooms, tubs, and attic spaces filled with holiday decorations. She stated that Croft found four guns and ammo that were taken. A property receipt was filled out. They drove the guns to Walterboro where Agent Worley took them. McAllister stated she did take a buccal swab from Buster.

During the cross, it was noted there were 3 or 4 bedrooms at Moselle. When Harpootlian asked her if any of the tubs or sinks were swabbed for blood, she replied, "No, sir. There was no blood visible to me."

"Any evidence of any bloody clothes or shoes?"

"No, sir."

At 4:00 p.m. that day, the jury was dismissed until 11:30 a.m. the following day, as there would be more "in-camera" testimony.

Michael Gunn with Forge Consulting going over evidence.

The "in-camera" testimony involved Michael Gunn with Forge Consulting. He testified that his relationship with Alex Murdaugh had begun in a professional capacity but later became a friendship. He did five insurance settlement structures with Alex over the years. He was aware of the boat case and that Alex was being sued because of it.

When asked about the events surrounding PMPED's discovery of Alex's financial fraud, Gunn said Lee Cope called him and asked if Forge Consulting ever banked at Bank of America. He said they hadn't in several years. Bank of America was where Alex's fake Forge account was set up. Gunn was told by Cope about the phony Forge account, and he was surprised. When shown checks that went to the fake Forge account, Gunn testified none of them had gone to the legitimate Forge Consulting account. He stated that Forge Consulting LLC did a full investigation into it after Cope notified him of the fraud.

Chapter Thirty-Three
What Are Friends For?

The most heartbreaking testimony on Day 6 was the "in-camera" testimony of Chris Wilson, a man who considered Alex Murdaugh his best friend. He looked totally broken on the witness stand. We have gone over some of his testimony earlier in the book. This is a recap of his lengthy time on the stand.

Chris Wilson testifies to his involvement with Alex.

Chris Wilson testifies that Alex Murdaugh admitted he had stolen money and had been addicted to opioids for 20 years. Wilson told the court that he was informed on September 3, 2021, by PMPED attorney Lee Cope that Murdaugh had been stealing money from the law firm.

Wilson testified about the Ferris vs Mack Trucks settlement case that Alex approached him about. It was a products liability case and Alex reached out to Chris to act as co-counsel with him. "It wasn't a jury trial," Wilson said, "it was bench trial. There are no appeals in a bench trial." The trial was in Ridgeland County and Alex did the closing arguments. "We were in COVID," Wilson added.

"There were two verdicts," he said. "$4 million for Ferris and $1.5 for his wife. $792,000 in fees went to Alex, and $791,000 went to me."

The disbursements for the fees and the expenses for that case were made in March of 2021. Alex told Chris he wanted to put his in annuities, and the checks made directly to him, not to PMPED (where they should have gone). He told Chris he had already cleared it with PMPED. Chris wrote out three checks to Alex: $192,000, $225,000, and $375,000. Alex sent someone to pick up the checks.

"He made a lot of money," Chris said. "He made more than I did. Alex was the producer at his firm.

It was shortly after that, Annette Griswold at PMPED started noticing something was wrong when the firm received the expense check for the case, but not the attorney fees. The rest has been gone over earlier in the book.

In August of 2021, Wilson runs into Alex at a Hilton Head conference. Alex had managed to give Wilson back $600,000 of the Ferris fees, but he still owed him $192,000. Wilson had to put his own money in a trust in order to tell Seckinger he was holding the fees she thought were missing. At the conference, Wilson asks Alex for the $192,000 he owes him. Alex told him he was selling property and his dad died and left him some money. He said he was dealing with Maggie's estate. On August 17, 2021, Wilson gets Alex to sign a Promissory Note saying he owns Wilson $192,000 and that it will be repaid within 60 days. Wilson never got that money.

Waters brings Wilson to September 3, 2021, and asks what happened? Wilson said he met Murdaugh at his parents' home in Almeda. He goes over Alex's story of drugs and that he had lied to him.

'I was so mad. I had loved the guy for so long, and I probably still love him a little bit, but I was so mad.'

Chris Wilson and Alex both cry during Wilson's heartbreaking testimony.
Photo courtesy of *Law & Crime*.

Wilson is emotional as he tells the court he doesn't know how he didn't see these things happening with his friend.

"He told me that he had been stealing money." Murdaugh said he had 'shit me up.' He said he had 'shit a lot of people up.'

Wilson later found out that Murdaugh had been shot in the head.

'What in the devil is going on?' Wilson said. 'I thought he had tried to kill himself.'

While Alex has reached out to Wilson, Wilson hasn't spoken to Murdaugh since that day on Miss Libby's porch in Almeda. One of the texts Alex sent to Wilson, said: So sorry for the havoc I created. I'd do anything to make it right.

Chris Wilson finished his "in-camera" testimony by saying Alex told him that the $600,000 Alex gave to Chris so that he would tell Seckinger the money was there, actually came from Palmetto State Bank. Lafitte had covered the loan "off the books." Alex had already blown through $792,000 in just a couple of months. He was shy the balance of $192,000. Alex told Chris he was getting another loan from Palmetto to re-finance Edisto when Maggie died. Had Wilson just given the court a darn fine motive for murder? If Maggie had turned him down for that re-finance loan, as she owned half of Edisto and her name would be needed on the paperwork, did Alex kill her in order to get the money he so desperately needed?

At the conclusion of Wilson's testimony, the Prosecution argues that the jury should hear Wilson's testimony.

Creighton: 'For the jury to understand the reality of what he was facing, they have to understand the extent of what was going to be exposed.'

Day 7, February 3ʳᵈ

Jan Malinowski, the CEO and President of Palmetto State Bank is also heard outside the jury's presence. He is not a happy camper as he takes the stand, and the grim reaper expression remains with him throughout his testimony. He states he is the CEO now, but Russell Lafitte had been the prior CEO. It was not lost on the court that Lafitte had been found guilty of six charges of fraud and embezzlement in November of 2022. It hung like a black cloud over the proceedings. The judge and courtroom had just heard from Alex's best friend and how Alex had "shit him up." Russell Lafitte, another man who considered Alex a friend, and had helped him numerous times with loans to bail him out of overdrafts and financial issues, was now looking down the barrel of a long prison sentence. Lafitte was on home arrest awaiting sentencing and petitioning for a new trial.

Jan Malinowski, CEO of Palmetto State Bank

During Jan Malinowski's testimony, it was clear that Alex was not the only one feeling the wrath of the Palmetto State Bank CEO and a member of its Board of Directors. As he poured out the loans given to Alex over the year by Lafitte, it was obvious that many had not been authorized. Lafitte had covered a $350,000 overdraft in Alex's account August 6, 2021, without a loan application or going through the usual channels. On August 9, 2021, another $400,000 from Lafitte to Alex to cover another overdraft. Creighton Waters made the comment," Quite possibly the most generous overdraft policy ever seen!" Where was all that money going?

On August 17, 2021, a meeting was held with the Board of Directors to go over the loans made to Alex. At that point, it was over $3.5 million. The bank had to charge off loans made to Red Beard LLC and Zero United LLC. Malinowskit testified that Alex did make a few payments on those loans. It was noted that Alex was telling Palmetto he was trying to sell his farm (Moselle) to repay his debts. On April 22, 2021, Alex wanted an appraisal done on Edisto, supposedly for a remodel of the home there. The note on the mortgage had matured and there was money owing. Malinowski testified that the loan was not going toward a remodel. It was to pay off the existing mortgage on Edisto (so Alex could see it), but Maggie was never told that. She went about her remodeling plans, even buying a pair of $5,000 curtains.

Alex had maxed out a $1 million dollar line of credit the bank extended. It was clear Alex was looking at the two properties at Edisto and Moselle as his pledge to get more money. Yet, Moselle was in Maggie's name, and she owned half of the Edisto Beach house. Had she declined Alex's wishes to use the properties for collateral, or outright sell them? Was it a motive for murder?

It was said that Maggie was house hunting in the desirable area of Hilton Head, SC, which would put her directly on the ocean. While Blanca said in her testimony that Maggie was having a lot of work done on the Edisto house in preparation for a big July 4th party she was hosting there, was there more to it? Was she getting it fixed up to sell, precipitating a move to Hilton Head? Was a divorce on the table? It would be a good reason not to let Alex refinance Edisto and take out a second mortgage. It's hard to sell a house that is mortgaged to the hilt.

On June 7, 2021, Alex had his father, Randolph III, down as a co-borrower as he continued to look for funds. It was that same day he asked Jeannie Seckinger what he had in his 401K. It was the same day Maggie and Paul were murdered.

On Jim Griffin's cross, something staggering was mentioned. It was stated that Maggie was scheduled to meet with the appraiser at Edisto Beach on June 8, 2021. One day after she was murdered. It was an odd thing for Griffin to bring up. His purpose was to show Alex's intentions were good; he was trying to use Edisto to secure a loan. But the loan was for nefarious reasons, not the ones stated. Maggie may have believed the appraisal was in preparation to sell her beloved home and move to Hilton Head, not to put a second mortgage on it to bail Alex out of trouble and get rid of the boat crash lawsuit.

Lafitte did give Alex a loan of $750,000 for an Edisto remodel, but $350,000 went to Chris Wilson, and the other $400,000 went toward covering his overdraft at the bank. Meanwhile, Maggie is happily purchasing new décor and paying workmen at the beach house. The most damning testimony here was that it was stated Edisto Beach was solely in Maggie's name at the time of her death, according to Colleton County Deed Records.

Throughout Malinowski's testimony, Alex popped hard candies and looked uninterested. He watched his former friend's testimony with the detachment of one removed from the damning statements being made about him.

Tony Satterfield on the witness stand.

It was the next witness to take the stand that evoked the most emotion from the gallery, and later the jury. Because Tony Satterfield's testimony revolved around Alex's insurance fraud, the jury was once again absent. He would be back in Week 3 of the trial when the Judge ruled to allow it in.

Gloria Satterfield's oldest son, Michael Tony Satterfield sat in the witness chair, adjusted the microphone and waited, glancing occasionally at his counsel, Eric Bland, who nodded silent encouragement to the young man.

Tony testified that his mother, Gloria Satterfield, had worked for the Murdaughs for over 20 years. She did everything: cleaned, babysat, ran errands, and whatever they needed to have done. When asked what happened to his mother, Tony replied, "She fell and hit her head at Alex's house at Moselle." Tony briefly goes over Alex approaching him and his brother Brian after their mother's funeral and offering to sue himself, as it was his dogs who caused her fall. He assured them his insurance policy he had on Moselle would pay for an accident. He recommended Corey Fleming to represent them in the case and he was sure he could get them some money.

"I thought Alex was our attorney the whole time," Tony said. They were further removed from the case when Alex convinced them to let Chad Westendorf become the Personal Representative instead of Tony, as Westendorf knew how to navigate the complicated case better than Tony would have. Tony agrees, believing Alex has their best interests at heart. Tony said he only met Westendorf once. He was also never told about an additional umbrella company that would pay out millions. He was only told of the property insurance with Lloyds of London with a possible payout of $505,000.

Tony called Alex several times asking how the case was coming along. He had received a notice from the trailer company and his mother's medical bills were piling up. When Alex would take the call, he assured him he was trying to get $100,000 each for Tony and his brother, Brian.

A newspaper article came out, stating Alex had won the $505,000 Lloyds of London lawsuit. Tony called him in June of 2021, "Around the time that Maggie and Paul were murdered," and Alex said it would be settled by the end of the year. In truth, he already had the money. Tony was never told about the Nautilus umbrella policy that also paid up to $3.8 million. The two brothers never saw a dime of any of the payouts.

Tony Satterfield hugging his attorney, Eric Bland after his time on the stand.

This author had the privilege of interviewing Gloria Satterfield's younger son for this book. His section is presented earlier. He and his brother Tony are incredible young men. Despite the payout they eventually received, they both have jobs. Their Aunt Ginger manages their money for them. Brian has the heart of an angel, and it was a fear of the family's that people would prey on that and ask him for money. While speaking with him over the phone, he was nothing but goodness and laughed often. There was no hint of malice or feeling sorry for himself due to Alex's treatment of them. He did break into tears often when speaking of his mother. Frankly, in my humble opinion, there is no sentence a court could impose on Alex Murdaugh that would equal the pain he has caused so many. Even when speaking with his son Buster from jail, he was bragging about winning Slim Jim's and some other food items in a card game, ecstatic with his prize. It is an insight into a man without remorse or guilt.

Carson Berney, with the South Carolina Attorney General's Office testified next and ran down a forensic accounting of Alex's statements that had been presented to the State Grand Jury and were partly responsible for Alex sitting at the Defense table at this time. He presented a rundown of loans and payments Alex made from 2011 to the time he was incarcerated. Among all the checks was one made for a GMC Yukon in the amount of $75,000. Curtis Eddie Smith was paid regularly in sums ranging from $4k to $132k. The checks to Eddie were written out to 10 variations of Smith's name.

Thomas Darnell, a fingerprint expert for SLED was next. He gave the court a quick lesson in the difference between fingerprints, which are primarily moisture (sweat), and a latent fingerprint, which means it is hidden or invisible to the eye. They have to use special techniques to see latent prints, such as Super Glue fume tents, light, some black powder, and fluorescent dye stains, he said. He went to explain a non-porous surface would be a gun, cartridge, etc. Porous would be paper, etc.

He tested the .300 Blackout shell casings, and no fingerprints were found. He listed other things he tested such as the Super Eagle Benelli shotgun, Paul's cell phone, other guns—all resulted with no fingerprints found. It was a letdown for the spectators.

Harpootlian cross-examined the expert and said there were no notes saying the doorknob to the feed shed had been fingerprinted. He also pointed out that the Benelli shotgun was held by Alex, yet no fingerprints are found.

The next three witnesses were only on the stand long enough to testify from whom they had taken buccal swabs: C.B. Rowe, Connor Cook, Roger Davis, Anthony Cook, Morgan Doughty, Miley Altman, Randy Murdaugh, Alan Gonzales, John Marvin, Buster Murdaugh, and Alex Murdaugh.

Paul Greer, the SLED firearms examiner spent some time on the witness stand. In a quiet, yet unflappable delivery, he went over his findings for the courtroom.

Greer went over the ballistics evidence collected at the murder scene. Using Worley's diagram and the markers placed by law enforcement that night, he listed them for the jury:

Markers 2-7: all fired S & B .300 Blackout casings.

Marker 9: fired Federal shotgun shell (found behind feed room door)

Marker 10: fired Winchester shotgun shell (" ")

Marker 8: a bullet found near tire track impressions in the hangar.

Marker 13: bullet fragments in gravel

A bullet was found in the bedding of a doghouse near Maggie.

24 bird shot pellets collected from the feed room.

1 piece of bullet on hair and dress of Maggie Murdaugh

48 birdshot pellets from Paul's shoulder and head at autopsy

1 plastic wadding from the shoulder & 1 from the head of Paul

Greer testified that the black .300 Blackout AR-15 found on the property (Buster's gun) had to be fed bullets manually, they did not feed automatically. He testified that the .300 casings found by Maggie, the flower bed area around the stairs to the gunroom at the Moselle property, and at the family shooting range "were loaded into, fired, and ejected by the same rifle." This was powerful testimony that the defense had tried to keep out.

Paul Greer holds up the Benelli shotgun Alex retrieved from the house during his 911 call.

When Jim Griffin approached the witness, he was determined to dilute his testimony about the matching casings.

"Your field would be considered an art, would it not?" he asked, his mouth twisted to one side.

Without missing a beat, Greer answered calmly, "Our field is an applied science. Only the arranging of the lighting to analyze evidence under a microscope could be considered artistic." If the members of the gallery could have applauded, they would have.

Griffin plows on, by pointing out that Greer received Buster's AR-15 on June 10th, 2021, and he gave his report to SLED on the same day. Dive teams were out then looking for the guns.

"Did you tell SLED never mind—I've found the murder weapons?"

"No, sir," Greer said simply.

After a little clean-up by the prosecution, along with reiterating how the casings found around Maggie, matched those from the Moselle flower bed and shooting range, Greer was allowed to step down.

Chapter Thirty-Three
Week Three of Trial Testimony

Week three of the trial started off with an explosive witness. The man who put Alex Murdaugh's feet to the flame, and indeed his immediate family's as well, took the stand. Mark Tinsley settled in with a determined look on his face for his "in-camera" testimony. This was the attorney for the Beach family who was asking for millions in damages in a civil suit against the Murdaughs. Alex had juggled, strategized, lied, and hidden assets as he tried to outmaneuver the attorney who was about to speak out against him.

Attorney Mark Tinsley

As Creighton Waters led Tinsley through the salient points of the Beach lawsuit, it became clear that an obstruction of justice suit was also in the crosshairs. It was brought up how Renee and Phillip Beach were not allowed to go beyond the yellow tape to see the boat from which their daughter was ejected. They couldn't even stand near the water to watch the rescue efforts. Yet, Maggie and Randolph III were practically escorted to the boat. He mentioned that Buster Murdaugh had a duplicate ID made and it was this ID with which Paul bought all that alcohol and chugged it before the boat even took off from his grandfather's river house.

Tinsley said that Murdaugh's attorney at the time, Danny Henderson, showed him Alex's insurance policy on the boat, totaling $500k that he would split with the victims. What Henderson did not say was that Nautilus Insurance had an open claim against Alex for the Satterfield case, as did Lloyd's of London. Neither policy was going to pay a dime for the boat crash. In short, Alex was underinsured.

In October of 2020, Alex tells Tinsley he's broke. Tinsley cried "Bulls87t!" He knew of Alex's lifestyle and that he was winning some big cases. At that time, he did not know of the fraudulent settlements and the millions blown. Tinsley filed a motion to compel, meaning, the court would order Alex to show all his financials. It was akin to the sounding of a death knell—literally.

November of 2020, the Beach family announced it wanted accountability for the death of their daughter. Paul had never admitted to driving the boat while intoxicated, in fact, he had tried to pin it on Connor Cook. Whether through a settlement or a trial, they wanted to be treated as more than an inconvenience for the Murdaugh family. Alex finally said he could "cobble together" $1 million. It was rejected. Tinsley next move would be to subpoena the financial records.

The Status Conference on the lawsuit was scheduled for May 11, 2021. However, both Mark Tinsley and Alex's new attorney, John Tiller, were dealing with cancer. The motions hearing was moved to June 10, 2021. John Tiller died from his illness before the hearing took place.

The shock and horror of the double murders of Maggie and Paul Murdaugh brought it all to a grinding halt. Mark Tinsley testified on the stand that he would have settled for Alex's offer of $1 million if it was proved a vigilante had been responsible for their deaths, and/or was after Alex as well.

In September of 2021, Satterfield settlement inquiries were sent to Eric Bland, the attorney for the Satterfield boys. The pressure was still on, especially after the fake roadside suicide attempt. His statement that he had wanted Eddie Smith to kill him so that his only surviving Buster could have the $10 million life insurance payout was all a lie. There was no insurance policy.

"We expected Alex to settle," Tinsley said. "No real money had been offered. We were going to trial. I cared about putting pressure on Alex."

If Mark Tinsley felt that the pressure he mentioned led to the murders of Paul and Maggie, he did not convey that. Instead, he and Creighton Waters hammered home that despite the Defense trying to compel him to admit that the June 10th hearing was just that, a hearing, and that other hearings and a trial were way down the road, Tinsley let it be known that the June 10th hearing was the beginning of the settlement and Danny Henderson looking into Alex's finances. It was only the sound of a gavel, and Alex's decade of fraud and theft would be laid bare. It would probably have gone beyond that. The money trail would lead to drug dealings and prison.

Tinsley finished by saying he would have worked out a payment plan with Alex, which entailed him signing over the Edisto Beach house and Moselle.

The hatred from camp Murdaugh during Mark Tinsley's testimony was palpable. Whether Buster Murdaugh flipped off the attorney is up for debate. Leave it to say, he was not a popular witness with Alex or his family.

Ronnie Crosby during the Murdaugh murder trial.

Ronnie Crosby looked like a man whose heart was still broken over the events responsible for the Murdaugh murder trial. Not only had he been friends with Maggie and Paul, but Paul had also been at his home often and shot hogs on his property. The murders were still a shock to him, and he was also dealing with the fact that a man he considered his friend and co-worker at PMPED had lied to him and robbed millions from the firm. He had hurried to Moselle the night of the murders to comfort Alex and support him.

Ronnie testified that throughout those long hours that evening and into the morning, although many of the attorneys who rallied around Alex asked him for the details of the night's events, he never once said he had gone down to the kennels. The kennel video is played again, and Ronnie Crosby identifies Alex as the voice calling for the dog, only minutes before Maggie and Paul were gunned down.

At the end of Crosby's "in-camera" testimony, Judge Newman rules that he will allow all the financial testimony presented while the jury was absent. Those witnesses would take the stand again at a later time and tell it all over again while the jury was in attendance. It will not be repeated in this book, as their testimony was basically the same the second time around.

Muchelle "Shelley" Smith was next. We have covered much of her testimony concerning Alex's movements the night of the murders, and his activity when he arrived at his father's house with a blue vinyl "tarp" a few mornings after Randolph III's funeral. On the witness stand, the caregiver for Miss Libby looked nervous and sad. It was obvious she would rather have been anywhere but here, with Alex Murdaugh in her eyeline.

A large blue raincoat was shown to Shelley. "Could this have been what you saw the morning Alex Murdaugh arrived at the house at 6:30 a.m. carrying something in his arms?" Meaders asked her. She admitted it looked like it could be the blue vinyl object she saw. It was bundled up in his arms and it was hard to tell.

Objections about "leading the witness" were hurled from the Defense table over this particular subject. Meaders stepped back and asked the questions again. Shelley confirmed that Alex had never arrived at Mr. Randolph's house at that hour of the morning before. She testified to his arriving in the black truck, leaving in Mr. Randolph's white truck, and then fifteen minutes later, bringing back the white truck and finally leaving in the black one he had arrived in initially.

This testimony about the two trucks has baffled many. Alex is at his father's house early with a blue vinyl object, and he takes it directly upstairs to the bedroom level (where no one has stayed in years), comes down without it, and goes outside. A blue raincoat is found in September of 2021, balled up behind a box in the upstairs closet. It is tested by SLED and found covered with GSR on the *inside*.

Prosecuting Attorney Meaders showing Shelley Smith a blue tarp.

Alex announces, "I'm leaving," to Shelley as he exits the house. She peeks through the blinds in Miss Libby's room on the main floor that faces the side yard. She sees Alex leave in Mr. Randolph's white truck. Randolph III passed away several days earlier. His funeral service was at the house and there is a catering truck and a canopy still set up on the lawn. It is blocking Shelley's view of the black truck.

Fifteen minutes later, he is back with the white truck and leaves in the black truck he came in. When Shelley looks outside, she sees an ATV parked at the side of the house. She testifies it is usually kept at Mr. Randolph's smoke house.

The entire revolving door of trucks is confusing. Let's see if this works: Alex arrives in Buster's old Ford F-150. This truck does not have the newer tracking devices that Alex's SUV and Maggie's Mercedes have. There will be no breadcrumbs to follow to Mr. Randolph's house. Besides, SLED has Alex's and Maggie's cars still impounded. Shelley says he "pounds on the side of the house, under Miss Libby's window," and says, "I'm here." No phone calls this time, like he did the night of the murders. Shelley states she did not know he was there until he pounded on the wall. It was 6:30 am when he slapped the wall, but she did not know how long he had been there before that. The ATV has been moved during his visit. And he is entering with an oversized blue vinyl object which he takes upstairs.

Did Alex pull up in the old black truck, walk the short distance to the smoke house, retrieve two murder weapons wrapped in a blue raincoat, put the guns into Randolph's white truck, take the raincoat inside and hide it, come out and take off in the white truck?

As Alex is leaving the GSR-laden raincoat behind, it would intimate that he is probably not going to bury the weapons. If he were, he would leave them in the incriminating raincoat and dig a hole. But, if he is planning on dumping them in the water, where a raincoat could surface and float along, that's a different story.

He is gone 15 minutes in the white truck, including round trip. Could he have taken the guns to his brother John Marvin's hunting property only minutes from Randolph's house, with its miles of swamp land and rivers? He has been staying at John Marvin's and Randy's properties since the murders. He had plenty of time to scout out the perfect place to dump the guns in one of the marshes or rivers.

He then drives Randolph's truck back to his dad's house and leaves again in the black Ford F-150.

To cap it off, while Alex is upstairs hiding the blue raincoat in the closet at Randolph's house, he takes a blue tarp that was lying folded on top of a box of dishes and spreads it out on Miss Libby's old recliner upstairs, to trick Shelley into thinking that was what she had seen him carry in. Barbara Mixon, who works the morning shift testified she did not see it on the recliner, but Miss Shelley had. Miss Libby's room used to be upstairs, but since her illness, a room with her usual bed and a hospital bed were moved to the first floor near the kitchen for convenience. No one goes upstairs. Shelley said she hadn't been upstairs in two years. Barbara Mixon may not have seen it until Alex folded it up and replaced it atop the box of dishes. We do see a photo of such a tarp on top of a box in a closet when SLED takes photos in September and finds the raincoat. Alex is at the house on September 3rd when he's talking to Chris Wilson on the front porch. Did he return the tarp to the box of dishes then?

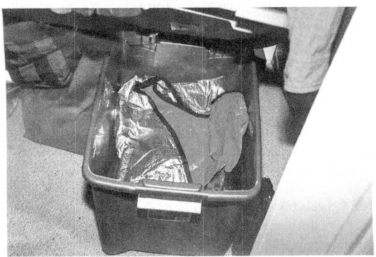

Blue tarp folded on top of dishes in a plastic tub in the 2nd floor closet at Randolph's home.

Are the guns somewhere on John Marvin's hunting property? They may have been moved many times before Alex's incarceration in October of 2021.

Shelley breaks down when asked how long Alex was there visiting his mother the night of the murders. She testifies 15-20 minutes. When asked why she is crying, she has to admit he wanted her to say he was there 30-40 minutes. He also gave her money to help with her upcoming wedding expenses and offered to put in a word at the school where she worked part-time to get her a better job or more pay. She was so upset by his wanting her to change her testimony that she called her brother who was the Assistant Chief of Police in Varnville. It was a hard testimony to watch.

It was brought to the attention of the court that the Defense had interviewed and recorded Shelley Smith just prior to the trial. The Judge ordered that the recording be turned over to the State.

Special Agent Kristen Moore addressed the court from the witness stand and testified to finding the blue raincoat at the Almeda house in a coat closet on the second floor, balled up behind a box. The blue tarp was folded atop a box of miscellaneous dishes in the north bedroom on the second floor. She admitted during Griffin's cross that SLED did not test the blue tarp and the stains on the blue raincoat were not blood.

Paul's friend William McElveen took the stand and testified about Paul spending time with him in Charleston after the boat crash. He spent summers with Paul at Edisto Beach. He said Paul was the life of the party, a loyal friend, and he was always there when you needed him. He said Paul used his cell phone a lot and would call his friends daily. William said Maggie was "a super sweet lady." She liked William because she thought he was a good influence on Paul, and she didn't worry about Paul getting into trouble when he was with William. He said he had spent the night at Moselle around 30-40 times. He said the last time he saw Paul was at the Windjammer Bar in Charleston on June 5th, two days before he was murdered.

Jaimie Hall with the West Columbia Police Department was the next witness. She was the evidence custodian dealing with GSR and other findings. She prepares the evidence to be tested for GSR. She testified that when she took Alex's white T-shirt from the evidence bag it had a strong odor of laundry detergent. Officer Rutland had noticed the detergent smell as well while seated behind Alex in SLED Agent Owen's car the night of the murders.

On October 5, 2021, the blue raincoat was brought in for testing. She testified that particle lifts were done by Megan Fletcher on the entire jacket; inside and out.

Jeannie Seckinger was recalled to the stand to present the testimony she he given while the jury was not in attendance. We will not repeat it here as it was presented in a previous chapter. It needs to be pointed out here, that Creighton Waters crafted a strategic attack against Alex Murdaugh for his financial crimes while he had the PMPED CFO back on the stand. Ad nauseam, Waters went over each and every client associated with the law firm that Alex had swindled. While most of us watching the court proceedings on television were "shouting no more financial stuff!" We learned later there was a reason for it. Seckinger went over each settlement fraud, the amount stolen, and how much the law firm was paying each client back out of their own pockets. She made the ominous statement, "We are still paying some of them." Waters strategy for this lengthy testimony would hit home during his attack when Alex Murdaugh took the stand to testify on his own behalf.

Following Jeannie Seckinger, Ronnie Crosby again took the stand to go over his testimony that the jury did not hear the first time.

SLED agent Megan Fletcher took the stand for the much-anticipated results of the GSR testing on Alex's clothes and the raincoat. With her master's in forensic chemistry and a BA in Biochemistry, she was deemed an expert before she began her testimony.

Megan Fletcher identifies evidence at the trial.

Agent Fletcher's findings were as follows:
- She noticed a strong smell of laundry detergent when she removed Alex's T-shirt from the evidence bag.
- Fletcher examined the lifts from the shorts and shirt. The T-shirt had some stains on the lower left side. The shorts were visibly clean.

- The shirt tested positive for firing a gun or holding a gun. Multiple particles were found on the right sleeve and right chest areas.
- The shorts showed 2 particles on the right side of the groin area. The left side showed 1 particle. Both sides of the shorts showed more on the right side.
- No GSR was found on the neon tennis shoes.
- These items were all a Priority Request and tested on June 8, 2021, the day after the murders.
- 1 particle of GSR was found on the seat belt buckle of Alex's SUV.
- The blue raincoat showed GSR particles on the outside of the raincoat, and significant amounts on the inside—over 52 particles inside and out. They stopped counting on the inside after 34. There was a lot more there.
- 1 particle of GSR on the outside of the hood—3 on the inside.
- No GSR found inside the raincoat pockets.
- 1 particle was found on Alex's right hand.
- Both the shirt and the shoes were wet.

Annette Griswold, Alex's ex-paralegal took the witness stand. She had also been heard "in-camera" in her prior testimony. The jury was now present, and she repeated her earlier testimony against her former boss. This testimony is in a previous chapter.

Michael Gunn, who had also been questioned "in-camera" went over his testimony again about his association with Alex. Gunn is the Principle at Forge Consulting. He testified he had no knowledge of Alex's fake Forge account, nor had he done business with the Bank of America where the fake Forge account's business was conducted for years.

As the day wore on, the courtroom and the home audience were buzzing. Eddie Curtis Smith was on the witness list, and it was hinted that he might testify today. One news outlet said Eddie had made a statement from jail that Alex had confessed to him about the murders of Maggie and Paul. The courtroom was packed in anticipation as each witness came and went.

The next witness Attorney Conrad with the Prosecution called was not Eddie, but Brian Hudak, a SLED special agent in computer crimes, such as cell phones, electronic devices, and a car's GPS system. Just as he was about to begin, Judge Newman stopped him and asked the jury to please leave the courtroom. It was so abrupt that many wondered what was going on. Then, in a clear, calm voice, Judge Newman said everyone would have to "evacuate the building, until we see what's going on." He asked the gallery to quietly exit the building through the back doors leading to the horseshoe-shaped staircase outside the building. Alex and his defense team were immediately taken out the side door, while the Murdaugh family was led out another door into the hallway.

It's a Bomb Threat!

The gallery is evacuated from the Colleton County Courthouse during a called-in bomb threat.

It didn't take long for the word to get out that a bomb threat had been phoned into the Clerk of Courts at the courthouse. The South Carolina Law Enforcement Division (SLED) said that Colleton County Courthouse personnel received the threat, and that the agency is investigating along with the Colleton County Sheriff's Office. Police dogs were brought in to help sweep the courthouse, and court staff and attorneys were allowed back in around 2:30 p.m.

after the building was cleared. The anonymous caller was said to be a male. No other news was forthcoming at that time.

The morbid humor that usually follows a traumatic event was swift in coming. Someone posted in a Murdaugh Facebook group: "I guess Cousin Eddie got his one free call." While it was meant to be funny, many wondered if it was a coincidence that the call came in on the day many believed Eddie Smith would be called to the stand.

According to *Crime Online*, an inmate in South Carolina's Ridgeland Correctional Institute is being charged with making the bomb threat that temporarily halted Alex Murdaugh's murder trial earlier this month.

The Colleton County courthouse was evacuated on February 8 after courthouse personnel received the bomb threat, as *Crime Online* previously reported. The trial was halted until about 2:30 p.m. while the South Carolina Law Enforcement Division's bomb squad searched the premises. They found nothing, and the trial resumed at about 2:30, although it ended early that day, two hours later.

Colleton County deputies say 32-year-old Joey Coleman made the call, telling a clerk there was a "bomb in the judge's chamber," the Colleton County Sheriff's Office said in a statement.

According to the sheriff's office, SLED agents and Colleton County detectives traced the call to the Ridgeland Correctional Institute in Jasper County, about 35 miles from the courthouse in Walterboro. State Department of Corrections personnel tracked the call to a cell phone in Coleman's possession.

Joey Coleman made the bomb threat call, Feb. 8th.

511

"An initial forensic examination of the phone confirmed the components were a match to the device used to call in the bomb threat to the courthouse," the sheriff's office statement said.

An inside source told this author that the bomb threat had nothing to do with Cousin Eddie's testimony. It was a Comedy of Errors that is just one more surreal moment in this twisted tale. As it turns out, Alex Murdaugh's murder trial was not the only business being conducted that February 8 in the Colleton County Courthouse. It was also Family Court Day. It was nicknamed "Baby Daddy Day" by the court clerks. These proceedings go after the Deadbeat Dads who are reneging on their parental responsibilities to pay child support.

On this day, one such father who was scheduled to appear was in the Ridgeland Correctional Institute. In other words, he was in jail. He was on the docket that day to appear and answer for the late child support payments. This gentleman asked one of his cellmates at the jail to call the Clerk of Courts and announce a bomb was in the building so that he wouldn't have to appear. Enter Joey Coleman. Joey got on a cell phone that had been given to him and began dialing the courthouse. The calls repeatedly went to a voice prompt that no one answered. An hour went by as a nervous Coleman dialed the Clerk of Courts again and again. Finally, out of desperation, he punched in Prompt #2 and the call went to a different department where the woman on the other end about had a heart attack when Coleman told her there was a bomb in the courthouse. The judges were notified, and the Murdaugh trial came to an abrupt halt. And now you know the rest of the story.

When court resumed, a dubious Brian Hudak once again took the stand and gave his short statement that the On-Star module and Infotainment system of Alex's SUV had undergone an FBI examination. Short and sweet. He stepped down.

Dwight Falkofske with the FBI was sworn in as an electronics engineer specializing in electronic analysis and automotive forensics. He testified that Alex's 2021 Chevy Suburban had encrypted data that requires a key. It took a year to de-crypt it.

Falkofske educated the jury by telling them the Suburban Infotainment System was linked to phones by Bluetooth. They contained call logs and some location data.

He went over the various confusing things going on with Alex's car when it was shown going in and out of park so often. Here is his timeline:

- 9:03 pm. Boot-up sequence
- 9:04 pm. Starting up
- 9:06:44 pm. Power up process
- 9:06:48- 9:06:49 Engine running.
- 9:06:50 Taken out of park.
- 9:22:45 Went into park.
- 9:43:05 out of park (this shows Alex is at mother's 21 minutes)
- 9:43:59 park
- 9:44:54 out of park (Alex stopped for one minute at the end of his mother's driveway)
- 10:00:36 out of park (Alex is back at Moselle house)
- 10:01:17 out of park (heading for kennels)
- 10:01:29 in park
- 10:01:30 out of park
- 10:01:43 into park
- 10:04:47 powering down
- 10:04:49 out of park
- 10:05:55 in park
- 10:11:45 out of park (going to house for gun during 911)
- 10:12:38 into park (arriving at house for gun)
- 10:13:39 out of park (heading back to kennels)

The timeline shows Alex made it to his mother's that night in 16 minutes. It was typically a 20-minute drive. It took him the same 16 minutes to return home to Moselle. Later testimony would show he was driving in excess of 80 miles an hour on dark back roads. The frequent changes in "park" mode within seconds of each other were never really explained.

Chris Wilson was back on the stand to repeat his earlier testimony when the jury was not in attendance. It was an emotional retelling of a friendship he thought was solid and how Alex had admitted to "Shitting him up." Waters showed no mercy to the defendant as he pushed Wilson to state how devastated he was to this day about what Alex had done to everyone who trusted him. Wilson went over the Ferris fees and how everything came crashing down on Alex when he could no longer hide them from his law firm or "his best friend."

The emotions continued with the testimony of Gloria Satterfield's oldest son Tony. Once again, the brave young man took the witness stand, this time in front of a rapt jury. Those in the gallery stated many of the jurors were crying as Tony reiterated what Alex had done to his family. Without emotion, Tony calmly went through Water's questions. He never played it up for sympathy---just succinctly answered the questions.

It was once again put to the jury how clients of Alex Murdaugh considered him to be on their side—their hero in their time of need. Many thought of him as a friend. It was Tony Satterfield's testimony that he and his little brother thought of Alex as family that ripped through the jury. Tony's mother had raised Alex's two sons, Paul and Buster. Tony thought they were important to Alex, because of that 20+ year relationship their mother had with the family. While Alex spent their money and dragged them along, they were served eviction papers for their trailer home that Tony had tried to tell Alex about. They became homeless and lived with various relatives. It was the acts of a man without conscious or soul.

If public opinion against Dick Harpootlian had been lukewarm, it was his treatment of Tony Satterfield that pushed it to *Tilt*. Harpootlian had already insulted one of the State's witnesses who had been presented as a SLED Special Agent. He asked her sarcastically, "What's so special?" But it was with Tony Satterfield that many people watching from home threw unbreakables at their television screen, this author included.

As Tony twisted in his seat, Dick Harpootlian strode to the podium and callously asked the young man, that despite all he and his little brother had gone through—the loss of their mother and her income, the loss of their home, the stress of the accumulating medical bills and Alex lying to them and stealing their $4.5 million dollar settlement—

hadn't they actually come out better? "They ended up receiving $6.5 in a judgement, thanks to their attorney Eric Bland, correct?" The court was silent. The shocked look on Tony Satterfield's face was apparent as he looked to Eric Bland, who was seated in the audience, for help. Was he supposed to answer that? Harpootlian's fall from grace at that moment was complete. He appeared rarely for the duration of the trial and walked back to his seat with the angry gazes of several jurors following him. Many in the gallery stated later that Tony's testimony evoked the most emotion of anyone who took the stand. Several jurors wiped their eyes.

Jan Malinowski, the new CEO of Palmetto State Bank (after Russell Lafitte was fired and eventually found guilty on all six counts of financial fraud levied against him) testified to the Lafitte side of Alex's schemes. He had also given his prior testimony "in-camera," and was now before the jury. This was also reported in a prior chapter.

Another "in-camera" witness retook the stand. Mark Tinsley, the attorney for the Beach family in their lawsuit against the Murdaughs, Parker's Kitchen and others, went over his previous testimony again for the now seated jury. It was pretty much the same as his first time on the stand. Tinsley testified that he subpoenaed Randolph III's, Alex's, and John Marvin's phone records from the day of the boat crash to show a collusion going on that would show obstruction of justice in the case. He said whether or not the June 10th Motion to Compel Hearing was pushed back due to the murders of Maggie and Paul; it would have still gone forward.

Blanca Simpson was back, looking as apprehensive and sad as her first go-around on the stand. She leaned forward throughout her testimony, her mouth inches from the microphone, and her eyes fixed on whoever was questioning her. Attorney Meaders handled her with kid gloves and was a good choice to lead her through his questions. Meaders tended to take a more grandfatherly approach to the witnesses, often touching them on the arm or hand, as if to settle them a little.

Of all the witnesses who were privy to the Murdaugh's private life, it was their housekeeper, Blanca Simpson. The world sat riveted to her testimony, hoping for a smoking gun (literally) or some inside information. Much of what she had to say was mentioned earlier, but there were also some odd moments she recounted in the final days of the murder and the investigation.

Blanca testified that besides being at the Murdaugh's beck-and-call for housekeeping and errands, she also had 5 children of her own. Her husband is a police officer in Hampton, she said. In 2007, she worked every other day for the Murdaughs at the Holly Street house in Hampton. She testified that someone had tried to burn it down, and she came more regularly after that to help. In 2015, Blanca had a stroke and was in rehab. After she recovered, Maggie asked her to come back shortly after the boating accident in 2019. Blanca would clean the house, cash checks, and run errands. One got the impression that the check cashing was so that Maggie could pay the staff in cash. It left many wondering if this was a tax move, to forego employee benefits, or other reasons to avoid a paper trail of employment data.

In 2019, the Murdaughs were still living on Holly Street, she said. They sold it and moved full-time to Moselle in 2020. She and Maggie became close and would talk about personal things.

Blanca was asked to talk about the weekend of the murders. Maggie and Paul were murdered on Monday, June 7, 2021. She said she had seen Paul the Friday before at Moselle. She had worked there most of the afternoon and was getting ready to go home to her family. Paul walked in the door with a large laundry basket of dirty clothes. Blanca was coming out of the laundry room when he came toward her with the clothes.

"What's up, Miss B?" Paul asked smiling.

"Boy, if you think I'm going to wash all those dirty clothes, you're wrong," she said, good-naturedly.

Paul gave her a smile and said, "Oh, come on Miss B. I need them for the weekend."

Blanca finally told him to pull out a few that he needed, and she stayed late to wash them for him. Her face looked pained as she remembered it was the last time, she saw him.

Monday, the day of the murders, Blanca said she was supposed to work at Moselle. Maggie texted her and asked to stop at the grocery store to get Alex some of his favorite orange Capri Sun fruit drinks. She went to Lion King and couldn't find them.

Maggie told Blanca she had to go to a doctor's appointment in Charleston and asked Blanca if she would cook. She told Blanca she had left some food in the refrigerator and probably wouldn't be back in time to cook it. Maggie said Alex had asked Paul to come fix "the sunflower mess" that C.B. made when he over sprayed the sunflowers. Blanca said Maggie told her Alex said there was going to be a hunt that weekend and he wanted it cleaned up.

"Paul likes the way you cook," Maggie added in her phone call with Blanca. Blanca cooked the dinner and texted Maggie that it was on the stove, and she was leaving. This was about 3:30. She had to pick up her son from school. [The texts and timeline are in a previous chapter.]

Blanca testified that Maggie sounded like she didn't want to come home that night. Work was going on at the Edisto Beach house. Maggie was planning a big July 4th party.

Blanca said when she arrived at Moselle that day, she didn't see Paul. He hadn't come yet. Maggie had already gone. She said Alex was still in bed. She was there a couple of hours before he got up and got dressed for work. She described what he was wearing as he prepared to leave for work:

"He had a pair of khaki pants, a greenish-I call it seafoam—polo shirt, and he put a blue sports coat over it. He put his shoes on on the way out the door. He was wearing his work shoes—a pair of brown leather shoes. The polo is a short-sleeved shirt. As he put his coat on, and he was getting ready to walk out, "I said, "Alex, hold on, your collar is sticking up,' and I fixed it for him." She said the polo had three buttons at the top.

Blanca said she made cubed steak, green beans, and rice for dinner, and left.

She heard about the murders the next morning. Alex called her and said in a shaky voice, "B...they're gone." She thought at first, he meant Maggie had gone back to Edisto and Paul had gone back to Okatie. When she asked him what he meant, he said, "They're gone, B. They're dead." She testified that she dropped the phone in shock and her husband picked it up. She finally told him she would be right over. Alex told her he was at Almeda at his parents' house. He asked her to go to the Moselle house, go in the front door, and "straighten it up the way Maggie would like it." He told her people would be stopping by with food and stuff.

Alex seemed adamant that she would go in the front way to the house. Blanca said she normally took the kennel entrance when she came to work.

"It was hard," she said in a shaky voice to the jury. "I knew she wasn't going to be coming back and I didn't want to move her stuff. It was such a weird feeling. I felt cold."

When she went into the kitchen, "I stopped in my tracks. There were no pots on the stove. Maggie usually left the pots on the stove." She found them, with leftover food still in them, in the refrigerator. When she went to the laundry room, she saw Maggie's pajamas laid neatly on the floor in the middle of the entrance to the laundry room. On top of the neatly folded pajamas was a pair of Maggie's folded underwear. Blanca said she had never seen Maggie leave her clothes like that on the floor of the laundry room floor.

Blanca looked uncomfortable as Attorney Meaders led through the next question. "Was there something odd about that," he asked gently, already knowing the answer, and the housekeeper's reticence about answering it.

In a hushed voice, Blanca said, "Miss Maggie didn't wear underwear with her pajamas. The underwear was fresh and still had fold marks. They were clean," she said, her eyes looking at the attorney for guidance.

The odd situations continued as she entered Alex and Maggie's master bedroom. Maggie's clothes were next to the big garden tub. By the shower was a slight puddle on the floor and a pair of khaki pants, like the ones Alex wore to work that day. On the floor of the bedroom closet was a wet towel with a clean t-shirt next to it that looked like someone had yanked it down from the folded T-shirts on the closet shelf. Blanca said Alex had a lot of white t-shirts, especially ones with restaurant logos on them. The white T-shirt Alex is wearing when law enforcement arrives the night of the murders has a Black Sheep logo over the left pocket. Blanca said she picked up the T-shirt and placed it back with the other clean T-shirts on the closet shelf. It was clean.

Blanca said she washed the khaki pants that were lying on the bathroom floor by the shower.

"Do you recognize those pants in Exhibit 7?" Meaders asked. She was shown the still of Officer Greene's bodycam video showing Alex in the white T-shirt and cargo shorts the night of the murders.

"Yes, sir. They were kept in the third drawer or fourth drawer. One drawer had shorts he would wear on the weekend, the dressier ones." He didn't wear the shorts shown in the bodycam very often.

Blanca is shown the SnapChat video Paul took the night of the murders showing Alex in his khaki pants, pair of house loafers, and a Columbia shirt that was kept in the closet. He had a few of them, different colors, she said. She described it as a "seafoam" greenish-aqua color.

"After June 7, did you ever see that shirt again?" Meaders asks her. "No sir. There was a pink one, a white one, and a baby blue one in the closet. It wasn't there anymore. The house loafers were not there again. I never saw them again. They were usually kept in the closet."

He had Speery shoes, or boat shoes. "They used to sit in the closet. I didn't see them in the closet again," after June 7, 2021.

Men's Speery shoes. They are cloth-covered and were also called "boat shoes," by Blanca.

Blanca stayed on at Moselle after the murders of June 7th. She was present for the large gathering of mourners following the funerals of Maggie and Paul. She doubtless helped serve and clean up for a hundred of the Murdaugh's friends and family filled the Moselle house where Maggie and Paul had enjoyed so many memorable times together. Alex offered Blanca a deal that was hard to pass up. He could no longer abide staying at the house. He asked her if she and her husband would stay there and look after the grounds work and maintenance. Alex offered them $1500 a week and free accommodation.

When many raised their eyebrows at being paid $1500 a week, Blanca pointed out it took two days to mow the lawn and it was a vast property. We know C.B. Rowe stayed on until the roadside shooting incident, so they did have help with the remainder of the farm. Blanca fed Grady and Bubba. We don't know what became of the hunting dogs that were also housed at the kennels.

Blanca was asked about Bubba's pen and his habit of chasing the bird fowl on the property. She said Bubba had his own pen—the second one over from the feed room. On the night of the murders, he was found in the wrong pen. He and Grady, the other family dog, had switched pens. Alex claimed he didn't put the dogs up that night after Maggie let the two dogs out to run after dinner. Blanca said Bubba would catch guineas and chickens. It would take several attempts to get the bird away from Bubba.

A stuffed chicken in Bubba's pen.

Bubba died sometime after the murder trial. It was a report that stirred the feelings of many who saw the dog as a four-legged hero in this sad saga. If he had not run off with the chicken, we would not have heard Alex yelling for him on that damning kennel video. Paul raised Bubba from a puppy and the dog was featured in many family photos. Maggie would take Bubba and Grady with her to Edisto on occasion. It was her habit to "run the dogs" when she was at Moselle as they were kept in the dog kennel pens a lot. Mr. Davis, the dogs' caretaker said Maggie was "a dog lover." Alex seemed to only take an interest in the dogs when they were used for hunting. Davis said Bubba would listen to Alex more than the others.

Paul Murdaugh holding Bubba as a puppy. Photo from Maggie Murdaugh's FB page. Courtesy of cherishedkellybrown.org.

Watercolor of "Bubba and the Chicken," by Sali Parker Morris. Sali is an artist and art instructor from Hampton, SC. This is her tribute to what many call a Hero in the Murdaugh murders sage.

You can order a print of this beautiful full-color art piece at Sali's Art Page on Facebook and at carolinapaintings.com. This author put her autographed copy in her office as a reminder of this poignant part of the story.

Blanca went on to testify about a small building she called "the little house." It was a small 2-bedroom house in Hampton by Randy Murdaugh's home. Alex had her move all his clothes and toiletries to the "little house" after the murders. He was bouncing around between his brothers' homes and his in-laws in Summerville. Alex would go to the "little house" to get what he needed. He stayed there a few times as well.

August 10, 2021, two months after the murders, and the afternoon after Alex's third interview with SLED (when they confirmed he was their only suspect), Alex walked into the "little house" where Blanca was at the moment, and said, "B…I need to talk to you. I got a bad feeling. You know I was wearing a Vinnie Vine shirt." Blanca got a sick feeling. It was obvious he was asking her to state he was wearing a shirt other than the Columbia shirt she saw him wearing in the Snapchat video Paul took the evening of the murders. During her testimony, Blanca was asked to look at the SnapChat video. She identified the shirt he was wearing in the video Paul took of Alex playing with the tree as the Columbia shirt, not a Vinny Vine brand shirt.

On September 4, 2021, Alex asked Blanca to send him a copy of the insurance cards. He said, "I need the cardboard ones." These were medical cards that were still in Maggie's purse. This is the day he was shot in the head at the roadside shooting.

After the roadside shooting, Blanca and her husband stopped living at Moselle. C.B. Rowe quit as well. The sad property sat empty, the grass growing longer, as if to cover the remnants of a once happy family. Yet, many questioned if they were as happy as the myriad photographs displayed.

John Marvin Murdaugh, Alex's younger brother, took over managing the abandoned property. We do not know if ground workers were hired to help with the massive 1,700 acres. Most photos of the house and kennels show tall weeds. The kennel walkway where Paul lay that dreadful night is filled with pine needles and debris in recent photos. As mentioned, Moselle sold shortly after Alex's murder conviction and the proceeds were divided up.

The last family photo of the Murdaughs was taken a few days before.
the murders of Maggie and Paul.

Randy Murdaugh called Blanca and asked her if she would pick up Maggie's Mercedes from the Impound Lot at the Sheriff's office. This was obviously before the September 4th roadside shooting as Alex was driving the Mercedes at the time. Randy asked Blanca to clean it out. It seemed all the heartbreaking tasks were left to Murdaugh's prior housekeeper. Once again, she had to be among Maggie's things and relive the pain of losing her. Some pillows and fabric swatches Maggie had gotten for the Edisto Beach remodel were still in the car.

Blanca testified that she found Maggie's wedding ring under the front passenger seat. It struck her as odd. Not much was made of the find during the trial. It was only mentioned briefly. No one asked her if she had seen Maggie wearing it lately? Or if she was in the habit of taking it off. Maggie had had a pedicure that day. It's possible she had a manicure as well and left the ring in the car for safekeeping. This author has lost a ring during a manicure, so I get it. The nefarious meaning could be that the killer removed it from her finger rather than risk it being stolen when put into evidence or at the autopsy. Was that why Randy asked Blanca to clean the car? Alex had asked him to, knowing what Blanca would find and that she would dutifully give it back to him. Alex said he turned Maggie onto her side to "Check her." Had he rolled her to take the ring from her left hand that was tucked beneath her?

523

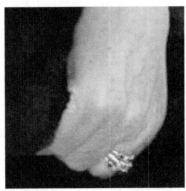
Maggie's Wedding Ring

When asked about her close relationship with Maggie, Blanca admitted her late employer confided in her during the days leading up to the murders. Blanca testified that Maggie told her she was very worried about the $30 million Mark Tinsley and the Beach lawsuit were asking for. "We don't have it," Maggie cried to her housekeeper and friend. "I would give everything I have to make it go away." Maggie also told Blanca that she didn't think Alex told her about everything.

Blanca said Maggie never went down to the kennels at night. She would take the dogs with her or alternate them in the last few months. When asked, she said she didn't see any bloody clothes at the house or anywhere else. She agreed Paul and Alex were always on their phones. (This was to underscore the strange one hour of silence with Alex's phone between 8:09 pm and 9:09 pm the night of the murders.)

Dick Harpootlian cross-examined Blanca. He got her to admit that when it came to Maggie, Alex "adored her. She was his all. I never saw them have arguments. They disagreed on remodel issues. Maggie just wanted him to sit still for 10 minutes and listen to her."

Harpootlian led her through what she found at the Moselle house the morning of the murders. She said the dishes were in the sink and the pots and pans of leftover food were in the refrigerator. She did not notice how much food was still in the pots.

"Do you know if anybody (relatives there that night) cleaned up?"

"No, sir."

"There were 12-15 people there at the house the night of June 7th," he told her. As Blanca was not there, she had no way of knowing what went on.

Blanca admitted the cell phone service at the kennels was sporadic. "It's touch and go," she said.

Harpootlian asked her about Alex talking to her at the "little house" concerning what he was wearing the day of the murders.

"Did Alex tell you he had spoken to SLED earlier that day about what he was wearing?" Harpootlian asked.

"He sounded like he was trying to convince me about what he was wearing that day," Blanca answered softly.

Blanca said Alex was there because he, Randy, and Buster were going golfing, and he needed clothes. But it was obvious the housekeeper thought he had a different reason for seeing her.

Harpootlian asked about the vehicles at Moselle. She said Paul would take "Dolly," the F-250, or his own truck when he went to the kennels. Sometimes the golf cart. She said the golf cart was gas-powered.

Blanca testified that Alex wore a 2XL. "He had a few items that were large," she said. She added that she had never seen the rain jacket in evidence.

"Alex had too many raincoats to count," but not that one, she said.

(This might be a good place to underscore the inventory found on Alex's boat the morning of the boat crash in February 2019. A raincoat is listed as part of the inventory found on board. We know Maggie, Randolph, and John Marvin all had access to the boat that day, and its belongings were probably returned to Alex later. Was this the raincoat Alex brought into the house a few days after Randolph's funeral? The one coated with GSR on the inside?)

Blanca testified that Alex kept clothes at the office and in his car. She testified she sent the text about "dinner is on the stove. I'm leaving now," at 3:28 pm the day of the murders. She saw Paul's truck at the kennels as she left. This is significant. She must be speaking about "Dolly," the F-250. Paul's own truck is in for repairs, and he will be arriving around 7:00 pm driving his Uncle John Marvin's white truck.

Alex said he and Paul rode the property that night in two trucks: the black one and the white one. Why two trucks? Perhaps Paul met him at the house when he arrived from Okatie that evening, or somewhere on the property. Alex then was driving the black truck, the one they found .300 Blackout cartridges in. The one Harpootlian objected to when the truck was mentioned during the trial as "being irrelevant."

Blanca said she was sad for Maggie. Ever since the boat crash, people were rude to her in Hampton. She preferred staying in Edisto.

Harpootlian went over what Blanca was privy to the morning after the murders when she was at the house at Moselle. She saw no police at the house that morning. They were down at the kennels. Several agents came through later that afternoon. Some went upstairs to the other bedrooms and found a shotgun shell on Paul's nightstand. Blanca admitted a towel on the floor was not unusual.

"SLED took his clothes, so would you assume he had to wear other clothes when he went to his mother's house to stay the morning after the murders…even that shirt you said you never saw again?"

She admitted there was no blood on the towel or the khaki pants. No bloody footprints. She said she did rinse the shower down and wash the khaki pants *after* SLED left. The pants were left there and not taken into evidence.

Belinda Rast was next on the stand. She is a CAN in home health care and hard of hearing. She was a caregiver for Miss Libby as well. "She doesn't know if she has gone to the bathroom or not," Rast testified. They monitor her around the clock. She sits with Miss Libby from 8 pm to 8 am weekdays and 7 pm. to 9 am every other weekend.

Belinda Rast, one of Miss Libby's caregivers.

"This is my 5th year with Miss Libby," she said. "Miss Libby is like family."

Rast testified that Shelley Smith had asked Belinda to switch with her for the day of June 7th, 2021. Shelley had plans with a friend and wanted a different day off, and so she asked Rast, who would have been working that night, to switch with her. If she hadn't, it would have been Ms. Rast with her limited hearing that would have been sitting with Miss Libby the night of the murders.

Ms. Rast said Paul came to see his grandparents more than the other grandchildren. He would get his grandmother ice cream and go over memories with her to help her with her dementia. She said Alex didn't come very often in her 8 pm – 8 am shift. She said she had seen him do that maybe 6 times in the five years she had been there. Rast said she helped Mr. Randolph too.

Belinda Rast testified that Alex and Maggie dropped by the night before the murders on June 6, 2021.

"Alex and Miss Maggie both came by. They brought doughnuts."

"Why did they bring doughnuts?" Attorney Fernandez asks.

"Because Mr. Randolph asked for some doughnuts."

"Did Mr. Randolph like doughnuts?" Fernandez asks sweetly.

"Well, they were Kripsy Kremes... (courtroom erupts in laughter) ...you couldn't get them anywhere in our area."

Rast testified they didn't see Mr. Randolph. He was asleep and they let him sleep. When Rast told him later that Maggie and Alex dropped by at 9 pm, he was surprised and asked why so late? She told him it was because he had asked for doughnuts. "He just seemed surprised," she said.

Miss Libby is given her medicine at 8 pm and she sleeps after that. She is full care now. Miss Libby would sometimes not know her sons were there. Miss Libby was told Mr. Randolph died and she was taken to his funeral. She seemed to have forgotten later on that he was gone and stopped calling for him.

Dick Harpootlian questions Belinda Rast. He got her to say it was "unusual" for Alex to stop by that late, not "strange" as the State put it. Rast said that in 2021, Miss Libby would stare at the television, but she wouldn't play along with the game shows like she used to. She said Paul had a calming effect on Miss Libby.

Supervisory Special Agent Mathew Wilde with the FBI in Rock Hill, South Carolina, testified next about the cellular service data collected during the investigation of the double murders. He was asked by Agent Hightower to see which cell phone towers near Moselle pinged during the phone data collected from Maggie, Paul, Alex, Marti Cook (Connor Cook's father), and C.B. Rowe. Maps showing the different areas around Moselle pinging off the phone data were shown to the jury. They show Paul at the dove fields where the sunflowers were sprayed around 7:30 pm the night of the murders. It also showed Paul arrived at Moselle that night at 7:05 pm. It shows him at the kennels at 8:40 pm that night. From 7:45 pm to 7:56 pm, the cell phone sector shows Paul around the kennels. At 8:06 pm, he is moving from the kennels toward the house. At 8:08 pm, he is at the house.

At 8:35:07 pm he is moving again toward the kennels and arrives there at 8:38:07. At 8:44:45 the kennel video is filmed. The 10:18 pm sector shows Paul's phone is still at the kennel where it remained until removed by SLED agents.

Maggie's phone was not of much help. It showed no calls were answered after 7:50 pm as she leaves the Walterboro area driving to Moselle. It does show she was in the Charleston area from 4:25 pm to 7:05 pm. It shows a small number of steps going into the house when she arrives at 8:17 pm., and a small number when she leaves after dinner: only about 40 steps. It appears she is going to and from her car parked at the front steps. It does not show over 200 steps taken like it does with Paul as he leaves the house and arrives at the kennels. It appears Paul walked to the kennels after dinner, and Maggie rode in a car to get down there, most likely her Mercedes.

Alex's cell phone data aligns with his activities, placing him either at Moselle, or driving to and from Varnville when he went to see his mother the night of the murders.

What is of interest is the data showing where Alex was the days after the murders, according to cell tower triangulates.

- June 8: Mostly Moselle
- June 9: 7:52 am – 8:36 am—Almeda (parent's house)
- June 10: Almeda
- June 11: Almeda
- June 12: Almeda

- June 13: Almeda
- June 14: 12:04 am – 9:53 am Almeda
- June 14: 10:26 am – 12:29 pm—Somerville (Maggie's parents' house)
- June 15: Somerville to Hampton, Almeda

Alex said he could not have been at his parents' house in Almeda at 6:30 am the morning he was seen coming into the house with a blue tarp because he was in Somerville at Maggie's parents' house that day. Shelley said he "came in the day after, or maybe the next day" after Mr. Randolph's funeral. The funeral was Sunday, June 13, 2021. The food truck was still there and the canopy for the service in the side yard at Randolph's house. On June 14th, Alex was at Almeda from 12:04 am – 9:53 am, according to cell towers. That means 6:30 am puts him in the Almeda area, not Somerville during the time Miss Shelley said he came inside with the tarp. He didn't ping in Somerville until 10:26 am that morning. He's back in Hampton and Almeda the next morning after visiting Somerville.

The cell phone tower data proved C.B. Rowe and Marti Cook were not in the area during the window of time the murders were believed to have occurred. Attorney Barber for the defense asks if Eddie Smith's phone was checked, and Agent Wilde says that it was, but he doesn't have that data with him.

Nathan Tuten, the younger brother of Nolan Tuten, and a good friend of Buster and Paul Murdaughs was next on the witness stand. He has a degree in Criminal Justice from USC and is currently with the Walterboro Police in the road patrol division.

Nathan said he was childhood friends with Paul. Paul was a good friend, loyal, "salt of the earth." He was a reliable friend and on the phone all the time. Maggie was one of the sweetest ladies and was like a second mother to him. He lived with Paul in his Freshman year in the cabin by the hangar at Moselle.

After the boat crash, when Paul was attending college in Columbia, he didn't to go home (Moselle) that often. He testified that the original entrance to the property was by the hangar. The entrance to the house was created a couple of years after they took possession of Moselle. He said Alex and Maggie usually used the main entrance, while the kids usually used the hangar entrance. He said Maggie and Alex would typically stop by the kennel area on their way out from the house.

Nathan Tuten testifying during the trial.

Tuten testified that in February of 2019 he began working as a "runner" for PMPED. He was a courier for documents, helped the paralegals, and other duties. He said he cashed checks for Alex at Palmetto State Bank and would bring the money to him at the law office. Tuten said he did this frequently. He said there were multiple people in Alex's office when he brought in the cash. He mentioned Corey Fleming, Chris Wilson, and Greg Alexander (the Yemassee Police Chief and Alex's close friend). A few weeks before the murders, Alex stopped asking him to cash checks, Tuten said. Jeannie Seckinger was his immediate supervisor and Tuten testified he helped her look for discrepancies.

On July 4th, 2021, Nathan drove Alex to the airport for a Florida vacation with his in-laws. Tuten said Alex said that he wanted to clear Paul's name and "beat the boat case." He was asked by the Prosecution to repeat that last statement, that Alex was only interested at that time, a month after the murders, of "beating the boat case." Tuten confirmed his statement.

Nathan Tuten left PMPED in May of 2022.

During the re-direct in the testimony, Tuten admitted the kennel and hangar areas were well lit. Fans were left on for the dogs. He said the dog beds were put up on top of their houses until the pad area dried after being hosed down, and then they were put back on the floor. He said Paul kept his phone in his back pocket. (Will Loving testified that Paul kept his phone in his front pocket. It's an interesting sidenote.)

Chapter Thirty-Four
Week Four of Testimony

The fourth week of the trial saw two jurors released because of COVID-19. Defense attorney Dick Harpootlian made much about the damage the virus could do to the courtroom, recommending fewer people in the gallery, spaced six feet apart, and masks. Judge Newman finally allowed for masks and asked that boxes of COVID face masks be brought in for any who wanted one. Harpootlian grabbed one and put it on. Only a few in the gallery availed themselves. After two minutes, Harpootlian took his off and never used it again.

It was now Day 16 of the trial. A projected 3-week trial had now rolled into 4, with 6 weeks rumored as the wrap-up point. The jury was inundated with graphic autopsy photos, DNA findings, and emotional testimony from Maggie Murdaugh's sister, Marion Proctor. It was not an easy week.

Rachel Ngien, a forensic scientist with SLED gave testimony on DNA and serology (blood). Her job was to test for evidence and forward her findings. The salient points were:
- Alex's Chevy Suburban tested positive for blood on the steering wheel. It was a mixture of his and Maggie's DNA.
- Alex's shorts—several stains tested—Left interior pocket was positive for blood.
- Alex's shoes—2 stains positive plus the left shoelace.

- The Benelli shotgun Alex retrieved from the house tested positive for blood where shells are loaded into the gun.
- No tests done on Paul or Maggie's clothes.
- Additional serology and Hema trace was done on Alex's T-shirt, shorts and shoes.
- Hematrace swabs from the Ford F-250—45 swabs negative for blood.

Sarah Zapata testifies of DNA findings.

Sarah Zapata, SLED Forensic Scientist in the DNA department took the stand to go over the findings submitted by Ngien:
- 24 buccal swabs tested.
- .300 Blackout cases—single source—Maggie Murdaugh (one of the casings was found underneath her right knee)
- Shotgun shells in feed shed—single source—Paul DNA
- Feed Room doorknob exterior—single source—Paul
- Benelli Camo Super Eagle Shotgun—loading chamber—mixture of Alex and Maggie's. Maggie's blood was the reddish-brown debris on the receiver.
- Paul's cell phone—not enough information
- Suburban steering wheel—mixture of Maggie and Alex's blood with Maggie's being 30x higher)
- Left and right fingernail clippings of Maggie: L) C.B. Rowe and Maggie. Rowe's was an infinitesimal amount that could

have come from touching something at the hangar with his DNA on it)

- Left and Right fingernail clippings Paul—Only Paul
- Alex's shirt—mixture of DNA from Maggie, Paul, Alex, and Nolan Tuten. (Nolan said he hugged Alex the night of the murders and his DNA was found on the shoulder area of the shirt).
- No human blood on Alex's shirt, only touch DNA.
- Shorts—front left interior pocket—mixture of 3 people— Alex, Maggie, and Paul
- Shoes—single source: Alex
- Raincoat: 2 swabs (interior cuffs, hood, etc.) No DNA profile.

During the cross, it was brought up that Maggie had been at a nail salon that day. It was to point out that 3 alleles of male DNA had been found under her nails. It may have come from the nail salon.

The blood spatter evidence said to be found on the T-shirt Alex was wearing had been blocked from testimony. It had been touted as the smoking gun since *People Magazine* first aired the story in June of 2021. The issue with the evidence was the chain of custody and findings. Pictures of the "blood spattered shirt" were sent to Tom Bevell in Oklahoma, a blood spatter expert. He said that to the naked eye, he did not see any blood on the shirt. SLED decided to take the shirt to Bevell in person, making the trip to Oklahoma, where Bevell tested it "in his garage laboratory" and, low and behold, he found over 100 areas showing blood spatter evidence. He said it was indicative of the mist that comes as blowback when a shooter is standing close to the point of impact.

Bevell said he used Photo Shop to brighten up the areas so he could see them better and therefore changed his original report. It was a no-win for the Prosecution. The discrepancy between the two reports was too vast and it reeked of tainted evidence and testimony. Judge Newman would not allow it in.

The DNA testimonies were a huge letdown to the armchair sleuths hoping for something that showed definitively who fired the murder weapons. No bloody clothes, no DNA on the feed shed door other than Paul's. The .300 Blackout casings had been tested together in a diffused liquid, which baffled us all. Only Maggie's DNA showed up as her bare knee had been lying on top of one of the casings. The tiny bit of blood found on Alex in his pocket, and Maggie's blood on the steering wheel of his SUV could all be explained away. He admitted to touching Paul and Maggie to see if they had a pulse when he found them slaughtered. The fact that Paul's brain was on the sidewalk, and bits of Maggie's brain were clearly visible on the grass, did not deter Alex from checking for a pulse. The white T-shirt spattered in blood was not to be.

The only thing that jumped out to this author during Zapata's testimony was the myriad areas of Alex's T-shirt that had Maggie's DNA on it. Three official witnesses testified the shirt smelled of laundry detergent and it looked "fresh out of the dryer." The defense tried to dismiss the DNA as "Maggie probably hugged him." Perhaps, or was Maggie trying to stop him from slaughtering her son?

Up next was who many dubbed "the happy pathologist." With almost childlike glee, Dr. Ellen Riemer went over the gore put before the jury members in graphic photos and testimony. She was clearly a fan of her chosen career. At times, her cheerful delivery did hit the wrong note with those who heard and saw what the photos portrayed: the catastrophic damage that had been done to Paul and Maggie the night of the murders.

Using posterboards with male and female diagrams, Dr. Ellen Riemer, a forensic pathologist from the Medical University of South Carolina, detailed to jurors the wounds on Maggie and Paul Murdaugh. She performed autopsies on both bodies. Riemer testified that Paul could have survived the first shotgun blast to the chest had he received medical treatment. The second shot to Paul was a severe fatal injury to the head.

Paul Murdaugh would have had his arms by, or near, his side when the first shot was fired and showed no defensive wounds, Riemer said. Pauls' face had scratches consistent with a forward fall where he was unable to brace himself. The jury was shown autopsy photos of Paul Murdaugh.

Riemer explained Maggie Murdaugh's injuries in just as much detail, telling jurors that she had five gunshot wounds from at least four gunshots. Stippling around Maggie Murdaugh's wounds indicated the first two shots had been fired from within three feet, Riemer said. Riemer testified the shot fired into Maggie Murdaugh's ribcage went downward, going through her abdominal wall, pancreas, toward the back, through the kidney and exited the back. She was standing. The pain likely would have caused her to bend over or fall to her hands and knees, setting up the first of two fatal shots to the head.

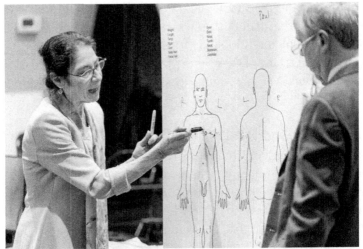

Forensic Pathologist Dr. Ellen Riemer demonstrates wounds to Paul Murdaugh's body as Creighton Waters looks on.

Dr. Riemer posited that Maggie was first shot in the thigh. As she backed away from her attacker, she was shot in the abdomen, the bullet traveling to her pancreas. Both shots showed stippling, meaning the shooter was 3' or less away. The pain of this shot would have caused her to double over, and possibly drop to the ground. Diagrams show Maggie on her hands and knees, her right hand holding her up, the left hand pressed against her stomach. Riemer said the shooter then came around behind her and crouched, firing up under her. The bullet could have gone through her wrist before entering the body and traveling upward through her left breast, until it exploded into her brain, severing her spinal cord. Maggie is now flat on the ground, her right arm straight ahead of her bent at a slight angle, her left arm bent beneath her, her legs straight. The shooter came around to the front of her and shot one more .300 Blackout round into her head.

Riemer testified that Maggie was killed with either four or five shots. The reason for the discrepancy is that shot number four could have gone through her wrist and into the body. If not, then the wrist wound was due to a single shot of its own, making it five shots instead of four.

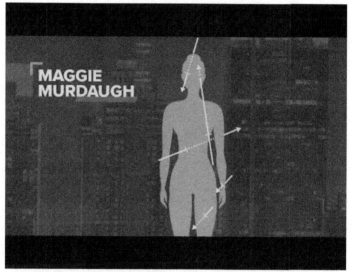

Diagram of Maggie Murdaugh's bullet trajectories.

Paul was thought to be standing at an angle in the feed room with his right arm toward the door. The first shotgun blast hit the left side of his chest, entered his upper armpit area, and sprayed pellets through his left arm. He then moved slowly to the open doorway, dripping blood from his left arm as he did so. His head tipped to the left and slightly bent over, the second shotgun blast entered his left shoulder, went up under his left jaw and exploded into his brain. It blew out a large piece of his skull, ejecting the brain with it. The brain hit the ceiling and landed next to his left leg on the cement where he fell. Due to the instantly fatal blast, he fell forward dead, his face hitting the gravel next to the cement walkway lining the kennels. His arms were bent beneath him.

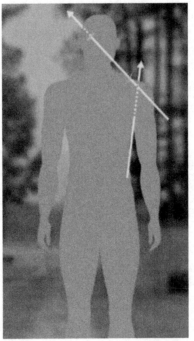

Diagram of Paul Murdaugh's Trajectories

Crime Scene diagram of shotgun wadding from the second shot fired at Paul Murdaugh at Marker #1. The blood is from the wounds he sustained during the first shot as he walked slowly to the open doorway.

Reimer said the first shot to Paul was likely very close; within 3 feet due to stippling on his chest. The wadding from the shotgun shell was imbedded in his left armpit area. The wadding from the second blast was on the feed room floor not far from where he was standing. It was marked with Marker #1 on Agent Worley's crime scene diagram.

During Dick Harpootlian's cross-examination of Dr. Riemer, the Defense tried hard to get her to say that Paul's wounds from the second shotgun blast could have been reversed. They posited the shooter shot him in the *top* of the head and the gas from that blast blew his brain out, and the remaining pellets traveled out his jaw, ending in a splayed-out area on his left shoulder. Riemer negated it as a possibility. There would be soot on top of his head from such a close-up shot. The wounds showed the blast entered his shoulder *first* and traveled up into this head. They spent a good portion of her testimony going back and forth over this diagnosis. Her findings also showed that there were no drugs or alcohol in Paul's stomach, only caffeine.

Maggie's stomach contents also showed only caffeine and food contents that matched Paul's: both were gray in color.

The courtroom had a much-needed reprieve after all the gory autopsy evidence and unrelenting testimony of Maggie and Paul Murdaugh's last moments on earth. The camera panned to a weeping Alex Murdaugh and the pained faces of family members throughout the grueling and graphic overview.

Roger Dale Davis ambled up to the stand, looking every bit a southern 'good-ole-boy' and acting like he would have preferred to be sitting in a front porch rocker. Roger Dale Davis is a Hampton resident and lives 1 ½ miles from Moselle. Four years ago, he was asked to clean the dog kennels: 7 am in the morning and again 3:30-4:00 pm in the afternoon. He said it took him about 45 minutes each time to clean out the pens. His duties were to feed the dogs and chickens, wash out the pens, put the dog beds on top of their houses while cleaning, and put them back down in the afternoon in the summer.

Roger Dale Davis talks dogs and hoses.

Roger Dale Davis is a Hampton resident and lives 1 ½ miles from Moselle. Four years ago, he was asked to clean the dog kennels: 7 am in the morning and again 3:30-4:00 in the afternoon. He said it took him about 45 minutes each time to clean out the pens. His duties were to feed the dogs and chickens, wash out the pens, put the dog beds on top of their houses while cleaning, and put them back down in the afternoon during the summer.

Davis said Maggie was laid back and talked a lot about dogs. She would show up and say, "I'm going to the beach. I'm taking Bubba and Grady with me."

Davis testified that Paul was wild and crazy, but he would work hard. He'd work on the tractor, anything his Daddy asked him to.

"Alex was very particular," Davis said. "He wasn't easy to get hold of." He said he saw Paul and Maggie more often. Paul was usually in his white F-150 or the white F-250. Maggie drove the black Range Rover until she got the Mercedes. "She always drove those," he said.

Davis testified that dogs were usually locked up. Sometimes Maggie would take them up to the house for a couple of hours and then put them back.

Attorney Fernandez showed Davis a photo of the kennels and the way the hose was wound up the night of the murders. He said he always wound it so that there were no kinks in it, and the nozzle was pointing down. "Somebody used the hose after I did," he said. "That nozzle it too far up."

Dog kennel hose with the nozzle "too far up."

Davis testified he was at the kennels around 4 p.m. on June 7, 2021, just hours before the murders. He said no one else was at Moselle while he was there, and he was finished around 4:30 p.m.

The dog keeper was asked to show the jury which pens the dogs were usually in. He drew out a rough diagram, labeling each pen.

Crime Scene photo of kennels. The hose can be seen in the center of the pens. Paul's draped body is at the top end of the walkway. Photo courtesy of Courtroom Pool photos.

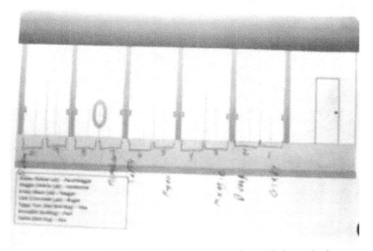

Dog pen diagram. Davis labeled the pens in which each dog was typically kept. Feed room door is at the right.

Davis gave the following summary of which dog was usually in which pen:

1. Grady (Black Lab)
2. Bubba (Yellow Lab)
3. Maggie (Yellow Lab)
4. Empty pen
5. Cash (Rogan's dog)
6. Tappy Toes
7. Armadillo
8. Empty
9. Empty
10. Dolly

Through crime scene photos, Davis pointed out places along the kennel run where water would pool. When asked, he said water wouldn't pool around the feed room or in front of Grady and Bubba's pens because the sun would hit it and dry it out quickly. Davis was shown a photo of that area after the murders, and he said there was too much water in the photos based on when he left.

Crime scene photo of water on the cement walkway in front of the feed room and the first two pens. Photo courtesy of Joshua Boucher. Courtroom Pool photo.

Davis testified that another thing he thought was strange was that the dog beds weren't put back down. In a still shot from the kennel video, you can see the neon green hose stretched out across the path. Davis said he wound it up and put it back. Many believe they hear running water on the dog kennel video. Had Maggie unwound the hose and either filled up the buckets or was washing out Grady and Bubba's pens again before she left? Is that why the beds are on the doghouse roofs? Had she been murdered before she could put the hose back and finish what she was doing? We know now that she probably died within five minutes of the kennel video being filmed.

Davis said he never saw a gun left in the feed room, and he was always in there getting food for the dogs. He said Paul did leave guns in the golf cart, side by side (Polaris Ranger), and sometimes in the truck during hunting season. None of the trucks were ever locked on the property, and the keys would be left inside them.

During Jim Griffin cross-examination, Davis admitted that Ronnie Freeman had quit. This was the groundskeeper who was supposedly privy to Gloria Satterfield's "trip-and-fall accident." He said Paul wasn't usually very careful about how he wrapped the hose back up. Yes, sometimes the dogs would knock their water buckets over.

Griffin got Davis to admit he had never heard Alex raise his voice to Maggie. He describes them as "Lovey Dovey." He said Alex couldn't shoot an injured dog. He would ask Davis to "put the dog down." Davis said he heard no gunshots from his house 1 ½ miles away that night. "I went straight home after I left Moselle at 4:30 pm.

Davis says he was careful not to let water puddle in front of the feed room door. The water would run up under the door and it would cause rot. There was sealant along the door jamb.

"Paul and Alex like to hunt and fish together and drink beer together. I didn't see Buster as much," he testified.

"Bubba was rambunctious. He would listen to Alex. Shock collars, dog feed, chicken feed, and medicine were kept in the feed room."

"Maggie would walk, ride the golf cart, ride the bike…She would run the dogs behind the golf cart sometimes."

The dogs weren't let in the house because Buster had allergies. A rooster would taunt the dogs and aggravate them to death. They started chasing the rooster and chickens after that. "Grady or Bubba ended up getting the rooster."

Attorney Fernandez got Davis to admit Alex hunted animals to dilute the testimony that Alex couldn't put the dog down. Davis also said the cement walkway in front of the kennels sloped down so the water would run off. Maggie would have put the dog beds down from the roofs.

"My bedtime all depends," he said in response to being asked about his nighttime routine. "My routine, either get home around 4 or 5 o'clock, I get a shower, and I'm in my recliner the rest of the day. That's it. *Done!*"

The courtroom laughs and we get a rare smile from Alex Murdaugh.

Attorney Fernandez asks Dale Davis his final question, "On the afternoon of June 7th, when you were out there at the kennels, did you see any firearms lying around?"

"I did not see any firearms."

Carson Burney, a forensic accountant with the South Carolina Attorney General's Office, testified that the money known as the Ferris fees was gone just months after it hit Murdaugh's accounts.

Burney testified the first deposit from the fees came on March 10, 2021, and the last of the $792,000 was out of the account by May 25, 2021.

Around $500,000 of that money went to Curtis Eddie Smith, Burney said. Smith is accused of attempting to shoot Murdaugh in a failed insurance fraud attempt on Labor Day of 2021.

Burney testified that not only did Alex blow through the Ferris fees of $792,000 in less than two months, but he was also in dire straits. To show the situation Alex was in on June 7, 2021, the day of the murders, Burney said Murdaugh did not have the $10 million to satisfy Tinsley for the boat case; he did not have the $4 million he stole from Satterfield's boys, and they were getting restless; he did not have the final $192,000 of the &792,000 to repay Chris Wilson. Griffin pressed that half a million of that $792,000 went to Eddie Smith.

Finally, it was brought to the attention of the jury that on June 7, 2021, Alex had no liquid assets. His only option was to mortgage or sell the Edisto Beach house and/or Moselle. As both were in Maggie's name, it wasn't lost on the jurors that should Maggie die, Alex could come into some money. But property payouts don't come until after the closing. No, but property can be leveraged for a loan.

There was a hush in the courtroom when the next witness was called. All turned to watch a beautiful woman with a pained expression walk toward the witness stand. She was dressed in a modest tan V-neck sweater over a white shirt. Her thick ash blonde hair was pulled back in a chignon. All about her was an air of grace and, on this day, sadness.

Marion Proctor, Maggie's sister.

Marion Proctor was Maggie Murdaugh's older sister; they are five years apart. She lives in Charleston, South Carolina with her husband Bart. They have three daughters.

Marion said that she and Maggie would talk almost every day. "Maggie was sweet, free-spirited, and up for anything," she said. "She loved her boys and her parents. She's a girl's girl but would fish with Alex and the boys. She loved being on a boat. She was a big Gamecocks fan. She was my girl's favorite aunt. She loved being a stay-at-home mom. Once she and Miss Libby had a little shop in town. She went to all her son's sports."

Marion said Paul was "a sweet boy. There was a kind side to him. He would bring them a load of wood."

When asked how she viewed the Murdaugh's lifestyle, Marion said that Maggie wasn't involved in the family finances. "They had a comfortable life, not a lavish life," she said. She smiled when she said "Maggie's checkbook was kept on the floor of her car with all of her bills. She was not organized."

Marion said Maggie felt the Hampton community had turned against her after the boat crash. Paul was getting a lot of hate. It was part of the reason Maggie stayed at Edisto Beach. They had sold the Holly Street house, so that left Edisto and Moselle. She was looking in Hilton Head for a house in the Bluffton area. She found a house she loved. Alex told her the timing wasn't right with the boat crash case going on.

Marion testified that Alex asked Maggie to come home to Moselle the night she died. "She didn't really want to go. She said they were going to Almeda to see Randolph. She had maintenance work going on at Edisto and she really didn't want to go." Marion begins crying when she admits she encouraged her sister to go and support Alex due to Randolph's failing health. "I told her to go," she sobbed. It would be something she would always regret.

Maggie and Marion. Exhibit 554. Courtroom Pool photo.

"Bart got a text from Randy that night, saying there had been a tragedy," she said, dabbing at her eyes with a handkerchief. "When Bart called Randy, he told him what happened." They gathered up their things and went to Summerville to tell Maggie and Marion's parents that Maggie and Paul were dead. "Mom had just had knee replacement surgery," Marion said. Marion and Bart went to Moselle the next morning. She was at Moselle every day until after the funeral. She hugged Alex and cried.

547

"He told me that Maggie and Paul didn't suffer much," she said, her face twisted with pain. Then he said, "Whoever did this must have thought about if for a really long time."

Marion said it was routine for Alex to fall asleep on the couch after dinner. She then added that she thought it was strange they didn't go to Almeda to see Randolph when that was the whole reason Maggie came.

Her next statement was filled with tears and a look of confusion and pain. "Alex would talk about the boat crash. He said his number one goal was to clear Paul's name. My number one goal was to find out who killed my sister!" It struck Marion as such an odd thing for him to say.

She went on to say that "We were all afraid. We didn't know what was going on. But Alex didn't seem to be afraid. He was working on getting Buster back into law school."

Marion said Maggie wanted to give the boys AR's that Christmas of 2016. "They loved to shoot hogs."

When Jim Griffin stood to cross-examine Marion, he did it with tenderness. He was choked up as well. He got her to say how good Alex was to her parents, and that Alex and Maggie had a great family life. He pressed to say Maggie didn't go see Miss Libby very often, but she did make no-salt dinners for Randolph.

"Randolph was at Almeda, but he went into the hospital in Savannah at 4 – 4:30 pm that day, so it wasn't that unusual that they didn't end up going to Almeda to see him, right?"

Marion said that she and Alex never talked about the murders. He never wondered who could have done it. "I thought it was odd," she said sadly. "We thought it was about the boat crash until September, and then things changed a little bit."

Marion testified that dogs did not stay in the house at Edisto Beach or Moselle. They had dog beds and water on the porch at times. She said Paul loved Moselle and hoped to take it over someday. She said Alex and Maggie had a good relationship. "It wasn't perfect, but she was happy."

Creighton Waters on re-direct asked Marion, "What happened in September to change your mind?"

"Alex was shot," she said. She said she heard he had been shot and taken to Savannah Hospital and was okay. She was told he had been fired from the law firm for stealing money. "Initially, I thought he might be dead, and the family was being targeted." But then the things came out that he had done. Events about the roadside shooting were not true.

Marion said Maggie called Paul "Little Detective" because he was trying to keep his dad in check for his pill addiction. Paul was determined to find the pills, and he did find some, she said.

"Were you aware that Alex carried a gun after the murders?" Griffin asked her on his re-cross. "He always carried a gun," Marion countered. She was shown a photo of the blue raincoat and asked if she had ever seen it. She said she had never seen it before.

The testimony the jury did not hear from this witness was that Alex had had an affair during his marriage to Maggie. "It was 15 years ago," Marion Proctor told the judge out of the hearing of the jurors. "Maggie even kicked Alex out of the house due to her suspicions at the time of the affair." She said Maggie never completely did get over it. Judge Newman decided not to allow the testimony as he said it was too far removed in time and it might confuse the jury.

Marian Proctor reaches out to hug her nephew Buster Murdaugh after she testified in his father Alex Murdaugh's murder trial at the Colleton County Courthouse in Walterboro, Tuesday, Feb. 14, 2023. (Grace Beahm Alford gbeahm@postandcourier.com | Grace Beahm Alford/The Post and Courier/Pool)

On Wednesday, February 15, 2023, Judge Newman held a one hour "in-camera" (jury not present) hearing between the Defense and the State. Creighton Waters wanted Alex's faked roadside shooting evidence admitted. "What the defendant said (about the shooting) wasn't true," Waters argued. It shows a "consciousness of guilt." He was trying to prove that he was targeted and someone else killed Maggie and Paul.

In the end, the Judge ruled against allowing it in, saying it falls outside the scope and goes against Rules 404 and 403. "It's a bridge too far," Judge Newman said. (This is interesting, as Marion Proctor just alluded to the roadside shooting and that it was faked.) Judge Newman did allow the insurance fraud evidence, which was a huge strike against Alex Murdaugh's credibility and his lack of conscience when it came to scamming his clients, friends, and even his family.

The Defense team however, made a mistake when *they* opened the door for the roadside shooting during their cross-examination of the next witness: SLED investigator David Owen.

Owen, an agent for the South Carolina Law Enforcement Division, was made the lead investigator on the shootings after the agency took control of the investigation from the Colleton County Sheriff's Office. Owen had front row seats throughout most of the investigation. He was present for all three of Alex' in-person interviews.

Agent Owen testified that in the early morning hours after Alex's 911 call, he interviewed Alex in Owen's Dodge Durango. After the interview, he allowed Alex fifteen minutes alone with Buster at the house before he came in to collect the clothes Alex was wearing. Buster had just arrived after hearing the bad news about his mother and brother.

"I did look around at the house," Owen said. "Nothing seemed out of place. Nolan Tuten was there, and he was on the couch." Owen said 8-10 people were there. SLED's team had arrived and were processing the crime scene. Alex's "dark Suburban" was towed the next morning. Owen stayed all that night until 9:30 or 10 am, the morning after the murders. He was back again around 2 pm. June 8th. C.B. Rowe arrived and Owen interviewed him. Rowe said he had taken his father to the hospital that day (of the murders) and he wasn't there. He interviewed Dale Davis (dog caretaker) and Rogan Gibson (that Alex had so desperately tried to get hold of).

The SLED agents canvassed the neighbors in the next few days. They were few and far between. Any hopes of front door video surveillance cameras came to naught. The house at Moselle was searched again the next day by other SLED agents.

Alex was interviewed a second time at John Marvin's hunting property on June 10th. Owen said in both interviews, Alex showed no signs of intoxication. It was clear in what Alex told him that he had not gone down to the kennels the night of the murders. On June 15th, they searched the Moselle property and ponds. They took Maggie's Mercedes and searched it (missing a large diamond ring under the passenger seat).

Owen testified that Alex called him on July 28th and wanted his car. They couldn't let him have it. He wanted some clothes and his golf clubs because he was going on vacation. When Alex returned, he asked how the investigation was going and a meeting was arranged at a SLED office in Columbia. Alex arrived with Corey Fleming and soon realized he wasn't running the show. Agent Owen was using the meeting to interview Alex for a third time. That interview is transcribed in full in a previous chapter of this book.

Spectators in the gallery that day mentioned the jury's reaction to the long interview. At first, they were rapt with attention. But as it went on for over an hour, they began fidgeting and losing interest. It was noted that they often looked over at Alex at the Defense table as the video was played, judging his reactions to what had become very pointed questions put to him by Agent Owen.

One of the biggest takeaways from that third interview was Alex now stretching the time he had visited his mother that night to 45 minutes to an hour. He had said 30-40 minutes in a previous interview. Shelley Smith had been interviewed by then, and she said he was there 15-20 minutes. During this interview, Alex has spoken to Rogan Gibson and realized Rogan heard him at the kennels at 8:40 pm while talking to Paul on the phone. Alex now needs to be seen at his mother's house earlier and longer than before stated. The problem with this is his timeline is locked in by GPS and Infotainment information, plus the time he made the 911 call.

Many wondered why the kennel video wasn't played during the August 11, 2021, interview for Alex as he sat in Owen's office. For the simple reason it had not been extracted from Paul's phone until April of 2022. SLED got the information on April 8, 2022. Until then, 8 months after Alex's third interview, no one knew about the kennel video. This was not just the word of Rogan Gibson saying he heard Alex on the phone at 8:40 pm the night of the murders—a statement Alex contested, saying Rogan was mistaken—this was a video, and you can clearly hear Alex's voice yelling for Bubba the dog. Maggie's voice and Paul's are also on the video. They would be gunned down within 3 to 5 minutes of that video ending.

During cross examination Owen was asked by attorney Jim Griffin if he was aware that Murdaugh was paying up to $50,000 per week for drugs from Eddie Smith. Griffin went on to say that Smith was skimming money from Murdaugh that was meant for a drug gang, offering the debt as a motive for someone other than Murdaugh to be behind the killings.

Defense attorney Jim Griffin asks SLED special agent David Owen about his Grand Jury report during Alex Murdaugh's trial for murder at the Colleton County Courthouse on Wednesday, February 15, 2023. (Joshua Boucher | jboucher@thestate.com) Courtroom Pool.

Jim Griffin had a lot of clean-up to do in his cross of Agent Owen. The jury had heard a lot of damning evidence against Alex in the third interview just played for the court. Not surprisingly, he played the "sloppy police work card," and pointed out that Agent Owen had lied to Alex during the interview to illicit information. Agent Owen twisted his mouth. "I'm allowed to use trickery to illicit a response," Owen said, nonplussed.

Griffin began his battery of questions:

- Alex was "in the circle "since Day One, correct?
- Whoever killed Maggie and Paul would have biological matter all over them, correct?
- No murder weapons were found on the route to Almeda, correct?
- The searches of the waterways…nothing, correct?
- You didn't even search Almeda (Randolph's home) until late
- September, correct? Then you found a raincoat with GSR.
- The raincoat did not test for blood, just GSR, correct?
- Nothing wet had been found in the Suburban, correct?
- There was no trace evidence of blood found in the Moselle house, correct?
- Alex gave his full permission to search the house and property, correct?
- "Did you ever ask Alex Murdaugh for that blue shirt, khaki pants, and shoes seen in the SnapChat video?" "No."
- "Do you recall what Alex put on after he handed you his clothes from the night of the murders?" "No."
- "Did you pick up the khaki pants found lying on the bathroom floor the night of the murders?" "No."

A few volleys were fired back by Owen. He made it a point to say Alex contacted Nolan Tuten that night and tried to get him to get hold of Rogan Gibson. Had Alex seen Rogan's texts and calls coming in on Paul's phone when Alex took if from Paul's body and then put it on his dead son's backside?

Owen mentioned the several shotguns found on the property that were loaded in a similar manner with a combination of buckshot and turkey shot, in other words, matching the ammo that killed Paul.

Agent Owen said Maggie and Paul were murdered between 8:50 pm and 9:06 pm. He pointed out the GPS on Alex's phone places him in Randolph's back yard the night of the murders for several minutes *before* he calls Shelley Smith and says, "I'm here. Let me in." What was he doing back there? The smoke house and a small shed are near where the GPS dot fell.

It was brought up that C.B. Rowe lied about the reasoning for his absence from Moselle on the day of the murders. He was not taking his father to the hospital. He was looking for another job and didn't want Alex to get mad at him and fire him before he had another job lined up.

Griffin brings up a notorious drug gang that ran a huge operation out of Walterboro. He said Alex was dropping $50k a week for drugs and Eddie Smith needed to get money to the gang for the pills.

Owen argued that the gang wasn't worried about the money because they knew they would get paid. He said neither Smith nor the Cowboys gang was mentioned in any of the three interviews he conducted with Murdaugh.

Many podcasters took to the air to show their surprise that the notorious Cowboys gang of Walterboro had been called out in a courtroom. They had been known as the Sandhill Drug Gang previously, and their reputation for violence was well known.

The fact that no life insurance was found for either or Maggie or Paul was pushed forward by Griffin as a reason against Alex killing them. There was no financial profit from their deaths.

After the Aug. 11 interview, Murdaugh was the only known suspect, Owen said. Owen said the inconsistencies between the interviews were significant to his investigation.

"It wasn't one inconsistency," Owen said. "It was several inconsistencies over a period of time repeated."

The jury has heard about those inconsistencies throughout the trial from witnesses like Alex's mother's caretaker Shelley Smith who said Murdaugh was only at the home for 15 - 20 minutes and later tried to sync up the stories by telling her he was at the home for 30 or 40 minutes.

Owen pointed out the inconsistency in Murdaugh's recollection of time spent visiting his mother that night by saying Murdaugh started by saying he was at the home for a little while before changing the story to 25 or 30 minutes in the second interview, and finally 45 minutes to an hour in the third interview.

During cross examination, Griffin worked to discredit SLED's investigation. The defense has said previously they thought SLED's investigation never considered anyone other than Murdaugh as a suspect in the case.

During Attorney Meaders re-direct, we see a very real possibility for why no blood (other than the tiny amount of Maggie's found on the steering wheel) was found in Alex's Suburban. If he had put bloody clothes in there to dispose of at his mother's house that night, there should be something in the car. Meaders asked in what seemed like a throwaway question, "Can you put something in a cooler in the back of a car?" he asked. It was left hanging for the jury to digest. It was mentioned that C.B. Rowe said a cooler was kept in the Skinning shed, which is only steps from the hangar and kennels.

Hangar area where the murders happened. The Skin Shed is the small building, upper middle right at the edge of the photo.

In State's Exhibit 191, we see a photo of the Skinning shed with a picnic table beside it. On the table is a cooler. Beer cans are scattered around the ground.

The cooler (arrow) from trial exhibit 191 is on a picnic table by the skinning shed. Courtroom Pool photo.

Mark Ball mentions seeing the cooler by the shed June 8th, the morning after the murders. He says beer cans were scattered around on the ground as if someone had hastily dumped them out from the cooler. C.B. Rowe testified that the Murdaugh's would often unload their boats here. Was this the cooler from Alex's boat that Paul crashed on Archer's Creek? A raincoat was also in that boat's inventory. One other thought. Is that partially why there is so much water in the kennel area? Did Alex wash the cooler out before putting it back on the picnic table after returning from his mother's house that night?

David Grubbs with the South Carolina Attorney General's Office was next on the witness stand for the prosecution. He is an expert in computer forensics and cell phone extractions. He testified that Paul's phone had died four times in the week prior to his death. He would frequently let the battery get down to zero before recharging it. On the night of the murders, Paul's phone was at only 2% power at the time of his death. At 10:18 pm that night, Paul's phone came back on (lit up) for several seconds. Any incoming text or alert will cause a phone to light up for a few seconds, Grubbs testified. The last text that came in was from Rogan Gibson. It simply said, "Yo." Rogan had been texting and calling Paul to get the kennel video Paul shot. He never saw it until a year later. Paul's phone finally died at 10:34 pm the night Paul died.

Attorney Conrad for the Prosecution asked Grubbs a chilling question that was not lost on the audience. "You could see that text from Rogan by looking at the phone, correct?" he asked. "Yes, you could," Grubbs replied. It's that little window of text we are familiar with that shows you a snippet of communication coming in before you "click" on it. To the courtroom, it showed Alex saw that text from Rogan despite not being able to open Paul's phone. He tried to get Rogan to return his texts and calls for hours after that.

Grubbs testified that Maggie's phone finally stopped transmitting any data, including motion detection, at 9:08 pm. It was at that time the phone was supposedly dumped on the roadside. Grubbs testified that Maggie's phone was locked from 8:53 pm to 9:08 pm the night of the murders. It remained locked until found the next morning. "From 9:07-9:31 pm, the phone was locked, and it wouldn't record an orientation change," Grubbs testified. In other words, if someone had thrown Maggie's phone out of the window of a truck, the motion sensor that would have shown an orientation change would not have been activated.

Kenneth Kinsey Takes the Stand

The state called Dr. Kenneth Kinsey to the stand Thursday morning. Kinsey was to be their big gun in the reconstruction of the crime scene and events that happened the night of the murders. Kinsey is the Chief Deputy at the Orangeburg Sheriff's Office. He quipped when he took the stand that he had come all the way from Orangeburg, a small town about an hour away. He is a Crime Scene Reconstruction Expert and Technician. The one downfall to Kinsey's testimony was that he wasn't called by SLED to the crime scene at Moselle until the following year. He did his own measurements of the hangar area, where Maggie and Paul were found, bullet trajectories, building and equipment placement, etc.

The Defense had filed a motion to block Kinsey's testimony before the trial began on the basis of blood spatter evidence in Kinsey's report. Prosecutors never mentioned the T-shirt blood spatter during their questioning of Kinsey.

Prosecutor Creighton Waters questions witness Kenneth Kinsey during Alex Murdaugh's trial for murder at the Colleton County Courthouse on Thursday, February 16, 2023. Joshua Boucher/The State/Pool (Joshua Boucher | jboucher@thestate.com)

Kinsey testified to the locations of Paul and Maggie Murdaugh on the night of the murders as well as the potential location of the shooter. Kinsey said Paul Murdaugh was standing about five feet inside the feed room when he was shot the first time in the chest. Paul would have then turned and walked toward the door of the feed room when he was shot fatally a second time, Kinsey said.

"The breach of the shooter's shotgun would have been inside the door for the first shot and the shooter would have been located outside and to the right of the feed room door during the second shot," Kinsey said.

Kinsey testified that most of the pellets from the first shot went out the window behind Paul. "He was moving slowly, and droplets went straight down his arm and dripped off his fingers," he said. He put the feed room dimensions at 10 feet deep. "You could follow the droplets to the door," Kinsey said. In one of Kinsey's recreation photos, he placed a mannequin digitally in the photo to show where Paul was and his position when the first shot was fired.

Kinsey's crime scene recreation showing where Paul would have been standing when the first shot was fired that struck him in the chest and left arm. Courtroom Pool photo.

Kinsey said his arms were down. 20-25 wounds were found in his left arm. 9 shotgun pellets in buckshot were to the chest. There was stippling to the chest which means the gun barrel was close; three feet or less away. The gun was inside the door, as witnessed by the shotgun shell ejecting to the right, hitting something and then rolling beneath the feed room door. He said Paul "was real close to the door exit when the second shot was fired. His feet were just inside the door." Kinsey said Paul was 5'8" tall.

"The shooter was just to the right of the feed room door outside," he said, "for the second shot." Paul's shoulder was just outside the door. The second shot to his left shoulder, jaw, and head was birdshot.

The Defense would question the angle and distance of the second shot to Paul Murdaugh, arguing that a shot fired at an angle of approximately 135 degrees would require the shooter to be really low to the ground or bent over. They questioned earlier testimony that it was fired from three feet away. Kinsey testified that he had no way of knowing the exact distance or placement because he did not have the actual shotgun used and instead used blood spatter and damage to the door to draw his conclusions before adding he thought the distance was closer to two feet.

Kinsey said Maggie had three non-fatal injuries: shots to her wrist, left thigh, and the one to the ribcage. The two fatal wounds were the ones through her breast that went into her head, and the shot to the top of her head. He said the shooter shot her thigh and stomach quickly; both had stippling that put him/her only 4 – 5 feet away from Maggie. He agreed with Dr. Riemer that Maggie would have bent over after the shot that went through her stomach and pancreas. He said five or six cartridges were used during the assault on the 52-year-old woman.

One of the most compelling pieces of evidence presented by Dr. Kinsey was his statement that the small patch of mud found on the back of Maggie's leg came from the mud on the tire of the Polaris Ranger only a few feet from the feed shed. He showed the jury photos of the pattern in the tire mud on the Polaris and how it matched the imprint in mud on the back of Maggie's leg. He said she was standing at the time the first shot went through her thigh and she probably backed into the tire behind her. "She was facing the feed room door," he said. He stated he saw no signs of defensive wounds on either victim from his examination of the autopsy and crime scene photos. He also said the shooter was holding the shotgun parallel to the ground with the first shot, about 4'7" from the ground. During the second shot, the gun was held "really low." The shooter was three feet or closer, Kinsey testified. He said he was hired in October of 2022 and looked at evidence in November of that year.

Kinsey demonstrated on Creighton Waters how the shots to Paul and Maggie were inflicted. Using a long dowel rod, he positioned Waters' head slightly to the left and bent forward for the second shot that exploded Paul's head. Waters even crouched on all fours on the floor in his suit to allow Kinsey to show the jury where the shooter was for each of Maggie's wounds. After "shooting" the Prosecutor with the dowel rod, Kinsey gently shoved the attorney all the way to the floor with his foot to put Waters in Maggie's final position for the fatal head shot.

Dr. Kenneth Kinsey positioning Creighton Waters head to show the angle of the second shot that exploded the top of his head. Courtroom Pool.

Dr. Kinsey's warm "down home, 'Aw Shucks Ma'am'" approach during his testimony made him a courtroom favorite. He was never flustered during cross-examination. He never impugned SLED's own measurements and diagrams, merely had his own opinion about the crime scene. He was so popular, that SLED brought him into the Stephen Smith investigation in April of 2023 to aid in reconstructing the crime scene of the young man's death.

Special Agent Ryan Kelly sat down in the witness chair and adjusted the microphone that had been the bane of each witness's testimony. It was too short, and one had to continually lean over it to be heard. Taller witnesses finally sat sideways and mouthed their answers over their left shoulders.

Creighton Waters led Agent Kelly through a series of questions. Thanks to the defense opening the door for the roadside shooting incident, Kelly was able to discuss and play his phone interview with Alex as he sat in a room at the treatment center in Atlanta with his attorneys Griffin and Harpootlian. That interview was documented in an earlier chapter in the book.

561

In a phone interview with South Carolina Law Enforcement Division Agent Ryan Kelly from Sept. 13, 2021, Murdaugh admitted to lying about the circumstances surrounding the Sept. 4, 2021, shooting on Salkehatchie Road when he told investigators his SUV had a flat on the side of the road and an unknown man stopped and shot him in the head. Murdaugh went as far as to have a composite sketch drawn of the man, he claimed shot him. In the phone interview, Murdaugh admits to having an 18–20-year addiction to prescription painkillers and said he thought it would be easier on his family if he was dead.

One of the salient points Kelly made was to say Randy Murdaugh was at the Savannah hospital with Alex when Agent Kelly arrived the day of the shooting on Old Salkehatchie Road in Hampton. He went over the lies Alex told him that day, that Murdaugh admitted to in the phone interview. He said when the Mercedes was searched the day of the roadside shooting, Alex had his Assistant Solicitor's badge in the car. A tan folding knife was found across the street from the Mercedes the following day on September 5th. Alex and Eddie's prints were found on the knife.

Kelly said the fancy Mercedes had what is called a "run flat" feature, meaning that even with a puncture, it will run for a while; close to another 50 miles or more. Alex could have made it to a gas station or repair shop with the puncture that he said he had to pull over and fix the day he was shot.

Agent Kelly testified that Randy Murdaugh called Agent Owen and told him Alex had paid a nurse at the hospital and was calling unknown phone numbers. Keep in mind that Randy and the law firm were aware Alex had been stealing from them at the time he was visiting Alex in the Savannah Hospital. Perhaps he was looking out for the law firm's reputation, or he had just had it with his little brother.

Someone in the Murdaugh family provided Kelly with Curtis Eddie Smith's phone number and it matched the numbers Alex had been calling from the hospital. The video surveillance from St. John's Church had come in, showing Eddie's blue Chevy truck driving by at 1:25 pm the day of the roadside shooting. Alex's Mercedes is seen following right behind him. Only five minutes later, Eddie's truck is seen going the opposite direction. Whatever went down at the "shooting" happened within only five minutes.

Eddie, known to the public as "Cousin Eddie," as he purported to be a distant cousin of Alex Murdaugh, lived in Walterboro. Agent Kelly and another agent went to Eddie's house on September 7, 2021, three days after the roadside shooting. They had a search warrant for Eddie's house. They found narcotics in the garage, a drug reference guide, and 3 ½" spiral notebook with pill identifications, and numbers, "like a ledger," Kelly testified. Several hundreds of thousands of dollars were found in Eddie's bank account, yet he lived in a humble home.

Dick Harpootlian cross-examines Agent Ryan Kelly.

Agent Kelly went over salient points in the phone interview with Alex that had been played for the jury. In the interview, Murdaugh tells Kelly that he didn't pay Smith to shoot him and only ever paid him for drugs, at times spending $40,000 or more. Murdaugh was pressed on if he owed any drug dealers money, and he told Kelly that he did not.

Kelly asks if Smith had any connection to the Moselle murders and Murdaugh tells him no. Kelly testified that no evidence indicated Smith was involved in the shootings.

Just the Facts, Ma'am

Twenty days into the trial, SLED Agent Peter Rudofski put the hammer down on Alex's timeline the night of the murders. He presented 43 pages of GPS points, phone calls, text messages, and orientation data detailing the movements of Alex, Maggie, and Paul Murdaugh on June 7, 2021.

Rudofski's testimony created a minute-by-minute timeline that shows inconsistencies with Murdaugh's recollection of events from that night.

The data showed deleted phone calls and text messages on Murdaugh's phone, and a lack of steps taken between 8:09 pm and 9:02 p.m. the night of the murders. Alex's phone showed no activity at all for almost an hour in that time frame. It was the only time his phone had been so documented.

Prosecutors gained data from Murdaugh's Chevy Suburban OnStar system Friday and investigators were able to establish that only 20 seconds had elapsed between Murdaugh's arrival at the kennels and his 911 call. It was hotly disputed by the State that Alex could have arrived at the kennels that night, seen his wife and son lying in pools of blood in his headlights, exited the car, gone over to Maggie and checked for a pulse, then crossed to Paul, try to turn him over, replace his phone that "popped out of his pocket," return to the car and dial 911, all in the 20 second window. Murdaugh later said he did all those things while on the phone to the dispatcher, not before the call was placed.

The timeline data for Alex Murdaugh for June 7, 2021, was given to the jury as follows:

- 12:07 pm: Alex leaves for work, turns right on Moselle Road, 12 mph.
- 12:08 pm.: Driving on Moselle Road, 55 mph.
- 12:24 pm: Arrives at Law Firm, 60 mph.
- 6:24 pm: Leaves work, 8 mph, then 42 mph
- 6:42 pm: Alex arrives at Moselle home.
- 9:07 pm: Alex leaves for Almeda
- 9:08 pm: 42 mph; 45 mph after Maggie's phone location
- 9:13 pm: 68 mph to Almeda
  70 mph into Varnville (reached a maximum 74 mph)
- 9:22 pm: Arrives at Alameda
- 9:22:39 Alex's car goes into the grass & outbuildings.
- 9:43:18 pm: Leaving Almeda

- 9:45:22 pm: Goes onto highway (80 mph to Moselle)
- 10:05 pm: Leaves for kennels
- 10:06 pm: 911 Call

Agent Peter Rudofski testifying during Murdaugh trial.

The timelines for Alex, Maggie, and Paul were listed in a previous chapter. This data was to focus on the speeds Alex was traveling. Data recovered also shows the Suburban driving at a high rate of speed on his way to and from his mother's house reaching a maximum speed of 80 mph.

Defense attorney Phillip Barber worked to poke holes in Rudofski's interpretation of the data suggesting that Murdaugh could have hit that speed by passing a car on the two-lane road. Rudofski didn't take the bait and said he was just looking at the data.

Rudofski pointed out that Alex paused for a minute toward the end of Randolph's driveway on his way back to Moselle. Alex claims he dropped his phone inside the SUV and stopped to pick it up.

The state ended the day by showing the jury a voicemail from Paul Murdaugh about Maggie Murdaugh finding pills in Alex Murdaugh's bag and a search history showing Maggie Murdaugh had tried to identify the pills.

With that, the State rested. There was a bit of a letdown that a few witnesses were not called. The absence of Cousin Eddie was keenly felt, and many had hoped C.B. Rowe would be called to the stand.

There was a brief recess for "housekeeping matters." The prosecution looked over the evidence presented. As is typical of most trials, the defense called for an acquittal, saying the prosecution had not met its burden of proof. The Hail Mary was denied by Judge Newman. It barely registered on the faces at the defense table. It was a long shot, but worth taking.

The courtroom readied itself for what the Defense had in store. It had been a long trial already. Many were hoping for a succinct parade of witnesses. The rumor mills were buzzing about whether or not Alex Murdaugh would take the stand.

Chapter Thirty-Four
Alex Murdaugh Takes the Stand

Alex Murdaugh's defense team had an uphill battle. The weeks leading up to the trial saw blogs and podcasts saying the State was coming to bat with one hand tied behind their backs. Dick Harpootlian, a seated Senator, would roll over Creighton Waters like a June bug. But as the trial progressed, it was the underdog that showed the most bite. Waters' rapid-fire questioning was often a welcome relief after Harpootlian's faltering examinations. The State's team of lawyers were well-selected, each having their area of expertise. There were times when the Defense's questions and statements actually helped the Prosecution's case.

The first witness called for the Defense was Colleton County Coroner Richard Harvey. He said he was notified by a detective at 10:30 pm the evening before of the murders and he arrived at Moselle at 11:04 pm. He said he often attends murder scenes. He stated that he took photographs of the feed room. "It had not been processed by SLED yet," he testified.

The coroner released the death certificates of Maggie and Paul saying they both died at 9:00 pm that night. He said he checked both bodies as they lay there at the crime scene. He determined their time of death by placing a hand in both of their armpits to gauge their temperature. He checked for signs of rigor mortis, which is when the joints stiffen. Rigor starts within 1-3 hours, he stated. He said both bodies were covered with sheets when he got there. He said he doesn't use a rectal thermometer to determine body temperature. He

567

also 9:00 pm was a "guesstimate." Harvey also said it had not rained hard by that time and both of the victims' hair was dry.

The coroner failed to mention that he asked one of the officers at the scene to take the photographs of the bodies because he "had contaminated his gloves."

Shalane Tindal with the Colleton County Sheriff's Office was called to the stand. She was asked about the immediate news release on June 8th saying, "At this time, there is no danger to the public..." Tommy Crosby was SLED's Public Information Officer (PIO). Tindal said it was a joint effort with SLED to put out the notification one day after the murders. Mr. Crosby removed the "no danger to the public" from subsequent releases. On the morning of June 8, before 10 am, SLED had already redacted the hasty announcement.

Week Five of the Trial

As the courtroom readied itself for the fifth week of trial, Judge Newman had a little business to attend to. He asked Alex's attorney about a Tweet Jim Griffin had put out a couple of days prior. Griffin was retweeting an article in the *Washington Post* that had found issues with the crime scene investigation of the Murdaugh murders, basically saying it was shoddy police work. Judge Newman said he just found out about it and was not pleased with Griffin. He reminded Griffin of Rule 3.6 and treated the seasoned attorney as a child about to be sent to the corner for bad behavior. A chastened Jim Griffin apologized to the court and said it wouldn't happen again. Judge Newman said, that while it wasn't against the law, "It doesn't pass the feel test." With the reprimanding over, Griffin called the Defense's next witness.

When Buster Murdaugh's name was read out to the courtroom, a buzz could be heard from the gallery. It was as if a celebrity was walking up to the witness stand. Here was the elusive sole surviving child of Alex Murdaugh's. Not much was known about Buster. There were the usual snarky remarks concerning his expulsion from college for cheating off a classmate's paper. That rumor was followed by Alex trying to buy his son's way back into the

University. The shadow of Stephen Smith's death still hung like a cloud over the ginger like a storm that never quite burst but was always threatening.

Those watching the trial from their cozy recliners at home had noticed how often Buster had tried to catch his father's eye at the trial each time Alex rose and was escorted out at the end of the day. Sometimes, Alex looked his way and nodded or shot his son a thumbs up. Often, the ex-attorney was busy schmoozing with the security guards or other attorneys. Many had heard the myriad jail house phone calls between Buster and Alex, this author included. Buster never failed to answer the phone, even when Alex called him several times a day. He would sound tired and a little put out at times, but he always took his dad's calls.

Buster Murdaugh on the stand for his father's murder trial.

The 26-year-old son of Alex Murdaugh took his seat on the stand, adjusted his jacket and the microphone, and leaned toward it with perfect poise. His eyes were laser focused on whomever was doing the questioning.

Jim Griffin led Buster through some trivial details. He was living in Hilton Head with his girlfriend Brooklyn. He was born in Savannah, Georgia. The Murdaughs moved to Hampton in 2000. He was into sports, fishing, hunting, and the outdoors, although he admitted Paul had been more of the outdoorsman than himself. He said Paul played basketball and softball. His dad, Alex, had coached every Little League team in which the brothers participated.

They bought Moselle around 2012. He was a sophomore at Wade Hampton High School at the time. Buster spoke about the home on Holly Street and said Hurricane Mathew had knocked palm trees over onto the house. He said he went frequently to the Edisto Beach house. When the Murdaughs sold Holly Street and made Moselle their permanent residence in 2014, Buster said he had started college and was living on campus.

Buster described the Moselle property in a way that many had not appreciated. It was 1,700 acres with swampland, road systems, 20 deer stands, duck stands, etc. There was a duck pond. Friends were always coming there to hunt. Buster described the cabin that sat near the hangar at the kennel entrance to the property. He said the summer of his sophomore year, he and Rogan Gibson, and Nolan Tuten had lived in the cabin. He went on to say there were a lot of guns at Moselle. 12-, 16-, 20-, and 28-guage shotguns, rifles, AR's, etc. He admitted that guns were left at the shed, in golf carts and trucks, etc. Paul left guns on the property more than anyone else. He carried them in his truck. Paul never locked his truck, Buster said.

Buster went over the two AR-15 .300 Blackouts he and Paul were given one Christmas. "Mine was black and Paul's was tan," he said. "Mine had a Benelli MOJO brand sticker on it. Paul would borrow my gun, but he wasn't good about putting it back." There was no emotion as Buster talked about Paul. It was a clear and concise recitation of facts. He had shown little to no emotion throughout the trial, even during the grueling forensic evidence dealing with his mother's and brother's slain bodies.

Maggie and everyone took the kennel entrance to the property, Buster stated. The mailbox was there, and Amazon delivered to the shed near the kennels. He said his mother preferred Edisto in the summer of 2021 and Buster went there a lot. In the Spring of 2021, Buster said he was living in an apartment in Columbia but split his time with Moselle. In the summer, he was usually in Columbia or Rock Hill. Brooklyn, his girlfriend lived in Rock Hill, he clarified. He said Paul spent the spring of 2021 in his apartment in Columbia where he was going to school. That summer, he was living with their

Uncle John Marvin in Okatie where he was working for his uncle's heavy equipment rental company.

Buster said the Murdaughs would go with the Brandstatter's (Maggie's parents) to Key West, and they all gathered for Christmas. May of 2021, there was a baby shower at Lake Kiwi for their oldest cousin. It was the last photo taken of the four of them before the murders took place. He said that Randolph was called "Handsome." Almeda, where Randolph and Miss Libby's house was located, was about 20 minutes from Moselle. They called Miss Libby 'M.' He said he didn't have any set schedule for visiting his grandparents. Maggie would go once and a while. Paul went regularly.

The crux of the questioning began when Jim Griffin asked Buster where everyone parked when they went to visit "Handsome" and "M" in Almeda. Buster said there was a car park at the end of the driveway where you could park. He said at night, they would pull around to the back side of the house where the back door was. This was all grass. Griffin shows Buster photos of the GM tracking dots placing Alex in the side yard the night of the murders when he came to see his mother. Buster said that was where they usually park. He pointed out the "Cook Shed" (what most were calling the Smoke House) and said it was an open room with couches and a TV for Randolph to do cookouts. To the right of the cook house was an old shed. Both buildings were about 10-20 yards from the back door.

Randolph III's side yard. Miss Libby's window is seen.

Smoke house (left) and old shed (right) in Randolph's side yard where GPS coordinates place Alex's Suburban that night. It's about 10- 20 yards to the back door where Alex entered on the night of June 7th.

Buster testified that he talked to his mother and father every day, sometimes multiple times a day. He said he had called him at 9:10 pm, the night of the murders. He said that was normal. He stated the cell phone service at the hangar and the house was spotty because both buildings had metal roofs.

(This is probably why Maggie had her cell phone in one spot during the 911 call for Gloria Satterfield's call. Maggie asked the dispatcher if she could "get off the phone and get down there" to where Gloria was, probably because she knew the call would drop if she moved from the sweet spot on the front porch.)

Buster said it was not unusual for his dad to leave his phone at the house. He said his dad and Paul were always misplacing their phones. In a further attempt to help his dad out, Buster said Bubba would listen to Alex more than others. They sometimes used a shock collar on the dogs. Next came the shower Alex took the night of the murders. "He took showers a lot. It's hot out there," Buster said. He went on to say he knew very little about his dad's pills. He knew his mom and brother had found pills. In 2018, at Christmas time, his dad had gone into rehab. He tried detoxing at home a few times. "He was always sorry and apologetic," Buster said.

He said their family handled disputes civilly. There was never any violence. He testified that he was in Columbia at school when the boat crash happened in 2019. He said Paul got hit pretty hard after that. People would yell at him from cars when he is walking down the sidewalk. His mom read all the negative stuff on social media and distanced herself from Hampton, staying more at the Edisto Beach house. She started shopping in Walterboro.

(I spoke to a native of Hampton that said Maggie would go into the little shops or the post office in Hampton wearing a lot of diamonds and sometimes fur. This woman remembered thinking, "What are you doing wearing all that jewelry like that? You're a walking target." Others I spoke with said Maggie was never really happy in Hampton. She gave the locals the feeling that she couldn't relate to them and preferred Charleston or the larger towns and cities.)

Jim Griffin asked Buster if he was sued for the boat crash?

"Yes, sir." Alex was sued, Maggie's estate had been sued. He said his mother was very anxious about the civil suit for the boat crash. Mark Tinsley posted, and was going around saying, he wanted $40 million. Buster said his dad didn't seem overly anxious about it. He said there was a civil suit and a criminal suit against Paul and the others named in the two cases. The family didn't think Paul was driving the boat, Buster said.

He went over the two weekends leading up to the murders. The Memorial Day/Birthday party was gone over. His mom had made his dad's cake. The next weekend was a baseball tournament in Columbia. He and his girlfriend, and his mom and dad went. It was a regional game and a big deal. He said his mom and dad spent the night of June 5th in Columbia and June 6th went back to Moselle. (This would have been when they brought the Krispy Kreme doughnuts to Randolph.)

Buster said he learned about the murders when "My dad called me and asked if I was sitting down. He told me my mother and brother had been shot. I was in shock." He said his girlfriend Brooklyn hurriedly packed their stuff. They got to Moselle around 2 am. He said his dad "was destroyed." Buster falters somewhat during this part of his testimony. He shoots a sideways glance toward his father at the Defense table a couple of times. Alex is crying.

Buster lists the people in the house when he arrived: his Uncles Randy and John Marvin, Chris Wilson, Corey Fleming, law firm partners, Nolan Tuten and others. He said they stayed for about three or four hours at Moselle and then left to stay at Almeda. His dad was wearing a T-shirt. Buster helped him pack to leave. He said he grabbed him some T-shirts, shorts, and some toiletries. A T-shirt may have fallen on the floor in the closet when he hastily yanked down clothes. He said they went back to Moselle the next morning. They got there early and showered there. Buster said he was with his dad every day after that. On June 8, they were at Almeda or John Marvin's property called Greenfield. It's only a couple of minutes from Almeda. (Almeda was often used to refer to Randolph and Miss Libby's home.)

On June 10th, Randolph died, he said. That was a Thursday. His mom and Paul's funeral was on Saturday, and then on Sunday was Randolph's. In the beginning of the next week on June 14th, they went to Summerville and stayed until the 17th. They left to go to Lake Kiwi. It was Alex, his mom's grandparents, aunt and uncle and their kids. He eventually went back to work in Rock Hill. He said his dad offered him some protection or to carry a gun, or a security detail. He and his dad announced a reward for $100,000 in a news release. The expiration date was September 30, 2021. He said he wasn't sure why there was an expiration date.

"Did Alex ever come back home for his clothes or belongings?" Griffin asked.

"No, sir," Buster said. He had clothes at Almeda, Okatie, Edisto, in his car, at Randy's...

Griffin shows Buster the SnapChat video and asks him if he recognizes the light blue shirt his father is wearing. He does, and says, "It's not a Columbia shirt." Buster went on to say he never saw his dad buy "Vinny Vine" shirts. He said his dad stayed sometimes at the "little house" that was between John E. Parker's and Randy's residences.

Jim plays the segment of the second interview that his father gave in Agent Owen's car at John Marvin's Greenfield. He asks Buster if he hears Alex say, "I did him so bad." Buster says he hears, "*They* did him so bad." He said his dad said the same thing the night of the murders at the house when he and Brooklyn arrived.

When Attorney Meaders made the cross, he asked Buster about parking on the grass near the back door of his grandparents' house.

"Would you ever go there at 6:30 in the morning?" he asked.

"I would if I was going hunting," Buster said.

"When did you find out your family's finances were bad?" Meaders asked.

"September 4th." (The day of the roadside shooting.)

Meaders brought up the boat crash. "Your brother used your I.D.?"

"Yes. It frustrated me sometimes," Buster said, with just a touch of heat.

Buster is asked about that jail house phone call where Alex asked him if he would like to go hunting at Moselle since the deer feeders were full and there were probably a lot of deer running around. Buster said he told him he didn't want to go there. Alex is unwavering in the call, oblivious to the fact Buster's mother and brother were murdered there. "How about dove huntin'?" Alex presses. "No." Buster says. "Do you mind if Jim goes dove huntin' then?" Alex asks his son, meaning his attorney Jim Griffin. "I don't care," Buster says, sounding frustrated and ready to get off the phone.

During the re-direct, Jim asked Buster if Maggie would take the dogs to Edisto Beach with her? "She would if she was staying multiple nights there," he said. He added there was work going on there now, so the dogs were kenneled at Moselle.

Buster Murdaugh had done his best to undo all the previous testimony that had been damaging to his father. He explained it all away. He had been composed, answered every question with the words, "No sir" or "Yes sir." It was clear he loved his father. He had lost his mother and brother. He was still looking at a lawsuit because of his little brother's drunken carelessness. Rumors of his involvement in Stephen Smith's death were worse than ever as one documentary and podcast after another came out. It was at a fever pitch during the trial of his father. Paparazzi were camped out by the condo he shared with Brooklyn in Hilton Head. They hid in bushes and followed the couple on dog walks. It was relentless.

As Buster waited to sign paperwork, his father took advantage of his being led from the courtroom and brushed his son's side. It was a touching but surreal moment. Crime scene evidence of the murders was only a table away.

Alex Murdaugh touches his son on the way out of the courtroom.

Dick Harpootlian next questioned his own forensic engineer to offset the impressive testimony of the State's witnesses on what happened the night of June 7, 2021.

Mike Sutton, a forensic engineer and expert in reconstructing accidents was called to the stand. He testified he had done work on 50 shooting reconstruction cases. It was his testimony that elicited a great deal of satire during the prosecution's cross-examination.

Sutton went to the crime scene in October of 2022, 18 months after the murders of Maggie and Paul. He took measurements and went over SLED's evidence. In a Power Point display, Sutton went over the defects in the doghouse and quail pen, using little figures armed with rifles, shooting green laser lights, to demonstrate his two-shooter theory. Each "shooter" was placed to align with the proposed trajectory it would take to line up with the doghouse and quail pen holes.

Mike Sutton demonstrates for Dick Harpootlian the bullet trajectories necessary to match the defects in the doghouse and the quail pen.

Mike Sutton's Power Point recreation showing 2 "shooters" by the doghouse where Maggie's body was found. The trajectory lines are going to the quail pen. Photo courtesy of the Courtroom Pool photos.

Sutton pointed out that the bullet defect to the doghouse near Maggie's body was 5 ½" up from the ground, going down slightly to the left. The quail pen bullet defect, he said, was 4' up from the ground going upwards.

"The shooter was not holding the rifle at shoulder height," Sutton said. "He shot from the hip." He stated that Alex Murdaugh is 6'3" or 6'4" tall. It's 25" up to his kneecap, Sutton pointed out. It was unlikely a tall person made the quail pen shots. It was more likely someone who was 5'2" – 5'4" made the shots for the shooter to have ejected shell casings where they were marked.

Sutton continued on with his "little person shooter theory," as he went over Paul's wounds. In the feed room, it showed a 3'11" upward trajectory, again proving the shooter had the shotgun closer to hip level.

Sutton was also responsible for running a sound test on January 5, 2023, to see if shots fired at the kennel could be heard from the house. He established that due to the pine trees' interference, ambient noise within the house, such as an air-conditioner and/or a television set playing, it was entirely possible the sounds of gunshots would not be heard.

Attorney Fernandez tore into Sutton's diagrams and theory that the person(s) responsible for the bullet defects in the doghouse and quail pen were "5'2" midgets." Throughout his cross, he came back to the "midget" vigilantes as the murder suspects. It was a preposterous theory, and many wondered how desperate the defense was to even present it as a possibility. Fernandez also pointed out that Sutton had worked with Jim Griffin on the boat crash case. His parting comment rang in the jury's ears as the court ended for the day:

"Is an AR-15 with a short barrel called a pistol?" he asked the gun expert. Fernandez wanted to put the thought into the jurors' minds that when Alex Murdaugh said he and Paul had been shooting at bottles with pistols as they toured the property less than two hours before Paul was shot, it could have been a short-barrel AR. And an AR-15 was used in the murder of Maggie Murdaugh. .300 Blackout cartridges were found in the black Ford F-150 that Alex said was one of two vehicles he and Paul toodled around in that night. Was the AR-15 in the truck afterwards, along with ammo? Is this why the defense was so eager to keep that truck out of the testimony concerning ammunition found in the various vehicles on the property?

A low-point for Defense Attorney Dick Harpootlian was when he took an AR-15 from evidence and leveled it at Creighton Waters, who was seated at the Prosecution table. Harpootlian grins and laughingly said, "Tempting," during his examination of Sutton's gun testimony. With the gory crime scene fresh in everyone's mind, it seemed in incredibly poor taste. It was probably a decision the veteran attorney regretted later. It seemed that he was often scrambling during the trial to make-up points for his inadequate knowledge of the courtroom technology, and disorganized materials needed during testimony. Leveling an AR-15 rifle from evidence at his nemesis, may have been his worst move.

Defense attorney Dick Harpootlian jokingly aims AR-15 at the prosecution table, as Sutton looks on.

On Wednesday, February 22, Day 22 of the trial, Jim Griffin asks the judge to limit the cross-examination of Alex Murdaugh, should he take the stand the following day, as to how much the State could go into his financial crimes. He wanted a ruling on that now. Judge Newman says he won't stipulate such a ruling.

"Can he assert the 5th?" Griffin asks.

"I won't give you advice," Judge Newman answered. And that was that.

The courtroom and home audiences were both shocked and eager that Alex Murdaugh was going to take the stand in his own defense. It would open him up to Creighton Waters' machine-gun questions and have him testify to the world concerning all of his lies "under oath."

Mark Ball, Alex's ex-law partner at PMPED (now the Parker Law Group) settled into the witness chair. His testimony was an eyewitness account of the early hours of the murder investigation of June 7, 2021.

Mark Ball testifies during the Murdaugh trial.

Ball said he and his wife Lisa arrived near the kennels at 10:52 pm that night, less than an hour after Alex's 911 call. He said he pulled into Moselle at the kennel entrance by the mailbox. He parked by Officer Green's car, the first officer on the scene that night. The ambulance was by the hangar, he testified. Randy Murdaugh was there, Barry McCroy with Fire and Rescue, and 2 EMTs. It was obvious Ball knew many of the officials at the scene as he rattled off their names.

"Sheriff Buddy Hill was there. He was telling officers that they needed to block off the entrance. It didn't get blocked. People just kept piling in," Ball said. He stated the weather was misty and foggy. It was drizzling off and on with a floating fog, heavy at times.

Mark Ball became heated in his testimony when he mentioned seeing Paul's body. "Water was dripping off of the kennel roof and dripping on Paul, puddling on the cement. Paul was a good young man and quite frankly, it pissed me off," Ball said. "Randy was on the phone, walking around. "Alex was devastated. He was crying. I told him we'd get through it," Ball said. Alex said to him, "Look at what they did, look at what they did!"

Ball said SLED came within an hour to an hour and a half after he got there. He said all the lawyers from the firm were there with the exception of maybe 2 or 3. All of Alex's family was there. Coroner Richard Harvey showed up and told everyone to go to the house. Ball was worried about that directive.

"Where does the crime scene stop and start?" he asked. It was perhaps one of the most salient questions proffered that evening. The issue seemed irrelevant to those documenting the kennel area, and so everyone went to the house.

Ball described what happened at the Moselle home: The den and kitchen are connected, he said. He and Lee Cope (law firm partner) put the pots in the refrigerator. Folks were cleaning up. It was around 1:30 or 2 in the morning. He and his wife left at 3:30 or 4:00 am. Ball was not to get much sleep. Randy Murdaugh called him at 8:00 am and asked him if he knew of someone who could clean up the feed shed. He said John Marvin had tried and couldn't do it. Ball sent him some names the coroner gave him.

Ball testified that he was there when SLED asked Alex for the clothes he had on. "My own clothes were uncomfortably damp," Ball said. He saw Alex drop his clothes in a bag. There may have been more than one bag, he didn't remember.

Mark Ball verified what others had said, that the morning after the murders, on June 8th, SLED had already released the scene. It was shocking to most that it was let go so quickly. Ball said Solicitor Duffy Stone was there (he took Randolph III's place when "Handsome" stepped down). A deputy and SLED agent were there as well. Ball said he looked into the feed room. There were pellets on the floor, blood, and still some of Paul's remains. He said he could tell the pellets were #2 birdshot.

Ball walked over to the SLED agent and asked, "Are you sure about releasing it already? Parts of his skull are in there." "We got all we need," the agent replied.

"There was a piece of Paul's skull the size of a baseball still lying there," Ball said. "It really infuriated me."

C.B. Rowe pulled up to the hangar, Ball testified. He had a jug of Clorox in the bed of the truck. Randy had asked him to help with the cleaning of the feed room. Ball took pictures of Rowe's vehicle and the Clorox and turned them over to SLED. "It just looked odd," Ball said. "Two people had been killed and there's Clorox around."

"Did you see any coolers on the property around there?" Jim Griffin asked him.

"I did. When I walked around the bottom part between the hangar and the skinning shed, there was an open cooler there. It looked like a Yeti style cooler. I can't tell you if it was a Yeti or not, but it was one of those thicker coolers. There were probably a dozen beer cans around it. It looked like somebody had unloaded a boat or something and just thrown them out of the boat and left them."

(Alex sold the boat after the crash. Were the things at the skinning shed the items from the boat? If so, it would put the raincoat right there, handy for wrapping guns, and a cooler with which to transport bloody clothes. Mark Ball seems to be the only one "on the ball" during this investigation.)

Ball said he showed SLED an AR-15 in the gun room. There were 3 shotguns on the pool table along with ammunition. Blanca said she put all the guns back when was asked to clean up.

Mark Ball mentioned Alex's removal from the law firm on September 3rd, and the roadside shooting on September 4th. He then said he and Ronnie Crosby were asked to pick up Maggie's jewelry and have it cleaned. "There was a diamond bracelet in pieces," he said. "I don't remember if her wedding ring was there."

Alex asked Blanca while he was in rehab or jail, to sell Maggie's things on Posh Mark. Locals were appalled to see her favorite jackets and other pieces of clothing being sold by the housekeeper. Rumors that Blanca was pocketing the money were unfounded. Alex probably needed the money for buying commissary goods, or who knows what else.

Jim Griffin asks Mark Ball how he saw Alex now. "After September 3rd, I can't say I know that person," he said sadly. Alex betrayed us (the law firm) when he stole the money."

The shocking part of this direct questioning of Mark Ball by Jim Griffin is that Jim is Alex's Defense attorney. Yet, Griffin leads Ball to talk about the cooler, which no one else had. Although Ball said SLED didn't take the cooler, or seem to pay much attention to it, it still did more damage than good to the Defendant. He even allows Ball to state how he feels about Alex now, although they had once been good friends and co-workers.

Creighton stood to cross-examine the Defense's witness. Ball said he had known Alex for 34 years. He was a law partner with him for 27 years.

Ball mentioned that Randy's truck was impounded as well as Alex's and Maggie's. Waters then turned him to the night of the murders.

"Did you talk to Alex about what happened that night?" he asked. Ball had been sitting next to Alex on the couch that night and into the following morning.

Ball said Alex told him he laid down on the couch and fell asleep. Alex told him that same story three times in the coming days. He told the other law partners the same thing. He never said he went down to the kennels. Ball noticed inconsistencies in Alex's recounting of events. "He said he checked Maggie first, and then he said it was Paul first."

The law firm had to shut down after the murders, Ball said. "We were on heightened alert." He never saw Alex on the phone trying to find out what happened to his wife and son. Ball said Alex went to Ronnie Crosby's house with a bag that had a pistol in it. He left the bag there when he left. "Typical Alex, Buster, and Paul fashion," Ball said. (Or did it underscore that the gun was a prop and Alex wasn't really concerned someone was after his family?) "He didn't seem worried about Buster's safety," Ball said.

Waters then led Ball through the financial frauds that we have covered here and Jeannie Seckinger's testimony went over. He ended that segment of his testimony by saying "We've paid north of $12 million" to the victims of Alex's settlement frauds.

Marco Cooke was called next to try and dilute the danger the June 10th motion to compel hearing would have been to Alex. Cooke was Alex's attorney for the boat case after John Tiller passed away from cancer. While the Defense tried hard to play down potential threats to Alex if that hearing had gone through, Creighton Waters pushed back. He pointed out that Cooke wasn't heavily involved between Tiller and Mark Tinsley (the Beach family's attorney) until May of 2022. Was he aware that there was a Declaratory Judgment from Philadelphia Insurance saying they would not cover Alex for the boat wreck? Were you aware Alex was stealing all that money?

"No," Cooke answered.

"If the hearing had gone forward, the order could have been issued for Alex to produce his financial records, correct?"

The Defense countered by asking if Alex would have had to turn the financials over immediately? "No," Cooke answered. Waters was back with his closer: "It would have happened eventually."

The Defense called Kenneth Zeriecie to the stand. He is a crime scene specialist in forensic science and has been for 29 years. Harpootlian used him mainly to point out all the shoddy investigative procedures by law enforcement the night of the murders, including no protective footwear worn, an officer stepping into the feed shed to cover Paul with a sheet (a tarp would have been better, he said), Paul and Maggie's clothes should have been submitted, better photography procedures, etc.

Attorney John Meaders' cross-examined the witness and asks him, "When did you do the Power Point display you presented here today?"

"A week ago," Zeriecie answered. "Didn't you prepare another Power Point display that showed the mud on the back of Maggie's calf?" Meaders asked him. "Yes." "Where is it?" "Mr. Harpootlian decided not to use it," he answered.

Meaders hammered on. "You have not read all the reports in this case?" "No." "Did you do a report for this case?" "No." He took notes on his computer and handwritten notes. Meaders tells him he would like to see them. "Were you ever at the crime scene?" "No."

Jim Griffin next called a name that had been heard often throughout the trial. Barbara Mixon's phone number showed up three times on Maggie Murdaugh's cell phone log the day of the murders. Ms. Mixon worked for the Murdaughs for 42 years and was involved with the housekeeping and partial care of Miss Libby, Alex's mother. Barbara said she spoke with Maggie every day.

Barbara Mixon, housekeeper and caregiver for Miss Libby.

Mixon testified that she felt like the Murdaughs were her family. She worked Monday, Tuesday, Wednesday, and Friday, sometimes Saturday and Sunday, if needed. She always worked 8 am – 3 pm. "Maggie didn't come during the week," she said. "Maybe on a Friday."

On the day of the murders, Mixon said she spoke with Maggie. She said John Marvin came to the house to take Mr. Randolph to the doctor. She said she called Alex on June 7th and said, "Your mama is very agitated. Can you come help me?" She said Miss Libby was agitated because Mr. Randolph had been taken to the doctors again. (It had already been testified that Miss Libby was generally unaware of what was going on around her.) She said she called Alex at 3:58 pm that day.

"I was sittin' on the porch and a police car came and said Alex found them shot," Mixon said when asked how she found out about the murders.

Mixon testified that Mr. Randolph passed on June 10. His funeral was on Sunday. "The next day, Monday, I got there five to eight. The same on Tuesday. On Wednesday, again, it was five minutes to

8 am. "I relieve Shelley Smith each time. I never saw a blue tarp laid out at the house," Mixon said.

Attorney Meaders got to the heart of what everyone else was thinking when he cross-examined Barbara Mixon.

"You love Alex?" he asked her.

"I love all of them. They're like my children."

"When did you first tell that story about your conversation with Alex?" Meaders asked, concerning Mixon saying she called Alex and asked him to come help her with Miss Libby because she was agitated about Mr. Randolph going to the doctor.

"I don't remember," Barbara said.

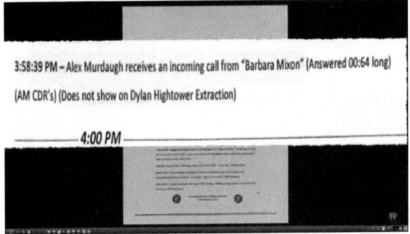

Evidence presented showing Barbara Mixon called Alex Murdaugh at 3:58 pm. The call is answered by Alex. It lasts 64 seconds. It states in parentheses that it does not show up on Dylan Hightower's Extraction report. What date was the call made?

Mica Sturgis, the Defense's answer to the phone orientation and steps presented by the State's witness, was up next. He had looked over the evidence provided by the State and the phone extractions. Sturgis plotted out Alex and Maggie's steps and distance on two charts that were placed on the ELMO for the jury. It was noted that the steps taken could happen anytime within the start and stop times; not that they started at the start time and stopped at the stop time.

Mica Sturgis, digital forensics expert for the defense.

Alex Murdaugh Steps and Distance

Entry	Start	Stop	time (seconds)	steps	distance (meters)
26	7:55:32	8:05:07	575	270	203.13
27	8:05:35	8:09:52	257	74	54
28	9:02:18	9:06:47	240	283	208.3
29	9:22:39	9:32:14	575	195	138.39
30	9:35:55	9:45:37	582	60	44.71
31	9:56:57	10:06:57	600	231	173.42
32	10:06:57	10:16:37	580	594	443.89
33	10:18:53	10:28:05	552	525	391.39

Alex's steps and distance on the night of June 7, 2021, beginning at 7:55 pm and ending when police arrived around 10:18 pm.

Maggie Murdaugh Steps and Distance

Entry	Start	Stop	time (seconds)	steps	distance (meters)
4	8:17:41	8:18:29	47	38	27.29
5	8:30:40	8:33:28	168	43	31.61
6	8:53:15	8:55:32	137	59	31.25

Maggie's steps and distance June 7th, between 8:17 pm and 8:53 pm.

Sturgis testified that if the phone screen is off, the orientation change from portrait to landscape, or vice versa, won't show up. He said it takes very little motion to cause a phone to light up. He said Maggie's database indicated her phone screen was off when Alex passed by where the phone was thrown by the side of the road.

Attorney Conrad, the State's technical expert, handled the cross of Sturgis. He pointed out that there were no steps recorded on Alex's phone between 8:09 pm – 9:02 pm that night. An entire hour of no activity on a phone that had been very active that day. Conrad got Sturgis to admit that for a phone to change orientation, it had to have human involvement. All the orientation changes that showed up on Maggie's phone after she was probably dead, could have come from it being jostled around in someone's pocket. He also pointed out that there is no activity on Maggie's phone from 8:55 pm – 9:03 pm, like someone put the phone down in a vehicle or a golf cart.

The words "golf cart" did not fall on deaf ears. It was the first time it had been hinted at as a possible vehicle used that night. What did the State know that the rest of the world didn't…at least, not yet.

Nolan Tuten was on the stand next. We have covered some of Nolan's testimony in earlier segments of the book. He was Paul's best friend and helped him sight in the replacement AR-15 a few months before the murders. While some saw Nolan's testimony as just a lead-up to the main attraction of Alex Murdaugh taking the stand, it couldn't be further from the truth. Nolan Tuten had much to offer.

Nolan Tuten, Paul's best friend, on the stand.

Nolan went over how he had checked on the sunflowers in the dove field around 10 or 11 am the morning of the murders and found them dying after C.B. Rowe over sprayed them. He and Paul were supposed to till them under the evening of the murders, but Nolan got hung up at work and didn't come. He went over the guns at Moselle and how Paul's favorite shotgun was a Benelli Super Eagle 3, Buster's was a Super Eagle 2, and Alex's was a Super Eagle 1.

Perhaps the most important part of Nolan Tuten's testimony, aside from his testimony concerning sighting in the AR-15 and the casings found near the back door to Moselle that matched those found by Maggie's body, was his involvement with the sunflowers at Moselle.

Tuten testified that he helped Paul with the farm work. He said that the Thursday or Friday before the murders on Monday, C.B.

Rowe, the Moselle groundskeeper, had sprayed the sunflowers in the dove field at Moselle. He had over sprayed them, and they were dying. This was important because the sunflowers attract the doves and the hunting season for them was coming up. Paul had been there the previous Friday when he asked Blanca to wash his clothes, and perhaps he saw Rowe spraying them. Paul asked Tuten if he would stop by the morning of the murders and look at them.

Tuten said he went by the dove field around 10 or 11 am and they did look like they were dying. He called Paul and told him. Paul asked him if he would come and help him till them under so they could be replanted. Tuten said he would meet him at Moselle that evening and help him. Paul drove up from Okatie to help his Uncle John Marvin out with the switching of the vehicles when John Marvin took his father to the doctors that afternoon. Tuten ended up backing out as he was working late in Columbia. He said he and Paul decided to do it "sometime that week."

He said Paul sent him a SnapChat video that evening around 7 pm to show him the highboy was leaking and broken. A highboy is a piece of farm equipment used in spraying crops. It may be that Paul was showing that the sprayer may have been leaking and that's why there was too much chemical on the sunflowers. It does show that Paul is at the hangar where the highboy is kept around 7:00 pm, which is when he arrives at Moselle from Okatie, give or take a minute. It also shows he was interested in the sunflowers that night.

Tuten said his mom called him between 10:30 – 11:00 pm that night and said something had happened at Moselle. It took him 20-25 minutes to get there. He saw first responders and Maggie's and Paul's bodies under sheets. When he got to Alex, the first thing Alex said was, "The boat wreck, the boat wreck, the f$#king boat wreck," and then "He asked me to call Rogan Gibson," Tuten testified.

Tuten said he saw the black Ford F-150 at the house that morning when he checked the dove fields. He said Paul would often clean his truck out at the kennels, and he had turned it into for service on Friday, the same day he was at Moselle with his dirty laundry. Was the shotgun or AR-15 taken from his truck that evening and left in the hangar area? Tuten identifies Alex's voice on the kennel video and is excused.

Judge Newman turned his gaze to the Defense table and asked, "Does your client need to confer with you anymore before he takes the stand?"

Dick Harpootlian stands and says, "Your honor, he doesn't want to talk to me. Hurts my feelings but there you go. He would like to use the bathroom before he testifies." The court took a 10-minute break. When Alex returns to the table, he borrows Chapstick from Jim Griffin and applies it to his lips. This is against the rules. It is considered contraband. No one knows what may be in the Chapstick. It was commented on by the Murdaugh FB community, but it seemed to get past the judge and prosecution.

After Judge Newman went over Alex's rights with him and was convinced Alex was taking the stand at his sole discretion, despite his attorneys advising against it, the world buckled up for what promised to be an Oscar-worthy performance. Alex did not disappoint. He repulsed a lot of people with his effusive crying and dripping snot but did not disappoint. One juror put tissue in her ears during Murdaugh's first day of testimony, and on the second day, she put a pink blanket over her head. She was quickly dubbed "blanket lady" by social media who found it not only funny but bewildering. Why did Judge Newman allow such actions? Moreover, how daunting was it to Alex Murdaugh to see a juror react to his theatrics in such an overt manner. Just another day at the Colleton County Courthouse and the Alex Murdaugh Murder Trial.

Alex Murdaugh being sworn in for his time on the stand.

Jim Griffin, Alex Murdaugh's long-time friend and attorney must have swallowed hard as he approached the podium in readiness to question his client. Alex taking the stand was a mistake. He knew it was a mistake, Dick Harpootlian knew it was a mistake, and most of those watching were waiting to see if the whole thing exploded. Only Alex Murdaugh was confident in what he was doing. The man that Mark Ball said, "could talk to a fence post." A man who had been depicted as an expert in swaying a jury or entering a room and glad-handing everyone in sight. There was no doubt in Alex Murdaugh's mind that he could look that jury in the eye and convince them of his innocence.

Griffin went over the main points with Alex:

- Paul got home a little before 7 pm. Alex got home shortly before.
- Maggie arrived at Moselle a little after 8:00 pm. Alex said he and Paul were at the shop at the hangar when Maggie got the mail, passed the kennels, and went to the house. (This is new.)
- Alex left Paul at the shed and went to the house to see Maggie and took a shower. (New. Alex knows the SnapChat video shows him wearing different clothes than the ones he is wearing when law enforcement shows up after the 911 call, and so he tells Owen in Interview 3 he changed clothes before dinner. Now he's added a shower.)
- He and Paul unloaded and washed the bulldozer. (New.)
- Paul was already eating when he got out of the shower. Maggie fixed him a plate. They ate in front of the TV. Maggie was eating on a TV tray. (New.)
- After dinner, Paul "moved on." He was somewhere around the house. Maggie wanted to go to the kennels and "I didn't want to go right then." (His statement is new.)
- She rode down with Paul. (New) He does not say in which vehicle.
- Alex felt badly that he didn't go when Maggie asked him to, so he went down in the golf cart to the kennels. (New.)

- Maggie had let the dogs out. (Grady and Bubba) "Bubba would mark every tree behind the kennels," Alex said. Grady was chasing guinea fowl. Bubba caught a chicken. (New.)
- Alex got the chicken out of Bubba's mouth and headed out. He went back to the house in the golf cart. (New.)
- Bubba had a shock collar on, he said. (New.)
- Alex lay down on the couch. The TV is on.
- Alex said he spoke with Barbara Mixon that day and she told him his mother was agitated. He went to check on his mom.
- Alex said he parked "Left of the back door" at his mom's house. Knocked on the back door. Shelley didn't hear him, so he called her on the house phone. Shelley let him in. (New. The part about knocking on the door first. It is to make it look like Alex didn't call Shelley just to establish an alibi for his timeline when his phone records are checked. It also buys him a couple of minutes from his arrival in the yard.)
- He sat on his mother's hospital bed. His mom was awake. (Shelley said she was asleep and didn't wake up while he was there.) She wasn't agitated. "I just talked to her," Alex said. Shelley said he was propped up on the other bed and was looking at his phone the whole time. He did hold Miss Libby's hand when he arrived.
- Maggie wasn't planning on going with him that night. Maggie preferred to visit Randolph.
- There are several entrances to Moselle.
- Alex said there was no reason to go to the kennels when he left for his mom's. He left through the main gate.
- He tried to call Maggie 2 times, no answer. He texted her after that. "It didn't concern me because she was with Paul," Alex said. Spotty phone service at the kennels.
- Drove straight back to Moselle from Almeda.
- Alex stopped in his mom's driveway because he dropped his phone between the console and the seat.
- "Were you disposing of guns or bloody clothes?" Griffin asks. "No, sir."
- Comes back through main gate and went to the house. The lights were on in the house, but Maggie and Paul weren't

there. Stayed in the house for several minutes. (GPS data shows he was there one minute)

- Alex went to the kennels. "I'm not positive but I think I tried to call them."
- Griffin asks Alex what he did with Paul. "I was on the side that was away from my car," he said, when stating which side of Paul, he was kneeling over.
- "Did you see any messages on Paul's phone?" Griffin asks.
- "No, sir."
- Griffin plays 911 call for all to hear.
- Alex says the dogs were in the kennels and he did not roll up the hose. (New.)
- When asked why he said, "Paul, I should have known," during the 911 call, Alex says it was because of the boat crash threats.
- Griffin shows Alex the gun he got from the house during the 911 call. Alex said he grabbed one off the pool table.
- Griffin points out there were .16-gauge shells in this .12-gauge shotgun. Alex knows better. He was just really scared and traumatized.
- "I'm about 100 yards from my house," when at the kennels, Alex said. It's 1100 feet.
- Alex brings up the boat crash threats to Paul. "My son (Buster) knows who was threatening him."
- Griffin points out the 911 call at the 10:13:38 mark. The dispatcher tells Alex not to touch them. "I already touched them," Alex tells her. He said he touched them both before he went to the house for the gun.
- "Did your son make a report about the threats?" Griffin asks him. "Yes. I never thought there was a formal request or police report." He made a report on campus to the Dean of Students. (New.)
- "Did you call family?" Griffin asks.
- "I called Randy and John Marvin. And Rogan. We call him Ro."
- "Had you seen Rogan's name on Paul's phone?" Griffin asks.

- "No," Alex answers, and "I didn't Facetime him."
- Alex is asked if he saw Michael Gunn's text with a photo of a woman in a bikini with the text message, "She brought the heat," or if he Googled Whaley's Restaurant in Walterboro after the 911 call while waiting for law enforcement? Alex says "No," to the bikini text and that he must have butt-dialed Google for Whaley's restaurant while calling family.
- Another call was to Brian White, a wedding photographer and videographer. "I certainly wasn't calling him," Alex said. "I haven't talked to him in years."
- Alex said Maggie's blood on the shotgun from the house and on the Suburban steering wheel came from him touching her to check for a pulse.
- Paul didn't clean his guns often, hence the GSR on Alex's hand from the shotgun he got from the house.
- "Was there any high velocity blood spatter on your shirt?" Griffin asks him. "No, there was no high velocity blood spatter on my shirt," Alex said. (As that testimony was blocked from the trial, it's odd that Griffin brings it up here.)
- Alex said he took another shower at Moselle the morning of June 8th when they came back from Almeda. (Blanca was the first one there that morning and there was already water on the bathroom floor and a damp towel in the closet.)
- Alex said Maggie's phone had the Find My Phone app. "I knew there would be GPS data on her phone," he said. (Could the jury read that as the reason for trying to get rid of the phone?)
- It's brought up that from June 9th back, Maggie's GPS data was erased.
- Alex went over where he stayed after the murders: "I stayed with Buster & Brooklyn every night." June 8th, he stayed at Greenfield with Jim, Liz, Buster, Brooklyn, Randolph's friend and his wife. Stayed there through Sunday.
- Alex said Maggie and Paul's funerals were Friday, Randolph's was Sunday. Buried all three on Sunday.
- The following week: Monday, after the funeral, he went to Summerville by himself. Buster went to, maybe in a different car. (Which makes it convenient to stop by

Randolph's house with the blue raincoat before heading to Summerville.) Monday, Tuesday & Wednesday: stayed in Summerville. He then went to Greenville for his niece's baby's birth. He went to Lake Kiwi.

- Jim Griffith asked him if the morning of June 16, a Wednesday, "Did you go to Almeda at 6:30 a.m.?" "I was in Summerville," Alex said. (That's wonderful, but it was June 14th he went to Almeda at 6:30 am with the raincoat, not June 16th.)

- "Did you take a blue tarp into your dad's house the week following your dad's funeral?" Griffin asked. "The week after?" Alex asks. "No." "Anytime?" Griffin asks him a little frustrated. "I don't remember. I know Shelley has that in her mind. I don't remember."

- Alex said he told Shelley to tell SLED the truth about how long he was there that night (of the murders)." Shelley said Alex was trying to get her to say he was with his mom 30-40 minutes instead of the 15-20 minutes he was there.

- Alex said it was his idea for the August 11th interview at the SLED office. He wanted to find out what was going on. "You thought the meeting was to give you an update?" Griffin asks. "Yes." At the conclusion of the meeting, he's told he's a suspect.

- Alex said the clothes he was wearing that day didn't become an issue until the splatter on his T-shirt was found to be a lie.

- Alex said the "little house" by John E. Parker's was about 70 yards from Randy. He had clothes everywhere, including Chechessee (the river house).

- Griffin asks Alex about Jeannie Seckinger and Chris Wilson wanting the Ferris fees. He said he wasn't concerned about it. Moselle appraised for $3.3 million plus the timber value. $1.9 million was owed on it. Yes, Moselle was 100% in Mag's name. (He is now calling Maggie, Mag's and Paul is Paul Paul with sounds like Paw Paw.)

- The house at Edisto Beach had $250k owed on it. It had a $700k plus value. It was 50% Alex's.

- Alex got into his drug addiction. 2002 he began taking hydrocodone for a football knee surgery. That moved into oxycodone from 2008-2009. He went to detox 3 times; the first time was December 2017. He tried to detox at home. Mags helped him. He was at Sunrise Detox in Atlanta, GA when the phone interview with Agent Kelly was taken. Normally, he would stay 7 days. September 2021 went to rehab in Florida (after the roadside shooting). Today, he has been drug free for 535 days.

- On September 3rd, he was confronted by his brother Randy and Danny Henderson for stealing funds from the law firm and his clients. He admitted to the fake Forge account and drug addiction. He was forced to resign.
- September 4th, he met with Chris Wilson at Almeda. "I wanted to go and meet Corey Fleming to confess. I gave my pills to Randy and Danny. I got nervous and called someone to bring me more pills. "I changed my mind and asked him to shoot me," Alex said. "I knew how humiliating it would be for my son, Buster. I had a lot of insurance on me. I had a $4 million and an $8 million life insurance policy." (Even under oath, this man lies.)
- Alex said Paul was ADDHD.
- Griffin holds up the two guns that were in evidence (but never found to be the murder weapons) and asks Alex if he shot his wife with the guns or any guns? "I did not shoot my wife and or Paul."
- If Alex is found "Not Guilty" he has access to Maggie's estate.

Creighton Waters was like a hunting dog who smelled meat all day. When it was his turn to have a go at Alex, he leapt from his chair and was ready. He went over the Murdaugh legacy of Alex's family acting as Solicitors for almost 100 years. He pointed out Alex was a successful trial lawyer making millions of dollars in fees. He was President of the Trial Lawyers Association in 2013. He did jury trials.

Waters zeroed in on a poignant point. Alex had cases where the Black Box and OnStar data was used. He knew all about cell tower triangulation, call logs, computer evidence and other technology. Alex had used them all in his cases. Translation: Alex knew how to play the technology the night of the murders, leaving his phone at home for over an hour to avoid dropping breadcrumbs of data, and to be careful with the GPS tracking.

Waters pointed out that Alex had been with PMPED from 1998-2021. "Do you think your family is prominent in this community?" he asked him. "Yes, sir." "You've had a long association with law enforcement. You're the Volunteer Assistant Solicitor. You have a lot of friends in the law enforcement circuit. You have 2 badges for Assistant Solicitor. You've put evidence together for trials. You had blue lights in your vehicle. (Alex points out that the law firm owned the car he was driving then. He got the Suburban in 2020.) Alex said that Andy Strickland said it was okay to have the blue lights.

"Did you have your solicitor badge at the hospital the night of the boat wreck" "I don't remember." Waters shows Alex a photo of him at the hospital with his badge hanging out of his side pocket. "That gave you some leverage with law enforcement, correct?"

"You went to Morgan's room in the ER. You went to Connor's room," Waters said, lunging forward as he did when making his points. He looked like he was fencing. "I never told anyone not to cooperate with law enforcement," Alex said about the boat crash.

In the Spring of 2021, there is an investigation launched into Alex's conduct at the hospital the night of the boat crash. Andy Strickland lost his job as sheriff a few months prior to Alex becoming aware of the investigation into Alex's obstruction of justice charges. Andy was his friend, Waters pointed out and let Alex put the lights in his car. There was a financial indictment of Andy Strickland in the fall of 2020.

While Alex tried to blame his opioid addiction for his problems, Waters said Alex's land deals started going wrong in 2008. The prosecuting attorney then began going over each fraud case Alex handled while putting the settlements into his own bank account. His stealing increased as it went toward June 7, 2021.

"Did it increase after the boat crash?" Waters hammered.

"No, sir, I don't agree with that," Alex said.

"In 2019, after the boat crash, you stole $3.7 alone. You stole more money that year than any other year!" Waters yelled. "Since 2015 had your income decreased?" He goes over the years from 2014 – 2019 to show his earnings for his legitimate income were decreasing.

"I love and still love the people I stole from," Alex said in one of his more audacious moments.

Waters continued to hammer home each fraudulent settlement and the money he pocketed. Even with all that, Alex borrowed 5 and 6 figures from his father, borrowed money from John E. Parker, from his brother Randy. He would pay them back with more stolen money. Waters told Alex that he stole the Ferris funds in March because he needed more money before his usual payout in December from the firm. He exhausted that $792,000 in only two months.

Alex sat there, turned sideways in the chair, eyeing the attorney over his left shoulder as he spoke into the much-too-short microphone. At times, his eyes were like two dark marbles, and his face twisted into cruel expressions that flashed quickly before he regained control. Thursday ended. The next day, Waters was stalking the floor in front of the jury like a caged tiger.

One of the many faces of Alex Murdaugh during his testimony. When Creighton Waters would turn his back during questioning, the mask often fell away.

Waters next brought up the growing control over his pill addiction by his family. Maggie found pills one month before she was murdered. Alex had gone in for cataract surgery and she was out in the car. She looked through his computer bag and found pills in May 2021. She texted Paul about it, who in turn texted his dad and said they weren't happy about it and needed to talk. Waters said Maggie and Paul had been watching him like a hawk for years. (It harkened back to Gloria Satterfield finding a bag of pills taped under Alex's bed on Holly Street in 2018, only a couple of days before Gloria "fell."

Alex admitted that "Mag's, Paw Paw, and Bus all found pills."

"You had to admit you were at the kennels because of the kennel video, isn't that, right?" Waters accused. "We all heard your story about the kennels for the first time yesterday. About the golf cart, washing the bulldozer, etc. Your own lawyer was repeating your story of napping on the couch in a documentary on TV November 2022. (Jim Griffin appeared on the HBO documentary and supported Alex's version of the original story that he never went down to the kennels.)

And then, Jeannie Seckinger cornered him in his office the morning of June 7th, Waters said. John E. Parker wasn't going to loan any more money if it's proven he stole the Ferris money. On June 6th, the day before the murders, he said Alex was in the hotel in Columbia while his family was at the game, going through withdrawals.

Prosecuting attorney Creighton Waters in attack mode
during his cross-examination of Alex Murdaugh.

And now, the moment the courtroom and viewing audience had been waiting for: Alex's breakdown of his timeline the night of the murders, using his "new story," as Waters called it.

- Alex left the house shortly after noon for work. He worked on an Energy case at work. Danny Henderson wanted his report on the boat case, so he worked on that too. Had the meeting with Jeannie Seckinger.
- Left work a little after 6:00 pm. Got home at 6:45 pm.
- He and Paul rode the property. Shot a pistol.
- He told law enforcement he did not see a Blackout rifle while they were driving around. "We were not looking for hogs," Alex said. "They're in the swamp during the day."
- Alex said he was by himself when he left for the house after riding around with Paul. Paul was at the shop at the kennels.
- It only takes a minute to get to the house from the kennels. It's 2 minutes by golf cart.
- Alex now said he arrived at the kennels before Paul filmed the video. Paul was in the kennel driveway, he said, playing with Cash (Rogan's dog), and then he went into the dog pen.
- He did not talk to Maggie about going to Almeda.
- "Did you talk with Paul about Cash's tail before going to Almeda?" Waters asked. "No."
- Maggie was by the pines and chicken coop. He pulled the golf cart into that space between the feed shed and the chicken coop. He said he may have talked to Mag's and Paw Paw while he sat in the cart. He couldn't remember anything they talked about. He was only down there a couple of minutes when Bubba came running by with a chicken in his mouth. He came to him and Mag's by the kennels.
- The kennel video is at 8:45:45.
- Alex said he had the chicken out of Bubba's mouth within 10 or 15 seconds. He walked to put the chicken up on the pen, but he couldn't remember where he put it down, if there was blood on it, or if it was alive.
- Alex said he got back in the golf cart, and "I got outta there!"
- "I was getting ready to do what I didn't want to do," he said ominously. That statement was never cleared up.
- "Did you say Goodbye? Did you talk with Paul about Cash's tail?" All of Alex's answers were evasive. It was the last time he would see his wife and son alive, and he could not remember a single thing he said to them.

601

- I was thinking, "It's hot outside and I'm going back."
- Waters points out it would take 30 seconds to say Goodbye…be back in a minute, going to see mom. None of that happened.
- "This is the first time this is being told openly," Waters says to Alex.
- 8:47 is the time Alex said he left the kennel area heading back to the house and the air-conditioning. It's two minutes to the house in the golf cart. He parked the cart in front of the house "Where Mark Ball saw it," he said. Mark said he saw it to the left of the house when it is usually parked to the right of the front steps. Alex says he parks it facing the other way because the outlet is to the right rear to charge it. Blanca said it was gas-powered.

Golf cart parked in front of Maggie's Mercedes.

- Laid down on the couch and dosed for a short time.
- "9:02 pm, you're up and moving!" Creighton says, pacing in front of the jurors. It was now Alex's phone that came back to life after being silent for an hour.
- "Did you have the tan Blackout and shotgun on the cart?" Waters asks.

- "No."
- "You thought you heard a car pull up when you were in the house, but you didn't hear Blackout shots?" Waters asked sarcastically. Plus, there's a wild cat outside.
- "The dogs weren't barking in the pine trees," Alex said, "because they didn't see anyone they didn't know." (This was probably not his smartest admission.)
- "Did you have any knowledge of Cash's tail before you went down there?" "No."
- "Was there any blood on the chicken?"
- "I don't believe so."
- "Did you wash your hands?"
- "I don't believe so."
- "Did Maggie use the hose?"
- "At that time? No."
- "You don't remember the last conversation you had with Maggie?" Waters asked incredulously.
- Paul's cell phone pings at the house at 8:08 pm when he goes there for dinner after riding around with Alex.
- "Where'd you put your phone at the house?" Waters asked. This is when Alex's phone goes quiet. "Did you put it in the Suburban?" "No."
- Alex said he went in the white pickup truck from the shop and left Paul there after riding around.
- 8:17 pm: Maggie disconnects phone from Mercedes as she arrives for dinner. She takes 38 steps. Alex said Maggie got the mail and came into the kennel entrance past where he and Paul were at the shop. That's impossible if he and Paul are already at the house before she arrives.
- Alex says Paul arrived at the house after Mags and Alex, which does not line up with Paul's phone data. "He was not inside the house when I got into the shower," Alex states.
- 8:38 pm: Paul is at the kennels again.
- 8:44:45: Kennel video
- 8:49 pm. Maggie's and Paul's phones lock forever.
- 9:02 pm – 9:05 pm: Alex's phone comes to life, and he takes more steps than he has at any other time in those 4 minutes.

Creighton hammers him about what he was doing. "Did you go to the bathroom? "No." "Were you on the treadmill?" "No." Alex doesn't remember what he was doing as he readied himself to go to Almeda to see his mother. In that timeline, he is also making all these phone calls, including missed calls to Maggie who is only a short distance away.

- "Did you delete phone calls between June 7th and June 10th, including any during those 4 minutes?" Waters pounds.
- "I did not intentionally delete phone calls," Alex said. (Note the "intentionally.)
- Waters asserted that Alex made all the calls to and from Almeda the night of the murders to establish an alibi.
- Maggie was planning to stay at Edisto June 7th, but "You called her to come home," Waters said. Marion, Maggie's sister, said that as well.
- Maggie texted Blanca and said, "Alex wants me to come home."
- 9:22 pm: Alex arrives at Almeda, making calls along the way to Chris Wilson and John Marvin and others.
- 9:24 pm: Alex calls Shelley on the house phone to let him in
- Alex told Shelley at a later date to say he had stayed longer.
- "You talked to Blanca about the clothes you were wearing," Water said. "It made her feel uncomfortable."
- In the August 11th interview with Owens, he showed you the Snap Chat video and showed you what you were wearing.
- 9:42 – 9:43 pm: Alex is on his way back to Moselle.
- 10:00 pm: Turns into Moselle
- 10:05 pm: Alex is at the house.
- Went to the kennels and saw the bodies and jumped out of the car. Went back to the car and called 911 and then "did what I did."
- "You told law enforcement you checked the bodies *before* you called 911," Waters yelled.
- 10:05:57 pm: Alex's Suburban arrives at the kennels.
- 10:06:14: Only 20 seconds later, he calls 911. He could not possibly have checked their bodies, rolled Paul over, etc. in 20 seconds.

- Waters shows Alex his first interview with Owens the night of the murders where Alex told the agent he checked the bodies before calling 911.
- Alex called Randy, John Marvin, and Rogan (the boy around the corner) after he hung up from 911. But Rogan wasn't home. That's why his dog Cash was being boarded at the kennels. Rogan was in Beaufort.
- Alex said he had a pocketful of pills in his shorts and that's why he lied to SLED that night. He was paranoid because he had pills on him, and because he knew they always looked at the husband first, and the one who discovered the bodies. He also said he thought Agent David Owen was a different David...one who had gone after his friend.
- Alex said he "chucked the pills in the bathroom" when they took my clothes.
- "Not telling the whole truth is the same as telling a lie," Waters said.
- "The boat wreck is why Paul is dead," Alex repeated.

(If you look at the context of that sentence, Alex is telling the truth. The boat wreck is why there are lawsuits which are demanding to see Alex's financial records. His fraud schemes and stolen money would have been laid bare. So, yes. The boat wreck is why Paul is dead.)

- Alex said he left the golf cart facing to the left. In a crime scene photo, the cart is facing to the right in front of Maggie's Mercedes near the front door. (The golf carts are usually kept over by the bushes to the right of the door. In the photo, the cart is near the front steps in front of Maggie's car. There were plenty of other places to park it. Had he put the cart back after the murders and brought Maggie's car up after that? Did Maggie go down to the kennels in her Mercedes? Did Alex take the ring from her finger and throw in under the seat as he brought the car back to the house after he killed them?)

- The June 10th SLED interview was at John Marvin's Greenfield property. Between June 10th and the August 11th SLED interview at their office, Alex was not working at all.
- Alex borrowed $250k from John E. Parker to cover the Ferris fees. He borrowed $350k from Palmetto State Bank to cover the Ferris fees. He had to convince Chris Wilson to cover the remaining $192k for the Ferris fees.
- Alex couldn't get a loan against Moselle, but he could against Edisto. Hence, the appraisal.
- The replacement AR-15 was missing 6 months before the murders at Christmastime, Alex said.
- "You now know it was there at Turkey season, in April of 2021," Waters said, calling him out on another lie.
- September 3, 2021: the law firm called Alex out on the stolen fees. He even stole his brother Randy's check for $125k at the firm, said he lost it, and had them cut him another check.
- September 6: An interview at the Savannah Hospital after the roadside shooting where he spoke to Agent Kelly and a sketch artist to turn out a drawing of his assailant.
- "The bad guys are back again and targeted you only two hours after Chris Wilson confronted you," Waters stated.
- John E. Parker lost $477k because of Alex.
- Alex sent a text to Tony Satterfield April 21, 2021, saying that he was still working on the case, even though he had gotten the money in March and spent it.
- "I have lied well over a decade," Alex admitted.

When Jim Griffin stood for his re-direct, Alex gave it one more chance to pour on the tears for the jury. He had cried throughout most of the trial, especially when describing what he saw when he discovered his wife and son slaughtered. "I have seen what y'all have seen," he cried to the jurors, never taking his eyes off him. He meant all the gory photographs in the exhibits. It was a smart move.

They had seen Paul's and Maggie's brains shot out. What father and husband could do that? That was Alex's hope.

Alex Murdaugh's face during most of his testimony when he was facing the jurors and testifying about the brutal murders. Often his nose ran, unchecked. It was a lot and seemed to go on forever.

That face would show many masks during his 10-hour testimony that spanned two days. It was often when Creighton Waters made a powerful point and turned his back, that Alex forgot to cry.

Creighton Waters vs Richard Alexander Murdaugh

Chapter Thirty-five
Countdown to a Verdict

On Monday, February 27, 2023, The State of South Carolina vs Richard Alexander Murdaugh entered the sixth and final week. Buster and John Marvin Murdaugh had been in the courtroom every day. Buster's girlfriend Brooklyn was in attendance each day, along with Alex's sister Lynn. Sometimes Lynn's daughter was there or John Marvin's wife Liz. Randy Murdaugh attended 3 or 4 times.

Behind the prosecution's table sat several SLED agents. Behind them were journalists, reporters, and authors. The gallery saw some familiar faces on a regular basis: Joe McCulloch (Connor Cook's attorney), Mark Tinsley (the Beach family lawyer), podcasters and YouTubers, all madly scribbling away, their programs bringing the latest Breaking News each night or shortly after. The witness' testimony was dissected with glee as each social media mouthpiece put their own spin on the day's revelations. The trial's highlights made it to the big players. *Fox News, Dateline, CNN, HBO*, and outlets worldwide were all plastering the airwaves with the grizzly details of this now famous trial.

Before the Defense's witnesses were brought forward that morning, Dick Harpootlian requested a "jury view." He asked Judge Newman to schedule a day that the jury could go to Moselle and see the kennel area for themselves. He said it would be helpful to see the small area in which the murders took place and the distance from the kennels to the house.

Creighton Waters argued against it. His biggest objection was that the property had changed in the past two years since the murders. It was also adding more time to a trial that had already run twice as long as anticipated. In the end, Judge Newman agreed to the jury view. It would come at the end of trial testimony.

Dr. Jonathan Eisenstat was called. The expert in Forensic Pathology was the Defense's answer to the Prosecution's Dr. Riener. They had a new theory about how Alex's youngest son lost his life.

Dr. Jonathan Eisenstat was asked to review the reports of Dr. Ellen Riemer and said he agreed on four of the five shots that hit Maggie Murdaugh. Riemer said one of the shots traveled through Maggie's chest and into her brain. Eisenstat said he believed it was traveling in the other direction.

Eisenstat's testimony about the fatal shot differed from the medical examiner who examined Paul's body.

"There's no skull here," Eisenstat said. "That's probably the area where the shotgun was pressed against the head, and we've got all of these fractures. In medical terms, we call it multiple cumulated fractures. This is textbook contact range shotgun wound to the head."

Dr. Riemer told jurors on Feb. 13 that she believed the shot was fired from a lower angle and went *up* through Paul's shoulder and through his head.

Dr. Eisenstat demonstrating for Savannah Goude how
he believed the shot to Paul's head was delivered.

Eisenstat testified that he believed the fatal shotgun blast that killed Paul Murdaugh was a close contact shot to the back of his head fired downward.

For Maggie's injuries, Dr. Eisenstat also disagreed with Dr. Riener on some points but agreed with her on others.

1. The stippling on Maggie's thigh showed the shooter was 1' – 3' away when the shot was fired.
2. The entrance wound to her upper torso went through a number of organs and exits out of her body lower and to the left. (This may have been the bullet that entered the doghouse.)
3. Her left wrist and forearm—the bullet entered the back of the wrist.
4. The shot at the back of her head caused an injury to the brain stem. She would die instantly.

Eisenstat differed on the shot that hit Maggie when she was down on all fours:

5. Wound to her left breast and left chin was shot from the top of the head and went down. Riemer said the bullet went up through her breast, under her chin and into her brain, blowing off her earlobe and earring.

The Prosecution's cross brought up some salient points. Dr. Eisenstat did not do a report. He was not the one who performed the autopsy; Dr. Riemer did. The blood-spattered containers on the shelf in the feed room to the right of the door showed a clear area of demarcation where the blood was blocked by the door frame when Paul received the second shot. If was shot from the head down, the blood evidence did not match up.

That the shot to Paul was made with the shotgun to the top of his head was agreed upon by Tim Palmpagh, another forensic scientist who was the Defense's next witness. Palmpagh gained some notoriety as a blood spatter analyst in the famous Staircase murder trial with Michael Peterson as the suspected killer.

Palmpagh went as far as suggesting that two shooters were involved in the murders. Palmpagh said he thought Paul was shot first and that he had no idea it was coming, first in the chest and then the back of the head. He said anyone in close proximity would have heard that, including Maggie.

Tim Palmpagh testifies in Murdaugh trial.

Palmpagh said things happened fairly quickly and very close together. He said the shooter was likely stunned with biological material in their eyes, possibly injured. It would have taken time to recover from that before engaging in another meaningful assault and shooting Maggie.

"To me, it's structurally difficult for a shooter to have two long guns, and no practical reason for that to happen," Palmpagh said. "Add that to what I believe happened to the shooter who fired first with the shotgun, and I think it tips in favor of the probability of two shooters."

Palmpagh also backed up the Defense's assertation that SLED's investigation into the shootings could have been better and said they probably missed evidence. He did agree with earlier testimony about Paul Murdaugh having no defensive wounds.

"Maggie faced her shooter the entire time," Palmpagh said. It was a sobering statement for those who thought the Defendant was guilty. How would a wife feel as her husband unilaterally executed her, one bullet at time as she backed away from him. This along with the probability that she had just seen her son's head explode. "She moved a little, but not much," he said.

Palmpagh pointed out the dozens of head hairs on the back of Maggie's leg showed she wasn't moved after the last shot.

It was the Defense's two-shooter theory. Maggie would have heard the shots at Paul and come running. The second shooter would have gunned her down, as the first shooter would have been stunned by the amount of biological matter splattering him from shooting Paul in the top of the head. The Prosecution pointed out that the only pellet defects were to the top of the feed room door, none found at the bottom of the door.

Alex Murdaugh's very affable and likeable younger brother, John Marvin was next on the stand. He was smiling as he sat down and made eye contact with the jurors. He looked comfortable as if preparing for a fireside chat. As he was led into questions about the day of the murders, he quickly dissolved into tears.

John Marvin Murdaugh during his testimony about the murders.

Jim Griffin greeted John Marvin like an old friend. Indeed, the two knew each other well. John Marvin said he was overseeing Moselle for now. It was disgraceful to see tourists taking selfies in front of the feed shed.

Paul was very close to John Marvin. His uncle had given him a job at his big farm equipment rental property in Bluffton. It was partly to keep Paul out of trouble for the summer while he wasn't in college. It was also a place where Paul felt safe from the hatred toward him in the Hampton area since the boat crash.

"We had a very special relationship," John Marvin said, his voice cracking at times. "We called him Little Rooster. We always called him Paw Paw (to underscore Alex's new use of his son's name during his testimony). When he worked for me, I called him Paul or Paul Terry." He said Paul had worked two summers for him prior to 2021. "Whatever was asked of him, he would do."

John Marvin said Paul and Buster would come to his hunting property called Greenfield near Almeda to hunt. He had a great relationship with Buster and Paul. They went to sporting events.

(It is John Marvin who appears in many of the photos Maggie Murdaugh posted on her FB page. One rarely saw Randy Murdaugh.)

John said Alex and Maggie had a good marriage. Like all marriages, it had its hiccups. At their football parties and tailgates, they would put out a spread. (He left out the part about the affair Alex had years before during their marriage. Marion Proctor said it still bothered Maggie. Rumors of an affair swirled around Alex up to and including Maggie's funeral.)

John Marvin said the Monday of the murders he took his father Randolph to Savannah to see his doctor. "He was having major breathing problems," he said. When the doctor saw him, he said he has to go to the hospital because of the breathing. The doctor thought it was pneumonia. "We were optimistic that it was only that," John said. "I sent out emails about what the doctor said, and Randy sent out texts." The next day, Tuesday, Randolph was sent home in an ambulance on Hospice Care. There was nothing more they could do for him.

The switching of the cars was gone over. John Marvin asked Paul to drive Miss Libby's car back to Almeda and pick up his truck and bring it back the next morning to Bluffton. John had met Randy in Ridgeland and got in Miss Libby's car to take his father to the doctor. Randy took John Marvin's truck to Almeda and picked up his own truck there. John didn't want to be stuck in Miss Libby's car, so he asked Paul to drive it up and bring him back his truck. Paul's truck was at Jimmy Butler's repair shop in Varnville.

(Was this Paul Murdaugh's undoing? If John Marvin had not asked him to get his truck, would Paul have been safe in Bluffton the night of the murders? He went to Moselle to look after the sunflowers since he was already in Almeda and had dinner with his mother. Rogan had him check on his dog while he was there.)

When Alex called John Marvin that night, saying "Maggie and Paul have been hurt badly," he took off from Okatie. As he had no car now, he took Paul's old farm truck, which "really was a piece of junk." On the way, Randy or Alex called him and said, "The sheets are being put over them."

Paul's old truck gave out on him. He called Greg Alexander, and he came and picked him up and took him to Moselle. "We went in the main gate and came around," John said. "I jumped out and ran to Alex and hugged him and cried." We got there around 11:00 pm. We didn't go to the house until late; around 2 or 3 am."

He said people were cleaning up the house. Putting pots and pans in the refrigerator, etc. They spent the night at Almeda. Alex was wearing shorts and a T-shirt."

John Marvin's next statement would underscore the water and wet towel Blanca found the next morning *before* Alex came back: "I'm pretty sure he showered before they left for Almeda."

As Alex's little brother went over what he saw the morning after the murders, he held a handkerchief to his eyes and cried.

"Later at the house that morning, a lot of people showed up, so I went down to the kennels. I reached out to a law enforcement friend of mine, and he said the crime scene had been cleared and I could go in the shed.

"I could see where Maggie had been. I walked over to the feed room. It had not been cleaned up. I started cleaning. I called Randy and he said to stop cleaning, it wasn't healthy. Mark Ball came and told me to leave. He said they would clean up. Mark got me back to the house. The lawyers were all there talking and questioning things."

Someone told John Marvin that Maggie's phone was missing. Buster had Find My Phone. He saw Maggie's phone and pressed it. It pinged right outside the property. John said he didn't know SLED but went up to two of their agents and showed them Buster's phone was showing where Maggie's phone was. They found the phone. John called Alex and asked him for the passcode and Alex gave it to him. It opened the phone.

John said he escorted Agent Kate McAllister through the house. She took her gun and badge off to be considerate to the family. After that, John Marvin became a liaison between Agent Owens and the family.

"Were you asked if law enforcement could search Almeda?" Griffin asked him. "No."

John said Alex brought up the boating accident multiple times that night and the next day. He said Alex said, "They did him so bad," many times following the murders. (It has always interested this author that it was only Paul "they did so bad." Maggie's brains were blown out as well.)

John said that Michael Paul is John Marvin's best friend. (This is the man many suspected of involving John Marvin with obstruction after the boat crash. John hauled away the Murdaugh boat on a trailer, which many saw as inappropriate.) According to John, Michael asked him if the murders could have been related to the boat crash.

Further clean-up for his brother came when John Marvin agreed that the family pulled around back of their mother's house because it made it easier to go in the back door near her bedroom.

On Labor Day weekend of 2021, John said he and Randy took Alex to a detox facility near Atlanta. "Alex was sweating, thrashing around, he wasn't able to control it," John said. "He had diarrhea in his pants in the car." He said they also took Alex to the Orlando rehab center. On the way, he would sleep in the car and wake up like he was having nightmares.

John Marvin went over the raincoat evidence. He said David Owens came up to him in September and said they found a blue raincoat on the Almeda property. Later, he said they found it at the top of the stairs. They asked him if he recognized the photo of the raincoat, and John Marvin said, "No."

Randy, Lynn, and John Marvin were asked to listen to the kennel video. They recognized their brother's voice. They were all shown the raincoat and none of them had seen it before. They were told blood was found all over the white T-shirt Alex was wearing.

While cleaning the kennel on June 8th, John Marvin said to Paul, "I love you and I'll find out who did this to you."

"Have you found that person?" Griffin asks.

"I have not."

Attorney Conrad for the Prosecution did the cross.
"When did you find out your brother was at the kennel?" he asked.
"August 12, 2022, is when I heard the kennel interview," John answered.

John said Paul drove a white Ford F-150 Platinum, the same as John Marvin. John said he saw his truck parked at the house in the front. The keys were in the ignition.

He said he didn't remember Blanca getting there the morning of June 8th, but it was after him. (Blanca said she was the first one there that morning.)

SLED asked Buster about the blue rain jacket. Buster said he didn't recognize it. SLED asked if Randolph owned the blue jacket. Buster answered, "If it's over $15, no it isn't."

With that, the Defense rested.

After the defense rested its case, the State said they had four or five witnesses to call in their reply case. Lead Prosecutor Creighton Waters said he believed they could get through the witnesses Tuesday. Defense attorney Dick Harpootlian was skeptical about the claim, saying Waters has often underestimated the amount of time needed in the case.

"I'll be happy, I'll be ecstatic if it happens," Harpootlian said. Monday marked the beginning of week six in the trial which was expected to last three weeks.

Once the State has concluded its reply case, jurors will be taken to the Moselle property to see the crime scene. Harpootlian suggested the trip, but also raised the issue of safety at the property stating that dozens of trespassers were on the property taking selfies in front of the feed room over the weekend. Judge Clifton Newman assured both sides that the property would be secured before the jury was allowed to travel there.

After the visit to Moselle, the jurors will begin to hear closing arguments.

On Tuesday, February 28th, the sixth week of a long and drawn-out trial began. Anticipation was high. Would Alex Murdaugh be found guilty of killing his wife and son? The jurors were restless; some showing definite signs of wear and tear. They had seen photos that would haunt their nights and cause them to question their own safety in a relationship.

As was typical with the morning routine of the trial, Dick Harpootlian again raised objections to Creighton Waters calling 7 reply witnesses. "Many have already testified," Harpootlian stated, his typical hand motions rising and falling like gentle waves. "If they raise new issues, we have a right to reply." Judge Newman told him his concerns were "duly noted," and then he said quietly, "Call your next witness."

Waters brought Ronnie Crosby back to the stand. He asked Crosby to tell him about his close relationship with Paul Murdaugh. With a great deal of sadness, he said they rode around his property and looked for hogs. The hogs were tearing up his crops and property, Crosby explained.

"What would you carry when you were looking for hogs?" Waters asked him. Crosby said they would carry a rifle day or night…some kind of long gun.

"Paul was fond of the .300 Blackout. You can see hogs in the daytime," Crosby said, a point used to discredit Alex's statement on the stand that the hogs don't come out in the daytime; they stay in the swamp. "I've killed 100's in the daytime," Crosby said.

"Did Alex have a good relationship with law enforcement?"

"Yes," Crosby said, "more than the rest of us, except his father."

When asked about Alex's statements the night of the murder, Crosby confirmed that Alex said he checked the bodies *before* calling 911.

Crosby said Alex told him that he didn't believe anybody on the boat did it, just someone threatening Paul because of the boat crash.

Waters led Crosby into the financial arena. He brought up Barrett Boulware.

"Barrett needed money in June 2018," Crosby said, "because of his illness. "Barrett and Alex were very close." He said Alex told him that Barrett had sold Moselle to him for $5 because "Barrett owed me the money anyway." Ronnie said he did a couple of land transactions with Barrett.

"Barrett was Stage 4 colon cancer," Crosby said. "His wife didn't have enough money for the hospital or a hotel to stay near him during his treatments. Barrett wanted to sell some property to help with the expense."

He died in September. Alex was stealing money while this was going on. There was a $70k check due to Barrett that Alex stole. More money was taken after Barrett died. $250,000.

Waters brought up Alex's allegation that the reason he lied to Agent Owen the night of the murders, while seated in his car at Moselle, was because he was paranoid. One of the reasons was because he thought Agent David Owen was the man involved in the case against his good friend, Chief Gregory Alexander. That agent was David Williams. Waters shows Crosby photos of both David Owen and David Williams. They look nothing alike.

Dick Harpootlian took on the hapless-looking Ronnie Crosby.

"Did you ever ride around Moselle with Alex?" he asked.

"For dove hunting," Crosby responded. "You wouldn't take an AR-15 on a dove hunt."

Crosby described the dove field: it's a few hundred yards from the house, he said. This is the area where the sunflowers had been over sprayed.

Harpootlian asks Crosby if he agrees that people involved in traumatic accidents, where they've lost a loved one, sometimes get details wrong.

"In my experience," Crosby said, "they try to remember details as best they can to help with the investigation." (This author would add, they usually have the final moments of their time with their loved one burned into their memory and replay it often.)

Harpootlian suddenly went on the attack. He yelled at Alex's ex-law partner,

"You aren't angry with Alex Murdaugh for stealing all that money?"

Showing a flash of anger himself, Ronnie Crosby answered, "You're headed in the wrong direction, and I resent you implying I'm testifying here because of this. I have no feelings about it, and I had to work on it."

Creighton Waters next brought up the happy pathologist, Dr. Ellen Riemer. She looked as poised as before. The court was ordered to "seal the monitors," code for covering up the laptop monitors at the Defense's and State's tables—there are going to be graphic photos. It wasn't just to spare Alex, but the gallery, who was directly behind both of the lawyers' tables.

Dr. Riener said she had done 5500 autopsies. She did an independent autopsy at the request of the coroner on Maggie and Paul. She was shown an autopsy photo of Maggie.

"Was the shot top down or bottom up on the head wound that went through the left breast and wrist?" Waters asked.

"Bottom up," she said, with absolute certainty.

When they went over Paul's wounds, it was hard to listen to. With the disconnected objectivity of a pathologist who had seen it all, Riener went over what would have happened should the fatal head shot have been delivered from the top of the head, instead of going up through the shoulder first and into the head.

She said if the contact wound had been to the top of the head, the associated gas explosion would have displaced his eyes from the orbital cavity. "He wouldn't have a face left," she said, as Alex rocked and cried in his chair at the Defense table.

Riener made some good points when defusing the Defense's expert pertaining to the second shot fired at Paul. The entrance wound was clearly the shoulder and not the head, she said. "The Styrofoam wadding particles are evident in the shoulder shot which means the pellets hit the shoulder first," she testified. "No way it was a contact wound to the top of the head."

Dick Harpootlian addressed the pathologist and tried one final time to discredit her testimony. Riener is shown a photo of a gunshot wound where some of the packing material is seen on the skin.

"Why didn't you include that in your report?" he asks her.

"I take notes to put into my autopsy report," she said.

The matter wasn't settled to either team's satisfaction.

Thomas C. Smalls, the Sheriff of Hampton County for 19 years took the stand. He said he retired December 31, 2022. Smalls said he had known Alex for years. Creighton Waters asked him about the blue lights Alex said Smalls had allowed him to install in a personal vehicle. The Sheriff said he never gave Alex permission to do so.

When asked if the prior Sheriff had ever received anything about the threats Paul was receiving concerning the boat crash, Smalls said he did not.

When Jim Griffin cross-examined him, Smalls reiterated, "I never had any knowledge that he had a blue light in his vehicle."

The witnesses came and went in a timely manner. Paul McManigal was called again. He went over a phone's behavior again for the jury.

"Raise to wake is when a phone is lifted or a notification comes in and it lights up," he said. "If the screen is off, it won't show an orientation change." He stated that if the phone is violently picked up, it won't light up. If someone is moving more aggressively, it won't light up. The accelerometer registers movement. He said he performed many tests to see how the phone behaved.

"If the phone is thrown like a Frisbee, 9 out of 10 times, it won't light up," he said.

Attorney Butler for the Defense stepped up to question the digital forensic specialist.

"Did you record any of your experiments you did with the phone?" he asked.

"No. It did not cross my mind to video record the experiments."

"What phone did you use in these experiments?" Butler asked.

"I used an iPhone 14 like Maggie's, just a little newer," he said.

He had to admit there was no data on the Raise to Wake information. He also admitted that if a phone is picked up aggressively, there are times it does light up.

Attorney Conrad tried to undo the damage of the Defense's questioning when he asked the witness again that if the phone is thrown with a Frisbee toss, not hand-over-hand, with a more aggressive handling of the phone, the light did not come on most of the time.

"That's correct," McManigal stated.

Butler took his final jab, "How many times do you need to run this test to determine reliability?"

"More than 10," McMonigal said.

Mark Ball was called. In this author's mind, *he* should have been called, the "Little Detective."

Waters asked him, "Prior to the murders, did Alex voice any distrust of SLED?"

"No, sir. He interacted with law enforcement regularly."

It was pointed out that Alex got the Suburban 6 months before the murders in December 2020. The blue lights had been installed in his previous Suburban.

The habit of hogs was brought up again. It was apparent that the State believed Alex and Paul had shot at hogs while they were riding the property the day of the murders. They were trying to show the AR-15 was already in the truck that was used on Maggie. The State was hoping to make it clear to the jury that Paul loved hunting for hogs, not just shooting at a bottle as Alex testified. And, if they were looking for hogs to shoot, there would be an AR-15 in the vehicle. The vehicle they surmised was the black Ford F-150.

"Hogs come out all times of the day," Ball testified. "The more pressure you put on them, they go nocturnal." He agreed that a .300 Blackout was used for hog hunting.

Waters asked Ball what Alex had said to him about his movements when he pulled up and "found his wife and son shot"?

"He said he went to Maggie, then went to Paul and rolled Paul over. The second time he told me, he said he went to Paul first and then Maggie, and then called 911. He never said he went to the kennels that night."

Ball said he had known Alex for 34 years. "I didn't know about the stealing. I didn't know any of that," he said.

Jim Griffin cross-examined the lawyer who was now with the reformed Parker Law Group. Griffin went over how the firm, which was PMPED at that time, confronted Alex on Labor Day weekend. Ball said he has not spoken to Alex since Labor Day 2021. "He was in jail or rehab," he said.

Griffin brought up that SLED was investigating Alex in the Obstruction of Justice clause in the boat crash. His point was that would be reason enough for Alex to distrust SLED and be "paranoid" when they questioned him after the murders.

Alex was planning a vigorous campaign to clear Paul's name. He didn't say I distrust SLED, or Beaufort County, or DNR. He thought it was a defensible case. (Did that mean Paul did not have to die?)

It was brought out that Billy Hill and others recused themselves during the murder investigation because they knew Alex.

Ball testified that Paul had hunting dogs. There was a swamp and the Old Salkehatchie River behind the Moselle house.

Ball said he had killed over 1,000 hogs. He also sets traps for them. He said he usually has a gun while riding the property.

"You wouldn't use a thermal scope in the daytime," he said.

He said Alex got emotional when his dad received the coveted Order of the Palmetto Award. It was Griffin showing that Alex was not the monster being portrayed to the court.

When the notice to the public was made the morning after the murders that there "was no danger to the community," Ball said he got on the phone to Sheriff Smalls and asked, "What was that about?" He said because they didn't have any threats against anyone else.

Despite that, Ball said they locked the doors at the law firm for months. (Today, several lawyers in that same building have long guns and pistols in their office since the double murders went down.)

Creighton Waters wrapped it up by stating that Colleton County continued to assist on the case even though they recused themselves. Solicitor Duffy Stone and a chief assistant were out at the crime scene the next two days after the murders. In August 2021, Duffy Stone recused himself from the investigation.

The crowd favorite, Dr. Kenneth Kinsey, was back on the stand. He smiled warmly at the courtroom as if everyone was a dinner guest at his home. Attorney General Allan Wilson stepped up for the State to question the expert.

The points of Kinsey's testimony were succinct. While showing respect to Mr. Sutton, who had provided the courtroom with "midgets" shooting long guns in his diagrams, Kinsey settled it humbly.

"Mr. Sutton's methods are flawed," he said. You can't rationalize that the green lines of trajectories Sutton presented in the diagrams necessitate a 5'2" – 5' 4" shooter.

"I have zero confidence in the angle of the bullet in the quail pen," Kinsey said. "I have more confidence in the angle of the impact in the doghouse wall. It is board/wood, not weathered cardboard like the quail pen," he said.

The location of the cartridge cases determined where the Defense's expert had placed the animated people in their diagram.

"There are a lot of variables," Kinsey said. "Ejections from guns don't always eject the same. It was a dynamic crime scene. Both the shooter and the victim were moving. The shell casing is moving as they're ejected."

Kinsey said Maggie's head was pointing in the direction of the kennels.

He then stated that Paul's head wound could not have been a contact wound pointing down. There were no defects in the cement, framing or door frame.

Kinsey said the gun that killed Maggie was a family-owned gun. (The casings match the weathered casings in the flowerbed and shooting range.)

Kinsey stipulated that crime scene carnage is not cleaned up by law enforcement. There are companies that do that. (Yet Randy had C.B. Rowe and the other groundskeeper do it. Why? To have it hauled away and burned?)

Finally, in what many have appreciated about Dr. Kinsey, he said, "I cannot include or exclude 2 shooters."

When Griffin did his cross, it did him no favors. When he tried to get Kinsey to admit Paul was taken by surprise in the feed room due to the lack of defense wounds, Kinsey answered ominously, "Or someone he was real comfortable with."

There was a short recap of the events by the Attorney General. With that, it was over. The Rebuttal phase of the trial rested. There would be no other witnesses. The jury had heard all they would hear in the way of evidence for or against Alex Murdaugh's guilt or innocence. They had heard it all, now they would see the crime scene for themselves.

The Jury Goes to the Crime Scene

Judge Newman was good for his word. A security detail had been dispatched to 4147 Moselle Road in preparation for the "jury view." He also gave strict rules to the jury they were to obey.

- They would depart the next morning at 9:30 a.m. in various vehicles driven by law enforcement.
- They were not to talk to each other on the way.
- They cannot ask questions while there to anyone but Judge Newman.

- After the viewing, they will return to the courtroom to hear Closing Arguments.
- The judge reminded them that the murders were June 7, 2021. It is now March 1, 2023. Things will have changed at the property.

The jury was taken in several vehicles to the property. The media lined the road near Moselle but were kept at a safe distance. Due to the juror's right to anonymity, the photos showed only their cars arriving at the scene. After they returned to the courtroom, the cameras were allowed onto the property for a short period to take pictures.

The media lined Moselle Road as the jurors arrived at the property.

Law enforcement guarding kennel entrance during jury view.

A desolate kennel area during the jury view outing. All of the farm equipment and ATVS have been removed.

A view from inside the feed room looking out. All the cladding has been removed and the area power washed. The quail pen can be seen across the outside pathway, under the hangar.

Some thought Maggie's bike had been deliberately placed where it seen here in the photograph, outside the Moselle home. Photo by Andrew J. Whitaker with the *Post and Courier*.

When the jurors returned, the crime scene was fresh in their minds, the final segment of the 6-week-long murder trial commenced. Creighton Waters with the State would be first up for Closing Arguments. He hit the jury with the points he felt were pertinent for them to come to a guilty verdict:

- The means, motive, opportunity, and Alex's actions afterward betray him.
- Alex has been able to avoid accountability his entire life.
- The boat crash set in motion everything.
- The pace of his stealing increased. It was all coming to a head.
- The Ferris case had been his saving grace for much-needed money.
- Then came Tinsley's Motion to Compel that was scheduled for June 10th, three days after the murders.
- In May 2021, the law firm started seeing red flags.
- On June 7th, Seckinger confronts him in his office. At the same time, he hears his dad is going back to the hospital.

Alex is $376,000 in the hole in the bank. His dad can't bail him out this time and the law firm is onto him.

- The timeline of the murders puts Alex at the kennels.
- He had the use of family weapons.
- All his lies and guilty actions afterwards.
- The murders would mean everything goes away. The hearing goes away. Everyone will rally around him and forget about the missing fees.
- John E. Parker and Palmetto State Bank help Alex out with even more loans after the murders. That lasted a couple of months until they found the Ferris check in his office.
- September 4, 2021, Chris Wilson confronts him. He wants to know what's going on. He wants his $192k Alex owes him. 2 hours later, the roadside shooting.
- Accountability was at his door, so he gets shot by a stranger as he is changing a tire.
- His own brother finds out about the drugs.
- His prominence in the community was all a lie.
- In May, just before the murders, Maggie and Paul find pills in a computer bag. They are watching him like a hawk.
- April 2022, they finally unlock Paul's phone where they find the incriminating kennel video.
- The badge hanging out of Alex's pocket at the hospital after the boat crash where he is telling everyone to keep their mouths shut.
- The blue lights for a personal vehicle.

The morning of Thursday, March 2, 2021, before the Defense could offer their Closing Argument, the Judge addresses a concern. A juror is accused of talking to someone outside the trial. Two people supposedly talked to the juror and she offered her opinion about the evidence presented during the trial. SLED interviewed the people who said they had spoken with her. One of them had been a witness during the trial.

Juror #785 is brought out from the jury room. The judge went over the allegations toward her and said she would have to be removed. He thanked her for her service. He said that since she has been officially removed from the jury, she cannot go into the jury room to retrieve her personal items. He asks her what she has in the room and a bailiff will get it for her. She tells him she has a purse, a bottled water, and "a dozen eggs." Judge Newman smiles and seems surprised she brought eggs to the trial. She said she had brought them to share with the other jurors.

"Alright then, we'll have the bailiff retrieve your purse and your bottled water," he said kindly.

She then informed him she wanted the eggs too. It was basically, "You're kicking me out of here. I'm takin' my eggs with me!"

She was replaced by Juror #254. They were down to only one more alternate. It was a good thing the Defense's Closing was all there was left.

Jim Griffin gave his closing. To many it was obvious the air had gone out of the Defense. Harpootlian sat staring at the table before him, lost in thought.

Griffin's points were these:

- You must begin a trial by presuming the defendant innocent.
- The State must prove guilt beyond a reasonable doubt.
- When Officer Green rolled up, Alex was standing yards from 2 dead bodies in pools of blood, and he had just put down a shotgun.
- At this time "there's no danger to the public."
- SLED failed miserably at their job.
- Tire impressions not preserved.
- The hair in Maggie's hand never examined.
- No fingerprints in the feed room belonging to Alex.
- No footwear impressions in the feed room and on the cement, apron belonging to Alex.
- No DNA off Maggie's or Paul's clothing.
- "Unless we find someone else, it's going to be Alex!"
- Maggie's phone was found on the side of the road.
- Alex's phone and car did not travel at the same time as Maggie's phone. He could not have tossed her phone out the window.
- Last minute OnStar data from General Motors.
- Maggie's data from phone by June 16th could have been overwritten and lost.

- June 10th, Alex's phone had a surface extraction.
- Griffin plays a clip from Blanca's testimony: "He adored her. He loved her."
- Griffin plays a clip from Dale Davis: "They were lovey dovey. I've never seen him raise his voice to her or the boys."
- Why would Alex Murdaugh on June 7th execute his wife and son?
- The State's theory is, "Storm's a-comin'!" His financial house of cards is about to be exposed. Jeannie Seckinger will stop asking questions for a time. The boat case is coming up. His dad is back in the hospital.

This is their theory for "beyond reasonable doubt."

- Paul was a "Little Detective" and he found pills.
- Blue tarp at Almeda was on the chair and then it wasn't.
- The State tried to compress the timeline.
- Mud from the Polaris tire.
- Maggie ran toward her baby.
- An Apple phone or any phone, if you pick it up, it lights up.
- Alex drove by Maggie's phone at 9:08 p.m.
- Alex butchered Maggie and Paul without any blood evidence on him.

Testimony that makes no sense:
- Griffin goes over the slideshow of Maggie's phone data.
- At 9:08 p.m., Alex drives by Maggie's phone. He does not speed up.
- Why would he speed back? He'd want to make it look like he was gone longer.
- He has Maggie's password to her phone. He could have answered his own text and phone calls to make her look like she was still alive.
- Why take Maggie's phone and not Paul's?
- If they had secured Maggie's phone in a Faraday bag, the data would have been secure.

- Alex left Moselle at 9:07 p.m. 17 minutes from 8:50 p.m. (time of death) -9:07 p.m. to get rid of evidence and blood.
- "They did him so bad," is brought up again.
- Bodycam footage has Alex asking for a police officer in Columbia to watch over Buster. (Buster was in Rock Hill.)
- As for all of Alex's inconsistent statements? [Griffin gets emotional here]. "*Alex* was running to his baby!" He can't remember the sequences as to when he placed the 911 call—before or after he checked them.
- He has Maggie and Paul's DNA on his shirt from when he checked them. But no blood.
- Maggie's blood is on the steering wheel and shotgun because he checked her and got blood on his fingers.
- Alex lied about being at the kennels because:
    1- He is under investigation by SLED for Obstruction of Justice in the boat crash case.
    2- He thought Agent Owens was Agent David Williams who prosecuted his friend Gregory Alexander.
    3- He had a lot of financial crimes that were coming to light.
    4- Opioid pills and addiction.

Griffin wound up his segment of the Defense's Closing Argument by telling the jurors, "Soon, you will have the most powerful voice in this courtroom. On behalf of Alex, of Buster, of Maggie and my friend Paul, I ask you not to compound one tragedy with another and enter a verdict of Not Guilty! Thank you."

Attorney John Meaders was given the opportunity for a rebuttal. It was the State's case, and they were afforded the last word. He was an interesting choice for the closing. Some wondered why Creighton Waters, or the Attorney General had not chosen to voice the last words the jurors would hear before going into deliberations. His grandfatherly approach had registered well with the jury, composed mainly of down-home workers and locals. It was said later by some news outlet that it was not a sophisticated jury one might see in a big city.

Meaders walked back and forth throughout his closing comments, his eyes on the jury, studying their reactions as he spoke. He left them with the final things to consider:

- "There's not a book on how to be a juror. You have to decide what's credible. What's believable. Use your common sense."
- They put the law enforcement on trial. It's all a smoke screen.
- He lied about being down at the kennels.
- Circumstantial evidence became real evidence.
- They blame everybody but Alex.
- Buster wasn't his first thought after the murders. It was focusing on other things.
- He didn't tell Buster to stay where he was and get protection. (He brings him to the crime scene.)
- He doesn't get anybody over to his mom's.
- He asked Shelley about her wedding and her job to get her to say he had been there 30-40 minutes.
- Blanca loved Maggie. June 7th, Blanca is texting her. Maggie didn't want to go to Moselle. Marion regretted encouraging her to go.
- Blanca helped Alex with his shirt collar the morning of the murders. The clothes in SnapChat are what he was wearing. In August, he tries to convince her to say he was wearing a Vinnie Vine shirt.
- He changed his shoes.
- She never saw the Speery shoes or shirt again.
- He was clean, even though he said he turned Paul over and checked Maggie.
- You can't take the number of pills Alex said he was taking.
- "When he took the stand, he corroborated he was a liar."
- Family-owned guns.
- These are giving you real evidence:
    1- The casings found by Maggie are from the AR-15 Paul sighted in by the house. That gun is missing.
    2- Paul's phone video puts his father at the kennels only minutes before he and Maggie are murdered.

- "Your best witness are the dogs."
- Bubba died and is with Paul now.
- "Your greatest power is your power to choose," Meaders said. "It stops here!"

Judge Newman gave his charge to the jury. He went over their choices for a verdict and admonished them to rely on evidence presented and not emotion. They were sent off to deliberate.

The courtroom cleared. Everyone thought it would be a long, grueling process of dissecting all the evidence and coming to a verdict. It was 3 o'clock in the afternoon. Lawyers who were close enough to their offices checked in to get caught up on paperwork. Restaurants filled again. Newscasters were betting it could be days before a verdict was reached.

This author breathed a sigh of relief that all the testimony was over. My notes filled three spiral notebooks to the brim. I got up and stretched, walked to my home office to check emails, and return a week's worth of phone calls, and other housekeeping details. Just as I came back through the living room, where the TV was still running, I stopped in my tracks. I looked at the screen with my mouth hanging open. They were saying the jury was back with a verdict! It was only 6:21 pm.

I grabbed up my notebook again and sat there with my heart pounding. That was so fast! Not usually a good sign for the Defendant. Alex and his lawyers must have thought the same thing for when they were ushered back to their seats at the Defense table, their expressions were somber. The courtroom cameras zeroed in on the row where the Murdaugh family was seated. It was hard to read their expressions. Alex's sister Lynn pressed her lips together nervously. John Marvin looked weary from it all. Buster was stoic as always. He may as well have been watching a lecture on the mating call of chimpanzees. His girlfriend Brooklyn looked sad and a little tired. Randy Murdaugh was not there.

The hot Thursday evening in downtown Walterboro was about to explode with sounds other than that of cicadas. Once the jury was seated again, Judge Newman asked the Clerk of Court to stand with the verdicts in hand. Judge Newman read over each of the juror's four verdicts.

Jim Griffin, Alex Murdaugh, and Dick Harpootlian as the Verdict is read.

"The defendant will rise," Judge Newman, said. "Madame Clerk, you may publish the verdict."

"Docket #20222 GS15 000552, the State vs Richard Alexander Murdaugh, indictment for murder: Verdict: Guilty, signed by the Floor Lady. March 2, 2033.

"Indictment for Murder: Verdict: Guilty.

"Indictment of Possession of a Weapon during the commission of a violent crime: Verdict: Guilty.

"Indictment of Possession of a Weapon during the commission of a violent crime: Verdict: Guilty.

Guilty on all four counts. Dick Harpootlian asked for an individual polling of the jurors. All answered it was their verdict.

Jim Griffin and Dick Harpootlian showed no visual reaction. They looked defeated and tired. Jim Griffin, in a lifeless voice that knew the answer ahead of time, asked for a mistrial. The judge asked the State for their answer to that. Creighton Waters said the case went properly to the jury and their verdict was proper.

Judge Newman said there was an overwhelming amount of evidence, and the jurors were charged to base their verdicts solely on that evidence. "The evidence of guilt is overwhelming, and I deny the motion."

"Mr. Murdaugh, you have now been found guilty of two counts of murder involving your wife and your son, two counts of possessing a weapon during the commission of a violent crime, the burden now comes upon the court to impose a sentence. Given the lateness of the hour, and the victim's rights that must be taken into consideration and complied with under the victim's bill of rights, and considering what I think may be a number of people with something to say regarding sentencing, we will defer sentencing to a later date. The minimum sentence for murder is 30 years. The maximum sentence is life imprisonment as to each count. The weapons charge is up to five years which has to be concurrent if a life sentence is imposed."

Judge Newman asks the Defense and State when they would like sentencing to begin. Both say that 9:30 am the following morning would work. "Alright, the Defendant will now be taken into custody and taken to the Colleton County Sheriff's Department."

Alex is handcuffed. "And he may be taken away, Judge Newsman said, without further delay.

Alex leaves the courtroom without glancing at his family.

Judge Newman at a rare moment. Was it a "Help Me, Jesus," or "Thank goodness this trial is over," moment?

Friday, March 3, 2023. Sentencing.

Alex Murdaugh was led into the courtroom in a jailhouse jumpsuit. His family was once again in attendance, and once again, Randy Murdaugh was absent.

Alex flanked by his attorneys while waiting for sentencing.

The State stood and voiced their reasons for a life sentence to be imposed on the defendant. "He's a cunning manipulator," Waters said emphatically.

Dick Harpootlian said, "He has no priors. The family has had to suffer in the public eye."

Sadly, not one of Alex's family stood to speak on his behalf and to ask for leniency. No victim statements came from the other side as well. It seemed a very hollow and sad ending to so much tragedy and grief.

Before sentencing was passed, Alex was afforded the opportunity to say something.

His head bobbing, he licked his lips, and with emotion said, "I'm innocent. I would never hurt my wife Maggie and I would never hurt my son Paw Paw."

Judge Newman took center stage. He told Alex and his counsel to step up before his bench for sentencing. His words were stinging and filled with contempt for the man standing before him. There would be no mercy shown.

"This has been one of the more troubling cases, not just for me as the judge. But also, for the Defense team and the State, and for all of the citizens of this community, all the citizens in the state, and as we've seen based on the media coverage, throughout the nation. You have a wife who's been killed. Murdered. A son who has been savagely murdered. A lawyer: a person from a respected family who has controlled justice in this community for over a century. A person whose grandfather's portrait hangs at the back of the courthouse, that I had to have ordered removed in order to ensure that a fair trial was had by both the State and the Defense.

"And I sat through the trial, not only the trial, but also as the presiding judge of the Great Grand Jury, bond hearings, search warrants---I've had to consider many things. I'm also assigned to preside over 99 other cases.

"It's also particularly troubling, Mr. Murdaugh, that as a member of the legal community, a well-known member of the legal community, you've practiced law before me, and we've seen each other at various occasions throughout the years. It was heartbreaking for me to see you go through the media from a grieving father who lost a wife and a son to the person indicted and convicted of killing them. And you've engaged in such duplicitous conduct, here in the courtroom, here on the witness stand, and as established by the testimony, throughout to this moment in time.

"As appeals are probably or absolutely expected, I would not expect a confession of any kind. I have yet to find a defendant and go there and go back to that moment in time before they decided to pull the trigger. When they opted to commit the most heinous crimes known to man. This case qualifies under our Death Penalty statute. Two or more people being murdered.

"I do not question the decision by the State not to pursue the Death Penalty. As I sit here in this courtroom and look around at many of the portraits of the many judges, your family, including you, have prosecuted others in this courtroom who received the Death Penalty, probably for lesser conduct.

"Reminds me of the statement you made on the witness stand, "Oh what a tangled web we weave..." What did you mean by that?"

"That once I started lying, I couldn't stop," Alex says brokenly.

"The question is, when will it end?" Judge Newman asked. "It's already ended for the jury. They've concluded you lied and lied throughout your testimony.

"Within your own soul, you'll have to deal with it. And I know you have to see Paul and Maggie in the nighttime when you're attempting to go to sleep. I'm sure they come and visit you."

"All day and every night," Alex interjected, head bobbing.

"I'm sure they will continue to do so, and the last time they looked you in the eyes, as you looked the jury in the eyes. You had such a lovely family, including you, and to go from that to this.

"Your law license was stripped from you. You've turned from lawyer to witness.

"I would never under any circumstances hurt my wife Maggie and my son Paw Paw," Alex said brokenly.

"And it may not have been you. It may have been the monster you became after taking all the pills, but we'll leave that at that," Judge Newman said.

"There are other victims whose cases deserve to be heard. This case has jumped it. You will never have the opportunity to argue another case. Anything further?" (Both sides say, "No, Your Honor."

"Mr. Murdaugh, I sentence you to the State Department of Corrections for each of the murder indictments: for the murder of Maggie Murdaugh, I sentence you to a term for the rest of your natural life. For the murder of Paul Murdaugh, whom you probably loved so much, I sentence you to prison for murdering him for the rest of your natural life. Those sentences will run consecutively. That is the sentence of the court, and you are remanded to the State Department of Corrections. The officers may carry forth with their jurisdiction."

Alex is led from the courtroom. Again, he does not look back at his family.

It was over. Alex's family remained stoic and resigned. There were no tears. It was a shocking feeling to find resolution in a case so filled with lies, twists, and turns. There was a sense of sadness at all the unnecessary loss, not just for Maggie and Paul, but the other victims the judge mentioned. Paul and Maggie's killer had been found guilty and sentenced. Would other victims associated with the Murdaugh name find the same closure?

637

As the security detail from the Colleton County Sheriff's Office led Alex outside and past the media staked out by the van that would carry him to jail, zealous shouts were hurled at him from a few bystanders. One accusation was hard to miss: a man pressing his way forward through the crowd yelled, "Your son's next, Murdaugh! Buster is next!"

Attorney John Meaders smiles at the sign displayed outside the courthouse on March 3, 2021, as Alex is driven away to begin his prison sentence.

Chapter Thirty-Six
Other Cases

Although the double murder trial had ended with the resolution many had hoped for, other cases swirling around the Murdaugh name were still ongoing. Some were in shadows; others were put before the bar and their fate swiftly meted out.

Stephen Smith's Body is Exhumed

On April 1, 2023, people driving along Sandy Run Road saw a tall black vinyl drape blocking their view of Gooding Cemetery. The body of Stephen Smith was being exhumed, with only a handful of people present. Sandy Smith, Stephen's mother, stood in a long white coat, her hands clasped together as the backhoe bit into the dirt that had covered her son's grave for almost eight years. His headstone was moved to the side and sat on 2' x 2' boards. A few members of the media were there, snapping photos and shooting footage. There were no photos of Stephen's casket shared on the internet, only a green mortician's blanket covering the hole as the body was carried away. Stephen was taken by police escort to Tampa, Florida, where a second autopsy was declared a success by investigators, who say new evidence was collected. It all happened over the weekend, and he was reinterred on Sunday.

Smith, 19, was found dead with deep gashes to his forehead, three miles away from his vehicle on July 8, 2015, in the middle of a dark country road in Hampton County, S.C. His death was initially ruled a hit-and-run, but now authorities believe his death was a homicide.

639

Forensic expert Dr. Kenneth Kinsey, who was hired as a private investigator by Sandy Smith's legal team, gave an autopsy update to *NewsNation* on Tuesday.

"I do know it was a success. They say they did collect evidence, it was very good documentation, and everybody was upbeat about the information that was collected," Kinsey said. "And that's not always the situation when you exhume someone after so many years."

Dr. Michelle DuPre said, "Stephen was still in his medical scrubs he had been buried in, with Dr. Stephen Smith embroidered over the pocket." It was Stephen's dream to become a doctor, and while he was killed before he could realize that dream, he had begun nursing school. Dr. DuPre said the body was amazingly well preserved. "We got what we needed," she said. "A pathologist and forensic anthropologist, who looked at the bone fractures, worked together on a complete and thorough autopsy," DuPre said.

Kinsey went on to say the final autopsy report was not yet ready, but he said, "I'm very, very excited about the report coming and the pathologists were very upbeat."

After Stephen was laid to rest for a second time, his mother, Sandy Smith, shared a photo with the "Justice for Stephen N. Smith Family" page on Facebook on Sunday. "My baby is back in his final resting place. Thank you again to all of you who helped make this possible," the post said.

On Monday morning, Sandy Smith announced through the family's attorneys that she is allocating a $35,000 reward from monies raised from a GoFundMe for information leading to an arrest in connection with Stephen's death. Proceeds from that crowd funding campaign raised upwards of $120,000. The money was used to cover the costs of the exhumation, transport to Tampa and back, and the fees for an independent autopsy by several participants.

"We hope that this reward will encourage anyone with information to come forward and provide the critical details needed to solve this case," Attorney Ronnie Richter said in a statement.

Smith's case was initially investigated by the South Carolina Highway Patrol before going cold in 2016, according to *FITSnews*. In that investigation, the Murdaugh name — a powerful local family known for their longstanding law firm — was mentioned dozens of times as possibly being connected to his death, *FITSnews* reported.

Buster Murdaugh — the surviving son of convicted murderer Alex Murdaugh — and Smith were high school classmates. However, authorities have never accused anyone in the Murdaugh family of being connected to the killing, and last month, Buster vehemently denied that he had anything to do with Smith's death.

A green mortician's blanket covers the grave after Stephen Smith's body was exhumed. His headstone is on the left waiting to be returned to its rightful place.

Sandy Smith posing at the head of Stephen's grave after he was reinterred. "My baby is back in his final resting place," she said. Seashells were placed atop the fresh dirt leading to the flowers newly placed there.

As of the writing of this book, mid-May 2023, the results from the autopsy have not been revealed. There was some momentum toward mid-April when two people of interest were brought in for questioning. Shawn Connelly and Patrick Wilson were names already in the limelight from the original investigation. Shawn was the young man who said he was drunk on the night of Stephen's death and "hit something in the road." He said he went back the next morning to see what he hit and saw police everywhere. He asked an officer what happened and was told a young man had been hit and left in the middle of the road. Shawn told his friend Patrick Wilson about it, and Patrick told the man who was dating his mother at the time, Darrell Williams. Darrell said Patrick was so upset after telling him about it, that he went outside and threw up. Darrell told a Hampton County Police Officer about the exchange. When Corporal Duncan interviewed Darrell Williams concerning the conversation, he repeated the information and added, Randy Murdaugh told me to call the police with the information.

Everyone was abuzz that something was finally happening in the Stephen Smith case. Many believed Shawn and Patrick were being "leaned on" to give up evidence concerning someone else involved in Stephen's death. Then, just as suddenly as it started, it stopped. Buster Murdaugh released a statement saying, "I have tried my best to ignore the vicious rumors about my involvement in Stephen's Smith's tragic death that continue to be published in the media as I grieve over the brutal murders of my mother and brother," Murdaugh said. "I love them so much and I miss them terribly."

And so, we wait for news from SLED. Dr. Kenneth Kinsey has walked the area where Stephen's body and his car were found. He is a crime scene reconstruction expert that held the courtroom spellbound during Alex Murdaugh's murder trial. Will the autopsy report reveal new evidence? Will the Smith family finally get some resolution to the mystery surrounding Stephen's death?

The Moselle Property Sells

COLLETON COUNTY, S.C. — WJCL—March 25, 2023
This week, two men, James A. Ayer and Jeffrey L. Godley, purchased the infamous Moselle property where Maggie and Paul Murdaugh were shot to death in June 2021.

It comes just a few weeks after disgraced attorney Alex Murdaugh was convicted of the double slayings in a trial that drew headlines around the world.

According to court records, the money will be divided as follows:

$530,000: Buster Murdaugh, Alex's surviving son
$290,000: John Marvin Murdaugh, Alex's brother
$100,000: Attorney Joe McCulloch, who represents Connor Cook in a civil suit against Buster
$275,000: General fund

Mark Tinsley, who represents several of the boat crash victims and the family of Mallory Beach, will also receive a significant share of the funds.

WJCL spoke to Tinsley on Friday, who said there still has to be one more hearing to finalize payments. He said it is more of a formality.

An estate sale was held for the furnishings and personal items that had once been used by the Murdaugh family in their Moselle home. An estimated 3,000 people showed up for an auction of items from the Moselle estate on Thursday — three times the normal crowd, Emily McGarry, who works for the auction house, told *CBS News*.

A Yeti cup, which typically sells for about $35, was bought for $400. Other bidders bought a sofa set for $30,000, while a pair of longhorns that had hung on a wall sold for $10,000, she said. The purchaser of the sofa set told the *Island Packet* that he didn't believe buying the furniture was "morbid" or "cold-hearted."

"That money is going to help the victims of these people who went through a very dark time in their life and were wronged," the buyer, Phillip Jennings of Soperton, Georgia, told the publication.

Proceeds from the auction will go to the Moselle Estate and paid out as per the settlement agreement. As mentioned earlier in this book, many of the high-ticket items from the Moselle property had been sold off before the court froze Buster and Alex Murdaugh's accounts. The heavy farm equipment sales had fetched close to $700,00, along with other assets from the hangar area. It is believed Alex asked his housekeeper to sell of many of Maggie's expensive fashions and accessories on PoshMark, after he was arrested. Alex asked Ronnie Crosby and Mark Ball to have Maggie's jewelry cleaned, ostensibly to sell it.

A leather couch set with Maggie's initials on the pillows was one of the items from Moselle up for bid at the estate sale. The couch is probably the one from the rec room where Alex said he lay down for a nap while his family was being murdered.

Cousin Eddie is Released on Bond

By Nick Neville
Published: Apr. 3, 2023, at 6:12 PM MDT
COLUMBIA, S.C. (WIS) - A South Carolina judge has reinstated bond for Curtis "Eddie" Smith, an alleged accomplice of convicted killer Alex Murdaugh.

He faces charges stemming from his accused involvement in Murdaugh's failed suicide-for-hire plot on Labor Day weekend of 2021, along with several money laundering charges in connection with some of Murdaugh's alleged financial crimes.

In June 2022, the South Carolina Grand Jury indicted him on four counts of money laundering, three counts of forgery, trafficking methamphetamine 10-28 grams, one count of unlawful possession of a Schedule II narcotic, possession of marijuana, and two counts of criminal conspiracy.

Judge Clifton Newman set his previous bond at $250,000 but revoked it a few months later.

Newman said Monday at the Richland County Courthouse that Smith must adhere to the same conditions that were in place prior to his bond being revoked.

He will be placed on house arrest, have GPS monitoring, and will undergo regular drug testing. Smith will be allowed to go to work and church, however.

"There must be strict compliance with it," Newman said. "No deviation, no leniency, no latitude in any way."

Smith, a distant cousin of Murdaugh's, acknowledged the seriousness of that order.

"I understand the significance of these cases as tied in with Alex Murdaugh, and I totally understand the importance of the letter of my bond," he said.

Smith's bond was previously revoked because Newman ruled that he had lied about how much money he had, and he had violated the terms of his house arrest.

"He's looking forward to getting out, he is understanding his need to follow the letter of the court's order as opposed to maybe the general intent," Jarrett Bouchette, Smith's defense attorney, told reporters after the hearing. "We're confident that he's going to do that, and confident we're going to be prepared to defend the remainder of the charges and decide what the state wants to do, and in what order the state wants to do, or the court wants to do for that matter."

Smith's lawyers requested the bond reconsideration hearing. State prosecutor John Meaders agreed with the defense's position, citing Smith's cooperation throughout the murder investigation of Maggie and Paul Murdaugh.

"Obviously, your honor, in revoking his bond, did the right thing," he said. "There's no question about that. And I am certainly not questioning that. Since that time, in my involvement with Mr. Zelenka, he has cooperated completely, and we are asking your honor to take that into consideration."

Meaders said Smith was prepared to testify in the Murdaugh murder trial.

"Based upon my years of experience, I think he would have testified truthfully," he said.

The rumor mill ground out unfounded information that Eddie was going to testify that Alex confessed the murders to him the day of the roadside shooting. The day Eddie was supposed to testify in the Murdaugh double murder case was the day the bomb threat was called in. He was never mentioned as a witness again after that. He was said to be ill, and based on what he looked like when he appeared for the bond hearing, it may have been true. Smith had been in jail for 235 days. He gained 55 pounds due to lack of exercise and said he has not been able to get the medical treatment he needs.

Curtis Eddie Smith looking heavier and having trouble walking during his bond reinstatement hearing.

Bouchette believes his client will be vindicated as more evidence is revealed. "As we've seen, as this last year to two years played out, a lot of things have changed, and a lot of the evidence has come to light, so we think that's going to continue to happen over the next six months to a year," he said.

Corey Fleming and Russell Lafitte

Alex's other partners in crime were also seeing their day in court.

CHARLESTON, S.C. (WCSC) – November 23, 2022.

A federal jury convicted Russell Lafitte, the former CEO of Palmetto State Bank whom prosecutors accused of conspiring with Lowcountry attorney Alex Murdaugh on all six charges Tuesday night.

Lafitte, 51, faced six counts related to financial crimes. Each charge holds a maximum sentence of up to 30 years in prison with a $1 million fine.

Judge Richard Gergel extended Lafitte's bond, saying he has been compliant. He sets 14 days for post-trial motions.

The jury began deliberating around 10 a.m. Tuesday and they came to a decision at 9:30 p.m. He is on house arrest until sentencing.

Russell Lafitte exits the court after a guilty verdict is handed down.

Lafitte was back to secure a new trial on April 10, 2023, nearly five months after his conviction of helping disbarred attorney Alex Murdaugh steal money from clients. Lafitte's attorneys sought to convince U.S. District Judge Richard Gergel that their client, the former chief executive of Palmetto State Bank, deserved a new trial because Murdaugh vouched for Lafitte's innocence after the trial was over. The judge ruled Murdaugh's words weren't enough to reverse the jury's conclusion that Lafitte was guilty of conspiracy, wire fraud, bank fraud and misapplication of bank funds.

In typical Alex Murdaugh fashion, he dumped his friend Russell when he needed him most. Lafitte's initial legal team tried to call Murdaugh to testify at the November trial, believing he'd take responsibility for the thefts. But Murdaugh, 54, invoked his Fifth Amendment protection from self-incrimination and didn't take the stand. Yet, when it came time to save his own hide, Alex admitted to his financial crimes during his own trial in hopes of persuading the jury that he was being honest about those crimes, therefore, they must think he was being honest when he said he did not kill his wife and son. It didn't work. It took his jury three hours to find him guilty. Lafitte's jury took almost four times longer to deliberate and pass judgement on the former banker.

Corey Fleming is set to go on trial in September 2023.

Next up is Corey Fleming, Alex's other accomplice, whose trial is slated for September 11, 2023. Judge Clifton Newman will again preside. Fleming is facing multiple charges tied to one of the financial schemes allegedly perpetrated by Alex Murdaugh. That scheme pertains to the three-headed fraud perpetrated on the Satterfield boys where Fleming acted as their lawyer, helping Murdaugh to get away with millions while the young men got nothing.

But Wait, There's More

According to *Fox News*, **Alex Murdaugh** is accused of swindling his former law firm out of more than $2 million then failing to report the illegally earned income, according to a new indictment from a South Carolina grand jury.

The 54-year-old is charged with two fresh counts of willful attempt to evade or defeat a tax.

In 2020, Murdaugh legitimately earned $1,147,342 from his former firm Peters, Murdaugh, Parker, Elzroth & Detrick (PMPED) and then stole another $1,112,734 from the firm and clients' settlement funds but never filed a tax return, the indictment alleges.

Alex Murdaugh was taken to the Colleton County Courthouse for sentencing on Friday, March 3, 2023. He owes the state $67,624 for that year, the filing says.

In 2021 – the same year he murdered his wife, Maggie, 52, and his son Paul, 22 – he earned $86,069 from PMPED and allegedly embezzled another $1,000,333.

Again, he failed to file a tax return, allegedly robbing the government of $64,948, bringing his tax evasion counts to two.

Alex had been in prison only two months, after being convicted of killing his wife and son, when he hatched one of his more diabolical schemes yet. It wasn't enough to steal almost $4 million dollars from Gloria Satterfield's sons in March of 2021, Alex now decided to reach out through the bars of prison and hit them again.

"My Dogs Did Not Trip Gloria Satterfield."

On May 3, 2023, Alex Murdaugh claimed in a federal court filing that he lied when he told his insurance companies that the family dogs caused his late housekeeper Gloria Satterfield to trip and fall.

Satterfield died Feb. 26, 2018, after supposedly tumbling on the steps of the family's main residence at the family's former South Carolina hunting estate known as Moselle.

"No dogs were involved in the fall of Gloria Satterfield," Murdaugh's lawyers wrote in his reply to the Nautilus Insurance

Company's fraud lawsuit against him. "After Ms. Satterfield's death, the Defendant invented Ms. Satterfield's purported statement that dogs caused her fall to force his insurers to make a settlement payment."

According to *Fox News* Nautilus sued Murdaugh, his former friend and ex-attorney Cory Fleming, and others for fraud after they allegedly pocketed $3.8 million from Nautilus and $505,000 from Lloyd's of London that should have gone to the Satterfield children.

Nautilus has accused Murdaugh of hatching an insurance fraud scheme by encouraging the Satterfield children to sue him, then lining his own pockets. Murdaugh told the Satterfield boys that a settlement hadn't been reached, as he and his co-conspirators allegedly spent the windfall.

In the reply, Murdaugh's lawyers point out that the Satterfield's recovered over $7.5 million based on the allegation that the disbarred attorney had stolen insurance money that should have gone to them.

Tony Satterfield (left) who testified against Alex during the double murder trial in early 2023. He is with his late mother, Gloria Satterfield.

The Satterfield estate wasn't entitled to the funds in the first place if Murdaugh lied about the circumstances of the fall, the document contends.

Lawyer Eric Bland, who represents the late housekeeper's family, alleges that Murdaugh is lying yet again to avoid a judgment against him and to encourage Nautilus to sue the Satterfield estate. The attorney added that none of the $7.5 million settlement came from Nautilus. The Satterfield family has a $4.3 million judgment against Murdaugh, which he voluntarily signed.

"He's not to be believed. He's a convicted murderer and a known liar," said Bland.

On May 16, 2023, Alex released another statement from prison via his attorneys, saying he now wants his entire confession removed. His attorneys are now blaming his statement about dogs on his opioid addiction, saying it is the same lies he told while scamming his other clients. Alex wants out of Nautilus' lawsuit completely, saying if that huge $4.2 million lawsuit it eliminated, more of that money can be spread out to the other victims waiting in line for compensation. And the Grinch's heart grew three sizes that day...not.

As of this writing, no update has been released of whether SLED will order an exhumation of Gloria Satterfield's body. Murdaugh's latest allegation that it wasn't his dogs that caused his housekeeper to "trip and fall" raises the question, then what did happen? The Satterfield family gave their consent in 2022 for the exhumation. It is a hard call, especially for Gloria's sons. Her youngest son Brian told this author he doesn't want her exhumed. Everyone's hearts go out to these boys who have been through so much...and now this.

Alex is delaying the court case for the Satterfield money, saying prison conditions make it hard for him to prepare his defense.

This is only the beginning of the many schemes Alex Murdaugh will perpetrate from within his tiny prison cell. It will go on beyond the release of this book. Many have speculated already that Alex is trying to smack the Satterfield lawyers, Eric Bland and Ronnie Richter. He says now he was coerced into giving his statements. I'm not sure how you back that up. As this author proved in the chapters on Gloria Satterfield, you can clearly hear Alex's voice during the 911 call Maggie made when Gloria fell. Alex was right there and told many people he was there when EMS arrived. So, at what time was anyone in authority present in those few short minutes to coerce him into anything? It's just part of Alex's crazy delusions, such as claiming a stranger shot at him while he was fixing a flat. It is unfortunate that his attorneys continue to back up his ongoing opioid malfunction excuse.

Michael Virzi Gives a Local Attorney's Perspective

Michael Virzi, Ethics Lawyer

Michael Virzi is an Ethics Lawyer practicing in Columbia, South Carolina. He also teaches Legal Research, Analysis and Writing I & II and Professional Responsibility at the University of South Carolina. Michael has also taught upper-level courses in Advanced Legal Writing and Fundamentals of Law Practice and Professionalism. He has an insider's perspective on what has been going on with the various Murdaugh undertakings. It was important to this author to hear from an ethics expert how he views Alex Murdaugh and the machinations surrounding him.

"I'm an ethics lawyer and that means that I just counsel lawyers in professional discipline proceedings. Like any profession, you know, whether it's a doctor, a plumber, or an esthetician who does something wrong, there's a licensing board where you can file a complaint against that. Someone is investigated and it's not a civil suit where there's money to be awarded and it's not a criminal case where someone goes to jail; it's just administrative where the person might lose their license, or that their license is suspended, or they may be subject to monitoring, or just be reprimanded like, if you do it again, you'll lose your license temporarily or permanently, it's that kind of administrative.

"In lawyer discipline cases, like I was just describing, I am the lawyer's lawyer. I am their counsel, advocating for that. Defending them in a trial, but a small percentage of them go to trial. You're defending them in the process. You're convincing the disciplinary authority that: A) they didn't do it, or B) what they did does not violate the rules, or C) that their punishment should be minimized. It's providing them with whatever defense is appropriate to that case, but that's about 1/3 of what I do. Another third of what I do is serve as an expert witness in civil legal malpractice cases like the various lawsuits against Alex Murdaugh and Corey Fleming and their law firms.

"I'm an expert witness in several of them. I've just given six or seven affidavits of the Murdaugh stuff," Virzi said.

"The other third of what I do is just providing private ethics advice to lawyers and law firms, you know, if they want to know is this a conflict of interest, can I do this, can I not do this, or what's the proper ethical way to go about doing this, that kind of thing. Actually, there are a dozen lawyers around our state that do that kind of work. Most of them do it in conjunction with something else. Like for example, I teach at the law school, and I do that on the side. There are a lot of lawyers that do, say, personal injury work and plaintiffs' attorneys who also do ethics work, and there are lawyers who do a lot of administrative defenses. They're defending doctors and plumbers and estheticians, and also lawyers. Like I said, there's only 10 or 12 of us; one of them is a commercial real estate lawyer who also does ethics work on some.

"They say lawyers make their money in the gray areas, you know, that's because the answers aren't clear and black and white, and obvious. If they were, a lot of people who need lawyers to help with things wouldn't if the answers were simple, but in terms of stumping me like, "Wow, I've never seen anything like this before, this one's way up there!" [Murdaugh case]

This author asked Mr. Virzi, "At what point do you cross the line from ethics to Illegal and even into criminal?"

"Well, I don't think there's a line to be crossed. I think there's a lot of overlap. It's a Venn diagram. There are things that are illegal and if a lawyer were to do them it would not be unethical, like speeding. There are things that are criminal and not unethical, and there's a whole lot of things that are criminal that are also unethical, like stealing a client's money. And then, you have things that are not criminal but they're still illegal; they're civilly actionable like negligence.

I asked Mr. Virzi: "Michael, in the Murdaugh cases, there were leaks springing everywhere. The tap dancing he's had to do with this, I don't know how he slept at night."

"Well, you know," Michael said, "one of the things that came out in discovery in those cases was emails between him and Russell Lafitte, the president of the bank right where he [Alex Murdaugh] would say, "OK, I got this new settlement in. I'm sending you $750,000 in this case. The first thing you need to do is pay off the money we borrowed in the prior case. OK, you tell me how much that we owe on that one and then here's what you do with the rest of the money."

I opined, "For someone in the legal field, he doesn't seem all that savvy to me; he left such a paper trail. It all seems really reckless. It's as if he believed that they were above it all and it didn't matter. They were never going to have to account for anything they did.

"That's the sense I got," Michael said. "I mean it was such a fiefdom, you know, and his family had run 100 years and there was no higher authority around there. How many crime scenes did his family members clean up?"

It's a chilling thought that reminds us of the recent twist in the Gloria Satterfield case and the open investigation into the death of Stephen Smith. In the realm of Alex Murdaugh, life was expendable, except for his own.

Love Behind Bars

It is a strange anomaly that certain women are attracted to convicted killers, even serial killers. Ted Bundy received so many letters professing love and support during his incarceration, that he practically needed a press secretary. Is it a feeling of forbidden love? A tantalizing way to touch someone dangerous through the mail system, knowing he/she is out of reach? It's hard to quantify. What we do know is the convicted killer is getting his share of love notes as he sits in an 8' x 10' cell in maximum security.

"I think I love you," wrote Nicole K. on March 12, according to messages obtained by *FitsNews* through a public records request. "I think about you all day every day."

The message was sent just 10 days after a Colleton County jury convicted the scion of a once-powerful legal dynasty of gunning down his wife, Maggie, 52, and son, Paul, 22, to hide his decade-long financial schemes.

The admirer sent another message the next day shortly after midnight. "I swear on my life and on my soul I'll never say a single word to anyone important or not important. I genuinely care for you," she gushed.

The messages, which Murdaugh received during his brief stay at the intake facility Kirkland Correctional Institution, were mostly from women.

Lacie, who described herself as a "small town girl from Missouri," sent Murdaugh six messages. "I am unable to get you off my mind," she wrote March 6. "I do want you to know that you are loved and cared for."

Love letters in prison.

In subsequent missives, Lacie expressed concern for Murdaugh's distress at being "locked in a concrete room all day, every day" and her belief in his innocence.

"I am here if you want to talk. Or vent. XXLacie," she wrote, undeterred by Murdaugh's silence.

According to *Fox News*, other fans of the convicted killer hailed from Louisiana, Florida, and Tennessee — some offering to put cash in his commissary, help with legal research for his appeal, or send a photo "to put a face to a name."

Shianne D. called herself a "bored 31-year-old female" who thought Murdaugh could use a "non-judgmental friend."

He received 26 messages in two weeks, according to the log, including a pitch from a *Netflix* producer for *"Murdaugh Murders: Southern Scandal."* The producer for the show, which aired in the middle of the trial, was identified as Mike Gasparino by *FitsNews*.

"We feel at this point its [sic] very important to have your voice in the remember (sic) of our series," wrote Mike G. "Our first 3 Episodes was (sic) viewed by 40 million households and also 75 million hours watched in just 10 days. Those numbers will continue to rise. We believe you can have the largest platform on TV if you are willing to speak to us."

Alex has continued to petition to be moved to the general population in prison. He may want to rethink that. Prison has its own code of ethics, and it is well known that men who murder wives and children find themselves suddenly on the wrong end of a "shank."

There will be more breaking news, of that we can be certain. For this author, it was a challenge to write this book with new information coming in each day. I likened it to Jack climbing a beanstalk that was forever growing ahead of him. Now that the giant has fallen, perhaps the law enforcement of South Carolina can chop down that insidious tower of lies, fraud, and murder. There's always hope.

4147 Moselle Road from the right side. Two golf carts were usually parked to the left of the tree and faced the house.

Moselle a year after the murders. The grass has died, and weeds cover the once manicured grounds. The staircase (to the right of pine tree) is where Paul Murdaugh stood one humid afternoon in April 2021 with his good friend Will Loving and placed against the railing an AR-15 .300 Blackout rifle that would only two months later be used to gun down his mother on that same property. It is also the site of Gloria Satterfield's purported fall. It happened at the front steps to the left and out of sight of this photo. Stephen Smith had attended parties here, as had Mallory Beach. The Murdaugh home has been nicknamed the "Murder House" by many. Who could blame them?

Chapter 39

Was Paul Murdaugh Supposed to Die?

While researching this book and listening attentively to the 6-week-long murder trial of Alex Murdaugh in the spring of 2023, something kept nagging me. It began with *People Magazine's* article in June 2022 when Dick Harpootlian is quoted concerning the release of Paul's famous kennel video. The video had only been discovered 2 months earlier in April. Harpootlian's choice of words jumped out at me immediately. He said, "You can hear Alex talking to Maggie. Paul is having a good time…" I thought, why isn't he saying Alex, Maggie and Paul are talking together in the video? He goes on to say it shows a lighthearted exchange about a chicken. Why is Paul separated in his description?

Harpootlian says it again during a Motion's Hearing with Judge Newman. He uses the exact same words. Could it be Alex wasn't aware Paul was there? Bear with me while I present a premise that, admittedly, flies in the face of the conclusions of witnesses presented during the trial. This is only my theory, but one I will back up. In some cases, the evidence could go either way.

Let's begin with what we know. According to Blanca Simpson, the Murdaugh's housekeeper, Maggie called her the morning of June 7, 2021, and asked her to pick up some Orange Capri Suns for Alex. Later, after Alex gets the call from Randy about Randolph, Maggie tells Blanca that Alex wants her to come home because his father Randolph III is back in the hospital. Randolph had been in the hospital the previous Friday and Alex had stayed overnight with him there. Maggie also tells Blanca that Alex asked Paul to come home to take care of the sunflower mess C.B. Rowe made when he over sprayed the sunflowers.

We are limited on the cell phone data from that day because the expert's testimony begins the data timeline after Alex leaves for work at 12:06 pm, shortly after lunch. Maggie's, Paul's, and Alex's phone extraction logs are all presented from that time period on. Blanca says she speaks with Maggie before she arrives at Moselle that morning. Alex is still in bed and remains there for two hours after she arrives. Since she helps him with his shirt collar as he heads out the door at 12:06 pm, we know she has been there at least until 10:00 that morning. She testified she had no set hours, and she did not give an exact time Maggie called her earlier or when she arrives at the house. Even the screenshot of Maggie's calls that day does not show one to Blanca, but it may have been earlier than this photo shows.

Maggie's calls Monday June 7 & John Marvin the next day when John helped find her missing phone.

We also see in that photo of Maggie's calls, that she tries four times to reach Barbara Mixon, who was caring for Miss Libby that day. It may have been to ask how Randolph is doing, rather than ask Alex. All calls lasted 4-8 seconds, which sounds like Maggie's calls went to Voicemail.

Maggie tells Blanca she does not want to come home because she is having work done at Edisto Beach. She tells Blanca she left food in the refrigerator. Would Blanca please fix dinner as she won't be back in time? Blanca says, "Sure, I'll do it."

Based on Blanca's testimony, we know Alex has asked Paul to come home and take care of the sunflowers. Paul calls Nolan Tuten to please stop by Moselle that morning and see if the sunflowers are indeed a mess. Nolan stops by around 10 or 11 that morning and sees they are dying. He calls Paul and tells him that. That also is too early to show up on the phone logs presented in court during the trial.

In the meantime, John Marvin and Randy have arranged for John to drive up from Okatie and meet Randy in Ridgeland. Randy will have Randolph III in Miss Libby's car as Randolph is too ill to climb up into Randy's truck. Randy's truck was left behind at Miss Libby's when he picked up Randolph. John Marvin drives his white pick-up truck to Ridgeland where Randy trades places with him. Randy drives off in John Marvin's truck, John takes the wheel of Miss Libby's car and drives his father to his doctor's appointment. The doctor is alarmed at how labored Randolph's breathing is and orders him into the hospital. He is diagnosed with pneumonia.

Randy drives John Marvin's truck back to Miss Libby's and takes his own truck. John Marvin, after taking his father to the hospital, drives Miss Libby's car back to Okatie and arrives at 5:00 pm when he sees Paul in the front yard playing with John's kids. John is now stuck with Miss Libby's car, since Randy left his truck at Miss Libby's. He asks Paul if he will drive Miss Libby's car up to Almeda, leave it at Miss Libby's, and grab his truck and bring it back in the morning. Paul says "Okay." Paul's own truck went in for repairs the previous Friday.

Paul drives toward Moselle around 6:17 pm. The phone data shows his movements and others:

5:30-6:09 p.m.: Paul Murdaugh's phone places him in Okatie.

6:04:11 p.m.: Paul Murdaugh calls Will Loving.

6:04:25 p.m.: Will Loving calls Paul Murdaugh.

6:08:57 p.m.: Paul Murdaugh calls "Dad." No record of the call is found on Alex Murdaugh's phone.

6:09:48: Maggie Murdaugh texts Paul saying she's getting a foot massage.

6:20:53 p.m.: Marian Proctor calls her sister Maggie's phone. Maggie texts Marian saying she can't talk and she's getting a foot massage.

6:23:27 p.m.: Paul texts his mom asking what Blanca cooked for dinner. She replies, "country fried steak and macaroni and cheese."

6:24 p.m.: Alex Murdaugh's vehicle leaves the PMPED law firm, headed to Moselle.

6:25:35 p.m.: Alex Murdaugh's phone receives a call from Jay Parker.

6:17-6:53 p.m.: Paul's phone shows him traveling from Okatie to Moselle.

6:40:01 p.m.: Paul Murdaugh calls "PA" (Alex Murdaugh's phone). The call lasts 2 minutes and 29 seconds. There is no call log for it in Alex Murdaugh's phone.

6:42 p.m.: Alex Murdaugh's vehicle arrives at Moselle.

6:43 p.m.: Alex calls his wife's phone. The call lasts 104 seconds. There is no call log for it in the data extractions of Alex's phone.

6:53:44 p.m.: Paul Murdaugh's phone calls John Marvin Murdaugh.

7:04 p.m.: Paul Murdaugh is at Moselle.

7:05 p.m.: Alex texts Maggie, "Paul says you are getting pedi!! Call when you get done."

7:00:06 p.m.: Paul texts CB Rowe asking if he's coming to the property the next day.

7:07-7:50 p.m.: Maggie's phone places her traveling from the North Charleston area, taking Highway 17, towards Moselle.

7:09:43 p.m.: Maggie Murdaugh calls Courtney Shelbourne. The call lasts 3 seconds.

7:09:43 p.m.: Maggie Murdaugh calls "Mom." The call lasts 8 minutes and 17 seconds.

7:14:13-7:22:19 p.m.: Paul Murdaugh's phone records 208 steps taken.

7:15:35-7:21:52 p.m.: Alex Murdaugh's phone records 200 steps taken.

7:18:40 p.m.: Maggie Murdaugh calls "Barbara." The call lasts 2 seconds.

7:18:44 p.m.: Alex Murdaugh texts CB Rowe stating, "Call me pls."

By this log, it looks like Paul is leaving Okatie around 6:09 pm and arriving at Moselle at 7:04 pm which is just about right. It's roughly a one-hour drive from Okatie to Moselle. Along the way, Paul tries to get his father a couple of times. The first one to "Dad" is at 6:08 pm. It goes unanswered and is found deleted from Alex's phone later. Paul calls him again at 6:40 pm and connects. That call lasts roughly 2 minutes and a half. He is obviously driving toward Moselle at this time. We do not know what that call was about. It too was deleted off Alex's phone. We do not know if Paul told Alex Nolan Tuten was coming to help him fix the sunflowers. Nolan said he would come and help Paul that evening to plow them under for replanting. Nolan at some point tells Paul he is hung up at work and can't come.

Paul sends Nolan a SnapChat a little after 7 pm from Moselle showing him that the valve of the Highboy is leaking. As these machines are used for spraying, it may be what was used by C.B. Rowe to overspray the sunflowers on Friday.

Alex arrives at Moselle at 6:42 pm, around 20 minutes before Paul does. Alex obviously sees Paul a few minutes after he arrives, and Paul tells him Maggie is getting a pedicure. Alex texts Maggie at 7:05 pm saying, "Paul says you are getting a pedi!! Call when done."

What is also obvious is that Paul has already talked with Alex around 7:00. He may have told his father then that Nolan Tuten wasn't coming to help with the sunflowers. As we do not see a call or text to Paul from Nolan in the timeline above, Nolan must have contacted him earlier than 6:00 pm to say he was hung up at work and couldn't come.

At 7:00:06 pm, Paul texts C.B. Rowe asking if he's coming to the property the next day. C.B. does not respond. He was supposed to work at Moselle that day but didn't show up. He claimed later he was taking his father to the hospital. In actuality, he was looking for another job. According to Alex's testimony on the stand during his murder trial, he and Paul went first to the dove field after Paul arrived. It is only minutes from the kennel area where the Highboy is. This is where the dead sunflowers are. Paul's phone records 208 steps between 7:14-7:22. He may be walking the sunflower aisles and his phone is either in his hand or in his pocket. Alex's phone also records 200 steps during this time period.

At 7:18 pm, Alex texts C.B. and says, "Call me pls." C.B. does not respond. The two continue to show steps. Paul is receiving texts from friends.

7:39:55 p.m.: It appears Paul Murdaugh records the video of his father with the tree here. He sends it as a Snapchat video about 15 minutes later.

7:41:23-7:48:49 p.m.: Alex Murdaugh's phone records 29 steps.

7:45-7:56 p.m.: Paul's phone places him by the kennels on the Moselle property.

[Paul is now back at the kennels. We do not see Alex's phone placing him at any location at this time.]

7:50 p.m.: Maggie's phone is in Walterboro, roughly a half hour away from Moselle. It's the last location data pulled from her phone.

7:50:03 p.m.: Maggie calls "Barbara." The call lasts 8 seconds.

7:55:44-8:05:28 p.m.: Paul Murdaugh's phone records 262 steps.

7:55:32-8:05:07 p.m.: Alex Murdaugh's phone records 270 steps. [It appears Paul and his dad are still together as their steps and time lapse are almost identical.]

7:56 p.m.: Paul sends a SnapChat video he filmed earlier. Alex is seen standing by a little tree at Moselle as it flops over.

8:05:35-8:09:52 p.m.: Alex Murdaugh's phone records 54 steps.

8:05:46-8:15:24 p.m.: Paul Murdaugh's phone records 303 steps.

8:06 p.m.: Paul's phone begins moving from the kennels to the main house. (The previous log shows Paul taking 303 steps during this time. Did he walk back to the house? Alex left before him. John Marvin's white truck that Paul drove to Moselle is seen at the house after the murders. Therefore, it seems reasonable that Alex drove his Suburban up to the house. Maggie is not there yet.)

8:07:20 p.m.: Paul Murdaugh sends a Snapchat message to several friends.

8:09-9:02 p.m.: Alex's phone records no steps or data during this one-hour time frame, indicating he was not moving with the phone in his possession. He later told investigators he was sleeping during that time.

[For almost a full hour, Alex's phone is void of movement or any phone data.]

8:11:08-8:31:15 p.m.: Maggie Murdaugh's phone is locked. She unplugs it from her car at about 8:15 p.m. It is probably when she arrives at the Moselle house.]

8:14-8:35 p.m.: Paul Murdaugh's phone puts him at the main house.

8:15:55-8:21:45 p.m.: Paul's phone records 140 steps.

8:17-8:18 p.m.: Maggie Murdaugh's phone records 38 steps taken.

[This may be when she exits the car and walks up the steps and into the house.]

8:19:23 p.m.: Paul Murdaugh receives a Snapchat message from "Ansley Wilson," stating "He's got the magic touch."

8:23:33 p.m.: Paul sends a Snapchat message to "Marlene Robinson," stating, "He's hurt."

8:24:08 p.m.: Paul sends an iMessage to Meagan Kimbrell stating, "Meagan."

665

8:28:07 p.m.: Paul receives an iMessage from Meagan Kimbrell stating, "We're u avoiding me."

8:28:35 p.m.: Paul responds to Meagan Kimbrell with, "When?"

8:28:54 p.m.: Paul receives an iMessage from a Mrs. Morgan stating, "I have not received anything back yet. Did you get the lease email?"

8:29:06 p.m.: Paul receives an iMessage from Meagan Kimbrell stating, "You didn't send me any movie recommendations."

8:29:36 p.m.: Paul responds, "Haha I didn't have a good one. Wills might."

8:30-8:33 p.m.: Maggie Murdaugh's phone records 43 steps taken.

[Here we may have Maggie leaving the house to probably get into a vehicle to go down to the kennels. It appears dinner is over. Paul looks as if he spent the dinner texting back and forth to friends and a Mrs. Morgan.]

8:31 p.m.: John Marvin Murdaugh sends a text to several family members, including Alex and Maggie, which reads, "I plan to go over to visit dad tomorrow afternoon. Is anyone else planning to go?" Maggie Murdaugh's phone did not unlock for the notification until 8:49:26 p.m. Alex Murdaugh reads his text from John at 1:44 p.m. the following day. [Maggie may have left the phone in the Mercedes or whatever she drove down, or somewhere else at the kennels. It is obvious that Alex is not very worried about his dad's health at this time. He waits until the next day to read his brother John Marvin's text concerning their father.]

8:32:10 p.m.: Paul receives a call from Lucile Boyle. The call is not answered.

8:32:25-8:42:11 p.m.: Paul's cell phone records 283 steps taken. (Is Paul walking back down to the kennels?)

8:38 p.m.: Paul's phone places him by the kennels.

(Looking at Paul's 283 steps taken between 8:32-8:42 pm, it looks as if Paul walked down to the kennels. It would seem he did not move around much once he got there. He may have gone straight to Rogan Gibson's dog's pen, talked to Rogan, tried to Facetime Rogan to show him the dog's tail (which did not go through), took a video of the dog's tail, and walked to the feed room to send the video where the cell service may have been better.)

8:40:20 p.m.: Paul calls longtime friend Rogan Gibson asking if something is wrong with the tail of Gibson's dog, who was staying in the Murdaugh kennels. The call lasts 4 minutes and 14 seconds. It is during this call that Rogan hears Alex's voice in the background, so Alex is at the kennels by 8:40:20 p.m. He testified in court he took a golf cart down after Maggie left the house.)

8:41:38 p.m.: Paul receives a Snapchat message from Rogan Gibson.

8:44:34 p.m.: Paul Murdaugh initiates a FaceTime call with Gibson. It lasts 11 seconds and fails to send.

8:44:55 p.m.: Paul records a video for Gibson at the kennels, showing the dog. Three voices are heard in the video. Multiple witnesses testify that those voices are Paul, Maggie, and Alex Murdaugh.

8:47:55 p.m.: Paul sends an iMessage to Meagan Kimbrell stating, "Haha kidding."

8:48:05 p.m.: Paul again sends an iMessage to her, stating, "Star was born is the movie."

8:48:29 p.m.: Meagan Kimbrell texts Paul, "No I need something happy" and "Don't like watching sad movies."

8:49:01 p.m.: Paul Murdaugh's phone is locked. [He will be shot in the next several seconds.]

8:49:26 p.m.: Maggie Murdaugh's phone unlocks, and she reads another text in the group chat about Randolph Murdaugh.

[This is the last time Maggie reads her phone messages. It is now that she probably hears shots coming from the feed shed.]

8:49:28 p.m.: Maggie Murdaugh's phone accesses an application and implements orientation change to landscape.

[Landscape mode on a phone is lying flat. Maggie probably dropped the phone and hurried to the feed shed where she was shot in the thigh. As she backs away, she is shot three to four more times and dies by a small doghouse at the hangar overhang.]

8:49:31 p.m.: Maggie Murdaugh's phone is locked and not unlocked until it's found a quarter mile away the next afternoon.

8:49:35 p.m.: Rogan Gibson texts Paul about the dog's tail, "See if you can get a good picture of it. MaryAnn wants to send it to a girl we know that's a vet. Get him to sit and stay. He shouldn't move around too much." The text goes unread.

Investigators believe Maggie and Paul Murdaugh are killed around 8:50 p.m. near the kennels. Paul is shot twice with a shotgun, once in the chest and once in the head. Maggie is shot 4-5 times with .300 Blackout ammo from an AR-style rifle. Two of those shots struck her in the head.

The best evidence presented at the trial was the dog kennel video. If you listen to it and watch it carefully, you can ascertain several things:

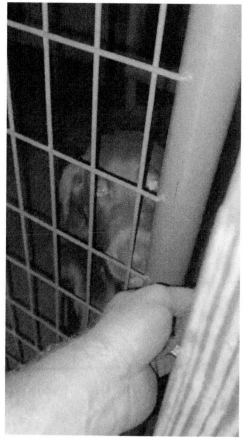

Paul opening Cash's dog pen to film the kennel video.

- It is dark out. You can see the camera light from Paul's phone reflect from the cement pad in the dog pen. You can see darkened conditions outside the pen.
- You can hear crickets in the first few seconds of the video. Then there is the sound of water. A quick glimpse outside the pen shows the green hose is stretched out, not wound up the way Dale Davis left it four hours before. We know from hearing Maggie's voice next that she is standing not too far

from Paul and is probably washing down the two dog pens while the dogs are running loose. They may have messed up their pens again after Davis left, and I believe she ran them before she planned to head back to Edisto Beach that night.

- Alex testified that Maggie asked him to go to the kennels with her and he said "No." After she left, he felt guilty and jumped in a golf cart (which is usually parked around a large pine tree to the right of the front steps if you're facing the house.) He says he drives down to the kennels and parks the golf cart between the feed shed and the chicken coop. He says he may have talked to Maggie and Paul from the golf cart. (Creighton Waters cannot get Alex to remember what he said to his wife and son during his last conversations with them ever.) Alex said Maggie was in the pine trees behind the kennels running the dogs. He testified that Paul was playing with Cash, Rogan's dog, in the pathway. (We have only Alex's word for any of this.)

- Paul is quietly trying to wrangle Cash's dog within the pen to where he can get a shot of a lump on the dog's tail. We do hear Alex say, "What's wrong with the dog?" It's unclear if that statement is made to Paul or Maggie. Paul mumbles something that sounds like, "It's not that bad." It's hard to tell. Maggie, sounding very near, yells, "Oh, he's got a bird in his mouth." You hear Alex, farther away, "Bubba!" Alex supposedly is chasing the dog. Maggie yells, "It's a guinea!" Paul says softly, "It's a chicken." Alex is heard from a distance also saying, "It's a chicken." A few seconds later Paul says softly, "Hey Bubba." It seems the dog is running around, happy with his chicken. Alex yells from further away, "Bubba, come here!" We do not know where Alex went.

- Paul, finishing the short 57-second video, walks past four pens to the feed room where he goes inside. Before he can send the video to Rogan, he answers a couple of texts to a girl checking on movie plans. It is the last text Paul sends.

- Maggie has finished with the hose but has not put the dog beds back down from where she placed them on their dog houses until the cement dries. She may have walked the short distance to her car and looked at her phone as she waited for the pen to dry. She sees John Marvin's text about his dad. It is the last time she uses her phone.

If Alex went off around the hangar to chase Bubba, is this when he retrieved the AR-15 rifle and came back around the corner near the end of the kennels? Was it in the black Ford F-140? Agent Owen mentions that the black truck is at the kennels during his interview with Alex shortly after the 911 call. Maggie was at the kennels with the hose when Alex ran off after the dog. Did he come around to where she had been last, so that he could come up behind her? But she is finished and has walked to her car. As Alex walks along the kennels toward the other end where her car would have been parked, he passes the feed room. The light is on. It is here, things went down.

If you look at the ballistics testimony from the trial, and especially Agent Worley's diagram, you can see this is a chaotic scene. Something has gone wrong. There is a bullet strike in the gravel right outside the feed room. It is marker #13 in the diagram. It is never spotlighted during the trial, but I feel it's important. It means the AR-15 shot into the ground there. Why? There is also no casing marked next to it. Did it eject into the golf cart which is parked nearby? Maggie's DNA is found on the front and back of Alex's freshly washed shirt. Was she up against him as she wrestled for the gun, or even pulling on his shirt?

As Alex walks past the feed shed, does something happen? Does Maggie see the AR-15 and yell something at him? Paul may have his Benelli shotgun with him in the shed. He stops texting and turns to see his father just outside the door with possibly the AR raised to shoot. Paul grabs his shotgun that may have been standing next to him with his left hand, grabbing the barrel first to lift it. Alex runs into the room and grabs the butt of the gun before Paul can shoulder it and yanks it away from his son, at the same time, accidentally firing. The shot skids across Paul's chest, under his left arm which may still be slightly raised, and out the window.

Maggie is screaming and running at Alex who has the AR-15 in one hand and Paul's shotgun in the other. She may have tried to get the shotgun from him or is struggling with him when Paul walks slowly to the doorway, blood dripping from his arm. His head is leaning slightly forward and to the left. His left shoulder is just outside the doorway. Maggie and Alex are struggling over the shotgun. When Alex or Maggie yank down on it, it goes off again, the blast entering Paul's left shoulder at a low angle and traveling up under his jaw and into his head where it explodes the skull. During the struggle for the guns, the AR-15 goes off, shooting a bullet into the gravel. (Marker #13)

Maggie screams, and backs away as Alex drops the shotgun and aims the AR-15 at her. He shoots her in the thigh. It is a through and through shot which exits the rear of her thigh and sails into the hangar where it is found near tire imprints. She falls against the Polaris ATV, which is right there, the mud from its tire leaving an imprint on the back of her thigh.

Polaris ATV on the right. The feed room is directly across from it to the right and outside this photo. Maggie's blood is the dark discoloration in front of the right front tire. (Note how dark it is.) Courtesy of Courtroom Photo Pool.

This again shows a chaotic scene. Based on the stippling found on the shot to her thigh, Alex is only 3' or less from her. Yet, he only shoots her in the thigh. Is she still impacting the gun somehow? Her

672

hands were not tested for GSR. As she backs up, Alex is right there and shoots again, this time finding his target by hitting her in the ribcage. This wound too shows stippling. In rapid order, he gets off the other two or three shots. The one to the ribcage goes through organs and out her back, probably into the small doghouse near where her body is found. Which bullet went into the quail pen inside the hangar? Again, a chaotic scene. The final two shots find their way into her brain. Her broken earring was found near the Polaris.

I want to point out something I mentioned earlier in the book: the hangar lights are not on when the first responders arrive. Even the first photos taken are in the dark. Maggie and Paul's bodies are blurred in the photo below. You can see light coming from the feed shed to the right, and some light coming from inside the hangar work shed to the left. That's it, except for flashlights and headlights.

Bodycam shot of dark hangar with bodies still there.

Photo after the hangar lights are turned on. Maggie's body is beneath the sheet under a canopy in front of the Polaris.

Why weren't the hangar lights on when Maggie and Paul were at the kennels? Did Alex want it to be dark there? The light from the feed room would have been enough for Maggie to see while she cleaned the pens, and I believe she was going to leave in a few minutes to go back to Edisto Beach. Paul was almost finished, and she may have said she'd drop him at the house before she leaves.

Here is my point. I don't believe Alex knew Paul was at the kennels. In all three of his SLED interviews, he says he didn't know where Paul went after dinner. Frankly, I don't believe Alex ate dinner with them. Not once could he remember the dinner conversation. He finally says they ate on TV trays in front of the TV. He said Paul had already started dinner when Alex got out of the shower. On page 250, Alex says he didn't know where Paul went, "outside somewhere." Page 259, "Paul was going to set up to plant sunflowers." Page 304, "Don't know where Paul went, but he left the house." Alex talks about the sunflowers in each interview. Page 592, Alex says, "Paul was somewhere around the house."

All the vehicles are accounted for at the house after dinner. I believe Maggie rode down to the kennels in her Mercedes, and as I've shown, based on steps taken, I think Paul walked down. If Alex saw John Marvin's truck at the house when he took the golf cart down, did he think Paul was in the house somewhere? Possibly up in his room? Or, when he arrived at the kennels in the golf cart, did he not see Paul, confirming he wasn't down there and that he was at the house? I believe that due to the darkening conditions outside, no hangar lights, Maggie blocking the view of Cash's pen (as she was between that pen and Alex in the golf cart), the sound of rushing water hitting the cement as she washed out the pens, and her yelling about the bird in Bubba's mouth, that Alex may not have seen Paul in the dark pen trying to get a picture of the dog's tail. Paul is very quiet. He never yells out anything. Maggie is near him, but Alex is not and runs after the dog. When he returns with the AR-15, Paul is inside the shed.

What we see is that Alex gets Paul there to handle the sunflowers. C.B. Rowe is supposed to be there that day working. But he doesn't show up. Maggie is in Charleston. I doubt Blanca noticed or cared, and Paul is at Okatie. Alex told Agent Owen that Paul got along with C.B. and was working with him. It is clear that Alex was trying to throw C.B. under the bus as a possible murder suspect. He tells Agent Owen about the Black Panther murder raid in the first interview shortly after the murders. Was the plan to get Paul up there to make sure C.B. would stay late and work with Paul plowing under the sunflowers? If they were running the tractor, a gunshot wouldn't have been heard over it. Alex probably thought he would kill Maggie in one shot. I don't think it went the way he planned.

With C.B. on the property, and Paul making sure the work was being done properly, Alex has his plan in action. He knows Maggie will go down to the kennels to run the dogs before she goes back to Edisto. Alex is trying to get C.B. there when he texts him at 7:18 and says, "Call me pls." C.B. isn't answering him or Paul. Alex drives around with Paul to make sure Paul is where he knows he is until its dinner time. They've already seen the sunflowers during that drive. There is no need for Paul to go back out there and it will be dark soon. Alex probably figures Paul will chill out at the house and take a shower after working all day at John Marvin's equipment rental company. If C.B. is using the tractor, the tractor will have to be returned to the hangar at some point, right where Maggie's body is found. The only hiccup is Paul would be with C.B. He could be his alibi. Perhaps Alex figures all he needs is for C.B. to be on the property and he can say Paul wasn't with him at every minute. It's no more of a hare-brained scheme than the roadside shooting or

Gloria's dog-trip fall is. We do know Alex brings C.B. up a lot, and he may have had Eddie start the rumor that C.B. and Maggie were fooling around at the hangar. It came out after the murders.

If Alex planned to shoot Paul as well as Maggie, why not just shoot Paul with the AR-15 the minute he saw him in the feed shed? One shot to the head or chest and he'd be dead. Why two messed up shots from odd angles spaced a minute or more apart? He could have shot him before Paul lifted the shotgun to shoot. Why was it important for Alex to say he saw Paul playing with Cash in the pathway when he pulled up on the golf cart? Paul couldn't possibly have been playing with the dog. His phone shows him arriving at the kennel at 8:38. He called Rogan two minutes later to tell him about the dog's tail. That was at 8:40. When he hangs up, he tries to shoot a Facetime that doesn't work. So, at 8:45, Paul films the kennel video. You see him arrive at the kennel pen and open the door in that video. He hasn't been chasing a rambunctious puppy around the grounds trying to film his tail. But Alex needed people to believe he saw Paul because there was no way he could have shot his son on purpose. But I don't think he did. I think Paul was in the wrong place at the wrong time.

Maggie was going to divorce Alex. They were living apart. She was spending money like a bandit. She bought a brand-new $80,000 Mercedes on December 10, 2020, only six months before she was murdered. Her sister Marion said Maggie had found a house in Hilton Head she really liked. Maggie was spying on Alex's pill use and involving Paul in being the "Little Detective." Paul was hardly at Moselle, except for weekends. He was working for his uncle in Okatie when school was out, and he was about to lease a house with his friends for the school term. Alex could hide the pills from Paul.

And, most important of all, I don't believe Maggie was going to let Alex use the Edisto Beach house as collateral for a loan he desperately needed. A loan Russell Lafitte said he could get him with some collateral. Alex just wanted money so he could get out of the boat crash case before they looked at his financials and discovered what he had been doing. He called Jennie Seckinger that afternoon around 4 pm to ask how much he had in his 401k. It was probably Seckinger cornering him in his office and demanding to know where the Ferris fees were, and Randolph (Alex's personal piggy bank) going back into the hospital, which made Alex ramp up his plans. If you look at it, he didn't try to get Maggie out to Moselle until that afternoon. He is trying to Facetime her at her massage. She tells Blanca at 3:48 pm, "Alex wants me to come home and I don't want to. The door is open at Edisto. I trust the Mexicans will lock up." Does this look planned to you? Doesn't he try to get C.B. Rowe there at the last minute as well? Dr. Kenneth Kinsey, the crime scene reconstruction expert in the trial, stated in May 2023 that the crime scene felt to him as though it was planned at the last minute.

Paul and Buster are an extension of Alex. Maggie is a wife he has tired of and who is going to divorce him. He has a mistress (or 2 or 3). Alex is a narcissist to the highest degree. He is not going to destroy an extension of himself, and Paul and Buster were Alex Murdaugh's sons. He told everyone he was going to get Paul's name cleared from the boat crash. Yes, part of it was to get out of the lawsuit, but it was more than that. Jim Griffin, Paul's attorney, said the boat case was "defensible." Based on the early interviews from the kids onboard the boat that morning, I believe he may have had a chance at "reasonable doubt." Morgan drew Connor at the wheel in her drawing for DNR. Connor said he didn't know who was driving. Anthony said he didn't know, only that Paul was driving when they left Luthor's. Morgan was under a blanket when they hit the bridge. Connor was drunk as well as Paul and refused a sobriety test at the hospital. Only Miley said she saw Paul at the wheel the last time she looked, but she also yelled, "Connor!" just before they hit the bridge. I do believe Alex thought that with a good old Hampton jury, who always ruled in favor of a Murdaugh, they could win. He was trying to keep the trial in Hampton and not Beaufort.

In the photo on the following page, I have placed the white golf cart between the feed room and the chicken coop. Maggie is at the dog pens, and Paul is inside the feed room. Alex is chasing Bubba around the hangar. Based on the footwear patterns matching Maggie's sandals that SLED agents saw in the dirt in the left hangar overhang, it's possible her car was parked just under the overhang as it was threatening rain. She may have left her cell phone in the call while washing out the dog pens and walked to it to check the last text message she would read before running to the feed shed when shots are fired. Everything happened in a very small area around the hangar and kennels.

Diagram of Maggie at dog pens, Paul inside the feed shed, and Alex
chasing Bubba. The golf cart is between the chicken coop and feed room.
Diagram by Rebecca F. Pittman

I believe Paul was just to make sure C.B. Rowe, who liked Paul,
was going to be there that night to take the fall for Maggie's death.
The same way Connor was set-up for Mallory's death, the same way
the dogs were blamed for Gloria's fall, the same way Shawn
Connelly was set-up for Stephen Smith's death, and the same way
Eddie Smith was set-up for the roadside shooting. This is Alex's
MO. Find a patsy to blame it on.

Alex thought Paul was somewhere else. Is that why he is heard on
the 911 call, as he bends over his dead son's body, saying, "I should
have known?"

Alex could not tell Creighton Waters during his time on the
witness stand one thing Maggie and Paul said at dinner, or while at
the kennels. The time at the kennels is very short; only about ten
minutes or less from the time Rogan heard Alex and Maggie's voice
while on a phone call with Paul at 8:40 pm until they were dead by
8:50 pm. If Bubba hadn't run off with a chicken, it may be that Alex
was just going to pull up in the golf cart and shoot her after she put
the dogs back in the pen. We know the two dogs were put back into
the wrong pens, and the dog beds were still on top of their houses.
The hose was wound up hastily with the nozzle too high up, unlike
how Davis left it, neatly wound with the nozzle pointing down. The
hangar lights were off. Alex is the only person who knows. It is

possible he knew Paul was there but not that he had gone to the feed room. This is only one author's opinion.

I do believe Alex put his bloody clothes and shoes in the cooler that was by the skinning shed and put them in the back of the Suburban. I think he took the big raincoat that may have been in the boat crash and rolled the two guns into it and put it into the car. He drove them to his mother's house and put them somewhere near the smoke house until he took care of them later. Those clothes may have gone up in smoke, along with the bloody evidence from the feed room, in the fire near Randy Murdaugh's house the morning after the murders.

C.B. Rowe and another workhand were given the task of cleaning up the feed room the morning after the murders. Mark Ball saw a large jug of bleach in the back of C.B.'s truck. The crime scene had been released. In later photos, it appears the interior cladding has been removed from the walls. Who knows what may have been inside that abandoned little house near Murdaugh property down Highway 278 that burnt to the ground as law enforcement and the Hampton Fire Department looked on?

The morning after the murders. You can see a large dump truck behind the tractor inside the hangar. To haul away sections of the feed room?

Kennels and open door to the feed room as seen by the jury during their "Jury View."

The dove fields where the sunflowers are, are at the left of this photo. The Moselle house is in the center. The kennels are down the road that turns right in this picture. The kennels are less than a minute drive to the house.

Chapter Forty
A Different "View" Altogether

Remote Viewing is the process of using one's clairvoyance and intuitive abilities to perceive details of a specific target. The target can be anything from a missing person to a distant location, and even something more abstract, but one thing in common is that the viewer is never revealed the identity of the target until they finished their session. Remote Viewing adheres to specific protocols in order to structure the viewer's feedback, but a full session can take many forms. Keywords and descriptors, sketches, and feelings from all senses are recorded. This project is using the TransDimensional Remote Viewing Protocol taught by Michelle Freed.

INTRODUCTION:
In February 2023, Michelle Freed and Rebecca Pittman discussed designing a remote viewing project to gather additional information to help Rebecca's research in the Alex Murdaugh case for her upcoming book. Michelle led a team of four of her students, each given a codename, and the only information they were pried with was that it was related to "True Crime". The following are excerpts from their sessions.

Target #5709 1907
Date: Feb 17th

Four Viewers:
Firehorse
GiGi Pink
Pixie
Gracie Hart

Method: TDRV
Group Name: BECRVG
Instructor: Michelle Freed
butterflyeffectcenter.com/

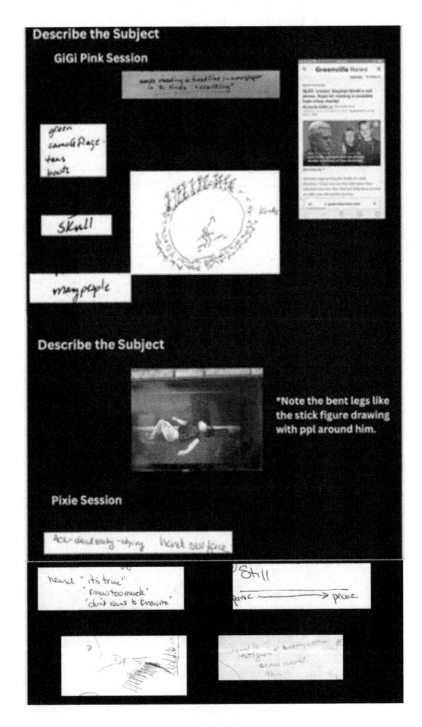

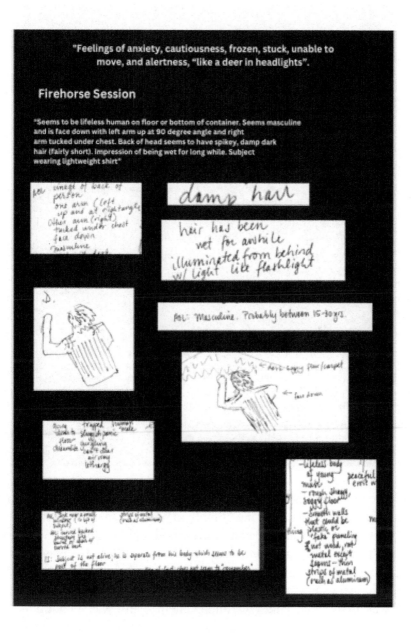

Firehorse Session

"Perceived that Subject was going to meet someone at the location and arrived with another person (perhaps a friend "Second Person") known to him (he felt comfortable being with him in a lifelong friends kind of way). Second Person also seems like 15-20 year old male. Perceived from Subject that they entered the structure, Subject entered first; Second Person behind and to the right of him.

Seems like Subject entered the structure quickly and confidently as though he had been there before. They were surprised by something. Seems like Second Person ran out. Subject did not have time to be afraid. Struck from left (blind-sided as he was looking forward into the dark-it was dark inside)."

Feed Back Session [ZOOM Recording]:
Below are impressions the viewer got during the feed back session when they were informed of their tasking and the target.

"Camo netting, scuffling in dirt, hunting garb, old heavy wood like a chair falling apart, leg of chair maybe used as a club, splintered.

Subject is VERY ANGRY. His anger turns on like flipping a switch. Others are afraid of him. Something with his hands, fingers spread out and grasping. Smell of dead animal inside the cabin-like structure. Metal roof. Hard wood floor. Dark. White Ford pickup truck.

The first blow stunned him. He wasn't dead yet.. Possibly two wounds."

Please keep in mind that when Michelle approached me, she did not want any information from me other than what I wanted them to focus on, which was a location I had in my mind and anything they could see about the subject(s) involved. She knew only that it was a true crime case. That's all. They could have zeroed in on any crime, anyplace. Any subject. Yet, they saw a southern region with tall pines and even mentioned South Carolina. Their victim was a young male between 15-20 years of age. He was hit in the head. The person who struck him was very angry, like a switch had flipped. He did something with his hands; fingers spread out and grasping. All of the viewers saw the attacker wearing camouflage like hunting garb.

The headline on Page 2 blew my mind. The report was sent to me in February 2023. It says, "Words in a newspaper headline. Two lines. "cracking." The headline in the *Greeneville News* came out in April, two months later! It reads, "SLED "cracks" Stephen Smith's phone. The rape kit is still missing." There is no way that is a coincidence. When I saw the headline, I ran to my home office where I had printed out the viewing reports two months earlier and showed it to my husband. That made me a believer without the rest of reports.

This is for your consideration and it's a part of the subconscious mind many don't understand, me included. But these reports were too incredible for me not to share them with you. The CIA uses remote viewing. I have been to lectures where the top experts in the world have discussed it. According to them, the Russians have been "Remote Viewing" us for years. It is a surreal concept to grasp.

I want to thank Michelle and her team for taking the time to produce copious reports. This is only a sampling of all the work they did. They were only given a target number and a goal: Where is the location, what do you see around it, what do you see concerning the subject or subjects involved. The most chilling for me was the follow-up meeting. They still did not know who the victim was. 3 of the 4 viewers said the victim was not dead with the first blow. He was blindsided and struck. He died later, possibly from a second wound.

Recommended Media for Murdaugh Information

Books:

- *Murdaugh She Wrote: A Tale of High Crimes in the Lowcountry,* and *Murdaugh She Wrote: After the Trial,* by Kathleen McKenna Hewston
- *Tangled Vines,* by John Glatt
- *The Fall of the House of Murdaugh,* by Michael DeWitt
- *Wicked Hampton County,* by Michael DeWitt
- *Behind the Doors of Justice: The Murdaugh Murders,* by Becky Bloom Hill

Podcasts:

- *Impact of Influence: The Murdaugh Family Murders and Other Cases*
- *Murdaugh Murders Podcast/Eric Alan YouTube*
- *Lovely Law Firm*

News Outlets:

- *FitsNews*
- *Law & Crime*
- *Crime TV*
- *Greeneville News*
- *The Island Packet*
- *The State Newspaper*
- *Channel 5 TV, SC*
- *Hampton County Guardian*
- *The News and Courier*

Documentaries:

- *Murdaugh Murders: Deadly Dynasty,* Prime Video
- *Low Country: The Murdaugh Dynasty,* HBO Max
- *Murdaugh Murders: A Southern Scandal,* Netflix

- *20/20: Fall of the House of Murdaugh,* Hulu
- *American Greed: "The Decline of a Dynasty"* and *"A Legacy of Fraud"*
- *Dateline: The Trial of Alex Murdaugh* and *Dark Waters*
- *CNN Special: The Murdaugh Murders,* CNN
- *48 Hours, The Murdaugh Mysteries,* YouTube and CBS

More documentaries are on the drawing board with rumors of another *Netflix* series falling in September 2023.

Inside the Hampton County Courthouse is where each of the Murdaugh family solicitors and lawyers have tried cases before the bench. Sergeant William Reid was kind enough to give this author a tour of the courtroom where three generations of Randolph Murdaugh portraits hang. Sergeant Reid's career in the Criminal Justice system is long and varied. He's been in law enforcement since 1987. After going into different arenas in his field, he graduated from the Criminal Justice Academy at the age of 55. Among his careers was a stint with the South Carolina Department of Corrections or "Department of Corruption," Reid laughed. Reid witnessed Alex Murdaugh in his role as prosecutor and said he was laid back and always spoke to people. "He treated people as if he knew them," Reid said. "That's his talent."

Sergeant William Reid at the Hampton County Courthouse.

Author's Page

Rebecca F. Pittman is a bestselling author in several genres. Her *History and Haunting* series of books are featured on TV, radio, podcasts, and newspaper outlets. *Mysteries Decoded* and *Legend Hunter* featured her book *The History and Haunting of Lizzie Borden*. Dan Ackroyd's *Hotel Paranormal* featured her documentation on *The History and Haunting of Lemp Mansion*, and several of her books show up on *The Scariest Places on Earth*.

Her *Countdown to Murder Series* is also a popular series. *Countdown to Murder: Pam Hupp*, was featured on *St. Louis Live* where Ms. Pittman and the lead detectives and prosecuting attorneys discussed the case. She has appeared on *Coast to Coast AM* twice for her *The History and Haunting of the Stanley Hotel* and other books. She is featured monthly on international radio and podcast forums.

Besides writing, Ms. Pittman is a game creator. Following her stint as an Escape Room creator and operator, she delved into creating card and board games. Her *Lizzie Borden Paranormal Card Game* regularly sells out from her website. Next up is a series of games under her new flagship, *"It Haunts Me."*

Ms. Pittman is diving into a murder mystery ghost story next, *When Shadows Walk.* Her juvenile fiction book *T.J. Finnel and the Well of Ghosts* has been compared to *Harry Potter* and *Fablehaven* for its mystery, paranormal, and creative characters.

Rebecca is a wife and the proud mother of four sons and a grandmother to 9 grandchildren. They are her joy. She makes her home in Colorado. Sign up for her free newsletter at www.rebeccafpittmanbooks.com.

Other Books & Games by Rebecca F. Pittman

Non-Fiction

- The History & Haunting of the Stanley Hotel (1st & 2nd)
- The History & Haunting of the Myrtles Plantation
- The History & Haunting of Lemp Mansion
- The History & Haunting of Lizzie Borden
- The History & Haunting of Salem: The Witch Trials & Beyond
- The History & Haunting of the Palace of Versailles
- How to Start a Faux Painting & Mural Business (1st & 2nd)
- Scrapbooking for Profit (1st & 2nd)
- Troubleshooting Men: *What* in the World Do They Want?
- Countdown to Murder: Pam Hupp
- Countdown to Murder: Alex Murdaugh

Fiction:

- T. J. Finnel and the Well of Ghosts (Juvenile/Adult)
- When Shadows Walk (Coming Fall 2023)
- The Diamond Peacock Club (Coming 2024)

Games:

- The Lizzie Borden Paranormal Card Game (Available on the website: www.rebeccafpittmanbooks.com)
- The Murdering Wives Club (Coming soon)
- It Haunts Me (Subscription Paranormal Game, Coming Soon)

Other Cases

Printed in Great Britain
by Amazon

34222745R00393